Ravikumar, Y V,
Oracle Database upgrade
and migration methods :
2017.
33305238917177
la   09/11/17

D0556116

Oracle Database Upgrade and Migration Methods

Including Oracle 12c Release 2

Y V Ravikumar (Oracle ACE and OCM)

K M Krishnakumar (OCP)

Nassyam Basha (Oracle ACED and OCM)

Foreword by Mike Dietrich

Oracle Database Upgrade and Migration Methods

Y V Ravikumar
Chennai, Tamil Nadu, India

K M Krishnakumar
Bangalore, Karnataka, India

Nassyam Basha
Nellore, Andhra Pradesh, India

ISBN-13 (pbk): 978-1-4842-2327-7
DOI 10.1007/978-1-4842-2328-4

ISBN-13 (electronic): 978-1-4842-2328-4

Library of Congress Control Number: 2016963204

Copyright © 2017 by Y V Ravikumar, K M Krishnakumar and Nassyam Basha

This work is subject to copyright. All rights are reserved by the Publisher, whether the whole or part of the material is concerned, specifically the rights of translation, reprinting, reuse of illustrations, recitation, broadcasting, reproduction on microfilms or in any other physical way, and transmission or information storage and retrieval, electronic adaptation, computer software, or by similar or dissimilar methodology now known or hereafter developed.

Trademarked names, logos, and images may appear in this book. Rather than use a trademark symbol with every occurrence of a trademarked name, logo, or image we use the names, logos, and images only in an editorial fashion and to the benefit of the trademark owner, with no intention of infringement of the trademark.

The use in this publication of trade names, trademarks, service marks, and similar terms, even if they are not identified as such, is not to be taken as an expression of opinion as to whether or not they are subject to proprietary rights.

While the advice and information in this book are believed to be true and accurate at the date of publication, neither the authors nor the editors nor the publisher can accept any legal responsibility for any errors or omissions that may be made. The publisher makes no warranty, express or implied, with respect to the material contained herein.

Managing Director: Welmoed Spahr
Lead Editor: Celestin Suresh John
Technical Reviewer: Brian Peasland
Editorial Board: Steve Anglin, Pramila Balan, Laura Berendson, Aaron Black, Louise Corrigan, Jonathan Gennick, Robert Hutchinson, Celestin Suresh John, Nikhil Karkal, James Markham, Susan McDermott, Matthew Moodie, Natalie Pao, Gwenan Spearing
Coordinating Editor: Prachi Mehta
Copy Editor: Kim Wimpsett
Compositor: SPi Global
Indexer: SPi Global
Artist: SPi Global

Distributed to the book trade worldwide by Springer Science+Business Media New York, 233 Spring Street, 6th Floor, New York, NY 10013. Phone 1-800-SPRINGER, fax (201) 348-4505, e-mail orders-ny@springer-sbm.com, or visit www.springeronline.com. Apress Media, LLC is a California LLC and the sole member (owner) is Springer Science + Business Media Finance Inc (SSBM Finance Inc). SSBM Finance Inc is a **Delaware** corporation.

For information on translations, please e-mail rights@apress.com, or visit www.apress.com.

Apress and friends of ED books may be purchased in bulk for academic, corporate, or promotional use. eBook versions and licenses are also available for most titles. For more information, reference our Special Bulk Sales–eBook Licensing web page at www.apress.com/bulk-sales.

Any source code or other supplementary materials referenced by the author in this text are available to readers at www.apress.com. For detailed information about how to locate your book's source code, go to www.apress.com/source-code/. Readers can also access source code at SpringerLink in the Supplementary Material section for each chapter.

Printed on acid-free paper

Contents at a Glance

About the Authors...xvii

About the Technical Reviewer xix

Acknowledgments...xxi

Foreword xxiii

■Chapter 1: Getting Started 1

■Chapter 2: Database Upgrade Methods 19

■Chapter 3: Comparison of Upgrade Methods.. 151

■Chapter 4: Upgrade Using a Database Backup 169

■Chapter 5: Oracle Database Migration.. 213

■Chapter 6: Migrating Oracle Database from Non-ASM to ASM Environments... 279

■Chapter 7: Oracle GI and Oracle 12*c* Database Upgrades in
   RAC Environments 323

■Chapter 8: Database Upgrades in Data Guard Environments 381

■Chapter 9: Database Upgrades in EBS Environments...................................... 425

■Chapter 10: Multitenant Database Upgrades.. 447

■Chapter 11: Pluggable Database Migrations 491

■Chapter 12: Oracle Database Patching Strategies.. 503

■Chapter 13: Database Downgrades 547

■Chapter 14: Oracle Database Upgrades in Oracle Database Release 12.2 565

Index... 603

Contents

About the Authors...xvii

About the Technical Reviewer xix

Acknowledgments..xxi

Foreword xxiii

■Chapter 1: Getting Started..1

Why Are Database Upgrades Necessary? 1

    New Innovations..3

    Bug Fixes..3

    Supporting Environment..4

    Certification 4

    Database Support Level..4

Benefits of a Database Upgrade 4

Hurdles That Affect the Database Upgrade Decision...5

Types of Database Upgrade..6

Things to Consider Before Upgrading 7

Engineers Involved in the Upgrade Activity 9

    Database Administrator 10

    Storage Administrator..11

    System Administrator 11

    Network Administrator..11

    Solution Architect 11

    Application Team 12

Upgrade Compatibility Matrix..12

Best Practices for a Database Upgrade 14

Database Migration 16

    Situations That Demand a Migration 16

    Things to Consider Before Migration 17

What This Book Covers 17

Summary 17

■Chapter 2: Database Upgrade Methods 19

Oracle Binary Relinking 19

    Relinking Process 20

    Known Issues 21

Database Upgrade Methods 21

The Database Upgrade Assistant 22

    Prerequisites for the DBUA 23

    Upgrade Compatibility Matrix 24

    Pre-upgrade Checks 25

    Activities Performed by the DBUA 26

    Best Practices with the DBUA 26

    Upgrade Steps 28

    Sample Restore Script 31

    12c DBUA New Features 42

    DBUA Upgrade Steps 54

    How to Make Sure the Upgrade Is Successful 56

    DBUA in Silent Mode 57

    Comparison Between 11g R2 DBUA and 12c R1 DBUA 59

Database Manual Upgrade 61

    Pre-upgrade Tasks 62

    Execution Method 63

    Recommended Steps for the Source Database 66

    Upgrade Steps 71

    12c Upgrade Script Execution 73

    Parallelism 73

Phases 74

Post-upgrade Steps 75

Comparison Between 11*g* R2 and 12*c* R1 79

Traditional Export/Import 81

Compatibility Version Matrix 81

Upgrade Steps 82

Data Pump 85

Parallel 85

Upgrade Steps 87

Transportable Tablespace 90

Things to Consider 91

Prerequisites to Perform Transportable Tablespace 91

Upgrade Steps 92

Limitations 97

Advantages 98

Database Upgrade Using Oracle GoldenGate 98

Planning Phase with Oracle GoldenGate 98

Configuration Setup at the Source Database (Oracle 11*g*) 105

Configuration Setup at the Target Database (Oracle 12*c*) 111

Configuration Setup at the Target Database (Oracle 12*c* for Oracle GoldenGate 12*c*) 113

High Availability or Fallback Option Using the Source Database (Oracle 11*g*) 119

Configuration Setup at Target Database Oracle 12*c* and Implementing Bidirectional
Data Replication Between Target Database (pdb12*c*) and Source Database (Oracle 11*g*) 120

Configuration Setup at Source Database Oracle 11*g* and Implementing Bidirectional
Data Replication Between Target Database (pdb12*c*) and Source Database (Oracle 11*g*) 123

Summary 126

Create Table As Select (CTAS) 126

CTAS vs. COPY 127

Advantages of CTAS 127

Disadvantages with CTAS 127

How Does CTAS Work? 127

Requirements 128

Parallel Usage with CTAS... 130

Order By with CTAS... 130

Summary 131

Database Upgrades Using Transient Logical Standby 131

Create a Restore Point... 135

Enable Supplementary Logging... 136

Upgrade of Logical Standby Database... 136

Manual Upgrade Using the 12c Method 137

Switchover.. 137

Initiate Flashback 138

Convert Logical to Physical Standby.. 138

Starting MRP.. 138

Switchover 138

Full Transportable Export/Import.. 139

Prerequisites 140

Upgrade Steps 140

Summary.. 149

■Chapter 3: Comparison of Upgrade Methods.. 151

The DBUA 151

Features.. 151

Limitations.. 152

Manual/Command-Line Upgrade 152

Features.. 153

Limitations.. 153

Comparison of the DBUA and Manual Processes 154

Traditional Export/Import and Data Pump 155

Features.. 155

Limitations 155

Data Pump.. 155

Transportable Tablespaces 156

    Steps in Summary 156

Features 157

    Limitations 157

Full Transportable Export/Import 157

    Features.. 157

    Limitations 158

Transient Logical Standby 158

    Switchover Best Practices... 159

    Features.. 159

    Limitations 159

Oracle GoldenGate 160

Comparison of All Methods 161

Real Application Testing 161

    Benefits of Using RAT 162

How to Choose the Best Upgrade Method... 162

    Database Downtime 163

    Getting Additional Storage... 165

    Number of Actions and Required Skill Set.. 165

    Total Time Allotted 166

    Unsupported Features 166

    Number of User Objects... 166

    Source Database Version.. 166

    Change of Platform... 167

Summary.. 167

■Chapter 4: Upgrade Using a Database Backup 169

Introduction 169

What Are the Various Backup Techniques? 170

Cold Backup (Traditional) 171

Hot Backup (User-Managed) 180

Logical Backup (expdp/impdp) 190

Prerequisites 191

Objects Count 191

Check NLS Settings 192

Datafiles and Metadata 193

Check the Invalid Objects from the Target Database 194

Registry Components at the Target Database 194

Create Triggers of the SYS Schema 195

Database Export Using expdp 196

Importing the Database (impdp) 197

RMAN Backup 201

Summary 211

■Chapter 5: Oracle Database Migration 213

Traditional Export/Import 213

Export 214

Output 215

Import 216

Output 216

Data Pump 217

Data Pump Working Process 218

Features 218

Partition 220

Merge 221

Departition 221

REMAP_DATAFILES 222

REUSE_DATAFILES 222

REMAP_TABLESPACE 222

Transportable Tablespaces 223

Oracle GoldenGate 228

    Environment Setup 228

        Oracle GoldenGate Setup on the Source Database 229

        Oracle GoldenGate Setup on the Target Database 230

        Configure Oracle GoldenGate on the Source Database 232

        Changes in Parameters in the Source Database 233

        Start Oracle GoldenGate Manager 239

        Configure Oracle GoldenGate on the Target Database 243

        Method 2: Initial Load with Bulkload 246

Oracle GoldenGate 228

CTAS 249

Transport Database 252

    Migrate Steps 253

Heterogeneous Standby Database 268

Oracle Streams 270

Summary 277

■Chapter 6: Migrating Oracle Database from Non-ASM to ASM Environments 279

Scenario 1: Moving datafiles online from a non-ASM location to an ASM location 281

Scenario 2: Migrating an Oracle Database 12c CDB with PDBs from a
non-ASM to ASM using EM 13c 297

Scenario 3: Migrating an Oracle Database 12c CDB with PDBs from a
non-ASM to ASM using RMAN 310

    Summary 321

■Chapter 7: Oracle GI and Oracle 12c Database Upgrades in
RAC Environments 323

Run the CVU Pre-upgrade Check Tool 324

Running the Oracle RAC Configuration Audit Tool (ORAchk) Tool 326

Execution Steps for ORAchk 326

Consider Real Application Testing 328

Performing a Rolling Upgrade Using Oracle GI 328

Scenario 1: Upgrading Oracle 11g RAC (11.2.0.3.0) to Oracle 12c RAC (12.1.0.2.0) 341

Scenario 2: Manual upgrade of Oracle 11g RAC (11.2.0.3.0) to
Oracle 12c RAC (12.1.0.2.0) 369

Scenario 3: Upgrading of Oracle 11g RAC (11.2.0.3.0) to
Oracle 12c RAC (12.1.0.2.0) with GI and Database using EMCC 13c.................... 378

Summary.. 380

■Chapter 8: Database Upgrades in Data Guard Environments 381

Upgrading Data Guard from 11.2.0.4 to 12.1.0.2 382

Pre-upgrade Steps 382

Review of the Pre-upgrade Log..384

Upgrade the Data Guard Environment 389

Post-upgrade Tasks 405

Summary 410

Rolling Database Upgrades Using DBMS_ROLLING in 12c................................. 410

Rolling Upgrades in 11g vs. DBMS_ROLLING in 12c..410

DBMS_ROLLING: 12c 411

Summary.. 424

■Chapter 9: Database Upgrades in EBS Environments...................................... 425

Prerequisite Steps 425

Pre-upgrade steps.. 426

Upgrade Steps.. 427

Post-upgrade Steps.. 427

Example.. 428

Apply the Prerequisite Patches to the Apps Home 438

Apply the Prerequisite Patches to the Database Home 438

Shut Down the Application Process...439

Execute cr9idata.pl..439

Drop the sys.enabled$indexes Table 439

Execute the Pre-upgrade Scripts..439

Check the Database Components' Status 440

Check the Invalid SYS/SYSTEM Schema Objects.. 440

Drop the MGDSYS Schema 440

Upgrade the Database to the 12c Version 441

Post-upgrade Steps for an EBS Database Upgrade 442

Summary... 445

■Chapter 10: Multitenant Database Upgrades.. 447

Multitenant Architecture... 448

Move the Lower-Version Database to the Multitenant Architecture............................ 450

Container Database Upgrade 454

Database Upgrade Assistant 458

Manual Database Upgrade or Command-Line Upgrade 463

Upgrade Steps.. 468

Post-upgrade Tasks 479

Pluggable Database Upgrade 479

Summary... 489

■Chapter 11: Pluggable Database Migrations 491

The Need for Migration.. 491

Migration Steps... 492

Same Endian Format 492

Different Endian Format 496

Summary... 502

■Chapter 12: Oracle Database Patching Strategies.............................. 503

What a Patch Contains 504

inventory.xml 504

actions.xml 506

How Patching Works 506

Central Inventory... 506

Re-creation Steps... 509

How to Remove from the Central Inventory... 511

Local Inventory 512

Using the Opatch Tool 513

Types of Patches 516

Patch Set Update (PSU) 516

Security Patch Update (SPU) 516

Bundle Patches 517

One-Off Patches 517

Proactive Bundle Patches 517

Conflicts 517

Overlay Patches 517

Patch Apply Strategies (Online and Offline Patching) 518

Patch Apply Steps 524

Applying Patch in Offline Mode 524

Patching in Online Mode 527

Post-Patch Steps 528

Patch Rollback 528

Opatch Debug 529

PSU and SPU Patching 529

PSU Patch Apply Steps 530

How to Confirm the PSU Patch Apply Is Successful 532

PSU Rollback 533

SPU Patching 535

Patch Apply Steps in RAC and Data Guard Environments 537

Patching in an RAC Environment 537

Patching in a Data Guard Environment 539

PSU/SPU Patch Apply in a Data Guard Environment 540

Datapatch 540

Queryable Patch Inventory 542

■Chapter 13: Database Downgrades 547

Limitations of Downgrading 547

Downgrade Steps for Multitenant Databases.. 550

Downgrade Steps Using Database Flashback.. 554

Upgrade Steps.. 554

Downgrade Steps.. 555

Downgrade Steps Using Database Flashback for Multitenant Databases 558

Upgrade Steps.. 558

Downgrade Steps.. 559

Known Issues 563

Summary... 563

■Chapter 14: Oracle Database Upgrades in Oracle Database Release 12.2 565

Upgrading to the 12.2 Release (12.2.0.1.0).. 565

Pre-upgrade Checks: What's New in 12.2 565

Steps.. 566

Upgrade Emulation... 570

Database Upgrade Assistant 573

Upgrade Steps.. 574

DBUA in Silent Mode.. 583

New 12.2 DBUA Features 583

Manual Database Upgrade/Command-Line Upgrade....................................... 583

Upgrade Steps.. 586

Post-upgrade Tasks.. 588

Oracle 12.2 New Manual Upgrade Features... 590

Pluggable Database Upgrade 590

Pluggable Database Upgrade Steps 591

Manual Upgrade of Pluggable Database in 12c R2 596

Target 12.2 Environment 597

Start PDB12cR2 in Upgraded Mode.. 598

Downgrade 12.2 to Earlier Versions 598

Prerequisites 599

Downgrade Steps for the Entire Container Database 599

Summary 601

Index 603

About the Authors

Yenugula Venkata Ravikumar (YVR) is an Oracle ACE and Oracle Certified Master (OCM) with 18 years of experience in the banking, financial services, and insurance (BFSI) verticals where he has played various roles such as senior database architect and production DBA. He is also an OCP in Oracle 8i, 9i, 10g, 11g, and 12c and is certified in Oracle GoldenGate, RAC, performance tuning, and Oracle Exadata. He continuously motivates many DBAs and helps the Oracle community by publishing his tips, ideas, suggestions, and solutions on his blog. He has written 50+ OTN articles on Oracle Exadata, Oracle RAC, and Oracle Golden Gate for OTN-Spanish, OTN-Portuguese, and OTN-English; 20+ articles for Toad World; 2 articles for UKOUG; 3 articles for OTech Magazine; and 2 articles for Redgate. He is a regular Oracle speaker at @OTN, NYOUG, AIOUG, Sangam, and IOUG. He also designed, architected, and implemented a core banking system (CBS) database for the central banks of two countries: India and Mahe, Seychelles. Learn more from his profile at Laser-Soft.

K M Krishnakumar is a database administrator with 12 years of experience with Oracle Database (8i to 12c). He has a master's degree in business administration from Anna University, Chennai. He started his career in 2004 as an Oracle database administrator and has been working with Oracle Corporation for the last six plus years. He has expertise in Oracle Database installation, patching, upgrades, migration, backup and recovery, and high availability. He is skilled with Oracle technologies such as Oracle Data guard, Real application clusters, RMAN, Oracle Database Cloud Service. He has performed many real-time production database installations, upgrades, and migrations. In addition, he has delivered sessions on database upgrades through various channels and is certified in Oracle 12c administration. He actively participates in Oracle communities and has contributed to community articles. He is reachable at kmkittu2005@gmail.com.

Nassyam Basha is a database administrator. He has about 10 years of IT experience, with the last eight years as a production Oracle DBA. He currently works as a senior principal consultant at Data Intensity. He is a post-graduate who has a master's degree in computer applications from the University of Madras.

He started working with dBase and FoxPr and has participated in several projects with FoxPro and Oracle Database starting from Oracle 7. He is an Oracle 11*g* Certified Master and was awarded the Oracle ACE Director title from Oracle. He is skilled with Oracle technologies such as Data Guard, RMAN, RAC, Cloud Control, and performance tuning. He has completed hundreds of Data Guard setups with major Data Guard–related issues on all platforms and has worked with business-critical production databases. He actively participates in Oracle-related forums such as OTN with a status of Super Hero, participates in Oracle Support with the title of Guru, and acts as an OTN moderator. He also has written numerous articles for OTN and Toad World with the status of Master, Legend, Guru, and Celebrity. He maintains an Oracle technology–related blog (www.oracle-ckpt.com) and is reachable at nassyambasha@gmail.com.

About the Technical Reviewer

Brian Peasland has been in the IT field for over 20 years and has worked as a computer operator, operations analyst, systems administrator, application developer and for more than half of his career as a database administrator. He holds a B.S. in computer science and a M.S. in computer science, specializing in database systems. Additionally, Brian holds OCP DBA credentials for Oracle 7.3, 8, 8*i*, 9*i*, and 10*g*, . Brian has been a member of SearchOracle.com's Ask The Experts since 2001. He regularly contributes to the My Oracle Support and Oracle Technet communities. He can be followed on Twitter on @BPeaslandDBA and maintains a blog at http://www.peasland.net. He is the author of "Oracle RAC Performance Tuning" on Rampant TechPress.

Acknowledgments

Above and beyond all others, I thank the Almighty and my parents, N.Abdul Aleem and Rahimunnisa. Without their support I wouldn't have been able to be what I am today. A special thanks to my family; my wife Ayesha and my daughter and my lucky charm, Nassyam Yashfeen Fathima. I would also like to thank my brother, Nawaz Basha, who was supportive all the time; my niece, Fathima Zehra; my nephew, Yaseen; and also Zaheer, Ahamed, Farhana, Riyana, and all my family members.

I would also like to express my gratitude to the Oracle professionals Syed Jaffar Hussain, Chinar Aliyev, shahabaz(TZ), Emre Baransel, Michael Seberg, Francisco Munez Alvarez, Bjoern Rost, Ameer Zaheer Ahmed, Javid Ur Rehman, Ahmed Ullah (XoraSoft.com), Gulzaman Khan, the AIOUG team, Ezra, and all my friends.

I thank my clients and colleagues who provided me with invaluable opportunities to expand my knowledge and shape my career.

My heartfelt appreciation goes to the technical reviewer of this book, Brian Peasland, for the time he spent reviewing this book. I would like to thank the Apress team for giving us the opportunity to write this book and their support throughout. Last but not least, I would like to say a big thanks to my friends and co-authors, Krishnakumar and YV Ravikumar, for their contribution to the team and great direction. Finally our big thanks to Mike Dietrich for writing book forward and indeed we delighted with his write up.

—Nassyam Basha

I would like to thank the Apress team who worked patiently until the end to produce an excellent book. This book is the result of unremitting hours of working, and I hope you will find it extremely helpful. I thank the entire team for making it possible.

I would like to express my gratitude to my colleagues Umesh Ashwathanaryana Rao and Roderick Manalac for performing a technical review of my content. Also, I would like to thank Brian Piesland for the technical review of the entire book.

I would like to convey my sincere thanks to Jaikishan Tada, Vikash Palisetti and Mohammed Salim Akbani for their great support and special thanks to my management team for their support and encouragement.

Above all, I want to thank my wife, Swetha Ramesh, for standing beside me throughout my career and helping to complete this book in spite of all the time it took me away from her. Her support and feedback helped me a lot to complete this book. I also want to thank my parents Mohanram and Lalitha and rest of my family members, especially my brother, Ramkumar, who supported and encouraged me to complete this book.

Also, I want to thank my friend Koushik Suresh who has been my motivation for continuing to improve my knowledge and move my career forward. I would like to thank my friend Velu Natarajan for his guidance in my DBA carrier.

Finally, last but not the least, this book is dedicated to the Oracle database administrators around the world who work 24/7 in production environments.

All kinds of feedback, comments, and ideas are warmly welcomed. Any suggestions regarding the improvement of this book will be acknowledged.

—K M Krishnakumar

I am grateful to God who gave us all the strength, courage, perseverance, and patience in this sincere and honest attempt of knowledge sharing.

This first book of mine would not have been possible without the following:

Shri Yenugula Venkata Pathi and Smt. Yenugula Krishnakumari, my parents, for instilling in me good thoughts and values. They encouraged me to work hard and always be a step ahead in learning new things.

B. Suresh Kamath, my mentor, my guru, my strength, and my guide, who has inspired me for the last 20 years. He is an immensely talented and technically sound individual. He taught me how to be well-read with no compromises. He led by example in being content yet hungry of knowledge. He motivated me to go that extra mile in attempting and experimenting newer technologies/environments and in being regularly out of my comfort zone.

Anitha Ravikumar, my wife, for being immensely tolerant with me. "Behind every successful man, there is a woman," as they say. I believe she is the embodiment of this well-known belief.

Naveen Shenoy R, my illustrator, who has been instrumental in giving visual life to my book. "A picture is worth a thousand words," as they say. The technically complex subject I have covered in this book has been simplified well by scores of illustrations and diagrams.

My friends and colleagues, for backing me up and sharing with me their knowledge, laughter, joy, wisdom, and strengths. I received continuous encouragement from each one, and most of them were instrumental in shaping me into what I am.

The reader, for picking up this book. I have attempted to be as simple and straightforward as possible when sharing this knowledge, and I truly believe that it will help you, the reader, to steadily deep dive into various interesting concepts and procedures. I would also like to express my gratitude to the Oracle professionals Murali Vallath, Binay Rath, Syed Jaffar Hussain, Nassyam Basha, Krishnakumar, Laura K Ramsey, Javid Ur Rehman, Muni Chandra, AIOUG team, Sangam OUG and all my friends.

—Y V Ravikumar

Foreword

Upgrading or migrating an Oracle Database is a simple task, isn't it? Well, in theory it is - once the best path and approach has been chosen. But often there are many options and possibilities. Important questions will have to be answered at first such as about downtime requirements or the size of the database once it comes to migrations. And sometimes a mixture of techniques will lead to the best possible solution.

I deal and work with database upgrades and migrations for almost 15 years now, from tiny but business critical systems to environments with thousands of databases. And I get asked these "simple" questions several times a week. Now with Oracle Database 12c and the Multitenant option there's even more variety to select from. Database upgrades and migrations may sound like a simple topic - but there are a lot of things to take into consideration.

This book, written by Nassyam Basha, Y V Ravikumar and K M Krishnakumar will guide you through the entire process. From finding the best upgrade or migration strategy for your specific environment to all the details of each method, its advantages and the potential pitfalls. It includes considerations for standby databases as well as for Real Application Clusters and Automatic Storage Management. And it covers also the move to the new Oracle Multitenant architecture, and finally the very important patching topic.

Everything is looked at from a true hands-on perspective by real world experts making this book an extremely helpful guide through all the various approaches.

I'd like to congratulate Nassyam Basha, Y V Ravikumar and K M Krishnakumar to this excellent book. It's must-have for every DBA dealing with upgrades, migrations and patching.

Mike Dietrich
Master Product Manager Database Upgrades and Migrations
ORACLE Corporation

CHAPTER 1

■■■

Getting Started

Welcome to the upgrade realm! In today's world, people use software every day for various purposes, and it is embedded in the many devices that we all use; this includes the operating system, a database, a mobile application, and so on. This software helps us complete our jobs quickly, reduces our workloads, and provides ease of access. At the same time, our expectations of software in general get higher every day. To meet this need, software needs to be updated. In fact, all software needs to be upgraded periodically to achieve longevity in the software industry, and you will find that the software that has survived for a long time has seen many upgrades. This might be because the software creator wanted to introduce new features, address existing bugs, or satisfy demands from its dependent and supporting environment. By contrast, software that is not regularly upgraded will lose its value, and slowly it will fade from people's memory.

In this book, we talk about upgrading Oracle Database, including the commencement of its journey, the necessity for its upgrade, the upgrades it has seen so far, and the methods to upgrade your databases to the latest version. This book discusses each upgrade and migration method in detail and will help you choose the right process for your environment. It also explores the best practices of each upgrade method, which will help you to complete your upgrade effectively with less downtime in mission-critical environments.

Oracle Database was released in 1979, with initial version 2. Later it was upgraded to 3, and so on. Currently the commonly used latest version is Oracle 12c R1 (12.1.0.2.0). During its upgrade journey, it has introduced a rich set of features such as high availability (HA), Real Application Clusters (RAC), Automatic Storage Management (ASM), Recovery Manager (RMAN), Global Data Services (GDS), data compression, Real Application Testing (RAT), and cloud computing.

Why Are Database Upgrades Necessary?

We'll talk about why upgrades are necessary through a real-life example. Consider how the storage for media files and media players has changed over the years (see Figure 1-1).

© Y V Ravikumar, K M Krishnakumar and Nassyam Basha 2017
N. Basha et al., *Oracle Database Upgrade and Migration Methods*, DOI 10.1007/978-1-4842-2328-4_1

Figure 1-1. *Necessity of upgrade*

During the initial days of music, people listened to songs on records using a gramophone. Technically, it used an analog sound-recording medium. In a way, it was not user-friendly because both the storage and the player were huge in size. It was difficult to carry the device and had to be listened to using the large speaker attached to the gramophone. Smaller record players were eventually introduced, but they were still pretty nonportable.

Later, to reduce the complexity, the tape recorder and cassette tape were introduced. A tape recorder was easy to handle, and because of its simplicity, the majority of people started using them instead of record players. Some of tape recorders had provisions for earphones as well, with which the listening could be privatized and confined to one or two listeners. Still, cassette tapes were lacking storage space, which made people carry more tapes. Inventory for tapes was also a problem. Audio clarity was reduced with increased recordings on a tape, and accessing the songs randomly was difficult because storage was in a sequential form. The cassettes and tape within were prone to physical damage with magnetic effect, overlooping of tapes while playing, and so on.

Later, the media was upgraded to compact discs. The audio became digital, which improved the quality. In addition, compact discs had more storage compared to cassette tapes. Also, as audio compression formats improved, more songs in various audio formats could be stored on each disc. The downsides were the difficulty of carrying disc players and the continuous need of electricity. Finally, the discs were prone to physical damage from scratches.

Compact media players were introduced in the market after compact discs. This created a revolution in the media player industry. They were small in size, easy to carry, and available in multiple storage sizes. Once they were charged, they could play continuously as long as the charge lasted. The problem of carrying the storage medium was avoided as the storage and player were combined into one small device. Also, the problems of physical damage to the storage devices could be avoided. The only problem now was maintaining songs within the storage available. Refreshing the songs with the listener's latest favorites and playlists had to be done with the proper software. This problem was not considered trivial, but this media remains a favorite of many music listeners. A similar idea applies to storing songs on mobile phones enabled with audio players.

In recent times, the trend has moved a step ahead by introducing access to online music, in the cloud. There is no need for local storage space, and any media player that can connect to the Internet can play the audio files. The media player can even be a mobile device or tablet. This technology change also makes it easy to share audio files with others. Playlists can be made on the fly, and searching through archives for favorites is easy.

Through this real-life example, you can observe the factors that create a need for upgrades. They include making access more user friendly and improving the quality, convenience, storage optimization, and online facilities.

You'll now see the factors that create the need for a database upgrade.

New Innovations

New innovations are essential reasons to upgrade. Innovations are required to simplify and improve existing functionality, enhance a product, and add new features. They modernize a product. The new features make the product stand unique among others, which eventually leads to long survival in the competitive database market. It gives new experiences to users.

Oracle Database has traveled from version Oracle 2 to Oracle 12c. Each release has provided many new features. Table 1-1 lists some features released in the latest versions.

Table 1-1. *New Features of Recent Database Releases*

Oracle Version	New Features
Oracle 8i	Statspack, global temporary tables, locally managed tablespaces (LMT), Recovery Manager (RMAN), standby database
Oracle 9i	Automatic Undo Management (AUM), Oracle Managed Files (OMF), resumable space allocation, multiple block sizes, advanced replication, Data Guard, and default temporary tablespace
Oracle 10g	Automatic Storage Management (ASM), Automatic Workload Repository (AWR), temporary tablespace groups, new memory parameters, BIG file and SYSAUX tablespaces, cross-platform transportable tablespace, and Data Pump
Oracle 11g	Automatic Memory Management (AMM), Flashback Data Archive, Data Repair Advisor, automatic SQL tuning, Database Replay, Active Data Guard (ADG), SQL Performance Analyzer, and edition-based redefinition
Oracle 12c	Multitenant database, cloud computing, data redaction, full database caching, in-memory aggregation, table recovery, fast active DUPLICATE, cross-platform backup and restore, and JSON support

Without a database upgrade, applications cannot leverage these new features. Along with the new features listed in Table 1-1, each release has enhanced the existing features. For example, RMAN has been enhanced in each version since its release.

Bug Fixes

When software doesn't perform the expected functionality, that improper behavior is called a *bug*. Oracle releases intermediate patches, or *bug fixes*, to address the bugs in its database software. But sometimes bugs that require a fix at the code level will be fixed in the next higher version. In general, the higher version will include fixes for bugs seen in lower versions.

Supporting Environment

Oracle Database works with many other applications, including Oracle applications and other vendors' applications. When those applications get upgraded, they could have new demands and might look for new enhancements in Oracle Database. To support the surrounding environment and continue the existing relationship, the database may require an upgrade.

Certification

The compatibility between applications/software and Oracle Database is called *certification*. Any software that works with Oracle Database has its own compatibility matrix. For example, Windows 7 requires the database version to be a minimum of 10.2.0.5.0, and Windows 10 requires at least 11.2.0.4.0. If the operating system gets upgraded, then the associated database also needs to be upgraded.

Oracle 12c R1 (12.1.0.2.0), has been certified with the latest operating systems such as Windows 10 and Oracle Enterprise Linux 7.

Database Support Level

Oracle Database has three levels of support: Premier, Extended, and Sustained. When a database version is released, it will be in the Premier support level, where you get all kinds of support including patches and updates and new bug fixes. Once the Premier support period is over, the database will enter the Extended support level. With Extended support, new patches and bug fixes will be released only for licensed customers of Extended support. Once the Premier support duration is over, the customer needs to pay additional costs to acquire Extended support. After completing the Extended support period, the database version will move to Sustained support, where new enhancements will not be offered. Newly discovered bugs will not be patched. Each database release will pass through these three phases. There will be a definite period for each release in each support level.

Upgrading is necessary to keep your database on a version that is always covered under Premier support. To summarize, your database requires upgrades for the following reasons:

- To invite new features and functionalities released in the higher version

- To get bug fixes released in the higher version

- To sustain a relationship with the supporting environment

- To stay with Oracle Premier support

Benefits of a Database Upgrade

You just saw why upgrades are necessary; let's spend some time here to explore the benefits of them.

- *New* features: Using the new features, you can add lots of innovations and improvements to your existing environment. Using Oracle 9i, you could build HA using RAC, and using Oracle 10g, you could build HA with Automatic Storage Management. Oracle 12c has introduced a multitenant architecture that businesses can use to achieve better consolidation and provisioning. On Windows platforms, Oracle 12c has given provision to start the services through the Oracle Home user, who does not need to be an administrator.

- *New* functionalities: Using new functionality, you can enhance your capabilities. This will even help the existing functions to perform better. For example, the Oracle multisection backup enables you to take a backup of large datafiles by dividing them into multiple sections, which can be backed up by multiple channels. This will improve the speed of the backup. This feature was available only for full backups of databases and datafiles until 11g R2. In Oracle 12c, RMAN supports multisection incremental backup. By using the same RMAN incremental backup, speed can be improved. In Oracle 12c, Data Pump has introduced the option to perform no logging while importing tables and indexes, which will reduce archive log generation. Using Oracle 11g enhanced compression, space can be saved, and performance can be improved.

- *Bug fixes*: Major bugs will be fixed in subsequent releases. The database will get all the required bug fixes in one shot.

- *Stay with supporting environment*: The database will maintain compatibility with its companions such as the operating system, application server, and web server.

- *Oracle* Premier *support*: Oracle Database will stay in Premier support always. You can also get all the bug fixes and intermediate patches.

- *Reduce cost*Database Upgrade: By using new features such as Advanced Compression and Flex Cluster, the resource can be optimized. The database administrator (DBA) also saves time while using new features, which helps lower the cost of maintaining and developing database solutions.

Hurdles That Affect the Database Upgrade Decision

The moment you hear *database upgrade*, you may think of the following questions:

- What does it mean to upgrade? How am I going to benefit?

- My application is working fine with the current database version, so why should I upgrade it? What if I don't upgrade?

- After upgrading, will my application perform better or worse?

- Will it have any negative impact on my existing business?

- How much cost is involved in this upgrade process?

- Does the upgrade require database downtime? If so, how do I perform the upgrade with less or near-zero downtime?

- If I upgrade now, do I need to upgrade again in the future?

These queries are commonly asked when thinking about upgrading. This book will answer all of these questions, and it will help you find the right path to upgrade your environment.

These are the main obstacles when upgrading:

- *Database downtime*: The major hurdle to decide about a database upgrade is the downtime. Downtime means the database will not be available for external user access or applications. Database downtime is required to upgrade a database to a higher database version. Basically, a database upgrade happens in one of two ways. Either the application/user data moves along with database dictionary to the higher version or only the application/user data is moved to the higher data dictionary. The data dictionary will have all information about the database, including database components, features, and options. In the first method, the data dictionary gets upgraded to the higher database version. Here the user data will not be touched, and downtime is required to upgrade the data dictionary. In the second method, you move the user data from the source database to the higher-version database, which has its own data dictionary. Downtime is required to move the data to the higher database version. The amount of downtime differs between these methods. In the current eventful world, whether you can afford downtime is not an easy decision. Downtime is the major factor when choosing a suitable upgrade method. In this book, we will discuss each upgrade method along with its expected downtime.

- *Upgrade-dependent environment*: The upgraded higher database version may demand upgrades to its associated operating system or web server or application server, and so on, which would add additional actions for the dependent environment. It may also add extra licensing costs. Upgrading the dependent environment also may add additional database downtime.

- *Application compatibility*: Existing applications that access the database may not be compatible with the upgraded database version. Some code changes may be required in an application. Based on the application type, you have to plan the strategies with the upgrade/migration.

- *Test environment*: Performing the upgrade directly in a production environment is not advisable. The database upgrade should be implemented/tested first in a preproduction or test environment to observe the results. This will help you in many ways. You could calculate the required downtime for upgrade, the issues faced during upgrade, and their required action plans. The test environment should be similar to production in all aspects (CPU, memory, and so on) to get accurate results. An organization has to spend money to get the proper environment for testing.

- *Cost involved*: Cost doesn't mean only the value of money. It also means the time and effort required for the database upgrade. A database upgrade involves many phases such as planning, testing, implementing, and post-upgrade testing. Each phase requires a certain amount of time to complete. Also, testing usually will happen in the dev ➤ test ➤ QA ➤ prod environment. An organization should consider this cost factor before proceeding to upgrade.

Types of Database Upgrade

Database upgrades come in two types: release upgrades and patch set upgrades. We'll cover what both of these are (see Figure 1-2).

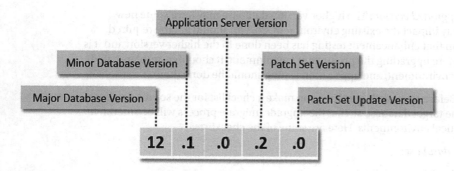

Figure 1-2. *Oracle Database version information*

- *Release upgrade*: This is an upgrade with a major and minor database version. An example is upgrading from 10.2 to 11.2 or from 11.1 to 11.2.

- *Patch set upgrade*: This includes applying patch sets to existing releases. An example is upgrading 10.2.0.1.0 to 10.2.0.5.0. Oracle 11*g* R2 patch set upgrades are considered release upgrades.

In addition, you need to decide whether you are going to upgrade the whole database to the higher database version or extract only the user data from the database and move it to the higher database version.

Every database has a metadata dictionary. This dictionary will have information about database objects (tables, indexes, view, synonyms, function, procedures, triggers, and so on), users, and the physical structure of the database. It also has information about database features and installed options. You can say it is the heart of the database and this dictionary is stored in the system tablespace. You can upgrade the data dictionary to a higher version, which will make changes in the dictionary according to the higher version. During this upgrade, existing dictionary objects (tables, functions, and procedures) will be modified, and new objects will be created. According to the higher version, new users and roles will be added to the existing database. Here we will not be touching on user data. But you should check the upgrade compatibility matrix discussed later in this chapter for more information.

If you choose the alternate method, extracting data from the database, then the source database dictionary will not be changed. You will be moving the user data along with the metadata to the higher database dictionary.

You will be performing one of the previously mentioned upgrade methods, which are discussed in detail in Chapter 2.

Things to Consider Before Upgrading

You should consider the following items before upgrading:

- *Purpose*: You need to define the purpose of doing this upgrade. What are you looking for, and is it to get bug fixes or new features or to achieve a support level or all of it? Though you will get all of these benefits with an upgrade, you should know more about your theme for the upgrade. For example, some bug fixes will be fixed with patch sets like 12.1.0.2.4. In that case, the upgrade should not end with the major release (12.1.0.2.0) upgrade. You will need to apply PSU 12.1.0.2.4 after that.

- *Application compatibility with the higher database version*: Will your application work fine with the upgraded database version? Consider doing regression testing before performing an upgrade. You can also use the Oracle Database 12*c* Real Application Testing option, which addresses these issues head-on with two features that complement each other: Database Replay and SQL Performance Analyzer.

- *Bugs with upgraded version*: The higher-version database may have some new bugs that may impact the existing environment. So, you should get the required confirmation that enhancement testing has been done in the higher version and it is bug free. Before upgrading the production environment, it should be implemented in a testing environment, and application testing should be done there.

- *Checklists*: Before starting this activity, you make a checklist for the source database as well as the target database so that the upgrade/migrate process will be smooth in mission-critical environments. Here are some of the checklists:

  - *Source database*:

    - Check for invalid objects.

    - Check for duplicate objects in schemas like SYS and SYSTEM.

    - Collect accurate performance statistics from the source database before starting this activity.

  - *Target database*:

    - Check the certification matrix on My Oracle Support.

    - Check for the latest patch set for the newer version of Oracle.

    - Apply the latest PSU, recommended bundled patches (BPs) for the newer version of Oracle.

    - Check interim patches (IPs) for known issues for the newer version of Oracle.

- *Benefits*: How much will the higher versions benefit your environment? It is the final measurement that gives justification for your upgrade.

- *Upgrade methods*: Which upgrade method suits your environment? After doing a thorough study of the upgrade methods, you will be able to find the right one for your environment.

- *Number of databases*: How many databases are you planning to upgrade? This attribute is required to calculate the total time required for the upgrade. In a 12c multitenant architecture, you can upgrade the older version of databases to a nonpluggable database and then migrate as pluggable databases (PDBs) in the container database (CDB) to make use of common memory and background processes for better resource utilization, agility, and rapid provisioning. You need to calculate how much memory you have to allocate to the container database level based on the number of pluggable databases.

- *Backup*: Once you have decided to proceed with the database upgrade, the foremost activity is taking a database backup. The backup could be a cold backup or hot backup or RMAN backup. The backup should be consistent enough to restore the database to a valid state.

- *Fallback options*: What fallback options have you planned? If the upgrade is not successful or doesn't meet your expectation, you may decide to go back to the old version. In that case, what options have you chosen to revert the changes? Are you going to rely on the database backup or create a flashback restore point as a fallback option? In the case of the Oracle GoldenGate method, you can use the bidirectional option from a higher version of Oracle Database to a lower version of Oracle Database to make use of the older version of the database as the fallback option, for reporting purposes, and for backup operations.

- *Test environment*: It is essential to test the database upgrade and observe the behavior of applications with the upgraded database. You should have the test environment ready to examine the upgrade steps before doing it in a production environment. Some organizations consider testing it in multiple test environments to investigate more. They record all upgrade steps and issues seen during the implementation. Once all the issues are sorted out, they will proceed to the production upgrade.

- *Budget/cost*: Here the budget includes the software license cost, human resources, and the additional cost of required software and hardware.

- *Team involved in* the *upgrade*: These include the storage administrator, database administrator, system administrator, and network administrator along with the application team.

Engineers Involved in the Upgrade Activity

The major roles in an upgrade are played by the database administrator, network administrator, and storage administrator (see Figure 1-3). Also, the application team and solution architects play a role to complete the upgrade effectively.

Figure 1-3. *Engineers involved in the upgrade activity*

Database Administrator

The DBA performs a crucial role in a database upgrade. The DBA is the one who knows the environment well and its demands. The DBA is the right person to choose the appropriate upgrade method. Let's spend some time here getting to know the DBA's role and responsibilities during the upgrade activity.

In general, the database administrator performs daily maintenance tasks such as monitoring database health, taking a backup and validating it, performance monitoring, calculating database size growth, and estimating future storage need. In addition, the DBA takes on the additional role of new installation, patching and upgrades, enabling high availability, and creating Disaster Recovery sites (DR). The DBA is the one who identifies the necessity of an upgrade, finds appropriate time to upgrade the database considering the impact to the business; creates proper plans, and executes the database upgrade process. The DBA knows the benefits that get imported into the environment while upgrading to a higher version. The DBA communicates with management and gets approval to proceed with the upgrade.

The DBA's planning will involve choosing an appropriate upgrade method, calculating the required downtime, executing pre-upgrade tasks, identifying required resources, testing the upgrade in a preproduction environment, evaluating performance through proper application testing, performing precautionary steps, and communicating to management and the application team about the events.

Before starting the upgrade activity, the DBA will draft a check list of activities, document the upgrade steps, and verify periodically to know whether everything was completed at the expected deadline. The DBA is the one to report the status to management and the application team. Sometimes the DBA may have to work 24/7 to complete the task successfully. The DBA may need to involve Oracle global customer support to evaluate the plan and seek help in case of any unexpected issues.

The whole upgrade process will go on for several weeks based on the environment. Usually the DBA allocates some amount of time for planning and testing it in a preproduction environment. In some organizations, DBAs even test the upgrade in multiple preproduction environments to ensure the reliability and verify how their applications behave with the newly upgraded database. Sometimes when the operating system demands a database upgrade, then database compatibility has to be checked after the upgrade.

Storage Administrator

The database upgrade may demand additional storage for testing. Pre-upgrade tests like Real Application Testing require database clones to be created for which additional storage will be required. RAT will perform load testing on the upgraded database. Also, some of the upgrade methods discussed in this book require additional storage to perform a database upgrade. Those methods will create clone databases to reduce the downtime required for an upgrade.

The storage administrator will discuss with the database administrator and collect storage requirements such as the type, how much storage, the size, and how much time is needed.

System Administrator

The system administrator plays a crucial role in the database upgrade activity. The system administrator's typical duties will be related to monitoring system memory usage and I/O rate and configuring, troubleshooting, and performing maintenance activities. During a database upgrade, the higher-version database may require more memory, which may demand an increase in system memory. Sometimes the database may get migrated to a different data center as part of upgrade, so the system administrator is responsible for configuring the new site for the database.

The system administrator also has to ensure that system resources are free and system performance doesn't affect the database upgrade. Installing a higher database version requires the root user to execute some scripts for which system admin presence is mandatory.

Network Administrator

The network administrator is responsible for designing and planning the network, setting up the network, and maintaining and expanding the network. During the upgrade activity, the network administrator will ensure there is a proper connectivity between the servers involved in the upgrade. The network administrator will be monitoring the network speed. His role is crucial for a database upgrade in a high availability environment.

Solution Architect

In addition to the previously mentioned people, there are some other people who contribute when necessary. The Solution architect designs the whole system architecture. The Solution architect has extensive knowledge about the environment and its upcoming demands. His contribution is more in deriving project cost. The Solution architect knows how the upgrade will benefit the environment and recommends the right time to perform the upgrade. The Solution architect is the person who will be able to talk about the application compatibility with the upgraded database version.

The Solution architect's role will be predominant during the planning phase. The Solution architect talks with the DBA and arrives at a conclusion for the project cost, time required to perform it, required resources, and the backup plan.

Application Team

Finally, the application team confirms that the upgraded database is compatible with the applications. The application team acceptance is vital to conclude the upgrade. They will be testing the applications for functionality, performance, new features, scalability, and high availability. The application team will incorporate the necessary changes required on the application side. The application team will also test the functionality of the applications/modules with different approaches. They first test with databases upgraded in a test environment. Once they approve this, the upgrade will proceed to the go-live phase.

Upgrade Compatibility Matrix

Different database versions have different sets of features. When you upgrade a database along with database dictionary, you need to check their compatibility matrix. It is always advisable to upgrade to the latest database version, which will help to get the latest features and bug fixes and stay with Premier support for a long time.

Because of version compatibility, for some upgrade methods (which perform upgrade with database dictionary) it may not be possible to upgrade the database directly to the latest version. You may need to jump temporarily to an intermediate version and then upgrade to a higher version from there. While reviewing the upgrade methods, consider this upgrade compatibility.

Table 1-2 shows an upgrade compatibility matrix for a direct upgrade to 11g R2.

Table 1-2. *Direct Upgrade to 11g R2*

Source Database Version	Target Database Version
9.2.0.8.0	11.2.0.X.X
10.2.0.2.0 or Higher	11.2.0.X.X
11.1.0.6.0 or Higher	11.2.0.X.X
11.2.0.1.0 and above	11.2.0.X.X

In Oracle Version 11.2.0.X.X, the fourth digit denotes the patch set version. Its value is from 1 to 4. The fifth digit denotes the patch set update. It can be from 1 to the latest PSU.

Table 1-3 shows the database version required for an intermediate upgrade to reach Oracle 11g R2.

Table 1-3. *Intermediate Upgrade for 11g R2*

Source Database Version	Intermediate Database Version	Target Database Version
10.2.0.1.0	10.2.0.2.0	11.2.0.X.X
9.2.0.7.0 and lower	9.2.0.8.0	11.2.0.X.X
9.1.0.3.0 and lower	Source database version → 9.1.0.4 0 → 10.2.0.2.0 or higher OR Source database version → 9.2.0.8.0	11.2.0.X.X
8.1.7 and lower	Source database version → 8.1.7.4 → 10.2.0.2.0 or higher OR Source database version → 9.2.0.8.0	11.2.0.X.X

■ **Note**   Here, ➤ denotes the database upgrade.

Table 1-4 shows an upgrade compatibility matrix for a direct upgrade to 12*c*.

Table 1-4. *Direct Upgrade to 12c R1*

Source Database Version	Target Database Version
10.2.0.5.0	12.1.0.X.X
11.1.0.7.0	12.1.0.X.X
11.2.0.2.0 and higher	12.1.0.X.X

In Oracle version 12.1.0.X.X, the fourth digit denotes the patch set value. Its value is from 1 to 2. The fifth digit denotes the patch set update. It can be from 1 to the latest PSU.

Table 1-5 shows the database version required for an intermediate upgrade to reach to the Oracle 12*c* R1 version.

Table 1-5. *Intermediate Upgrade for 12c R1*

Source Database Version	Intermediate Database Version	Target Database Version
11.2.0.1.0	Upgrade to 11.2.0.2.0 or higher	12.1.0.X.X
11.1.0.6.0	11.1.0.6.0 → 11.1.0.7.0	12.1.0.X.X
10.2.0.4.0 and lower	Source database version → 10.2.0.5.0	12.1.0.X.X
9.2.0.8.0 and lower	Source database version → 10.2.0.5.0	12.1.0.X.X
8.1.7 and lower	Source database version →8.1.7.4 → 10.2.0.5.0	12.1.0.X.X

Best Practices for a Database Upgrade

These are guidelines for completing an upgrade successfully in less downtime without any intermediate issues. These guidelines are generic to all upgrade methods. Method-specific best practices are discussed in detail in Chapter 2.

- *The importance of database backups*: Before making any changes in a database, it is mandatory to take a backup. The backup can be a cold backup or hot backup or RMAN backup. The backup should be consistent enough to restore the database to a reliable state.

- Consider Figure 1-4, which shows the importance of a power backup. Any organization would suffer if an electric power backup was not available. Almost all corporate companies have an uninterrupted power supply to provide an electric power backup to continuously function.

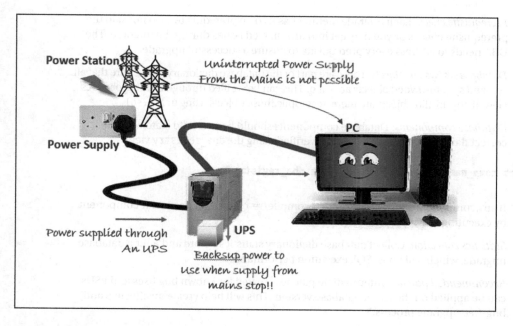

Figure 1-4. *Importance of a backup*

- If possible, test the integrity of the backup in a test environment. If it is an RMAN backup, validate the backup using the restore validate preview command.

- *Certification*: Make sure that the target database version is installed on the certified platform. Skipping this step may create unexpected issues during the upgrade steps.

- *Binary relinking*: After the higher database software installation, verify the installation log. Ensure there are no errors. Binary integrity has to be ensured. Sometimes binary executables are damaged after installation or not properly linked with operating system libraries. To ensure the binary executables are in the right shape, perform the relinking. This re-creates the Oracle executables by linking them with the operating system libraries. There should not be any error in the relink output to guarantee binary. We will discuss this more in Chapter 2.

- *Prerequisite check*: Each upgrade method has its own prerequisites. Do not skip the prerequisite checks or you may get into unexpected issues during the upgrade. The DBA needs to address every prerequisite to ensure a successful upgrade.

- *Database sys/system objects*: These are part of the database dictionary. Make sure that all sys- and system-owned objects are valid. This can be verified through the dba_objects view. If any invalid objects are there, recompile those objects using utlrp.sql.

- *Database components*: Database components should be in a valid state with the correct database version. This can be verified using the dba_registry view.

```
SQL> select comp_name, version, status from dba_registry;
```

- If any component status is not valid, recompile/re-create that particular component by executing the appropriate SQL scripts.

- *Statistics collection*: Collect database dictionary statistics before and after a database upgrade, which will boost SQL execution performance.

- *Recommended patches*: Intermediate patches created for known bug fixes and PSUs can be applied on the target database version. This will help create an effective and bug-free upgrade process.

- *Application testing*: Before performing an upgrade in a production environment, test it in an alternate environment and ensure that the application is compatible with the target database version. Oracle has provided the feature Real Application Testing to test applications with the target database version in a real-time manner.

- *Review application manual*: Applications such as eBiz have specific requirements to apply some patches according to the database version. Apply the appropriate patches in the database home before proceeding with the upgrade.

Database Migration

Situations sometimes demand moving a database to a different environment for which you need to make changes in the current database. The change in environment might be moving to a different operating system or the same operating system with a different flavor, different hardware, different storage architecture, character set change, and so on. This process of moving to a different environment with the same or different attributes is called a *database migration*. This process usually occurs when moving a database to a different data center or when replacing existing hardware. Note that a migration can happen with or without a database upgrade.

Situations That Demand a Migration

These are situations where you will need to do a migration:

- *Storage migration*: The database is getting moved to different storage. For example, the database storage has been changed to ASM disk or file system.

- *Operating system migration*: The database-hosting operating system may require changes.

- *Hardware change*: You might need to migrate to different hardware such as moving Oracle on Linux to Oracle Exadata or a cloud environment.

- *Bit conversion*: This means changing database hosting operating system bit, like moving from Linux x86 (32-bit) to Linux x86-64 (64-bit).

- *Multitenant*: You can move the database to an Oracle 12*c* multitenant architecture to achieve better resource utilization, rapid cloning, rapid provisioning, and consolidation.

Things to Consider Before Migration

You will want to consider the following when doing a migration:

- *Backup*: This is the foremost activity. Before making any changes in the database, take a database backup.

- *Application compatibility*: How will the application react to the migrated database? Suppose an application may be 32-bit and the database now moves to a 64-bit architecture. What additional steps are required to continue the relationship?

- *Known issues in the new environment*: What are the known issues so far in the migrate environment for Oracle Database? If any known issues are there, what are the patches/workarounds available to solve them? In AIX, you could observe relink issues for Oracle databases. Patches are available to resolve that.

- *Character set*: When you migrate a database to a different character set, its compatibility needs to be checked.

- *Testing*: Before performing a migration to production, test it in an available test environment and ensure the data integrity.

What This Book Covers

Finally, what you can expect from this book?

This book will explain the database upgrade process and the available methods. It explains each upgrade method with detailed steps. As we always recommend upgrading to the latest version, most of the steps and examples in this book talk about upgrading to Oracle 12*c*; at the same time, we won't forget about intermediate upgrades. We will use the Enterprise edition for all upgrade scenarios.

We also discuss known issues and best practices to finish the upgrade in an effective manner.

You may wonder whether the upgrade process ever gets upgraded. The answer is yes. The upgrade process keeps getting improved with every release. Up to Oracle 11*g* R2, the Database Upgrade Assistant (DBUA) and manual upgrade process were going in a serial manner. In Oracle 12*c* there is the option to run the upgrade execution with parallel processes to improve the performance, reduce the downtime, and make use of CPU resources effectively. In Oracle 10*g* Data Pump was introduced. This is an enhanced version of the traditional export (exp)/import(imp). In Oracle 12*c* a new upgrade method called *full transportable export/ import* to upgrade an entire database was introduced. This method will support multitenant container databases and pluggable databases. An advantage of this method is it supports cross-platform upgrades.

Summary

This chapter introduced you to database upgrades and migrations and their necessity. It also explored the roles and responsibilities of the engineers involved in the upgrade process.

CHAPTER 2

■ ■ ■

Database Upgrade Methods

In Chapter 1, we discussed database upgrades and their benefits. In this chapter, you will explore all the available upgrade methods.

As part of the first step of an upgrade, you install the binaries for the higher database version. They can be installed on the same server or on a different server. Before performing any upgrade steps in the source database you need to make sure that the higher-version binaries are installed and are not physically corrupted because having inaccurate binaries can create issues during the upgrade. So, you'll spend a little time in this chapter to make sure that your target environment doesn't have any binary issues.

You may wonder what we mean by incorrect binaries or physical binary corruption. During the installation of any Oracle version on the Unix platform, first the installation binaries (delivered with software media) will be placed at installation location, and then relinking is performed. This relinking process creates executables by compiling the Oracle binary object files with the operating system (OS) libraries. If the linking between the Oracle software binaries and OS libraries was not done properly, then the executables will not be created appropriately. Also, if some executables in the Oracle Home are removed mistakenly or replaced by incorrect binaries, then the binaries will not be in good shape. The Windows software is delivered in the form of dynamic link libraries (DLLs), relinking does not come into the picture when using Windows.

Oracle Binary Relinking

On Linux/Unix platforms, the Oracle software is delivered in the form of object files that are compressed into archive files. These files will be linked, or compiled, with operating system libraries to generate executables. This linking process happens during the installation. You might have observed that many prerequisite OS packages are asked for during the installation. These packages deliver the required libraries for the Oracle relinking. If you ignore these packages, the installation will end up having relink issues.

Consider how the sewing machine works in Figure 2-1. It takes material and thread as inputs and creates the link between them; at the end, you get a wearable shirt as the output. Similarly, some Oracle software object files will be linked with operating system libraries to create executable Oracle binaries.

© Y V Ravikumar, K M Krishnakumar and Nassyam Basha 2017
N. Basha et al., *Oracle Database Upgrade and Migration Methods*, DOI 10.1007/978-1-4842-2328-4_2

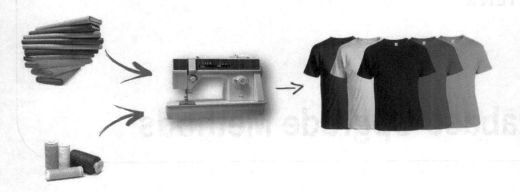

Figure 2-1. *Example of relinking process*

Suppose some necessary prerequisites are not met and you see a relinking error during installation. You don't need to stop or terminate the installation. You can do the relinking even after installation. In other words, you can ignore the error and allow the remaining installation process to complete. Later you can investigate the error and install the missing OS packages and then perform the relinking, which will re-create the executables in an appropriate manner.

The relinking process will compile the Oracle binaries with the OS libraries and generate the executables. If the relinking output is fine, then you can say that the executable binaries are in good shape. You can verify the relink log at `$ORACLE_HOME/install/relink.log`. It is advisable that you perform the relinking followed by a binary backup before making any changes in the Oracle Home.

Relinking Process

Set the environment variables properly to the required Oracle Home and then stop all the services of that Oracle Home including the databases, listener, Enterprise Manager (EM), and so on.

Invoke the `relink` command from the Oracle Home `bin` directory as the Oracle installation owner, as shown here:

```
$cd $ORACLE_HOME/bin
$pwd
/u01/app/oracle/product/11.2.0/bin
$ls -l relink

$./relink all
```

In Oracle 10*g* R2, when relinking, you have the option to relink all components or specific components such as `oracle`, `network`, `client`, `client_sharedlib`, `interMedia`, `ctx`, `precomp`, `utilities`, `oemagent`, `ldap`, `has`, `em`, and so on. In Oracle 11*g* R2, this list has been reduced to the options `all` and `as_installed`. This is because since 11*g* R2, all database options get installed by default and enabled as part of installation. A custom installation allows you to specify which options need to be enabled during installation.

The relinking process will regenerate the Oracle executables. Before replacing the existing executables, the process will rename them, as in `<Executable_name>0`. You may find some executables in the `bin` directory ending with 0. This denotes that relinking has been performed and these are the backup files.

As relinking is related to operating system libraries, when the operating system gets updated, the Oracle binary has to be relinked since the OS libraries would have been updated.

From Oracle 11*g* R2, relinking can be done through runInstaller as well.

```
cd $ORACLE_HOME/oui/bin
Syntax
./runInstaller : -relink -maketargetsxml <location of maketargetsxml> [-makedepsxml
<location of makedepsxml>] [name=value]
```

The order in which relinking has to be performed is listed in $ORACLE_HOME/inventory/make/makeorder.xml.

```
Eg:
oracle@localhost:/oradata$ cd /u01/app/oracle/product/12.1.0/dbhome_1/oui/bin
oracle@localhost:/u01/app/oracle/product/12.1.0/dbhome_1/oui/bin$ ./runInstaller -relink
-maketargetsxml $ORACLE_HOME/inventory/make/makeorder.xml -logLocation /u01/app/oracle/
product/12.1.0/dbhome_1/install/
Starting Oracle Universal Installer...
Checking swap space: must be greater than 500 MB.   Actual 4094 MB    Passed
Preparing to launch Oracle Universal Installer from /tmp/OraInstall2015-11-01_07-36-52AM.
Please wait ...oracle@localhost:/u01/app/oracle/product/12.1.0/dbhome_1/oui/bin$
```

Known Issues

In AIX you might see the following warnings:

```
ld: 0711-773, ld: 0711-783, ld: 0711-319, ld: 0711-415, lc: 0711-224,
ld: 0711-324, ld: 0711-301, ld: 0711-345.
```

These warnings are specific to the AIX platform and can be ignored.

Some of the Oracle binaries are owned by root. For example, the jssu and extjob files in $ORACLE_HOME/bin are owned by root.

Relinking regenerates Oracle executables with Oracle Home owner permissions. If any executables are expected to have different permissions, then they have to be changed manually after relinking. For example, since jssu and extjob are owned by root, after relinking the library permissions should be changed to root manually.

Database Upgrade Methods

Oracle has provided many methods to upgrade a database. During the upgrade, either the database dictionary is upgraded to a higher version or only the user and application data is moved from the lower-version database to the higher-version database. The following upgrade methods perform either one of these types of upgrades:

- The Database Upgrade Assistant (DBUA)

- Manual upgrade

- Export/import

- Data Pump

- Transportable tablespace (TTS)

- GoldenGate
- Create Table As Select (CTAS)
- Transient logical standby
- Full transportable export/import (12*c*)

We'll now discuss each method in detail.

The Database Upgrade Assistant

The DBUA is one of the most proficient tools provided by Oracle. DBUA is mostly used in industries to upgrade the database. This tool upgrades database dictionary along with user data to higher version. It is a GUI tool to perform the upgrade tasks automatically with multiple user-friendly options. It can also be invoked in silent mode.

The DBUA tool will get installed by default along with the database server software, and it will be located in $ORACLE_HOME/bin. It will be owned by the software installation owner; hence, the DBUA should be invoked only by the Oracle Home owner.

Make sure the Oracle environment variables are set to the right Oracle Home and invoke dbua.

```
$ cd $ORACLE_HOME/bin
[oracle@Server bin]$ ls -l dbua
-rwxr-xr-x. 1 oracle oinstall  dbua
[oracle@Server bin]$ ./dbua
```

Figure 2-2 shows the DBUA Welcome screen.

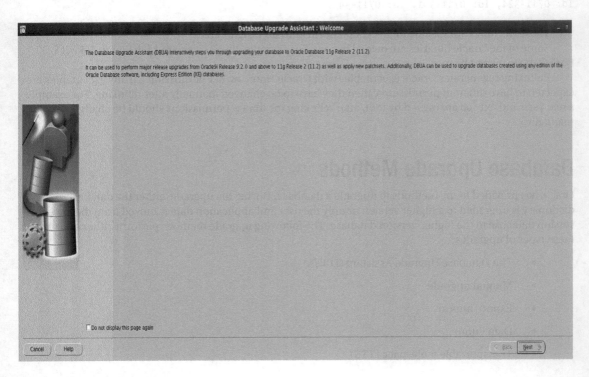

Figure 2-2. *DBUA Welcome screen*

Here are the features of DBUA:

- The GUI interface offers several options to perform an upgrade.

- The DBUA performs prerequisite checks at the beginning and provides the results and recommendations.

- All database components get upgraded at once.

- The DBUA will create the necessary tablespaces and schemas according to the higher version.

- The database time zone version also can be upgraded by the DBUA.

- It has option to take a database backup. In the background the DBUA invokes RMAN to take a backup. Using this backup, the DBUA can restore the database if any issues occur during the upgrade and you want to go back to the old version.

- The database files can be moved to a different location during the upgrade.

- The DBUA can be invoked in silent mode where the GUI interface is not possible.

- When using the DBUA, executing pre-upgrade scripts manually is optional.

- Fixup scripts before and after the upgrade are created by the DBUA in 12*c*.

- In 12*c*, the DBUA performs the upgrade in multiple phases with parallelism.

- The DBUA works for databases in any kind of environment such as Data Guard and RAC (from 9*i*).

Prerequisites for the DBUA

Because the whole database with the dictionary gets upgraded, version compatibility between the source and the target has to be checked before invoking the DBUA.

Upgrade Compatibility Matrix

Through the DBUA, a direct upgrade to 11g R2 version is possible to versions 9.2.0.8.0, 10.1.0.5.0, 10.2.0.2.0 and higher, and 11.1.0.6.0 and higher. Other database versions require intermediate upgrades, as shown in Table 2-1.

Table 2-1. *Upgrade Compatibility Matrix to 11g R2*

Source Database	Intermediate Upgrade	Target Database
7.3.3 (lower)	7.3.4 ➤ 9.2.0.8	11.2.x
8.0.5 (or lower)	8.0.6 ➤ 9.2.0.8	11.2.x
8.1.7 (or lower)	Source database version ➤ 8.1.7.4 ➤ (10.2.0.2 or higher) or Source database version ➤ 9.2.0.8.0	11.2.x
9.0.1.3 (or lower)	Source database version ➤ 9.0.1.4 and higher ➤ (10.2.0.2 or higher) or Source database version ➤ 9.2.0.8.0	11.2.x
9.2.0.7 (or lower)	Source database version ➤ (10.2.0.2 or higher) Or Source database version ➤ 9.2.0.8.0	11.2.x
10.2.0.1.0	10.2.0.1.0 ➤ 10.2.0.2.0	11.2.x

For a direct upgrade to a 12c version, the source database version should be either 10.2.0.5.x or 11.1.0.7.x or 11.2.0.2.x and higher. Other database versions require an intermediate upgrade to reach 12c, as shown in Table 2-2.

Table 2-2. *Upgrade Compatibility Matrix to 12c*

Source Database	Intermediate Upgrade	Target Database
7.3.3 (lower)	7.3.4 ➤ 9.2.0.8 ➤ 10.2.0.5	12.1.x
8.0.5 (or lower)	8.0.6 ➤ 9.2.0.8 ➤ 10.2.0.5	12.1.x
8.1.7 (or lower)	8.1.7.4 ➤ 10.2.0.5	12.1.x
9.0.1.3 (or lower)	9.0.1.4 ➤ 10.2.0.5	12.1.x
9.2.0.7 (or lower)	10.2.0.5	12.1.x
10.2.0.4 (or lower)	10.2.0.5	12.1.x
11.1.0.6	11.1.0.7	12.1.x
11.2.0.1	11.2.0.2 or higher	12.1.x

Pre-upgrade Checks

Before invoking the DBUA, you should perform the following pre-upgrade checks. This will help you avoid unexpected issues during the upgrade.

✓   Install the target database version on the certified platform. Ensure the binaries are in good shape by performing binary relinking.

✓   The DBUA is a GUI tool, so if the DBUA is invoked from a remote server, then the display variable has to be set properly in Unix environments to redirect the GUI interface. The DBUA has also the option to operate in silent mode.

✓   The DBUA should be invoked by the Oracle Home owner.

✓   The source database should be accessible by the DBUA to perform the pre-upgrade checks. This means the DBUA can perform an upgrade only when the source and target Oracle Homes are on the same server.

✓   Since the DBUA will access the source database to validate the prerequisite upgrade checks, you should have the source and target Oracle Home owned by the same operating system user. That will also allow the DBUA to start the source database if it is down. If both are owned by different users, then you may get the error PRKH-1014, "Current user <user> is not the same as owner <owner> of oracle home." If it is a must that the source and the target should be owned by different owners, then grant the appropriate permission to the Oracle datafiles so that they will be read and writable by both the users. In one way, it can be done by making the same primary group for both the owners and that primary group will be having read-write permission on the datafiles. Specify the log directory while invoking the DBUA as follows: dbua -logdir <directory>. This directory should have permission for both the owners.

✓   For the "datafile move" option, as part of the upgrade (without OMF), the DBUA will accept only one target location. Hence, make sure that the source database doesn't have the same datafile name in a different location. Having it like that will generate an error during the upgrade.

✓   If you are upgrading the 9*i* database, ensure there is no tablespace named SYSAUX. It should be created only in the 10*g* version. If you have tablespace already by the name of SYSAUX in 9*i*, then you will get an error message during upgrade, as shown in Figure 2-3.

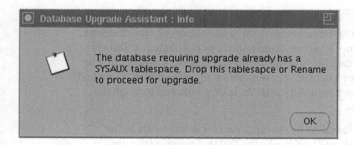

Figure 2-3. DBUA message for SYSAUX tablespace presence

✓ Make sure there are no datafiles that require recovery or that are in backup mode.

✓ Disable cron jobs that may get executed during the upgrade window.

✓ Ensure the SYS and SYSTEM schema default tablespace is SYSTEM.

✓ The DBUA reads the oratab file to get the list of databases installed on the server. This file should have the proper permission.

✓ The time zone version of the target Oracle Home should have a higher or equivalent time zone version of the source database.

Activities Performed by the DBUA

Here are some of the manifest activities performed by the DBUA:

✓ *Collect existing database details*: The DBUA will read the oratab file and get the list of existing installed databases on this server. Up to 11g R2, the DBUA lists all databases along with their versions. In 12c R1, it collects the Oracle database details along with their status and kind of instance.

✓ *Execute prerequisites*: The DBUA will execute the prerequisite script on the source database. If the source database is not active, it will start the database, execute the script, and display the results.

✓ *Collect the component details*: Collect the details of all database components that require an upgrade. Deprecated components will not get upgraded.

✓ *Back up*: The DBUA can take a database cold backup. The 11g R2 DBUA takes a backup image copy, and the 12c R1 DBUA takes a backup as the backup set.

✓ *Upgrade*: It will invoke the appropriate upgrade script based on the source database version. If there are any errors and it is not able to proceed upgrade, it will provide options to roll back the upgrade changes.

Best Practices with the DBUA

Though the DBUA will perform all the upgrade tasks automatically, it is better to complete some potential DBUA tasks manually before invoking the tool. Remember, when the DBUA is invoked, the database downtime starts. So, completing certain possible tasks before invoking the DBUA will reduce its workload and decrease the downtime.

Here are the possible tasks to do in advance:

✓ *Back up*: Taking a backup is the first step before making any changes in the database. Take a complete database backup. It can be a cold backup or hot backup or RMAN backup. The backup should be capable of restoring the database to a valid state. The DBUA also has the option to take a backup. But remember, once the DBUA is invoked and starts the upgrade steps, the downtime starts. So, taking a backup through the DBUA will add more downtime.

✓ *Execute the pre-upgrade script*: Execute any pre-upgrade scripts manually in the source database even though this will be done by the DBUA. Executing the pre-upgrade scripts in advance followed by the required corrective actions will help the DBUA to pass the pre-upgrade step easily.

✓ The pre-upgrade script can be executed multiple times. Evaluate the pre-upgrade script execution results. Resolve warnings and errors. Implement the recommended changes. When the DBUA invokes the pre-upgrade script, you will get error-free output.

✓ In 11*g* R2, the pre-upgrade script is $ORACLE_HOME/rdbms/admin/utlu112i.sql.

✓ In 12*c* R1, the pre-upgrade script is $ORACLE_HOME/rdbms/admin/preupgrd.sql. Preupgrade.sql will call utluppkg.sql internally to create SQL packages in the source database, which collects database information and produces log files if you want to execute preupgrd.sql from a different location and then copy utluppkg.sql along with preupgrd.sql.

✓ Some portion of the pre-upgrade output is shown here. More details are covered in the "Database Manual Upgrade" section.

```
Oracle Database Pre-Upgrade Information Tool 01-23-2016 08:48:56
Script Version: 12.1.0.2.0 Build: 006
**********************************************************************
  Database Name:  PRIM
  Container Name:  Not Applicable in Pre-12.1 database
  Container ID:  Not Applicable in Pre-12.1 database
  Version:  11.2.0.3.0
  Compatible:  11.2.0.0.0
  Blocksize:  8192
  Platform:  Linux x86 64-bit
   Timezone file:  V14
**********************************************************************
**********************************************************************
                         [Component List]
**********************************************************************
--> Oracle Catalog Views                 [upgrade]  VALID
--> Oracle Packages and Types            [upgrade]  VALID
--> JServer JAVA Virtual Machine         [upgrade]  VALID
--> Oracle XDK for Java                  [upgrade]  VALID
--> Oracle Workspace Manager             [upgrade]  VALID
--> OLAP Analytic Workspace              [upgrade]  VALID
--> Oracle Enterprise Manager Repository [upgrade]  VALID
--> Oracle Text                          [upgrade]  VALID
--> Oracle XML Database                  [upgrade]  VALID
--> Oracle Java Packages                 [upgrade]  VALID
--> Oracle Multimedia                    [upgrade]  VALID
--> Oracle Spatial                       [upgrade]  VALID
--> Expression Filter                    [upgrade]  VALID
--> Rule Manager                         [upgrade]  VALID
--> Oracle Application Express           [upgrade]  VALID
--> Oracle OLAP API                      [upgrade]  VALID
```

✓ Collect dictionary statistics in the source database before invoking the DBUA.

✓ Before starting the upgrade, make the nonadministrative tablespaces read-only so that in the fallback plan you need to restore only the SYSTEM, SYSAUX, and UNDO tablespaces.

✓ If possible, put the database into noarchivelog mode. This will reduce the required storage. This option is not applicable to a transient logical standby upgrade, which you'll see in the "2.6" section.

Upgrade Steps

We'll first discuss the 11g R2 DBUA, and later you will see the new features and improvisations released in the 12c release.

Set the environment variables ORACLE_HOME and PATH to the 11g R2 Oracle Home. Some additional environment variables declaration could be required, but they are specific to your operating system. Invoke dbua from the $ORACLE_HOME/bin directory.

```
$cd $ORACLE_HOME/bin (on windows %ORACLE_HOME%/bin)
$dbua
For Windows
Move to directory %ORACLE_HOME%\bin directory
Double click on 'DBUA' file.
```

As shown in Figure 2-4, this page allows you to choose the Oracle database for upgrade.

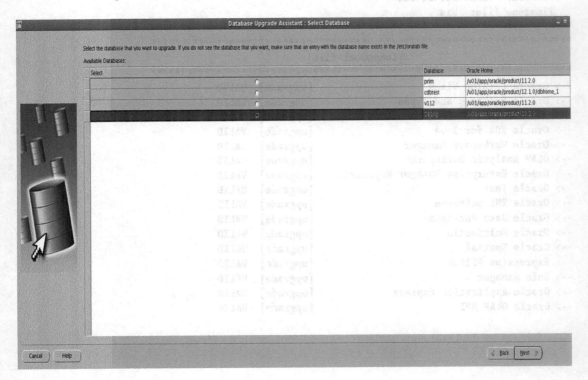

Figure 2-4. *DBUA, database selection page*

The DBUA reads the oratab file at the default location to show a list of Oracle databases available in this Oracle Home. Its default location in Solaris is /var/opt/oracle, in Linux is /etc, and in Windows is HKEY_LOCAL_MACHINE\systems\CurrentControlset\Services\Oracleservice<SID>.

It will show all the databases installed on the server along with its Oracle Home.

If it doesn't display databases, it means oratab doesn't exist, it doesn't have the proper permission, or the database entry is missing in the oratab file.

Clicking Next will collect the database information and perform a prerequisite check, as shown in Figure 2-5.

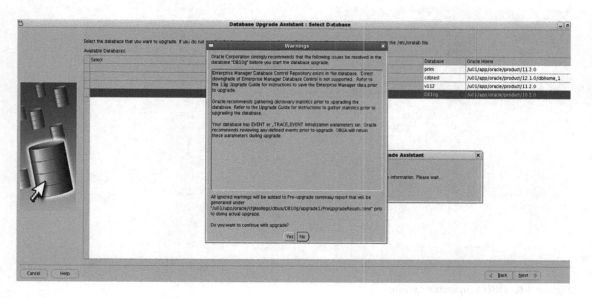

Figure 2-5. *DBUA, pre-upgrade results*

The DBUA will perform the prerequisite checks at the source database. In case the source database is down, then it will start the source database and execute an XML version of the pre-upgrade script utlu112x.sql.

If there are any errors, they will be displayed here.

When the pre-upgrade script is executed, a directory will be created to store the DBUA logs at $ORACLE_BASE/cfgtoollogs/dbua/$ORACLE_SID/upgrade<n>, where n denotes the number of upgrade attempts done for that database. If you get any issue in the DBUA steps, refer to the file trace.log available in this folder. Pre-upgrade execution also creates a results file called Pre-upgradeResults.html file and a log file called Pre-upgrade.log.

Existing database schema names will be recorded in Pre-upgrade.log, and this information will be used to lock new users created during the upgrade.

In Figure 2-6 you can see the DBUA upgrade options. The DBUA has the option to recompile objects at the end of the upgrade, disable archiving, and do a time zone upgrade.

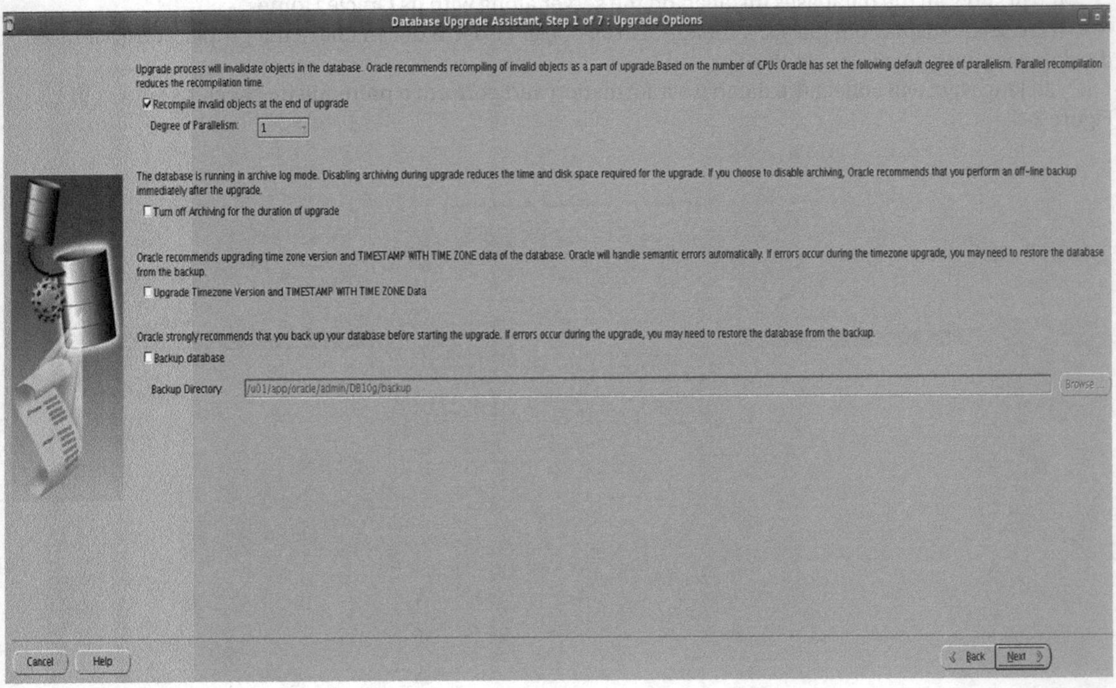

Figure 2-6. *DBUA, upgrade options*

An option is available to turn off archive logging, which will avoid the need to store the required archive logs. The database will be changed to noarchivelog mode before the upgrade starts and reverted to archivelog mode after the upgrade. You have other functionality too:

- *Recompile invalid objects at the end of upgrade*: During the upgrade some SYS- and SYSTEM-owned objects might have become invalid, which could affect dependent database components. Recompiling invalid objects will validate those SYS objects.

- *Upgrade time zone data*: Each database release carries updates to handle time zone data; each database release will have its own time zone version. So, when the database gets upgraded, its time zone version also has to be upgraded. The DBUA can upgrade the time zone while doing the upgrade. Before 11*g* R2, it was expected that you would upgrade the time zone version of the source database before the upgrade. Later, the provision was given to upgrade the time zone after the database upgrade. By default, the 11*g* R2 Oracle Home has time zone version 14. If the source database has a time zone version less than 14, then it needs to be upgraded. It can be also done later manually, but the DBUA automates the process. Remember, if the source database Oracle Home has a time zone version higher than 14, then the same time zone version should be installed at the 11*g* R2 Oracle Home.

The DBUA also has the option to back up the database. This is a cold backup. The DBUA will shut down the database and copy the datafiles, control files, and redo logs to the backup folder. This creates SQL scripts for shutdown, startup, and restore.

Sample Restore Script

The following restore script is created while taking a backup for the 10*g* database:

```
ORACLE_HOME=/u01/app/oracle/product/11.2.0; export ORACLE_HOME
ORACLE_SID=DB10g; export ORACLE_SID
/u01/app/oracle/product/11.2.0/bin/sqlplus /nolog @/oradata/DB10g/backup/shutdown_DB10g.sql
echo You should Remove this entry from the /etc/oratab: DB10g:/u01/app/oracle/product/11.2.0:Y
echo -- Copying Datafiles....
/bin/cp /oradata/DB10g/backup/redo01.log /oradata/DB10g/redo01.log
/bin/cp /oradata/DB10g/backup/redo02.log /oradata/DB10g/redo02.log
/bin/cp /oradata/DB10g/backup/redo03.log /oradata/DB10g/redo03.log
/bin/cp /oradata/DB10g/backup/sysaux01.dbf /oradata/DB10g/sysaux01.dbf
/bin/cp /oradata/DB10g/backup/system01.dbf /oradata/DB10g/system01.dbf
/bin/cp /oradata/DB10g/backup/temp01.dbf /oradata/DB10g/temp01.dbf
/bin/cp /oradata/DB10g/backup/undotbs01.dbf /oradata/DB10g/undotbs01.dbf
/bin/cp /oradata/DB10g/backup/users01.dbf /oradata/D310g/users01.dbf
/bin/cp /oradata/DB10g/backup/control01.ctl /oradata/DB10g/control01.ctl
/bin/cp /oradata/DB10g/backup/control02.ctl /oradata/DB10g/control02.ctl
/bin/cp /oradata/DB10g/backup/control03.ctl /oradata/DB10g/control03.ctl
echo -- Bringing up the database from the source oracle home
ORACLE_HOME=/u01/app/oracle/product/10.2.0; export ORACLE_HOME
ORACLE_SID=DB10g; export ORACLE_SID
unset LD_LIBRARY_PATH; unset LD_LIBRARY_PATH_64; unset SHLIB_PATH; unset LIB_PATH
echo You should Add this entry in the /etc/oratab: DB10g:/u01/app/oracle/product/10.2.0:Y
cd /u01/app/oracle/product/10.2.0
/u01/app/oracle/product/10.2.0/bin/sqlplus /nolog @/oradata/DB10g/backup/startup_DB10g.sql
```

During the restore, the datafiles will be moved from the backup location to the original location, and the startup script will be fired. You can notice /bin/cp is called to restore files to the old location. This cp executable should exist at the /bin directory or the restore will not happen. In Windows, services need to be re-created to point to the correct Oracle Home manually.

As shown in Figure 2-7, the DBUA provides the option to move datafiles as part of the upgrade. The destination location might be a file system or ASM. This option helps if you want to move datafiles to a new location as part of the upgrade process. In the upgrade process, this movement activity will happen at the end of the upgrade. Once the database components are upgraded, in the post-upgrade process, the control file and datafiles will be moved to the new location.

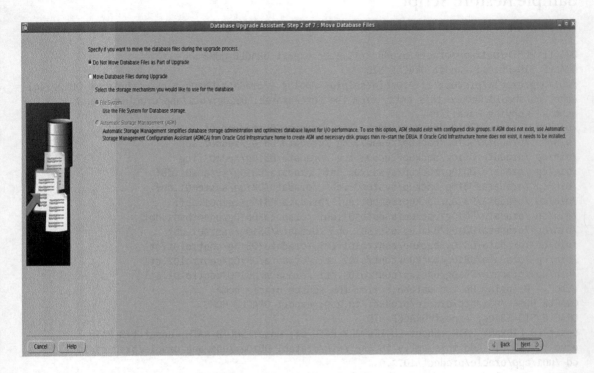

Figure 2-7. *DBUA, moving database files during upgrade*

If you choose to move the database files, then the next screen will look like Figure 2-8.

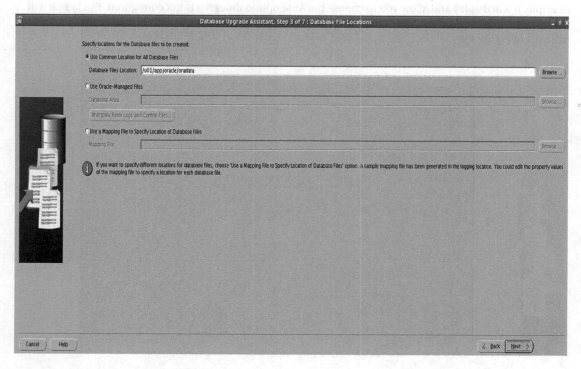

Figure 2-8. *DBUA, database file locations*

Internally the DBUA calls the database package dbms_backup_restore, which has the functions Copycontrolfile and Copydatafile. Through that, files will be copied to the new location, and old files will be removed. The new location can be common for all datafiles, or mapping can be done to each datafile. While choosing the common location, remember there should not be datafiles with the same name in different locations. Having the same name will raise errors. OMF naming conventions also can be used to specify the new location. The Dbms_backup_restore.getOMFFileName procedure will be used to move the datafiles to a new location with the OMF format.

The DBUA generates these SQL files to perform this activity: rmanCopyControlFile.sql, rmanCopyDatafile.sql, and rmanSwitchDatafile.sql. The output will be stored in RmanCopy.log.

In the DBUA, the listed options are static. You need to choose options based on your environment. For example, it will display and allow you to choose the ASM option though it is not configured. But later it will throw an error saying that the DBUA is not able to connect to the ASM instance. You could see the error message in Figure 2-9.

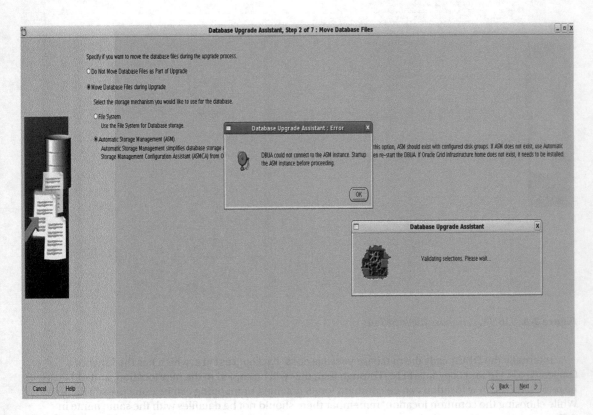

Figure 2-9. *DBUA, error message for ASM instance*

The DBUA allows you to change or define the Fast Recovery Area location, which is shown in Figure 2-10.

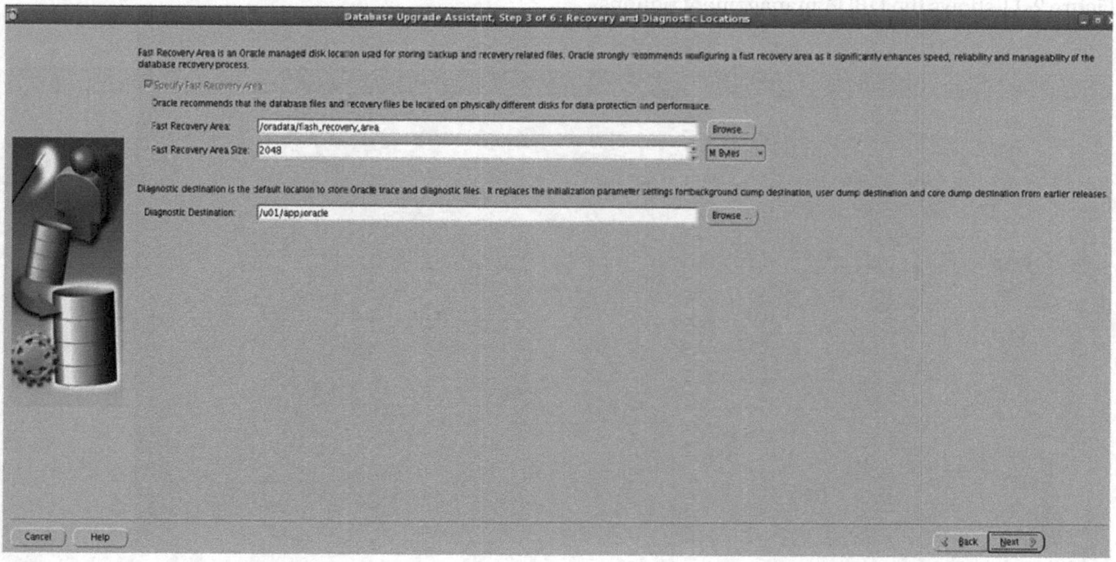

Figure 2-10. *DBUA, recovery and diagnostic locations*

For EM configuration, the DBUA provides the option to make this upgraded database be part of EM Grid Control or EM Database Console. The database can be monitored and managed using one of these. Figure 2-11 shows the DBUA management options.

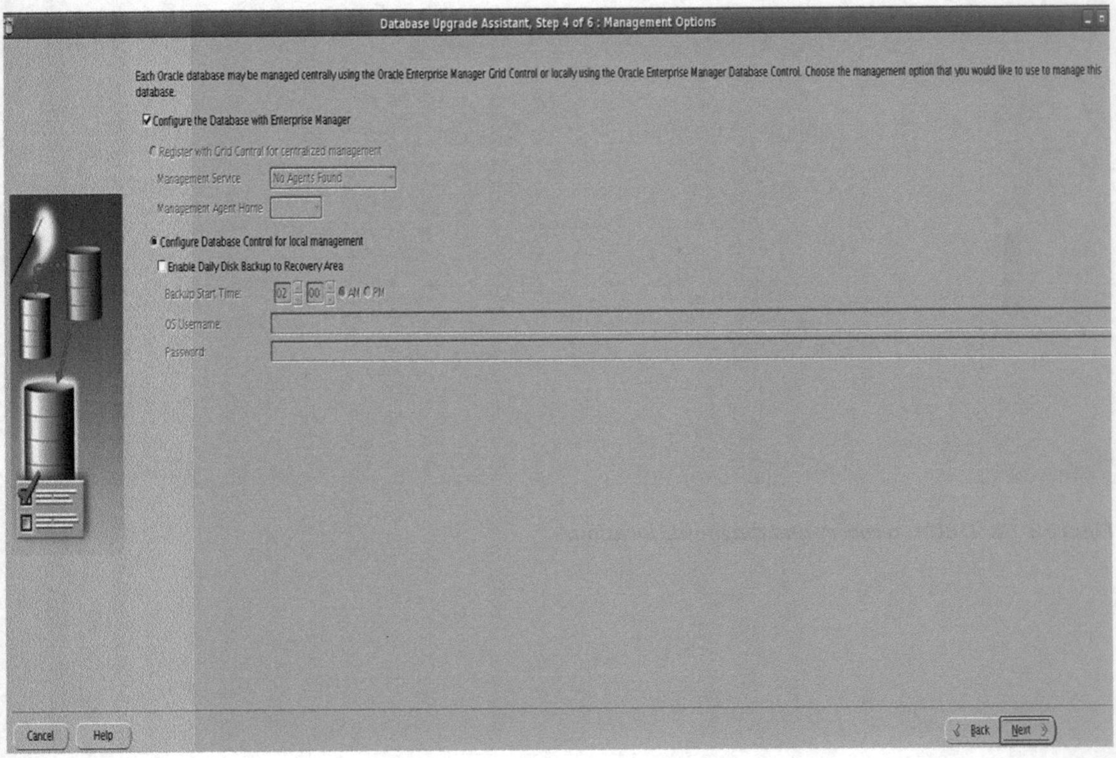

Figure 2-11. *DBUA, management options*

The next screen shows the database upgrade summary page, as shown in Figure 2-12 and Figure 2-13.

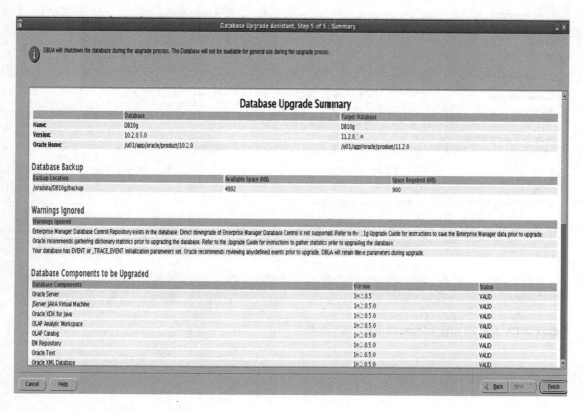

Figure 2-12. *DBUA, upgrade summary*

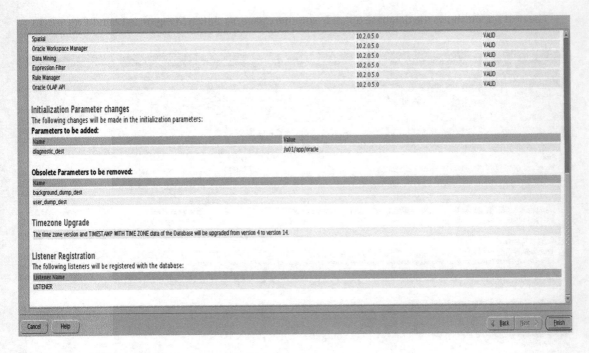

Figure 2-13. *DBUA, upgrade summary, continued*

Clicking the Finish button will start the database upgrade (Figure 2-14).

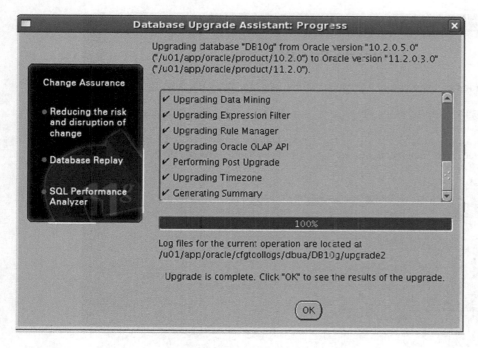

Figure 2-14. *DBUA, finishing the pgrade progress*

After all the upgrade steps are complete, click OK to see the upgrade results, as shown in Figure 2-15.

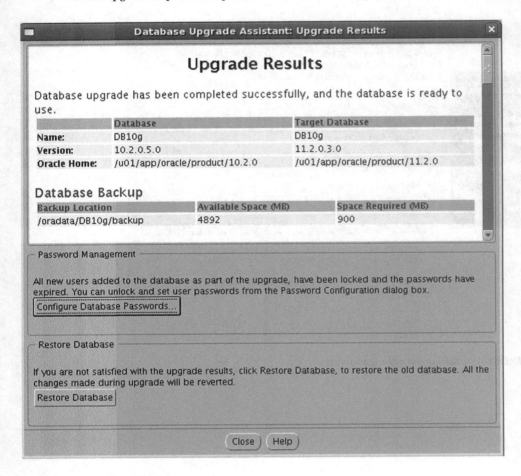

Figure 2-15. *DBUA, upgrade results*

If you plan to go back to an old version, click Restore Database (Figure 2-16). This will restore the cold backup taken by the DBUA and start the database in the old Oracle Home. If the backup is not taken through the DBUA, then you need to manually restore the backup. The DBUA only rolls back the changes made in config files like /etc/oratab. You will see the Restore Settings Only button.

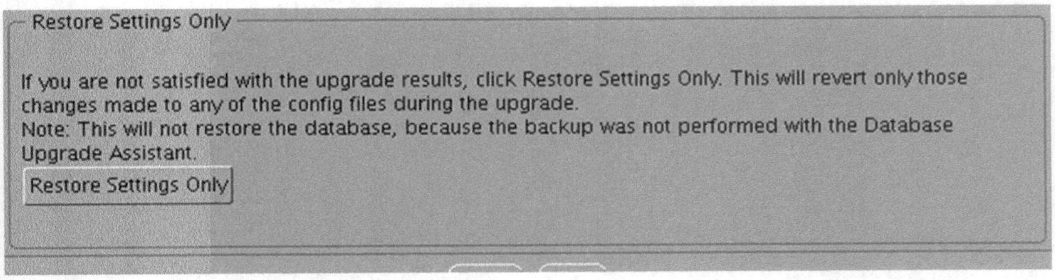

Figure 2-16. *DBUA, restore settings*

Table 2-3 lists all the DBUA logs. All the database component upgrade details will be stored in Oracle_Server.log.

Table 2-3. *DBUA Logs*

STEP NAME	LOG FILE NAME
PRE-UPGRADE	Backup.log
ORACLE SERVER	Oracle_Server.log
JSERVER JAVA VIRTUAL MACHINE	Oracle_Server.log
ORACLE XDK FOR JAVA	Oracle_Server.log
OLAP ANALYTIC WORKSPACE	Oracle_Server.log
OLAP CATALOG	Oracle_Server.log
EM REPOSITORY	Oracle_Server.log
ORACLE TEXT	Oracle_Server.log
ORACLE XML DATABASE	Oracle_Server.log
ORACLE JAVA PACKAGES	Oracle_Server.log
ORACLE INTERMEDIA	Oracle_Server.log
SPATIAL	Oracle_Server.log
ORACLE WORKSPACE MANAGER	Oracle_Server.log
DATA MINING	Oracle_Server.log
EXPRESSION FILTER	Oracle_Server.log
RULE MANAGER	Oracle_Server.log
ORACLE OLAP API	Oracle_Server.log
COLLECTING INFORMATION FROM DATABASE	CloneDataGatheringStep.log
MODIFYING & SHARING ORACLE INSTANCE	CloneInstanceStep.log
COPYING DATABASE FILES	CloneRmanCopyStep.log
SWITCHING DATABASE FILES	CloneDatabaseSwitchStep.log
POST UPGRADE	PostUpgrade.log
TIMEZONE UPGRADE	UpgradeTimezone.log
GENERATE SUMMARY	generateSummary.log

12c DBUA New Features

In 12c, the DBUA tool has been enhanced to include many useful options (see Figure 2-17).

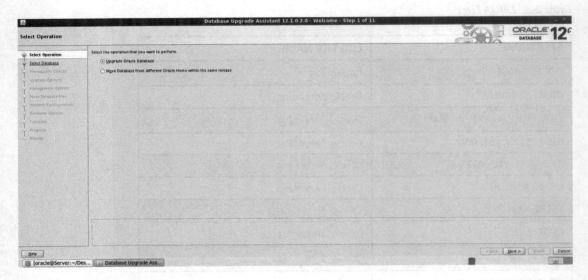

Figure 2-17. . DBUA, initial screen

As shown in Figure 2-17, DBUA 12c will have two options on the first screen.

> *Upgrade Oracle Database*: A lower-version database can be upgraded to the 12c version. The upgrade compatibility matrix is applicable to the source database. If the 12c Oracle software is the Enterprise Edition, then the source database can be either from the Standard Edition or from the Enterprise Edition. If the source database is in Standard Edition, it will automatically be converted to the Enterprise Edition as part of the upgrade. If the 12c Oracle software is Standard Edition 2, then the source Oracle Home should be from Standard Edition. Remember to move the Enterprise Edition to the Standard Edition, the only option is export/import.

> *Move Database from different Oracle Home with the same release*: This option is to move the 12c Oracle database from another Oracle Home to the current Oracle Home. Moving from the 12c Standard Edition to the Enterprise Edition can be done. This is a new option provided in 12c.

The next page (Figure 2-18) gives you the option of choosing the Oracle database for upgrade.

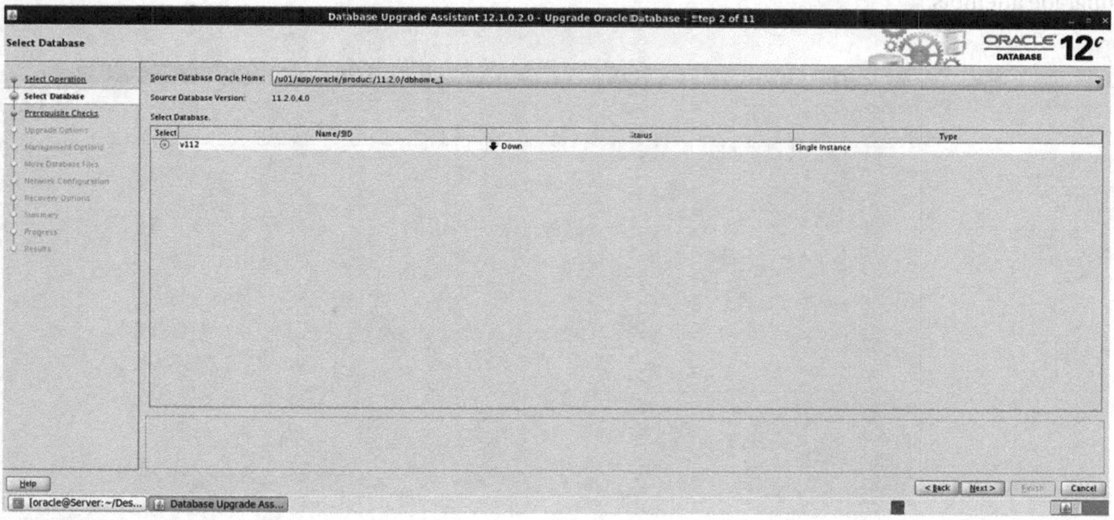

Figure 2-18. *DBUA, database selection*

Here the listing of Oracle databases is improved. The source database Oracle Home drop-down list shows a list of the Oracle Homes available on this server. Once the Oracle Home is chosen, it lists all the databases available in that Oracle Home along with their status.

When the pre-upgrade script is executed (Figure 2-19), the directory will be created to store the DBUA logs called $ORACLE_BASE/cfgtoollogs/dbua/$ORACLE_SID/upgrade<n>, where n denotes the number of upgrade attempts.

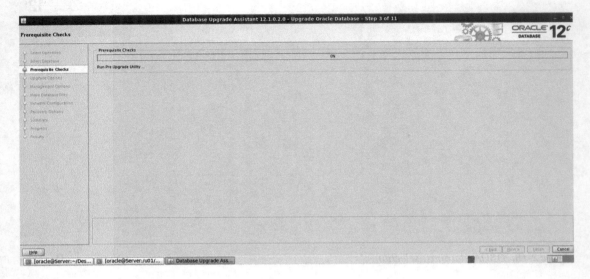

Figure 2-19. *DBUA, pre-upgrade execution*

The DBUA will perform a prerequisite check at the source database.

If the source database is down, it will start the source database and execute the pre-upgrade script Pre-upgrade.sql (Figure 2-20). It displays the validation results and its severity. This page has a Check Again button to execute the prerequisite check again. Unlike 11g R2, here a separate pre-upgrade script for the DBUA is not available. Preupgrd.sql will be executed with the argument XML.

Here are some of the prerequisite checks:

- ➢ Source and target database version.

- ➢ Available free space of tablespaces SYSTEM, SYSAUX, UNDO, and the temp tablespace. These tablespaces will extend during upgrade. Also, the mount point of these tablespaces will be verified.

- ➢ Enabled database options in the chosen database.

- ➢ Supported upgrade version check.

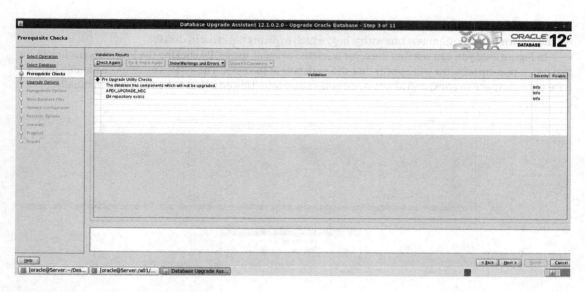

Figure 2-20. *DBUA, pre-upgrade results*

A prerequisite check analyzes the database, and the results will be either information or an error.

Information will be for user observation, and if any actions are required, then that will be taken care of by the DBUA. To get the details of informational messages, click Info.

The message in Figure 2-21 shows information about the EM database control repository, which is deprecated in 12*c*, and hence it will be removed as part of the upgrade. There are no manual actions required. But if it is removed manually prior to the upgrade, you can save downtime. This window also shows steps for removing the EM repository.

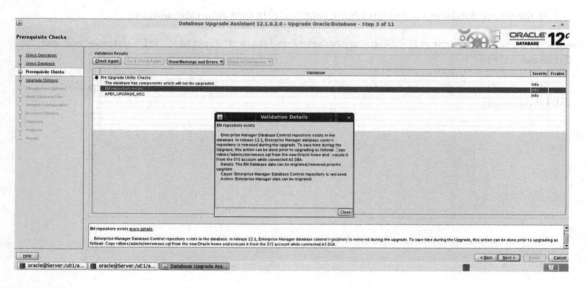

Figure 2-21. *DBUA, pre-upgrade validation results*

An error mostly requires manual attention. To get the details of the error, click that error, and the details will be shown in the bottom text box with a link, which explains the error in detail.

In Figure 2-22 you can see that the error is related to space usage. By clicking the More Details link in the text box, a pop-up window will appear that shows details of the error. The system tablespace datafile doesn't have enough space to grow, and also it is not auto-extensible. This error has to be corrected manually.

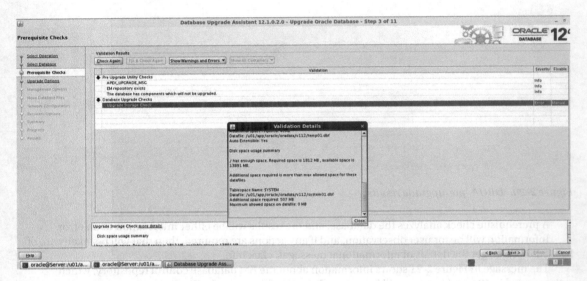

Figure 2-22. *DBUA, pre-upgrade validation (error) details*

In the source database, either increase the datafile size or turn auto-extensible on.

```
SQL> alter database datafile '/u01/app/oracle/oradata/v112/system01.dbf' autoexetend on;
Database altered
```

Click the Check Again button and see whether the error has disappeared from the prerequisite validation results.

The error message disappeared (Figure 2-23) after revalidating the prerequisite checks. The database is good to go to the next step.

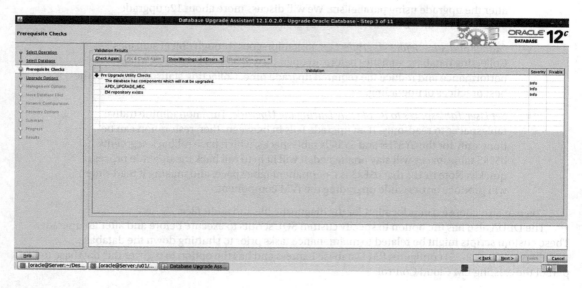

Figure 2-23. *DBUA, pre-upgrade results*

Figure 2-24 shows the Upgrade Options page, which lists some best practices.

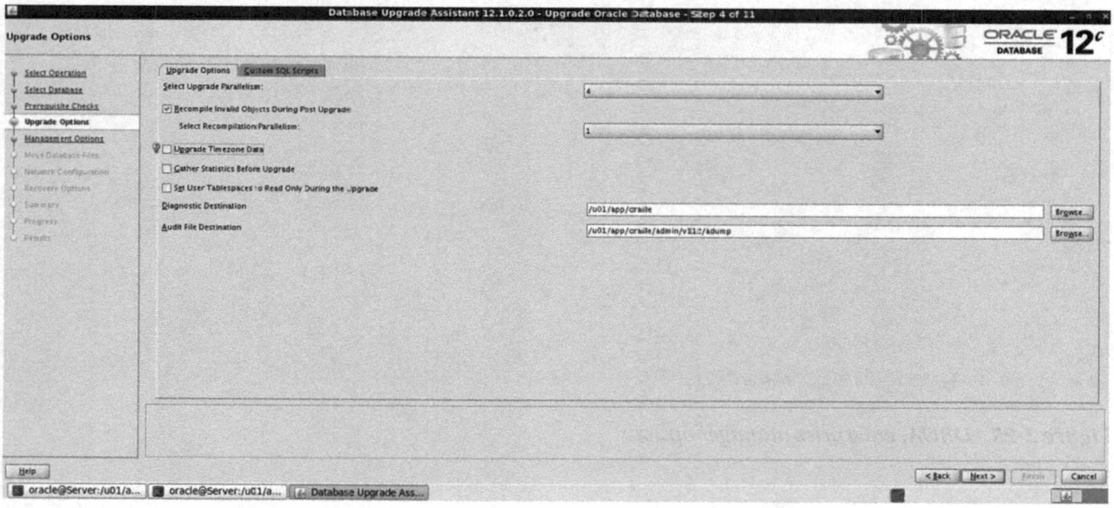

Figure 2-24. *DBUA best practices*

Here are the relevant options:

- *Recompile Invalid Objects During Post Upgrade*: You can recompile invalid objects after the upgrade using parallelism. We will discuss more about 12*c* upgrade parallelism in the "Database Manual Upgrade" section.

- *Gather Statistics Before Upgrade*: SQL execution goes through object statistics. Collecting database statistics before an upgrade will help to boost execution performance and reduce the required upgrade time. Collecting statistics is one of the best practices of upgrading.

- *Set User Tablespaces to Read Only During the Upgrade*: Turn nonadministrative tablespaces to read-only. If an upgrade fails in between, then restoration can be done only for the SYSTEM and SYSAUX tablespaces, which have rollback segments. USERS tablespaces will stay unaffected. It will help to roll back the upgrade process quickly. Note in 12*c* that USERS is a permanent tablespace, and making it read-only will produce errors while upgrading the JVM component.

You can also choose a new location for the diagnostic file and audit files.

The DBUA also has the option to specify custom SQL scripts to execute before and after an upgrade. These custom scripts might be related to maintenance tasks prior to shutting down the database.

Step 5 (Figure 2-25) configures EM Database Express and has the option to register this database to be part of the existing EM Cloud Control.

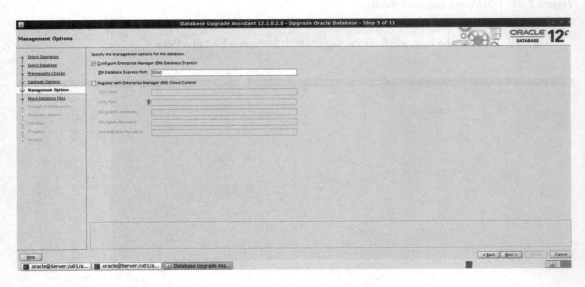

Figure 2-25. *DBUA, enterprise manager options*

Step 6 (Figure 2-26) talks about the additional options available as part of the upgrade.

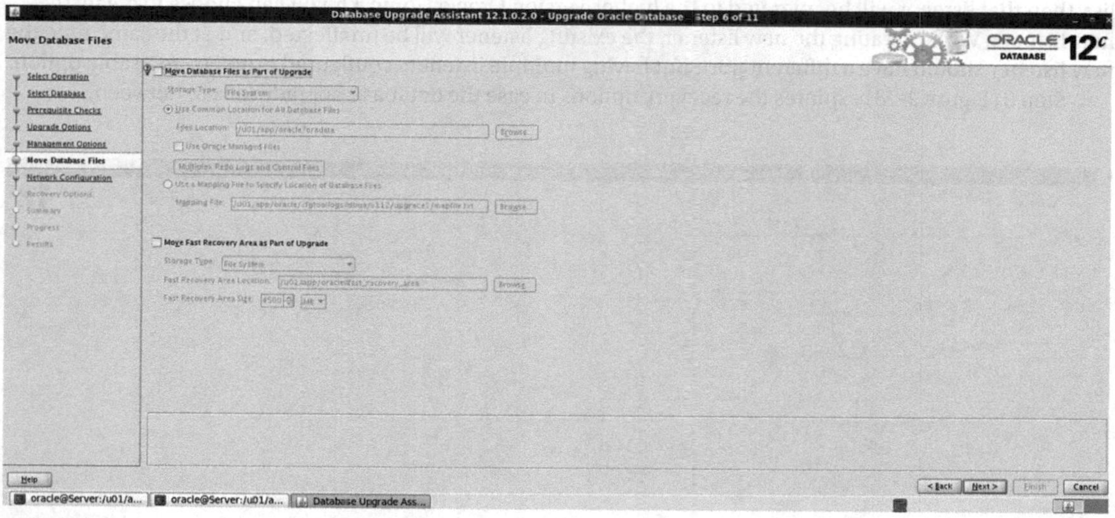

Figure 2-26. *DBUA, upgrade options*

Move Datafiles as Part of Upgrade

Like 11*g* DBUA, it invokes the `dbms_backup_restore` package to move datafiles to a new location. But while choosing a common location, remember there should not be datafiles with the same name in a different location, which may overwrite datafiles.

Step 7 (Figure 2-27) talks about network configuration.

Figure 2-27. *DBUA, listener configuration*

This is a new feature in DBUA 12*c*. It lists the existing listeners and their status. It gives you the option to choose the desired listener for the upgraded database. If the source Oracle Home listener is chosen from the list, then that listener will be migrated to the higher-version Oracle Home. Or you can choose to create the new listener. While creating the new listener, the existing listener will be unaffected, and at the same time the new listener should have a different port. But having multiple listeners configured is not an advisable option.

Step 8 (Figure 2-28) explores the recovery options in case the database upgrade fails in between.

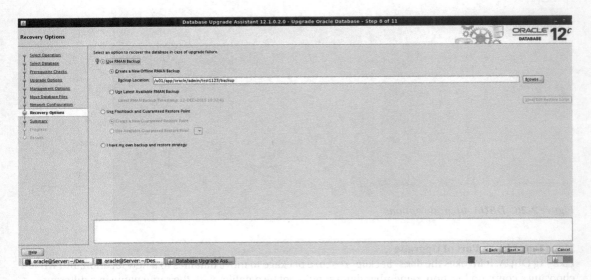

Figure 2-28. *DBUA, recovery options*

Remember in the DBUA method if the upgrade fails, there is no alternate way to restart. You have to start the upgrade again after restoring the source database backup. It is also not possible to upgrade a DBUA failed database. On this screen, the DBUA provides options to restore the database to the old state.

The DBUA is integrated with RMAN to provide the recovery option.

Create a New Offline RMAN Backup
A new RMAN backup will be taken by the DBUA before starting the upgrade. The backup location can be chosen, and this backup will be taken as the RMAN backup set. This backup will be used to restore if the DBUA fails during the upgrade. If the backup is already available, RMAN has the option to choose that as well for recovery. A check box is available to choose the latest available RMAN backup. The DBUA reads the control file and retrieves the backup piece of information.

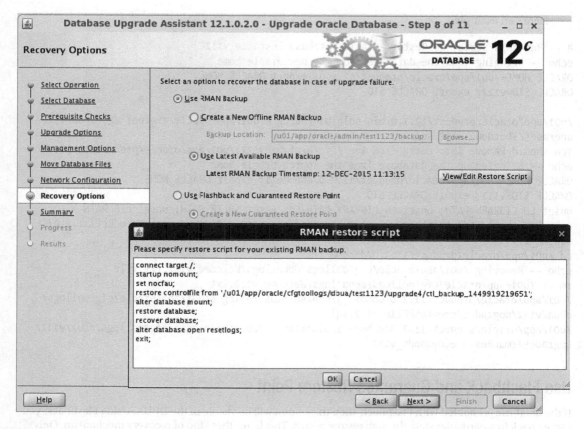

Figure 2-29. *. DBUA, RMAN restore script*

If you want to use a different RMAN backup, click View/Edit Restore Point. The RMAN restore script will be visible in a text box, and you can make changes here. The control file will be backed up before starting the upgrade, which will have the information about the latest backup. Remember, you need to ensure that a sufficient backup is available to do the restore. The DBUA will not validate the backup or check the availability of the archived log backup to restore. The DBUA copies the latest control file to $ORACLE_HOME/cfgtoollogs/dbua/<$ORACLE_SID>/upgrade<n>. The control file will have all the backup information. Using that database can be restored. If you want to edit the script, that is possible. You can place your own restore script there.

During the upgrade, the DBUA will create the file rmanRestoreCommands_<$ORACLE_SID>. It will have the edited script, and it will be used for recovery purposes. But remember in any case the control file will be backed up at $ORACLE_HOME/cfgtoollogs/dbua/<$ORACLE_SID>/upgrade<n>.

For the restore, the DBUA will call <$ORACLE_SID>_restore.sh, which will create the environment settings and call the RMAN restore command.

Here's an example:

```
# -- Run this Script to Restore Oracle Database Instance v112
echo -- Bringing down the database from the new oracle home
ORACLE_HOME=/u01/app/oracle/product/12.1.0; export ORACLE_HOME
ORACLE_SID=v112; export ORACLE_SID

/u01/app/oracle/product/12.1.0/bin/sqlplus /nolog @/u01/app/oracle/cfgtoollogs/dbua/v112/
upgrade5/shutdown_v112.sql
You should Remove this entry from the /etc/oratab: v112:/u01/app/oracle/product/12.1.0:N
echo -- Bringing up the database from the source oracle home
ORACLE_HOME=/u01/app/oracle/product/11.2.0/dbhome_1; export ORACLE_HOME
ORACLE_SID=v112; export ORACLE_SID
unset LD_LIBRARY_PATH; unset LD_LIBRARY_PATH_64; unset SHLIB_PATH; unset LIB_PATH
echo You should Add this entry in the /etc/oratab: v112:/u01/app/oracle/product/11.2.0/
dbhome_1:Y
cd /u01/app/oracle/product/11.2.0/dbhome_1
echo -- Removing /u01/app/oracle/cfgtoollogs/dbua/logs/Welcome_v112.txt file
rm -f /u01/app/oracle/cfgtoollogs/dbua/logs/Welcome_v112.txt ;
/u01/app/oracle/product/11.2.0/dbhome_1/bin/sqlplus /nolog @/u01/app/oracle/cfgtoollogs/
dbua/v112/upgrade5/createSPFile_v112.sql
/u01/app/oracle/product/11.2.0/dbhome_1/bin/rman  @/u01/app/oracle/cfgtoollogs/dbua/v112/
upgrade5/rmanRestoreCommands_v112
```

Use Flashback and Guarantee Restore Point

If the database is enabled with Flashback, then this option will be visible in the DBUA. Using Flashback, you can go back to a particular state through restore points. This is another kind of recovery mechanism. Only the guaranteed restore point will be considered. If any existing guarantee restore point is available, that can also be chosen. The database will be restored to the chosen restore in the case of an upgrade failure.

When choosing the Flashback option, you should not have selected the Move Datafiles or Fast Recovery option. Flashback cannot roll back DDL changes.

Step 9 (Figure 2-30) is the Summary page. It summarizes all the selected options with an edit provision. Using Edit, you can go back to any step to make changes.

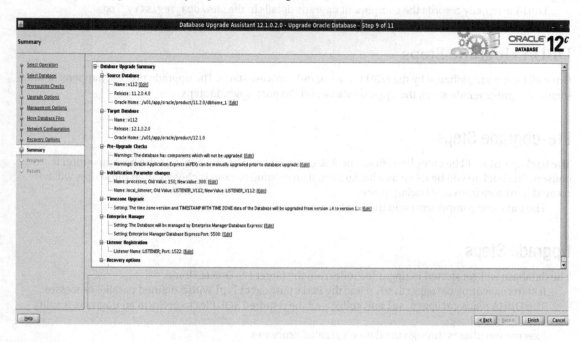

Figure 2-30. *DBUA, upgrade summary*

Click Finish once the upgrade options are confirmed. The database upgrade starts from here. Figure 2-31 shows the Progress page.

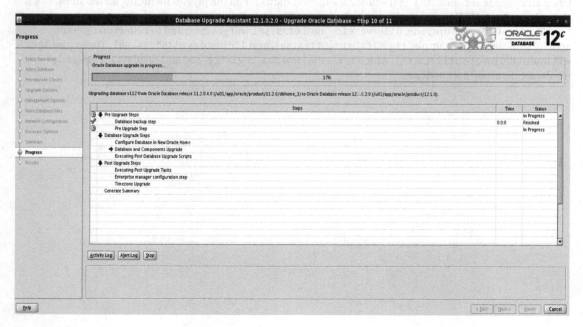

Figure 2-31. *DBUA upgrade progress, progress*

The progress bar will show the status of the database upgrade by percentage. You can monitor the upgrade through the activity log and the alert log. These logs will get modified dynamically.

DBUA internally records the component upgrade details in the view `dba_registry_log`.

DBUA Upgrade Steps

Once all inputs are gathered by the DBUA, the upgrade process starts. The upgrade process happens in three stages: the pre-upgrade steps, the upgrade steps, and the post-upgrade steps.

Pre-upgrade Steps

The backup tasks will be completed first. The RMAN backup will be taken in case the backup option is chosen. The backup will be taken as a backup set. If an existing backup is chosen, then the scripts will be created to restore from that backup pieces.

The database components and their status will be collected.

Upgrade Steps

The database will get started in upgrade mode from the target 12*c* Oracle Home.

It starts executing `catupgrd.sql` using the Perl utility `catctl.pl` with a defined parallel processes.

The DBUA reads `catupgrd.sql` and collects all the required SQL files to perform an upgrade. It splits the SQL files into phases.

Execute the phases through the defined parallel processes.

Post-upgrade Steps

Once an upgrade is completed, you will see a Finished status for all the phases including all the steps. Click Cancel to exit the DBUA window. You can also use the Upgrade Results button to view the upgrade results.

As part of the post-upgrade, `utlu<version_number>s.sql` will get executed to collect an upgrade activity summary. For example, 11*g* R2 calls `utlu112s.sql`, and 12*c* invokes `utlu121s.sql`. These packages will internally invoke `utlusts.sql`, which reads the view `dba_registry_log` and displays the upgrade results for database components.

Figure 2-32 shows the Results page.

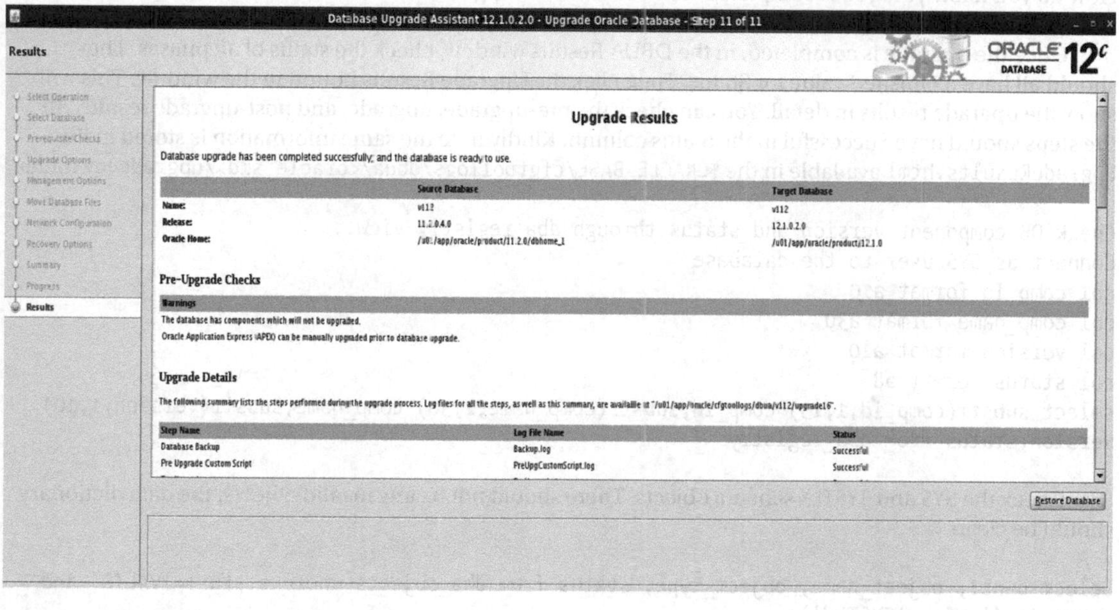

Figure 2-32. DBUA, upgrade results

If you are not OK with the upgrade results, you have the Restore Database option to restore to the old version.

Table 2-4 lists the 12 DBUA logs.

Table 2-4. DBUA Logs

STEP NAME	LOG FILE NAME
DATABASE BACKUP	Backup.log
PRE-UPGRADE	PreUpgrade.log
RDBMS UPGRADE	Oracle_Server.log
COLLECTING INFORMATION FROM DATABASE	CloneDataGatheringStep.log
MODIFYING AND STARTING ORACLE INSTANCE	CloneInstanceStep.log
COPYING DATABASE FILES	CloneRmanCopyStep.log
SWITCHING DATABASE FILES	CloneDatabaseSwitchStep.log
ALL UPGRADE STEPS	catupgrd<0>.log to catupgrd<n-1>.log n=number of parallel processes
POST UPGRADE	PostUpgrade.log
ENTERPRISE MANAGER CONFIGURATION	emConfigUpgrade.log
TIMEZONE UPGRADE	UpgradeTimezone.log
GENERATE SUMMARY	generateSummary.log

How to Make Sure the Upgrade Is Successful

How do you know your job is completed after the database upgrade? This is one of the major questions a DBA gets. It is pretty simple.

Once the upgrade is completed, in the DBUA Results window, check the status of all phases. They should all have a Finished value for Status. Then click the Upgrade Results button in the window. This will show the upgrade results in detail. You can check the pre-upgrade, upgrade, and post-upgrade results. All the steps should have Successful in the Status column. Kindly note the same information is stored in file UpgradeResults.html available in the $ORACLE_BASE/cfgtoollogs/dbua/<oracle_sid>/upgrade<n> folder.

```
Check DB component version and status through dba_registry view..
Connect as SYS user to the database
col comp_id format a10
col comp_name format a30
col version format a10
col status format a8
select substr(comp_id,1,15) comp_id,substr(comp_name,1,30) comp_name,substr(version,1,10)
version,status from dba_registry
```

Check the SYS and SYSTEM schema objects. There should not be any invalid objects; the data dictionary should be clean.

```
Select owner, object_name, object_type, status from dba_objects where status!='VALID' and
owner in ('SYS', 'SYSTEM');
```

Review all the log files. Ensure there are no warnings or errors present in the logs.

Limitations

The DBUA accesses the source database to perform prerequisite checks; hence, it requires the source and target databases to be accessible on the same server and on the same platform.

The source database must have passed the database upgrade compatibility matrix. If a direct upgrade to target the database version is not possible as per the matrix, then the source database should be upgraded to a possible intermediate version and then upgraded to the destination target version from there.

The DBUA cannot perform an upgrade using the existing database backup.

The DBUA recommends the source and target Oracle Home owned by the same user. This is because the DBUA will perform the prerequisite checks on the source database. To access the source database, the DBUA requires the proper privileges. In general, the source datafiles will have read-write permission for the owner and read permission for the group.

The DBUA cannot work on the upgrade's failed/uncompleted databases.

While choosing a database, the DBUA collects all the database details. Those details will be static, and they will be used by the DBUA during its life cycle. Dynamic changes on the source database will not be considered by the DBUA. For example, after executing the pre-upgrade checks, if you take a backup at the source database, then that will not be visible in the recovery options of the DBUA. Even if you rerun the pre-upgrade check, the dynamic changes will not be considered.

The DBUA has the option to perform a recovery in the case of a failure using the existing latest RMAN backup. But it will not check that the required backup pieces are available.

Once the DBUA is invoked and starts progressing, it cannot revert the upgrade process. It can be rolled back only by the recovery mechanism.

Running more than one DBUA at the same time is not recommended as the DBUA updates the central inventory. It is not advisable to update the central inventory at the same time by multiple processes.

Known Issues

Here are some known issues:

- If the DBUA is terminated during the upgrade, it cannot be invoked again. The DBUA cannot be invoked on an upgraded failed database. In 12c you can expect error ORA-00904, "CON_ID: invalid identifier" when the DBUA is invoked on the 12c failed upgrade database.

- The DBUA status bar sometimes may not reflect the exact progress. The status percentage bar gets modified in stages. Some stages take more time, and some take less. So, based on status percentage, you cannot judge the exact upgrade progress.

- Suppose you have datafiles with the same name at a different location and you have chosen to move the datafiles as part of the upgrade (without OMF and the mapping file) in the DBUA, then it may overwrite the datafiles when moving to the new location.

- If preupgrd.sql doesn't exist physically or doesn't have the expected permission, the DBUA may get hung in a pre-upgrade execution state.

- If the Flashback option is not chosen for the recovery options, then you can choose to move the datafiles or the Flash Recovery Area as part of the upgrade.

- If the archive log is enabled, ensure you have allocated enough Fast Recovery Area size (db_recovery_file_dest_size), or if the recovery area becomes full during the upgrade, then the DBUA will wait for more allocation. But it will not report it via any message box or record it in any logs. It will look like hung state. You need to verify it through the alert log.

- At the end of 100 percent completion in the DBUA, you see only the Cancel button with an enabled status. The Finish button will be in a disabled status. You need to click Cancel and come out of the DBUA.

DBUA in Silent Mode

Though the DBUA operates in GUI mode, it can also be invoked in silent mode. It accepts the required inputs as arguments and performs the upgrade in a silent manner.

```
dbua   -silent [<command> [options *  ]]
```

Here's an example:

```
Dbua -silent -sid <oracle db name>
```

You can find all the available commands and options using the following:

```
Dbua -help
```

Here are some of the most used arguments:

- sid <System Identifier>
- oracleHome < Source Database Oracle Home >
- oracleBase < Database Oracle Base >
- diagnosticDest < Database Diagnostic Destination >
- sysDBAUserName <user name with SYSDBA privileges>
- sysDBAPassword <password for sysDBAUserName user name>
- autoextendFiles <Autoextend database files during upgrade. Datafiles will be reverted back
to -their original autoextend settings after upgrade.>
- useASM < Whether Database Is Using Automatic Storage Management>
- newRecoveryArea < Recovery Area for Moved Database>
- newRecoveryAreaSize < Recovery Area Size (MB) for Moved Database>
- backupLocation < directory to back-up your database before starting the upgrade>
- initParam < a comma separated list of initialization parameter values of the format
name=value,name=value.>
- recompile_invalid_objects <true | false>

With 12*c*, these additional options are available:

- degree_of_parallelism < number of CPU's to be used for parallel recompilation>
- auditFileDest < Database Audit File Destination >
- preUpgradeScripts < a comma separated list of SQL scripts with their complete
pathnames. These scripts will be executed before the upgrade and it will store results in
PreUpgCustomScript.log>
- changeUserTablespacesReadOnly <Change user tablespaces read only for the duration of the
upgrade.>
- gatheringStatistics <Gathering statistics before upgrade database.>
- upgrade_parallelism < number of CPU's to be used for parallel upgrade>
- recoveryAreaDestination <destination directory for all recovery files>
- createGRP <To create a guaranteed restore point when database is in archive log and
flashback mode>
- useGRP <To restore the database using specified guaranteed restore point>
- useExistingBackup <To restore database using existing RMAN backup>
- listeners <To register the database with existing listeners, specify listeners by comma
separated -listenerName:Oracle Home. Listeners from lower release home are migrated to newer
release home. Specifying -listeners lsnrName1,lsnrName2, DBUA searches specified listeners
from GI home (if configured), target home and source home.>
- createListener <To create a listener in newer release Oracle Home specify
----listenrName:lsnrPort>

Comparison Between 11g R2 DBUA and 12c R1 DBUA

As you have seen, the upgrade steps involved in the DBUA of 11g R2 and 12c R1 have some differences. It will help to know how the DBUA has been improved in 12c R1 (Table 2-5).

Table 2-5. *DBUA Preupgrade Comparison Between 11g R2 and 12c R1*

	Oracle 11g R2	Oracle 12c R1
Pre-Upgrade		
Number of options in initial screen	Only 'Upgrade database to 11gR2 version'	It includes 'Upgrade to 12cR1' and also move database from different oracle home to current oracle home in same release.
Listing source databases	It will list all available databases in oracle server (as per /etc/oratab)	It has improved look and feel. The oracle home details will be listed in drop down box. Once oracle home is chosen, database associated with that oracle home will be listed
Source database Status (Active/shutdown)	Will not be shown in Preupgrade screen	Source database active status and type of instance (single or RAC) will be shown
Preupgrade script	Utlu112x.sql	Preupgrd.sql executed with –XML option
Preupgrade output	Warnings will be listed and option to continue or cancel the upgrade	Warnings will be listed with their severity (Info, warning, error) and whether it is fixable by DBUA or Manual
Option to fix the warnings by DBUA	No	Fixable warnings will be taken care by DBUA
Validation details on warnings or error	It will show only the error details	It will show more details about the warning/error and how to resolve it
Re-execute the Preupgrade script	Invoke DBUA again to perform the check	'Check again' button available to re-execute the Preupgrade script

Table 2-6 shows the DBUA options.

Table 2-6. *DBUA Options Comparison Between 11g R2 and 12cR1*

	Oracle 11g R2	Oracle 12c R1
DBUA Options		
Parallelism	Not available	Number of parallel process can be chosen to perform upgrade
Audit file destination	Not available	New location can be chosen for Audit file destination
Gather statistics before upgrade	Not available	Dictionary statistics can be gathered before upgrade
Set user tablespaces to read only	Not available	User tablespaces set to read only. It will reduce the time in case we want to go back to old version as part of recovery mechanism.
Custom scripts execution	Option available to execute at post upgrade	Option available to execute at Preupgrade and post upgrade stage
Ignore errors during script execution	Errors during custom script execution cannot be ignored	Option available to specify ignorable errors for custom scripts execution
Listener configuration	Not applicable	We can choose any existing listener that upgraded database will become part of or create new listener in higher version
RMAN backup	It is a Cold backup	Backup taken as RMAN Backup set
Backup size	Since it is image copy the size will be same as Database size	Since it is backup set, size of database backup will be same as records
Choosing any other available RMAN backup	Not possible	Option is available.
Flashback Guaranteed restore point	Not available	New Guaranteed restore point can be created or existing restore point can be used.

Table 2-7 shows the Upgrade Activity screen.

Table 2-7. *DBUA Activity Comparison Between 11g R2 and 12cR1*

	Oracle 11g R2	Oracle 12c R1
Upgrade activity screen		
Monitoring DBUA through DBUA	Checking progress bar	Along with progress bar 'Activity log' button available to monitor the upgrade
Viewing alert log from DBUA	Not available	'Alert log' button available to monitor the alert log recordings
Upgrade Execution	Serial	Parallel
Execution method	Catupgrd.sql executed as a single file	Upgrade activity is split into phases
Logs	Oracle_Server.log	Along with oracle_server.log each parallel process will have catupgrd<parallel process number>.log

Database Manual Upgrade

A database can be upgraded manually by executing the upgrade steps one at a time at the command line. This section shows the tasks involved in a manual database upgrade, including prerequisite checks, upgrade steps, and post-upgrade steps.

We have spent some quality time with the Database Upgrade Assistant in this chapter. It is a good time to know the concepts involved in the manual upgrade method.

As the name implies, all the upgrade tasks are done manually. You may ask why a manual method is required when you have a good automated tool (the DBUA) for upgrade that performs all the tasks automatically.

Yes, the DBUA is a good tool to perform all the tasks, but it has some limitations.

- The source and target database should be running on the same server.
- The source and target database should be owned by the same owner.
- If the DBUA fails in the middle of the upgrade process, it cannot be restarted.
- You cannot execute multiple database upgrades at the same time through the DBUA.

To overcome limitations, you can use the manual upgrade method. Since all tasks are done manually, these limitations can be overcome.

Prerequisites for Manual Database Upgrade

These are the prerequisites:

- The source database version must pass the upgrade compatibility matrix to move to a higher database version.
- The pre-upgrade script should have been executed in the source database, and the errors and warnings listed in the output should be corrected. The target database home should not have any binary issues.
- A database backup should have been taken for the fallback mechanism.
- The datafiles should not be in recovery mode.

- All database components should be in valid state, and there should not be any SYS/SYSTEM schema invalid or duplicate objects.

- The time zone version of the source database home should be lesser or equal to the target database home of the time zone version.

- There should not be any active customer triggers when the manual upgrade is in progress.

There are three stages in performing a manual upgrade: pre-upgrade, upgrade, and post-upgrade. In this section, we will use the 11g R2 and 12c R1 databases as the target version to explain the steps.

Pre-upgrade Tasks

Before upgrading, you need to check whether your database is ready for upgrade. Do you require any changes in the database for upgrade? This section explains the tasks you do before the upgrade.

The pre-upgrade step involves evaluating the source database for the upgrade. This phase can be done when the source database is online; there's no need to have downtime.

Pre-upgrade Script Execution

The foremost step of a manual upgrade is executing the pre-upgrade script. Each database version has a pre-upgrade script to evaluate the source database for upgrading to its version. This pre-upgrade script contains SQL statements to evaluate and project the results. It is kind of a verification before you proceed with the upgrade. Each database has a different set of requirements, and this pre-upgrade script is built based on those version requirements. For example, the 12c version requires more memory allocation than 11g R2; it doesn't require the OLAP component, and the EM Database Console is deprecated in 12c R1. Also, the time zone version differs between the database versions.

The pre-upgrade script is smart enough that it collects the database details and evaluates them. In the case of any unexpected things, then they will be projected as warnings or errors based on their severity. Warnings can be given the least priority. But it is based on a kind of warning message. Errors should be given high priority, and they should be addressed before proceeding with the upgrade process or you will get into unwanted issues. The pre-upgrade output has lots of other useful information; hence, Oracle recommends executing the pre-upgrade script though you planned to upgrade through the DBUA.

The pre-upgrade script execution is mandatory for a manual upgrade. It will store the collected source database details in tables that will be referred to during the actual upgrade. If you miss the pre-upgrade script, then the manual upgrade will fail.

The pre-upgrade script is available in the $ORACLE_HOME/rdbms/admin directory. The directory is the same for all platforms. Suppose the database is getting upgraded from 11g R2 to 12c R1; then ORACLE_HOME refers to the 12c installation home. If the higher database version binary is not installed yet, you can download the pre-upgrade scripts from the My Oracle Support (MOS) note "How to Download and Run Oracle's Database Pre-Upgrade Utility (Doc ID 884522.1)." This is applicable only for Oracle-licensed users.

The pre-upgrade script up to 11g R2 had a naming convention like utlu<version>i.sql. For example, for 11g R2 it's utlu112i.sql and for 10g R2 it's utlu102i.sql, and only one script is provided to perform pre-upgrade checks.

If you have installed the higher-version Oracle Home already, then copy the pre-upgrade scripts into some temporary location and execute them from there. This is to avoid disturbing the higher-version binaries. In 12c R1, the pre-upgrade scripts are Preupgrd.sql and utluppkg.sql. Both have to be copied to the temporary location.

Execution Method

Move the current directory to the pre-upgrade script location.

```
Cd <Preupgrade script location>
Connect as sysdba user in source database
SQL> connect sys/<password> as sysdba
SQL> spool <location>/Preupgrade_ouput.log
SQL> @<Preupgrade script>
SQL> spool off
```

Until 11*g* R2, the script execution will not create any spool file; hence, you need to set the spool file before execution.

The pre-upgrade first checks the source database for the version, to see whether it's compatible, for its block size, and for platform information.

- *Tablespace*: Statistics about the SYSTEM, UNDO, and SYSAUX tablespaces. What is the tablespace size? Does it have enough free space to grow, or does it have the option to be auto-extensible if additional free space is required?

- *Flashback*: Is Flashback enabled in database? If so, what is the size limit, and how much has it been used?

- *Parameters*: Any existing parameter that needs to be updated or that is now deprecated or any parameter that has been renamed

- *Components*: Status of all database components

- *Warnings*: About time zone, invalid objects, EM repository, standby database, recycle bin

- *Recommendations*: Suggestions before performing a database upgrade such as collecting data dictionary statistics

12*c* Pre-upgrade Execution Method

Until 11*g* R2, the pre-upgrade script was represented in a single file, and you will have SQL statements to verify the prerequisites. In 12*c* you have two scripts: Preupgrd.sql and utluppk.sql. Both are expected to be present in the same location.

In 12*c* R1, Preupgrd.sql will invoke utluppkg.sql, and this SQL file has procedures and functions to evaluate the source database. Execution output will be spooled in the log file, and in addition, 12*c* creates a fixup script for pre- and post-upgrade execution.

Move the current directory to the pre-upgrade script location.

```
Cd <Pre-upgrade script location>
Connect as sysdba user in source database
SQL> connect sys/<password> as sysdba
SQL>@preupgrd.sql {TERMINAL|FILE} {TEXT|XML}
```

The output can be shown in the terminal, or it can be saved to a log file. By default it gets stored in logs.

The TERMINAL option will not log the output. With the TEXT option, it will show all executions, results, and recommendations in the terminal, and the XML option will show the results in XML format in the terminal.

The FILE option logs the output into log files, and it creates fixup SQL scripts for before and after the upgrade. The TEXT option will show only errors in the terminal, and the rest of the information will be in the log file. The XML option will record output in an XML file called upgrade.xml. This will get stored in the logical directory PREUPG_OUTPUT_DIR. This directory should have been created already if the FILE and XML options are used or you will get error message that PREUPG_OUTPUT_DIR is not writable and the output will be shown in the terminal. Actually, this option is used by the DBUA tool.

By default the FILE and TEXT options will be used.

Among the two scripts, Preupgrd.sql will check the database open status, type of database (whether it is a multitenant container database or a pluggable database), platform information (it has to create the Pre-upgrade directory to store logs because that platform information is required), and the existence of utluppkg.sql in the current directory.

The Utluppkg.sql script creates the dbms_preup package in the source database. This package has procedures to collect the required information from the source database.

The 12c pre-upgrade execution will create three files: Pre-upgrade.log (the spooled output file), pre-upgrade_fixups.sql, and post-upgrade_fixups.sql. All these files are created in the $ORACLE_BASE/cfgtoollogs/<$ORACLE_SID>/Preupgrade folder. If there are any errors found in the source database, then they will be reported in the output terminal window.

Here's an example:

```
1) Check Tag:     COMPATIBLE_PARAMETER
   Check Summary: Verify compatible parameter value is valid
   Fixup Summary:
    ""Compatible" parameter must be increased manually prior to upgrade."
   +++ Source Database Manual Action Required +++
2) Check Tag:     FILES_NEED_RECOVERY
   Check Summary: Check for any pending file recoveries
   Fixup Summary:
    "Recover or repair these files prior to upgrade."
   +++ Source Database Manual Action Required +++
3) Check Tag:     PURGE_RECYCLEBIN
   Check Summary: Check that recycle bin is empty prior to upgrade
   Fixup Summary:
    "The recycle bin will be purged."
```

These errors must be resolved before proceeding with the upgrade.

Preupgrade.log

This has prerequisite check information the same as 11g R2 and presents the output in a formatted way. It lists a summary with the warnings and errors at the end.

Pre-upgrade Fixup Script

The fixup script will guide you through the tasks to do before the upgrade. It has details of identified warnings and errors and their fix-up methods. Details include the name of that warning/error and its description, severity, action, and fixup summary.

Here's an example:

```
-- **************** Fixup Details ********************************
-- Name:          OCM_USER_PRESENT
-- Description: Check for OCM schema
-- Severity:      Warning
-- Action:        Fixup routine
-- Fix Summary:
--      Drop the ORACLE_OCM user.
```

This message is related to OCM_USER. It is a warning. The action displays as Fixup Routine. It means executing the fixup SQL script will perform the necessary action.

Some fixup warnings/errors require manual intervention, as shown here:

```
-- Name:          DEFAULT_PROCESS_COUNT
-- Description: Verify min process count is not too low
-- Severity:      Warning
-- Action:        ^^^ MANUAL ACTION REQUIRED ^^^
-- Fix Summary:
--      Review and increase if needed, your PROCESSES value.
```

The previous message is related to the process count. The process parameter value is not enough for the higher version, so it needs to be increased. It is a warning message. The upgrade can proceed by ignoring this warning. But increasing this value is recommended, and it has to be done manually.

Basically, the fixup script executes the dbms_preup procedure to perform the fixup routine. In this case, the fixup action requires some additional SQL script execution, and then executing the fixup script will show a warning.

Here's an example:

```
-- **************** Fixup Details ********************************
-- Name:          EM_PRESENT
-- Description: Check if Enterprise Manager is present
-- Severity:      Warning
-- Action:        Fixup routine
-- Fix Summary:
--      Execute emremove.sql prior to upgrade.
dbms_preup.run_fixup_and_report ('EM_PRESENT');
```

Though there is a fixup routine to remove the EM Database Console, manual intervention is required to execute emremove.sql. Executing the fixup script will show the following:

```
Check Tag:      EM_PRESENT
Check Summary: Check if Enterprise Manager is present
Fix Summary:    Execute emremove.sql prior to upgrade.
**********************************************************************
```

```
Fixup Returned Information:
WARNING: --> Enterprise Manager Database Control repository found in the database. In Oracle
Database 12c, Database Control is removed during the upgrade. To save time during the
Upgrade, this action can be done prior to upgrading using the following steps after copying
rdbms/admin/emremove.sql from the new Oracle Home
     - Stop EM Database Control:
      $> emctl stop dbconsole
     - Connect to the Database using the SYS account AS SYSDBA:
     SET ECHO ON;
     SET SERVEROUTPUT ON;
     @emremove.sql
   Without the set echo and serveroutput commands you will not be able to follow the progress
of the script.
```

Perform the recommended actions before proceeding with the upgrade.

Post-upgrade Fixup Script

Post-upgrade fixup scripts are provided to check for invalid database objects, components that are not upgraded, and the existence of old time zones. Mostly the fixup actions have to be performed manually.

Recommended Steps for the Source Database

Here are the recommended steps for the source database.

Database Backup

The foremost activity before upgrading is taking a database backup. The backup can be a cold backup or a hot backup or an RMAN backup. RMAN makes the backup task easier. It is easy with RMAN to validate the backup and ensure that the necessary backup is available to restore.

If the database upgrade is not successful, you should have a backup plan to restore the database to the original version.

Statistics Collection

During an upgrade, optimizer statistics will be collected for dictionary tables that lack statistics. Collecting statistics before the upgrade will reduce the execution time of the upgrade scripts and in turn database downtime.

Connect as the sysdba user to the database.

```
Sql> Exec dbms_stats.gather_dictionary_stats;
```

Time Zone Version

Each database has its own time zone version. For an upgrade, the source database should have a lower or equivalent time zone version compared to the target database. If the source database has upgraded its time zone version, which is higher than the target database, then that same or higher time zone version should be installed in the target database home.

```
Sql> select filename, version from v$time_zone_file;
```

Datafile Status

Datafiles in the source database should be in available status; they should not be in backup or recovery mode. Having a file in another mode would not be a consistent state and would demand recovery.

```
Sql> select * from v$recover_file;
Sql> select name, status from v$datafile where status='RECOVER';
Sql> select file#, status from v$backup where status='ACTIVE';
```

At the same time, datafiles that don't have redo and undo can be placed in a read-only state. If an upgrade fails and recovery is required, then only datafiles with redo and undo can be restored. You don't need to restore the whole database. This is considered a best practice.

```
Sql> select * from v$backup where status! ='NOT ACTIVE';
```

CONNECT Role

The CONNECT role privilege has the following privileges for versions lower than 10g R1:

```
GRANTEE                         PRIVILEGE                           ADM
------------------------------  ----------------------------------  ---
CONNECT                         CREATE VIEW                         NO
CONNECT                         CREATE TABLE                        NO
CONNECT                         ALTER SESSION                       NO
CONNECT                         CREATE CLUSTER                      NO
CONNECT                         CREATE SESSION                      NO
CONNECT                         CREATE SYNONYM                      NO
CONNECT                         CREATE SEQUENCE                     NO
CONNECT                         CREATE DATABASE LINK                NO
```

But from 10g R2, it has only the Create Session privilege. Hence, after upgrading the database, the users who had the CONNECT role in 9i will have only Create Session in 10g R1, and the other privileges will be lost.

Database Link with Password

From 10g R2, by default the password associated with database links will get encrypted. If the database is upgrading from versions less than 10g R2, then kindly note that the database link passwords will be encrypted during the upgrade, and you cannot retrieve the password values.

So, before proceeding with an upgrade from, say, 9*i* or 10*g* R1, take a backup of the database link create scripts.

```
select dbms_metadata.get_ddl('DB_LINK','Link_name','Owner') from sys.dual;
or
select  'CREATE '||DECODE(su.name,'PUBLIC','public ')||'DATABASE LINK '||chr(10)
||DECODE(su.name,'PUBLIC',Null, 'SYS','',SU.NAME||'.')|| sl.name||chr(10)
||'CONNECT TO ' ||sl.userid || ' IDENTIFIED BY "'||sl.password||'" USING
'''||sl.host||''''
||chr(10)||';' TEXT
From sys.link$ sl, sys.user$ su
Where sl.owner#=su.user#;
```

If you decide to go back to the old version through the downgrade procedure, then the password-encrypted database link has to be dropped. At that time, you will require the password to re-create the database links.

Materialized Views

Materialized views are used to replicate data to remote or local sites. The new data will be a local copy of the remote data or a subset of the data such as the rows/columns of a table. Unlike normal views that store only queries, materialized views will store the data locally. This view gets refreshed at periodical intervals through jobs. Before you proceed to the database upgrade, these materialized view refreshes should get completed so that the dictionary will be free for the upgrade.

To know the ongoing materialized view refreshes, execute the following query:

```
select s.obj#,o.obj#,s.containerobj#,lastrefreshdate,pflags,xpflags,o.name,o.owner#,
bitand(s.mflags, 8)
from obj$ o, sum$ s
where o.obj# = s.obj# and o.type# = 42 AND bitand(s.mflags, 8) = 8;
```

Disable Database Vault

If the source database home is enabled with Database Vault, then disable the Data Vault option in the target database Oracle Home before starting the database in upgrade mode. This is applicable to 11*g* R2. When upgrading to 12*c* R1, by default Data Vault will be disabled in the target Oracle Home.

To disable Data Vault, shut down the Oracle database and all related services and execute the following as the Oracle Home owner:

```
$ cd $ORACLE_HOME/rdbms/lib
$ make -f ins_rdbms.mk dv_off ioracle
```

When upgrading the database to 12*c* R1 that uses Oracle Label Security (OLS) and Oracle Database Vault, you must first run the OLS preprocess script, olspre-upgrade.sql, to process the aud$ table contents. The OLS upgrade moves the aud$ table from the SYSTEM schema to the SYS schema. The olspreupgrade.sql script is a preprocessing script required for this move. The script olspreupgrade.sql is available in the 12*c* ORACLE_HOME/rdbms/admin directory. Execute it at the source database as the SYS user.

Sysaux Tablespace

The tablespace SYSAUX was introduced in 10g. If you are upgrading from a 9i database, then the SYSAUX tablespace has to be created when the database is started in upgrade mode using the 10g/11g version. If the tablespace named SYSAUX already exists in the 9i database, you better drop the tablespace after moving objects to different tablespace or rename it to a different name before the upgrade.

Also, when SYSAUX gets created manually in a 10g/11g database. it is expected to be with extent management local and segment space management auto.

```
create tablespace SYSAUX datafile '<datafile>'
size 500M reuse
 extent management local
segment space management auto
 online;
```

Disable Cron or Scheduled Jobs

If there are any scheduled jobs, disable the scheduling until the upgrade gets completed. The database should be free from user modifications while the backup is running.

Sys and System Tablespace

The SYS and SYSTEM schema should have the default tablespace as SYSTEM. The upgrade is performed through the SYS user, and the data dictionary is installed in the SYSTEM tablespace. Having a different default tablespace will throw an error during execution.

```
Sql> select username, default_tablespace from dba_users where username='SYS' or
username='SYSTEM';
```

Recycle Bin

Empty the recycle bin as the sysdba user.

```
SQL> purge dba_recyclebin;
```

Outstanding Distributed Transactions

Before upgrading, outstanding distributed transactions should be committed and resolved. You can find the outstanding distributed transactions through dba_2pc_pending.

```
Sql> select * from dba_2c_pending;
```

If there are any transactions through the previous query, check the status of the transactions through the State column. Automatic recovery usually takes care of all the distributed transactions. If it is not automatically resolvable, use the DBMS_TRANSACTION.PURGE_LOST_DB_ENTRY procedure to purge transactions.

Flash Recovery Area

If the source database has archive log enabled and Flash Recovery Area (FRA) has been configured, then ensure that sufficient free space is available for FRA to accommodate archived logs generated during the upgrade. Failure to provide the sufficient space will cause the upgrade to hang.

Audit User and Roles

Oracle 12*c* has supplied the user AUDSYS and the roles Audit_admin and Audit_viewer. If these users are already in the database before upgrading to 12*c*, then error ora-1722, "invalid number," will be thrown. Drop or rename this user and roles before upgrading to 12*c*.

PROVISIONER, XS_RESOURCE, XS_SESSION_ADMIN, XS_NAMESPACE_ADMIN, and XS_CACHE_ADMIN are Oracle-supplied roles in 12.1. Hence, these existing user or role names in the database must be dropped before upgrading.

SYSBACKUP, SYSDG, and SYSKM are Oracle-supplied users in 12.1, and CAPTURE_ADMIN is the Oracle-supplied role in 12.1. Hence, these existing user or role names in the database must be dropped before upgrading.

EM_EXPRESS_BASIC and EM_EXPRESS_ALL are Oracle-supplied roles in 12.1. Hence, these existing user or role names in the database must be dropped before upgrading.

GSMCATUSER, GSMUSER, and GSMADMIN_INTERNAL are Oracle-supplied users in 12.1, and GSMUSER_ROLE, GSM_POOLADMIN_ROLE, GSMADMIN_ROLE, and GDS_CATALOG_SELECT are Oracle-supplied roles in 12.1. Hence, these existing user or role names in the database must be dropped before upgrading.

Creating Flashback Restore Point

Using the Flashback mechanism, the database can go back to a particular state. This feature can be used during upgrade. It is a faster option to go back to the previous state using a restore point. Before upgrading, create a flashback restore point so if any issue occurs, then you can go back to the state before upgrading. Remember, there should not be any compatibility parameter change during the upgrade to use this procedure. Also, DDL changes such as moving datafiles to a different location cannot be rolled back during flashback. We will discuss the steps in detail in Chapter 13.

Authenticated SSL Users

Check whether the database has any externally authenticated SSL users using the following query:

```
SQL> SELECT name FROM sys.user$ WHERE ext_username IS NOT NULL AND password = 'GLOBAL';
```

If there are rows returned and the source database is 9.2.0.*x* or 10.1.0.*x*, then you need to upgrade these users after the database upgrade. This is discussed in the "Post-upgrade" section.

Hidden/Underscore Parameters

Check for any hidden/underscore parameters using the following query:

```
SQL> SELECT name, value
from SYS.V$PARAMETER
WHERE name LIKE '\_%' ESCAPE '\' order by name;
```

Remove the setting of all the hidden parameters. After upgrading, it can be enabled again. Some parameters will have become obsolete in the higher version. It needs to be verified before enabling it in the higher version after the database upgrade.

PSU Patches Installation

Oracle releases patch set update (PSU) patches every quarter for supported Oracle database versions. This type of patch has bug fixes for identified vulnerabilities and security fixes. This type of patch is cumulative, which means applying the latest patch will also install all PSU fixes released so far. So, apply the latest PSU patch on a higher binary version; it will apply bug fixes identified for that version.

You can find the available PSU patches and their bug fixes from the Oracle support site. Remember that only Oracle-licensed users can download and apply the patch. You will learn more about patching in Chapter 12.

Until now you have seen the recommended tasks to perform an upgrade effectively. We'll now discuss the upgrade steps.

Upgrade Steps

Once the pre-upgrade steps are completed and you have ensured that there are no warnings or errors in the report, you can proceed with the upgrade. The following best practices will help you perform the upgrade in an efficient manner.

First shut down the database at the source Oracle Home and also stop all Oracle-related services. This means the database should be cleanly shut down.

Change the environment variables to point to the higher-version Oracle Home. The usual environment variables are ORACLE_HOME, PATH, and LD_LIBRARY_PATH. Also, modify the /etc/oratab file to modify the Oracle Home location for the database SID.

Here's an example:

```
DB10g:/u01/app/oracle/product/10.2.0/dbhome_1:N
```

DB10g is the Oracle SID. Its Oracle Home is /u01/app/oracle/product/10.2.0/dbhome_1; N denotes not an automatic startup.

Change the Oracle Home path to the higher database home.

Here's an example:

```
DB10g:/u01/app/oracle/product/11.2.0/dbhome_1:N
```

Executing the oraenv file (for the CShell it will be coraenv) and specifying DB10g will set the CShell Oracle environment to 11.2.0.

Copy the parameter file from the source Oracle Home to the higher-version Oracle Home. If any changes for the parameter are recommended by the Preupgrade script, then perform it after copying it to the target database home.

Also, you can copy tnsnames.ora, the password file, and the listener file to the new Oracle Home.

If Datafiles Stay in the Same Location After the Upgrade

In this scenario, the datafiles stay in the same location; hence, you can directly start the database in upgrade mode using the higher version.

On the higher-version binaries, create the password file for this Oracle SID.
Here's an example on Unix:

```
Cd $ORACLE_HOME/dbs
```

```
Orapwd file=orapw<service_name>  password=<sys password> entries=<number of sysdba users
allowed>
```

You can also specify the values of other additional parameters of the orapwd command.

In Windows, along with the password file, you need to create a service for the database. If the upgrade happens on the same server, then first remove the service through the following command:

```
Oradim –delete –sid <service name>
```

Here the oradim binary belongs to the old Oracle Home.

To create a new service, execute the following:

```
Oradim –new –sid <service name> -password <sys password> -startup <Auto/Manual>
```

Ensure the operating system variables point to the new Oracle Home before executing the previous commands.

Start the database in upgrade mode. The database could be started with the pfile or the spfile.

```
Sql> startup upgrade pfile=<init file name along with location>
```

This will start the database in upgrade mode. If the compatible parameter is changed in the init parameter, remember you cannot downgrade the database after upgrade or lower the compatible parameter value later.

If the Datafiles Location Is Different from the Source

You may want to change the datafile location as part of the upgrade. If so, before starting the database in the higher version, first copy the datafiles to new location. You need to modify its location in the control file. Execute this SQL query to change the location of each datafile while the instance is in mount state. Ensure the control_files parameter in the init file points to the new location of control files.

```
Sql> alter database rename file '<old location>' to '<new location>';
```

Once all files are renamed, open the database in upgrade mode.

```
Sql> alter database open upgrade;
```

Execute the Upgrade Script

As you know, upgrading the database is to internally upgrade the data dictionary. It has to upgrade each individual component of the database to a higher version. For that, it has to check the source database version first and then execute the SQL scripts responsible for upgrading the individual database components.

You will be calling catupgrd.sql, which will call the required SQL scripts internally. Let's first discuss the 11g R2 upgrade, and later you will see the new features introduced in the 12c release.

Connect to the database as the SYSDBA user. The `catupgrd.sql` script should be executed as the SYSDBA user.

```
cd $ORACLE_HOME/rdbms/admin
Sql> @catupgrd.sql
```

Remember, if you execute the `catupgrd.sql` script without the pre-upgrade execution, then you will get an error. The reason is that the pre-upgrade will update the database information in the history table, and that will be used by the upgrade scripts. For example, the time zone information will be updated in the `registry$history` table. If the pre-upgrade script is not executed, then the time zone information will be missing in the history table, and the upgrade will fail with the error ora-01722, "Time zone invalid number."

The upgrade execution will validate the source database version, and it will call the respective upgrade SQL scripts. The upgrade SQL script's execution output has to be spooled manually. The upgrade progress will be stored in history tables. At the end of the upgrade, "summary of upgrade progress" will be displayed. During that time, the information stored in history tables will be used to display the progress, such as how much time was spent for each individual database component to upgrade, the total time spent for database upgrade, and any errors reported during the upgrade.

After `catupgrade.sql`, restart the database and then execute `catuppst.sql`, which will perform the remaining upgrade actions that don't require the database to be in upgrade mode. `catuppst.sql` will record the upgrade activity in the `registry$database` table and also execute post-PSU scripts. You don't need to execute post-PSU scripts separately if the PSU is installed in the target database home before the database upgrade.

12*c* Upgrade Script Execution

In 12*c*, the upgrade script execution has been improved. Until 11*g* R2, the script execution happened in a serial manner. This means each database component will get upgraded in serial execution. This way will take more time. Also, if there are any issues during upgrade and the `catupgrd.sql` execution gets terminated, then you need to start the upgrade again from the scratch. This means you need to again execute `catupgrd.sql`. This will reexecute all the upgrade steps from the beginning even though some of the initial steps were successful. You may also get a unique constraint violation error as some constraints are already in place and it has been retried to create. These two difficulties are overcome in the 12*c* version. Let's discuss the new features first and later you will see how they play a role in the 12*c* upgrade.

Parallelism

The file `catupgrd.sql` internally calls many SQL scripts to upgrade the database components. Some of the SQL scripts can be run in parallel. In other words, they can be executed by parallel processes. Because of parallel processing, the amount of time required to execute the scripts will get reduced. In 12*c* you can specify the number of parallel processes to execute `catupgrd.sql`. By default it is 4, and it can go up to maximum of 8. You can specify the value based on the available CPU space. To enable parallel processes, Oracle 12*c* has introduced the Perl utility `catctl.pl` (Catalog Control Perl Program).

First, the details of all SQL scripts required to upgrade will be collected, and then it will be split into multiple phases based on the dependency involved in the SQL scripts. Each phase will be operated by the parallel process.

To create a parallel process and to create multiple phases, 12*c* has a Perl script called `catctl.pl`. To compile this Perl script, Perl binaries are available in ORACLE_HOME.

Phases

From 12*c* the SQL scripts required for upgrade are split into phases based on the dependency between them. A phase is a set of SQL files chosen to execute in a parallel (using multiple SQL process) or serial manner (a single SQL process). If you open catupgrd.sql or catproc.sql, you will notice the following lines along with the SQL files:

```
@@cmpupgrd.sql     --CATFILE -X
--CATCTL -S
@@catresults.sql
--CATCTL -R
--CATCTL -M

-X denotes SQL file contains multi processing
-S denotes to execute sql file in serial manner
-R denotes Reconnect to database
```

First catctl.pl collects details of all the SQL files and splits them into phases. With a specified number of parallel processes, it executes each phase.

This phase model provides a feature that catctl.pl can call any phase as a starting one. Suppose the upgrade failed in the 40th phase, then the retry can start from the 40th phase. There is not necessary to start from scratch like 11*g* R2.

```
catctl [-u username] [-n processes] [-d directory]
               [-t table] [-l directory] [-s script] [-N PDB processes]
               [-e] [-p startPhase] [-P endPhase] [-i identifier]
               [-c quotedSpaceSeparatedInclusionListOfPDBs]
               [-C quotedSpaceSeparatedExclusionListOfPDBs]
               [-x] [-M]   filename
```

The following are the most commonly used arguments:

- n: The number of processes to use for parallel operations
- d: The directory containing the files to run
- l: The directory for spooled output logs (if it is not specified, it will create a spool file in the current working directory)
- S: The serial upgrade
- p: The start phase (to start from a particular phase)
- P: To stop upgrade execution on a particular phase
- i: The identifier for spooled logs
- x: To postpone the post-upgrade script

We discuss the multitenant-related arguments c, C, and N in Chapter 10.

To upgrade to 12*c*, invoke catctl as follows:

```
cd $ORACLE_HOME/bin
$ORACLE_HOME/perl/bin/perl catctl.pl -n 4 -l /u01/app/oracle/upgrade_log catupgrd.sql
```

Here 4 parallel processes is used and log directory is /u01/app/oracle/upgrade_log

The Final argument is catupgrd.sql

In case present directory is not $ORACLE_HOME/rdbms/admin directory, then use –d option

Since we are invoking catctl. pl from rdbms/admin directory, we haven't used –d option

Here is the output:

```
********************************************************************************
catctl.pl version: 12.1.0.2.0
Oracle Base           = /u01/app/oracle

Analyzing file catupgrd.sql
Log files in /u01/app/oracle/upgrade_log
catcon: ALL catcon-related output will be written to /u01/app/oracle/upgrade_log/catupgrd_
catcon_17249.lst
catcon: See /u01/app/oracle/upgrade_log/catupgrd*.log files for output generated by scripts
catcon: See /u01/app/oracle/upgrade_log/catupgrd_*.lst files for spool files, if any
Number of Cpus        = 1
SQL Process Count     = 4


-------------------------------------------------------
Phases [0-73]
Serial   Phase #: 0 Files: 1     Time: 203s
Serial   Phase #: 1 Files: 5     Time: 42s
Restart  Phase #: 2 Files: 1     Time: 1s
Parallel Phase #: 3 Files: 18    Time: 22s
Restart  Phase #: 4 Files: 1     Time: 0s
Serial   Phase #: 5 Files: 5     Time: 19s


********************************************************************************
```

This shows the number of phases: 73. This includes each phase, the number of files involved in that phase, and the execution time of that phase.

The upgrade SQL execution output will be stored in catupgrd<0>.log to catupgrd<n-1>.log where n is the number of parallel processes. Each parallel process will create a separate output logfile.

Once the upgrade is completed, the database will be shut down and need to be started manually.

Post-upgrade Steps

Here are the post-upgrade steps.

Upgrade the Time Zone After the Database Upgrade

Right now only the database is upgraded. You need to upgrade the time zone to a higher version. Oracle 12*c* has time zone version 18. Check the current database time zone version. If it is less than 18, then it has to be upgraded to 18.

```
Steps
Verify the timezone version of database
SQL> select * from v$timezone_file;

FILENAME                       VERSION    CON_ID
--------------------           ---------- ----------
timezlrg_14.dat                14         0
```

Check database primary timezone version

```
SQL> select property_name, substr(property_value,1,30)value
  2   from database_properties
  3   where property_name like 'DST%';

PROPERTY_NAME
--------------------------------------------------------------------------------
VALUE
------------------------------
DST_UPGRADE_STATE
NONE

DST_PRIMARY_TT_VERSION
14

DST_SECONDARY_TT_VERSION
0
```

You can see the time zone–related files in the $ORACLE_HOME/oracore/zoneinfo folder. The folder will have all the time zone version files starting from 1 to the latest version, 18.

To upgrade the time zone, first shut down and start the database in upgrade mode.

```
SQL> shutdown immediate
Database closed.
Database dismounted.
ORACLE instance shut down.

SQL> startup upgrade
ORACLE instance started.

Total System Global Area   234881024 bytes
Fixed Size                   2922904 bytes
Variable Size              176162408 bytes
Database Buffers            50331648 bytes
Redo Buffers                 5464064 bytes
Database mounted.
Database opened.
```

Begin the timezone upgrade

```
exec dbms_dst.begin_upgrade(<Higher version>);
SQL> exec dbms_dst.begin_upgrade(18);

PL/SQL procedure successfully completed.
```

Shutdown the database and start it in normal mode

```
QL> shutdown immediate
Database closed.
```

```
Database dismounted.
ORACLE instance shut down.

SQL> startup
ORACLE instance started.

Total System Global Area  234881024 bytes
Fixed Size                  2922904 bytes
Variable Size             176162408 bytes
Database Buffers           50331648 bytes
Redo Buffers                5464064 bytes
Database mounted.
Database opened.
```

Truncate sys.dst$error_table and sys. dst$error_table. These tables will record the errors seen during the time zone upgrade. You truncate them before starting the upgrade.

Execute dbms_dst.upgrade_database procedure which performs timezone upgrade

```
Sql> desc dbms_dst.upgrade_database
Argument Name                    Type                     In/Out Default?
------------------------------   ----------------------   ------ --------
 NUM_OF_FAILURES                 BINARY_INTEGER           OUT
 UPGRADE_DATA                    BOOLEAN                  IN     DEFAULT
 PARALLEL                        BOOLEAN                  IN     DEFAULT
 CONTINUE_AFTER_ERRORS           BOOLEAN                  IN     DEFAULT
 LOG_ERRORS                      BOOLEAN                  IN     DEFAULT
 LOG_ERRORS_TABLE                VARCHAR2                 IN     DEFAULT
 ERROR_ON_OVERLAP_TIME           BOOLEAN                  IN     DEFAULT
 ERROR_ON_NONEXISTING_TIME       BOOLEAN                  IN     DEFAULT
 LOG_TRIGGERS_TABLE              VARCHAR2                 IN     DEFAULT
```

```
Example:
SQL> declare
  2  n number;
  3  begin
  4  dbms_dst.upgrade_database(n,true,true, true, true,'SYS.DST$ERROR_TABLE',true,true,'SYS.
DST$TRIGGER_TABLE');
  5  end;
  6  /
PL/SQL procedure successfully completed.
```

After successful execution check tables sys.dst$error_table and sys. dst$error_table

```
SQL> select  count(*) from dst$trigger_table;
  COUNT(*)
----------
       0
```

```
SQL> select  count(*) from dst$error_table;

  COUNT(*)
----------
         0
```
End the upgrade procedure
```
SQL> declare
  2  n number;
  3  begin
  4  dbms_dst.end_upgrade(n);
  5  dbms_output.put_line('Number of failures: '||n);
  6  end;
  7  /

PL/SQL procedure successfully completed.
```

> Here argument 'n' denotes number of failures
> Check the timezone version

```
SQL> select * from v$timezone_file;
FILENAME             VERSION    CON_ID
-------------------- ---------- ----------
timezlrg_18.dat      18         0

SQL> select property_name, substr(property_value,1,30)value
  2   from database_properties
  3  where property_name like 'DST%';

PROPERTY_NAME
--------------------------------------------------------------------------------
VALUE
------------------------------
DST_UPGRADE_STATE
UPGRADE

DST_PRIMARY_TT_VERSION
18

DST_SECONDARY_TT_VERSION
14
```

> Primary version has been changed to latest 18 version.
> Edit /etc/oratab and change the ORACLE_HOME value to higher version oracle home

```
<ORACLE_SID>:<ORACLE_HOME>:N
```

Upgrade Statistics Table

If there are any statistics tables created already using the DBMS_STATS.CREATE_STATS_TABLE procedure, then upgrade it using the following:

```
SQL> execute  DBMS_STATS.UPGRADE_STAT_TABLE('<Owner>','<Name of Statistics table>');
```

Enable Database Vault

To enable the optional Data Vault, shut down the Oracle database and all related services and execute the following as the Oracle Home owner:

```
$ cd $ORACLE_HOME/rdbms/lib
$ make -f ins_rdbms.mk dv_on ioracle
```

Upgrade Externally Authenticated SSL Users

If the database is upgraded from 9.2.0.x or 10.1.0.x and the database has externally authenticated SSL users, then execute the following command to upgrade those users:

```
ORACLE_HOME/rdbms/bin/extusrupgrade --dbconnectstring <hostname:port_no:sid> --dbuser <db
admin> --dbuserpassword <password> -a
```

This step is not necessary for databases 10.2.x and higher

Enable Hidden Parameter

Before upgrading, hidden parameters were removed. Some parameters would have become obsolete in the upgraded version. Review all the parameters and set them appropriately.

Comparison Between 11g R2 and 12c R1

We discussed the manual upgrade steps of 11g R2 and 12c R1. Let's now compare the differences in both the methods, which will help you know the improvisations included in 12c R1. Table 2-8 compares the 11g R2 and 12c R1 upgrade steps.

Table 2-8. Manual Upgrade Comparison Between 11g R2 and 12c R1

	Oracle 11g R2	Oracle 12c R1
Pre-upgrade Step		
Scripts	utlu112i.sql	Preupgrd.sql and utluppkg.sql.
Spooled output	Manual spooling is required	Default spooling and terminal output.
Fixup scripts	Not available	Pre- and post-fixup scripts will be created.
Execution method	utlu112i.sql has all scripts	Preupgrd.sql will call utluppkg.sql, which has the procedures and functions to collect database details.
Multitenant	Not applicable	Applicable for multitenant environment.
Upgrade step		
Scripts	catupgrd.sql	catupgrd.sql and catctl.pl.
Parallelism	Not supported	Parallelism using available CPU processes.
Upgrade execution	Serial	Parallel and serial.
Upgrade time	High	Less due to parallelism.
Number of phases	Single phase	Multiple phases.
In case catupgrd.sql failed in between	Execute catupgrd.sql again from the beginning	Execute from the failed phase.
Utilizing available CPU	Less	Optimized.
Execution output	Manual spooling required	Output automatically spooled for every parallel processes.
Stopping catupgrd.sql at particular step	It should not be stopped in between	Using the catctl -P option, you can stop execution to a particular phase.
Post-upgrade step		
utlrp.sql execution	Serial	Parallel

Traditional Export/Import

A traditional export/import was one of commonly used method until the 9*i* database to transfer data between different databases. It extracts objects from the database and creates a dump file that can be imported into another database. The databases involved in the transmission can be with the same or a different version. It can be even a different platform or with a different character set. For an upgrade, you transfer the data from a lower-version database to a higher-version database.

■ **Note**   The data is copied into a dump file, and it gets imported into the target database. There are no changes in the source database.

The export utility is available in the Oracle Home as exp under the $ORACLE_HOME/bin directory, and the import utility is available as imp under the $ORACLE_HOME/bin directory.

The import utility is backward compatible. It means it can import the dump taken from lower than its database version.

Compatibility Version Matrix

Traditional export/import utilities are available from version 5. You may ask whether you can take an export at version 5 and import the dump into version 12*c*. The answer is yes. You can export from a lower version and import it into a higher version. Another question is when you extract data as a dump file, can you take a dump at a higher version and import it into a lower version? For some compatible version combinations, you can do that. But the dump should be taken with the lower/target version executables. To import the dump from 9.2.0.1 to 9.0.1, the export dump should have be taken from 9.0.1 executables. Connect the 9.2.0.1.0 database from the 9.0.1 export executable and take the dump.

Table 2-9 discusses the possible combinations.

Table 2-9. *Source and Target Version Compatibility for Export/Import*

Source Version/Target Database Version	9.2	10.2	11.2	12.1
8.0.6	8.0.6	8.0.6	8.0.6	8.0.6
8.1.7	8.1.7	8.1.7	8.1.7	8.1.7
9.0.1	9.0.1	9.0.1	9.0.1	9.0.1
9.2.0	9.2.0	9.2.0	9.2.0	9.2.0
10.1.0	10.1.0	10.1.0	10.1.0	10.1.0
10.2.0	9.2	10.2	10.2	10.2
11.1.0	9.2	9.2	11.1	11.1
11.2.0	9.2	9.2	11.2	11.2

Here are the prerequisites for performing the upgrade:

- The target database should have been created in a higher version, and the necessary PSU patches should have been applied.

- While taking a full database export, the tablespaces definition will be exported. So, while importing the dump into the target database, those tablespaces will get created. But if the target database has a different physical directory structure, then pre-create those necessary tablespaces.

- While taking the export, the binary exp executable should be from the source database version or a version lesser than the source database version.

For example, if the 11g R2 exp binary is used to take a backup of the 10g R2 database, then the following export will be terminated with an error:

```
EXP-00008: ORACLE error 942 encountered
ORA-00942: table or view does not exist
EXP-00024: Export views not installed, please notify your DBA
EXP-00000: Export terminated unsuccessfully
```

- Copy tnsnames.ora to the target Oracle Home. This is an optional step.

Upgrade Steps

Here are the upgrade steps:

1. Create a physical directory to store the dump and logs.

   ```
   $mkdir /u01/app/oracle/exp_backup
   ```

2. Take the export dump using the source exp utility.

   ```
   cd /u01/app/oracle/exp_backup
   $ORACLE_HOME/bin/exp
   ```

It will ask for login details and other export-related arguments.
You can also specify all the required arguments while invoking exp as follows:

```
$ORACLE_HOME/bin/exp system/manager file=<dumpfile name> log=<logfile name> full=y
```

The following are the other useful parameters:

- FILESIZE: Exports the dump file size. Dump files will be created in this dump size.

- Grants: Exports grants information.

- Statistics: Analyzes objects.

In the following example, you take the backup of the 9i (9.2.0.8.0) database. You have created new the tablespace tbstest (datafile location: /u01/ app/oracle/oradata/oracle9i/tbstest01.dbf) and the schema usertest.

```
$exp system/<password> file=db9i_bkp.dmp log=db9i_bkp.log full=y statistics=none
```

Export: Release 9.2.0.8.0 - Production on Sun Jan 31 08:54:34 2116
Export done in US7ASCII character set and AL16UTF16 NCHAR character set
server uses WE8ISO8859P1 character set (possible charset conversion)
Here you are about to export the entire database:

```
. exporting tablespace definitions
. exporting profiles
. exporting user definitions
. exporting roles
. exporting resource costs
. exporting rollback segment definitions
. exporting database links
. exporting sequence numbers
. exporting directory aliases
. exporting context namespaces
. exporting foreign function library names
. exporting PUBLIC type synonyms
. exporting private type synonyms
. exporting object type definitions
. exporting system procedural objects and actions
. exporting pre-schema procedural objects and actions
. exporting cluster definitions
. about to export SYSTEM's tables via Conventional Path ...
. . exporting table            AQ$_INTERNET_AGENTS          0 rows exported
. . exporting table        AQ$_INTERNET_AGENT_PRIVS         0 rows exported
. . exporting table                   DEF$_AQCALL           0 rows exported
.
.
. . exporting table                      TABTEST     1000000 rows exported
. exporting synonyms
. exporting views
. exporting referential integrity constraints
. exporting stored procedures
. exporting operators
. exporting indextypes
. exporting bitmap, functional and extensible indexes
. exporting posttables actions
. exporting triggers
. exporting materialized views
. exporting snapshot logs
. exporting job queues
. exporting refresh groups and children
. exporting dimensions
. exporting post-schema procedural objects and actions
. exporting user history table
. exporting default and system auditing options
. exporting statistics
Export terminated successfully without warnings.
$ls
db9i_bkp.dmp  db9i_bkp.log
```

The export dump is available, so now let's import it into the 12*c* (12.1.0.2.0) database. Remember, if you upgrade data along with the data dictionary, then the minimum required version is 10.2.0.5.0. Here you move only data; hence, the upgrade compatibility matrix doesn't come into the picture. The 12*c* database can be a nonmultitenant database or a pluggable database.

```
12 database name:  pdb1 (pluggable database)
12c database version: 12.1.0.2.0
```

Since the target database server doesn't have the same physical directory structure as the 9*i* database server, importing the dump will throw an error for 9*i* tablespaces, and also users present in the 9*i* database but not in 12*c* will be given an error.

So, 9*i* tablespaces and users that are not present in the 12*c* database have to be created in the 12*c* pluggable database pdb1 before import.

First you will set the environment variables to the 12*c* home and invoke the imp utility.

```
imp system/sys@pdb1  file=db9i_bkp.dmp log=db9i_db12c_imp.log full=y commit=y

Connected to: Oracle Database 12c Enterprise Edition Release 12.1.0.2.0 - 64bit Production
With the Partitioning, OLAP, Advanced Analytics and Real Application Testing options
Export file created by EXPORT:V09.02.00 via conventional path
import done in US7ASCII character set and AL16UTF16 NCHAR character set
import server uses WE8MSWIN1252 character set (possible charset conversion)

. importing SYSTEM's objects into SYSTEM
```

First it performs character set conversion. Then it will try to import system objects and then create tablespaces, users, roles, sequences, synonyms, and tables. Then it imports objects into other schemas.

Ensure you have enough free space in the tablespace or that auto-extensible is on to extend the space. If the import fails, it can be invoked again. This will throw errors for the objects that are already imported. To ignore those warnings, include the ignore=y argument.

Check whether the tablespace tbstest and table usertest exist.

```
SQL> select tablespace_name, file_name from dba_data_files where tablespace_name='TBSTEST';
TABLESPACE_NAME                 FILE_NAME
-----------------------------   ---------------------------------------------
TBSTEST                         /u01/app/oracle/oradata/CDBTEST/PDBFTIMP/tbstest01.dbf
SQL> select owner, tablespace_name from dba_tables where table_name='TABTEST';
OWNER                           TABLESPACE_NAME
-------------                   ---------------------------
USERTEST                        TBSTEST
```

Here are some known issues:

- Traditional export/import is deprecated from 11*g*.

- It was not developed to handle large databases.

- If the datafile path is different in the target database, then the tablespaces should have been created before import.

- The import will directly import the objects. It will not check whether those objects are valid to the target database version. Some objects will have been deprecated or not required for the target database version.

- Traditional export/import will consume more time compared to other methods.

Data Pump

Data Pump was introduced in Oracle 10*g*. It is an enhanced version of the traditional export/import. Data Pump is a server-side utility. It means most Data Pump operations happen on the server side, and the export backup can be initiated only on the database server by creating a logical directory. Like traditional export, it has utilities to export and import. They are expdp and impdp. Both utilities resemble the traditional export and import in the interface, but though the interface is the same, they are totally different. Traditional export backup cannot be imported using the Data Pump import utility. Data Pump has new features that the traditional method doesn't provide. We will discuss a little about some new features and then move on to the steps for an upgrade using Data Pump. In this chapter, export and import denotes Data Pump export and import.

Parallel

This is one of the best features of Data Pump. This parameter specifies the maximum number of active threads that can do the job on behalf of Data Pump. By default it will have a value of 1. Modifying it will help to optimize the resource utilization. The value of this parameter should be less than or equivalent to the number of the Data Pump file set. Each active worker in the parallel process mode exclusively writes on one file at a time. Having more parallel processes than the Data Pump file set will create an adverse effect.

```
$ expdp system/sys directory=expdp_dir dumpfile=full%u.dmp parallel=3
```

The previous command will create three dump files by each individual parallel process.

Network_link

You can perform export and import over the network. If the target database can connect to the source database, then this option can be utilized. The database link has to be created from the target to the primary, and that link data will be transferred to the target database. There are no dump files involved in this method. expdp will not be invoked; the logical directory doesn't need to be specified.

```
$ impdp scott/tiger network_link=DB10g tables=salgrade commit=y
```

Here the 10*g* database is connected via the database link, and the table salgrade has been imported to the current database from the source database.

Remap Datafile

In a traditional export, while importing the full database backup, if the datafile location in the target is different, then the tablespace creation will fail. You should create those tablespaces up front before doing an import. In Data Pump, this difficulty is ruled out. You can specify the remap_datafile parameter to create datafiles in a different location. The Remap_tablespace option is also available to remap tablespaces during import.

Estimate_only

This option is used to estimate the space required by the export.

```
$ expdp system/manager estimate_only=y
```

The total estimate using the BLOCKS method is 704 KB.

The dump file name is not required to execute this command. By default, the log file export.log will be created while executing this command. If you don't require a log file, then specify Nologfile=y along with the previous command.

Version

This is one of the good features of Data Pump. It denotes the version of database objects to be exported. It is used when the target database has a lesser compatibility level than the source database. Suppose 11g database has to be imported on the 10g database, and then you can make use of this parameter. Specifying the version will not export objects or datatypes when they are not compatible with the specified version value.

```
$ expdp system/manager directory=expdp_dir dumpfile=fulldb.dmp logfile=fulldb.log
version=10.0 full=y
Export: Release 11.2.0.3.0
ORA-39139: Data Pump does not support XMLType objects in version 10.0. TABLE_
DATA:"ORDDATA"."ORDDCM_DOCS" will be skipped.
```

The export binary version is 11.2.0.3.0, and the dump is taken for the 10.0 version. You can see the incompatible objects are reported with ORA-39139.

You may have doubt that a traditional export/import also can export objects in a higher version and import into a lower version. What is the advantage that Data Pump has with this version parameter?

Remember in the traditional method, if you want to import objects into a lower database version, then the export should have taken through that lower-version binaries. Suppose you want to import 11g objects into a 10g database; the export dump should have been taken through the 10g exp binaries. Or the dump cannot be imported. So, to take an export, you have to install the lower-version binaries on the source side, or the target site should have connectivity with the source database so that it can export the source database.

In Data Pump, that requirement has been overcome using the version parameter. Using this parameter, you can take an export of objects to the required version. You don't have any other requirement.

Stop and Reattach the Job

It is possible to stop and resume the job through Data Pump. The ATTACH command is used to continue the existing stopped export jobs. Here's an example:

```
oracle@localhost:/oradata/backup$ expdp system/manager directory=expdp_dir dumpfile=full_
db.dmp logfile=full_db.log  full=y
Export: Release 11.2.0.3.0
Starting "SYSTEM"."SYS_EXPORT_FULL_06":  system/******** directory=expdp_dir dumpfile=full_
db.dmp logfile=full_db.log full=y
```

A full backup has been initiated, and the backup is in progress. The job name is SYS_EXPORT_FULL_06. You stop the job using Ctrl+C.

```
Processing object type DATABASE_EXPORT/SCHEMA/SEQUENCE/GRANT/OWNER_GRANT/OBJECT_GRANT
^C
Export>
```

The Export prompt appears. Type **stop_job=immediate**, which stops the job and disconnects it from this session.

```
Export> stop_job=immediate
Are you sure you wish to stop this job ([yes]/no): y
```

Now we want resume the job. The reattach the job to the preferable session by just specifying username credentials and Job name as below

```
oracle@localhost:/oradata/backup$ expdp system/manager attach=SYS_EXPORT_FULL_06
Export: Release 11.2.0.3.
Job: SYS_EXPORT_FULL_06
  Owner: SYSTEM
  Operation: EXPORT
  Creator Privs: TRUE
  GUID:
  Start Time: <Data and Time it had started>
  Mode: FULL
  Instance: prim
  Max Parallelism: 1
  EXPORT Job Parameters:
  Parameter Name        Parameter Value:
     CLIENT_COMMAND        system/******** directory=expdp_dir dumpfile=full_db.dmp
logfile=full_db.log full=y
  State: IDLING
  Bytes Processed: 0
  Current Parallelism: 1
  Job Error Count: 0
  Dump File: /oradata/backup/full_db.dmp
    bytes written: 4,096
  Worker 1 Status:
  Process Name: DW00
  State: UNDEFINED
  Object Type: DATABASE_EXPORT/SYSTEM_PROCOBJACT/POST_SYSTEM_ACTIONS/PROCACT_SYSTEM
  Completed Objects: 4
  Total Objects: 4
  Worker Parallelism: 1
Type Continue_client to reinitiate the job
Export> continue_client
Job SYS_EXPORT_FULL_06 has been reopened at Saturday, 13 February, 2016 8:49
Restarting "SYSTEM"."SYS_EXPORT_FULL_06":  system/******** directory=expdp_dir
dumpfile=full_db.dmp logfile=full_db.log full=y
Processing object type DATABASE_EXPORT/SCHEMA/PROCACT_SCHEMA
```

Upgrade Steps

So far you have seen the new features released with Data Pump. Now let's move on to the steps to upgrade your database from a lower version to a higher version. Like a traditional export, you take a Data Pump backup on the source database and do the following:

1. In the source database server, create a logical directory to store the export dump.

2. The user who takes the export should have the Exp_full_database role.

87

3. Export the database with the `full=y` option.

4. The export dump will be stored at the logical directory created in step 1.

5. Move the dump to the target database server.

6. The user who imports the dump should have the role `Imp_full_database` role.

7. If datafiles have to be created and the directory structure is different, then specify the `remap_datafile` option.

8. If the target has the tablespace with the same name as the source database, then specify the `remap_tablespace` option.

9. Use the appropriate value for the `PARALLEL` parameter.

Here's an example:

Source database version: 10.2.0.1.0

We have created tablespace called 'TBS10G' at '/oradata/10.2.0.1.0/oradata/orcl/tbs10g01.dbf'

User 'DB10GUSER' has been created with default tablespace 'TBS10G'. Full database backup has been created using Expdp command.

```
Expdp command:
$$ expdp userid=\'sys/sys as sysdba\'  directory=data_pump_dir parallel=3 dumpfile=db10g%u.
dmp logfile=db10g.log full=y

Export: Release 10.2.0.1.0 - 64bit Production on Wednesday, 17 February, 2016 16:57:04

Copyright (c) 2003, 2005, Oracle.  All rights reserved.

Connected to: Oracle Database 10g Enterprise Edition Release 10.2.0.1.0 - 64bit Production
With the Partitioning, OLAP and Data Mining options
Starting "SYS"."SYS_EXPORT_FULL_01":  userid='sys/******** AS SYSDBA' directory=data_pump_
dir parallel=3 dumpfile=db10g%u.dmp logfile=db10g.log full=y
Estimate in progress using BLOCKS method...
Processing object type DATABASE_EXPORT/SCHEMA/TABLE/TABLE_DATA
Total estimation using BLOCKS method: 14.31 MB
Processing object type DATABASE_EXPORT/TABLESPACE
. . exported "SYSMAN"."MGMT_METRICS"                        553.3 KB    2578 rows
.
.
Master table "SYS"."SYS_EXPORT_FULL_01" successfully loaded/unloaded
****************************************************************************
Dump file set for SYS.SYS_EXPORT_FULL_01 is:
  /oradata/10.2.0.1.0/dbhome_1/rdbms/log/db10g01.dmp
  /oradata/10.2.0.1.0/dbhome_1/rdbms/log/db10g02.dmp
  /oradata/10.2.0.1.0/dbhome_1/rdbms/log/db10g03.dmp
Job "SYS"."SYS_EXPORT_FULL_01" successfully completed
```

Target database: We import this dump into 12c database to upgrade this database to 12c version.

Let's upgrade straightly to 12c pluggable database.

Target database version: 12.1.0.2.0

Target database name: PDB12c

We use IMPDP utility to import the database into 12*c* pluggable database. We create tns entry for pluggable database PDB12*c*. Remember the directory structure is different at target server. We don't have same directory path for datafiles as source has. Hence either we need to create same directory structure or use REMAP_DATAFILE parameter. Let's try to use REMAP_DATAFILE and import the dump.

```
The format of REMAP_DATAFILE is
REMAP_DATAFILE=source_datafile:target_datafile
```

We shall create par file as the number of arguments for impdp is huge

```
$cat imp10g.par
DIRECTORY=imp_dir
FULL=YES
DUMPFILE= db10g01.dmp, db10g02.dmp, db10g03.dmp
REMAP_DATAFILE="'/oradata/10.2.0.1.0/oradata/orcl/tbs10g01.dbf':'/u01/app/oracle/oradata/
CDB12C/tbs10g01.dbf'","'/oradata/10.2.0.1.0/oradata/orcl/users01.dbf':'/u01/app/oracle/
oradata/CDB12C/users01.dbf'"
logfile=DB10g_DB12c.log
```

In remap we have specified the different directory for users and tbs10g tablespace for target site.

```
$ impdp userid=\'sys@pdb12c as sysdba\' parfile=imp10g.par
Password:
Connected to: Oracle Database 12c Enterprise Edition Release 12.1.0.2.0 - 64bit Production
import done in WE8MSWIN1252 character set and AL16UTF16 NCHAR character set
export done in WE8ISO8859P1 character set and AL16UTF16 NCHAR character set
Starting "SYS"."SYS_IMPORT_FULL_01":  userid="sys/********@pdb12c AS SYSDBA" parfile=imp10g.par
Processing object type DATABASE_EXPORT/TABLESPACE
ORA-31684: Object type TABLESPACE:"SYSAUX" already exists
ORA-31684: Object type TABLESPACE:"TEMP" already exists
Processing object type DATABASE_EXPORT/PROFILE
Processing object type DATABASE_EXPORT/SYS_USER/USER
Processing object type DATABASE_EXPORT/SCHEMA/USER
ORA-31684: Object type USER:"OUTLN" already exists
ORA-31684: Object type USER:"ANONYMOUS" already exists
ORA-31684: Object type USER:"OLAPSYS" already exists
ORA-31684: Object type USER:"MDDATA" already exists
Processing object type DATABASE_EXPORT/ROLE
.
.
.
ORA-39082: Object type PACKAGE BODY:"SYSMAN"."MGMT_LOCK_UTIL" created with compilation warnings
ORA-39082: Object type TRIGGER:"SYSMAN"."MGMT_CREDS_INS_UPD" created with compilation warnings
Job "SYS"."SYS_IMPORT_FULL_01" completed
```

Check the tablespaces got created in target server.

```
SQL> select tablespace_name, file_name from cdb_data_files where tablespace_name='USERS' or
tablespace_name='TBS10G';
TABLESPACE_NAME
------------------------------
FILE_NAME
------------------------------------------------------------------------
USERS
/u01/app/oracle/oradata/CDB12C/users01.dbf

TBS10G
/u01/app/oracle/oradata/CDB12C/tbs10g01.dbf
```

Remember the impdp just imports the dump. It doesn't check whether the importing objects are valid or deprecated in 12*c*.

Transportable Tablespace

Transportable tablespace (TTS) is a mechanism to copy tablespaces between two different/same versions of databases. Using this method for a database upgrade, you can move nonadministrative tablespaces from a lower version to a higher version. There are two kinds of tablespaces present in the database: administrative tablespaces (SYSTEM, SYSAUX, UNDO, and TEMP) and nonadministrative tablespaces such as USERS and application-related tablespaces. In this method, the source database's nonadministrative tablespaces along with the datafiles will be physically moved to a higher database version, and the metadata of those datafiles will be imported to make it part of the higher-version database. The tablespace can be either dictionary managed or locally managed. This method can also move tablespaces across platforms. From an upgrade perspective, you will explore the steps to move tablespaces within the same platform. Doing an upgrade cross-platform will be covered in Chapter 5.

In general, this method will be used when the database is huge and doesn't meet the upgrade compatibility matrix. Unlike export/import or Data Pump, it will not extract and move data logically; instead, it moves datafiles physically to the target database. Extracting data and creating the dump file is a time-consuming process. Instead, copying all the datafiles and then adding those datafiles to the target database version will benefit you in many ways. There is no need to take a backup of each individual schema; the time taken will be less than with the traditional export/import or Data Pump.

The tablespaces involved in the TTS method are called the *transportable tablespace set*.

In this method, the source database is intact; you just place the tablespaces in read-only state for a short duration. The duration depends on the tablespace size and transfer speed between the source and target database destinations. Other than that, there are no changes in the source database.

This method was introduced in Oracle 8*i*. From Oracle 9*i*, the TTS method has been enhanced to support tablespaces with different block sizes.

From Oracle 10*g*, the TTS method has been further enhanced to support the transportation of tablespaces between databases running on different OS platforms (for example, Microsoft Windows to Oracle Linux or Oracle Solaris to HP-UX), which has same endian formats.

Oracle 10*g* R1 introduced cross-platform transportable tablespaces (XTTS), which allows datafiles to be moved between platforms of different endian formats.

From Oracle 10*g* R2, you can transport the whole database, which is called the *transportable database* (TDB).

From Oracle 11*g*, you can transport a single partition of a tablespace between databases.

You can query the V$TRANSPORTABLE_PLATFORM view to see all the platforms that are supported.

```
SQL> select * from v$transportable_platform order by platform_id;
```

Things to Consider

At the target site, the database should have been created with a higher version. The target database should not have a tablespace with the same name as tablespaces getting transported from the source database.

The tablespace sets needs to be self-contained for getting part of the TTS method. If the tablespace has objects that have dependent objects on some other tablespace, then that dependent object's tablespace also should be part of the TTS procedure. For example, partitioned tables/partitioned indexes may exist in different tablespaces. All tablespaces should be part of the transport tablespace set.

The character set and national character set of the source and target databases should be the same, or the source database character set should be a binary subset of the target database character set.

Administrative tablespaces (SYSTEM and SYSAUX) will not be transported.

TTS is might not be a suitable solution for applications that have more objects to rebuild. For example, partitions, subpartitions, partitioned indexes, and so on, will impact the TTS method in mission-critical database environments.

Prerequisites to Perform Transportable Tablespace

Find the schema details of objects that exist in the TTS.

```
SQL>Select distinct owner from dba_segments where tablespace_name='<tablespace name>';
```

These schemas must be created in the target database.

In target database check whether choosen tablespaces have the same name as tablespace getting transported.

```
SQL>select tablespace_name from dba_tablespaces where tablespace_name='<chosen tablespace for transport>';
```

Perform set integrity check for chosen tablespaces in source database

```
SQL>EXEC SYS.DBMS_TTS.TRANSPORT_SET_CHECK(ts_list => '<tablespace_name>,<tablespace_name>',
incl_constraints => TRUE);
```

While executing this procedure TTS violations are recorded in the view Transport_set_violations

```
SQL>Select * from transport_set_violations;
```

If there are any violations, they will be listed here.

```
Eg: ORA-39907: Index TEST.TTS_INDEX in tablespace TTS2 points to table TEST.TTS_TEST in
tablespace TTS1.
```

This shows that the table and index are in different tablespaces and both have to be considered for the transportable tablespace set.

Check the character set of the source and target databases. The database character sets of the source and target databases should be the same or the source character set should be a subset of the target character set.

```
SQL> SELECT value$ FROM sys.props$ WHERE name = 'NLS_CHARACTERSET';
```

The tablespaces should be online and read-only and should not require recovery.

```
SQL>select tablespace_name, status from dba_tablespaces where tablespace_name='<tablespace_name>';
```

Ensure that high network bandwidth is available between the source and target database servers or copying datafiles will consume more time and in turn increase database downtime.

As a best practice, ensure there are no invalid objects in the transportable tablespace. Having invalid objects may not create any issues, but the target database will get these invalid objects after upgrade.

The default Data Pump directory will not work for the Oracle 12c pluggable database architecture. Create an explicit data pump directory.

Figure 2-33 shows the sequence of steps for an upgrade.

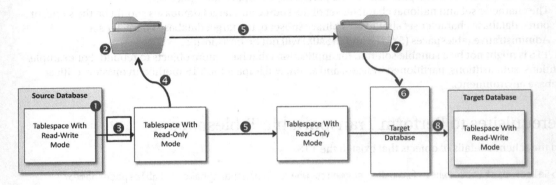

Figure 2-33. TTS upgrade steps

Upgrade Steps

① First ensure all the prerequisites are met in the source database and there are no violations reported.

② Create a directory object at the source and target databases to hold the metadata of the tablespaces.

```
SQL> connect / as sysdba
SQL> create directory tts_dir as ' <Directory location> ';
```

③ At the source database, make the chosen transportable tablespaces set to read-only (the following statement has to be executed individually for each tablespace involved in the TTS move):

```
SQL>alter tablespace <tablespace_name> read only;
```

Here the downtime starts for the tablespace (or tablespaces); or, you can say the downtime for the application depends on the number of tablespaces involved in this scenario.

④ Take export of metadata of chosen tablespace(s)

```
expdp userid=<username/password> directory=<Logical_directory_name> transport_
tablespaces=<tablespace_name> dumpfile=<Dump_file_name> logfile=<log_file_name>
```

Transport_tablespaces will carry tablespace information. In case multiple tablespaces are there then specify with comma seperator.

In case source database is lesser than Oracle 10gR1 then

```
exp userid=<username/password> transport_tablespace=y transport_tablespaces=<tablespace_
name> file=<Dump_file_name along with location> log=<log_file_name along with location>
```

⑤ Physically copy the datafiles of the chosen tablespaces and metadata dump file to the target database server. The target location for datafiles may have the same folder name or it can be different.

6 Ensure the required schemas are created with the required privileges in the target database.

7 Plug in the tablespace into the target database using Data Pump.

```
impdp userid=<username/password> directory=<Logical_directory_name>  dumpfile=<Dump_file_
name> logfile=<log_file_name> transport_datafiles='<datafile name along with location>'
```

Transport_datafiles will have datafile names along with location
In case you are upgrading to home lesser than Oracle 10g then

```
imp userid=<username/password> transport_tablespace=y datafiles='<datafile name along with
location>' tablespaces=<tablespace_name> file=<Dump_file_name along with location> log=<log_
file_name along with location>
```

8 Change the tablespaces to read-only to read-write mode at the target database and the source database. (The following statement has to be executed for each tablespace individually.) Downtime at the source database ends here once you make the tablespaces read-write.

```
SQL> alter tablespace <tablespace_name> read write;
```

The tablespaces at the source can be switched back to read-write after copying the datafiles and metadata dump to the target server. It may reduce the downtime at the source database server, but the source and target tablespaces may not be in sync.

Here's an example:

```
Source Database Version: Oracle 10g (10.2.0.5.0)
Source Database Name: DB10g
Target database Version: Oracle 11g (11.2.0.4.0)
Target database Name: Prim
Tablespaces to be transported: TTS1 and TTS2
```

Check the schema having objects in transported tablespace

```
sys:DB10g> Select unique owner from dba_segments where tablespace_name='TTS1';
OWNER
-----------------
TEST

sys:DB10g> Select unique owner from dba_segments where tablespace_name='TTS2';
OWNER
---------------
TEST
```

Schema 'TEST' has to be created in 11.2.0.4.0 database if not present there.

```
sys:prim>select username from dba_users where username='TEST';
no rows selected
```

The output shows the user TEST is not present and it has to be created. It's better to create the user TEST with the same privileges as in the source database. Using the following queries, the granted privileges can be identified:

```
sys:DB10g>select grantee, GRANTED_ROLE, ADMIN_OPTION, DEFAULT_ROLE from dba_role_privs where
grantee='TEST';
```

```
sys:DB10g>select GRANTEE, PRIVILEGE, ADMIN_OPTION from dba_sys_privs where grantee='TEST';

sys:DB10g>select PRIVILEGE ||' on '||owner||'.'||TABLE_NAME from dba_tab_privs where
grantee='TEST';
```

At Target Database:

```
sys:prim>create user test identified by test;
User created.
```

Grant the privileges retrieved from the above queries.
Ensure there is no tablespace in the name of TTS1 and TTS2

```
sys:prim>select tablespace_name from dba_tablespaces where tablespace_name='TTS1' or
tablespace_name='TTS2';

no rows selected
```

At Source Database:
Perform self integrity check for tablespaces TTS1 and TTS2

```
sys:DB10g>EXEC SYS.DBMS_TTS.TRANSPORT_SET_CHECK(ts_list => 'TTS1,TTS2',incl_constraints => TRUE);

PL/SQL procedure successfully completed.

sys:DB10g>Select * from transport_set_violations;
no rows selected
```

The result shows there are no violations and both the tablespaces can be transported.
Create the logical directory to store the export metadata. As this is an Oracle 10*g* R2 database, you use
Data Pump to export it.

```
$mkdir /u01/app/oracle/backup

sys:DB10g>create directory tts_dir as '/u01/app/oracle/backup';
Directory created.

sys:DB10g>Grant read, write on directory tts_dir to test;
Grant succeeded.
```

Put the tablespaces TTS1 and TTS2 to read only mode

```
sys:DB10g>alter tablespace tts1 read only;
Tablespace altered.

sys:DB10g>alter tablespace tts2 read only;
Tablespace altered.

oracle@localhost:~$ expdp userid=test/test directory=tts_dir transport_tablespaces=tts1,tts2
dumpfile=tablespace_metadata.dmp logfile=tablespace_metadata.log
```

As the TEST user has DBA privileges, you took an export using that user. You can also try with SYS or
SYSTEM or any other DBA user. The following is the command to take a backup using the SYS user:

94

```
expdp userid=\'sys/<password> as sysdba\' directory=tts_dir transport_tablespaces=tts1,tts2
dumpfile=tablespace_metadata.dmp logfile=tablespace_metadata.log
```

Copy the physical datafiles and metadata dump to target database server. To know physical datafiles and its location execute below query

```
sys:DB10g>select file_name from dba_data_files where tablespace_name='TTS1' or tablespace_
name='TTS2';
FILE_NAME
-----------------------------------------------------------------
/oradata/DB10g/tts101.dbf
/oradata/DB10g/tts201.dbf
```

Physical datafiles and tablespace_metadata.dmp (/u01/app/oracle/backup/tablespace_metadata.dmp) are copied to the location /oradata/prim in Oracle 11g (11.2.0 4.0) target database server.

```
Import the metadata
/oradata/prim$ impdp userid=test/test directory=tts_dir dumpfile=tablespace_metadata.
dmp logfile=tablespace_metadata_imp.log transport_datafiles='/oradata/prim/tts101.dbf','/
oradata/prim/tts201.dbf'
```

Check the impdp output. There should not be any error.
Verify whether these tablespace become part of database

```
SYS:prim> select tablespace_name, file_name  from dba_data_files where tablespace_
name='TTS1' or tablespace_name='TTS2';
TABLESPACE_NAME
----------------
FILE_NAME
-----------------------------------------------------------------------TTS1
/oradata/prim/tts101.dbf

TTS2
/oradata/prim/tts201.dbf

SYS:prim>  select tablespace_name, status from dba_tablespaces  where tablespace_name='TTS1'
or tablespace_name='TTS2';

TABLESPACE_NAME                  STATUS
------------------------------ ---------
TTS1                             READ ONLY
TTS2                             READ ONLY
```

Make the tablespaces (TTS1 and TTS2) from read only mode to read write mode in Oracle 10g (10.2.0.5.0) and Oracle 11g (11.2.0.4.0) databases

```
SYS:prim> alter tablespace tts1 read write;
Tablespace altered.

SYS:prim> alter tablespace tts2 read write;
Tablespace altered.
```

```
SYS:prim> select tablespace_name, status from dba_tablespaces  where tablespace_name='TTS1'
or tablespace_name='TTS2';
TABLESPACE_NAME                      STATUS
------------------------------- ---------
TTS1                                 ONLINE
TTS2                                 ONLINE
```

For upgrading to a 12*c* multitenant architecture, other methods like using the DBUA or a manual upgrade demand moving to a nonmultitenant architecture first and then migrating to a multitenant architecture. But by using the TTS method, you can directly transport datafiles to a 12*c* pluggable database.

Note that for 11*g* R2 you can make use of the default logical directories available in the database like DATA_PUMP_DIR (in the previous exercise you created the directory tts_dir explicitly). But in 12*c* you cannot use the default logical directory; you need to create the directory explicitly.

Let's see the steps with the previous example:

- *Source database version*: Oracle 10*g* (10.2.0.5.0)

- *Source database name*: DB10g

- *Target database version*: Oracle 12*c* (12.1.0.2.0) with the multitenant option

- *Target database name*: Container database (cdbtest) and pluggable database (pdbtts)

The prerequisites and TTS steps for the source database are the same. On the target, you will connect to the pluggable database (pdbtts) through the connection identifier.

We will create user 'TEST' if not present in pluggable database (pdbtts)

```
Provide the necessary privilege to the user 'TEST'
Create directory TTS_DIR
Grant privileges to the TTS_DIR for the user 'TEST'

SQL:PDBTTS> create directory tts_dir as '/u01/app/oracle/backup';
Directory created.

SQL:PDBTTS > grant read, write on directory tts_dir to test;
Grant succeeded.
```

Copy the physical datafiles and metadata dump to Oracle 12*c* oracle database server and invoke impdp command

```
impdp userid=test/test@pdbtts directory=tts_dir  dumpfile=tablespace_metadata.dmp
logfile=tablespace_metadata_imp.log transport_datafiles='/u01/app/oracle/oradata/CDBTEST/
tts101.dbf','/u01/app/oracle/oradata/CDBTEST/tts201.dbf'

SQL> select tablespace_name, file_name  from dba_data_files where tablespace_name='TTS1' or
tablespace_name='TTS2';
```

```
TABLESPACE_NAME
------------------------------
FILE_NAME
--------------------------------------------------------------------------
TTS2
/u01/app/oracle/oradata/CDBTEST/tts201.dbf

TTS1
/u01/app/oracle/oradata/CDBTEST/tts101.dbf

SQL> alter tablespace tts1 read write;
Tablespace altered.

SQL> alter tablespace tts2 read write;
Tablespace altered.
```

SQL> select tablespace_name, status from dba_tablespaces where tablespace_name='TTS1' or tablespace_name='TTS2';

```
TABLESPACE_NAME                    STATUS
------------------------------     ---------
TTS2                               ONLINE
TTS1                               ONLINE
```

Here are the known issues:

Sys owned objects should not exist in transportable tablespaces. If exists then violation will be reported

```
SYS:DB10g>  Select * from sys.transport_set_violations ;

VIOLATIONS
--------------------------------------------------------------------------------
Sys owned object  TEST in tablespace TTS1 not allowed in pluggable set
```

Downtime is calculated from the time source datafiles are moved to the read-only state. If network bandwidth is tiny, then the downtime will increase.

If any user object persists in the administrative tablespace, then it will not be transported in the TTS method.

Limitations

SYSTEM, UNDO, SYSAUX, and temporary tablespaces cannot be transported.

TTS will not move nonsegment objects such as PL/SQL procedures or packages. It needs to be manually extracted using the DBMS_METADATA.GET_DDL package and executed in the target database.

The source and target databases must use the same character set, and the national character set or target character set should be a superset of the source character set. If Automatic Storage Management (ASM) is used with either the source or destination database, you can use RMAN or dbms_file_transfer to transport the tablespace.

TTS does not support materialized views/replication or function-based indexes.

You can't do TTS when you are using Transparent Data Encryption (TDE) to protect the database.

The Binary_Float and Binary_Double datatypes are not supported if the database is Oracle 10g.

Advantages

Here are the advantages of this method:

- The source database remains unchanged in this method.

- Database downtime is less compared to the traditional upgrade methods.

- With TTS, bit conversion also possible.

- There's no need to take a database backup in this method, so you can reduce some of the steps in mission-critical database environments.

Database Upgrade Using Oracle GoldenGate

The current trend in IT of eliminating database downtime in production environments poses a significant challenge for IT organizations. You need to upgrade/migrate mission-critical database environments running on older versions of Oracle Database to newer versions of Oracle Database. When you upgrade/migrate, you have to provide continuous or near-continuous operations to application users/end users so that you can eliminate the impact on revenue as well as the reputation of the business operations.

This chapter explains how to upgrade with minimal downtime from Oracle Database 11*g* to Oracle Database 12*c* using Oracle GoldenGate. Oracle GoldenGate (OGG) is an Oracle product sold independently for Oracle Database and third-party database management systems. It is available for both Oracle Database Enterprise Edition (EE) and Oracle Database Standard Edition 2. When you upgrade/migrate, you have two choices; you can upgrade as a noncontainer database and you can convert as a pluggable database later in a container database or you can upgrade as a pluggable database (PDB) in a container database (CDB) in a multitenant environment. You can achieve these two methods through Oracle GoldenGate's real-time data integration and replication functionality with near zero-downtime. After the upgrade, you can check the data verification between the source database and the target database. You can use Oracle GoldenGate for application upgrades, database upgrades, hardware upgrades, and even endian changes.

This chapter will show how to eliminate database downtime minimally during a planned outage for database upgrades and migrations and how to minimize the clock time required to perform the entire database upgrade including data verification.

Using Oracle GoldenGate (OGG) in conjunction with Oracle database features, you can perform a rolling upgrade or a rolling migration from an older version of Oracle Database to a newer version of Oracle Database, with minimal application downtime, including the new multitenant architecture of Oracle 12*c*.

One of the major advantages of Oracle GoldenGate is you can implement uni/bidirectional replication between older versions of Oracle Database and newer version of Oracle Database. Both environments will support the application users. The application and end users will have options such as phased migration to the newer-version Oracle Database system, and switching over to the newer version of Oracle Database is completely transparent to the application users or with minimal downtime.

Planning Phase with Oracle GoldenGate

Oracle GoldenGate will not support all datatypes. In the planning phase, check the data types used in the source database with the application team. If datatypes that are not supported are found in the source database, you can plan for other arrangements for these data types.

In the planning phase, check the certification matrix for versions and platform support. Log in to My Oracle Support and click the Certifications tab. Specify the product, release, and platform.

Figure 2-34 shows an example of Oracle GoldenGate 12.2.0.1.0 being certified on Oracle Linux 6 (x86-64).

In the planning phase, you have to check and plan the storage space needed for Oracle GoldenGate trail

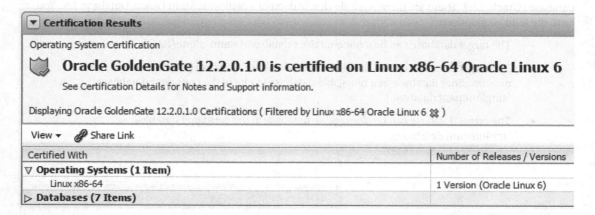

▼ **Certification Results**

Operating System Certification

Oracle GoldenGate 12.2.0.1.0 is certified on Linux x86-64 Oracle Linux 6

See Certification Details for Notes and Support information.

Displaying Oracle GoldenGate 12.2.0.1.0 Certifications (Filtered by Linux x86-64 Oracle Linux 6 ✖)

View ▼   🔗 Share Link

Certified With	Number of Releases / Versions
▽ **Operating Systems (1 Item)**	
Linux x86-64	1 Version (Oracle Linux 6)
▷ **Databases (7 Items)**	

Figure 2-34. *GoldenGate certification*

files in the source database as well as the target database and also calculate the memory requirements each process (extract, pump, and replicat processes).

Figure 2-35 shows the Oracle GoldenGate working functionality.

Here are some details:

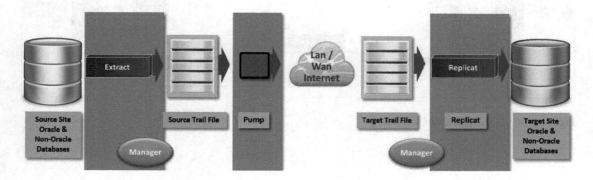

Figure 2-35. *Oracle GoldenGate working functionality*

- *Extract process*: Committed transactions are captured from the source database.

- *Trail file*: This stages the committed transactions for routing in a local trail file.

- *Pump process*: This distributes committed transactions to the target database (or databases).

- *Replicat process*: This applies committed transactions to the target database (or databases).

- *Manager process*: This is required to start and stop processes and is responsible for monitoring. It will be up and running in the source database as well as the target database.

Figure 2-36 shows ways to replicate data to Oracle 11*g* to Oracle 12*c* with high-level steps.

You can use the following ways to replicate a database from an older version to a newer version using Oracle GoldenGate. Set up database replication between the source database (Oracle 11*g*) to the target database (Oracle 12*c*). There are three possible Oracle database deployments in Oracle Database 12*c*. You have the following options:

- The target database can be a noncontainer database (stand-alone/RAC).

- The target database can be a noncontainer database, and later you can convert the noncontainer database as a pluggable database to one of the container databases (single-tenant database).

- The target database can be a pluggable database to the container database (multitenant database).

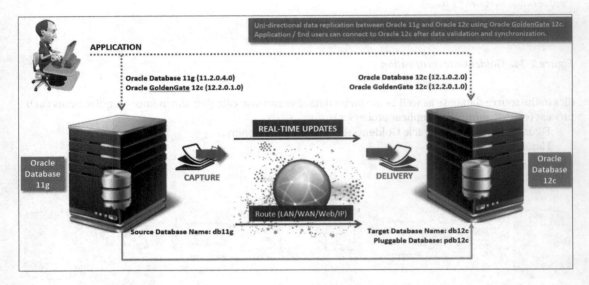

Figure 2-36. *GoldenGate unidirectional*

Implement a unidirectional (Table 2-10) between the source database (Oracle 11g) and the target database (Oracle12c). After application and end users connect to the target database (Oracle 12c), you can implement bidirectional (Table 2-11) to make use of the source database for backup and reporting purposes.

Table 2-10. *Database Version Before and After Upgrade*

Source Database		Target Database
BEFORE UPGRADE:		
Oracle Database 11g (11.2.0.4.0) Single Instance (db11g) With Oracle GoldenGate 12c(12.2.0.1.0)	Uni-Directional →	Oracle Database 12c (12.1.0.2.0) Multitenant Database (db12c) With pluggable database (pdb12c) With Oracle GoldenGate 12c(12.2.0.1.0)
AFTER UPGRADE:		
Oracle Database 11g (11.2.0.4.0) Single Instance (db11g) With Oracle GoldenGate 12c(12.2.0.1.0)	← Bi-Directional →	Oracle Database 12c (12.1.0.2.0) Multitenant Database (db12c) With pluggable database (pdb12c) With Oracle GoldenGate 12c(12.2.0.1.0)

Here are the configurations at the source database and the target database with high-level steps:

1. Create, configure, and apply any latest patches to the Oracle Database 12c environment in the target database server.

2. Create and configure the Oracle GoldenGate 12c environment in the target database server.

3. Create and configure the Oracle GoldenGate 12c environment in the source database server.

4. Build up the database copy with Data Pump or TTS with the system change number (SCN).

5. Restore the database backup in the new version of Oracle Database setup in the target database server.

6. Implement unidirectional data replication between the source database and the target database.

After unidirectional data replication, you can verify the data validation and synchronization using Oracle GoldenGate Veridata. This is optional but recommended for critical production database environments.

Shut down the application, restart it, and point to the target database server.

To achieve high availability or use the fallback option, you can implement bidirectional replication between these two database environments or upgrade the source Oracle Database 11g to Oracle Database 12c and start replicating the data between the newly upgraded source database and the target database server.

In either case, you can use the source database server for reporting and backup purposes instead of keeping the source database idle.

In this chapter, we have set up the environment as follows:

- Installed and configured the Oracle Database 11*g* (11.2.0.4.0) binaries with the Oracle database db11*g* as the source database.

- Installed and configured the Oracle GoldenGate 12*c* (12.2.0.1.0) binaries with the extract process (escott), pump process (pscott), and the manager process in the source database.

- Installed and configured the Oracle Database 12*c* (12.1.0.2.0) binaries with the Oracle database db12*c* as a container database with the pluggable database (pdb12c) in a target database.

- Installed and configured Oracle GoldenGate 12*c* (12.2.0.1.0) binaries with the replicat process (rscott) and the manager process in the target database.

- Create and configure the extract process (escott) on the source database. The extract process (ESCOTT) reads from the Oracle redo logs in the source database (db11g).

- Create and configure the Pump process (pscott) on the source database. The pump process (PSCOTT) will move captured transactions to the target pluggable database (pdb12*c*) in the container database (db12*c*)

- Create and configure the replicat process (rscott) on the target database. The replicat process (RSCOTT) will be used to sync up the source database as well as the target database.

- The replicat process (rscott) will be used to sync up both the databases based on the SCN. This SCN you will get prior to an Oracle export (exp).

- Export the data from the source database using the export utility.

- Import the data in the target database using the import utility.

- Start the replicat process (rscott) in the target database after the last CSN exported from the source database.

- Finally, check the transactions between the source and target databases.

Enter the new transactions in source database and check whether those transactions are in sync with the target database.

While installing Oracle GoldenGate 12*c* binaries, you have the option to select Oracle GoldenGate binaries for Oracle 12*c* and Oracle GoldenGate binaries for Oracle 11*g*.

Select the option to install Oracle GoldenGate for Oracle 12*c* for the target database.

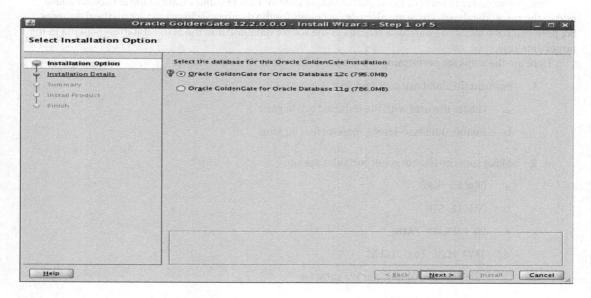

Figure 2-37. *GoldenGate installation option*

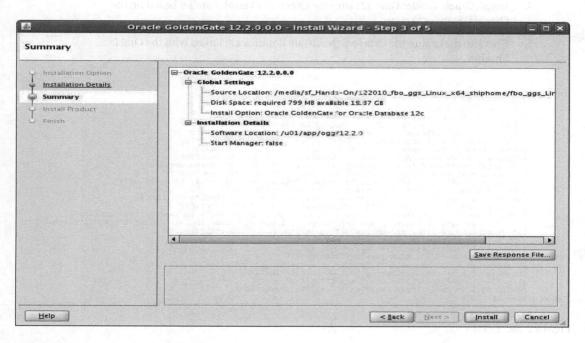

Figure 2-38. *GoldenGate installation summary*

Select the option to install Oracle GoldenGate for Oracle 11*g* for the source database (Figure 2-37).

Best practices say to set up a dedicated database user for Oracle GoldenGate in the source database and in the target database. There are also user accounts for the database schemas to set up the databases. So, here you have the SCOTT database schema in the source database and the SCOTT database schema in the target database.

Here are the steps for performing the Oracle GoldenGate 12*c* installation:

1. Perform the database prerequisites.

    a. Create the user with the required privileges.

    b. Enable database-level supplemental logging.

2. Make sure the environment variables are set.

    a. ORACLE_HOME

    b. ORACLE_SID

    c. LD_LIBRARY_PATH

    d. JAVA_HOME for JAGENT

3. Stage the Oracle GoldenGate 12*c* software.

    a. unzip <fbo for OGG>

4. Install Oracle GoldenGate 12*c* with the Oracle Universal Installer based on the Oracle Database version.

5. Check to make sure the Oracle GoldenGate libraries are linked with the Oracle libraries.

```
[oracle@ggnode1 12g]$ ldd ggsci
        linux-vdso.so.1 =>   (0x00007ffffc1ff000)
        librt.so.1 => /lib64/librt.so.1 (0x0000003fa9400000)
        libdl.so.2 => /lib64/libdl.so.2 (0x0000003fa7000000)
        libgglog.so => /u01/app/ogg/12g/./libgglog.so (0x00007f8abc940000)
        libggrepo.so => /u01/app/ogg/12g/./libggrepo.so (0x00007f8abc6ce000)
        libdb-6.1.so => /u01/app/ogg/12g/./libdb-6.1.so (0x00007f8abc2e9000)
        libggperf.so => /u01/app/ogg/12g/./libggperf.so (0x00007f8abc0b9000)
        libggparam.so => /u01/app/ogg/12g/./libggparam.so (0x00007f8abafaf000)
        libicui18n.so.48 => /u01/app/ogg/12g/./libicui18n.so.48 (0x00007f8ababbf000)
        libicuuc.so.48 => /u01/app/ogg/12g/./libicuuc.so.48 (0x00007f8aba93e000)
        libicudata.so.48 => /u01/app/ogg/12g/./libicudata.so.48 (0x00007f8ab9079000)
        libpthread.so.0 => /lib64/libpthread.so.0 (0x0000003fa7800000)
        libxerces-c.so.28 => /u01/app/ogg/12g/./libxerces-c.so.28 (0x00007f8ab8ab2000)
        libantlr3c.so => /u01/app/ogg/12g/./libantlr3c.so (0x00007f8ab8899000)
        libnnz11.so => /u01/app/oracle/product/11.2.0.4/db_1/lib/libnnz11.so (0x00007f8ab84cb000)
        libclntsh.so.11.1 => /u01/app/oracle/product/11.2.0.4/db_1/lib/libclntsh.so.11.1 (0x00007f8ab5a61000)
        libggnnzitp.so => /u01/app/ogg/12g/./libggnnzitp.so (0x00007f8ab530a000)
        libm.so.6 => /lib64/libm.so.6 (0x0000003fa7400000)
        libc.so.6 => /lib64/libc.so.6 (0x0000003fa6c00000)
        /lib64/ld-linux-x86-64.so.2 (0x0000003fa6400000)
        libstdc++.so.6 => /usr/lib64/libstdc++.so.6 (0x0000003fad400000)
        libgcc_s.so.1 => /lib64/libgcc_s.so.1 (0x0000003fab400000)
        libnsl.so.1 => /lib64/libnsl.so.1 (0x0000003fadc00000)
        libaio.so.1 => /usr/lib64/libaio.so.1 (0x0000003fa6800000)
[oracle@ggnode1 12g]$
```

Figure 2-39. *GGSCI*

6. Run the following commands from the command line in the Oracle GoldenGate (OGG) directory in the source database and the target database and look for any missing paths.

```
ldd mgr
ldd extract
ldd replicat
ldd ggsci
```

7. In GGSCI, run the CREATE SUBDIRS command for Oracle GoldenGate in the source database and the target database. This command creates subdirectories that you need for Oracle GoldenGate.

Configuration Setup at the Source Database (Oracle 11g)

Log in to the source database (db11g) as a SYS user and create the following steps for data replication between the source database (db11g) and the target pluggable database (pdb12c).

```
1 Create the GoldenGate tablespace 'tbsgg'
2 Create the user 'ogguser'
3 Assign the privileges for 'ogguser'
4 Add database level supplemental logging
5 Check database log mode
6 Set the database in 'FORCE LOGGING' mode
7 Grant dbms_flashback to the database schema 'SCOTT'
8 Set the parameter 'enable_goldengate_replication' to TRUE
9 Export the user 'SCOTT' data with System Change Number (SCN)
```

```
[oracle@ggnode1 ~]$ sqlplus /nolog
SQL*Plus: Release 11.2.0.4.0 Production on Wed Dec 23 11:18:49 2015
Copyright (c) 1982, 2013, Oracle.  All rights reserved.

SQL> connect sys/oracle@db11g as sysdba
Connected.

SQL> create tablespace tbsgg datafile '/u01/app/oracle/oradata/db11g/tbsgg01.dbf' size 10M
autoextend on;
Tablespace created.

SQL> create user ogguser identified by oracle default tablespace tbsgg temporary tablespace
temp account unlock;
User created.

SQL> grant connect,resource,dba,unlimited tablespace,select any dictionary to ogguser;
Grant succeeded.
```

If you need to restrict DBA privileges for the ogguser user, do the following:

```
SQL> alter database add supplemental log data;
Database altered.
```

```
SQL> alter database force logging;
Database altered.

SQL> alter system switch logfile;
System altered.

SQL> select supplemental_log_data_min from v$database;

SUPPLEMENTAL
--------------------
YES

SQL> show parameter enable_goldengate

NAME                                TYPE              VALUE
-----------------------------------------------------------------------------------
enable_goldengate_replication       boolean           FALSE
```

Note: If version of Oracle, 11.2.0.4 OR newer set the following parameter.

```
SQL> alter system set enable_goldengate_replication = TRUE scope=both;
System altered.

SQL> show parameter enable_goldengate

NAME                                TYPE              VALUE
-----------------------------------------------------------------------------------
enable_goldengate_replication       boolean           TRUE
```

Using the SQL*Plus prompt, you need to find the current Oracle SCN in the source database. (For the purpose of this example, you assume that there are no open transactions in the source database.) Make a note of SCN in the source database.

```
SQL> select dbms_flashback.get_system_change_number from dual;

GET_SYSTEM_CHANGE_NUMBER
--------------------------------------------
1004290
```

Grant DBMS_FLASHBACK package to user 'SCOTT'. You need to grant the package in order to use the FLASHBACK_SCN Parameter in the next step.

```
SQL> grant execute on dbms_flashback to scott;
Grant succeeded.
```

Now will use the Oracle System Change Number (SCN) as a marker and export the data from the source database for the user 'SCOTT'

```
[oracle@ggnode1 ~]$ exp scott/oracle flashback_scn=1004290 file=/u01/app/ogg/12g/scott.dmp
owner=scott
```

```
Export: Release 11.2.0.4.0 - Production on Mon Jan 4 15:11:38 2016
Copyright (c) 1982, 2011, Oracle and/or its affiliates. All rights reserved.


Connected to: Oracle Database 11g Enterprise Edition Release 11.2.0.4.0 - 64bit Production
With the Partitioning, OLAP, Data Mining and Real Application Testing options
Export done in US7ASCII character set and AL16UTF16 NCHAR character set
server uses AL32UTF8 character set (possible charset conversion)
. exporting pre-schema procedural objects and actions
. exporting foreign function library names for user SCOTT
. exporting PUBLIC type synonyms
. exporting private type synonyms
. exporting object type definitions for user SCOTT
About to export SCOTT's objects ...
. exporting database links
. exporting sequence numbers
. exporting cluster definitions
. about to export SCOTT's tables via Conventional Path ...
. . exporting table                     BONUS          0 rows exported
. . exporting table                      DEPT          4 rows exported
. . exporting table                       EMP         14 rows exported
. . exporting table                  SALGRADE          5 rows exported
. exporting synonyms
. exporting views
. exporting stored procedures
. exporting operators
. exporting referential integrity constraints
. exporting triggers
. exporting indextypes
. exporting bitmap, functional and extensible indexes
. exporting posttables actions
. exporting materialized views
. exporting snapshot logs
. exporting job queues
. exporting refresh groups and children
. exporting dimensions
. exporting post-schema procedural objects and actions
. exporting statistics
Export terminated successfully without warnings.
```

After the export has successfully completed, copy or move the export file, SCOTT.dmp, from the source OGG to the target OGG folder.

Here is the configuration setup at the source database, Oracle 11g, for Oracle GoldenGate 12c:

1 Create subdirectories for OGG
2 Create Extract process (escott)
3 Add local trail file for extract process (escott)
4 Create Pump process (pscott)
5 Add remote trail file and attach it to the pump process (pscott)
6 Create Manager process (mgr) with port information
7 Start extract, pump and manager process
8 Check the status of the processes using INFO ALL command

```
[oracle@ggnode1 12g]$ ./ggsci
Oracle GoldenGate Command Interpreter for Oracle
Version 12.2.0.1.0 OGGCORE_12.2.0.1.0_PLATFORMS_151101.1925.2_FBO
Linux, x64, 64bit (optimized), Oracle 11g on Nov 11 2015 01:38:14
Operating system character set identified as UTF-8.
Copyright (C) 1995, 2015, Oracle and/or its affiliates. All rights reserved.


GGSCI (ggnode1.oracle.com) 1> create subdirs

Creating subdirectories under current directory /u01/app/ogg/12g

Parameter files            /u01/app/ogg/12g/dirprm: created
Report files               /u01/app/ogg/12g/dirrpt: created
Checkpoint files           /u01/app/ogg/12g/dirchk: created
Process status files       /u01/app/ogg/12g/dirpcs: created
SQL script files           /u01/app/ogg/12g/dirsql: created
Database definitions files /u01/app/ogg/12g/dirdef: created
Extract data files         /u01/app/ogg/12g/dirdat: created
Temporary files            /u01/app/ogg/12g/dirtmp: created
Credential store files     /u01/app/ogg/12g/dircrd: created
Masterkey wallet files     /u01/app/ogg/12g/dirwlt: created
Dump files                 /u01/app/ogg/12g/dirdmp: created
```

Log in to the source database using the OGGUSER user for creating the extract process (escott), pump process (pscott), and manager process with PORT.

```
GGSCI (ggnode1.oracle.com as ogguser@db11g) 2> dblogin userid ogguser, password oracle
Successfully logged into database.
```

The following command adds the extract process (ESCOTT).

The TRANLOG option indicates that you are going to capture source database transactions from the Oracle redo logs to the local trail files in the source database.

The begin now option indicates a bookmark or checkpoint at this particular timestamp to begin capturing source database transactions.

```
GGSCI (ggnode1.oracle.com as ogguser@db11g) 3> add extract escott, tranlog, begin now
EXTRACT added.
```

The ADD EXTTRAIL command adds a trail file with the prefix ea, which will be written on the local machine and associates it to an extract process, ESCOTT.

The trail file will be created with the prefix and eight digits starting at 00000000. When the file reaches 10 megabytes, a new trail file will be created with an incremented count (ea00000001).

```
GGSCI (ggnode1.oracle.com as ogguser@db11g) 4> add exttrail ./dirdat/ea, extract escott,
megabytes 10
EXTTRAIL added.
```

The file is created in the directory named ea000000001.

```
[oracle@ggnode1 dirdat]$ pwd
/u01/app/ogg/12g/dirdat
```

```
[oracle@ggnode1 dirdat]$ ls -lrth
total 8.0K
-rw-r----- 1 oracle oinstall 1.5K Jan  6 15:40 ea000000001
```

The following command adds an additional extract process, called a *pump*. The pump process (pscott) reads from a local trail file and not a database's transaction log. The EXTTRAILSOURCE command points to the trail file that it will read from. Notice that it is the output trail from the ESCOTT process added earlier.

```
GGSCI (ggnode1.oracle.com as ogguser@db11g) 5> add extract pscott, exttrailsource ./dirdat/
ea
EXTRACT added.
```

The following ADD RMTTRAIL command adds a trail file with the prefix pa that will be written on the remote machine and attaches it to an extract process, PSCOTT.

```
GGSCI (ggnode1.oracle.com as ogguser@db11g) 6> add rmttrail ./dirdat/pa, extract pscott,
megabytes 10
RMTTRAIL added.
```

The following ADD TRANDATA command adds supplemental logging to the tables. Supplemental logging ensures that all the relevant information about update and delete operations are recorded in the Oracle redo logs so that Oracle GoldenGate can replicate the transactions for those tables correctly to the target database server.

```
GGSCI (ggnode1.oracle.com as ogguser@db11g) 7> add trandata scott.*
2015-12-23 11:43:15 WARNING OGG-00869  No unique key is defined for table 'BONUS'.
```

All viable columns will be used to represent the key but may not guarantee uniqueness. KEYCOLS may be used to define the key.

```
Logging of supplemental redo data enabled for table SCOTT.BONUS.
Logging of supplemental redo data enabled for table SCOTT.DEPT.
Logging of supplemental redo data enabled for table SCOTT.EMP.
2015-12-23 11:43:16 WARNING OGG-00869  No unique key is defined for table 'SALGRADE'.
```

All viable columns will be used to represent the key but may not guarantee uniqueness. KEYCOLS may be used to define the key.

```
Logging of supplemental redo data enabled for table SCOTT.SALGRADE.

Extract process (ESCOTT) will be configured to capture transactions against the source
Oracle 11g database

GGSCI (ggnode1.oracle.com as ogguser@db11g) 8> edit param escott
GGSCI (ggnode1.oracle.com as ogguser@db11g) 8> view param escott

extract escott
exttrail ./dirdat/ea
userid ogguser, password oracle
statoptions resetreportstats
tranlogoptions excludeuser ogguser
table scott.*;
```

Pump process (PSCOTT) send transaction's data to the Oracle GoldenGate 12c target site.

```
GGSCI (ggnode1.oracle.com as ogguser@db11g) 9> edit param pscott
GGSCI (ggnode1.oracle.com as ogguser@db11g) 9> view param pscott

extract pscott
rmthost ggnode2,mgrport 15000,compress
rmttrail ./dirdat/pa, format release 12.2
passthru
table scott.*;
```

Create the manager parameter file with port information. The mrg.prm parameter file is shown next.

The parameter PORT in the manager process is the TCP/IP communication port used by the manager process with other Oracle GoldenGate processes that require connections, such as the pump process.

```
GGSCI (ggnode1.oracle.com as ogguser@db11g) 10> edit param mgr
GGSCI (ggnode1.oracle.com as ogguser@db11g) 11> view param mgr

PORT 15500
PURGEOLDEXTRACTS ./dirdat/*,USECHECKPOINTS
```

Start the manager process and followed by extract (escott) and pump (pscott) processes
```
GGSCI (ggnode1.oracle.com as ogguser@db11g) 12> start mgr
Manager started.

GGSCI (ggnode1.oracle.com as ogguser@db11g) 13> info mgr
Manager is running (IP port ggnode1.oracle.com.15500).

GGSCI (ggnode1.oracle.com as ogguser@db11g) 14> start pscott
Sending START request to MANAGER ...
EXTRACT PSCOTT starting

GGSCI (ggnode1.oracle.com as ogguser@db11g) 15> start escott
Sending START request to MANAGER ...
EXTRACT ESCOTT starting
```

(OR)

We can start all the processes with single command

```
GGSCI (ggnode1.oracle.com as ogguser@db11g) 5> start er *

Sending START request to MANAGER ...
EXTRACT ESCOTT starting

Sending START request to MANAGER ...
EXTRACT PSCOTT starting
```

Now you can check the groups/processes status using the command INFO ALL from the GGSCI prompt.

```
GGSCI (ggnode1.oracle.com as ogguser@db11g) 16> info all


Program         Status          Group         Lag at Chkpt    Time Since Chkpt
MANAGER         RUNNING
EXTRACT         RUNNING         ESCOTT        00:19:57        00:00:00
EXTRACT         RUNNING         PSCOTT        00:00:00        00:00:00
```

Configuration Setup at the Target Database (Oracle 12c)

Log in to the target database (db12c) as a SYS user and create the following steps for data replication between the source database (db11g) and the target pluggable database (pdb12c):

```
1 Change the enable_goldengate_replication initialization parameter file
2 Create the GoldenGate tablespace 'tbsgg'
3 Create the user  'c##ogguser'
4 Check database log mode
5 Assign the privileges for 'c##ogguser'
6 Add database level supplemental logging
7 Set the database in 'FORCE LOGGING' mode
8 Assign dbms_goldengate_auth.grant_admin_privilege to the user 'c##ogguser'
9 Import the data in the user 'SCOTT' with System Change Number (SCN) taken from the source
  database (Oracle 11g)
```

```
[oracle@ggnode2 ~]$ sqlplus /nolog
SQL*Plus: Release 12.1.0.2.0 Production on Wed Dec 23 11:27:48 2015
Copyright (c) 1982, 2014, Oracle.  All rights reserved.


SQL> connect sys/oracle@db12c as sysdba
Connected.


SQL> show parameter golden


NAME                                    TYPE            VALUE
-------------------------------------------------------------------------------
enable_goldengate_replication           boolean         FALSE


SQL> alter system set enable_goldengate_replication =TRUE scope=both;
System altered.


SQL> show parameter golden


NAME                                    TYPE            VALUE
-------------------------------------------------------------------------------
enable_goldengate_replication           boolean         TRUE
```

```
SQL> select name,cdb from v$database;

NAME            CDB
----------------------------
DB12C           YES

SQL> create tablespace tbsgg datafile '/u01/app/oracle/oradata/db12c/tbsgg01.dbf' size 10M
autoextend on;
Tablespace created.

SQL> create user c##ogguser identified by oracle container=all;
User created.

SQL> alter user c##ogguser default tablespace tbsgg;
User altered.

SQL> grant connect,resource,dba,unlimited tablespace,create session,select any dictionary to
c##ogguser container=all;
Grant succeeded.

SQL> alter pluggable database pdb12c open read write;
Pluggable database altered.

SQL> alter database add supplemental log data;
Database altered.

SQL> select supplemental_log_data_min from v$database;

SUPPLEMENTAL
---------------------
YES

SQL> alter system switch logfile;
System altered.

SQL> alter database force logging;
Database altered.

SQL> exec dbms_goldengate_auth.grant_admin_privilege('C##OGGUSER',container=>'all');
PL/SQL procedure successfully completed.
```

Restore the SCOTT.dmp to the user 'SCOTT' in Pluggable Database (pdb12c) in Target Database

```
[oracle@ggnode2 ~]$ imp scott/oracle@pdb12c file=/u01/app/ogg/12g/scott.dmp full=y ignore=y

Import: Release 12.1.0.2.0 - Production on Mon Jan 4 15:30:34 2016
Copyright (c) 1982, 2014, Oracle and/or its affiliates.  All rights reserved.
Connected to: Oracle Database 12c Enterprise Edition Release 12.1.0.2.0 - 64bit Production
With the Partitioning, OLAP, Advanced Analytics and Real Application Testing options
```

```
Export file created by EXPORT:V11.02.00 via conventional path
import done in US7ASCII character set and AL16UTF16 NCHAR character set
import server uses WE8MSWIN1252 character set (possible charset conversion)
. importing SCOTT's objects into SCOTT
. . importing table                        "BONUS"          0 rows imported
. . importing table                         "DEPT"          4 rows imported
. . importing table                          "EMP"         14 rows imported
. . importing table                     "SALGRADE"          5 rows imported
About to enable constraints...
Import terminated successfully without warnings.
[oracle@ggnode2 ~]$
```

Configuration Setup at the Target Database (Oracle 12*c* for Oracle GoldenGate 12*c*)

Before that, make sure the Oracle GoldenGate libraries are linked with the Oracle libraries, as shown in Figure 2-40.

```
[oracle@ggnode2 ~]$ source 12c.env
[oracle@ggnode2 ~]$ cd $GG
[oracle@ggnode2 12g]$ ldd ggsci
        linux-vdso.so.1 =>  (0x00007fff3dd3c000)
        librt.so.1 => /lib64/librt.so.1 (0x0000003fa9400000)
        libdl.so.2 => /lib64/libdl.so.2 (0x0000003fa7000000)
        libgglog.so => /u01/app/ogg/12g/./libgglog.so (0x00007f81c0180000)
        libggrepo.so => /u01/app/ogg/12g/./libggrepo.so (0x00007f81bff0e000)
        libdb-6.1.so => /u01/app/ogg/12g/./libdb-6.1.so (0x00007f81bfb29000)
        libggperf.so => /u01/app/ogg/12g/./libggperf.so (0x00007f81bf8f9000)
        libggparam.so => /u01/app/ogg/12g/./libggparam.so (0x00007f81be7ee000)
        libicui18n.so.48 => /u01/app/ogg/12g/./libicui18n.so.48 (0x00007f81be3fe000)
        libicuuc.so.48 => /u01/app/ogg/12g/./libicuuc.so.48 (0x00007f81be07d000)
        libicudata.so.48 => /u01/app/ogg/12g/./libicudata.so.48 (0x00007f81bc8b8000)
        libpthread.so.0 => /lib64/libpthread.so.0 (0x0000003fa7800000)
        libxerces-c.so.28 => /u01/app/ogg/12g/./libxerces-c.so.28 (0x00007f81bc2f1000)
        libantlr3c.so => /u01/app/ogg/12g/./libantlr3c.so (0x00007f81bc0d8000)
        libnnz12.so => /u01/app/oracle/product/12.1.0.2/db_1/lib/libnnz12.so (0x00007f81bb9cd000)
        libclntsh.so.12.1 => /u01/app/oracle/product/12.1.0.2/db_1/lib/libclntsh.so.12.1 (0x00007f81b9a0e000)
        libons.so => /u01/app/oracle/product/12.1.0.2/db_1/lib/libons.so (0x00007f81b87c9000)
        libclntshcore.so.12.1 => /u01/app/oracle/product/12.1.0.2/db_1/lib/libclntshcore.so.12.1 (0x00007f81b8256000)
        libggnnzitp.so => /u01/app/ogg/12g/./libggnnzitp.so (0x00007f81b7778000)
        libm.so.6 => /lib64/libm.so.6 (0x0000003fa7400000)
        libc.so.6 => /lib64/libc.so.6 (0x0000003fa6c00000)
        /lib64/ld-linux-x86-64.so.2 (0x0000003fa6400000)
        libstdc++.so.6 => /usr/lib64/libstdc++.so.6 (0x0000003fad4c0000)
        libgcc_s.so.1 => /lib64/libgcc_s.so.1 (0x0000003fab400000)
        libmql1.so => /u01/app/oracle/product/12.1.0.2/db_1/lib/libmql1.so (0x00007f81b7500000)
        libipc1.so => /u01/app/oracle/product/12.1.0.2/db_1/lib/libipc1.so (0x00007f81b7181000)
        libnsl.so.1 => /lib64/libnsl.so.1 (0x0000003fadc00000)
        libaio.so.1 => /usr/lib64/libaio.so.1 (0x0000003fa6800000)
[oracle@ggnode2 12g]$ []
```

Figure 2-40. *GGSCI output*

Check the following commands also and look for any missing paths:

```
[oracle@ggnode2 ~]$ ldd extract
[oracle@ggnode2 ~]$ ldd replicat
[oracle@ggnode2 ~]$ ldd mgr
```

Here are the steps to be completed at the source database for Oracle GoldenGate 12c:

1. Create subdirectories for OGG.

2. Create GLOBALS and checkpoint table extract process (escott).

3. Create the manager process (mgr) with port information.

4. Create the replicat process (rscott).

5. Start the manager and replicat processes using the commit SCN.

6. Check the status of the processes using the INFO ALL command.

```
[oracle@ggnode2 12g]$ ./ggsci

Oracle GoldenGate Command Interpreter for Oracle
Version 12.2.0.1.0 OGGCORE_12.2.0.1.0_PLATFORMS_151101.1925.2_FBO
Linux, x64, 64bit (optimized), Oracle 12c on Nov 11 2015 03:53:23
Operating system character set identified as UTF-8.
Copyright (C) 1995, 2015, Oracle and/or its affiliates. All rights reserved.

GGSCI (ggnode2.oracle.com) 1> create subdirs

Creating subdirectories under current directory /u01/app/ogg/12g

Parameter files                 /u01/app/ogg/12g/dirprm: created
Report files                    /u01/app/ogg/12g/dirrpt: created
Checkpoint files                /u01/app/ogg/12g/dirchk: created
Process status files            /u01/app/ogg/12g/dirpcs: created
SQL script files                /u01/app/ogg/12g/dirsql: created
Database definitions files      /u01/app/ogg/12g/dirdef: created
Extract data files              /u01/app/ogg/12g/dirdat: created
Temporary files                 /u01/app/ogg/12g/dirtmp: created
Credential store files          /u01/app/ogg/12g/dircrd: created
Masterkey wallet files          /u01/app/ogg/12g/dirwlt: created
Dump files                      /u01/app/ogg/12g/dirdmp: created

Login to pluggable database (pdb12c) using 'c##ogguser' in container database (db12c).

[oracle@ggnode2 12g]$ ./ggsci

Oracle GoldenGate Command Interpreter for Oracle
Version 12.2.0.1.0 OGGCORE_12.2.0.1.0_PLATFORMS_151101.1925.2_FBO
Linux, x64, 64bit (optimized), Oracle 12c on Nov 11 2015 03:53:23
Operating system character set identified as UTF-8.
Copyright (C) 1995, 2015, Oracle and/or its affiliates. All rights reserved.

GGSCI (ggnode2.oracle.com) 1> dblogin userid c##ogguser@pdb12c, password oracle
Successfully logged into database PDB12C.
```

The PURGEOLDEXTRACTS parameter with the USECHECKPOINTS option instructs the manager process to purge the local trail files that have been processed by all extracts writing to or all replicats reading from those trail files.

```
GGSCI (ggnode2.oracle.com as c##ogguser@db12c/PDB12C) 2> edit param mgr
GGSCI (ggnode2.oracle.com as c##ogguser@db12c/PDB12C) 3> view param mgr
```

```
PORT 15000
PURGEOLDEXTRACTS ./dirdat/*,USECHECKPOINTS
```

This creates a checkpoint table used in the case of replicat recovery.

■ **Note**   The checkpoint table creation is tied to an entry in the GLOBALS file called CHECKPOINTTABLE GGS_ CHECKPOINT. The GLOBALS file is in the root OGG directory.

```
GGSCI (ggnode2.oracle.com as c##ogguser@db12c/PDB12C) 4> edit param ./GLOBALS
GGSCI (ggnode2.oracle.com as c##ogguser@db12c/PDB12C) 5> view param ./GLOBALS
CHECKPOINTTABLE c##ogguser.GGS_CHECKPOINT
```

A replicat that will deliver captured transactions from the source Oracle GoldenGate (OGG) 11*g* trail files to the target Oracle 12*c* database.

This file configures how to connect to the database and which tables to map and deliver data to. The parameter ASSUMETARGETDEFS statement means you're assuming that the target table structure is the same as the source table structure, which it is.

```
GGSCI (ggnode2.oracle.com as c##ogguser@db12c/PDB12C) 6> edit param rscott
GGSCI (ggnode2.oracle.com as c##ogguser@db12c/PDB12C) 7> view param rscott
```

```
replicat rscott
assumetargetdefs
discardfile ./dirout/rscott.dsc,purge
USERID c##ogguser@pdb12c,password oracle
map scott.*,target pdb12c.scott.*;
```

To refresh the configuration files related to the GLOBALS parameter, exit from the GGSCI prompt and log in again.

```
GGSCI (ggnode2.oracle.com as c##ogguser@db12c/PDB12C) 8> exit
```

```
[oracle@ggnode2 12g]$ ./ggsci
```

```
Oracle GoldenGate Command Interpreter for Oracle
Version 12.2.0.1.0 OGGCORE_12.2.0.1.0_PLATFORMS_151101.1925.2_FBO
Linux, x64, 64bit (optimized), Oracle 12c on Nov 11 2015 03:53:23
Operating system character set identified as UTF-8.
Copyright (C) 1995, 2015, Oracle and/or its affiliates. All rights reserved.
```

```
GGSCI (ggnode2.oracle.com as c##ogguser@db12c/PDB12C) 1> dblogin userid c##ogguser@pdb12c,
password oracle
Successfully logged into database PDB12C.
```

The following command creates a checkpoint table used in the case of replicat recovery.

■ **Note**   Checkpoint table creation is tied to an entry in the GLOBALS file called CHECKPOINTTABLE GGS_
CHECKPOINT. The GLOBALS file is in the root Oracle GoldenGate directory. This allows the checkpoint table to
be created under the user that is connected to the database during the process configuration, in this case
c##ogguser.

You can view the contents of the GLOBALS file from within the GGSCI command prompt with the SH
(shell) command.

```
GGSCI (ggnode2.oracle.com as c##ogguser@db12c/PDB12C) 2> add checkpointtable
No checkpoint table specified. Using GLOBALS specification (c##ogguser.GGS_CHECKPOINT)...
Logon catalog name PDB12C will be used for table specification PDB12C.c##ogguser.GGS_
CHECKPOINT.
Successfully created checkpoint table PDB12C.c##ogguser.GGS_CHECKPOINT.
```

This adds the replicat process and tells this process from which trail file to read. This trail file will be part
of the configuration of the pump from the OGG 11g side.

The replicat process (RSCOTT) will be accessing the trail file (pa000000002) from the following directory:

```
[oracle@ggnode2 12g]$ cd dirdat/

[oracle@ggnode2 dirdat]$ ls -lrth
total 8.0K
-rw-r----- 1 oracle oinstall 1.5K Jan  6 15:51 pa000000002

GGSCI (ggnode2.oracle.com as c##ogguser@db12c/PDB12C) 3> add replicat rscott, exttrail ./
dirdat/pa
REPLICAT added.
```

Start the manager process and check the status

```
GGSCI (ggnode2.oracle.com as c##ogguser@db12c/PDB12C) 4> start mgr
Manager started.

GGSCI (ggnode2.oracle.com as c##ogguser@db12c/PDB12C) 5> info mgr
Manager is running (IP port ggnode2.oracle.com.15000, Process ID 11267).
```

Once the import completes successfully, you can start your Replicat process using the SCN
number that you obtained earlier.

```
GGSCI (ggnode2.oracle.com as c##ogguser@db12c/PDB12C) 6> start rscott,aftercsn 1004290
```

```
Sending START request to MANAGER ...
REPLICAT RSCOTT starting
GGSCI (ggnode2.oracle.com as c##ogguser@db12c/PDB12C) 7> info all
```

Program	Status	Group	Lag at Chkpt	Time Since Chkpt
MANAGER	RUNNING			
REPLICAT	RUNNING	RSCOTT	00:00:00	00:00:04

Log in to the source database (db11*g*) using the SCOTT schema and add transactions to the table emp. Log in to the target pluggable database (pdb12*c*) using the SCOTT schema and check the transactions from the table emp.

```
[oracle@ggnode1 12g]$ sqlplus /nolog

SQL*Plus: Release 11.2.0.4.0 Production on Mon Jan 11 14:44:33 2016

Copyright (c) 1982, 2013, Oracle.  All rights reserved.

SQL> connect scott/oracle@db11g
Connected.
SQL> set lines 100 pages 1000
SQL> insert into emp values(&empno,'Oracle','GG',5,sysdate,12000,13,10);
Enter value for empno: 700
old   1: insert into emp values(&empno,'Oracle','GG',6,sysdate,12000,13,10)
new   1: insert into emp values(700,'Oracle','GG',6,sysdate,12000,13,10)

1 row created.

SQL> commit;

Commit complete.

SQL> select * from emp where empno=700;

    EMPNO ENAME      JOB          MGR HIREDATE        SAL       COMM    DEPTNO
---------- ---------- ---------- ----- --------- ---------- ---------- ----------
      700 Oracle     GG             6 11-JAN-16      12000         13        10

SQL> connect scott/oracle@192.168.2.106:1521/pdb12c
Connected.
SQL> select * from emp where empno=700;

    EMPNO ENAME      JOB          MGR HIREDATE        SAL       COMM    DEPTNO
---------- ---------- ---------- ----- --------- ---------- ---------- ----------
      700 Oracle     GG             6 11-JAN-16      12000         13        10

SQL> select con_id,name,open_mode from v$pdbs;

   CON_ID NAME                           OPEN_MODE
---------- ------------------------------ ----------
        3 PDB12C                         READ WRITE

SQL> []
```

Figure 2-41. *Verifying transactions*

Check the transactions count captured by the extract process (ESCOTT) at the source database.

Execute the command stats escott, total to get a snapshot of the records captured by the extract process in the source database at the GGSCI prompt.

```
GGSCI (ggnode1.oracle.com as ogguser@db11g) 2> stats escott, total


Sending STATS request to EXTRACT ESCOTT ...
Start of Statistics at 2016-01-11 16:11:38.
Output to ./dirdat/ea:
Extracting from SCOTT.EMP to SCOTT.EMP:

*** Total statistics since 2016-01-11 14:34:45 ***
        Total inserts                           1.00
        Total updates                           0.00
        Total deletes                           0.00
        Total discards                          0.00
        Total operations                        1.00
End of Statistics.
GGSCI (ggnode1.oracle.com as ogguser@db11g) 3>
```

Check transactions count processes by Pump process (PSCOTT)

```
GGSCI (ggnode1.oracle.com as ogguser@db11g) 3> stats pscott, total
Sending STATS request to EXTRACT PSCOTT ...
Start of Statistics at 2016-01-11 16:12:45.
Output to ./dirdat/pa:

Extracting from SCOTT.EMP to SCOTT.EMP:

*** Total statistics since 2016-01-11 14:34:46 ***
        Total inserts                           1.00
        Total updates                           0.00
        Total deletes                           0.00
        Total discards                          0.00
        Total operations                        1.00
End of Statistics.
GGSCI (ggnode1.oracle.com as ogguser@db11g) 4>
```

Check the transactions count delivered by the replicat process (RSCOTT) at the target database.

Execute the command stats rscott, total to get the number of records delivered by the replicat process in the target database at the GGSCI prompt.

```
GGSCI (ggnode2.oracle.com as c##ogguser@db12c/PDB12C) 2> stats rscott, total
Sending STATS request to REPLICAT RSCOTT ...
Start of Statistics at 2016-01-11 16:13:47.
```

Here's an example of replicating from SCOTT.EMP to PDB12C.SCOTT.EMP:

```
*** Total statistics since 2016-01-11 14:34:51 ***
        Total inserts                           1.00
```

```
        Total updates                                    0.00
        Total deletes                                    0.00
        Total discards                                   0.00
        Total operations                                 1.00
End of Statistics.
GGSCI (ggnode2.oracle.com as c##ogguser@db12c/PDB12C) 3>
```

High Availability or Fallback Option Using the Source Database (Oracle 11g)

Once the new version of the Oracle 12c database is ready after data replication and data synchronization from the source database (Oracle 11g), all the application users can connect to the Oracle 12c database and make transactions through the user SCOTT. To implement high availability or a fallback option, you can use the source database (Oracle 11g) as a standby database server as a fallback option. To make this environment ready to achieve high availability or a fallback option, you have to implement bidirectional data replication between the target database (Oracle 12c) to the source database (Oracle 11g). The advantage of Oracle GoldenGate works bidirectionally from higher versions to lower versions as well.

Figure 2-42 shows the steps for bidirectional data replication between Oracle 12c (pluggable database: pdb12c) to the Oracle 11g database (db11g).

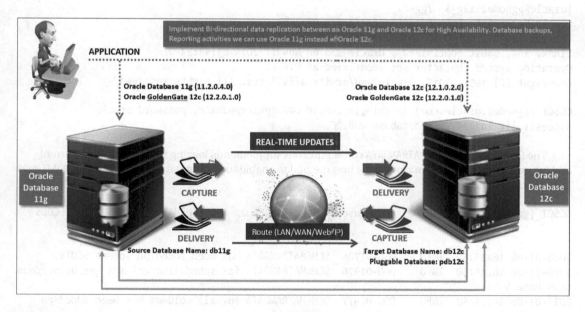

Figure 2-42. *GG between nonmultitenant and pluggable database*

Configuration Setup at Target Database Oracle 12*c* and Implementing Bidirectional Data Replication Between Target Database (pdb12*c*) and Source Database (Oracle 11*g*)

Add the new extract process (es01) and start it on the target database server (Oracle 12*c* database).

Add the new pump process (ps01) and start it on the target database server (Oracle 12*c* database).

The original source database server (the Oracle 11*g* database) will now act as the new target database server with the newly added replicat process (rs01) running on it.

It is a new unidirectional data replication in the reverse direction between the Oracle 12*c* pluggable database (pdb12c) and the Oracle 11*g* database (db11g).

You can verify the data synchronization using Oracle GoldenGate Veridata.

If there are any application compatibility issues in the target database server (the Oracle 12*c* database), perform the reverse switchover method; the application should be connected to the source database server (Oracle 11*g* database).

If there are no application compatibility issues with the target database server (the Oracle 12*c* database), you can perform database backup operations and application reporting activities using the source database server (the Oracle 11*g* database) since bidirectional is in place.

Log in to the container database (db12c) and the pluggable database (pdb12c) from the GGSCI command prompt using c##ogguser and perform the following steps:

```
[oracle@ggnode2 12g]$ ./ggsci
Oracle GoldenGate Command Interpreter for Oracle
Version 12.2.0.1.0 OGGCORE_12.2.0.1.0_PLATFORMS_151101.1925.2_FBO
Linux, x64, 64bit (optimized), Oracle 12c on Nov 11 2015 03:53:23
Operating system character set identified as UTF-8.
Copyright (C) 1995, 2015, Oracle and/or its affiliates. All rights reserved.

GGSCI (ggnode2.oracle.com) 1> dblogin userid c##ogguser@pdb12c, password oracle
Successfully logged into database PDB12C.
```

The following ADD SCHEMATRANDATA command adds supplemental logging to all tables, both current and future, of the SCOTT schema and is the best method to enable supplemental logging when both DML and DDL are concurrent:

```
GGSCI (ggnode2.oracle.com as c##ogguser@db12c/PDB12C) 2> ADD SCHEMATRANDATA SCOTT ALLCOLS


2016-01-06 16:15:50  INFO    OGG-01788  SCHEMATRANDATA has been added on schema SCOTT.
2016-01-06 16:15:50  INFO    OGG-01976  SCHEMATRANDATA for scheduling columns has been added
on schema SCOTT.
2016-01-06 16:15:50  INFO    OGG-01977  SCHEMATRANDATA for all columns has been added on
schema SCOTT.

GGSCI (ggnode2.oracle.com as c##ogguser@db12c/PDB12C) 3> dblogin userid c##ogguser@db12c,
password oracle
Successfully logged into database CDB$ROOT.
```

The following command registers the extract process (ES01) with the database. This option is called Integrated Extract Capture mode. Integrated Extract Capture mode directly interacts with the database log mining server and receives data changes in the form of logical change records (LCRs). Integrated Extract Capture mode is being used here against an Oracle 12c database, and with OGG 12c you don't need to create a trigger for DDL capture.

```
GGSCI (ggnode2.oracle.com as c##ogguser@db12c/CDB$ROOT) 3> register extract es01 database
container (pdb12c)
2016-01-06 16:17:15  INFO    OGG-02003  Extract ES01 successfully registered with database
at SCN 1724432.
```

The following command adds the extract process (ES01) with the following options:

- The INTEGRATED TRANLOG option indicates that you are going to capture transactions from the Oracle log mining server.

- The BEGIN NOW option indicates the bookmark or checkpoint at which this particular timestamp should begin capturing transactions.

```
GGSCI (ggnode2.oracle.com as c##ogguser@db12c/CDB$ROOT) 4> add extract es01 INTEGRATED
TRANLOG, BEGIN NOW
EXTRACT (Integrated) added.
```

■ **Note**   For Oracle GoldenGate 12c for Oracle Database 11.2.0 4.0 and above, Data Definition Language (DDL) functionality no longer requires a database trigger. The Integrated Extract option that you use for capturing Oracle GoldenGate 12c replicat is enabled with DDL delivery by default. But this DDL trigger is still required for Classic Capture.

When you use Classic Extract for the Oracle 12s database with a multitenant container database, you will get the following error:

View the error in GGSERR.log: ([oracle@ggnode2 12g]$ cat /u01/app/ogg/12g/ggserr.log)

2016-01-06 16:10:42 ERROR OGG-06220 Oracle GoldenGate Capture for Oracle, es01.prm: Classic Extract does not support multitenant container databases.

```
GGSCI (ggnode2.oracle.com as c##ogguser@db12c/CDB$ROOT) 5> add exttrail ./dirdat/ee, extract
es01, megabytes 10
EXTTRAIL added.

GGSCI (ggnode2.oracle.com as c##ogguser@db12c/CDB$ROO⁻) 6> add extract ps01, exttrailsource
./dirdat/ee
EXTRACT added.

GGSCI (ggnode2.oracle.com as c##ogguser@db12c/CDB$ROO⁻) 7> add rmttrail ./dirdat/pe, extract
ps01, megabytes 10
RMTTRAIL added.
```

■ **Note** In the extract process (ES01) and pump process (PS01) parameter files, the TABLE and MAP statements are slightly different. In the extract process (ES01) parameter file, the pluggable database (pdb12c) is being assigned with the SOURCECATALOG option. This option is used to switch the container and to use the pluggable database (pdb12c) for the tables.

The target side does not need the catalog option to specify the replicat process (RS01). The replicat process is logging into the pluggable database (pdb12c) directly.

```
GGSCI (ggnode2.oracle.com as c##ogguser@db12c/PDB12C) 8> edit param es01
GGSCI (ggnode2.oracle.com as c##ogguser@db12c/PDB12C) 9> view param es01

extract es01
exttrail ./dirdat/ee
userid c##ogguser@db12c, password oracle
LOGALLSUPCOLS
UPDATERECORDFORMAT COMPACT
SOURCECATALOG pdb12c
table scott.*;

GGSCI (ggnode2.oracle.com as c##ogguser@db12c/PDB12C) 10> edit param ps01
GGSCI (ggnode2.oracle.com as c##ogguser@db12c/PDB12C) 11> view param ps01

extract ps01
USERID c##ogguser@db12c, PASSWORD oracle
rmthost ggnode1,mgrport 15500,compress
rmttrail ./dirdat/pe
SOURCECATALOG pdb12c
table scott.*;

GGSCI (ggnode2.oracle.com as c##ogguser@db12c/CDB$ROOT) 12> start es01
Sending START request to MANAGER ...
EXTRACT ES01 starting

GGSCI (ggnode2.oracle.com as c##ogguser@db12c/CDB$ROOT) 13> start ps01
Sending START request to MANAGER ...
EXTRACT PS01 starting

(OR)

We can start all the processes in single command

GGSCI (ggnode2.oracle.com as c##ogguser@db12c/PDB12C) 14> start er *

Sending START request to MANAGER ...
EXTRACT ES01 starting

Sending START request to MANAGER ...
EXTRACT PS01 starting

GGSCI (ggnode2.oracle.com as c##ogguser@db12c/CDB$ROOT) 15> info all
```

Program	Status	Group	Lag at Chkpt	Time Since Chkpt
MANAGER	RUNNING			
EXTRACT	STARTING	ES01	00:00:00	00:05:15
EXTRACT	RUNNING	PS01	00:00:00	00:03:56
REPLICAT	RUNNING	RSCOTT	00:00:00	00:00:00

■ **Note**   Notice that the extract process (ES01) still reports a status of STARTING after running the GGSCI command INFO ALL. Since this extract process (ES01) is running in Integrated Capture mode, it requires extra startup time.

```
GGSCI (ggnode2.oracle.com as c##ogguser@db12c/CDB$ROOT) 15> info all
```

Program	Status	Group	Lag at Chkpt	Time Since Chkpt
MANAGER	RUNNING			
EXTRACT	RUNNING	ES01	00:05:19	00:00:03
EXTRACT	RUNNING	PS01	00:00:00	00:00:03
REPLICAT	RUNNING	RSCOTT	00:00:00	00:00:07

At this point, the extract process (ES01) and pump process (PS01) are configured at the pluggable database (pdb12c) and ready to take the transactions from the pluggable database (pdb12c) in the container database (db12c) to the Oracle 11g database (db11g).

Configuration Setup at Source Database Oracle 11g and Implementing Bidirectional Data Replication Between Target Database (pdb12c) and Source Database (Oracle 11g)

Log in to the source database (db11g) from the GGSCI command prompt using ogguser and perform the following steps:

1. Add the new replicat process (rs01) and start it on the source database server (the Oracle 11g database).

2. The replicat process (rs01) will deliver captured transactions from the target Oracle GoldenGate (OGG) trail files to the source database server (Oracle 11g database).

```
[oracle@ggnode1 12g]$ ./ggsci

Oracle GoldenGate Command Interpreter for Oracle
Version 12.2.0.1.0 OGGCORE_12.2.0.1.0_PLATFORMS_151101.1925.2_FBO
Linux, x64, 64bit (optimized), Oracle 11g on Nov 11 2015 01:38:14
Operating system character set identified as UTF-8.
Copyright (C) 1995, 2015, Oracle and/or its affiliates. All rights reserved.

GGSCI (ggnode1.oracle.com) 1> dblogin userid ogguser, password oracle
Successfully logged into database.
```

```
GGSCI (ggnode1.oracle.com as ogguser@db11g) 2> edit param ./GLOBALS
GGSCI (ggnode1.oracle.com as ogguser@db11g) 3> view param ./GLOBALS
CHECKPOINTTABLE ogguser.GGS_CHECKPOINT

GGSCI (ggnode1.oracle.com as ogguser@db11g) 4> exit

[oracle@ggnode1 12g]$ ./ggsci

Oracle GoldenGate Command Interpreter for Oracle
Version 12.2.0.1.0 OGGCORE_12.2.0.1.0_PLATFORMS_151101.1925.2_FBO
Linux, x64, 64bit (optimized), Oracle 11g on Nov 11 2015 01:38:14
Operating system character set identified as UTF-8.
Copyright (C) 1995, 2015, Oracle and/or its affiliates. All rights reserved.

GGSCI (ggnode1.oracle.com as ogguser@db11g) 1> add checkpointtable
No checkpoint table specified. Using GLOBALS specification (ogguser.GGS_CHECKPOINT)...
Successfully created checkpoint table ogguser.GGS_CHECKPOINT.
```

After adding the checkpoint table and GLOBALS parameter, check the data replication and synchronization between Oracle Database 12c (pluggable database pdb12c) and Oracle Database 11g (db11g). So, you can use Oracle Database 11g (db11g) for reporting and backup purposes in the environment. You can upgrade Oracle Database 11g to Oracle Database 12c also using Oracle GoldenGate 12c. Finally, your complete environment is upgraded to Oracle Database 12c with near zero-downtime using Oracle GoldenGate 12c.

```
GGSCI (ggnode1.oracle.com as ogguser@db11g) 2> add replicat rs01, exttrail ./dirdat/pe
REPLICAT added.

GGSCI (ggnode1.oracle.com as ogguser@db11g) 3> edit param rs01
GGSCI (ggnode1.oracle.com as ogguser@db11g) 4> view param rs01

replicat rs01
userid ogguser, password oracle
assumetargetdefs
discardfile ./dirout/rscott.dsc,purge
map pdb12c.scott.*, target scott.*;

GGSCI (ggnode1.oracle.com as ogguser@db11g) 6> start rs01
Sending START request to MANAGER ...
REPLICAT RS01 starting

GGSCI (ggnode1.oracle.com as ogguser@db11g) 7> info all

Program      Status      Group       Lag at Chkpt   Time Since Chkpt
MANAGER      RUNNING
EXTRACT      RUNNING     ESCOTT      00:00:00       00:00:09
EXTRACT      RUNNING     PSCOTT      00:00:00       00:00:08
REPLICAT     RUNNING     RS01        00:00:00       00:09:47
```

Now the bidirectional data replication is in place; it added the extract process (ES01), the pump process (PS01) in the Oracle 12c pluggable database, and the added replicat process (RS01) in the Oracle 11g database.

Replication data validation and synchronization between the target Oracle 12c database (pluggable database pdb12c) and source Oracle11g database (db11g)

You can check the data replication between the Oracle 12c database pluggable database (pdb12c) and the Oracle 11g database (db11g) for the user SCOTT. The same methodology holds for other schemas also.

```
[oracle@ggnode2 ~]$ sqlplus /nolog

SQL*Plus: Release 12.1.0.2.0 Production on Wed Jan 6 17:32:38 2016

Copyright (c) 1982, 2014, Oracle.  All rights reserved.

SQL> connect scott/oracle@192.168.2.106:1521/pdb12c
Connected.
SQL> show con_name

CON_NAME
------------------------------
PDB12C
SQL> show con_id

CON_ID
------------------------------
3
SQL> insert into emp values(&empno,'Oracle','GG',5,sysdate,10000,12,10);
Enter value for empno: 500
old    1: insert into emp values(&empno,'Oracle','GG',5,sysdate,10000,12,10)
new    1: insert into emp values(500,'Oracle','GG',5,sysdate,10000,12,10)

1 row created.

SQL> commit;

Commit complete.

SQL> set lines 100 pages 1000
SQL> select * from emp where empno=500;

    EMPNO ENAME      JOB            MGR HIREDATE         SAL       COMM     DEPTNO
---------- ---------- --------- ---------- --------- ---------- ---------- ----------
      500 Oracle     GG               5 06-JAN-16     10000         12         10

SQL> connect scott/oracle@db11g
Connected.
SQL> select * from emp where empno=500;

    EMPNO ENAME      JOB            MGR HIREDATE         SAL       COMM     DEPTNO
---------- ---------- --------- ---------- --------- ---------- ---------- ----------
      500 Oracle     GG               5 06-JAN-16     10000         12         10

SQL> []
```

Figure 2-43. *Replication between 11g and 12c pluggable database*

■ **Note** If the database is down for some reason, when you start up the container database, all the pluggable databases will not start up automatically. So, you have two choices here. One is you can write a trigger to start up the pluggable database when the container database is up and you can save the state of the pluggable database with the following command in the Oracle 12c database (12.1.0.2.0) version. So, when the container database is coming up, the pluggable database also starts up automatically.

SQL> alter pluggable database pdb12c save state;

Pluggable database altered

■ **Note** If you haven't implemented a trigger to start up the pluggable database and tried to connect to GGSCI, you will get the following error and the save state option is not available in the Oracle 12c database (12.1.0.1.0) version:

[oracle@ggnode2 12g]$ ./ggsci

GGSCI (ggnode2.oracle.com) 1> dblogin userid c##ogguser@pdb12c, password oracle

2016-01-08 12:23:21 INFO   OGG-05102 Retrying logon to Oracle database after previous attempt failed.

2016-01-08 12:23:26 INFO   OGG-05102 Retrying logon to Oracle database after previous attempt failed.

Summary

Finally, you have two databases! One is for application and end users upgraded to the new version of Oracle Database 12c and Oracle Database 11g for reporting and backup operations. If the application is working well with all the options with the upgraded Oracle version, then you can upgrade the previous source Oracle 11g database to Oracle Database 12c using OGG.

■ **Note** You can find up-to-date information regarding Oracle GoldenGate at the International GoldenGate Oracle Users Group (IGGOUG) at www.iggoug.org.

Create Table As Select (CTAS)

Each upgrade and migration method has limitations, so you should choose the relevant procedure in order to upgrade/migrate your database. In this section, you will see how the Create Table As Select method is used in upgrades.

For example, if the source database is in 9i or 10g on the Linux platform and you are moving to a new server and also upgrading to the 12c version, then you can assume the Oracle software 12c installed on the server and the database was created using the default settings. The goal is to move all the user objects from 9i to 12c. For the CTAS method, there are no restrictions in version or release either higher or lower because

CTAS works in DDL and DML statements, which are uniform query languages, such as CREATE TABLE AS SELECT. The flavor of CTAS is purely different from the procedures of the DBUA, manual upgrade, TTS, Data Pump, and others. The CTAS method is also widely used for reorganizing tables or moving to other tablespaces.

CTAS vs. COPY

CTAS is similar to COPY, but COPY has many limitations of the data types supported, and COPY is slower than CTAS. Apart from the COPY procedure, there are two other methods; they are direct load and the CTAS. Direct load works well, but the criteria are that the table structure should exist where you are trying to insert, but in case of CTAS of course it creates the table and also performs inserts into the table. The CTAS method works only when the table does not exist in the target database. If the table exists, then you can use the Insert Into (IIST) procedure.

Advantages of CTAS

Here are the advantages of CTAS:

- Reorganization
- Rename of the table name in the same command
- Resequence of the rows
- Fast response
- Support of data types
- Can skip undo and redo
- Parallel CTAS
- Support of table partitions
- Flexibility of merging of partitions with a single CTAS
- Storage clause changes

Disadvantages with CTAS

Here are the disadvantages of CTAS:

- Difficult to trace in case of large query or merged tables in single CTAS.
- Disk space required is double (if remote databases, then no worries).
- Tablespaces at the target should be available.
- Users/grants should be available prior to using CTAS.

How Does CTAS Work?

To understand how the CTAS method works, you will walk through a few tests to upgrade to the new version from the old server to the new server. This new database (NPRD) requires a connection with the old version database (R2B), which can be done using DB LINK.

Requirements

Here are the requirements:

- The database should exist at the target side (using the DBCA or manual method).

- You need to use DB LINK.

- Connectivity from the old-version database to the new version (Net service).

- Users should exist prior to using CTAS.

- Existing source tablespace at the new version database or mention the new tablespace in the CTAS command.

As per these requirements, the database can be either created using the DBCA or the manual method or cloned from another database, whichever applicable.

```
CREATE CONTROLFILE REUSE DATABASE "NPRD" RESETLOGS  NOARCHIVELOG
    MAXLOGFILES 16
    MAXLOGMEMBERS 3
    MAXDATAFILES 100
    MAXINSTANCES 8
    MAXLOGHISTORY 292
LOGFILE
  GROUP 1 (
    '/u01/app/oracle/oradata/NPRD/onlinelog/o1_mf_1_cbcpwc5k_.log',
    '/u01/app/oracle/fast_recovery_area/NPRD/onlinelog/o1_mf_1_cbcpwcb2_.log'
  ) SIZE 50M BLOCKSIZE 512,
  GROUP 2 (
    '/u01/app/oracle/oradata/NPRD/onlinelog/o1_mf_2_cbcpwcw3_.log',
    '/u01/app/oracle/fast_recovery_area/NPRD/onlinelog/o1_mf_2_cbcpwd18_.log'
  ) SIZE 50M BLOCKSIZE 512,
  GROUP 3 (
    '/u01/app/oracle/oradata/NPRD/onlinelog/o1_mf_3_cbcpwdlm_.log',
    '/u01/app/oracle/fast_recovery_area/NPRD/onlinelog/o1_mf_3_cbcpwdqk_.log'
  ) SIZE 50M BLOCKSIZE 512
-- STANDBY LOGFILE
DATAFILE
  '/u01/app/oracle/oradata/NPRD/datafile/o1_mf_system_cbcppfwd_.dbf',
  '/u01/app/oracle/oradata/NPRD/datafile/o1_mf_sysaux_cbcpljhj_.dbf',
  '/u01/app/oracle/oradata/NPRD/datafile/o1_mf_undotbs1_cbcpvbqr_.dbf',
  '/u01/app/oracle/oradata/NPRD/datafile/o1_mf_wmdata_cbcys05m_.dbf',
  '/u01/app/oracle/oradata/NPRD/datafile/o1_mf_users_cbcpv9fn_.dbf'
CHARACTER SET WE8MSWIN1252
;
```

Here is the new-version database:

```
SQL> show parameter db_name
```

```
NAME                     TYPE            VALUE
------------------    -----------    ----------------------------------
db_name                  string          NPRD
SQL> !hostname
ORA-C2
```

Old version Database

```
SQL> show parameter db_name

NAME                                    TYPE         VALUE
------------------------------------    -----------  --------------------------------
db_name                                 string       R2B
SQL> !hostname
ORA-C1.localdomain

SQL>
```

To upgrade to the new version, the database and structure should be ready; it can be created using the DBCA or manual database method. You are going to create only the user data but not anything related to system objects. For example, say you have the following table called WMT in the source database (OPRD) and you have to produce the same table or change of parameters into the target database.

```
SQL> select table_name,tablespace_name,initial_extent,next_extent,num_rows from user_tables
where table_name='WMT';

TABLE_NAME TABLESPACE_NAME    INITIAL_EXTENT NEXT_EXTENT    NUM_ROWS
---------- ---------------    -------------- -----------    ----------
WMT        WMDATA                     106496       57344     1000000

SQL> show user
USER is "WMUSER"
SQL>
```

You must establish a connection from the new-version database to the old database; for that you have to create a database link between the two databases. This database link you have to create on the target database, which points to the source database, as shown here:

```
SQL> create database link wmlink connect to wmuser identified by wmuser using 'oprd';

Database link created.

SQL> show user
USER is "WMUSER"
SQL>
```

This command is using the TNS service OPRD, which is the source database (old version: oprd). As discussed earlier, the tablespace, grants, and users should be created and ready to create the table. You have the table WMT in the source database, and to create the table in the target, the name can be the same or different, and the storage parameter can be same or it can be changed.

If the tablespace of the source does not exist, then it will consider writing into the default tablespace, so you have to ensure either the new tablespace is the same as created in the target database or specify the new tablespace name in the create statement.

```
SQL> create table wmtn as select * from wmuser.wmt@dbmigr;

Table created.

SQL> create table wmt tablespace wmdata as select * from wmuser.wmt@dbmigr;

Table created.

SQL> create table wmts storage(initial 200k next 50k) tablespace wmdata as select * from
wmuser.wmt@dbmigr;

Table created.
SQL>
```

CTAS provides great flexibility to alter the storage parameters and new tablespace name. A few other options in the upgrade process are covered next.

Parallel Usage with CTAS

The parallel clause can be used in creating a table using CTAS for performance reasons. For the partitioned table, when multiple partitions parse in one CTAS statement or for very huge tables, the parallel clause can be used.

When executing the create statement, you can specify parallel 8 or 10 manually. If the parallel clause is not mentioned, then it uses DOP based on the number of CPUs available. The parallel clause works even for partitioned tables and nonpartitioned tables.

```
SQL> create table wmtp parallel 5 tablespace wmdata as select * from wmuser.wmt@dbmigr;

Table created.
```

Order By with CTAS

The Order By clause is one more advantage of using CTAS to upgrade the database using the source data with database links. When using Order By, the sort will take place, and more temp will be used based on the sort operations. The parallel clause with Order By can improve performance greatly. If you use the Order By clause with any column, then the data will be arranged in either ascending or descending order depending on the choice given.

```
Source Database
SQL> show user
USER is "WMUSER"
SQL> select * from t;

        NO
----------
```

```
                 5
                 3
                 4
                 2
                 1

SQL>
```

Here is the target database (new version):

```
SQL> create table wmto tablespace wmdata as select * from wmuser.t@dbmigr order by no;

Table created.

SQL> select * from wmto;

        NO
----------
         1
         2
         3
         4
         5
```

The order in the source database is different, and the order in the remote database is different. Thus, you can simulate the CTAS using the various options, which helps to upgrade the database.

Summary

You've seen how to use the CTAS method in the upgrade method. Why would you use CTAS when there are various utilities and easier options available? The answer depends on the environment and the compatibility support. CTAS speaks purely in the SQL language. Again, the advantages and the disadvantages are common for every method; it's the DBA's call about which method should be used for a successful upgrade. You've also seen how to create tables over a remote database and the various options you can use to improve the performance of CTAS.

Database Upgrades Using Transient Logical Standby

Oracle has introduced an HA solution initially introduced as *standby* from 8i. It creates a clone database at a remote location, say, a disaster recovery (DR) site, and the cloned database stays up-to-date by applying recovery using the archive logs generated at the primary database and will be in sync with the primary database. The transactions happening in the primary database will get transferred to the disaster recovery database through archived logs. Oracle has improved the Data Guard functionality in 10g and 11g R2, and many new features are based on data protection in 12c. In the Data Guard configuration, the standby database will be applied with archive or redo log entries by the managed recovery process. For the high availability solution, it is highly preferred to have the same server configuration and database structure. Oracle Data Guard has two kinds of standby database. They are physical standby and logical standby.

- *Physical standby*: This standby database will be the exact replica of the primary database. Block by block, the data will be copied from the primary to the standby, which means the standby database has to be ready to act as the primary database in the case of any disasters. Once the archived log reaches the standby database, it will get applied through the Media Recovery Process (MRP). The physical standby database will be in either mount mode or read-only mode. The archived logs/redo log entries, which have primary database transactions, will be applied to the standby database through the MRP process. In an active Data Guard setup, the database can be opened in read-only mode and at the same time recovery will be running. It is especially useful for executing reporting jobs (select) or to offload the jobs from the primary.

- *Logical standby*: This standby database uses the SQL apply method. Just like a physical standby, it receives archived logs/redo logs, but it mines the received archived logs and converts its contents into SQL statements to be applied to the logical standby database. As it is not a block-by-block copy method, only user transactions will be transmitted between the primary and the standby. The SQL statement conversion gives the advantage of having the standby database in read-write mode. Since the standby database is in read-write mode, it adds luxuries to create additional new objects in standby, which may be helpful for reporting purposes. Anyway, it is not advisable to alter objects involved in the Data Guard activity, which means the objects that get updated via SQL Apply should not get altered.

Table 2-11. *Difference Between Physical and Logical Standby Database*

	PHYSICAL STANDBY	LOGICAL STANDBY
TRANSFER METHOD	Redo Log Apply	SQL Apply
DATABASE VERSION	Both Primary and Standby should be with same version	Primary and Standby cab be different version
ALLOWED DATATYPE	All Datatypes	Large Object is not allowed
STANDBY MODE	Mount or Read-Only	All modes including Read-Write
DBID	Same DBID for Primary and Standby	DBID is different
TRANSACTIONS	All sys and user transactions	Only user transactions
DATA UNIQUENESS	Not Required	Data uniqueness required at Table Level

Table 2-11 compares physical and logical standby.

In this method, the database upgrade is going to use both the physical and logical standby concepts to upgrade the database with less downtime. It is going to upgrade the data dictionary along with the data.

Here are the prerequisites for upgrade:

- It requires a high availability setup.

- It requires data uniqueness because the logical standby is involved.

- It requires additional storage for creating the standby database.

- Downtime is required while performing role switchover.

- Datatypes related to Bfile, Collections, Multimedia data types and large objects stored as secure files are not supported.

Figure 2-44 shows the upgrade steps.

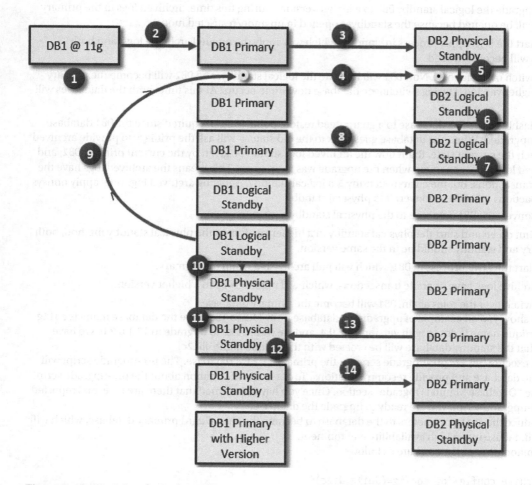

Figure 2-44. Transient logical standby steps

The database name is DB1.

① Ensure the database is in archivelog mode and Flashback is enabled.

② First make the DB1 database the primary database by adding the necessary parameters such as log_archive_config and log_archive_dest_2. In other words, you are creating a Data Guard setup, and in that, DB1 becomes primary database.

③ Create the physical standby database. The standby database can be created using the RMAN duplicate method or by using the primary database backup or basic SCP. Say that the standby database's unique name is DB2. So, DB1 and DB2 are part of Data Guard with the same database version, and both are in sync through the archive log transmission.

④ Create a guaranteed restore point at the primary and physical standby database. This guaranteed restore point will be used later to flashback.

⑤ Convert the physical standby database to a logical standby database and start the SQL Apply process. Now both the primary and standby databases are in sync.

⑥ Upgrade the logical standby DB2 to a higher version. During this time, archived logs in the primary database will be queued because the standby is opened in upgrade/restricted mode.

⑦ Start the SQL Apply process in standby, which will apply the queued archived logs, and both databases will become synced.

⑧ Switch over the roles. Now DB1 will become the logical standby, and DB2 will become the primary with the higher version. During switchover, database downtime occurs. At this time, both the databases will be in sync.

⑨ Flashback the DB1 database to a guaranteed restore point. This is required since the DB1 database has to be upgraded. When the database goes back to the old state, it will ask the primary to provide archived logs to reach the current state. Right now the archived logs should be given by the current primary DB2, and the archived logs were generated when the upgrade was in progress. This means the archived logs have the upgrade transactions. But the current standby is a logical standby. Applying archived logs only apply nonsys user transactions and hence convert it to physical standby.

⑩ Convert the DB1 database to the physical standby.

⑪ Shut down and start the physical standby in a higher version. In the physical standby method, both the primary and standby should be in the same version.

⑫ Start the MRP process in DB1, which will pull archive logs from the primary.

⑬ Archive logs have upgrade transactions, which will upgrade DB1 to a higher version.

⑭ Switch over the roles again. DB1 will become the primary database.

We'll show you an example of upgrading a database from 11.2 to 12c. Here the database name is db11g and the unique name is db11g with version 11.2.0.4, and we would like to upgrade to 12.1.0.2.0. We have decided that the standby database will be created with the unique name db12c.

First, execute the 12c pre-upgrade script in the primary 11.2.0.4 database. The pre-upgrade script will analyze the database and provide recommendations. To get more information about the pre-upgrade script, refer to the "Database Manual Upgrade" section. Once you have confirmed that there are no errors reported in the pre-upgrade script, you are ready to upgrade the database.

Introduce the init parameters to the database to become the Data Guard primary database, which will place the database into a high availability environment.

The mandatory parameters are as follows:

```
*.log_archive_config='dg_config=(db11g,d12c)'
log_archive_dest_1='location=use_db_recovery_file_dest valid_for=(online_logfile,all_roles)
db_unique_name=db11g'
*log_archive_dest_2='service="db12c" LGWR ASYNC db_unique_name="db12c" valid_for(online_
logfile,primary_role)'
*.log_archive_dest_state_2='enable'
*.fal_server=db12c
```

```
*.db_file_name_convert='/u01/app/oracle/oradata/db12c/','/u01/app/oracle/oradata/db11g/'
*.log_file_name_convert='/u01/app/oracle/oradata/db12c/','/u01/app/oracle/oradata/db11g/'
```

While preparing init parameter for primary database, let me create it for standby database as well. Along with basic parameters lets include DG parameters as below

```
*.log_archive_config='dg_config=(db11g,db12c)'
*.log_archive_dest_1='location=use_db_recovery_file_dest valid_for=(online_logfile,all_
roles) db_unique_name=db12c'
*.log_archive_dest_2='service="db11g" LGWR ASYNC db_unique_name="db11g" valid_for=(online_
logfile,primary_role)'
*.log_archive_dest_state_1='enable'
*.log_archive_dest_state_2='enable'
*.db_file_name_convert='/u01/app/oracle/oradata/db11g','/u01/app/oracle/oradata/db12c'
*.log_file_name_convert='/u01/app/oracle/oradata/db11g','/u01/app/oracle/oradata/db12c'
```

You need to create the clone database at the standby site. This can be achieved by restoring the primary database backup or creating the standby database using the duplicate method. The duplicate command creates the standby database by connecting to the primary database and at the end keeps the standby database in mount state. To perform the duplicate method, the standby database should be in nomount state, and both the primary and standby databases should be accessible through the listener.

Hence, create the static listener entry in the primary and standby databases and restart the listener. Also, create TNS entries for both the primary and standby databases.

```
(SID_DESC =
        (GLOBAL_DBNAME = db11g)
        (ORACLE_HOME = /u01/app/oracle/product/11.2.0/dbhome_1)
        (SID_NAME = db11g)
)
(SID_DESC =
        (GLOBAL_DBNAME = db12c)
        (ORACLE_HOME = /u01/app/oracle/product/11.2.0/dbhome_1)
        (SID_NAME = db12c)
)
```

From the RMAN prompt, connect the primary database as the target and the standby database instance as the auxiliary instance and execute the duplicate command.

```
$rman target sys/sys@db11g auxiliary sys/sys@db12c
Connected to target database: DB11G (DBID=365315951)
Connected to auxiliary database: DB11g (not mounted)
RMAN> duplicate target database for standby from active database nofilenamecheck;
```

The duplicate command creates the standby database in mount state.

Switch the log file from the primary and ensure both the primary and physical standby are in sync.

Create a Restore Point

Create a restore point at the primary and physical standby database. This restore point will be used for flashback later.

```
SQL> create restore point before_upgrade guarantee flashback database;
```

135

```
Restore point created.
```

The restore point will help to rewind the database to a certain time. Later you will move the database to the pre-upgrade state and you require a restore point to achieve that. Also, you will create the restore point as a guaranteed one. So, it will not get aged out, and even if flashback is disabled for any reason, the guaranteed restore point will live forever. It has to be manually deleted.

Enable Supplementary Logging

To prepare the primary database for logical standby support, you need to run the following package on the primary database so that it builds the log miner directory:

```
SQL> execute dbms_logstdby.build;
PL/SQL procedure successfully completed.

Convert to Logical standby
At standby execute Logical standby switchover command
SQL> alter database recover to logical standby keep identity;
Database altered.
```

Now the physical standby becomes the logical standby. Shut down the database and start it in read-write state. The database role can be confirmed by querying v$database.

```
SQL> select database_role from v$database;
DATABASE_ROLE
----------------------------
LOGICAL STANDBY

Start SQL Apply
 Start the SQL apply process at Logical standby database.
SQL> alter database start logical standby apply immediate;
Database altered.
```

After executing the apply statement, the logical standby will receive archive logs from the primary and mines it into SQL statements, which will be applied at standby. This process can be seen at the alert log.

Upgrade of Logical Standby Database

Once you have confirmed that the primary and logical standbys are in sync, you start the upgrade process to the logical standby database. The DBUA or Manual upgrade method can be used. In this example we use manual database upgrade method. Shut down the standby and start it in upgrade mode using the Oracle 12c Home. When the logical standby is in upgrade mode, the database will be in restricted mode. Hence, don't start the SQL Apply process; let the archived logs get stored at the standby site.

Since you have performed the prerequisites check at the beginning in the primary database, that step is not necessary here.

Copy the init parameter file and password file to 12c Oracle Home.

Start the database in upgrade mode in Oracle 12c Oracle Home.

```
SQL> startup upgrade
ORACLE instance started.
```

```
Total System Global Area    1660944383 bytes
Fixed Size                     2925072 bytes
Variable Size               1006636528 bytes
Database Buffers             637534208 bytes
Redo Buffers                  13848576 bytes
Database mounted.
Database opened.
```

Manual Upgrade Using the 12*c* Method

In 12*c* the manual upgrade has the option to upgrade database using the parallel processes. It can be achieved by using the Perl utility catctl.pl. The following command has been invoked from the $ORACLE_HOME/rdbms/admin directory:

```
$/u01/app/oracle/product/12.1.0/perl/bin/perl catctl.pl -n 4 -l /u01/app/oracle catupgrd.sql
```

In the previous command, the 12*c* Oracle Home is /u01/app/oracle/product/12.1.0.

```
Catctl.pl is located in /u01/app/oracle/product/12.1.0/rdbms/admin directory. It has to be
executed using perl binaries which is located at /u01/app/oracle/product/12.1.0/perl/bin
-n option specifies number of processes involved in upgrade process
-l specifies log location for upgrade log
```

Since you invoke the command from the rdbms/admin directory, you don't specify the location of the catupgrd.sql file.

The upgrade will be executed in phases. At the end of the manual upgrade, the database will shut down. Start the database in read-write mode and execute utlrp.sql to compile invalid objects. You can see some database components with the UPGRADED status after upgrade; executing utlrp.sql will change it to VALID.

After restarting database in read-write mode, enable SQL Apply. The transactions that happened in the primary during the upgrade period will get applied to the 12*c* logical standby database. Once you have confirmed that the 11*g* primary and 12*c* logical standby are in sync, initiate the switchover activity.

Switchover

Execute the switchover command first at the 11*g* primary to convert to the logical standby role.

```
SQL> alter database commit to switchover to logical standby;
Database altered.
```

Once 11*g* becomes the logical standby, execute the switchover command at the 12*c* database.

```
SQL> alter database commit to switchover to primary;
Database altered.
```

Confirm the database roles using the view v$database.

Initiate Flashback

Currently the primary 12*c* and logical standby 11*g* are in sync. But the 11*g* logical standby has to be upgraded to 12*c*. To achieve that, flashback the 11*g* database to the restore point created earlier. If you perform a flashback, then the state of the restore point will be available to you, in other words, the physical standby.

Shut down the 11*g* logical standby database and get it into mount state and then execute the flashback command.

```
SQL> flashback database to restore point before_upgrade;
Flashback complete.
```

Now the 11*g* logical standby goes back to the old state, and to get in sync with the primary, it will query the 12*c* primary database to send archive logs.

Convert Logical to Physical Standby

But it is the logical standby, and synchronization will happen only at the nonsys user level. The upgrade execution happened only at the sys level. So, to get upgrade transactions, the logical standby needs to be converted to the physical standby. So, convert the 11*g* logical standby to the physical standby.

```
SQL> alter database convert to physical standby;
Database altered.
```

Since the physical standby requires the same database version for the primary and standby, shut down the physical standby and start it using 12*c* Home to mount state.

Starting MRP

Start the managed recovery process; it will collect the archived logs generated from the restore point to until the current state of the primary. These archive logs have upgrade transactions. Hence, while applying archived logs, the current physical standby database dictionary will get upgraded to 12*c*.

```
SQL> alter database recover managed standby database using current logfile through next
switchover disconnect;
Database altered.
```

Ensure the standby is in sync with the primary database.

Switchover

Perform the switchover and you will see that both homes are on 12*c*, but the primary and standby are in opposite sites. So, you need to perform the switchover.

```
SQL> alter database commit to switchover to primary;
Database altered.
```

The current 12*c* physical standby can be shut down.

```
SQL> alter database commit to switchover to physical standby with session shutdown;
Database altered.
```

Here are the known issues:

- An upgrade using the transient logical standby method is available from 11.1.0.6.

- You can do a 12*c* manual upgrade; hence, all the prerequisites and known issues of the manual upgrade are applicable to this method

- Since flashback is happening, the compatibility parameter value should not be changed in the middle of upgrade. Hence, if the upgrade requires a compatibility parameter value change, then this method will not suit.

- If any archive log is deleted during the upgrade process, unexpected issues may occur.

Full Transportable Export/Import

As part of the upgrade methods, you have seen traditional export/import, Data Pump, and transportable tablespace. These methods can be used to upgrade databases to a higher database version such as 11*g* R2 and 12*c* non-CDB and pluggable databases. In addition to these methods, in 12*c* an exciting new feature called *full transportable export/import* has been introduced to make upgrading easier, more effective, faster, and more efficient than the other methods.

In traditional export/import, you extract the logical data and create it as the dump file. It is a time-consuming process because it has to extract each object with its metadata, and this method is not suitable for large databases. Also, if in upgrade process you want to have the source and target databases in sync, then there should not be any changes in the source database until the dump gets imported into the target's higher version. Downtime will be huge. This method got deprecated and didn't introduce new features/options in later versions. This method is recommended for 9*i* versions and older. Data Pump is an enhanced tool to perform export/import operations. It was introduced in 10*g*. It has lots of new features such as parallelism, stop and resume the export/import process, export through the network link (database link from target to primary), and exclude options for tablespaces. Unlike a traditional export, it is a server-side utility. The backup can be taken only at the server side using the database logical directory. It's a command-line utility, and it is easy to use. But again, for databases with a large number of objects, it has to extract data to create a dump file, and the performance is not that great.

The transportable tablespace method is much better in terms of performance compared to Data Pump. It is the fastest method to move massive user data to another database. Here, like traditional export/import, each individual object is not accessed. Datafiles are physically copied to the target location and that's why it takes less time to transfer the data. To make the copied datafiles part of the target database, the metadata of those tablespaces gets imported into the target database using Data Pump or traditional export/import. However, it requires complicated steps to move the metadata to the target database. Manual intervention is required to create the required schemas with the necessary privileges at the target database before import and to change datafiles to read-write at the end of import. Consider you have installed an application that has objects in the SYS schema. In the TTS method, those objects will not get exported. You need to export those objects separately and import them. Also, nonsegment objects like PL/SQL procedures and packages will not move to the target database in the TTS method. Using the DBMS_METADATA package, you need to get the PL/SQL source code and execute it on the target database.

To overcome the drawbacks of the Data Pump and transportable tablespace methods in 12*c*, the full transportable export/import has been introduced. It has features of both the Data Pump and transportable tablespace methods. It uses the command interface of Data Pump and along with that copies the datafiles physically as you do in the transportable tablespace method. As datafiles are copied physically, the data transfer time is less, and at the same time you use the Data Pump functionality to extract the metadata. Thus, full transportable export/import combines the ease of use of Oracle Data Pump and the performance of transportable tablespaces, resulting in a feature that makes database migration faster and easier. At the end of the transport, the required schema of objects and required nonsegment objects will be created automatically, and the datafiles will be switched back to read-write automatically.

Using the Data Pump network link functionality, it is possible to extract metadata from the source through the database link or network link at the target database. Using impdp you can get the required metadata for the target database; there is no need for expdp in this model. Using the exclude option, you can avoid exporting unnecessary tablespaces.

Prerequisites

Here are the prerequisites:

- The source database version is at least 11.2.0.3.0.

- The target database should not have user schemas that are the same name as the source database.

- The target database should not have a tablespace name that is the same as the tablespaces getting transported from the source database.

- The logical directory should be created in 12c. Default directories like DATA_PUMP_DIR cannot be used in 12c.

- If the particular tablespaces getting exported use the exclude or include option, then a self-contained check should be performed.

- For using the network_link parameter while using impdp, there should be a datalink link in the target database for the source database, and network connectivity should be there to the source database.

Upgrade Steps

The first step is to create a database in the target database version with the appropriate database components and tablespaces.

Kindly note there are two kinds of tablespaces available in a database: administrative tablespaces like SYSTEM, SYSAUX, UNDO, and nonadministrative tablespaces like USERS and application-related tablespaces. Data Pump will not export Oracle-supplied objects in an administrative tablespace like SYSTEM, SYSAUX, and UNDO.

In the source database, change the user tablespaces to read-only and take a Data Pump export, specifying the parameters Full=y and Transportable=Always. These parameters will denote that this Data Pump is taking a full transportable export dump. If the database version is less than 12c, in other words, is 11.2.0.3 or 11.2.0.4, then the version parameter has to be specified with the value Version=12.0. This value denotes that this generated dump will get imported into the 12c database. Here the metadata will be taken for the full database. If any user objects are stored in the administrative tablespace, those user objects and the metadata will be taken as part of the export.

The Data Pump log will show the necessary datafiles to be copied to the target database server. Copy those datafiles and metadata dump to the target database server and start impdp. For impdp you just specify the transport_datafiles parameter, which will carry the values of the datafile along with the location.

No other parameter is required because impdp is smart enough to identify that the dump is created as a full transportable export/import method. It can distinguish that the dump is created with the full transportable export/import option or conventional export.

After impdp, check the tablespaces and their status. Also check whether the required schemas are created automatically.

Here are the steps in detail:

```
Source datatbase version: 11.2.0.4.0
Source database name: orcl11g
Target database version: 12.1.0.2.0
Target database name: Container Database (CDB1) with Pluggable database (PDB2)
```

Source database

```
[oracle@TTS ~]$ sqlplus / as sysdba
SQL*Plus: Release 11.2.0.4.0 Production on Tue Jan 19 23:14:37 2016
Copyright (c) 1982, 2013, Oracle.  All rights reserved.
Connected to:
Oracle Database 11g Enterprise Edition Release 11.2.0.4.0 - 64bit Production
With the Partitioning, OLAP, Data Mining and Real Application Testing options

SQL> select name,open_mode from v$database;
NAME       OPEN_MODE
---------  --------------------
ORCL11G    READ WRITE

SQL> select tablespace_name,status from dba_tablespaces;

TABLESPACE_NAME                 STATUS
------------------------------- ---------
SYSTEM                          ONLINE
SYSAUX                          ONLINE
UNDOTBS1                        ONLINE
TEMP                            ONLINE
USERS                           ONLINE
TEST1                           ONLINE
TEST2                           ONLINE
```

Create a logical directory to store the metadata dump

```
SQL> create directory tts_dir as '/u01/app/oracle/backup';
```

Change the tablespace status from read-write to read-only before starting the TTS export. If the tablespace status has not changed to read-only, you will get an error message during export (expdp). After making it read only. You will not be able to make changes in objects stored in these tablespaces. In another way, you can say downtime starts from here.

```
SQL> alter tablespace USERS read only;
SQL> alter tablespace TEST1 read only;
SQL> alter tablespace TEST2 read only;

SQL> select tablespace_name,status from dba_tablespaces;

TABLESPACE_NAME                     STATUS
------------------------------      ---------
SYSTEM                              ONLINE
SYSAUX                             ONLINE
UNDOTBS1                           ONLINE
TEMP                               ONLINE
USERS                              READ ONLY
TEST1                              READ ONLY
TEST2                              READ ONLY
```

The status shows all the nonadmin tablespaces are read-only.
Copy all read only tablespace datafiles to target datafile location

```
Within server  ➤ $cp <source_location> <target_location>
Different server ➤ $scp <source_location> target_hostname:<target_location>
```

Take Datapump export. As this is 11.2.0.4 database we add version=12 parameter

```
$expdp userid=\'sys@DB11g as sysdba\' directory=tts_dir transportable=always full=y
version=12 dumpfile=exporcl.dmp logfile=exporcl.log
Export: Release 11.2.0.4.0 - Production on Sat Jan 2 11:30:03 2016
Copyright (c) 1982, 2011, Oracle and/or its affiliates.  All rights reserved.
Password:
Connected to: Oracle Database 11g Enterprise Edition Release 11.2.0.4.0 - 64bit Production
With the Partitioning, OLAP, Data Mining and Real Application Testing options
Starting "SYS"."SYS_EXPORT_FULL_01":  userid="sys/********@DB11g AS SYSDBA" directory=tts_
dir transportable=always full=y version=12 dumpfile=exporcl.dmp logfile=exporcl.log
Estimate in progress using BLOCKS method...
.
.
. . exported "SYSTEM"."REPCAT$_USER_PARM_VALUES"          0 KB       0 rows
. . exported "SYSTEM"."SQLPLUS_PRODUCT_PROFILE"           0 KB       0 rows
Master table "SYS"."SYS_EXPORT_FULL_01" successfully loaded/unloaded
******************************************************************************
Dump file set for SYS.SYS_EXPORT_FULL_01 is:
  /u01/app/oracle/backup/exporcl.dmp
******************************************************************************
Datafiles required for transportable tablespace TBS_TEST:
  /u01/app/oracle/oradata/DB11g/tbs_test01.dbf
```

```
Datafiles required for transportable tablespace TBS_TEST1:
  /u01/app/oracle/oradata/DB11g/tbs_test101.dbf
Datafiles required for transportable tablespace USERS:
  /u01/app/oracle/oradata/DB11g/users01.dbf
```

If you don't change tablespace are in read only status, once you execute expdp command, you will get below error details.

At the end log shows the expected tablespaces to be transferred to target side.

In case the expected tablespaces are not in read only then datapump will terminate with error

ORA-29335: tablespace 'TBS_TEST' is not read only

ORA-29335: tablespace 'TBS_TEST1' is not read only

ORA-29335: tablespace 'USERS' is not read only

Job "SYSTEM"."SYS_EXPORT_FULL_02" stopped due to fatal error at 04:53:48

```
Job "SYS"."SYS_EXPORT_FULL_01" successfully completed at Sat Jan 2 11:34:34 2016 elapsed 0 00:04:28

Target database (12c Container Database)
```

Pluggable database was created from seed (manual pluggable database creation)

```
SQL> create pluggable database pdb2
admin user test
identified by test
file_name_convert = ('/pdbseed/', '/pdb2/');
Pluggable database created.

SQL> show pdbs
    CON_ID CON_NAME                        OPEN MODE  RESTRICTED
---------- ------------------------------- ---------- ----------
         2 PDB$SEED                        READ ONLY  NO
         3 PDB1                            READ WRITE NO
         4 PDB2                            MOUNTED
SQL> alter pluggable database pdb2 open;
```

```
SQL> show pdbs
    CON_ID CON_NAME                              OPEN MODE  RESTRICTED
---------- ------------------------------------- ---------- ----------
         2 PDB$SEED                              READ ONLY  NO
         3 PDB1                                  READ WRITE NO
         4 PDB2                                  READ WRITE NO
```

Connect to pluggable database or change the current session container to pluggable database

```
SQL> alter session set container=pdb2;

SQL> show con_name
CON_NAME
---------
PDB2
```

Verify the default tablespaces created in the pluggable database. Remember, if the PDB was created through the DBCA, then the Users tablespace would have been created. That is a permanent tablespace for the pluggable database, and it cannot be deleted.

```
SQL> select tablespace_name from dba_tablespaces;
TABLESPACE_NAME
-------------------------------
SYSTEM
SYSAUX
TEMP
```

At target site copied metadata dump to /u01/app/oracle/backup
Create Logical directory for /u01/app/oracle/backup

```
SQL> create directory tts_dir as '/u01/app/oracle/backup';
Directory created.
```

Perform import by connecting to pluggable database through connection string

```
$impdp userid=\'sys@pdb2 as sysdba\'
directory=tts_dir
dumpfile=exporcl.dmp
logfile=tba_imp.log
version=12 transport_datafiles='/u01/app/oracle/oradata/CDB1/pdb2/users01.dbf',
                                '/u01/app/oracle/oradata/CDB1/pdb2/test01.dbf',
                                '/u01/app/oracle/oradata/CDB1/pdb2/test02.dbf'

Import: Release 12.1.0.2.0 - Production on Sat Jan 2 12:07:43 2016
Copyright (c) 1982, 2014, Oracle and/or its affiliates.  All rights reserved.
Connected to: Oracle Database 12c Enterprise Edition Release 12.1.0.2.0 - 64bit Production
With the Partitioning, OLAP, Advanced Analytics and Real Application Testing options
Master table "SYS"."SYS_IMPORT_TRANSPORTABLE_01" successfully loaded/unloaded
```

```
Source time zone is +00:00 and target time zone is -07:00.
Starting "SYS"."SYS_IMPORT_TRANSPORTABLE_01":  userid="sys/*******@pdb2 as sysdba"
directory=tts_dir dumpfile=exporcl.dmp logfile=tba_imp.log version=12 transport_datafiles='/
u01/app/oracle/oradata/CDB1/pdb2/users01.dbf','/u01/app/oracle/oradata/CDB1/pdb2/test01.
dbf','/u01/app/oracle/oradata/CDB1/pdb2/test02.dbf'
Processing object type DATABASE_EXPORT/PRE_SYSTEM_IMPCALLOUT/MARKER
```

Verify the tablespace name and status. You can see the tablespaces become read write by default.

```
SQL> show con_name
CON_NAME
------------------------------
PDB2

SQL> select tablespace_name,status from dba_tablespaces;
TABLESPACE_NAME                STATUS
------------------------------ ---------
SYSTEM                         ONLINE
SYSAUX                         ONLINE
TEMP                           ONLINE
TEST1                          ONLINE
TEST2                          ONLINE
USERS                          ONLINE

SQL> select owner, table_name, tablespace_name from dba_tables where owner='TEST';
OWNER      TABLE_NAME TABLESPACE
-----      ---------- ----------
TEST       T1         TEST1
TEST       T2         TEST2

SQL> select * from test.TAB_SYS;
         N
----------
         1
         1
         1
```

Objects in the SYSTEM tablespace have been exported along with the data, and they have been placed in the SYSTEM tablespace at the target site.

You can also import the metadata without taking an export at the source database. It can be achieved through the network_link parameter. This parameter has the name of the database link created from the target database to the source database. Along with that, you need to specify the parameters FULL and TRANSPORT_DATAFILES. If the source is 11.2.0.3 or 11.2.0.4, then the VERSION parameter has to be specified.

Let's create another pluggable database, pdbftimp.

```
SQL> create pluggable database pdbftimp admin user test identified by test;
Pluggable database created.
```

Connect to pluggable database and create a database link to source database 'DB11g'

```
[oracle@Server admin]$ sqlplus sys/sys@pdbftimp as sysdba
SQL*Plus: Release 12.1.0.2.0 Production on Sat Jan 2 13:49:38 2016
Copyright (c) 1982, 2014, Oracle.  All rights reserved.
Connected to:
Oracle Database 12c Enterprise Edition Release 12.1.0.2.0 - 64bit Production
With the Partitioning, OLAP, Advanced Analytics and Real Application Testing options

SQL> create database link dblink_db11g connect to system identified by manager using 'DB11g';
Database link created.

SQL> select count(*) from dual@dblink_db11g  ;
  COUNT(*)
----------
         1
```

The source datafiles are already copied to /u01/app/oracle/oradata/CDBTEST/PDBFTIMP after making it to read-only state.

Create a logical directory in 12c database. This is just for storing log file.

```
SQL> create directory datapump_imp_log as '/u01/app/oracle/backup_imp_log';
Directory created.
Invoke impdp command along with following parameter
Network_link - Database link created from 12c database to 11g database
Full =y and Transportable=always - This parameter denotes it is full transportable export/import
Transport_data_files - Datafiles with location which are copied from source database when
they were read only
Version - This is require when source database compatible setting is less than 12

impdp userid=\'sys@pdbexport as sysdba\'  directory=datapump_imp_log \
> logfile=full_tts_imp.log full=y transportable=always \
> version=12 network_link=dblink_db11g \
> metrics=y \
> transport_datafiles='/u01/app/oracle/oradata/CDBTEST/PDBFTIMP/users01.dbf',\
> '/u01/app/oracle/oradata/CDBTEST/PDBFTIMP/test101.dbf', \
> /u01/app/oracle/oradata/CDBTEST/PDBFTIMP/test01.dbf
```

Once the import is completed connect to pluggable database and check the newly added tablespaces.

```
SQL> select tablespace_name, status from dba_tablespaces;

TABLESPACE_NAME                 STATUS
------------------------------- ----------
SYSTEM                          ONLINE
SYSAUX                          ONLINE
TEMP                            ONLINE
TEST                            READ ONLY
TEST1                           READ ONLY
USERS                           READ ONLY
```

Make the tablespaces read write

```
SQL> alter tablespace test read write;

Tablespace altered.
SQL> alter tablespace test1 read write;
Tablespace altered.

SQL> alter tablespace users read write;
Tablespace altered.

SQL> select tablespace_name, status from dba_tablespaces;
TABLESPACE_NAME                  STATUS
-------------------------------- ---------
SYSTEM                           ONLINE
SYSAUX                           ONLINE
TEMP                             ONLINE
TEST                             ONLINE
TEST1                            ONLINE
USERS                            ONLINE
```

Here are the advantages over TTS:

- Metadata export becomes easy.

- There is no need to create the required schemas at the target database.

- There is no need to change tablespaces to read-write after import.

Here is known issue 1:

```
If Character set of both source and target database is not same, you will get the below error.
ORA-39123: Data Pump transportable tablespace job aborted
ORA-29345: cannot plug a tablespace into a database using an incompatible character set

Job "SYS"."SYS_IMPORT_TRANSPORTABLE_01" stopped due to fatal error
```

Here is the workaround:
Change the character set in the database, which should be the same in both databases.

```
SQL> shut immediate
SQL> STARTUP MOUNT;
SQL> ALTER SYSTEM ENABLE RESTRICTED SESSION;
SQL> ALTER SYSTEM SET JOB_QUEUE_PROCESSES=0;
SQL> ALTER SYSTEM SET AQ_TM_PROCESSES=0;
SQL> ALTER DATABASE OPEN;
SQL> ALTER DATABASE CHARACTER SET AL32UTF8;
ALTER DATABASE CHARACTER SET AL32UTF8
*
ERROR at line 1:
```

```
ORA-12712: new character set must be a superset of old character set

SQL> ALTER DATABASE CHARACTER SET INTERNAL_USE AL32UTF8;
Database altered.

SQL> shut immediate
SQL> startup
SQL> select * from v$NLS_PARAMETERS;
```

Here is known issue 2:

Metadata processing is not available.

```
[oracle@dbnode backup]$ impdp userid=\'sys@pdb1 as sysdba\' directory=tts_dir
dumpfile=exporcl.dmp logfile=tba_imp.log version=12 TRANSPORTABLE=ALWAYS transport_
datafiles='/u01/app/oracle/oradata/CDB1/29AEAE0BE9AA1379E0530100007FBF41/datafile/example01.
dbf'
Import: Release 12.1.0.1.0 - Production
Copyright (c) 1982, 2013, Oracle and/or its affiliates.  All rights reserved.
Password:
Connected to: Oracle Database 12c Enterprise Edition Release 12.1.0.1.0 - 64bit Production
With the Partitioning, OLAP, Advanced Analytics and Real Application Testing options
ORA-39006: internal error
ORA-39213: Metadata processing is not available
```

Here is the workaround:

Execute below procedure to avoid above error.
```
SQL> execute dbms_metadata_util.load_stylesheets
```

Here is known issue 3:

```
Inconsistences data files between source and target database
[oracle@dbnode backup]$ impdp userid=\'sys@pdb1 as sysdba\' directory=tts_dir
dumpfile=exporcl.dmp logfile=tba_imp.log version=12 transport_datafiles='/u01/app/oracle/
oradata/CDB1/29AEAE0BE9AA1379E0530100007FBF41/datafile/example01.dbf'
Import: Release 12.1.0.1.0 - Production on Tue Jan 19 17:58:28 2016
Copyright (c) 1982, 2013, Oracle and/or its affiliates.  All rights reserved.
Password:
Connected to: Oracle Database 12c Enterprise Edition Release 12.1.0.1.0 - 64bit Production
With the Partitioning, OLAP, Advanced Analytics and Real Application Testing options
ORA-39002: invalid operation
ORA-39352: Wrong number of TRANSPORT_DATAFILES specified: expected 2, received 1
```

Here is the workaround:

Don't create the tablespace in the target database when performing TTS import. Make sure to copy the required datafile from the source datafile location to the target datafile location to avoid this error.

Here is known issue 4:

```
Transportable import and TSLTZ issues while import (IMPDP)
```

```
[oracle@dbnode backup]$ impdp userid=\'sys@pdb1 as sysdba\' directory=tts_dir
dumpfile=exporcl.dmp logfile=tba_imp.log version=12 transport_datafiles='/u01/app/oracle/
oradata/CDB1/29AEAEOBE9AA1379E0530100007FBF41/datafile/example01.dbf'
Import: Release 12.1.0.1.0 - Production on Tue Jan 19 18:33:56 2016
Copyright (c) 1982, 2013, Oracle and/or its affiliates.  All rights reserved.
Password:
Connected to: Oracle Database 12c Enterprise Edition Release 12.1.0.1.0 - 64bit Production
With the Partitioning, OLAP, Advanced Analytics and Real Application Testing options
Master table "SYS"."SYS_IMPORT_TRANSPORTABLE_01" successfully loaded/unloaded
Source TSTZ version is 14 and target TSTZ version is 18.
Source timezone version is +00:00 and target timezone version is -07:00.
Starting "SYS"."SYS_IMPORT_TRANSPORTABLE_01":  userid="sys/********@pdb1 AS SYSDBA"
directory=tts_dir dumpfile=exporcl.dmp logfile=tba_imp.log version=12 transport_datafiles=/
u01/app/oracle/oradata/CDB1/29AEAEOBE9AA1379E0530100007FBF41/datafile/example01.dbf
Processing object type TRANSPORTABLE_EXPORT/PLUGTS_BLK
Processing object type TRANSPORTABLE_EXPORT/TYPE/TYPE_SPEC
Processing object type TRANSPORTABLE_EXPORT/PROCACT_INSTANCE
Processing object type TRANSPORTABLE_EXPORT/TABLE
ORA-39360: Table "OE"."ORDERS" skipped due to transportable import and TSLTZ issues.
ORA-39083: Object type TABLE:"OE"."WAREHOUSES" failed to create with error:
ORA-39339: Table "IX"."AQ$_ORDERS_QUEUETABLE_S" skipped due to transportable import and TSTZ issues.
ORA-39339: Table "IX"."AQ$_ORDERS_QUEUETABLE_L" skipped due to transportable import and TSTZ issues.
```

Here is the workaround:

Make sure the local time zone is equal in both database servers to avoid this error.

Summary

In this chapter, we discussed all the upgrade methods. We also explored their unique features, limitations, best practices, and known issues.

CHAPTER 3

■ ■ ■

Comparison of Upgrade Methods

You learned about the available upgrade methods in Chapter 2 in detail. Each method has unique features, prerequisites, steps, and constraints. You might be confused about how to choose the appropriate upgrade method for *your* environment. When choosing the right method, you need to know about the key features, limitations, and known issues of each method. In this chapter, you will analyze and compare all the upgrade methods in detail. This will give you an idea of which method is suitable for which environment.

The DBUA

The DBUA is an elegant utility that comes with the Oracle installation. It performs all the upgrade tasks automatically and requires minimal intervention. Once you have provided the inputs, such as the database name and Oracle Home, and you have started the upgrade, you can leave the database to the DBUA. This tool is smart enough to complete the upgrade with the specified options. It performs the pre-upgrade checks and displays the results. In addition to the basic upgrade process, it moves the datafiles as part of the upgrade, creates the new listener, provides fallback mechanisms such as the RMAN backup, and creates the flashback restore point.

Remember, the DBUA upgrades the data dictionary along with the user data to the higher version. The upgrade can be invoked only on a database that has passed the upgrade compatibility matrix. Based on the chosen source database version, it calls the appropriate script to perform the upgrade.

Features

These are some of the DBUA's features:

- The DBUA supports Real Application Clusters and Automatic Storage Management.

- The DBUA has the option to make the database part of an Enterprise Manager environment.

- The DBUA has the option to execute custom scripts before and after the upgrade.

- The DBUA can execute utlrp.sql to recompile invalid objects.

- If the GUI environment is not available, the DBUA can be invoked in silent mode. The DBUA can be scripted in silent mode with a response file.

- The DBUA records each upgrade activity. The upgrade output is recorded in different logs.

© Y V Ravikumar, K M Krishnakumar and Nassyam Basha 2017
N. Basha et al., *Oracle Database Upgrade and Migration Methods*, DOI 10.1007/978-1-4842-2328-4_3

- The DBUA has the option to include upgrade best practices such as making the user datafiles read-only before the upgrade. This option will be useful in the case of a fallback. With this option, only administrative tablespaces are required to be restored to the old version.

- Since all tasks are done automatically, the DBUA reduces the upgrade time and the chance of human errors.

- If an environment has multiple CPUs, then in 12*c* the DBUA automatically adds a Degree of Parallelism menu to the Recompile Invalid Objects screen.

- The DBUA keeps getting improved in each release. Until 8.0.6, it was handling only a single-instance database. Later it started handling a single instance and RAC databases. In 11*g* R2, the DBUA has the option to take an RMAN backup, and in 12*c*, the DBUA flashback restore point was introduced.

Limitations

These are some of the DBUA's limitations:

- The source and target databases must be on the same server; this is because the DBUA will access the source database using the source Oracle Home to perform the prerequisites check.

- The DBUA cannot perform a cross-platform migration.

- If multiple databases need to be upgraded, using the DBUA you need to upgrade databases one at a time. It is not recommended that you invoke multiple DBUA sessions at the same time on the same server.

- Dynamic changes will not be captured by the DBUA. While invoking the DBUA, it captures the source database details, and the collected information will be static all over the DBUA period. For example, a restore point, which is created after invoking the DBUA, will not be captured by the DBUA.

Manual/Command-Line Upgrade

As the name implies, in this method, all the upgrade tasks have to be done manually starting with the pre-upgrade steps. The prescribed step order has to be followed, and each step should be completed successfully before proceeding. In a manual upgrade, you need to execute each step carefully and observe its results. You will require debugging skills in case there are any issues.

Missing any upgrade step will create unexpected issues in further execution, and for this reason the DBUA is preferred. For example, missing the pre-upgrade step in a 11*g* R2 upgrade will terminate the upgrade execution with an ORA-01722, "invalid number," error. This is because the pre-upgrade process will update the internal tables that are referred to during the upgrade. Missing the pre-upgrade step means those tables won't be updated, and the upgrade process will not be able to proceed. So, make sure that each upgrade step is completed successfully without warnings or errors.

In a manual upgrade, `catupgrd.sql` is the script that takes care of upgrading database components. You can execute this script when the database is started in upgrade mode using the higher-version binaries. It will call other required scripts to perform the upgrade tasks. If the `catupgrd.sql` execution fails, you can execute the script again after making the necessary corrections. In the DBUA, if the upgrade fails while executing `catupgrd.sql`, then you need to restore the source database and try upgrading again. This is because the DBUA follows a series of steps, and you cannot force it to execute only `catupgrd.sql`. It has to start from the pre-upgrade part every time. This is the advantage of a manual upgrade over using the DBUA.

If the DBUA fails in between, then you can switch to a manual upgrade from there. The DBUA and a manual upgrade both will upgrade the data dictionary to the higher version. Also, in the manual upgrade, you can overcome some of the DBUA restrictions. For instance, the source and target databases do not need to be on the same server. If the source database is on a different server, then execute the pre-upgrade script there and move the database to the target server. Start the database in upgrade mode using the higher-version binaries and then follow the remaining upgrade steps.

For a manual database upgrade, the source and target database homes need not be owned by the same owner. After the pre-upgrade step, you can change the owner of the database files according to the target database home and then start the database in upgrade mode.

In a manual upgrade, you can take a copy of the source database and upgrade using that. In that case, the source database will be untouched. If any issue occurs, you can stop the upgrade and start the database in the source Oracle Home. Here you can consider the source database as a backup. You don't need a separate backup. Also, this will avoid restoration time. But this case is applicable only to a small database, because taking a copy of a big database will consume a lot of time (kindly note that the copy is done when the source database is shut down) and also require ample storage space.

If datafiles need to be moved from the file system to ASM, then this task should be done manually prior or after the upgrade. After moving the datafiles, the change has to be reflected in the control files. If multiple databases need to be upgraded, this can be done in parallel using the manual upgrade method. But remember that the upgrade is a resource-consuming activity. Hence, upgrading one database at a time is recommended.

Features

Here are the features of the manual upgrade method:

- Each step is executed manually. If there is a failure in any step, that particular step can be reexecuted. In the DBUA, if the upgrade fails, then it has to be started from the beginning.

- A manual upgrade is possible if the source and target database homes are owned by different operating system users.

- A manual upgrade can work even if the source and target database homes are located on different servers.

Limitations

Here are some limitations:

- The source and target database versions should have passed the upgrade compatibility matrix.

- You cannot skip the pre-upgrade step.

- Each upgrade step needs to complete successfully. It is best to document each upgrade step.

- The upgrade may take more time than the DBUA because all the tasks are done manually. Intermediate delays due to typos should be considered.

- You need to spool the upgrade execution into logs explicitly. If the upgrade fails, you need to walk through the logs to identify the cause.

Comparison of the DBUA and Manual Processes

Now that you have analyzed the pros and cons of both methods, let's compare the methods of using the DBUA versus doing an upgrade manually, both of which perform a data dictionary upgrade (Table 3-1).

Diagram 3.1 Comparison between DBUA and Manual upgrade

CATEGORY	DBUA	MANUAL UPGRADE
AUTOMATIC / MANUAL	All tasks are done automatically	All the steps have to be carried out manually
ORACLE HOME LOCATION	Source and Target database home should be in the same server	Source and Target database home can be in different servers
ORACLE HOME OWNERSHIP	Recommended to have Source and Target Oracle Home owned by same user	Source and Target database home can be owned by different users
PREUPGRADE STEP	Pre-upgrade step will be carried out by DBUA automatically	Pre-upgrade step should be carried out in source Oracle Database manually
ADDITIONAL OPTIONS FOR UPGRADE	DBUA has option to move data files to new location as part of upgrade	Moving data files has to be done manually and it may require recreation of control file
THE WAY IT WORKS	DBUA always start from Pre-upgrade script; We cannot bypass any upgrade step	In manual upgrade we can start upgrade from steps which were completed already
RESTART FEATURE	In case DBUA was stopped in the middle, we cannot restart again	catupgrd.sql can be executed multiple times
NECESSITY OF PREUPGRADE STEP	Executing Pre-upgrade script manually is optional for DBUA	Executing Pre-upgrade script is compulsory
TIME REQUIRED FOR UPGRADE	Since all tasks are done automatically, time taken for upgrade will be lesser than	Time consumed by manual will be comparatively higher than DBUA
MANUAL ERRORS	Chances of Manual Errors are less	Since all tasks are done manually, chances of Manual Errors like Skipping Steps, Missing to Observe Results can take place
GUI INTERFACE	It can operate with or without GUI	GUI Interface is not required for Manual Upgrade
DYNAMIC CHANGES IN DATABASE	Once DBUA is invoked, dynamic changes in database will not be observed by DBUA	Manual upgrade doesn't have any restriction

So, you have seen how to use the DBUA and how to do a manual upgrade; both upgrade the database dictionary along with the user data to the higher version. The rest of the methods will extract the user data and its metadata and then move it to the higher database dictionary. This means the higher-version database will have been created already.

Traditional Export/Import and Data Pump

Traditional export/import was introduced in Oracle version 5. In older Oracle versions up to 9*i*, it was commonly used to move data across databases and even across platforms.

Its steps are simple. It extracts data objects such as tables followed by their related objects (such as indexes and constraints) and makes a dump file. This dump will be imported into the target database. It is called as *client-server* utility. This means the export backup can be taken through the database client by connecting to the database server located remotely, or you can log in to the database server and take the dump there. This dump file is platform-independent. The dump can be imported across any platform, and the export can be done at the database level, schema level, and table level.

Only the imp tool can read the dump created by exp. The imp tool is smart enough to do all the required conversion on the data according to the target database while importing. It can do character set conversion, it can change the schema while importing, it can import only metadata, and it can overwrite existing objects.

The import utility has backward compatibility. It can import a dump file whose export utility version is lower or equivalent to the import utility version.

The export can be done from its own schema or from the SYS/SYSTEM user level using schema prefixes. To export its own schema, it requires you to have create session privileges. To export other schema objects, it requires the EXP_FULL_DATABASE privilege.

From an upgrade perspective, this method doesn't depend on the upgrade compatibility matrix; this is because you are not moving the data dictionary to a higher version. Only the data is getting moved. This means a 9*i* database can be imported on 12*c*.

Features

Here are its features:

- It is a simple way to transfer data between databases. It supports lower-version databases.

- It is a client-server utility. A backup can be taken either at the database client or at the database server.

Limitations

Here are its limitations:

- Traditional export/import is not built for large databases. It is deprecated in 11*g* R2. If your database size is small, then you can consider this method. The time taken to export and import is too long compared to other methods.

- If you want the source's and target's upgraded databases to be in sync, then you will have a longer downtime. The source database should stay unchanged until the import is completed successfully.

Data Pump

Data Pump is similar to traditional export/import, but is an enhanced method. It was introduced in Oracle 10*g*. It is a server-side utility, so a dump can be taken only at the server side in a logical directory. A dump taken with traditional export/import cannot be imported by Data Pump.

This method has lot of advantages over export/import. You will see some parameters related to upgrade, as shown here:

- `network_link`: Using this parameter, the export/import operations can be done over the network through the database link.

- `remap_datafile`: If the source and target have different naming conventions, then this parameter will be used. It changes the source datafile name to the target datafile name during import.

- `parallel`: This sets the number of active workers to complete the activity. It will increase the performance.

Data Pump is good at handling small and large databases.

The time taken to export and import is high. It may be lower compared to a traditional export/import, but it is longer than other methods.

Like the traditional method, if you want the source's and target's upgraded databases to be in sync, then the downtime increases.

Transportable Tablespaces

This method moves tablespaces across different databases. The target database version can be higher than the source. The datafiles associated with the tablespace will be physically copied to the target database home. To retain the consistency before copying datafiles, the tablespace will be placed in read-only mode.

This method is commonly used when the database is huge. Since it operates on the physical datafile, you don't need to worry about the number of objects residing in the tablespace. It will not touch logical objects. The downtime starts at the time the tablespace gets into read-only mode. The tablespace will stay in read-only mode until the datafile is copied to the target location and the metadata dump is taken. Here, copying the datafile to the target location may consume more time because it is based on network speed. Remember, the time spent on copying will contribute to the application downtime.

Steps in Summary

- As the first step, all prerequisites have to be passed.

- The chosen tablespaces should be self-contained.

- The required schemas should have been created at the target database.

- There should not be any tablespaces in the target with the same name as the tablespace getting transported from the source database.

- Exporting metadata to the target is complex in this method. If any objects are created in the SYSTEM tablespace, then those objects will not get transferred.

- After importing the tablespace metadata to the target, you need to switch back all the USER tablespaces to read-write.

Features

Here are its features:

1. Since datafile is physically copied to target database, the time taken to upgrade is very less.

2. Method is suitable for large size databases.

3. No need to worry about number of logical objects associated with the database.

Limitations

Here is a limitation:

- User objects located in the administrative tablespaces will not be transported.

- pl/sql procedures needs to be taken care manually.

- Required schema should be created manually before importing tablespace metadata.

Full Transportable Export/Import

To overcome the drawbacks of the transportable tablespace and Data Pump, full transportable export/import was introduced in 12c. But this method supports upgrading only from the 11.2.0.3.0 database.

Features

Here are the features:

- In Data Pump, you will see a performance issue because it takes more time to extract and create the dump file. The full transportable method resolves this by physically copying the datafiles to the remote location.

- In the transportable tablespace method, you will observe complexity in transferring the metadata. This full transportable method answers this by taking the metadata effectively through Data Pump.

- The metadata will contain schema creation scripts. Also, it exports user objects created in the administrative tablespace. This exports data as well as the metadata of those objects.

Also, using the network_link feature of Data Pump, the metadata can be retrieved directly from the source database. There is no need for a separate expdp step. This method is more effective compared to Data Pump and TTS, but it is applicable only to an upgrade to 12c, and also the minimum required source database version is 11.2.0.3.0.

Limitations

Here are the limitations:

- This method is available only from 12*c*.

- The source database should be 11.2.0.3.0 or higher, and the target database version should be 12.1.0.1.0 or higher.

Transient Logical Standby

If you want to reduce the downtime consumed during a database upgrade, then the transient logical standby method is one of the best procedures. Kindly note that this method will upgrade the data dictionary like the DBUA and manual upgrade methods. The upgrade compatibility matrix should pass. Also, you can use the DBUA or manual upgrade process intermediately as part of this method. As you are going to upgrade the dictionary, execute the pre-upgrade check scripts first in the source database.

First you introduce the primary database role to the source database. You add some parameters to make it part of the Data Guard setup. Then you create the physical standby database for this source database. This physical standby can be on the same server or a different server. Kindly note that to create the physical standby, you will require additional resources such as storage, CPU, and network bandwidth. The requirement is temporary. Once the upgrade is completed, the standby database can be removed, and its allotted resources will be freed.

The physical standby will be a block-by-block copy of the primary database; hence, this standby will be an exact replica of the primary. It will be in read-only or mount mode. It cannot be opened in read-write mode. The transactions of the primary will be applied to the standby through archived logs. The network speed plays a crucial role in this setup.

As a rule of thumb, the database version of the primary and the physical standby should be the same. You cannot upgrade the standby database to a higher version in this model. You convert the physical standby to the logical standby, which allows you to open the database in read-write mode and also can operate in the higher version to support a rolling upgrade. You can create a restore point here, which captures a snapshot of the database state.

The logical standby database will be upgraded to the higher version. This upgrade can happen through either the DBUA or manual method. Here you can observe why you executed the pre-upgrade script in the first step. When the pre-upgrade script was executed, you had only the source database. Later that database got cloned as the standby database. This means the pre-upgrade execution and corrections done at the source database are replicated to the cloned database. So, having successful pre-upgrade results in the first step to ensure that both the primary and standby databases are ready for an upgrade.

When the upgrade is happening at the logical standby database, it will be in upgrade mode, so recovery will not happen at the standby. The archived logs of the source database will be queued at this state. Once the logical standby is opened after the upgrade in the higher version, the archived logs will get applied. At the same time, the logical standby will have generated archived logs during the upgrade.

Until this state, the source database hasn't seen any outage. Currently, the source is still with the old version, the logical standby is with the higher version, and both are in sync. Switch over the roles between these databases. Here you see an outage. The current primary has to get the logical standby role. It needs to shut down and start as the logical standby database. Sessions connected to the primary have to log off and reconnect to the new primary database.

After switchover, the logical standby is at the lower version, and the primary is with the higher version. You need to upgrade the standby; it has to happen by applying archived logs generated while upgrading the old logical standby. To get those archived logs, you flash back the logical standby to the restore point created earlier. You can start the recovery here, but the logical standby will replicate only non-SYS schema changes; it will not replicate data dictionary changes. So, you convert the logical standby to the physical standby and start the recovery. Remember, after converting to physical standby, still it is with the lower version.

The physical standby will contact the current primary requesting archived logs to sync the database. The archived logs will have actual upgrade steps. So, to apply the archived logs to a physical standby, it should be in same binary version as the primary. Shut down the physical standby and start with the database binary version the same as the current primary database. Start the recovery. That will apply the archived logs, and in turn that will upgrade the standby database to the higher version.

Once the primary and the standby are in sync, switch over again. Here you see the next outage.

So, in total you see two switchovers in this method. The time taken to switch over the roles is considered downtime for this method. The switchover can be performed through the Data Guard Broker or through SQL commands. To reduce the downtime, you need to know what happens during switchover and follow the recommended best practices.

Switchover Best Practices

Verify there is no archive log gap between the primary and standby databases.

Make sure there are no active jobs.

Ensure the online redo log files of the standby are cleared. Though it happens using `Log_file_name_convert` as part of the switchover, making it clear prior will reduce the time required for this activity. If the redo log size is huge, it will take time to clear the logs.

Ensure the sufficient archive process (`Log_archive_max_processes`) is configured.

Check the `switchover_status` column value from v$database. The primary database should have the value To standby, and the standby database should have the value To Primary.

Before the switchover, ensure there is no application connectivity with the database.

By using these best practices, you can do the switchover in an effective manner. It will also help to avoid unexpected issues.

Features

Here are the features:

- It creates one of the shortest downtimes of the upgrade methods.

- The replicated/standby database can be used as a disaster recovery site.

Limitations

Here are the limitations:

- The character set check has to be done manually.

- Additional storage is required to keep the standby database.

- Additional network bandwidth is required if the standby database is created on the different server.

See Table 3-1 for a comparison of traditional export/import, Data Pump, TTS, and full transportable export/import.

Table 3-1. *Comparison Between Traditional Export/Import, Data Pump, TTS, and Full Transportable Export/Import*

EXPORT / IMPORT	DATAPUMP	TRANSPORT TABLESPACE (TTS)	FULL TRANSPORTABLE EXPORT / IMPORT
Logical backup of objects	Logical Backup of Objects	Physical Copy of Data Files	Physical Copy of Data Files
Time taken for upgrade is high	Time taken for Upgrade is lesser compared to traditional Export / Import	Upgrade Time is Less	Upgrade Time is Less
Character set conversion will be taken care automatically	Character Set conversion will be taken care automatically	Character Set check should be done manually	Character Set check should be done manually
Application objects in Administrative tablespace will be transferred automatically	Will be taken care automatically	Will not be transported	Will be taken care automatically

Oracle GoldenGate

Oracle GoldenGate provides low-impact capture, routing transactions, transformation, and delivery of database transactions across heterogeneous platforms. Oracle GoldenGate supports replication functionality for the databases such as Oracle, IBM DB2, Microsoft SQL Server, Teradata, Sybase, and MySQL.

Oracle GoldenGate supports operating systems such as Solaris, IBM AIX, Microsoft Windows, Oracle Enterprise Linux, Red Hat Linux, and HP-UX.

Oracle GoldenGate allows you to perform unidirectional, bidirectional, and active-active replication, with Conflict Detection and Resolution (CDR), between an Oracle 11*g* database and an Oracle 12*c* database so that you can use the older version of the database for backup purposes and reporting activities instead of keeping the source database idle.

Comparison of All Methods

Table 3-2 compares all the methods.

Table 3-2. Comparison of All Upgrade Methods

CATEGORY	DBUA	MANUAL UPGRADE	FULL TRANSPORTABLE EXPORT / IMPORT	TRANSPORTABLE TABLESPACE	TRANSIENT LOGICAL STANBY	DATA PUMP	GOLDEN GATE
UPGRADES SOURCE DATABASE DICTIONARY	✓	✓	✗	✗	✓	✗	✗
DOWNTIME	MORE	MORE	LESSER	LESSER	VERY LESS	MORE	NEARLY ZERO
REQUIRMENT OF HIGHER VERSION DATABASE	✗	✗	✓	✓	✓	✓	✓
SPEED	FASTEST	FASTEST	FASTER	FASTER	FAST	SLOW	SLOW
ACROSS PLATFORM	✗	✗	✓	✓	ONLY SUPPORTED COMBINATION	✓	✓
DIFFERENT SERVER	✗	✓	✓	✓	✓	✓	✓
NUMBER OF STEPS	VERY LESS	MORE	LESSER	LESSER	MORE	LESSER	MORE
CHANGE IN CHARACTERSET	✗	✗	ONLY SUPPORTED COMBINATION	ONLY SUPPORTED COMBINATION	✗	✓	✓
REQUIREMENT OF ADDITIONAL STORAGE	OPTIONAL	OPTIONAL	REQUIRE TO HOLD HIGHER VERSION DICTIONARY	REQUIRE TO HOLD HIGHER VERSION DICTIONARY	REQUIRE TO HOLD CLONE DATABASE	REQUIRE TO HOLD HIGHER VERSION DICTIONARY	REQUIRE TO HOLD CLONE DATABASE
MINIMUM VERSION TO UPGRADE TO *12c*	10.2.0.5.0	10.2.0.5.0	11.2.0.3.0	8.1.5	10.2.0.5.0	10g	8i

Real Application Testing

So far you have seen the differences between upgrade methods. Here we'll discuss a tool provided by Oracle to forecast the upgrade behavior in your current environment.

The Real Application Testing (RAT) tool is used to predict the outcome of changes performed in your environment. In other words, it enables the real-time testing of Oracle Database. Using this tool, you can measure the effect of changes that happened because of the upgrade.

In Chapter 1 we discussed that testing the upgrade in preproduction environments before moving to production is a best practice. You want to test the upgrade steps and see how the application behaves with the upgraded database in the current environment. Though you can test the upgrade in a preproduction environment, the test results might not be 100 percent similar to the results seen in production. This is because the realistic load of production is not re-created in the test environment. In that case, you cannot be sure how the real database will behave after the database upgrade. For example, production may see a performance degrade that is not observed in preproduction.

To overcome these issues, you can use the RAT tool. RAT captures the realistic workload of production, and it can be applied in a preproduction environmentafter performing the necessary changes.

It works as follows:

1. You will be creating a test database with a similar configuration as production. Having the test environment as close to the production environment in terms of hardware, platform, and resources will give you more accurate results.

2. Invoke the database replay capture activity at the source database; this will start capturing database metrics. Perform the necessary operations that should be tested in the upgraded database, such as load tests and EOD operation. To capture the workload, the database version should be 10.2.0.4 or higher.

3. The capture mechanism will record the necessary details and store them in the source database server. The capture activity's overhead is less. Mostly it will not impact normal database operations.

4. Once the workload is captured, move it to the test machine.

5. Perform the preprocessing on the captured workload. Preprocessing will translate the workload into replay files and create the necessary metadata to replay the workload. This preprocessing can be done in production, but doing the same at the test instance will reduce the workload in production.

6. Upgrade the test database to a higher version.

7. Invoke the database reply to apply the captured tests (production) to the test instance. Replay is supported only from 11g R1.

8. Execute replay reports, which will give you good comparison details on performance, data variation, and so on.

Data variation compares the query results in the source and the test instance.

Benefits of Using RAT

The following are the benefits of using RAT:

- Database replay is part of the Oracle database. So, there is no need to install it separately. But it does require a separate license.

- You can capture the load from production only once, and it can be replayed at the test instance as many times as required. If you feel like changing the index to improve performance, make the change and invoke the replay.

- The report will give you a clear explanation on many performance metrics.

- The time required to generate these results is less.

How to Choose the Best Upgrade Method

You learned about the upgrade methods in detail in Chapter 2 and saw comparisons of all of them in this chapter, including each method's unique features, prerequisites, steps, and limitations. Choosing the right method is like choosing a route on a road trip. Your destination could have different routes, and each could have different limitations. One route may have a longer distance but have fewer bumps and diversions. Another one may be closer but could have many hairpin curves. Another route may have the optimal distance but require paying toll charges. It is up to you to decide on the route based on convenience, available fuel, time to reach destination, and so on (see Figure 3-1).

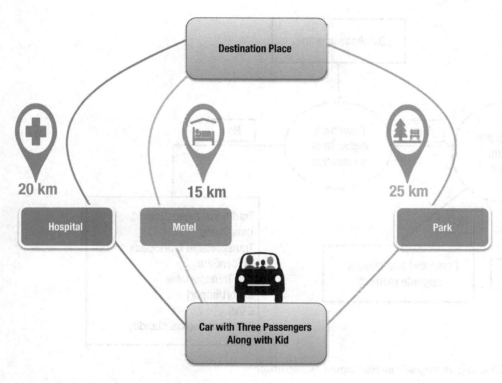

Figure 3-1. *Choosing best route to reach destination*

Choosing the appropriate upgrade method is like planning a convenient road trip. Like you have attributes in a road trip that help to decide your route, you have attributes to help you decide on an appropriate upgrade method. This section will discuss some of the attributes that will influence you when deciding on an upgrade method and also discuss generic guidelines for choosing each method.

The following are the most common influencing attributes:

- How much database downtime has been allotted for a database upgrade?

- Do you have the flexibility of getting additional storage?

- What are the number of actions and required skill set?

- How much total time has been allotted for the upgrade project?

- Are you changing the platform as part of the upgrade?

- What is the size of the database?

Database Downtime

Database downtime is one of the major attributes to consider when choosing an upgrade method (see Figure 3-2).

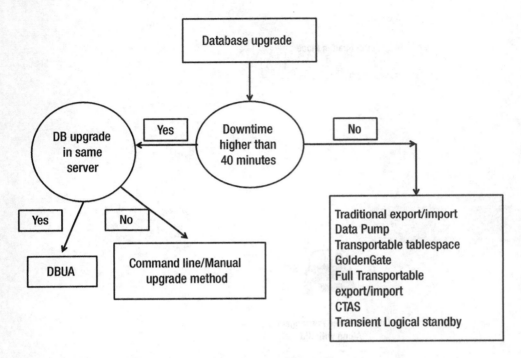

Figure 3-2. *Choosing an upgrade method based on downtime*

The database downtime for an upgrade depends on the number of database components enabled in that database. The DBUA and manual upgrade methods upgrade each database component, so for those methods, the downtime cannot be accurately measured. The DBUA and manual upgrade methods will require an average 40 minutes and more for completing the upgrade. If you can afford more than 40 minutes downtime, then you can choose the DBUA or manual upgrade method. At the same, if you follow the best practices of these methods, you can reduce the required downtime.

- Tasks such as taking a database backup, collecting statistics, and making user tablespaces read-only should be done before starting the upgrade. This will reduce the DBUA running time.

- Execute the pre-upgrade scripts manually and ensure the database is in an expected state to perform the upgrade.

- Deprecated parameters and database components can be removed in the source database, which will reduce the upgrade time.

- A time zone upgrade can be postponed based on application requirements.

- Make sure enough free space exists for tablespaces to extend during the upgrade. This will avoid issues related to space usage. The pre-upgrade output will show the details of the required free space.

- Ensure the FRA has enough free space to grow.

- In 12*c*, using parallel execution can make the upgrade process faster.

- Invite all involved teams when the upgrade is live. Have a web/audio conference active during the upgrade window so that if there are any issues, you can quickly get help from the respective teams.

- If the environment requires patches for bug fixes, install them on the target version before performing the upgrade, which will avoid the need for downtime after the upgrade.

- There could be some checklists derived after the upgrade is done in the test environment. Document those checklists and ensure they are implemented in production.

If you cannot afford much downtime, then the DBUA and manual command-line upgrade methods are not advisable. You need to look at one of the other upgrade methods. The GoldenGate method is a nearly-zero downtime method for database upgrades.

Getting Additional Storage

Storage is one of the influencing factors when choosing an upgrade method. As you know, the database upgrade happens in two ways. Either the database gets upgraded along with the dictionary or the data will be extracted and imported into the higher-version database.

When you upgrade the database along with the dictionary, you require the space to grow for the dictionary tablespaces SYSTEM and SYSAUX. These tablespaces will get new objects, and some of their existing objects will get modified. These changes are required to invite new features of the higher version into the existing data dictionary. The approximate required space can also be retrieved from the pre-upgrade output.

But when you choose the method of moving data to the higher-version database, a new database should have been created already in the higher version. This will have a higher-database version dictionary. You have many methods in this category. But in all methods, you will require additional storage to keep the higher-version dictionary. In addition to that, some methods require storage to keep an exact replica of the source database. For example, the transient logical standby method will require the logical standby database, which is an exact copy of the production database. If you are concerned with only downtime and storage doesn't matter, then you can choose an upgrade using the transient logical standby. This method will reduce the required downtime for an upgrade. The same is applicable to the traditional export/import method or Data Pump, which both require additional storage for keeping the higher-version database dictionary. Later during import, it will require storage for user tablespaces.

In the transportable tablespace and full transportable export/import method, the source database datafiles can be either copied or moved to the higher database version. The storage requirement is based on whether you keep the datafiles at the same location or move the datafiles to the higher version.

Number of Actions and Required Skill Set

The number of steps differ between each method, which can indicate the level of manual intervention that is required. Sometimes this is a factor while choosing the upgrade method. For example, an upgrade using the transient logical standby method takes more steps when compared to other methods. Each step in this method should be completed successfully to proceed. Not only does this method require upgrade knowledge, but it requires knowledge of database high availability. Thorough study of high availability concepts is required before choosing this method. This method also requires strong support from the network administrator if the target higher-version database will be placed on a different server. If the network connectivity is not consistent, the switchover may fail, which will lead to more downtime.

If you consider the GoldenGate method, technical expertise of GoldenGate is required. It also requires more actions to create the initial setup. Missing any steps may create issues during the upgrade.

A manual or command-line database upgrade requires more manual actions that need to be performed carefully. Skipping any step may create unexpected issues in further execution.

If you want to have less manual intervention, then the only suitable method is to use the DBUA. It does all the tasks automatically. You don't need to worry about any upgrade tasks. Keep it simple and pass it to the DBUA.

Total Time Allotted

The total time allotted for an upgrade project also sometimes becomes the deciding factor. This total time includes time spent for planning, testing, and upgrading the production database, as well as post-validation steps. Normally, the total allotted time is measured in weeks or months. If the number of actions is high, then it will consume a considerable amount of time. Suppose multiple teams are involved in an upgrade, this will consume time to arrive at the conclusion on action items and action plan for each team when any issues are seen. Definitely some buffer time has to be allocated to match the gap in communication between the teams. For example, in the transient standby method, you spent time for the logical standby creation, Data Guard broker configuration if required, switchover testings, and involving the network team to find out the data transfer speed.

Unsupported Features

Each method has its limitations. You have to analyze these limitations before choosing a suitable method for your environment. For example, in the transient logical standby method, you involve the logical standby database, which will not support some datatypes such as BFILE. If those datatypes are used, then you cannot use this method. For example, the DBUA will not support database upgrades across different servers. This means if you planned to move the database to different servers during upgrade, then the DBUA will not be a suitable choice. A manual upgrade could work in this case.

If an upgrade has to done with the database backup, then the DBUA method is not possible. Manual upgrade can work with cold backup, hot backup, and RMAN backup.

Suppose you have decided to upgrade and migrate the database to a different platform; the DBUA or manual method will not work.

TTS will not look at user objects stored in the SYSTEM tablespace. If by chance the database has more objects in the SYSTEM tablespace and your source database is 11.2.0.3.0, then you can choose the full transportable export/import method.

Number of User Objects

In some upgrade methods, you do a database upgrade by moving your database objects to a higher version. Can you consider the number of objects as a deciding factor when choosing the best upgrade method? The answer is yes.

Traditional export/import and Data Pump work on an object level. If the number of objects is high, then the time taken to export and import will increase with these methods. You can go for the TTS method of the full transportable export/import (if the source database version is 11.2.0.3.0 or higher).

Source Database Version

Methods such as transportable tablespace, transportable database, and Data Pump were introduced in Oracle 10g. If the source database is a version older than 10g, you need to look for other upgrade methods.

Full transportable export/import requires a source database version of at least 11.2.0.3.0.

For the DBUA and manual upgrade, the source and target compatibility matrix has to be verified.

Change of Platform

A platform change during upgrade will influence the method selection process. The DBUA and manual upgrade methods will not work across different platforms. The RMAN transport database method will not work if the endian format of the platforms is different. We will discuss this platform migration in detail in Chapter 5.

Summary

In this chapter, we covered the various methods of upgrade and their features. We also compared these methods to illuminate their limitations. To predict the upgrade behavior in a production environment, you can use the RAT tool. Also, we discussed the common influencing factors and their impact when choosing an upgrade method.

CHAPTER 4

■ ■ ■

Upgrade Using a Database Backup

From this chapter's title you might be thinking that you need to take a backup prior to upgrading or migrating, but where will the backup be used in the upgrade? Your second question may be about why you need to upgrade with a backup when the database is available? In this chapter, you'll dig into the answers to these questions, including why and when backups are required when upgrading.

Introduction

For starters, we'll discuss why you need a backup to upgrade a database.

> *Scenario*: You have a critical production database running, and for the customers, any downtime is challenging. At the same time, it is challenging to the DBA if the upgrade fails during the process for some reason or because of any unpublished bugs with the new Oracle RDBMS version or release. So, what is the solution to make the database available quickly?

> *Troubleshooting*: Let's consider you started fixing the upgrade issue, which is not in your hands all the time. You end up spending many hours on the job only to find that you have to restore the whole backup. What if the database size is 15 TB? How many hours would it take to restore the database and make it available for the applications?

> *Answer*: What if you restore the database as another copy and upgrade the database without touching the master copy? Consider what happens if the database is not up and running? If it's not, you have to apply the archive logs that are generated during the copy. If the upgrade fails, you can start the second copy, which means you are not disturbing the production database. If you are able to upgrade/migrate successfully, then you can destroy the second copy. There are pros and cons with this method. The disadvantages are maintaining the double space and the manual work involved in order to copy the entire database. The advantages outweigh these cons when it comes to the business and downtime.

Next, we'll discuss how a backup helps during a migration.

> *Scenario*: Let's say your current production database is running on a Windows server with 11.2.0.4 and you have to upgrade the database to 12.1.0.2 on the Linux x86_64 platform. What is the best method?

© Y V Ravikumar, K M Krishnakumar and Nassyam Basha 2017

N. Basha et al., *Oracle Database Upgrade and Migration Methods*, DOI 10.1007/978-1-4842-2328-4_4

Answer: There are many methods that can be used, such transportable tablespaces, switchover with heterogeneous Data Guard, expdp/impdp logical backups, and so on. Basically, in this scenario, you don't have to do anything with original production database; you are going to move the database into a different/new server using whatever method you choose. In most of the methods, a backup is necessary to move the database.

Finally, why is a backup required prior to upgrading?

Scenario: Let's say the current production database is 11.2.0.4 and is being upgraded to 12*c*. The various new features and options in the new 12c version (for example, the execution plan of the queries) may not same as 11*g*. How you are going to deal the situation?

Answer: A backup is a good idea (but never required) prior to the upgrade so that in case the upgrade goes terribly wrong and leaves the database in a state where it is no longer operational, the DBA can restore to a point in time just prior to the upgrade and resume normal operations.

With these few examples, you should now have an idea of how having a backup helps before and during the upgrade. This chapter will explain how to restore a database for upgrade purposes with the intention of not disturbing the production database and moving the database to a different server in the case of server migration. In addition, you will see the various methods available to build the database for an upgrade.

What Are the Various Backup Techniques?

From the beginning of the Oracle database evolution, various backup and restore techniques have been introduced in each version or release. In this chapter, you will use these frequently used methods to build a new database to upgrade. For example, all of these methods can be used to upgrade from 11.2.*x* to 12*c*, but you will see in depth which method is efficient to use in which cases. The following are the various methods used this chapter:

- User-managed cold backup
- User-managed hot backup
- Logical backup
- RMAN backup
- RMAN active duplicate

Now we will go through in detail how each technique works, In addition, we will use the following configuration for all the methods and assume that the RDBMS software is already installed on the servers:

Hostname	ORA-U1	ORA-U2
IP address	192.168.0.110	192.168.0.120
RDBMS home	11.2.0.4	12.1.0.1
Database name	ORC1	ORC1

Cold Backup (Traditional)

Database backups are critical to have in case of any hardware failure or human errors with the database. For example, a user may mistakenly delete a table or wrongly update a table that has critical data. In those cases, you have to depend on the backup to restore the deleted data. Early Oracle releases did not have the RMAN utility. Instead, you depended on the OS utility backup using the simple cp/scp commands. With this method, you have to copy all the control files, datafiles, and online redo logs. Before that, it was necessary to understand what a cold backup is. A *cold backup* means the database requires downtime to take the backup. The database is not running; therefore, it is cold. A cold backup is needed when there are major upgrades or migrations so that you can have a consistent database backup. There are many advantages of doing a cold backup, such as upon opening the database, there is no need to open it in resetlogs mode, and there is no recovery required to open it. On the other hand, the backup requires the exact space as the database size, because you are not taking a backup at the database block level. Instead, you are using working at the OS level. The database can be either in archivelog mode or in noarchivelog mode because you are performing a shutdown of the database and not expecting any changes.

Now you will see how to perform a cold backup and restore onto a different server. In the following example, the source version is 11.2.0.4, and the target server RDBMS home is 12c.

1) To perform the cold backup, the database can be either in archivelog mode or in noarchivelog mode, but the database should be down.

```
SQL> select * from v$version;

BANNER
--------------------------------------------------------------------------------
Oracle Database 11g Enterprise Edition Release 11.2.0.4.0 - 64bit Production
PL/SQL Release 11.2.0.4.0 - Production
CORE    11.2.0.4.0      Production
TNS for Linux: Version 11.2.0.4.0 - Production
NLSRTL Version 11.2.0.4.0 - Production


SQL> archive log list
Database log mode              No Archive Mode
Automatic archival             Disabled
Archive destination            USE_DB_RECOVERY_FILE_DEST
Oldest online log sequence     7
Current log sequence           9
SQL>
```

2) Before shutting down the database, gather the database files for which you have to take a backup.

```
SQL> select name from v$datafile
  2  union
  3  select name from v$controlfile
  4  union
  5  select member from v$logfile;
NAME
--------------------------------------------------------------------------------
/u01/app/oracle/fast_recovery_area/ORC1/control02.ctl
/u01/app/oracle/oradata/ORC1/control01.ctl
/u01/app/oracle/oradata/ORC1/example01.dbf
/u01/app/oracle/oradata/ORC1/redo01.log
/u01/app/oracle/oradata/ORC1/redo02.log
/u01/app/oracle/oradata/ORC1/redo03.log
/u01/app/oracle/oradata/ORC1/sysaux01.dbf
/u01/app/oracle/oradata/ORC1/system01.dbf
/u01/app/oracle/oradata/ORC1/undotbs01.dbf
/u01/app/oracle/oradata/ORC1/users01.dbf

10 rows selected.
 [oracle@ORA-U1 ~]$ cd /u01/app/oracle/oradata/ORC1/
[oracle@ORA-U1 ORC1]$ ls -ltr
total 1805924
-rw-r-----. 1 oracle oinstall  20979712 May 19 04:47 temp01.dbf
-rw-r-----. 1 oracle oinstall  52429312 May 19 04:49 redo01.log
-rw-r-----. 1 oracle oinstall  52429312 May 19 04:49 redo02.log
-rw-r-----. 1 oracle oinstall   5251072 May 19 04:49 users01.dbf
-rw-r-----. 1 oracle oinstall 328343552 May 19 04:49 example01.dbf
-rw-r-----. 1 oracle oinstall 524296192 May 19 04:54 sysaux01.dbf
-rw-r-----. 1 oracle oinstall  47194112 May 19 04:54 undotbs01.dbf
-rw-r-----. 1 oracle oinstall 775954432 May 19 04:54 system01.dbf
-rw-r-----. 1 oracle oinstall  52429312 May 19 04:54 redo03.log
-rw-r-----. 1 oracle oinstall   9748480 May 19 04:55 control01.ctl
[oracle@ORA-U1 ORC1]$ cd /u01/app/oracle/fast_recovery_area/ORC1/
[oracle@ORA-U1 ORC1]$ ls -ltr
total 9524
drwxr-x---. 2 oracle oinstall      4096 May 19 04:46 onlinelog
-rw-r-----. 1 oracle oinstall   9748480 May 19 04:56 control02.ctl
```

3) After gathering the database file information, execute the pre-upgrade script. Because you are taking a backup to upgrade the database, you need to make sure that the database has met all the upgrade prerequisites before taking the backup, and then you will shut down the database to take the backup. The pre-upgrade script will be available in the 12c Home. This script will evaluate the database and list the errors/warnings if any deviations are found. You learned more about the pre-upgrade script in Chapter 2.

```
SQL> @<Preupgrade script location>/preupgrc.sql
Prior to perform the copy ensure the database is not up and running, better to
crosscheck and then proceed to shutdown.

SQL> select name,open_mode from v$database;

NAME      OPEN_MODE
--------- --------------------
ORC1      READ WRITE

SQL> shutdown immediate;
Database closed.
Database dismounted.
ORACLE instance shut down.
```

4) Create the necessary directories to copy the files to the remote server.

```
[oracle@ORA-U2 ~]$ mkdir -p /u01/app/oracle/oradata/ORC1/
[oracle@ORA-U2 ~]$ mkdir -p /u01/app/oracle/fast_recovery_area/ORC1/
```

```
[oracle@ORA-U1 ORC1]$ scp * 192.168.0.120://u01/app/oracle/oradata/ORC1/
oracle@192.168.0.120's password:
control01.ctl                                                        100% 9520KB    9.3MB/s   00:00
example01.dbf                                                        100%  313MB  156.6MB/s   00:02
redo01.log                                                          100%   50MB   50.0MB/s   00:01
redo02.log                                                          100%   50MB   50.0MB/s   00:00
redo03.log                                                          100%   50MB   50.0MB/s   00:01
sysaux01.dbf                                                        100%  500MB  100.0MB/s   00:05
system01.dbf                                                        100%  740MB   92.5MB/s   00:08
temp01.dbf                                                          100%   20MB   20.0MB/s   00:00
undotbs01.dbf                                                       100%   45MB   45.0MB/s   00:01
users01.dbf                                                         100% 5128KB    5.0MB/s   00:00
[oracle@ORA-U1 ORC1]$ cd /u01/app/oracle/fast_recovery_area/ORC1/
[oracle@ORA-U1 ORC1]$ ls
control02.ctl   onlinelog
[oracle@ORA-U1 ORC1]$ scp control02.ctl 192.168.0.120:/u01/app/oracle/fast_recovery_area/ORC1/
oracle@192.168.0.120's password:
control02.ctl                                                       100% 9520KB    9.3MB/s   00:00
[oracle@ORA-U1 ORC1]$
```

5) After copying database, now you need to have the database configuration files
    and the network files to start the instance and for further connectivity.

    a) Create the init file and password file.

    b) To start the instance, you need to have the pfile in place, which you can
        copy from the 11g R2 server. Change the compatible parameter to 12.0.0.

    c) Copy the network configuration files from the source to the target under
        the directory $ORACLE_HOME/network/admin. Please note that the host
        names need to be changed as per the target server.

```
[oracle@ORA-U1 dbs]$ sqlplus / as sysdba

SQL*Plus: Release 11.2.0.4.0 Production

Copyright (c) 1982, 2013, Oracle.  All rights reserved.

Connected to an idle instance.

SQL> create pfile from spfile;

File created.

SQL> exit
Disconnected
[oracle@ORA-U1 dbs]$ scp initORC1.ora 192.168.0.120:/u01/app/oracle/
product/12.1.0/dbhome_1/dbs/
oracle@192.168.0.120's password:
initORC1.ora

100%  902      0.9KB/s   00:00
[oracle@ORA-U1 dbs]$ scp orapwORC1 192.168.0.120:/u01/app/oracle/product/12.1.0/
dbhome_1/dbs/
oracle@192.168.0.120's password:
orapwORC1
100% 1536      1.5KB/s   00:00
[oracle@ORA-U1 dbs]$
```

6) Modify the pfile to update the parameters and create the missing directories on
    the target server. Before that, the best practice is to add the database entry in the
    /etc/oratab file for easy access to the database and RDBMS home.

```
[oracle@ORA-U2 dbs]$ . oraenv
ORACLE_SID = [orcl] ? ORC1
The Oracle base remains unchanged with value /u01/app/oracle
[oracle@ORA-U2 dbs]$ echo $ORACLE_SID
```

```
ORC1
[oracle@ORA-U2 dbs]$ cat /etc/oratab |grep ORC1
ORC1:/u01/app/oracle/product/12.1.0/dbhome_1:N
[oracle@ORA-U2 dbs]$
[oracle@ORA-U2 dbs]$ cat initORC1.ora
*.audit_file_dest='/u01/app/oracle/admin/ORC1/adump'
*.audit_trail='db'
*.control_files='/u01/app/oracle/oradata/ORC1/control01.ctl','/u01/app/oracle/
fast_recovery_area/ORC1/control02.ctl'
*.db_block_size=8192
*.db_domain=''
*.db_name='ORC1'
*.db_recovery_file_dest='/u01/app/oracle/fast_recovery_area'
*.db_recovery_file_dest_size=4385144832
*.diagnostic_dest='/u01/app/oracle'
*.dispatchers='(PROTOCOL=TCP) (SERVICE=ORC1XDB)'
*.memory_target=629145600
*.open_cursors=300
*.processes=150
*.remote_login_passwordfile='EXCLUSIVE'
*.undo_tablespace='UNDOTBS1'

[oracle@ORA-U2 dbs]$ orapwd file=orapw$ORACLE_SID password=oracle entries=10
[oracle@ORA-U2 dbs]$ ls -ltr orapwORC1
-rw-r-----. 1 oracle oinstall 7680 May 19 06:44 orapwORC1
[oracle@ORA-U2 dbs]$

[oracle@ORA-U2 dbs]$ mkdir -p /u01/app/oracle/admin/ORC1/adump
[oracle@ORA-U2 dbs]$ mkdir -p /u01/app/oracle/fast_recovery_area
[oracle@ORA-U2 dbs]$ sqlplus / as sysdba
SQL*Plus: Release 12.1.0.1.0 Production

Copyright (c) 1982, 2013, Oracle.  All rights reserved.

Connected to an idle instance.

SQL> startup mount
ORACLE instance started.

Total System Global Area  626327552 bytes
Fixed Size                  2291472 bytes
Variable Size             440404208 bytes
Database Buffers          176160768 bytes
Redo Buffers                7471104 bytes
Database mounted.
```

```
SQL>
SQL> show parameter compatible

NAME                                     TYPE        VALUE
---------------------------------------- ----------- --------------------------------
compatible                               string      12.0.0
noncdb_compatible                        boolean     FALSE
SQL>
```

7) Now the database is ready to upgrade, which can be done with a manual upgrade. The DBUA requires access to the source database to execute a prerequisites check. Hence, with the DBUA method, it is not possible to upgrade a database using a cold backup. Refer to My Oracle Support note "Master Note For Oracle Database Upgrades and Migrations (Doc ID 1152016.1)." For this example, you are using the manual upgrade method.

8) There are various prerequisites to be performed prior to the upgrade, but this chapter's intention is not to show how to upgrade but to show how to use backups during the upgrade phase.

   To upgrade the database, you must start the database in the upgrade method when doing a manual upgrade.

Prior to opening the upgrade, if the original database is still being accessed by the users and expected to generate more archives, perform the following steps:

1) Perform the following at the command line: SQL> alter system switch logfile;.

2) Perform the following at the command line: SQL> shutdown immediate;.

3) Copy the newly generated archives to use for the new 12c database's recovery.

4) Catalog the archives using RMAN> catalog start with '/u01/archives'. Or, using the traditional method, you can register the log files.

5) Perform the following at the command line: RMAN> recover database;.

If no applications were started after the copying, then proceed with the following steps:

```
SQL> alter database open upgrade;

Database altered.

SQL>
```

9) From 12c, there are many features, and in the upgrade process there are various changes as well. Prior to 12c you used to run the script catupgrd.sql to upgrade the repository, but now this method is deprecated. To go into detail, Oracle uses the Perl script called catctl.pl, which calls catupgrade.sql and allows much scope for various options such as parallelism and so on.

In the following command, you are using the additional attribute –n, which refers to the parallelism, so that upgrade tasks will be performed faster.

```
[oracle@ORA-U2 ~]$ cd /u01/app/oracle/product/12.1.0/dbhome_1/rdbms/admin/
[oracle@ORA-U2 admin]$ /u01/app/oracle/product/12.1.0/dbhome_1/perl/bin/perl
catctl.pl -n 5 catupgrd.sql

Analyzing file catupgrd.sql
14 scripts found in file catupgrd.sql
Next path: catalog.sql
32 scripts found in file catalog.sql
Next path: catproc.sql
37 scripts found in file catproc.sql
Next path: catptabs.sql
61 scripts found in file catptabs.sql
Next path: catpdbms.sql
205 scripts found in file catpdbms.sql
Next path: catpdeps.sql
77 scripts found in file catpdeps.sql
Next path: catpprvt.sql
260 scripts found in file catpprvt.sql
Next path: catpexec.sql
26 scripts found in file catpexec.sql
Next path: cmpupgrd.sql
16 scripts found in file cmpupgrd.sql

[Phase 0] type is 1 with 1 Files
catupstr.sql

[Phase 1] type is 1 with 3 Files
cdstrt.sql         cdfixed.sql        cdcore.sql

[Phase 2] type is 1 with 1 Files
ora_restart.sql

[Phase 3] type is 2 with 18 Files
cdplsql.sql        cdsqlddl.sql       cdmanage.sql       cdtxnspc.sql
cdenv.sql          cdrac.sql          cdsec.sql          cdobj.sql
cdjava.sql         cdpart.sql         cdrep.sql          cdaw.sql
cdsummgt.sql       cdtools.sql        cdexttab.sql       cddm.sql
catldr.sql         cdclst.sql

[Phase 4] type is 1 with 1 Files
ora_restart.sql
```

```
[Phase 5] type is 1 with 5 Files
cdoptim.sql      catsum.sql      catexp.sql      cddst.sql
cdend.sql

[Phase 6] type is 1 with 1 Files
catpstrt.sql

[Phase 7] type is 1 with 3 Files
catptyps.sql      catpgrants.sql   catgwm.sql

[Phase 8] type is 1 with 1 Files
ora_restart.sql

[Phase 9] type is 2 with 60 Files
. . .
 . .
  .

dbmscred.sql     catcredv.sql     cataqsch.sql     catrssch.sql
catplug.sql      prvtsql.plb      prvtssql.plb     prvtlmd.plb
prvtlmcs.plb     prvtlmrs.plb     dbmslms.sql      prvthpu.plb
prvthpv.plb
. . .
 . .
  .
Using 5 processes.
Serial   Phase #: 0 Files: 1       Time: 92s
Serial   Phase #: 1 Files: 3       Time: 18s
Restart  Phase #: 2 Files: 1       Time: 0s
Parallel Phase #: 3 Files: 18      Time: 5s
. . .
 . .
  .

Serial   Phase #:54 Files: 1       Time: 110s
Serial   Phase #:55 Files: 1       Time: 331s
Serial   Phase #:56 Files: 1       Time: 12s
Grand Total Time: 2056s
[oracle@ORA-U2 admin]$
```

10) After the upgrade script has completed successfully, you can start the database in normal mode and of course from the 12*c* RDBMS Home. After starting the database in normal mode, you need to check the registry components' status and ensure they are valid. If they are not, then you have to run utlrp.sql to recompile the objects. The script can be called from the $ORACLE_HOME/rdbms/admin location.

```
 [oracle@ORA-U2 admin]$ sqlplus / as sysdba

SQL*Plus: Release 12.1.0.1.0 Production
```

```
Copyright (c) 1982, 2013, Oracle.  All rights reserved.

Connected to an idle instance.

SQL> startup
ORACLE instance started.

Total System Global Area  626327552 bytes
Fixed Size                  2291472 bytes
Variable Size             440404208 bytes
Database Buffers          176160768 bytes
Redo Buffers                7471104 bytes
Database mounted.
Database opened.
SQL> select name,open_mode from v$database;

NAME       OPEN_MODE
---------  --------------------
ORC1       READ WRITE
SQL> select comp_name,version,status from dba_registry;

COMP_NAME                                          VERSION     STATUS
-------------------------------------------------- ----------- ------
Oracle Application Express                         4.2.0.00.27 VALID
OWB                                                11.2.0.4.0  VALID
Spatial                                            12.1.0.1.0  INVALID
Oracle Multimedia                                  12.1.0.1.0  VALID
Oracle XML Database                                12.1.0.1.0  VALID
Oracle Text                                        12.1.0.1.0  VALID
Oracle Workspace Manager                           12.1.0.1.0  VALID
Oracle Database Catalog Views                      12.1.0.1.0  UPGRADED
Oracle Database Packages and Types                 12.1.0.1.0  UPGRADED
JServer JAVA Virtual Machine                       12.1.0.1.0  VALID
Oracle XDK                                         12.1.0.1.0  VALID
Oracle Database Java Packages                      12.1.0.1.0  VALID
OLAP Analytic Workspace                            12.1.0.1.0  VALID
Oracle OLAP API                                    12.1.0.1.0  VALID

15 rows selected.

SQL>
```

11) If you see in the previous output of registry components that a few of them are invalid, you must run utlrp.sql to validate the objects.

```
SQL> @?/rdbms/admin/utlrp.sql

TIMESTAMP
--------------------------------------------------------------------------------
COMP_TIMESTAMP UTLRP_BGN  2016-05-19 08:28:39
```

179

```
DOC>    The following PL/SQL block invokes UTL_RECOMP to recompile invalid
.  .  .
.  .
.
...Setting DBMS Registry 08:32:53
...Setting DBMS Registry Complete 08:32:53
...Exiting validate 08:32:53

PL/SQL procedure successfully completed.

SQL> select comp_name,version,status from dba_registry;

COMP_NAME                                           VERSION       STATUS
-------------------------------------------------- ------------  -----------
Oracle Application Express                          4.2.0.00.27   VALID
OWB                                                 11.2.0.4.0    VALID
Spatial                                             12.1.0.1.0    VALID
Oracle Multimedia                                   12.1.0.1.0    VALID
Oracle XML Database                                 12.1.0.1.0    VALID
Oracle Text                                         12.1.0.1.0    VALID
Oracle Workspace Manager                            12.1.0.1.0    VALID
Oracle Database Catalog Views                       12.1.0.1.0    VALID
Oracle Database Packages and Types                  12.1.0.1.0    VALID
JServer JAVA Virtual Machine                        12.1.0.1.0    VALID
Oracle XDK                                          12.1.0.1.0    VALID
Oracle Database Java Packages                       12.1.0.1.0    VALID
OLAP Analytic Workspace                             12.1.0.1.0    VALID
Oracle OLAP API                                     12.1.0.1.0    VALID

15 rows selected.

SQL>
```

As you can see in the previous output, after you run utlrp.sql, the components become valid. OWB will not be upgraded to 12c, but earlier versions of OWB could exist in Oracle 12c.

In conclusion, as you can see from the source database, you have taken a cold backup after performing a shutdown of the database, and then you have taken a backup of the target server using the scp (OS) method. So, after upgrading, the database is up and running from the 12c RDBMS Home from server ORA-U2. If your upgrade process fails with unrecoverable errors, then you can still start the database from the source server ORA-U1 any time to achieve a safe failback.

A cold backup can be performed either using RMAN or using an OS-level backup, but you will use the RMAN method for the other backup types.

Hot Backup (User-Managed)

The hot backup method is the same as a cold backup to perform a backup using the OS level, but in this method it is not necessary to shut down the database while taking a backup. Now the question is, how does the OS method (cp/scp) manage the ongoing updates to the database? The answer to that question is simple. Whenever you start a backup of the database or tablespace (alter database begin backup, alter tablespace users begin backup), the checkpoint will be initiated, the headers of the datafile (or datafiles) will be frozen, and further additional transactions will be generated into the redo; then the redo will be dumped into archive logs when the online redo log switches. To perform this method, the database should be in archivelog mode. Why is the database in archivelog mode? The answer is that you are achieving a backup without any downtime, and after restoring the database, you have to recover the database using the archive logs generated during the backup to make the SCNs consistent. This method was introduced prior to RMAN being introduced. The popularity of the traditional hot backup method has declined since RMAN was introduced to the world; however, this method still helps if you are upgrading from older Oracle versions. Follow these steps to use a hot backup to upgrade from 11.2.0.4 to 12.1.0.2:

1) Ensure the database is in archivelog mode. Prior to switching to archivelog mode, the database should be in mount status.

```
SQL> archive log list
Database log mode              No Archive Mode
Automatic archival             Disabled
Archive destination            USE_DB_RECOVERY_FILE_DEST
Oldest online log sequence     7
Current log sequence           9
SQL> shutdown immediate
Database closed.
Database dismounted.
ORACLE instance shut down.
SQL> startup mount
ORACLE instance started.

Total System Global Area    626327552 bytes
Fixed Size                    2255832 bytes
Variable Size               427820072 bytes
Database Buffers            188743680 bytes
Redo Buffers                  7507968 bytes
Database mounted.
```

Note: If we are archiving the logs means we have already enabled database in archive log mode and thus the redo data will be dumped into archive log files and also the location we have to set in log_archive_dest_1 and the value also visiables in "archive log list" command.

SQL> alter database archivelog;

Database altered.

SQL> alter database open;

Database altered.

```
SQL> archive log list
Database log mode              Archive Mode
Automatic archival             Enabled
Archive destination            USE_DB_RECOVERY_FILE_DEST
Oldest online log sequence     7
Next log sequence to archive   9
Current log sequence           9
SQL>
```

2) Gather the datafile, control file, and redo log file location.

```
SQL> select name from v$controlfile
  2  union
  3  select name from v$datafile
  4  union
  5  select member from v$logfile;

NAME
--------------------------------------------------------------------------------
/u01/app/oracle/fast_recovery_area/ORC1/control02.ctl
/u01/app/oracle/oradata/ORC1/control01.ctl
/u01/app/oracle/oradata/ORC1/example01.dbf
/u01/app/oracle/oradata/ORC1/redo01.log
/u01/app/oracle/oradata/ORC1/redo02.log
/u01/app/oracle/oradata/ORC1/redo03.log
/u01/app/oracle/oradata/ORC1/sysaux01.dbf
/u01/app/oracle/oradata/ORC1/system01.dbf
/u01/app/oracle/oradata/ORC1/undotbs01.dbf
/u01/app/oracle/oradata/ORC1/users01.dbf
[oracle@ORA-U1 ORC1]$ ls -ltr
total 1805924
-rw-r-----. 1 oracle oinstall  52429312 May 19 10:28 redo01.log
-rw-r-----. 1 oracle oinstall  52429312 May 19 10:28 redo02.log
-rw-r-----. 1 oracle oinstall 775954432 May 19 10:28 system01.dbf
-rw-r-----. 1 oracle oinstall  47194112 May 19 10:28 undotbs01.dbf
-rw-r-----. 1 oracle oinstall 524296192 May 19 10:28 sysaux01.dbf
-rw-r-----. 1 oracle oinstall   5251072 May 19 10:28 users01.dbf
-rw-r-----. 1 oracle oinstall 328343552 May 19 10:28 example01.dbf
-rw-r-----. 1 oracle oinstall  20979712 May 19 10:28 temp01.dbf
-rw-r-----. 1 oracle oinstall  52429312 May 19 10:32 redo03.log
-rw-r-----. 1 oracle oinstall   9748480 May 19 10:32 control01.ctl
[oracle@ORA-U1 ORC1]$ cd /u01/app/oracle/fast_recovery_area/ORC1/
[oracle@ORA-U1 ORC1]$ ls -ltr
total 9524
drwxr-x---. 2 oracle oinstall      4096 May 19 04:46 onlinelog
-rw-r-----. 1 oracle oinstall   9748480 May 19 10:33 control02.ctl
[oracle@ORA-U1 ORC1]$
```

3) Execute the pre-upgrade check script, preupgrd.sql. Ensure there are no errors or warnings in the pre-upgrade script output.

4) Perform the hot backup on the target database of 11g R2 and perform the backup/scp to the target server (ORA-U2) where the 12c RDBMS was already installed. Ensure the directory locations are created on the target server (ORA-U2) before performing a copy of the database files.

```
SQL> alter database begin backup;

Database altered.

SQL> select file#,status from v$backup;
```

```
        FILE# STATUS
---------- -------------------
             1 ACTIVE
             2 ACTIVE
             3 ACTIVE
             4 ACTIVE
             5 ACTIVE

SQL>
```

If the status is not Active, then end the backup and ensure all the datafiles are available; then retry enabling the backup. If any of the datafiles' status is Inactive, then this backup is not going to help you.

Now you create the necessary directories to copy the datafiles, control files, and redo log files.

```
[oracle@ORA-U2 ~]$ mkdir -p /u01/app/oracle/oradata/ORC1
[oracle@ORA-U2 ~]$ mkdir -p /u01/app/oracle/fast_recovery_area/ORC1/
[oracle@ORA-U2 ~]$
```

After creating the directories, you start copying the database files to the target server location, as shown here:

```
[oracle@ORA-U1 ORC1]$ scp *  192.168.0.120:/u01/app/oracle/oradata/ORC1/
oracle@192.168.0.120's password:
control01.ctl                                 100% 9520KB   9.3MB/s   00:00
example01.dbf                                 100%  313MB 156.6MB/s   00:02
redo01.log                                    100%   50MB  50.0MB/s   00:00
redo02.log                                    100%   50MB  50.0MB/s   00:01
redo03.log                                    100%   50MB  50.0MB/s   00:00
sysaux01.dbf                                  100%  500MB 166.7MB/s   00:03
system01.dbf                                  100%  740MB  92.5MB/s   00:08
temp01.dbf                                    100%   20MB  20.0MB/s   00:01
undotbs01.dbf                                 100%   45MB  45.0MB/s   00:00
users01.dbf                                   100% 5128KB   5.0MB/s   00:00
[oracle@ORA-U1 ORC1]$ scp /u01/app/oracle/fast_recovery_area/ORC1/control02.ctl 192.168.0.120:/
u01/app/oracle/fast_recovery_area/ORC1/control02.ctl
oracle@192.168.0.120's password:
control02.ctl                                 100% 9520KB   9.3MB/s   00:00
[oracle@ORA-U1 ORC1]$
```

After the copying to the server finishes, you create a test table so that you can test on the target server after the upgrade process to ensure all the changes are available after you perform the recovery.

```
SQL> select file#,status from v$backup;


        FILE# STATUS
---------- -------------------
             1 ACTIVE
             2 ACTIVE
             3 ACTIVE
             4 ACTIVE
             5 ACTIVE

SQL> archive log list
Database log mode               Archive Mode
```

```
Automatic archival             Enabled
Archive destination            USE_DB_RECOVERY_FILE_DEST
Oldest online log sequence     7
Next log sequence to archive   9
Current log sequence           9
```

We create a table to test whether it got transported via hot backup to target version.

```
SQL> create table upgtest as select * from dba_objects;

Table created.

SQL> alter system switch logfile;

System altered.

SQL> archive log list
Database log mode              Archive Mode
Automatic archival             Enabled
Archive destination            USE_DB_RECOVERY_FILE_DEST
Oldest online log sequence     8
Next log sequence to archive   10
Current log sequence           10
SQL>
```

Finally, you end the database in backup mode and proceed to open the database on the target server (ORA-U2) after recovering.

```
SQL> alter database end backup;

Database altered.

SQL> select file#,status from v$backup;

    FILE# STATUS
---------- ------------------
        1 NOT ACTIVE
        2 NOT ACTIVE
        3 NOT ACTIVE
        4 NOT ACTIVE
        5 NOT ACTIVE
```

5) You are done with the original database part except for the newly generated archives, which have to be copied for the new 12c database to use. Now you have to build the instance after you configure the pfile/spfile. Do not forget to create the password file and to configure the network parameters for connectivity use.

```
SQL> create pfile from spfile;

File created.

SQL> exit
```

```
Disconnected from Oracle Database 11g Enterprise Edition Release 11.2.0.4.0 -
64bit Production
With the Partitioning, OLAP, Data Mining and Real Application Testing options
[oracle@ORA-U1 dbs]$ scp initORC1.ora 192.168.0.120:/u01/app/oracle/
product/12.1.0/dbhome_1/dbs/
oracle@192.168.0.120's password:
initORC1.ora                                                 100%  902
0.9KB/s   00:00
[oracle@ORA-U1 dbs]$
```

Update the necessary directories as per the pfile locations to start the instance. There are many changes, but the upgrade procedure was covered in Chapter 2.

```
[oracle@ORA-U2 dbs]$ cat initORC1.ora
*.audit_file_dest='/u01/app/oracle/admin/ORC1/adump'
*.audit_trail='db'
*.control_files='/u01/app/oracle/oradata/ORC1/control01.ctl','/u01/app/oracle/
fast_recovery_area/ORC1/control02.ctl'
*.db_block_size=8192
*.db_domain=''
*.db_name='ORC1'
*.db_recovery_file_dest='/u01/app/oracle/fast_recovery_area'
*.db_recovery_file_dest_size=4385144832
*.diagnostic_dest='/u01/app/oracle'
*.dispatchers='(PROTOCOL=TCP) (SERVICE=ORC1XDB)'
*.memory_target=629145600
*.open_cursors=300
*.processes=150
*.remote_login_passwordfile='EXCLUSIVE'
*.undo_tablespace='UNDOTBS1'
[oracle@ORA-U2 dbs]$ mkdir -p /u01/app/oracle/admin/ORC1/adump
[oracle@ORA-U2 dbs]$ mkdir -p /u01/app/oracle/fast_recovery_area
[oracle@ORA-U2 dbs]$ . oraenv
ORACLE_SID = [ORC1] ?
The Oracle base remains unchanged with value /u01/app/oracle
[oracle@ORA-U2 dbs]$ cat /etc/oratab |grep ORC1
ORC1:/u01/app/oracle/product/12.1.0/dbhome_1:N
[oracle@ORA-U2 dbs]$
```

6) Start the database and perform the recovery. Whereas in the cold backup you started the database directly with the upgrade option, in this case you cannot start with the upgrade option. Instead, you have to perform the recovery by applying the necessary archivelogs/redo and have to open the database with the resetlogs option; then the new database incarnation will differ from the original database.

Update the entries in /etc/oratab for the ORACLE_HOME and ORACLE_SID settings so that it's easy to connect, as shown here:

```
[oracle@ORA-U2 dbs]$ sqlplus / as sysdba

SQL*Plus: Release 12.1.0.1.0 Production
Copyright (c) 1982, 2013, Oracle.  All rights reserved.
```

```
Connected to an idle instance.

SQL> startup mount
ORACLE instance started.

Total System Global Area  626327552 bytes
Fixed Size                  2291472 bytes
Variable Size             440404208 bytes
Database Buffers          176160768 bytes
Redo Buffers                7471104 bytes
Database mounted.

Target Server (ORA-U2)

SQL> archive log list
Database log mode              Archive Mode
Automatic archival             Enabled
Archive destination            USE_DB_RECOVERY_FILE_DEST
Oldest online log sequence     7
Next log sequence to archive   9
Current log sequence           9
SQL> select checkpoint_change# from v$database;

CHECKPOINT_CHANGE#
------------------
            963025

SQL> select min(checkpoint_change#) from v$datafile_header;

MIN(CHECKPOINT_CHANGE#)
-----------------------
                963899
```

The output of the checkpoint change helps in the next section when performing the recovery.

- *Source server (ORA-U1)*: In the previous output, the oldest sequence on the target database is 7, and hence you need to apply the archive logs until all the SCNs are in sync. So, you will copy the archive logs that are generated during the backup and also until the log switch after the ending backup mode.

```
SQL> select sequence#,name from v$archived_log where sequence# > 8;

 SEQUENCE# NAME
---------- ---------------------------------------------------------------------------
------------------
         9 /u01/app/oracle/fast_recovery_area/ORC1/archivelog/2016_05_19/o1_
mf_1_9_cmsw23rk_.arc
        10 /u01/app/oracle/fast_recovery_area/ORC1/archivelog/2016_05_19/o1_
mf_1_10_cmsxtzwc_.arc

 [oracle@ORA-U1 admin]$ scp /u01/app/oracle/fast_recovery_area/ORC1/
archivelog/2016_05_19/* 192.168.0.120:/u01/app/oracle/fast_recovery_area/ORC1/
archivelog/2016_05_19/
```

```
oracle@192.168.0.120's password:
o1_mf_1_10_cmsxtzwc_.arc                                    100%  998KB
998.0KB/s    00:00
o1_mf_1_9_cmsw23rk_.arc                                     100%   14MB
13.7MB/s    00:00
[oracle@ORA-U1 admin]$
```

- *Target server* (ORA-U2): After copying the archive logs to the target server, you start the recovery and you apply the archives, as mentioned earlier.

```
SQL> recover database using backup controlfile until cancel;
ORA-00279: change 963899 generated at 05/19/2016 10:44:19 needed for thread 1
. . .
. .
.
ORA-00289: suggestion :
/u01/app/oracle/fast_recovery_area/ORC1/archivelog/2016_05_19/o1_mf_1_10_cmsxtzw
c_.arc
ORA-00280: change 963899 for thread 1 is in sequence #10

Specify log: {<RET>=suggested | filename | AUTO | CANCEL}
/u01/app/oracle/fast_recovery_area/ORC1/archivelog/2016_05_19/o1_mf_1_10_
cmsxtzwc_.arc
ORA-00279: change 964903 generated at 05/19/2016 11:14:39 needed for thread 1
ORA-00289: suggestion :
/u01/app/oracle/fast_recovery_area/ORC1/archivelog/2016_05_20/o1_mf_1_11_%u_.arc
ORA-00280: change 964903 for thread 1 is in sequence #11
ORA-00278: log file
'/u01/app/oracle/fast_recovery_area/ORC1/archivelog/2016_05_19/o1_mf_1_10_cmsxtz
wc_.arc' no longer needed for this recovery

Specify log: {<RET>=suggested | filename | AUTO | CANCEL}
cancel
Media recovery cancelled.
```

Note: We are canceling the recovery because the generated sequences on source database during hot backup have to apply them until after the available archives, If any further archives generated and then proceed to apply, once you are aware that there are no more archives available then before that then pass the keyword "cancel".
```
SQL> alter database open resetlogs upgrade;

Database altered.

SQL>
SQL> select name,open_mode from v$database;

NAME      OPEN_MODE
--------- --------------------
ORC1      READ WRITE

SQL>
```

7) Now that the database is opened in upgrade mode, you will crosscheck the table that you created in step 3.

```
SQL> select count(*) from upgtest;

  COUNT(*)
----------
     86953

SQL>
```

8) Now you perform the database upgrade using the manual method like you performed earlier. In this output, you are going to truncate some additional logs to avoid the same information in this method.

```
[oracle@ORA-U2 ~]$ cd $ORACLE_HOME/rdbms/admin
[oracle@ORA-U2 admin]$ /u01/app/oracle/product/12.1.0/dbhome_1/perl/bin/perl
catctl.pl -n 5 catupgrd.sql

Analyzing file catupgrd.sql
14 scripts found in file catupgrd.sql
Next path: catalog.sql
32 scripts found in file catalog.sql
Next path: catproc.sql
37 scripts found in file catproc.sql
Next path: catptabs.sql
61 scripts found in file catptabs.sql
Next path: catpdbms.sql
205 scripts found in file catpdbms.sql
. . .
  . .
    .

Parallel  Phase #:40 Files: 10    Time: 7s
Restart   Phase #:41 Files: 1     Time: 0s
Serial    Phase #:42 Files: 1     Time: 3s
Restart   Phase #:43 Files: 1     Time: 0s
Serial    Phase #:44 Files: 1     Time: 2s
Serial    Phase #:45 Files: 1     Time: 2s
Restart   Phase #:46 Files: 1     Time: 0s
Serial    Phase #:47 Files: 2     Time: 6s
Restart   Phase #:48 Files: 1     Time: 0s
Serial    Phase #:49 Files: 2     Time: 0s
Restart   Phase #:50 Files: 1     Time: 0s
Serial    Phase #:51 Files: 2     Time: 1079s
Restart   Phase #:52 Files: 1     Time: 0s
Serial    Phase #:53 Files: 1     Time: 3s
Restart   Phase #:52 Files: 1     Time: 1s
Serial    Phase #:53 Files: 1     Time: 1s
Serial    Phase #:54 Files: 1     Time: 110s
Serial    Phase #:55 Files: 1     Time: 331s
Serial    Phase #:56 Files: 1     Time: 12s
```

```
Grand Total Time: 1923s
[oracle@ORA-U2 admin]$
```

9) After a successful upgrade, the database will shut down. Now you have to
start the database in normal mode, and you can check whether the registry
components are valid. If the components are invalid, then you have to reload
the object (you can follow the instructions from My Oracle Support for each
component). In this case, the components are valid, and only one component is
option-off, which is expected if not in use.

```
SQL> startup
ORACLE instance started.

Total System Global Area  626327552 bytes
Fixed Size                  2291472 bytes
Variable Size             440404208 bytes
Database Buffers          176160768 bytes
Redo Buffers                7471104 bytes
Database mounted.
Database opened.
SQL> select comp_name,version,status from dba_registry;
```

COMP_NAME	VERSION	STATUS
Oracle Application Express	4.2.0.00.27	VALID
OWB	11.2.0.4.0	VALID
Oracle Enterprise Manager	11.2.0.4.0	VALID
Spatial	12.1.0.1.0	VALID
Oracle Multimedia	12.1.0.1.0	VALID
Oracle XML Database	12.1.0.1.0	VALID
Oracle Text	12.1.0.1.0	VALID
Oracle Workspace Manager	12.1.0.1.0	VALID
Oracle Database Catalog Views	12.1.0.1.0	VALID
Oracle Database Packages and Types	12.1.0.1.0	VALID
JServer JAVA Virtual Machine	12.1.0.1.0	VALID
Oracle XDK	12.1.0.1.0	VALID
Oracle Database Java Packages	12.1.0.1.0	VALID
OLAP Analytic Workspace	12.1.0.1.0	VALID
Oracle OLAP API	12.1.0.1.0	VALID

```
16 rows selected.
```

10) Compile the invalid objects. It is expected that you will have invalid objects in any
upgrade, so it is a mandatory step to run the file utlrp.sql. If after running it there
are still invalid objects found, then you can run it as many times as necessary.

```
SQL> @?/rdbms/admin/utlrp.sql

TIMESTAMP
--------------------------------------------------------------------------------
COMP_TIMESTAMP UTLRP_BGN
```

```
. . .
. .
.
...Database user "SYS", database schema "APEX_040200", user# "117" 11:51:16
...Compiled 0 out of 2998 objects considered, 0 failed compilation 11:51:16
...263 packages
...255 package bodies
...453 tables
...11 functions
...16 procedures
...3 sequences
...458 triggers
...1322 indexes
...207 views
...0 libraries
...6 types
...0 type bodies
...0 operators
...0 index types
...Begin key object existence check 11:51:16
...Completed key object existence check 11:51:16
...Setting DBMS Registry 11:51:16
...Setting DBMS Registry Complete 11:51:16
...Exiting validate 11:51:16

PL/SQL procedure successfully completed.

SQL>
```

You have now completed the database upgrade using hot backup. After this, your major step is to share the new TNS entries to the customer/users who are allowed to connect in order to start the application.

Logical Backup (expdp/impdp)

Before continuing with logical backups, we'll cover the difference between physical backups and logical backups since this terminology is used repeatedly. For example, at the database level, you are probably familiar with *tablespace* and *datafile*. You can say that a tablespace is a set of datafiles, but here you can see the datafiles physically in a specific location like /u01/oradata/orcl/example01.dbf. The tablespace is not like this; it's just a logical notation. When it comes to the logical backup, in the early releases Oracle introduced export and import, and starting from Oracle 10*g* this technique was renamed Data Pump (expdp/impdp). These backup methods deal with logical objects such as the schema, table, and so on, but it is not concerned with the datafiles. That's why this method is called a *logical* backup. To use this method, the database can be either in archivelog mode or in noarchivelog mode. This method is more enhanced in 11*g* and also in 12*c*. This method works perfectly with the migrations of one platform to another platform and from a lower Oracle version/release to a major release (such as 12*c*). As stated earlier in the book, this method will also work where direct upgrades are not possible, for example, when going from 10.1.0.1 to 12.1.0.2.

Logical backup's great flexibility is the use of exp/imp prior to 10*g*. expdp/impdp from the 10*g* utilities can be used from and to any platform and from and to any database versions/releases. However, it is a must to check the export/import interoperability matrix from Oracle Support, but for this example there is no problem with compatibility, especially when exporting from 11*g* or 12*c* to 9*i*, and so on. In this example, you are upgrading a database from 11*g* to 12*c* directly by using the backup of the 11*g* database. To start the upgrade, there are few prerequisites.

1) The 12.1 RDBMS software needs to have been created already.

2) The database needs to have been created already on the 12*c* Home for the upgrade usage.

In the case of full database export and import, you must create an empty database initially, because while performing the export, the SYS and SYSTEM objects will not be created in the target database.

Prerequisites

Export/import is not as easy as other techniques because you have to take many things into consideration. You will now see what they are.

Registry Components

Let's suppose you are using a few additional registry components at the source database (11*g*). Then you must ensure these objects are loaded into the target database prior to the import into the 12*c* database. You can extract the list of components using the following view:

```
SQL> select comp_name,status,version from dba_registry;

COMP_NAME                             STATUS        VERSION
------------------------------------- ------------  ------------
OWB                                   VALID         11.2.0.4.0
Oracle Application Express            VALID         3.2.1.00.12
Oracle Enterprise Manager             VALID         11.2.0.4.0
OLAP Catalog                          VALID         11.2.0.4.0
Spatial                               VALID         11.2.0.4.0
Oracle Multimedia                     VALID         11.2.0.4.0
Oracle XML Database                   VALID         11.2.0.4.0
Oracle Text                           VALID         11.2.0.4.0
Oracle Expression Filter              VALID         11.2.0.4.0
Oracle Rules Manager                  VALID         11.2.0.4.0
Oracle Workspace Manager              VALID         11.2.0.4.0
Oracle Database Catalog Views         VALID         11.2.0.4.0
Oracle Database Packages and Types    VALID         11.2.0.4.0
JServer JAVA Virtual Machine          VALID         11.2.0.4.0
Oracle XDK                            VALID         11.2.0.4.0
Oracle Database Java Packages         VALID         11.2.0.4.0
OLAP Analytic Workspace               VALID         11.2.0.4.0
Oracle OLAP API                       VALID         11.2.0.4.0

18 rows selected.
```

Objects Count

Prior to upgrading, you must gather a list of objects of each schema and also a list of valid and invalid objects, because there may be many conflicts that result in invalid objects that fail to import. In that case, you have to again import the objects manually.

```
SQL> SELECT owner, count(*) FROM dba_objects WHERE owner IN ('CTXSYS', 'OLAPSYS', 'MDSYS',
'DMSYS', 'WKSYS', 'LBACSYS','ORDSYS', 'XDB', 'EXFSYS', 'OWBSYS', 'WMSYS', 'SYSMAN') OR owner
LIKE 'APEX%' GROUP BY owner ORDER by owner;

OWNER                        COUNT(*)
-------------------------   ------------
APEX_030200                      2561
CTXSYS                            389
EXFSYS                            312
MDSYS                            2011
OLAPSYS                           721
ORDSYS                           2513
OWBSYS                              2
SYSMAN                           3554
WMSYS                             333
XDB                              1170

SQL> SELECT owner, object_type, COUNT(*) FROM dba_objects  WHERE object_type LIKE 'JAVA%'
GROUP BY owner, object_type  ORDER BY 1,2;

OWNER                       OBJECT_TYPE            COUNT(*)
-------------------------   --------------------  ------------
EXFSYS                      JAVA CLASS                  47
EXFSYS                      JAVA RESOURCE                1
MDSYS                       JAVA CLASS                 544
MDSYS                       JAVA RESOURCE                3
ORDSYS                      JAVA CLASS                1877
ORDSYS                      JAVA RESOURCE               72
SYS                         JAVA CLASS               26607
SYS                         JAVA DATA                  323
SYS                         JAVA RESOURCE              864
SYS                         JAVA SOURCE                  2

10 rows selected.
SQL> select object_name,object_type,owner,status from dba_objects where status='INVALID' and
owner not in ('CTXSYS', 'OLAPSYS', 'MDSYS', 'DMSYS', 'WKSYS', 'LBACSYS','SYS','SYSTEM','ORDS
YS', 'XDB', 'EXFSYS', 'OWBSYS', 'WMSYS', 'SYSMAN','PUBLIC','ORDPLUGINS','ORACLE_OCM','IX','A
PEX_030200','DBSNMP');

no rows selected
```

Check NLS Settings

From the source database, you have to gather the NLS settings.

```
SQL> show parameter nls

NAME                                         TYPE        VALUE
-----------------------------------------    ----------  --------------------
nls_calendar                                 string
nls_comp                                     string      BINARY
```

```
nls_currency                    string
nls_date_format                 string     YYYY-MM-DD HH24:MI:SS
nls_date_language               string
nls_dual_currency               string
nls_iso_currency                string
nls_language                    string     AMERICAN
nls_length_semantics            string     BYTE
nls_nchar_conv_excp             string     FALSE
nls_numeric_characters          string
nls_sort                        string
nls_territory                   string     AMERICA
nls_time_format                 string
nls_time_tz_format              string
nls_timestamp_format            string
nls_timestamp_tz_format         string
```

Datafiles and Metadata

As discussed earlier, no SYS and SYSTEM objects will be imported because those objects will be available already when creating the database using the DBCA. So, you have to take care to create only the user tablespaces available except SYSTEM, SYAUX, and UNDO. If the path is the same, then the import will have the capability to create the tablespaces.

```
TABLESPACE_NAME                       BYTES STATUS        ONLINE_ FILE_NAME
------------------------------ ------------ ----------- ------- --------------------------
--------------------------------------------------------------------
EXAMPLE                           346030080 AVAILABLE   ONLINE  /u01/app/oracle/oradata/
ORC1/example01.dbf
SYSAUX                            534773760 AVAILABLE   ONLINE  /u01/app/oracle/oradata/
ORC1/sysaux01.dbf
SYSTEM                            796917760 AVAILABLE   SYSTEM  /u01/app/oracle/oradata/
ORC1/system01.dbf
UNDOTBS1                           47185920 AVAILABLE   ONLINE  /u01/app/oracle/oradata/
ORC1/undotbs01.dbf
USERS                               5242880 AVAILABLE   ONLINE  /u01/app/oracle/oradata/
ORC1/users01.dbf

SQL> set long 90000
SQL> select dbms_metadata.get_ddl('TABLESPACE','USERS') from dual;

  CREATE TABLESPACE "USERS" DATAFILE
  '/u01/app/oracle/oradata/ORC1/users01.dbf' SIZE 5242880
  AUTOEXTEND ON NEXT 1310720 MAXSIZE 32767M
  LOGGING ONLINE PERMANENT BLOCKSIZE 8192
  EXTENT MANAGEMENT LOCAL AUTOALLOCATE DEFAULT
NOCOMPRESS   SEGMENT SPACE MANAGEMENT AUTO
```

Check the Invalid Objects from the Target Database

Use the following to check for invalid objects:

```
SQL> select * from v$version;

BANNER                                                                   CON_ID
------------------------------------------------------------------------ ----------
--
Oracle Database 12c Enterprise Edition Release 12.1.0.1.0 - 64bit Production
0
PL/SQL Release 12.1.0.1.0 - Production
0
CORE    12.1.0.1.0        Production
0
TNS for Linux: Version 12.1.0.1.0 - Production
0
NLSRTL Version 12.1.0.1.0 - Production
0

SQL> select owner,count(*) from dba_objects where status='INVALID' group by owner;

no rows selected

SQL>
```

As you can see, there are no invalid objects found from the 12*c* target database. If you do find any invalid objects, then run the `$ORACLE_HOME/rdbms/admin/utlrp.sql` script.

Registry Components at the Target Database

After creating the database in 12*c* using the DBCA, you have to check that the registry components are loaded and which ones are missing. You must load the missing components if the components are in use at the source database.

```
SQL> select comp_name,status,version from dba_registry;

COMP_NAME                             STATUS       VERSION
------------------------------------- ------------ ------------
Oracle Database Vault                 VALID        12.1.0.1.0
Oracle Application Express            VALID        4.2.0.00.27
Oracle Label Security                VALID        12.1.0.1.0
Spatial                               VALID        12.1.0.1.0
Oracle Multimedia                     VALID        12.1.0.1.0
Oracle Text                           VALID        12.1.0.1.0
Oracle Workspace Manager             VALID        12.1.0.1.0
Oracle XML Database                   VALID        12.1.0.1.0
Oracle Database Catalog Views        VALID        12.1.0.1.0
Oracle Database Packages and Types   VALID        12.1.0.1.0
JServer JAVA Virtual Machine          VALID        12.1.0.1.0
Oracle XDK                            VALID        12.1.0.1.0
```

```
Oracle Database Java Packages          VALID       12.1.0.1 0
OLAP Analytic Workspace                VALID       12.1.0.1 0
Oracle OLAP API                        VALID       12.1.0.1 0
Oracle Real Application Clusters       OPTION OFF  12.1.0.1 0
```

16 rows selected.

Create Triggers of the SYS Schema

SYS objects will not be exported; hence, you have to gather the metadata of the triggers that belong to the SYS user.

```
OWNER                            TRIGGER_NAME                       TRIGGER_TYPE    TRIGGERING_
EVENT                   TABLE_OWNER    BASE_OBJECT_TYPE STATUS
-------------------------------- ------------------------------ ---------------- -------------
------------------------ ------------------------------ ---------------- ---------
SYS                              AW_DROP_TRG                        AFTER EVENT     DROP
SYS            DATABASE          ENABLED
SYS                              AW_REN_TRG                         AFTER EVENT     RENAME
SYS            DATABASE          ENABLED
SYS                              AW_TRUNC_TRG                       AFTER EVENT     TRUNCATE
SYS            DATABASE          ENABLED
SYS                              CDC_ALTER_CTABLE_BEFORE            BEFORE EVENT    ALTER
SYS            DATABASE          DISABLED
SYS                              CDC_CREATE_CTABLE_AFTER            AFTER EVENT     CREATE
SYS            DATABASE          DISABLED
SYS                              CDC_CREATE_CTABLE_BEFORE           BEFORE EVENT    CREATE
SYS            DATABASE          DISABLED
SYS                              CDC_DROP_CTABLE_BEFORE             BEFORE EVENT    DROP
SYS            DATABASE          DISABLED
SYS                              LOGMNRGGC_TRIGGER                  BEFORE EVENT    DDL
SYS            DATABASE          DISABLED
SYS                              XDB_PI_TRIG                        BEFORE EVENT    DROP OR
TRUNCATE                SYS            DATABASE         ENABLED
```

9 rows selected.

To extract the metadata then use dbms_metadata.get_ddl
package.--

```
  CREATE OR REPLACE TRIGGER "SYS"."LOGMNRGGC_TRIGGER"
BEFORE ddl ON DATABASE
 CALL logmnr_ddl_trigger_proc
ALTER TRIGGER "SYS"."LOGMNRGGC_TRIGGER" DISABLE
```

Also note that you can gather the list of grants is to users to objects owned by SYS or other schemas using the following spool query:

```
SELECT 'GRANT ' || privilege || ' ON ' || table_name || ' TO ' || grantee || ';' "GRANTS"
FROM dba_tab_privs WHERE owner = 'SYS' AND privilege NOT IN ('READ', 'WRITE') AND grantee IN
('TC') ORDER BY 1;
```

Database Export Using expdp

Now you are done with the prerequisites, and you can proceed with the backup using expdp at the source database of 11*g*. Before using expdp, you must create one directory so that the dump files will be stored in this location.

```
[oracle@ORA-U1 ~]$ mkdir -p /home/oracle/working_migr
[oracle@ORA-U1 ~]$ cd /home/oracle/working_migr
[oracle@ORA-U1 working_migr]$ sqlplus / as sysdba

SQL*Plus: Release 11.2.0.4.0 Production
Copyright (c) 1982, 2013, Oracle.  All rights reserved.

Connected to:
Oracle Database 11g Enterprise Edition Release 11.2.0.4.0 - 64bit Production
With the Partitioning, OLAP, Data Mining and Real Application Testing options

SQL> create directory migr as '/home/oracle/working_migr';

Directory created.

SQL> grant read,write on directory migr to system;

Grant succeeded.
```

Before starting the export of the backup ensure there are no applications are connected and better to set it into restricted mode as using with the command "alter system enable restricted session ;"
Apart from that it is highly recommended to set flashback_time so that we can fix constant SCN/Time to export until that time or else expected to face many issues such as snapshot too old error when searching for segment which is modified after the export or various other cases.

```
 [oracle@ORA-U1 working_migr]$ expdp system/oracle directory=migr dumpfile=bkp_11g_%U.dmp
logfile=bkp_11g_f.log full=y parallel=4  flashback_time=systimestamp

Export: Release 11.2.0.4.0 - Production
Copyright (c) 1982, 2011, Oracle and/or its affiliates.  All rights reserved.

Connected to: Oracle Database 11g Enterprise Edition Release 11.2.0.4.0 - 64bit Production
With the Partitioning, OLAP, Data Mining and Real Application Testing options
Starting "SYSTEM"."SYS_EXPORT_FULL_01":  system/******** directory=migr dumpfile=bkp_11g_%U.
dmp logfile=bkp_11g_f.log full=y parallel=4 flashback_time=systimestamp
Estimate in progress using BLOCKS method...
Processing object type DATABASE_EXPORT/SCHEMA/TABLE/TABLE_DATA
Total estimation using BLOCKS method: 359.5 MB
. . exported "SH"."COSTS":"COSTS_Q1_1998"          139.5 KB    4411 rows
. . exported "SH"."CUSTOMERS"                       9.853 MB   55500 rows
. . exported "SH"."COSTS":"COSTS_Q1_1999"          183.5 KB    5884 rows
. . exported "SH"."COSTS":"COSTS_Q1_2000"          120.6 KB    3772 rows
. . exported "PM"."ONLINE_MEDIA"                    7.752 MB       9 rows
. . exported "SH"."COSTS":"COSTS_Q1_2001"          227.8 KB    7328 rows
```

```
. . exported "SH"."COSTS":"COSTS_Q2_1998"                79.52 KB    2397 rows
. . .
.1.
.
Processing object type DATABASE_EXPORT/SCHEMA/EVENT/TRIGGER
Processing object type DATABASE_EXPORT/SCHEMA/MATERIALIZED_VIEW
Processing object type DATABASE_EXPORT/SCHEMA/JOB
Processing object type DATABASE_EXPORT/SCHEMA/DIMENSION
Processing object type DATABASE_EXPORT/SCHEMA/TABLE/POST_INSTANCE/PROCACT_INSTANCE
Processing object type DATABASE_EXPORT/SCHEMA/TABLE/POST_INSTANCE/PROCDEPOBJ
Processing object type DATABASE_EXPORT/SCHEMA/POST_SCHEMA/PROCOBJ
Processing object type DATABASE_EXPORT/SCHEMA/POST_SCHEMA/PROCACT_SCHEMA
Processing object type DATABASE_EXPORT/AUDIT
Master table "SYSTEM"."SYS_EXPORT_FULL_01" successfully loaded/unloaded
******************************************************************************
Dump file set for SYSTEM.SYS_EXPORT_FULL_01 is:
  /home/oracle/working_migr/bkp_11g_01.dmp
  /home/oracle/working_migr/bkp_11g_02.dmp
  /home/oracle/working_migr/bkp_11g_03.dmp
  /home/oracle/working_migr/bkp_11g_04.dmp
Job "SYSTEM"."SYS_EXPORT_FULL_01" completed with 1 error(s) at Sat May 21 18:16:31 2016
elapsed 0 00:02:43
```

Importing the Database (impdp)

You have the backup ready. Now, prior to performing the import, you must create the additional tablespaces, as you have already taken a backup of the metadata of the USERS tablespace, so these tablespaces need to be executed on the target database of 12c.

```
[oracle@ORA-U2 ~]$ mkdir -p /home/oracle/working_migr
[oracle@ORA-U2 ~]$
[oracle@ORA-U1 working_migr]$  ls -ltr
total 135180
-rw-r-----. 1 oracle oinstall 31014912 May 21 18:16 bkp_11g_01.dmp
-rw-r-----. 1 oracle oinstall 30924800 May 21 18:16 bkp_11g_02.dmp
-rw-r-----. 1 oracle oinstall 26251264 May 21 18:16 bkp_11g_04.dmp
-rw-r-----. 1 oracle oinstall 50110464 May 21 18:16 bkp_11g_03.dmp
-rw-r--r--. 1 oracle oinstall   107405 May 21 18:16 bkp_11g_f.log
[oracle@ORA-U1 working_migr]$ pwd
/home/oracle/working_migr
[oracle@ORA-U1 working_migr]$ scp * 192.168.0.120:/home/oracle/working_migr/
oracle@192.168.0.120's password:
bkp_11g_01.dmp                    100%    30MB   29.6MB/s   00:00
bkp_11g_02.dmp                    100%    29MB   29.5MB/s   00:01
bkp_11g_03.dmp                    100%    48MB   47.8MB/s   00:00
bkp_11g_04.dmp                    100%    25MB   25.0MB/s   00:00
bkp_11g_f.log                     100%   105KB  104.9KB/s   00:00
[oracle@ORA-U1 working_migr]$

SQL> select * from v$version;
```

```
BANNER                                                                        CON_ID
-------------------------------------------------------------------------- ----------
Oracle Database 12c Enterprise Edition Release 12.1.0.1.0 - 64bit Production        0
PL/SQL Release 12.1.0.1.0 - Production                                              0
CORE    12.1.0.1.0        Production
0
TNS for Linux: Version 12.1.0.1.0 - Production                                      0
NLSRTL Version 12.1.0.1.0 - Production                                              0

SQL>
SQL> create directory migr as '/home/oracle/working_migr';

Directory created.

SQL> grant read,write on directory migr to system;

Grant succeeded.

SQL>
```

The dumpfile names we can use wildcards instead of the dump file names by using the option %U and also for the faster import process we can enable parallelism by mentioning attribute parallel=4

```
[oracle@ORA-U2 working_migr]$ impdp system/oracle directory=migr dumpfile=bkp_11g_01.
dmp,bkp_11g_02.dmp,bkp_11g_03.dmp,bkp_11g_04.dmp logfile=imp_12c.log full=y parallel=4

Import: Release 12.1.0.1.0 - Production

Copyright (c) 1982, 2013, Oracle and/or its affiliates.  All rights reserved.

Connected to: Oracle Database 12c Enterprise Edition Release 12.1.0.1.0 - 64bit Production
With the Partitioning, OLAP, Advanced Analytics and Real Application Testing options
Master table "SYSTEM"."SYS_IMPORT_FULL_01" successfully loaded/unloaded
Starting "SYSTEM"."SYS_IMPORT_FULL_01":  system/******** directory=migr dumpfile=bkp_11g_01.
dmp,bkp_11g_02.dmp,bkp_11g_03.dmp,bkp_11g_04.dmp logfile=imp_12c.log full=y parallel=4
Processing object type DATABASE_EXPORT/TABLESPACE
ORA-31684: Object type TABLESPACE:"UNDOTBS1" already exists
ORA-31684: Object type TABLESPACE:"TEMP" already exists
ORA-31684: Object type TABLESPACE:"USERS" already exists
Processing object type DATABASE_EXPORT/PROFILE
Processing object type DATABASE_EXPORT/SYS_USER/USER
Processing object type DATABASE_EXPORT/SCHEMA/USER
ORA-31684: Object type USER:"OUTLN" already exists
ORA-31684: Object type USER:"ORDDATA" already exists
ORA-31684: Object type USER:"OLAPSYS" already exists
ORA-31684: Object type USER:"MDDATA" already exists
ORA-31684: Object type USER:"SPATIAL_WFS_ADMIN_USR" already exists
ORA-31684: Object type USER:"SPATIAL_CSW_ADMIN_USR" already exists
ORA-31684: Object type USER:"FLOWS_FILES" already exists
ORA-31684: Object type USER:"APEX_PUBLIC_USER" already exists
ORA-31684: Object type USER:"SCOTT" already exists
. . .
```

```
. .
  .
. . imported "APEX_030200"."WWV_FLOW_PAGE_PLUGS"           3.834 MB    7416 rows
. . imported "APEX_030200"."WWV_FLOW_STEP_PROCESSING"       1.248 MB    2238 rows
. . imported "APEX_030200"."WWV_FLOW_STEPS"                 570.5 KB    1754 rows
. . imported "APEX_030200"."WWV_FLOW_STEP_ITEMS"            3.505 MB    9671 rows
. . imported "APEX_030200"."WWV_FLOW_LIST_ITEMS"            590.3 KB    3048 rows
. . imported "APEX_030200"."WWV_FLOW_REGION_REPORT_COLUMN"  1.146 MB    7903 rows
. . imported "APEX_030200"."WWV_FLOW_STEP_VALIDATIONS"      611.4 KB    1990 rows
. . imported "APEX_030200"."WWV_FLOW_STEP_ITEM_HELP"        1003. KB    6335 rows
. . imported "APEX_030200"."WWV_FLOW_LIST_TEMPLATES"        73.32 KB     105 rows
. . imported "APEX_030200"."WWV_FLOW_STEP_BRANCHES"         508.6 KB    3255 rows
. . imported "SYSMAN"."MGMT_IP_REPORT_ELEM_PARAMS"          364.3 KB    1490 rows
. . imported "APEX_030200"."WWV_FLOW_STEP_BUTTONS"          472.4 KB    3513 rows
. . imported "SH"."FWEEK_PSCAT_SALES_MV"                    419.8 KB   11266 rows
. . .
. .
  .


ORA-39082: Object type TRIGGER:"APEX_030200"."WWV_BIJ_FLOW_SESSIONS" created with
compilation warnings
ORA-39082: Object type TRIGGER:"SYSMAN"."MGMT_CREDS_INS_UPD" created with compilation
warnings
Job "SYSTEM"."SYS_IMPORT_FULL_01" completed with 81 error(s) at Sat May 21 18:31:30 2016
elapsed 0 00:07:19
```

During the import, the warnings/errors are expected because of the already existing objects and a few dependencies. If they are related to user objects, then you must re-export and import the schema/objects. After the import process is completed, you can run the utlrp.sql script to recompile any invalid objects. This script can be executed more than once.

```
SQL> @?/rdbms/admin/utlrp.sql

TIMESTAMP
--------------------------------------------------------------------------------
COMP_TIMESTAMP UTLRP_BGN  2016-05-21 18:32:35

DOC>   The following PL/SQL block invokes UTL_RECOMP to recompile invalid
DOC>   objects in the database. Recompilation time is proportional to the
DOC>   number of invalid objects in the database, so this command may take
DOC>   a long time to execute on a database with a large number of invalid
DOC>   objects.
DOC>
DOC>   Use the following queries to track recompilation progress:
DOC>
DOC>   1. Query returning the number of invalid objects remaining. This
DOC>      number should decrease with time.
DOC>         SELECT COUNT(*) FROM obj$ WHERE status IN (4, 5, 6);
DOC>
DOC>   2. Query returning the number of objects compiled so far. This number
DOC>      should increase with time.
```

```
DOC>        SELECT COUNT(*) FROM UTL_RECOMP_COMPILED;
DOC>
DOC> This script automatically chooses serial or parallel recompilation
DOC> based on the number of CPUs available (parameter cpu_count) multiplied
DOC> by the number of threads per CPU (parameter parallel_threads_per_cpu).
DOC> On RAC, this number is added across all RAC nodes.
DOC>
DOC> UTL_RECOMP uses DBMS_SCHEDULER to create jobs for parallel
DOC> recompilation. Jobs are created without instance affinity so that they
DOC> can migrate across RAC nodes. Use the following queries to verify
DOC> whether UTL_RECOMP jobs are being created and run correctly:
DOC>
DOC> 1. Query showing jobs created by UTL_RECOMP
DOC>        SELECT job_name FROM dba_scheduler_jobs
DOC>           WHERE job_name like 'UTL_RECOMP_SLAVE_%';
DOC>
DOC> 2. Query showing UTL_RECOMP jobs that are running
DOC>        SELECT job_name FROM dba_scheduler_running_jobs
DOC>           WHERE job_name like 'UTL_RECOMP_SLAVE_%';
DOC>#
```

PL/SQL procedure successfully completed.

```
TIMESTAMP
--------------------------------------------------------------------------------
COMP_TIMESTAMP UTLRP_END  2016-05-21 18:32:47
```

```
DOC> The following query reports the number of objects that have compiled
DOC> with errors.
DOC>
DOC> If the number is higher than expected, please examine the error
DOC> messages reported with each object (using SHOW ERRORS) to see if they
DOC> point to system misconfiguration or resource constraints that must be
DOC> fixed before attempting to recompile these objects.
DOC>#
```

```
OBJECTS WITH ERRORS
-------------------
                  0
```

```
DOC> The following query reports the number of errors caught during
DOC> recompilation. If this number is non-zero, please query the error
DOC> messages in the table UTL_RECOMP_ERRORS to see if any of these errors
DOC> are due to misconfiguration or resource constraints that must be
DOC> fixed before objects can compile successfully.
DOC>#
```

```
ERRORS DURING RECOMPILATION
---------------------------
                        0
```

Function created.

```
PL/SQL procedure successfully completed.

Function dropped.

...Database user "SYS", database schema "APEX_040200", user# "98" 18:32:55
...Compiled 0 out of 2998 objects considered, 0 failed compilation 18:32:55
...263 packages
...255 package bodies
...453 tables
...11 functions
...16 procedures
...3 sequences
...458 triggers
...1322 indexes
...207 views
...0 libraries
...6 types
...0 type bodies
...0 operators
...0 index types
...Begin key object existence check 18:32:55
...Completed key object existence check 18:32:55
...Setting DBMS Registry 18:32:55
...Setting DBMS Registry Complete 18:32:55
...Exiting validate 18:32:55

PL/SQL procedure successfully completed.
```

RMAN Backup

The Recovery Manager released by Oracle with Oracle 8 is a phenomenal feature in terms of simplifying the backup and recovery procedure. Before the introduction of RMAN, it was never easy for the DBA to manage backups and recover in case of any failures. RMAN offers various features. The following are a few methods that can be used to refresh the database from one server to another server:

1) Traditional RMAN restore

2) RMAN duplicate (10g and later)

3) RMAN active duplicate (11g and later)

There are a few additional features and options available with the RMAN restore methods. In this case, you are upgrading from 11g to 12c, and hence you can use either of the first two methods. To upgrade the database to 12c, the source RDBMS version/release can be 10.2.0.5, 11.1.0.7, 11.2.0.2, or 12.1.0.1. (More information is available in Chapter 1.) In this chapter, you are upgrading the database from 11.2.0.4 to 12.1.0.1.

The RMAN method is not as complex; it's a straightforward technique. Initially you have to take a backup of the database, control file, and the archive logs.

First execute the pre-upgrade script preupgrd.sql in the source database and make sure the output doesn't have any errors or warnings.

```
RMAN> backup database format '/home/oracle/working_migr/FULL_11g_DB_%U' plus archivelog
format '/home/oracle/working_migr/ARCH_11g_DB_%U' ;
```

```
Starting backup at 21-MAY-16
current log archived
using channel ORA_DISK_1
channel ORA_DISK_1: starting archived log backup set
channel ORA_DISK_1: specifying archived log(s) in backup set
input archived log thread=1 sequence=9 RECID=1 STAMP=912249859
input archived log thread=1 sequence=10 RECID=2 STAMP=912251679
input archived log thread=1 sequence=11 RECID=3 STAMP=912290418
input archived log thread=1 sequence=12 RECID=4 STAMP=912301206
input archived log thread=1 sequence=13 RECID=5 STAMP=912444527
input archived log thread=1 sequence=14 RECID=6 STAMP=912445188
input archived log thread=1 sequence=15 RECID=7 STAMP=912449709
input archived log thread=1 sequence=16 RECID=8 STAMP=912449752
input archived log thread=1 sequence=17 RECID=9 STAMP=912451166
input archived log thread=1 sequence=18 RECID=10 STAMP=912451213
input archived log thread=1 sequence=19 RECID=11 STAMP=912451233
input archived log thread=1 sequence=20 RECID=12 STAMP=912452854
channel ORA_DISK_1: starting piece 1 at 21-MAY-16
channel ORA_DISK_1: finished piece 1 at 21-MAY-16
piece handle=/home/oracle/working_migr/ARCH_11g_DB_07r65r7m_1_1 tag=TAG20160521T190734
comment=NONE
channel ORA_DISK_1: backup set complete, elapsed time: 00:00:04
Finished backup at 21-MAY-16

Starting backup at 21-MAY-16
using channel ORA_DISK_1
channel ORA_DISK_1: starting full datafile backup set
channel ORA_DISK_1: specifying datafile(s) in backup set
input datafile file number=00001 name=/u01/app/oracle/oradata/ORC1/system01.dbf
input datafile file number=00002 name=/u01/app/oracle/oradata/ORC1/sysaux01.dbf
input datafile file number=00005 name=/u01/app/oracle/oradata/ORC1/example01.dbf
input datafile file number=00003 name=/u01/app/oracle/oradata/ORC1/undotbs01.dbf
input datafile file number=00004 name=/u01/app/oracle/oradata/ORC1/users01.dbf
channel ORA_DISK_1: starting piece 1 at 21-MAY-16
channel ORA_DISK_1: finished piece 1 at 21-MAY-16
piece handle=/home/oracle/working_migr/FULL_11g_DB_08r65r7q_1_1 tag=TAG20160521T190738
comment=NONE
channel ORA_DISK_1: backup set complete, elapsed time: 00:00:15
channel ORA_DISK_1: starting full datafile backup set
channel ORA_DISK_1: specifying datafile(s) in backup set
including current control file in backup set
including current SPFILE in backup set
channel ORA_DISK_1: starting piece 1 at 21-MAY-16
channel ORA_DISK_1: finished piece 1 at 21-MAY-16
piece handle=/home/oracle/working_migr/FULL_11g_DB_09r65r89_1_1 tag=TAG20160521T190738
comment=NONE
channel ORA_DISK_1: backup set complete, elapsed time: 00:00:01
Finished backup at 21-MAY-16

Starting backup at 21-MAY-16
current log archived
```

202

```
using channel ORA_DISK_1
channel ORA_DISK_1: starting archived log backup set
channel ORA_DISK_1: specifying archived log(s) in backup set
input archived log thread=1 sequence=21 RECID=13 STAMP=912452875
channel ORA_DISK_1: starting piece 1 at 21-MAY-16
channel ORA_DISK_1: finished piece 1 at 21-MAY-16
piece handle=/home/oracle/working_migr/ARCH_11g_DB_0ar65r8b_1_1 tag=TAG20160521T190755
comment=NONE
channel ORA_DISK_1: backup set complete, elapsed time: 00:00:01
Finished backup at 21-MAY-16

RMAN> backup current controlfile format '/home/oracle/working_migr/cf_%U';

Starting backup at 21-MAY-16
using channel ORA_DISK_1
channel ORA_DISK_1: starting full datafile backup set
channel ORA_DISK_1: specifying datafile(s) in backup set
including current control file in backup set
channel ORA_DISK_1: starting piece 1 at 21-MAY-16
channel ORA_DISK_1: finished piece 1 at 21-MAY-16
piece handle=/home/oracle/working_migr/cf_0br65r92_1_1 tag=TAG20160521T190818 comment=NONE
channel ORA_DISK_1: backup set complete, elapsed time: 00:00:01
Finished backup at 21-MAY-16
```

After finishing the RMAN backup, this backup can be copied to the target 12*c* server, and the location can be either the same or different. You need to restore and recover the database in the 12*c* Oracle Home and then start upgrading the database. You can use RMAN duplicate using a backup to restore the database on the new server. But the duplicate command will try to open the database with the resetlogs option at the end. Here the database is in the lower 11.2.0.4.0 version, and the binary is in the 12*c* version. You have to open the database in upgrade mode. To overcome this situation, 12*c* has provided a new option called NOOPEN with the duplicate command. When you use that option, RMAN will duplicate the database, but it will not open the database. After the duplicate activity, you can open the database in upgrade mode.

```
[oracle@ORA-U1 working_migr]$ ls -ltr
total 1420860
-rw-r-----. 1 oracle oinstall  257104384 May 21 19:07 ARCH_11g_DB_07r65r7m_1_1
-rw-r-----. 1 oracle oinstall 1177559040 May 21 19:07 FULL_11g_DB_08r65r7q_1_1
-rw-r-----. 1 oracle oinstall   10158080 May 21 19:07 FULL_11g_DB_09r65r89_1_1
-rw-r-----. 1 oracle oinstall       3584 May 21 19:07 ARCH_11g_DB_0ar65r8b_1_1
-rw-r-----. 1 oracle oinstall   10125312 May 21 19:08 cf_0br65r92_1_1
[oracle@ORA-U1 working_migr]$ scp * 192.168.0.120:/home/oracle/working_migr/
oracle@192.168.0.120's password:
ARCH_11g_DB_07r65r7m_1_1
100%  245MB 122.6MB/s   00:02
ARCH_11g_DB_0ar65r8b_1_1
100% 3584     3.5KB/s   00:00
cf_0br65r92_1_1
100% 9888KB   9.7MB/s   00:00
FULL_11g_DB_08r65r7q_1_1
100% 1123MB  86.4MB/s   00:13
```

```
FULL_11g_DB_09r65r89_1_1
100% 9920KB    9.7MB/s    00:00
[oracle@ORA-U1 working_migr]$
```

Prepare the auxiliary environment and create the necessary directories and the password file.

```
[oracle@ORA-U2 dbs]$ cat initORC1.ora
*.audit_file_dest='/u01/app/oracle/admin/ORC1/adump'
*.audit_trail='db'
*.compatible='12.1.0'
*.db_block_size=8192
*.db_domain=''
*.db_name='ORC1'
*.db_recovery_file_dest='/u01/app/oracle/fast_recovery_area'
*.db_recovery_file_dest_size=4385144832
*.diagnostic_dest='/u01/app/oracle'
*.dispatchers='(PROTOCOL=TCP) (SERVICE=ORC1XDB)'
*.memory_target=629145600
*.open_cursors=300
*.processes=150
*.remote_login_passwordfile='EXCLUSIVE'
*.undo_tablespace='UNDOTBS1'
[oracle@ORA-U2 dbs]$ ls -ltr *ORC1*
-rw-r-----. 1 oracle oinstall   24 May 19 06:42 lkORC1
-rw-r--r--. 1 oracle oinstall  580 May 19 10:52 initORC1.ora
-rw-r-----. 1 oracle oinstall 7680 May 21 18:24 orapwORC1
-rw-rw----. 1 oracle oinstall 1544 May 21 18:37 hc_ORC1.dat
```

Start the auxiliary instance in nomount mode from the 12c Home.

```
[oracle@ORA-U2 dbs]$ sqlplus / as sysdba

SQL*Plus: Release 12.1.0.1.0 Production
Copyright (c) 1982, 2013, Oracle.  All rights reserved.


Connected to an idle instance.

SQL> startup nomount
ORACLE instance started.

Total System Global Area  626327552 bytes
Fixed Size                  2291472 bytes
Variable Size             440404208 bytes
Database Buffers          176160768 bytes
Redo Buffers                7471104 bytes
SQL> exit
[oracle@ORA-U2 dbs]$ rman auxiliary /

Recovery Manager: Release 12.1.0.1.0 - Production
Copyright (c) 1982, 2013, Oracle and/or its affiliates.  All rights reserved.

connected to auxiliary database: ORC1 (not mounted)
```

```
RMAN> duplicate database to ORC1 NOOPEN nofilenamecheck backup location '/home/oracle/
working_migr/';

Starting Duplicate Db at 21-MAY-16

contents of Memory Script:
{
   sql clone "create spfile from memory";
}
executing Memory Script

sql statement: create spfile from memory

contents of Memory Script:
{
   shutdown clone immediate;
   startup clone nomount;
}
. . .
 . .
 .
renamed tempfile 1 to /u01/app/oracle/oradata/ORC1/temp01.dbf in control file

cataloged datafile copy
datafile copy file name=/u01/app/oracle/oradata/ORC1/sysaux01.dbf RECID=1 STAMP=912453997
cataloged datafile copy
datafile copy file name=/u01/app/oracle/oradata/ORC1/undotbs01.dbf RECID=2 STAMP=912453997
cataloged datafile copy
datafile copy file name=/u01/app/oracle/oradata/ORC1/users01.dbf RECID=3 STAMP=912453997
cataloged datafile copy
datafile copy file name=/u01/app/oracle/oradata/ORC1/example01.dbf RECID=4 STAMP=912453997

datafile 2 switched to datafile copy
input datafile copy RECID=1 STAMP=912453997 file name=/u01/app/oracle/oradata/ORC1/sysaux01.
dbf
datafile 3 switched to datafile copy
input datafile copy RECID=2 STAMP=912453997 file name=/u01/app/oracle/oradata/ORC1/
undotbs01.dbf
datafile 4 switched to datafile copy
input datafile copy RECID=3 STAMP=912453997 file name=/u01/app/oracle/oradata/ORC1/users01.
dbf
datafile 5 switched to datafile copy
input datafile copy RECID=4 STAMP=912453997 file name=/u01/app/oracle/oradata/ORC1/
example01.dbf
Leaving database unopened, as requested
Cannot remove created server parameter file
Finished Duplicate Db at 21-MAY-16

RMAN> exit

SQL> startup mount
```

```
ORA-32004: obsolete or deprecated parameter(s) specified for RDBMS instance
ORACLE instance started.

Total System Global Area  626327552 bytes
Fixed Size                  2291472 bytes
Variable Size             444598512 bytes
Database Buffers          171966464 bytes
Redo Buffers                7471104 bytes
Database mounted.
SQL> select name,open_mode from v$database;

NAME       OPEN_MODE
---------  --------------------
ORC1       MOUNTED

SQL> alter database open resetlogs upgrade;

Database altered.

SQL>
SQL> select name from v$tempfile;

NAME
--------------------------------------------------------------------------------
/u01/app/oracle/oradata/ORC1/temp01.dbf

SQL>
```

After the successful duplicate, the recovery is also included. Therefore, you can open the database in resetlogs mode. Now you have to check for the temp file availability. If there is no temp file created, then you can do it manually.

Now it's time to start the upgrade procedure.

```
[oracle@ORA-U2 admin]$ /u01/app/oracle/product/12.1.0/dbhome_1/perl/bin/perl catctl.pl -n 5
catupgrd.sql


Analyzing file catupgrd.sql
14 scripts found in file catupgrd.sql
Next path: catalog.sql
32 scripts found in file catalog.sql
Next path: catproc.sql
37 scripts found in file catproc.sql
Next path: catptabs.sql
61 scripts found in file catptabs.sql
Next path: catpdbms.sql
205 scripts found in file catpdbms.sql
Next path: catpdeps.sql
77 scripts found in file catpdeps.sql
Next path: catpprvt.sql
260 scripts found in file catpprvt.sql
Next path: catpexec.sql
```

```
26 scripts found in file catpexec.sql
Next path: cmpupgrd.sql
16 scripts found in file cmpupgrd.sql

[Phase 0] type is 1 with 1 Files
catupstr.sql

[Phase 1] type is 1 with 3 Files
cdstrt.sql         cdfixed.sql         cdcore.sql

[Phase 2] type is 1 with 1 Files
ora_restart.sql

[Phase 3] type is 2 with 18 Files
cdplsql.sql        cdsqlddl.sql        cdmanage.sql        cdtxnspc.sql
cdenv.sql          cdrac.sql           cdsec.sql           cdobj.sql
cdjava.sql         cdpart.sql          cdrep.sql           cdaw.sql
cdsummgt.sql       cdtools.sql         cdexttab.sql        cddm.sql
catldr.sql         cdclst.sql
. . .
. .
.
Using 5 processes.
Serial    Phase #: 0 Files: 1        Time: 92s
Serial    Phase #: 1 Files: 3        Time: 20s
Restart   Phase #: 2 Files: 1        Time: 0s
Parallel  Phase #: 3 Files: 18       Time: 6s
Restart   Phase #: 4 Files: 1        Time: 0s
. . .
. .
.

Restart   Phase #:39 Files: 1        Time: 0s
Parallel  Phase #:40 Files: 10       Time: 4s
Restart   Phase #:41 Files: 1        Time: 0s
Serial    Phase #:42 Files: 1        Time: 3s
Restart   Phase #:43 Files: 1        Time: 0s
Serial    Phase #:44 Files: 1        Time: 2s
Serial    Phase #:45 Files: 1        Time: 0s
Restart   Phase #:46 Files: 1        Time: 0s
Serial    Phase #:47 Files: 2        Time: 3s
Restart   Phase #:48 Files: 1        Time: 0s
Serial    Phase #:49 Files: 2        Time: 0s
Restart   Phase #:50 Files: 1        Time: 0s
Serial    Phase #:51 Files: 2        Time: 901s
Restart   Phase #:52 Files: 1        Time: 0s
Serial    Phase #:53 Files: 1        Time: 2s
Serial    Phase #:54 Files: 1
```

*** WARNING: ERRORS FOUND DURING UPGRADE ***

Due to errors found during the upgrade process, the post

upgrade actions in catuppst.sql have not been automatically run.

*** THEREFORE THE DATABASE UPGRADE IS NOT YET COMPLETE ***

1. Evaluate the errors found in the upgrade logs (*.log) and determine the proper action.
2. Execute the post upgrade script as described in Chapter 3 of the Database Upgrade Guide.

```
     Time: 116s
Grand Total Time: 1467s
[oracle@ORA-U2 admin]$
[oracle@ORA-U2 ~]$
```

The upgrade is completed, but there were few errors associated. You can fix these by reviewing the upgrade logs such as "unable to run catuppst as part of upgrade and various logs can be located in the mentioned directory at upgrade script." After that, you can check the registry components' status.

```
SQL> @?/rdbms/admin/catuppst.sql

Session altered.

Session altered.

Session altered.

TIMESTAMP
--------------------------------------------------------------------------------
COMP_TIMESTAMP POSTUP_BGN 2016-05-22 10:16:04

TIMESTAMP
--------------------------------------------------------------------------------
COMP_TIMESTAMP CATREQ_BGN 2016-05-22 10:16:04

PL/SQL procedure successfully completed.

catrequtlmg: b_StatEvt     = TRUE
. . .
. .
.
PL/SQL procedure successfully completed.

SQL> ALTER SESSION SET current_schema = SYS;

Session altered.

SQL> PROMPT Updating registry...
Updating registry...
SQL> INSERT INTO registry$history
  2    (action_time, action,
  3     namespace, version, id,
  4     bundle_series, comments)
  5  VALUES
```

```
 6     (SYSTIMESTAMP, 'APPLY',
 7     SYS_CONTEXT('REGISTRY$CTX','NAMESPACE'),
 8     '12.1.0.1',
 9     0,
10     'PSU',
11     'Patchset 12.1.0.0.0');

1 row created.

SQL> COMMIT;

Commit complete.

SQL> SPOOL off
SQL> SET echo off
Check the following log file for errors:
/u01/app/oracle/cfgtoollogs/catbundle/catbundle_PSU_ORC1_APPLY_2016May22_10_17_15.log

Session altered.

Session altered.

SQL>
SQL> select comp_name,status,version from dba_registry;

COMP_NAME                                  STATUS       VERSION
------------------------------------------ -----------  ------------------------------
Oracle Application Express                 VALID        4.2.0.00.27
OWB                                        VALID        11.2.0.4.0
Spatial                                    INVALID      12.1.0.1.0
Oracle Multimedia                          VALID        12.1.0.1.0
Oracle XML Database                        VALID        12.1.0.1.0
Oracle Text                                VALID        12.1.0.1.0
Oracle Workspace Manager                   VALID        12.1.0.1.0
Oracle Database Catalog Views              UPGRADED     12.1.0.1.0
Oracle Database Packages and Types         UPGRADED     12.1.0.1.0
JServer JAVA Virtual Machine               VALID        12.1.0.1.0
Oracle XDK                                 VALID        12.1.0.1.0
Oracle Database Java Packages              VALID        12.1.0.1.0
OLAP Analytic Workspace                    VALID        12.1.0.1.0
Oracle OLAP API                            VALID        12.1.0.1.0

16 rows selected.

SQL>
```

As you can see, the previous two components are in Upgraded status. This can be corrected by running the utlrp.sql script several times.

```
SQL> @?/rdbms/admin/utlrp.sql
```

```
TIMESTAMP
----------------------------------------------------------------------COMP_TIMESTAMP UTLRP_
BGN   2016-05-22 10:25:23
. . .
. .
.

OBJECTS WITH ERRORS
-------------------
                0

DOC> The following query reports the number of errors caught during
DOC> recompilation. If this number is non-zero, please query the error
DOC> messages in the table UTL_RECOMP_ERRORS to see if any of these errors
DOC> are due to misconfiguration or resource constraints that must be
DOC> fixed before objects can compile successfully.
DOC>#

ERRORS DURING RECOMPILATION
---------------------------
                0


Function created.


PL/SQL procedure successfully completed.


Function dropped.

...Database user "SYS", database schema "APEX_040200", user# "117" 10:26:02
...Compiled 0 out of 2998 objects considered, 0 failed compilation 10:26:03
...263 packages
...255 package bodies
...453 tables
...11 functions
...16 procedures
...3 sequences
...458 triggers
...1322 indexes
...207 views
...0 libraries
...6 types
...0 type bodies
...0 operators
...0 index types
...Begin key object existence check 10:26:03
...Completed key object existence check 10:26:03
...Setting DBMS Registry 10:26:03
...Setting DBMS Registry Complete 10:26:03
...Exiting validate 10:26:03


PL/SQL procedure successfully completed.

SQL>
```

This script can be run more than once; now you will check the registry components' status.

```
SQL> select comp_name,status,version from dba_registry;
```

```
COMP_NAME                               STATUS        VERSION
--------------------------------------- ----------    ---------------------------------
Oracle Application Express              VALID         4.2.0.00.27
OWB                                     VALID         11.2.0.4.0
Spatial                                 VALID         12.1.0.1.0
Oracle Multimedia                       VALID         12.1.0.1.0
Oracle XML Database                     VALID         12.1.0.1.0
Oracle Text                             VALID         12.1.0.1.0
Oracle Workspace Manager                VALID         12.1.0.1.0
Oracle Database Catalog Views           VALID         12.1.0.1.0
Oracle Database Packages and Types      VALID         12.1.0.1.0
JServer JAVA Virtual Machine            VALID         12.1.0.1.0
Oracle XDK                              VALID         12.1.0.1.0
Oracle Database Java Packages           VALID         12.1.0.1.0
OLAP Analytic Workspace                 VALID         12.1.0.1.0
Oracle OLAP API                         VALID         12.1.0.1.0

15 rows selected.
```

Summary

Customers may have various types of environments and various types of requirements based on criticality and availability. In this chapter, we explained how backups are useful for performing an upgrade as a fresh copy instead of disturbing the original database. The main reason to do this is so that if the upgrade fails with the backup copy, then immediately we can revert to the original database. In addition, we saw a few available options such as hot backup, cold backup, and logical backups in order to upgrade a database in a step-by-step manner.

CHAPTER 5

∎∎∎

Oracle Database Migration

Migration is the process of moving data from one database to another with changes in hardware, software, storage types, and so on. It is kind of like introducing your data to a new system. In Chapter 2 we discussed database upgrades where you just upgrade your database to a higher version, with no changes in hardware or the underlying platform. But that is not always the situation; besides upgrading, you may need to move to a different environment. This migration could be because of business needs such as mergers or acquisitions, to improve performance, or to reduce the cost or requirements of the application. Fortunately, Oracle has provided a rich set of tools and utilities for moving data across systems. This chapter gives you an overview of the different migration options provided by Oracle.

The following are the most commonly used migration methods:

- Export/import

- Data Pump

- Transportable tablespaces (TTS)

- GoldenGate

- Create Table as Select (CTAS)

- RMAN convert database

- Data Guard heterogeneous primary and standby

- Streams replication

As we discussed in Chapter 2, these methods either move data and the dictionary or extract data from the source database and import it into the target database. When we say *target database*, we mean a new database that has been created on the target migration server with the required Oracle database version. We will discuss each migration method and show examples.

Traditional Export/Import

Traditional export/import was commonly used to move data across databases on different platforms prior to Oracle 9*i*. Using this method, data can be exported and imported into any platform. The target database can have different hardware and software configurations. For example, an export dump taken on Windows can be imported into a database located on Solaris Sparc. There is no limitation on the platforms. In Chapter 2, you saw this method of database upgrade. In this chapter, we talk about how a database can be migrated across platforms using this method.

© Y V Ravikumar, K M Krishnakumar and Nassyam Basha 2017
N. Basha et al., *Oracle Database Upgrade and Migration Methods*, DOI 10.1007/978-1-4842-2328-4_5

Traditional export/import uses the exp utility to take an export backup. The backup taken by the exp utility is called a *dump*. It is a binary format file, and it can be imported by Oracle's imp utility. These exp and imp utilities are installed by default with the software installation, and they will be located in the $ORACLE_HOME/bin folder.

When the dump is getting imported, the imp utility internally performs all the required conversion. Endian format and character set conversion will be performed by imp internally. Since only the user data is extracted as the dump, this dump can be imported on a higher-version database. This means the dump taken on the 10*g* database can be imported on the 12*c* database. At the same time, the dump taken from the higher-version exp utility cannot be imported using the lower-version imp utility. This means the dump taken from the 11*g* database export utility cannot be imported on the 10*g* database.

An export can be taken at different levels, including the object level (tables, table partitions, and their dependent objects), schema level (all objects of schema), tablespace level (transportable tablespaces), and database level.

The export and import utilities can work on the client side and the server side. If you install the Oracle database client, these utilities will get installed. exp and imp can connect to the database server from the client to export or import the database. This means from the client machine you can extract the data from the server and create a dump file at the client machine.

Export/import is commonly used to properly convert the data for the new character set. But note that the target character set could be with the same character set or a superset of the source database character set otherwise data corruption may happen. Suppose you are migrating from character set A to character set B through export/import and there are some characters in the source that are not present in target character set B; then the replacement characters will be used. If character set B is a superset of character set A, then this issue will not occur.

Let's discuss the migration steps with an example.

- *Source*: Oracle database 10.2.0.5.0

- *Platform*: Linux x86-64

You want to migrate this database to a Solaris Sparc x64-bit server.

First you need to install the 11.2.0.3.0 software on the target server and create a new database.

Check the source and target character set, as shown here:

```
SQL> select value from NLS_DATABASE_PARAMETERS where parameter = 'NLS_CHARACTERSET';
VALUE
--------------------------------------------------------------------------------
UTF8
Destination database 11.2.0.3.0 characterset
SQL> select value from NLS_DATABASE_PARAMETERS where parameter = 'NLS_CHARACTERSET'   ;
VALUE
--------------------------------------------------------------------------------
AL32UTF8
```

The character set AL32UTF8 is a superset of the character set UTF8. So, exporting/importing between the source and target databases is possible.

Export

Here you have planned to migrate the whole database to the Solaris server. Hence, take an export backup at the database level in the Linux server.

The export/import compatibility matrix (the matrix table is available in Chapter 2) has been verified. The 11.2.0.3 database can import the dump taken by the 10.2.0.5.0 export utility.

To take a full-database export, the user doing the export should have the Exp_full_database role.

```
$ exp system/<password> file=10gexpdump.dmp log=10gexpdump.log buffer=100000 statistics=none
consistent=y filesize=100m
```

Here are the parameters:

- buffer: This specifies the size in bytes of the buffer used to fetch the rows. It is operating system–dependent. If it has a value of 0, then the export fetches only one row at a time.

- consistent: This makes it so that the data extracted by the export is consistent to a single point in time and doesn't change during the execution of export. The database will need sufficient undo to be able to support this option.

- filesize: This specifies the maximum size of export dump files. Once this threshold size is reached, the export will continue into another file. Export/import supports writing and reading from multiple dump files. Using this parameter dump, files can be placed into multiple locations. Since it creates multiple output files, you can use the %U option with file name parameters like file=10gexpdump%U.dmp. The output will look like 10gexpdump01.dmp, 10gexpdump02.dmp, and so on.

Output

Here's the output:

```
Connected to: Oracle Database 10g Enterprise Edition Release 10.2.0.5.0 - 64bit Production
With the Partitioning, OLAP, Data Mining and Real Application Testing options
Export done in US7ASCII character set and AL16UTF16 NCHAR character set
server uses UTF8 character set (possible charset conversion)

About to export the entire database ...
. exporting tablespace definitions
. exporting profiles
. exporting user definitions
. exporting roles
. exporting resource costs
. exporting rollback segment definitions
. exporting database links
. exporting sequence numbers
. exporting directory aliases
. exporting context namespaces
. exporting foreign function library names
. exporting PUBLIC type synonyms
. exporting private type synonyms
. exporting object type definitions
. exporting system procedural objects and actions
. exporting pre-schema procedural objects and actions
. exporting cluster definitions
. about to export SYSTEM's tables via Conventional Path ...
.
.
.
```

```
. . exporting table                    SALGRADE         5 rows exported
. exporting synonyms
. exporting views
. exporting referential integrity constraints
. exporting stored procedures
. exporting operators
. exporting indextypes
. exporting bitmap, functional and extensible indexes
. exporting posttables actions
. exporting triggers
. exporting materialized views
. exporting snapshot logs
. exporting job queues
. exporting refresh groups and children
. exporting dimensions
. exporting post-schema procedural objects and actions
. exporting user history table
. exporting default and system auditing options
. exporting statistics
Export terminated successfully without warnings.
```

Import

Copy the export dump to the target Solaris Sparc x64-bit server. Start the target 11.2.0.3.0 database.

Perform the import as follows:

```
$imp system/manager file=10expdmp.dmp log=10to11g.log buffer=100000 commit=y compile=y
constraints=y destroy=y full=y
```

Here are the parameters:

- **commit**: This specifies whether it should commit after each array insert. By default, the import commits only after loading each table.

- **buffer**: This determines the number of rows in an array inserted by the import. Its value denotes the size of the array in bytes.

- **compile**: This specifies whether the import will compile the procedure, function, or package during the import.

- **constraints**: This specifies whether the table constraints have to be imported. By default it will have a value of yes.

- **destroy**: The export contains the datafile names used in each tablespace. Specifying destroy=y directs the import to include the reuse option in the datafile clause of the create tablespace statement. This means the existing datafile in the target will be destroyed and reused by the import.

Output

Here's the output:

```
imp system/manager file=10expdmp.dmp log=10to11g1.log buffer=100000 commit=y compile=y
constraints=y destroy=y full=y ignore=y
import server uses AL32UTF8 character set (possible charset conversion)
IMP-00046: using FILESIZE value from export file of 104857600
. importing SYSTEM's objects into SYSTEM
.
.
.
. importing SYS's objects into SYS
. importing SYSMAN's objects into SYSMAN
. importing SYSTEM's objects into SYSTEM
. importing SYSMAN's objects into SYSMAN
. importing SYS's objects into SYS
. importing SYSTEM's objects into SYSTEM
. importing OUTLN's objects into OUTLN
. importing OLAPSYS's objects into OLAPSYS
. importing SYSMAN's objects into SYSMAN
. importing SYSTEM's objects into SYSTEM
About to enable constraints...
. importing OLAPSYS's objects into OLAPSYS
. importing SYSTEM's objects into SYSTEM
. importing OLAPSYS's objects into OLAPSYS
. importing SYSMAN's objects into SYSMAN
. importing SCOTT's objects into SCOTT
Import terminated successfully without warnings.
```

The import identifies that the export dump has a different character set and verifies whether it is possible to convert the character set according to the target. If it is possible, then it proceeds to import the dump. Or it will throw an error.

Data Pump

Until Oracle 9*i*, the export/import method was used to take a logical backup of the database. In 10*g* Oracle introduced a power logical backup tool called Data Pump. It is a server-side utility and has no client-side functionality like exp/imp does. This means the backup and restore can be initiated only on the database server. You already saw how this utility is useful for database upgrades in Chapter 2. In this section, we will discuss how this tool can be used for database migrations.

As you know, migration means moving a database to a different environment having a different platform with different hardware and software configurations. Like the traditional export/import, Data Pump has export/import utilities, called expdp and impdp, to do the export and import of objects. Data Pump is the next-generation export/import tool from Oracle. These utilities are created when the database software is installed, and they are located in the $ORACLE_HOME/bin directory. expdp extracts the logical objects from the database and creates a dump file. This dump file gets created at the specified directory object location. But remember, these dumps will be readable only by impdp. The user who invokes expdp should have read and write access to the directory object or expdp will fail.

As part of the migration activity, you can import the dump into a higher-version database. In general, the expdp version should be lower or equivalent to the impdp version, and the impdp version should ideally match the destination database's version. The backup taken by the higher-version expdp utility cannot be imported by the lower-version impdp. But this can be overcome with the VERSION parameter. By specifying the VERSION parameter while executing expdp, the backup will be created compatible to the specified database version. Suppose you are using a 10.2 database and you want to import its objects into the 10.1 database; then with expdb, you can specify VERSION=10.1. This will take the export of objects that are applicable to the 10.1 version. This means you can move databases between different database versions.

Data Pump will perform the required character set conversions during the import. Like the traditional export/import, Data Pump can take backups at the object level, schema level, and tablespace level. But Data Pump works differently compared to a traditional export/import.

Data Pump Working Process

When expdp is invoked by a user, it connects to the database by using the Data Pump API. Once a connection is established, a foreground process will be created at the database server level. This process creates a master control process (MCP) and advanced queues (AQ). The MCP is created for each Data Pump export and import job, and AQ will be used for communication between the processes. The MCP creates a pool of active worker processes to complete the job. The number of active processes depends on the parallelism defined for expdp execution. The MCP controls the Data Pump job by communicating with the client, performing logging operations, creating active worker process, and so on. This MCP divides the Data Pump job into multiple jobs and hands them over to the active worker process. The MCP has a process named ora_dmnn_<ORACLE_SID>, and the active worker process has a process named ora_dwnn_<ORACLE_SID>. You could see these processes get created once Data Pump execution starts, and they will expire once the job is completed.

During the expdp operation, a master table will be maintained in the schema that invokes the expdp utility. This table maintains one row per object with status information. If the operation is failed/suspended in between, Data Pump uses this table to restart the job. The table maintains all the information about the job; hence, it can be considered the heart of the Data Pump operation. This master table will be loaded into the export dump as the last step of the export activity, and then it will be removed from the schema. impdp will load this master table first into the schema that has invoked the import. The master table information will be used to sequence the objects that are getting imported.

Let's discuss the Data Pump features, and then we'll walk you through a migration procedure with an example.

Features

Here are the features:

- Data Pump can execute the export in parallel. The desired number of parallel processes can be specified.

    Note: Parallel export threads are possible only with Oracle Enterprise Edition. For other editions, the only degree of parallelism is one.

- It has the ability to detach and attach a job.

- It can restart a failed job.

- ESTIMATE_OPTION can be used to estimate the required disk space before the import.

- The NETWORK_LINK parameter can be used to get the data directly from the source database through database links. This avoids creating the dump file on disk and then transferring to the target system.

- It has the option to take the export backup for the old database version through the VERSION parameter. But this allows it to go back until version 10.1.

Example

Here's an example:

- *Source*: Oracle database 10.2.0.5.0

- *Platform*: Linux x86-64

- *Target*: Oracle database 11.2.0.3.0

- *Platform*: Solaris Sparc 64-bit server

Say you want to migrate this database to the Solaris Sparc x64-bit server platform. expdp has two steps.

1) In the source database server, create a physical directory to store an expdp dump and create a logical directory in the database mapping to that physical directory.

2) The physical directory in the source database is /u01/app/oracle/backup. The directory should have the proper permission to write dumps into that.

```
SQL> create directory datapump_dir as '/u01/app/oracle/backup';
Directory created.
```

In case expdp is called by different user then grant read, write permissions on this directory

```
SQL> grant read, write on directory datapump_dir to <User>;
```

2) Invoke expdp with the user that as the DATAPUMP_EXP_FULL_DATABASE role to take a full-database backup.

```
expdp system/manager directory=datapump_dir  dumpfile=10gexpdp.dmp
logfile=10gexpdp.log full=y
Starting "SYSTEM"."SYS_EXPORT_FULL_01": system/******** directory=datapump_dir
dumpfile=10gexpdp.dmp logfile=10gexpdp.log full=y
Estimate in progress using BLOCKS method...
Processing object type DATABASE_EXPORT/SCHEMA/TABLE/TABLE_DATA
Total estimation using BLOCKS method: 8.375 MB
Processing object type DATABASE_EXPORT/TABLESPACE
Processing object type DATABASE_EXPORT/PROFILE
Processing object type DATABASE_EXPORT/SYS_USER/USER
Processing object type DATABASE_EXPORT/SCHEMA/USER
Processing object type DATABASE_EXPORT/ROLE
Processing object type DATABASE_EXPORT/GRANT/SYSTEM_GRANT/PROC_SYSTEM_GRANT
Processing object type DATABASE_EXPORT/SCHEMA/GRANT/SYSTEM_GRANT
Processing object type DATABASE_EXPORT/SCHEMA/ROLE_GRANT
Processing object type DATABASE_EXPORT/SCHEMA/DEFAULT_ROLE
Processing object type DATABASE_EXPORT/SCHEMA/TABLESPACE_QUOTA
Processing object type DATABASE_EXPORT/RESOURCE_COST
Processing object type DATABASE_EXPORT/TRUSTED_DB_LINK
Processing object type DATABASE_EXPORT/SCHEMA/SEQUENCE/SEQUENCE
Processing object type DATABASE_EXPORT/SCHEMA/SEQUENCE/GRANT/OWNER_GRANT/OBJECT_GRANT
.
.
```

```
. . exported "SYSTEM"."SQLPLUS_PRODUCT_PROFILE"              0 KB        0 rows
. . exported "TSMSYS"."SRS$"                                 0 KB        0 rows
Master table "SYSTEM"."SYS_EXPORT_FULL_01" successfully loaded/unloaded
******************************************************************************
Dump file set for SYSTEM.SYS_EXPORT_FULL_01 is:
  /u01/app/oracle/backup/10gexpdp.dmp
Job "SYSTEM"."SYS_EXPORT_FULL_01" successfully completed.
```

You can observe the following information from the previous log:

- The job SYS_EXPORT_FULL_01 has been created for the export.

- The master table SYS_EXPORT_FULL_01 has been created and loaded into the dump.

- The total size for the dump has been estimated to be 8.375 MB before starting the dump.

```
Export dump would have been created at /u01/app/oracle/backup
```

Import

The utility impdp performs the Data Pump import activity. It is a superset of the traditional imp utility. It has all the features of the traditional import, and it has additional features such as the ability to exclude/include certain objects during import, import directly from the source database through a database link (which avoids exporting data), import with parallel active workers, remap the datafiles in case the target database allows a different directory structure, remap schemas, and transport the datafiles of the other database. The import can operate only on the dump exported by expdp. It will not work with a backup created with the traditional export utility.

As part of this migration example, install the 11.2.0.3.0 software on the target server and create a new database. The expdp dump has been copied to the target server. The database logical directory has been created in the target server to access the dump.

For importing the full database, impdp also should be invoked by a user with the role IMP_FULL_DATABASE_ROLE. The utility impdp will perform the character set conversion automatically. It is advisable to have the same target database character set as the source or have it be a superset of the source database character set. When a target is not the same or a superset of the source character set, then as part of the character set conversion, it needs to replace characters available in the target character set, which may create some logical data corruption.

We will discuss some of the possible changes that impdp can do during import.

Partition

Suppose in the migrating environment, you don't have Oracle partitioning option. For example, Oracle Standard Edition is not licensed for the partitioning option. So, during migration, either the existing partitions have to be merged or each individual partition can become an individual table. This is possible using the impdp option.

Example

For example, the source has a table called Test that has three partitions. During export, it exported all the partitions.

```
. . exported "USERTEST"."TEST":"P1_MAX"               131.7 KB      9981 rows
. . exported "USERTEST"."TEST":"P1"                    5.312 KB         9 rows
. . exported "USERTEST"."TEST":"P2"                    5.320 KB        10 rows
```

PARTITION_OPTIONS can be specified along with the IMPDP command. It has three options.

- None: There will be no conversion, and the same structure will be imported. This is the default.
- Merge: This merges all the partitions of a table.
- DEPARTITION: This converts each partition into a separate table.

Merge

Here's the code:

```
$impdp system/manager directory=datapump_dir dumpfile=user11g.dmp PARTITION_OPTIONS=merge
.
.
.
. . imported "USERTEST"."TEST":"P1_MAX"                   131.7 KB     9981 rows
. . imported "USERTEST"."TEST1":"P_MAX"                    131.7 KB     9981 rows
. . imported "USERTEST"."TEST":"P1"                        5.312 KB        9 rows
. . imported "USERTEST"."TEST":"P2"                        5.320 KB       10 rows
. . imported "USERTEST"."TEST1":"P1"                       5.312 KB        9 rows
. . imported "USERTEST"."TEST1":"P2"                       5.320 KB       10 rows

SQL> select table_name, partitioned from user_tables;

TABLE_NAME                      PAR
------------------------------- ---
TEST1                           NO
TEST                            NO
```

If you want to remove the partition for a specific table, you can use the TABLES argument during import.

Departition

Here's the code:

```
impdp system/manager directory=datapump_dir dumpfile=user11g.dmp partition_
options=departition
```

```
Departition option is used in case we want to convert each individual partition into
separate tables during import.
Starting " USERTEST"."SYS_IMPORT_FULL_02":  USERTEST/******** directory=datapump_dir
dumpfile=user11g.dmp partition_options=departition
Processing object type TABLE_EXPORT/TABLE/TABLE
Processing object type TABLE_EXPORT/TABLE/TABLE_DATA
. . imported " USERTEST "."TEST11G_P1"                     5.515 KB        9 rows
. . imported " USERTEST "."TEST11G_P2"                     5.523 KB       10 rows
. . imported " USERTEST "."TEST11G_P_MAX"                  131.9 KB     9981 rows
Job " USERTEST"."SYS_IMPORT_FULL_02" successfully completed
```

Verify the table creation through the User_tables view.

```
Sql> select table_name,partitioned from user_tables;

TABLE_NAME                       PAR
------------------------------   ---
TEST11G_P_MAX                    NO
TEST11G_P2                       NO
TEST11G_P1                       NO
```

REMAP_DATAFILES

If the migration environment doesn't have the same directory structure, then REMAP_DATAFILE can be used to create a datafile at a new location during the import.

```
DIRECTORY=imp_dp
FULL=YES
DUMPFILE= db12c.dmp
REMAP_DATAFILE="'/u01/app/oracle/oradata/TARKK1/tts01.dbf':'/u02/app/oracle/oradata/TARKK2/
tts01.dbf'"

$impdp userid=system/<password> parfile=db12c.par
```

This import will create a datafile in the /u02 directory. Alternatively, you can pre-create the tablespace, and it can be used for import.

REUSE_DATAFILES

This option can be used if the destination already has a datafile and you want to reuse it during the migration. During the import, the tablespace creation will reuse the existing datafile.

```
REUSE_DATAFILES=YES|NO

$impdp userid=\'sys as sysdba\'  directory=imp_dp dumpfile=full_db12c.dmp reuse_
datafiles=YES logfile=full_db_imp.log full=y
```

REMAP_TABLESPACE

When importing objects through impdp, it expects a tablespace name that is the same as the source database. If the migration environment doesn't have tablespaces with the same name, then the import will fail. For example, if the migration environment has a different naming convention for a tablespace, then the object import will fail as the expected source tablespace is not present. You can use Remap_tablespace to solve this.

Example

The source database has objects located in the tablespace source_tbs, and the target database has the tablespace dest_tbs and objects need to be imported into dest_tbs. So, use remap_tablespace=source_tbs:dest_tbs with impdp.

```
$impdp system/manager directory=imp_dp dumpfile=impdp_test.dmp remap_tablespace=source_
tbs:dest_tbs
```

```
Master table "SYSTEM"."SYS_IMPORT_FULL_01" successfully loaded/unloaded
Starting "SYSTEM"."SYS_IMPORT_FULL_01": system/********** directory=imp_dp dumpfile=impdp_
test.dmp remap_tablespace=source_tbs:dest_tbs
Processing object type TABLE_EXPORT/TABLE/TABLE
Processing object type TABLE_EXPORT/TABLE/TABLE_DATA
. . imported "SYSTEM"."IMP_TBS_TEST"                         5.070 KB        3 rows
Processing object type TABLE_EXPORT/TABLE/STATISTICS/TABLE_STATISTICS
Processing object type TABLE_EXPORT/TABLE/STATISTICS/MARKER
Job "SYSTEM"."SYS_IMPORT_FULL_01" successfully completed
```

Transportable Tablespaces

Transportable tablespaces (TTS) is one of the methods used for migrating databases to a different platform. You already saw its prerequisites and the limitations of this method in Chapter 2. There you performed the TTS steps to upgrade a database to a higher version. You also considered the source and the target on the same platform. In this chapter, we discuss how you can use TTS to migrate a database from one platform to a different platform. The target database version can be the same version or higher. In the TTS method, you copy/move tablespaces from the source database to the target database. When copying/moving the tablespaces, it will be in read-only mode. One big advantage of the TTS method is it can be used even though the source and target platforms have different endian formats, with a translation step to assist you. Let's discuss the migration steps with an example.

- *Source platform*: Solaris Sparc 64-bit; endian format: Big

- *Target platform*: Solaris operating system,(x86); endian format: Little

- *Source database version*: 11.2.0.3.0

- *Target database version*: 12.1.0.2.0

- *Tablespace to be transported*: TTS1

Here you will see a database migration along with an upgrade.

We will not spend much time here on the TTS concepts and the prerequisites because these were discussed in detail in Chapter 2. We are assuming the source has met all the prerequisites for TTS. The following are the migrate steps:

1) Check the self-integrity of the chosen tablespace.

   ```
   SQL> EXEC SYS.DBMS_TTS.TRANSPORT_SET_CHECK(ts_list => 'TTS1',incl_constraints =>
   TRUE);

   PL/SQL procedure successfully completed.

   SQL> Select * from transport_set_violations;
   no rows selected
   ```

2) Create the logical directory to store the metadata dump.

   ```
   SQL> create directory tts_dir as '/u01/app/oracle/backup ';
   Directory created.
   ```

3) Place the tablespace in read-only mode

```
SQL> alter tablespace tts1 read only;
Tablespace altered.
```

4) Take a metadata dump of the chosen tablespace tts1.

```
expdp userid=system/manager directory=tts_dir transport_tablespaces=tts1
dumpfile=tablespace_metadata.dmp logfile=tablespace_metadata.log

Export: Release 11.2.0.3.0 - Production
Connected to: Oracle Database 11g Enterprise Edition Release 11.2.0.3.0 - 64bit
Production
With the Partitioning, OLAP, Data Mining and Real Application Testing options
Starting "SYSTEM"."SYS_EXPORT_TRANSPORTABLE_01":  userid=system/********
directory=tts_dir transport_tablespaces=tts1 dumpfile=tablespace_metadata.dmp
logfile=tablespace_metadata.log
Processing object type TRANSPORTABLE_EXPORT/PLUGTS_BLK
Processing object type TRANSPORTABLE_EXPORT/TABLE
Processing object type TRANSPORTABLE_EXPORT/POST_INSTANCE/PLUGTS_BLK
Master table "SYSTEM"."SYS_EXPORT_TRANSPORTABLE_01" successfully loaded/unloaded
******************************************************************************
Dump file set for SYSTEM.SYS_EXPORT_TRANSPORTABLE_01 is:
/u01/app/oracle/backup/tablespace_metadata.dmp
******************************************************************************
Datafiles required for transportable tablespace TTS1:
/u01/app/oracle/oradata/Sol12c/tts1.dbf
Job "SYSTEM"."SYS_EXPORT_TRANSPORTABLE_01" successfully completed
```

5) Copy the tablespace datafiles and metadata dump to the target server.

6) Convert the copied datafile because the endian format is different. The conversion happens through the RMAN convert datafile command. Here you specify from which platform the datafile has been copied. Note that the conversion is happening on the target server.

```
RMAN> CONVERT DATAFILE
        '/u01/app/oracle/oradata/db12c/tts1.dbf'
        FROM PLATFORM="Solaris[tm] OE (64-bit)"
format  '/u01/app/oracle/oradata/db12c/tts_convert.dbf';

Starting conversion at target at 16-MAY-16
using channel ORA_DISK_1
channel ORA_DISK_1: starting datafile conversion
input file name /u01/app/oracle/oradata/Sol12c/tts1.dbf
converted datafile /u01/app/oracle/oradata/Sol12c/tts_convert.dbf
channel ORA_DISK_1: datafile conversion complete, elapsed time: 00:00:01
Finished conversion at target at 16-MAY-16
```

7) Import the metadata by specifying the converted datafile as an argument.

```
impdp userid=system/manager directory=tts_dir  dumpfile=tablespace_metadata.dmp
logfile=tablespace_metadata_imp.log transport_datafiles='/u01/app/oracle/oradata/
Sol12c/tts_convert.dbf'
Import: Release 12.1.0.2.0 - Production
Copyright (c) 1982, 2014, Oracle and/or its affiliates. All rights reserved.

Connected to: Oracle Database 12c Enterprise Edition Release 12.1.0.2.0 - 64bit
Production
With the Partitioning, OLAP, Advanced Analytics and Real Application Testing
options
Master table "SYSTEM"."SYS_IMPORT_TRANSPORTABLE_01" successfully loaded/unloaded
Source time zone version is 14 and target time zone version is 18.
Starting "SYSTEM"."SYS_IMPORT_TRANSPORTABLE_01":  userid=system/********
directory=tts_dir dumpfile=tablespace_metadata.dmp logfile=tablespace_metadata_
imp.log transport_datafiles=/u01/app/oracle/oradata/Sol12c/tts_convert.dbf
Processing object type TRANSPORTABLE_EXPORT/PLUGTS_BLK
Processing object type TRANSPORTABLE_EXPORT/TABLE
Processing object type TRANSPORTABLE_EXPORT/POST_INSTANCE/PLUGTS_BLK
Job "SYSTEM"."SYS_IMPORT_TRANSPORTABLE_01" successfully completed
```

In the previous exercise, the endian conversion happened on the target server. You converted the datafile according to the destination platform. Also, you transported the tablespace to a higher version on the target. This means you have performed an upgrade along with the migration. In this way, each individual datafile can be converted and plugged in to the target platform.

But remember, the TTS method will not move nonsegment objects such as PL/SQL procedures and packages. Those have to be manually created at the target database. For example, say the user has created a procedure in the source database, and the source code can be retrieved through this code:

```
select
  DBMS_METADATA.GET_DDL('PROCEDURE',uobj.object_name)
from
  user_objects uobj
where
  object_type = 'PROCEDURE';
```

The 12c database can also be a multitenant database, and the tablespace can be transported to a pluggable database.

In 12c TTS received a new feature: the datafile can be backed up as a backup set for transfer. Unlike the physical datafile, you copy this backup set. Taking the datafile as a backup set gives you many more benefits.

1) The backupset size will be smaller in size than the physical datafile copy because it will take a backup of only the used blocks.

2) It also enables you to use block compression to reduce the backup size.

    You will see the steps in detail. Say you move the tablespace from Linux to Solaris Sparc and both are 12c databases.

    1) Ensure all TTS prerequisites are met. The source and target database versions should be 12c.

    2) Place the tablespace in read-only mode.

3) Back up the tablespace to be transported through RMAN. Here you specify
   to which platform the datafile backup has to be taken. Also, you specify the
   Data Pump clause to indicate where the metadata dump of this tablespace
   should be created.

```
RMAN> BACKUP
TO PLATFORM 'Solaris Operating System (x86-64)'
FORMAT '/u01/app/oracle/tts_tbs.bkp'
DATAPUMP FORMAT '/u01/app/oracle/trans_ts_dmp%U%T.bck'
TABLESPACE tts12c;

Starting backup at 13-MAY-16
using target database control file instead of recovery catalog
allocated channel: ORA_DISK_1
channel ORA_DISK_1: SID=268 device type=DISK
Running TRANSPORT_SET_CHECK on specified tablespaces
TRANSPORT_SET_CHECK completed successfully

Performing export of metadata for specified tablespaces...
   EXPDP> Starting "SYS"."TRANSPORT_EXP_Linux12c ":
   EXPDP> Processing object type TRANSPORTABLE_EXPORT/PLUGTS_BLK
   EXPDP> Processing object type TRANSPORTABLE_EXPORT/STATISTICS/MARKER
   EXPDP> Processing object type TRANSPORTABLE_EXPORT/POST_INSTANCE/PLUGTS_BLK
   EXPDP> Master table "SYS"."TRANSPORT_EXP_Linux12c" successfully loaded/
unloaded
   EXPDP> ******************************************************************
***********
   EXPDP> Dump file set for SYS.TRANSPORT_EXP_ Linux12c is:
   EXPDP>    /u01/app/oracle/product/12.1.0.2.0/dbs/backup_tts_Linux12c_40546.
dmp
   EXPDP> ******************************************************************
***********
   EXPDP> Datafiles required for transportable tablespace TTS12C:
   EXPDP>    /u01/app/oracle/oradata/Linux12c/tts12c.dbf
   EXPDP> Job "SYS"."TRANSPORT_EXP_Linux12c" successfully completed
Export completed
channel ORA_DISK_1: starting full datafile backup set
channel ORA_DISK_1: specifying datafile(s) in backup set
input datafile file number=00005 name /u01/app/oracle/oradata/Linux12c/tts12c.
dbf
channel ORA_DISK_1: starting piece 1
channel ORA_DISK_1: finished piece 1
piece handle/u01/app/oracle/tts_tbs.bkp tag=TAG20160513T183531 comment=NONE
channel ORA_DISK_1: backup set complete, elapsed time: 00:00:01
channel ORA_DISK_1: starting full datafile backup set
input Data Pump dump file/u01/app/oracle/backup_tts_db12c_40546.dmp
channel ORA_DISK_1: starting piece 1
channel ORA_DISK_1: finished piece 1
piece handle/u01/app/oracle/trans_ts_dmp08r5gmcj_1_120160513.bkp
tag=TAG20160513T183531 comment=NONE
channel ORA_DISK_1: backup set complete, elapsed time: 00:00:01
```

4) Transport the backup sets to the target server.

5) Restore the backup at the target server using the RMAN restore command.
   Specify the dump file clause to import the metadata of the tablespace.

```
RMAN> RESTORE
2>      FOREIGN TABLESPACE tts12c to NEW
3>      FROM BACKUPSET '/u01/app/oracle/product/12.1.0.2.0/dbs/ tts_tbs.bkp'
4>      DUMP FILE FROM BACKUPSET '/u01/app/oracle/product/12.1.0.2.0/dbs/trans_
ts_dmp08r5gmcj_1_120160513.bck';

Starting restore at
using target database control file instead of recovery catalog
allocated channel: ORA_DISK_1
channel ORA_DISK_1: SID=25 device type=DISK

channel ORA_DISK_1: starting datafile backup set restore
channel ORA_DISK_1: specifying datafile(s) to restore from backup set
channel ORA_DISK_1: restoring all files in foreign tablespace TTS12C
channel ORA_DISK_1: reading from backup piece /u01/app/oracle/
product/12.1.0.2.0/dbs/tts_tbs.bkp
channel ORA_DISK_1: restoring foreign file 5 to /u01/app/oracle/oradata/db12c/
datafile/o1_mf_tts12c_cmd70mxt_.dbf
channel ORA_DISK_1: foreign piece handle/u01/app/oracle/product/12.1.0.2.0/
dbs/tts_tbs.bkp
channel ORA_DISK_1: restored backup piece 1
channel ORA_DISK_1: restore complete, elapsed time: 00:00:02
channel ORA_DISK_1: starting datafile backup set restore
channel ORA_DISK_1: specifying datafile(s) to restore from backup set
channel ORA_DISK_1: restoring Data Pump dump file to /u01/app/oracle/
product/12.1.0.2.0/dbs/backup_tts_db12c_98776.dmp
channel ORA_DISK_1: reading from backup piece /u01/app/oracle/
product/12.1.0.2.0/dbs/trans_ts_dmp08r5gmcj_1_120160513.bck
channel ORA_DISK_1: foreign piece handle /u01/app/oracle/product/12.1.0.2.0/
dbs/trans_ts_dmp08r5gmcj_1_120160513.bck
channel ORA_DISK_1: restored backup piece 1
channel ORA_DISK_1: restore complete, elapsed time: 00:00:03

Performing import of metadata...
    IMPDP> Master table "SYS"."TSPITR_IMP_Sol12c_aopw" successfully loaded/
unloaded
    IMPDP> Starting "SYS"."TSPITR_IMP_Sol12c_aopw":
    IMPDP> Processing object type TRANSPORTABLE_EXPORT/PLUGTS_BLK
    IMPDP> Processing object type TRANSPORTABLE_EXPORT/POST_INSTANCE/PLUGTS_BLK
    IMPDP> Job "SYS"."TSPITR_IMP_Sol12c_aopw" successfully completed Import
completed
```

In the previous example, you performed the conversion at the source server
itself using the To Platform option. You can also perform the conversion at the
target using the RMAN FOR TRANSPORT clause. On the source, take a backup of
tablespace tts12c using the For Transport option.

```
RMAN>
BACKUP
For transport
FORMAT '/u01/app/oracle/tts12c.bck'
DATAPUMP FORMAT '/u01/app/oracle/tts12c_dmp.bck'
TABLESPACE tts12c;
```

Copy the tablespace backup set and Data Pump backup set to the target server and restore it.

```
RMAN> RESTORE
2>     FOREIGN TABLESPACE TTS12c format '/u01/app/oracle/product/oradata/db12c/
tts12c.dbf'
3>     FROM BACKUPSET '/u01/app/oracle/product/12.1.0.2.0/dbs/ tts12c.bck'
4>     DUMP FILE FROM BACKUPSET '/u01/app/oracle/product/12.1.0.2.0/dbs/
tts12c_dmp.bck';
```

The conversion will happen at the target site, and the tablespace will be added to the target database.

Oracle GoldenGate

In this section we will demonstrate how to use Oracle GoldenGate to perform a database migration from the Oracle 11*g* R2 database to the Oracle 12*c* R1 pluggable database using the initial load in bulk load mode and Data Pump mode. The source database is running on Solaris 11 x86-64, and the target database is running on Oracle Enterprise Linux 6.

Environment Setup

Table 5-1 shows the setup.

Table 5-1. *GoldenGate Setup Details*

Source		Target	
OS	Solaris 11.3 x84-64	OS	Oracle Enterprise Linux 6.0
Oracle Database version	11.2.0.4 EE	Oracle Database version	12.1.0.2 EE
GoldenGate version	12.2.0.1.0	GoldenGate version	12.2.0.1.0
IP address	192.168.1.20	IP address	192.168.1.13
Database name	orcl2	Database name	orcl

Oracle GoldenGate Setup on the Source Database

You can download the Oracle GoldenGate 12*c* Solaris x86-64 distribution from the product page or from eDelivery. On the source machine, execute runInstaller from the Oracle GoldenGate 12*c* software kit, choose the Oracle GoldenGate for Oracle 11*g* option, and click the Next button as shown in Figure 5-1.

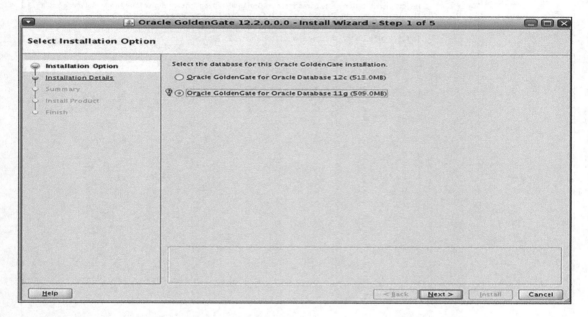

Figure 5-1. *GoldenGate installation option selection (11g)*

Choose the software location and specify the Oracle 11*g* database software home. The port by default is 7809; you can change this later. Click Next (Figure 5-2), and the installation will start.

229

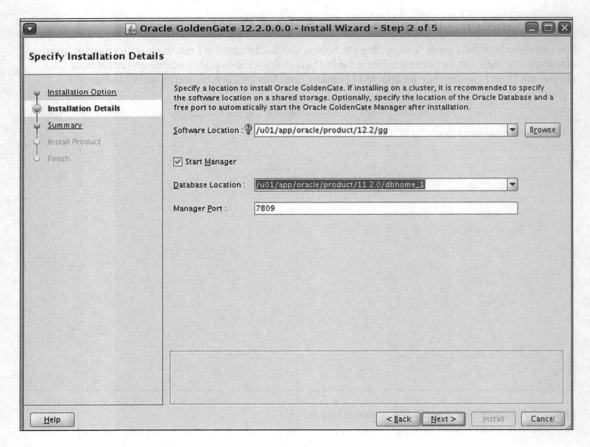

Figure 5-2. GoldenGate installation details on the source

Oracle GoldenGate Setup on the Target Database

Similarly, you can download the Oracle GoldenGate 12c Linux x86-64 distribution from the product page or from eDelivery. On the source machine, execute runInstaller from the GoldenGate 12c software kit, choose the Oracle GoldenGate for Oracle 12c option this time, and click the Next button (Figure 5-3).

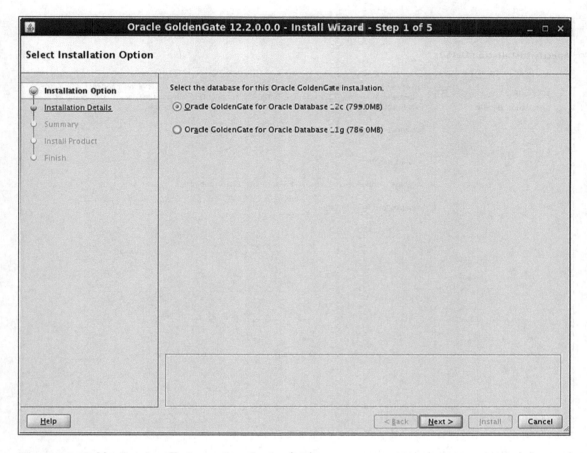

Figure 5-3. *GoldenGate installation option selection (12c)*

Choose the software location and specify the Oracle 12*c* database software home. The port by default is 7809 (Figure 5-4); you can change this later also.

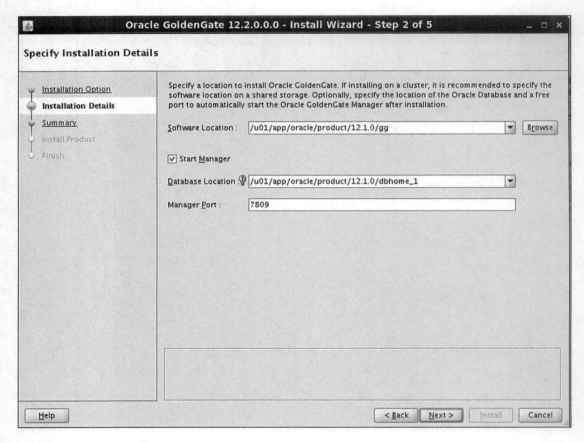

Figure 5-4. *GoldenGate installation details on target*

Click Next and the installation will start. After the installation is complete, click the Finish button.

Configure Oracle GoldenGate on the Source Database

Oracle GoldenGate 12*c* replication is using a mechanism that interferes with Oracle log mining. The log information must be complete; hence, the database must be in force-logging mode with supplemental logging enabled as follows:

```
oracle@orcl2:/u01$ sqlplus / as sysdba

SQL*Plus: Release 11.2.0.4.0 Production on Wed Jun 8 09:26:43 2016
Copyright (c) 1982, 2013, Oracle.  All rights reserved.
Connected to:
Oracle Database 11g Enterprise Edition Release 11.2.0.4.0 - 64bit Production
With the Partitioning, OLAP, Data Mining and Real Application Testing options
SQL> ALTER DATABASE FORCE LOGGING;
Database altered.

SQL> ALTER DATABASE ADD SUPPLEMENTAL LOG DATA (ALL) COLUMNS;
Database altered.
```

To maintain GoldenGate management on the source, you will create a user named GGS_ADMIN and grant all the necessary privileges as follows:

```
SQL> create tablespace ggs_admin_tbs
datafile '/u02/oradata/ORCL/ggs_admin_tbs01.dbf' size 100m
autoextend on next 100m maxsize unlimited;
Tablespace created.

SQL> create user ggs_admin identified by ggs_admin default tablespace ggs_admin_tbs;
User created.

SQL> grant dba to ggs_admin;
Grant succeeded.

SQL> conn ggs_admin/ggs_admin
Connected.

SQL> exec dbms_goldengate_auth.grant_admin_privilege('GGS_ADMIN');
PL/SQL procedure successfully completed.
```

Changes in Parameters in the Source Database

Here is the code:

```
SQL> alter system set enable_goldengate_replication=true scope=both;
System altered.
```

Usually during migration it's best to refrain from creating new objects such as tables or packages. However, sometimes this is not possible. Therefore, you must add in this particular case DDL replication support to the source database. The scripts are interactive, asking for the GoldenGate owner. In this case, this will be ggs_admin.

Execute the following scripts from the GoldenGate software installation path:

```
SQL> @marker_setup.sql
```

Marker Setup Script

You will be prompted for the name of a schema for the Oracle GoldenGate database objects.

■ **Note**   The ggs_admin schema must be created prior to running this script.

Enter the Oracle GoldenGate schema name: ggs_admin.

```
Marker setup table script complete, running verification script...
```

Enter the name of a schema for the GoldenGate database objects.
Set the schema name to GGS_ADMIN.

```
MARKER TABLE
```

```
----------------------------
OK

MARKER SEQUENCE
----------------------------
OK

Script complete.
SQL>
```

SQL> @ddl_setup.sql
Oracle GoldenGate DDL Replication setup script

Verify that the current user has the privileges to install DDL replication.
You will be prompted for the name of a schema for the Oracle GoldenGate database objects.

■ **Note**   For an Oracle 10*g* source, the system recycle bin must be disabled. For Oracle 11*g* and later, it can
be enabled.

The schema must be created prior to running this script.

```
Enter Oracle GoldenGate schema name:GGS_ADMIN

Working, please wait ...
Spooling to file ddl_setup_spool.txt

Checking for sessions that are holding locks on Oracle Golden Gate metadata tables ...
Check complete.
Using GGS_ADMIN as a Oracle GoldenGate schema name.
Working, please wait ...

DDL replication setup script complete, running verification script...
```

Enter the name of a schema for the GoldenGate database objects.

```
Setting schema name to GGS_ADMIN

CLEAR_TRACE STATUS:

Line/pos                                 Error
-------------------------------------    -------------------------------------
No errors                                No errors

CREATE_TRACE STATUS:

Line/pos                                 Error
-------------------------------------    -------------------------------------
No errors                                No errors
```

TRACE_PUT_LINE STATUS:

Line/pos	Error
No errors	No errors

INITIAL_SETUP STATUS:

Line/pos	Error
No errors	No errors

DDLVERSIONSPECIFIC PACKAGE STATUS:

Line/pos	Error
No errors	No errors

DDLREPLICATION PACKAGE STATUS:

Line/pos	Error
No errors	No errors

DDLREPLICATION PACKAGE BODY STATUS:
Line/pos	Error
No errors	No errors

DDL IGNORE TABLE

OK

DDL IGNORE LOG TABLE

OK

DDLAUX PACKAGE STATUS:
Line/pos	Error
No errors	No errors

DDLAUX PACKAGE BODY STATUS:
Line/pos	Error
No errors	No errors

SYS.DDLCTXINFO PACKAGE STATUS:
Line/pos	Error
No errors	No errors

```
SYS.DDLCTXINFO PACKAGE BODY STATUS:
Line/pos                                Error
-------------------------------------   ----------------------------------------------------
No errors                               No errors

DDL HISTORY TABLE
-------------------------
OK

DDL HISTORY TABLE(1)
-----------------------------
OK

DDL DUMP TABLES
-------------------------
OK

DDL DUMP COLUMNS
----------------------------
OK

DDL DUMP LOG GROUPS
----------------------------------
OK

DDL DUMP PARTITION
----------------------------------
OK

DDL DUMP PRIMARY KEYS
------------------------------------
OK

DDL SEQUENCE
----------------------
OK

GGS_TEMP_COLS
------------------------
OK

GGS_TEMP_UK
---------------------
OK

DDL TRIGGER CODE STATUS:

Line/pos                                Error
-------------------------------------   ------------------------------------------
No errors                               No errors

DDL TRIGGER INSTALL STATUS
```

```
----------------------------------------
OK

DDL TRIGGER RUNNING STATUS
-------------------------------------------
ENABLED

STAYMETADATA IN TRIGGER
-------------------------------------
OFF

DDL TRIGGER SQL TRACING
------------------------------------
0

DDL TRIGGER TRACE LEVEL
------------------------------------
NONE

LOCATION OF DDL TRACE FILE
-----------------------------------------------------------------------------------
/u01/app/oracle/diag/rdbms/orcl/ORCL/trace/ggs_ddl_trace.log
```

Analyzing installation status...

```
VERSION OF DDL REPLICATION
-----------------------------------------------------------------
OGGCORE_12.2.0.1.0_PLATFORMS_151211.1401

TATUS OF DDL REPLICATION
-----------------------------------------------------------------------------------
SUCCESSFUL installation of DDL Replication software components

Script complete.
SQL>

SQL> @role_setup.sql
GGS Role setup script
```

This script will drop and re-create the role GGS_GGSUSER_ROLE.

To use a different role name, quit this script and then edit the params.sql script to change the gg_role parameter to the preferred name. (Do not run the script.)

You will be prompted for the name of a schema for the GoldenGate database objects.

■ **Note** The ggs_admin schema must be created prior to running this script.

```
Enter GoldenGate schema name:GGS_ADMIN
Wrote file role_setup_set.txt

PL/SQL procedure successfully completed.
Role setup script complete
```

237

Grant this role to each user assigned to the extract, GGSCI, and manager processes, by using the following SQL command:

```
GRANT GGS_GGSUSER_ROLE TO <loggedUser>
```

where <loggedUser> is the user assigned to the GoldenGate processes.
```
SQL> grant ggs_ggsuser_role to ggs_admin;
Grant succeeded.
```

SQL> @ddl_enable.sql
```
Trigger altered.
```

You also add support to sequence replication as follows:

SQL> @sequence.sql

Enter the name of a schema for the GoldenGate database objects.

```
GGS_ADMIN
Setting schema name to GGS_ADMIN

UPDATE_SEQUENCE STATUS:
Line/pos                                    Error
----------------------------------------    ----------------------------------------
No errors                                   No errors

GETSEQFLUSH
Line/pos                                    Error
----------------------------------------    ----------------------------------------
No errors                                   No errors

SEQTRACE
Line/pos                                    Error
----------------------------------------    ----------------------------------------
No errors                                   No errors

REPLICATE_SEQUENCE STATUS:
Line/pos                                    Error
----------------------------------------    ----------------------------------------
No errors                                   No errors

STATUS OF SEQUENCE SUPPORT
--------------------------------------------------------------------------------
SUCCESSFUL installation of Oracle Sequence Replication support
```

The next step is the preparation of the source schema for replication. You need practically to add the first supplemental logging on the table level. This will enable you to complete the logging information regarding future transactions that will be issued against the table. To perform this operation, you should connect to the database first using DBLOGIN and then execute the command for adding the supplemental log on the table level, which is the ADDTRAN command.

```
GGSCI (orcl2 as ggs_admin@ORCL) 4> DBLOGIN USERID ggs_admin, PASSWORD ggs_admin
```

```
GGSCI (orcl2 as ggs_admin@ORCL) 4> add trandata scott.borus
2016-06-09 10:25:12  WARNING OGG-06439
```

No unique key is defined for the table BONUS. All viable columns will be used to represent the key but may not guarantee uniqueness. KEYCOLS may be used to define the key.

The logging of supplemental redo log data is already enabled for the table SCOTT.BONUS.

```
TRANDATA for instantiation CSN has been added on table 'SCOTT.BONUS'.
GGSCI (orcl2 as ggs_admin@ORCL) 5>

GGSCI (orcl2 as ggs_admin@ORCL) 7> add trandata scott.dept

Logging of supplemental redo data enabled for table SCOTT.DEPT.
TRANDATA for scheduling columns has been added on table 'SCOTT.DEPT'.
TRANDATA for instantiation CSN has been added on table 'SCOTT.DEPT'.
GGSCI (orcl2 as ggs_admin@ORCL) 8>

GGSCI (orcl2 as ggs_admin@ORCL) 10> add trandata scott.emp
Logging of supplemental redo log data is already enabled for table SCOTT.EMP.
TRANDATA for instantiation CSN has been added on table 'SCOTT.EMP'.
GGSCI (orcl2 as ggs_admin@ORCL) 11>

GGSCI (orcl2 as ggs_admin@ORCL) 12> add trandata scott.salgrade

2016-06-09 10:28:47  WARNING OGG-06439  No unique key is defined for table SALGRADE. All
viable columns will be used to represent the key, but may not guarantee uniqueness. KEYCOLS
may be used to define the key.

Logging of supplemental redo data enabled for table SCOTT.SALGRADE.
TRANDATA for scheduling columns has been added on table 'SCOTT.SALGRADE'.
TRANDATA for instantiation CSN has been added on table 'SCOTT.SALGRADE'.
GGSCI (orcl2 as ggs_admin@ORCL) 13>
```

■ **Note** Add supplemental logging at the schema level using the Oracle GoldenGate command ADD SCHEMATRANDATA.

Start Oracle GoldenGate Manager

For GoldenGate to be functional, you must have defined the Oracle libraries in the LD_LIBRARY_PATH environment variable. From the GoldenGate installation directory, issue the following command to initialize the GoldenGate environment:

```
oracle@orcl2:/u01/app/oracle/product/12.2/gg/./ggsci

GGSCI (orcl2) 2> start mgr
Manager started.
```

To check the status and availability of the manager, issue the info command as follows:

```
GGSCI (orcl2) 4> info mgr detail
Manager is running (IP port orcl2.7809, Process ID 12777).
```

Next you will configure the extract, Data Pump, and replicat process parameters. Oracle GoldenGate has three components involved in replication. From these, two are running on the source, and one is running on the destination. The first two are called *extract processes*; one is performing extraction (extract), and the second one is in charge of pushing the data over the network (Data Pump). Both process are manipulating and propagating the data through trails.

The Data Pump process continually scans the staging trail file, awaiting new data extracted by the extract process. The Data Pump process is packaged for routing via TCP/IP to the target database locations.

Trails are specific files that are filled continuously by the extract and Data Pump processes. What is important to know is that the extract is not interacting directly with the database. All transactions are extracted from online redo logs and archive logs (if the extract is configured in that way). On the destination is one process called *replicat*. Mainly this process is taking the data from the trail pushed by Data Pump and replicating the data in the destination database.

Define the extract process (scottext).

```
GGSCI (orcl2) 2> edit params scottext
EXTRACT SCOTTEXT
SETENV (NLS_LANG=AMERICAN_AMERICA.WE8ISO8859P1)
SETENV (ORACLE_SID=ORCL)
USERID ggs_admin, PASSWORD ggs_admin
discardfile dirrpt/scottext.dsc, purge, megabytes 200
statoptions reportfetch
EXTTRAIL dirdat/l3
table SCOTT.*;
sequence SCOTT.*;
```

Add the extract.

```
GGSCI (orcl2) 4> ADD EXTRACT SCOTTEXT, TRANLOG, THREADS 1, BEGIN NOW
EXTRACT added.
```

Define the extract trail characteristics such as name and maximum size

```
GGSCI (orcl2) 5> ADD EXTTRAIL dirdat/l3, EXTRACT SCOTTEXT, MEGABYTES 100
EXTTRAIL added.
```

Define the Data Pump process (scottdmp).

```
GGSCI (orcl2) 3> edit params scottdmp
extract SCOTTDMP
RMTHOST orcl, MGRPORT 7809
RMTTRAIL dirdat/l4
PASSTHRU
table SCOTT.*;
sequence SCOTT.*;
```

Add the Data Pump extract.

```
GGSCI (orcl2) 6> ADD EXTRACT SCOTTDMP, EXTTRAILSOURCE dirdat/l3
EXTRACT added.
```

Define the source of the extract trail.

```
GGSCI (orcl2) 7> GGSCI (orcl2) 6> ADD EXTRACT SCOTTDMP, EXTTRAILSOURCE dirdat/l3
EXTRACT added.
```

Define the remote trail characteristics such as the name and size.

```
GGSCI (orcl2) 10> ADD RMTTRAIL dirdat/l4, EXTRACT SCOTTDMP, MEGABYTES 100
RMTTRAIL added.
```

Start the extract process SCOTTEXT.

```
GGSCI (orcl2) 1> start scottext
Sending START request to MANAGER ...
EXTRACT SCOTTEXT starting
Start the data pump process SCOTTDMP:

GGSCI (orcl2) 11> start scottdmp
Sending START request to MANAGER ...
EXTRACT SCOTTDMP starting
```

Check their status with the info command as follows:

```
GGSCI (orcl2) 20> info all detail
Program      Status       Group      Lag at Chkpt        Time Since Chkpt
MANAGER      RUNNING
EXTRACT      RUNNING      SCOTTDMP   00:00:00            00:00:01
EXTRACT      RUNNING      SCOTTEXT   00:00:00            00:00:01
```

Prepare the tables on the target database.

We will demonstrate the use of Oracle GoldenGate 12c from the migration using the initial load with Data Pump method. For the initial load you need only to create the source tables with data at a certain point time (SCN); hence, on the source, you will perform an export using the flashback_scn option.

Check the current SCN of the database. The SCN will be used on the target as a starting point for replication.

```
oracle@orcl2:/u01/app/oracle/product/12.2/gg$ sqlplus / as sysdba
SQL*Plus: Release 11.2.0.4.0 Production on Thu Jun 9 10:44:24 2016
Copyright (c) 1982, 2013, Oracle.  All rights reserved.
```

This is connected to the following:

```
Oracle Database 11g Enterprise Edition Release 11.2.0.4.0 - 64bit Production
With the Partitioning, OLAP, Data Mining and Real Application Testing options

SQL> select to_char(current_scn) from v$database;
TO_CHAR(CURRENT_SCN)
-----------------------------------
1002822
```

Perform the export as follows using the flashback_scn option:

```
oracle@orcl2:~$ expdp dumpfile=export:scott_dump1.dmp logfile=export:scott_dump1.log
schemas=scott flashback_scn=1002822

Export: Release 11.2.0.4.0 - Production on Thu Jun 9 10:46:49 2016
Copyright (c) 1982, 2011, Oracle and/or its affiliates.  All rights reserved.
Username: / as sysdba

Connected to: Oracle Database 11g Enterprise Edition Release 11.2.0.4.0 - 64bit Production
With the Partitioning, OLAP, Data Mining and Real Application Testing options
FLASHBACK automatically enabled to preserve database integrity.
Starting "SYS"."SYS_EXPORT_SCHEMA_01":  /******** AS SYSDBA dumpfile=export:scott_dump1.dmp
logfile=export:scott_dump1.log schemas=scott flashback_scn=1002822
Estimate in progress using BLOCKS method...
Processing object type SCHEMA_EXPORT/TABLE/TABLE_DATA
Total estimation using BLOCKS method: 192 KB
Processing object type SCHEMA_EXPORT/USER
Processing object type SCHEMA_EXPORT/SYSTEM_GRANT
Processing object type SCHEMA_EXPORT/ROLE_GRANT
Processing object type SCHEMA_EXPORT/DEFAULT_ROLE
Processing object type SCHEMA_EXPORT/PRE_SCHEMA/PROCACT_SCHEMA
Processing object type SCHEMA_EXPORT/TABLE/PROCACT_INSTANCE
Processing object type SCHEMA_EXPORT/TABLE/TABLE
Processing object type SCHEMA_EXPORT/TABLE/INDEX/INDEX
Processing object type SCHEMA_EXPORT/TABLE/CONSTRAINT/CONSTRAINT
Processing object type SCHEMA_EXPORT/TABLE/CONSTRAINT/REF_CONSTRAINT
. . exported "SCOTT"."DEPT"                              5.929 KB       4 rows
. . exported "SCOTT"."EMP"                               8.562 KB      14 rows
. . exported "SCOTT"."SALGRADE"                          5.859 KB       5 rows
. . exported "SCOTT"."BONUS"                                 0 KB       0 rows
Master table "SYS"."SYS_EXPORT_SCHEMA_01" successfully loaded/unloaded
******************************************************************************
Dump file set for SYS.SYS_EXPORT_SCHEMA_01 is:
  /kit/scott_dump1.dmp
Job "SYS"."SYS_EXPORT_SCHEMA_01" successfully completed at Thu Jun 9 10:47:28 2016 elapsed 0
00:00:30
```

Transfer the data dump on the destination host using scp as follows:

```
oracle@orcl2:/kit$ scp scott_dump1.dmp oracle@orcl:export
oracle@orcl's password:
scott_dump1.dmp        100% ***********************************************************|
280 KB      00:00
```

On the destination, you will use the PDB called ORCL12_1. Create a network service name with the same name as follows:

```
ORCL12_1 =
  (DESCRIPTION =
    (ADDRESS_LIST =
      (ADDRESS = (PROTOCOL = TCP)(HOST = orcl)(PORT = 1521))
    )
```

```
  (CONNECT_DATA =
    (SERVICE_NAME = ORCL12_1)
  )
 )
```

Import the dump into the ORCL12_1 pluggable database (PDB) database as follows:

```
[oracle@orcl export]$impdp system/sys@orcl12_1 dumpfile=import:scott_dump1.dmp
logfile=import:scott_dump1.log

Import: Release 12.1.0.2.0 - Production on Thu Jun 9 10:57:41 2016
Copyright (c) 1982, 2014, Oracle and/or its affiliates.  All rights reserved.

Connected to: Oracle Database 12c Enterprise Edition Release 12.1.0.2.0 - 64bit Production
With the Partitioning, OLAP, Advanced Analytics and Real Application Testing options
Master table "SYSTEM"."SYS_IMPORT_FULL_01" successfully loaded/unloaded
Starting "SYSTEM"."SYS_IMPORT_FULL_01":  system/********@orcl12_1 dumpfile=import:scott_
dump1.dmp logfile=import:scott_dump1.log
Processing object type SCHEMA_EXPORT/USER
Processing object type SCHEMA_EXPORT/SYSTEM_GRANT
Processing object type SCHEMA_EXPORT/ROLE_GRANT
Processing object type SCHEMA_EXPORT/DEFAULT_ROLE
Processing object type SCHEMA_EXPORT/PRE_SCHEMA/PROCACT_SCHEMA
Processing object type SCHEMA_EXPORT/TABLE/PROCACT_INSTANCE
Processing object type SCHEMA_EXPORT/TABLE/TABLE
Processing object type SCHEMA_EXPORT/TABLE/TABLE_DATA
. . imported "SCOTT"."DEPT"                             5.929 KB       4 rows
. . imported "SCOTT"."EMP"                              8.562 KB      14 rows
. . imported "SCOTT"."SALGRADE"                         5.859 KB       5 rows
. . imported "SCOTT"."BONUS"                               0 KB        0 rows
Processing object type SCHEMA_EXPORT/TABLE/INDEX/INDEX
Processing object type SCHEMA_EXPORT/TABLE/CONSTRAINT/CONSTRAINT
Processing object type SCHEMA_EXPORT/TABLE/CONSTRAINT/REF_CONSTRAINT
Job "SYSTEM"."SYS_IMPORT_FULL_01" successfully completed at Thu Jun 9 10:57:47 2016 elapsed
0 00:00:05
```

Configure Oracle GoldenGate on the Target Database

Create the Oracle GoldenGate user with the availability across all containers as follows:

```
SQL> conn / as sysdba
Connected.

SQL> create user c##ggs_admin identified by ggs_admin;
Grant succeeded.

SQL> exec dbms_goldengate_auth.grant_admin_privilege('C##GGS_ADMIN',container=>'all');
PL/SQL procedure successfully completed.

SQL> alter system set enable_goldengate_replication=true scope=both;
System altered.
```

```
SQL> alter session set container=orcl12_1;
Session altered.

SQL> create tablespace ggs_admin_tbs
datafile '/u01/app/oracle/oradata/ORCL12/ggs_admin_tbs01.dbf' size 100m
autoextend on next 100m maxsize unlimited;
Tablespace created.

SQL> grant connect, select any dictionary to c##ggs_admin;
Grant succeeded.

SQL> alter user c##ggs_admin default tablespace ggs_admin_tbs;
User altered.
```

Next you will start the manager and configure the replicat process on the target as follows:

```
[oracle@orcl ggc]$ ./ggsci


Oracle GoldenGate Command Interpreter for Oracle
Version 12.2.0.1.1 OGGCORE_12.2.0.1.0_PLATFORMS_151211.1401_FBO
Linux, x64, 64bit (optimized), Oracle 12c on Dec 12 2015 02:56:48
Operating system character set identified as UTF-8.
Copyright (C) 1995, 2015, Oracle and/or its affiliates. All rights reserved.

GGSCI (orcl) 3> start mgr
Manager started.
```

Check the status and availability of the manager:
```
GGSCI (orcl) 6> info mgr detail

Manager is running (IP port orcl.7809, Process ID 9346).
```

The replicat process uses a table called the *checkpoint table* to maintain a record of its read position in the trail for recovery purposes. In the case of the pluggable database, the checkpoint table must be configured at the container level. Configure the checkpoint table for the replicat process as follows:

```
GGSCI (orcl) 2> dblogin userid c##ggs_admin@orcl12_1
Password:
Successfully logged into database ORCL12_1.

GGSCI (orcl as c##ggs_admin@ORCL12/ORCL12_1) 4> add checkpointtable orcl12_1.c##ggs_admin.
checkpoint

Successfully created checkpoint table orcl12_1.c##ggs_admin.checkpoint.

GGSCI (orcl as c##ggs_admin@ORCL12/ORCL12_1) 4>
```

Configure the replicat process parameters as follows:

```
GGSCI (orcl as c##ggs_admin@ORCL12/ORCL12_1) 29> edit params scottrep
```

```
REPLICAT SCOTTREP
ASSUMETARGETDEFS
HANDLECOLLISIONS
USERID c##ggs_admin@orcl12_1 PASSWORD ggs_admin
DISCARDFILE ./dirrpt/rprt.dsc, PURGE
DDL INCLUDE ALL
MAP SCOTT.*, TARGET SCOTT.*;
```

Define the replicat source trail; this trail is pushed by Data Pump from the destination.

```
ADD REPLICAT SCOTTREP, EXTTRAIL ./dirdat/l4, BEGIN NOW, CHECKPOINTTABLE ORCL12_1.c##ggs_
admin.checkpoint
GGSCI (orcl as c##ggs_admin@ORCL12/ORCL12_1) 17>
REPLICAT added.


GGSCI (orcl as c##ggs_admin@ORCL12/ORCL12_1) 22> start replicat scottrep, atcsn 1002822

Sending START request to MANAGER ...
REPLICAT SCOTTREP starting


GGSCI (orcl as c##ggs_admin@ORCL12/ORCL12_1) 24> info all

Program            Status          Group           Lag at Chkpt     Time Since Chkpt

MANAGER            RUNNING
REPLICAT           RUNNING         SCOTTREP        00:00:00         00:00:01
```

Check the replication. On the source, update the table emp as follows:

```
oracle@orcl2:/u01/app/oracle/product/12.2/gg$ sqlplus scott/tiger

SQL*Plus: Release 11.2.0.4.0 Production on Thu Jun 9 11:51:58 2016
Copyright (c) 1982, 2013, Oracle. All rights reserved.
Connected to:
Oracle Database 11g Enterprise Edition Release 11.2.0.4.0 - 64bit Production
With the Partitioning, OLAP, Data Mining and Real Application Testing options

SQL> update scott.emp set comm=1000 where ename='TURNER';
1 row updated.

SQL> commit;
Commit complete.

[oracle@orcl ggc]$ sqlplus system/sys@orcl12_1

SQL*Plus: Release 12.1.0.2.0 Production on Thu Jun 9 11:56:09 2016
Copyright (c) 1982, 2014, Oracle. All rights reserved.
Last Successful login time: Thu Jun 09 2016 11:13:29 +00:00
Connected to:
Oracle Database 12c Enterprise Edition Release 12.1.0.2.0 - 64bit Production
With the Partitioning, OLAP, Advanced Analytics and Real Application Testing options
```

```
SQL> select comm,ename from scott.emp;

COMM    ENAME
----------    -----------
            SMITH
     300    ALLEN
     500    WARD
            JONES
    1400    MARTIN
            BLAKE
            CLARK
            SCOTT
            KING
    1000    TURNER
            ADAMS
            JAMES
            FORD
            MILLER
14 rows selected.
```

On the target database, you should have the value replicated as follows:

```
SQL> select comm,ename from scott.emp where ename='TURNER';

COMM    ENAME
----------    ------------
1000    TURNER
```

Method 2: Initial Load with Bulkload

This method is suitable mostly if you can afford downtime during the upgrade or migration. Also, you can use it to replace the transport of data with dumps. On the target, you should have defined only the empty tables.

Perform an export on the source using the content parameter with a value of metadata_only.

Copy the data dump to the target and import it into the pluggable database ORCL12_1 as follows:

```
[oracle@orcl ggc]$ impdp system/sys@orcl12_1 dumpfile=import:scott_dump
logfile=import:scott_dump.log


Import: Release 12.1.0.2.0 - Production on Thu Jun 9 12:21:43 2016
Copyright (c) 1982, 2014, Oracle and/or its affiliates.  All rights reserved.

Connected to: Oracle Database 12c Enterprise Edition Release 12.1.0.2.0 - 64bit Production
With the Partitioning, OLAP, Advanced Analytics and Real Application Testing options
Master table "SYSTEM"."SYS_IMPORT_FULL_01" successfully loaded/unloaded
Starting "SYSTEM"."SYS_IMPORT_FULL_01":  system/********@orcl12_1 dumpfile=import:scott_dump
logfile=import:scott_dump.log
Processing object type SCHEMA_EXPORT/USER
Processing object type SCHEMA_EXPORT/SYSTEM_GRANT
Processing object type SCHEMA_EXPORT/ROLE_GRANT
```

```
Processing object type SCHEMA_EXPORT/DEFAULT_ROLE
Processing object type SCHEMA_EXPORT/PRE_SCHEMA/PROCACT_SCHEMA
Processing object type SCHEMA_EXPORT/TABLE/TABLE
Processing object type SCHEMA_EXPORT/TABLE/INDEX/INDEX
Processing object type SCHEMA_EXPORT/TABLE/CONSTRAINT/CONSTRAINT
Processing object type SCHEMA_EXPORT/TABLE/CONSTRAINT/REF_CONSTRAINT
Job "SYSTEM"."SYS_IMPORT_FULL_01" successfully completed at Thu Jun 9 12:21:51 2016
elapsed 0 00:00:05
```

Disable all the constraints on target.

Define the initial load extract as follows:

```
GGSCI (orcl2) 4> edit params orclext
EXTRACT orclext
SETENV (ORACLE_SID=ORCL)
USERID ggs_admin, PASSWORD ggs_admin
rmthost orcl, mgrport 7809
RMTTASK replicat, GROUP rep12pdb
table Scott.*;
```

Add the extract ORCLEXT as follows:

```
GGSCI (orcl2) 8> add extract orclext, sourceistable
EXTRACT added.
```

On the target, add the following line to the mgr parameters and restart it. This is a security option and allows remote commands from the destination Oracle GolderGate instance.

```
GGSCI (orcl) 8> edit params mgr
ACCESSRULE, PROG *, IPADDR 192.168.1.20, ALLOW

GGSCI (orcl) 11> stop mgr
Manager process is required by other GGS processes.
Are you sure you want to stop it (y/n)?y

Sending STOP request to MANAGER ...
Request processed.
Manager stopped.

GGSCI (orcl) 12> start mgr
Manager started.
```

Define the replicat parameters as follows:

```
GGSCI (orcl) 1> edit params rep12pdb
replicat REP12PDB
userid c##ggs_admin@orcl12_1, password ggs_admin
BULKLOAD
ASSUMETARGETDEFS
MAP SCOTT.*, TARGET SCOTT.*;
```

Add the replicat with the option SPECIALRUN. This option allows the source extract to start the replicat remotely; there's no need to start it manually.

```
GGSCI (orcl) 13> add replicat db2pdb, specialrun
REPLICAT added.
```

From the destination start the extract
```
GGSCI (orcl2) 9> start orclext
```

```
Sending START request to MANAGER ...
EXTRACT ORCLEXT starting
```

If you execute a tail on ggserr.log from the Oracle GoldenGate home on the target, you should see the initial load is executing and finishing with success.

```
2016-06-09 12:22:43  INFO    OGG-00996  Oracle GoldenGate Delivery for Oracle, rep12pdb.prm:
REPLICAT REP12PDB started.
2016-06-09 12:22:43  INFO    OGG-03522  Oracle GoldenGate Delivery for Oracle, rep12pdb.prm:
Setting session time zone to source database time zone 'GMT'.
2016-06-09 12:22:43  WARNING OGG-02760  Oracle GoldenGate Delivery for Oracle, rep12pdb.prm:
ASSUMETARGETDEFS is ignored because trail file  contains table definitions.
2016-06-09 12:22:43  INFO    OGG-06506  Oracle GoldenGate Delivery for Oracle, rep12pdb.prm:
Wildcard MAP resolved (entry SCOTT.*): MAP "SCOTT"."DEPT", TARGET "ORCL12_1".SCOTT."DEPT".
2016-06-09 12:22:44  INFO    OGG-02756  Oracle GoldenGate Delivery for Oracle, rep12pdb.prm:
The definition for table SCOTT.DEPT is obtained from the trail file.
2016-06-09 12:22:44  INFO    OGG-06511  Oracle GoldenGate Delivery for Oracle, rep12pdb.prm:
Using following columns in default map by name: DEPTNO, DNAME, LOC.
2016-06-09 12:22:44  INFO    OGG-06510  Oracle GoldenGate Delivery for Oracle, rep12pdb.prm:
Using the following key columns for target table ORCL12_1.SCOTT.DEPT: DEPTNO.
2016-06-09 12:22:44  INFO    OGG-00178  Oracle GoldenGate Delivery for Oracle, rep12pdb.prm:
owner = "SCOTT", table = "DEPT".
2016-06-09 12:22:44  INFO    OGG-06506  Oracle GoldenGate Delivery for Oracle, rep12pdb.prm:
Wildcard MAP resolved (entry SCOTT.*): MAP "SCOTT"."EMP", TARGET "ORCL12_1".SCOTT."EMP".
2016-06-09 12:22:44  INFO    OGG-02756  Oracle GoldenGate Delivery for Oracle, rep12pdb.prm:
The definition for table SCOTT.EMP is obtained from the trail file.
2016-06-09 12:22:44  INFO    OGG-06511  Oracle GoldenGate Delivery for Oracle, rep12pdb.prm:
Using following columns in default map by name: EMPNO, ENAME, JOB, MGR, HIREDATE, SAL, COMM,
DEPTNO.
2016-06-09 12:22:44  INFO    OGG-06510  Oracle GoldenGate Delivery for Oracle, rep12pdb.prm:
Using the following key columns for target table ORCL12_1.SCOTT.EMP: EMPNO.
2016-06-09 12:22:44  INFO    OGG-00178  Oracle GoldenGate Delivery for Oracle, rep12pdb.prm:
owner = "SCOTT", table = "EMP".
2016-06-09 12:22:44  INFO    OGG-06506  Oracle GoldenGate Delivery for Oracle, rep12pdb.
prm:  Wildcard MAP resolved (entry SCOTT.*): MAP "SCOTT"."SALGRADE", TARGET "ORCL12_1".
SCOTT."SALGRADE".
2016-06-09 12:22:45  WARNING OGG-06439  Oracle GoldenGate Delivery for Oracle, rep12pdb.prm:
No unique key is defined for table SALGRADE. All viable columns will be used to represent
the key, but may not guarantee uniqueness. KEYCOLS may be used to define the key.
2016-06-09 12:22:45  INFO    OGG-02756  Oracle GoldenGate Delivery for Oracle, rep12pdb.prm:
The definition for table SCOTT.SALGRADE is obtained from the trail file.
2016-06-09 12:22:45  INFO    OGG-06511  Oracle GoldenGate Delivery for Oracle, rep12pdb.prm:
Using following columns in default map by name: GRADE, LOSAL, HISAL.
```

```
2016-06-09 12:22:45  INFO    OGG-06510  Oracle GoldenGate Delivery for Oracle, rep12pdb.prm:
Using the following key columns for target table ORCL12_1.SCOTT.SALGRADE: GRADE, LOSAL,
HISAL.
2016-06-09 12:22:45  INFO    OGG-00178  Oracle GoldenGate Delivery for Oracle, rep12pdb.prm:
owner = "SCOTT", table = "SALGRADE".
2016-06-09 12:22:50  INFO    OGG-00994  Oracle GoldenGate Delivery for Oracle, rep12pdb.prm:
REPLICAT REP12PDB stopped normally.
```

You can also verify that on the destination you have the rows replicated. On the target, issue the
following:

```
[oracle@orcl Desktop]$ sqlplus scott/tiger@orcl12_1

SQL*Plus: Release 12.1.0.2.0 Production on Sat Jun 11 05:42:04 2016
Copyright (c) 1982, 2014, Oracle.  All rights reserved.
```

This is connected to the following:

```
Oracle Database 12c Enterprise Edition Release 12.1.0.2.0 - 64bit Production
With the Partitioning, OLAP, Advanced Analytics and Real Application Testing options
SQL> select count(*) from emp;
COUNT(*)
--------------
14

SQL> select count(*) from bonus;
COUNT(*)
--------------
 0

SQL> select count(*) from dept;
COUNT(*)
--------------
 4

SQL> select count(*) from salgrade;

COUNT(*)
--------------
 5
```

CTAS

Create Table As Select (CTAS) is one of the commonly used methods for database migration. It operates at
the object level. It is like collecting object structures along with data from the source database and importing
them into the target database.

1) This is a simple method; it collects records from the source database and transfers them to the target database via a database link. This means there should be network connectivity between the source and target databases while migrating the data.

2) It operates at the object level; there is no restriction in moving data. Remember, you are not migrating the dictionary in this method; only data is getting migrated to the new database.

3) There is no restriction on the endian format conversion. At the same time, you should consider the restrictions associated with the database link when operating between different database versions, and those restrictions are applicable to CTAS. For example, to create a database link between 10*g* and 12*c*, the minimum required version is 10.2.0.2.0. Otherwise, PL/SQL usage will fail. A database link between the 9*i* and 12*c* databases is not supported. While choosing the CTAS method, interoperability between the source and the target versions should be verified.

Let's see the steps with an example. Say you have a source database with the 10.2.0.4.0 version on a Solaris Sparc server and you need to migrate this database to a Linux x86-64 server. The endian format of the source and target platforms is different.

As a first step, you need to install the 10.2.0.4.0 database software on the Linux x86-64 server, and a new database should be created in that Oracle Home. Now you have the database on the source and target, and the data has to be moved from the source to the target database.

- *Source database name*: DB10SOL

- *Target database name*: DB10LIN

Create a database link from the target database to the source database. Both database servers have network connectivity. First you define a network connection string at the target tnsnames.ora file.

```
DB10SOL =
  (DESCRIPTION =
    (ADDRESS = (PROTOCOL = TCP)(HOST = <Host_name>)(PORT = <Port_number>))
    (CONNECT_DATA =
      (SERVER = DEDICATED)
      (SERVICE_NAME = DB10SOL)
    )
  )
```

Execute tnsping <tns_connection_string>, which is to check whether the source listener is reachable and the service is available.

Collect the list of objects needed to be migrated to the target database server. The objects might belong to the same schema or a different schema. In the process, objects can be migrated to the same schema or a different schema in the target server. But ensure that the schemas in the source and target database servers have same roles and privileges or the executing function or procedure will create errors after migration.

In this example, let's consider the objects are located in the schemas HR and FINANCE. These objects have to be migrated in the target database server 10.2.0.4.0 located on the Linux server. On the Linux server you have created the schemas HR and FINANCE with the same role and privileges.

To collect role information from the database, execute the following:

```
SQL > select * from dba_role_privs where grantee='HR' or grantee='FINANCE';
GRANTEE                        GRANTED_ROLE                   ADM DEF
------------------------------ ------------------------------ --- ---
```

HR	RESOURCE	NO	YES
HR	CONNECT	NO	YES
FINANCE	DBA	NO	YES

On the target database server, the same schemas have been created, and the necessary privileges have been granted.

```
SQL> create user HR identified by hr;
User created.
SQL> grant connect, resource to hr;
Grant succeeded.
SQL> grant create database link to hr;
Grant succeeded.
SQL> create user finance identified by finance;
User created.
SQL> grant dba to finance;
Grant succeeded.
```

Create a database link from the target schema to the source schema. Connect to the HR schema of the target database and create a database link. This database link will be owned by HR.

```
SQL> create database link DB10SOL connect to hr identified by hr using 'DB10SOL';
Database link created.
```

Instead of creating a database link at each individual schema, you can create a public database link in any DBA user and then access objects through a database link. For example, a public database link can be created by a DBA user for the system schema associated in the source database. This link is available to all users in the target database.

```
Sql> create public database link DB10SOL connect to system identified by manager  using
'DB10SOL';
Database link created.
```

Connect to the HR schema, and using this public database link, access the source database HR schema.

```
select object_name from dba_objects@db10sol where owner='HR';
OBJECT_NAME
--------------------------------------------------------------------------------
DEPT
EMP
BONUS
SALGRADE
DEPTNO_IDX
ADDITION
```

Once the database link is created, you are ready to do the migration.
Use create table as select records from the source HR schema table through a database link.

```
SQL> create table dept as select * from HR.dept@DB10SOL;
Table created.
```

Like the previous example, all tables can be created at the target HR schema.

251

Tables can indexes on one or many columns. Indexes associated with tables can be collected from the user_indexes view, and its DDL statement can be retrieved through dbms_metadata.get_ddl by passing the index name as an argument.

The index creation statement has to be retrieved through the dbms_metadata package.

```
select DBMS_METADATA.GET_DDL('INDEX',<INDEX_NAME>') from dual;
```

Here's an example:

```
select DBMS_METADATA.GET_DDL('INDEX','DEPTNO_IDX') from dual;
DBMS_METADATA.GET_DDL('INDEX','DEPTNO_IDX')
--------------------------------------------------------------------------------

  CREATE INDEX "HR"."DEPTNO_IDX" ON "HR"."DEPT" ("DEPTNO")
  PCTFREE 10 INITRANS 2 MAXTRANS 255 COMPUTE STATISTICS
  STORAGE(INITIAL 65536 NEXT 1048576 MINEXTENTS 1 MAXEXTENTS 2147483645
  PCTINCREASE 0 FREELISTS 1 FREELIST GROUPS 1 BUFFER_POOL DEFAULT)
  TABLESPACE "USERS"
```

This index creation statement can be executed on the target database schema HR. The HR schema could have other objects such as procedures, functions, and packages. The objects owned by the HR schema can be collected using user_objects.

The procedure, function, and package DDL can be collected from the user_source dictionary view in the source database.

```
select text from user_source where name='ADDITION';
TEXT
--------------------------------------------------------------------------------
procedure addition as
 i number;
begin
for i in 1..10000 loop
 insert into dept values (i,'computer','bangalore');
end loop;
commit;
end;
8 rows selected.
Execute the collected DDL statements in target database to create the objects.
```

We can also use DBMS_METADATA to collect source code of required objects.

Transport Database

The transport database method is commonly used for migrating databases across platforms having the same endian format. Unlike TTS, here the whole database will be migrated to a different platform. You don't need to operate on an individual tablespace like you do in TTS. This method was introduced in 10g. Though the endian format is the same, you cannot simply copy the datafiles to the target server. The datafiles have to go through a conversion process. Tablespaces will be converted according to the destination platform using RMAN commands. The conversion can happen at the source server or at the destination server.

Let's see the requirements of this method.

- The source and target platforms should have the same endian format.

- Redo logs and control files need to be re-created on the target server.

- The tempfile belonging to the locally managed temporary tablespace cannot be transported. The temporary tablespace can be re-created once the transfer is over.

- The source database should be in read-only mode.

- The password file cannot be transported. It has to be created newly on the target server. When the convert command is executed, it will show the user in the password file.

- External tables and directories cannot be transported. You can check these nontransferable objects using procedures before the transfer. Also, the convert command output lists these objects' information.

Here are the preparatory steps:

1) Execute the DBMS_TDB.CHECK_DB procedure to identify whether the database can be migrated to the target platform.

```
SQL> set serveroutput on
SQL> DECLARE db_ready BOOLEAN;
BEGIN
db_ready := DBMS_TDB.CHECK_DB('Solaris Operating System (x86-64)', DBMS_TDB.
SKIP_NONE);
END;
PL/SQL procedure successfully completed.
```

In this example, the source platform is Linux x86-64, the target platform is Solaris x86-64, and the output shows no errors. This means this database can be migrated to the target Solaris x86-64 platform.

2) Check for external objects, which need to be re-created after the migration.

```
SQL> declare x boolean; begin x := dbms_tdb.check_external; end;
  2  /
The following external tables exist in the database:
SYS.OPATCH_XML_INV
The following directories exist in the database:
SYS.ORACLE_OCM_CONFIG_DIR2, SYS.XMLDIR, SYS.ORACLE_OCM_CONFIG_DIR, SYS.XSDDIR,
SYS.DATA_PUMP_DIR, SYS.OPATCH_INST_DIR, SYS.OPATCH_SCRIPT_DIR,
SYS.OPATCH_LOG_DIR, SYS.ORACLE_BASE, SYS.ORACLE_HOME
PL/SQL procedure successfully completed.
```

Migrate Steps

You will see walk through the steps with an example.

- *Source platform*: Linux x86-64

- *Destination platform*: Solaris x86-64

- *Database version*: 12.1.0.2.0

Here are the steps:

1) Check the platform endian format of the source and target database servers. Both should have the same platform.

```
PLATFORM_NAME                        ENDIAN_FORMAT
------------------------------       --------------
Linux x86 64-bit                     Little
Solaris Operating System (x86-64)    Little
```

2) Execute DBMS_TDB.CHECK_DB and ensure that the output is successful.

3) Execute dbms_tdb.check_external and note the objects that require attention.

4) Shut down the database and open it in read-only mode.

```
SQL> shutdown immediate
Database closed.
Database dismounted.
ORACLE instance shut down.
SQL> startup mount
ORACLE instance started.

Total System Global Area  448790528 bytes
Fixed Size                  2925456 bytes
Variable Size             272632944 bytes
Database Buffers          167772160 bytes
Redo Buffers                5459968 bytes
Database mounted.
SQL> alter database open read only;
Database altered.
```

5) Do the conversion at the source platform. Connect to the RMAN prompt at the source database and execute the conversion script. In the script, you specify the following:

   • transport script: This script will be created dynamically during execution, and it will have commands required at the destination side during transport.

   • to platform: This is the destination platform information.

   • db_file_name_convert: This is where the converted datafiles should be placed.

```
RMAN> CONVERT DATABASE NEW DATABASE 'Sol12'
transport script '/u01/app/oracle/product/tds12c/convert/transportscript'
2> 3> to platform 'Solaris Operating System (x86-64)'
4> db_file_name_convert '/u01/app/oracle/product/tds12c/' '/u01/app/oracle/
product/tds12c/convert/'
5> ;
Starting conversion at source
using target database control file instead of recovery catalog
allocated channel: ORA_DISK_1
channel ORA_DISK_1: SID=13 device type=DISK
```

```
External table SYS.OPATCH_XML_INV found in the database
Directory SYS.ORACLE_HOME found in the database
Directory SYS.ORACLE_BASE found in the database
Directory SYS.OPATCH_LOG_DIR found in the database
Directory SYS.OPATCH_SCRIPT_DIR found in the database
Directory SYS.OPATCH_INST_DIR found in the database
Directory SYS.DATA_PUMP_DIR found in the database
Directory SYS.XSDDIR found in the database
Directory SYS.ORACLE_OCM_CONFIG_DIR found in the database
Directory SYS.XMLDIR found in the database
Directory SYS.ORACLE_OCM_CONFIG_DIR2 found in the database
User SYS with SYSDBA and SYSOPER privilege found in password file
User SYSDG with SYSDG privilege found in password file
User SYSBACKUP with SYSBACKUP privilege found in password file
User SYSKM with SYSKM privilege found in password file
channel ORA_DISK_1: starting datafile conversion
input datafile file number=00001 name=/u01/app/oracle/product/tds12c/system01.dbf
converted datafile=/u01/app/oracle/product/tds12c/convert/system01.dbf
channel ORA_DISK_1: datafile conversion complete, elapsed time: 00:00:25
channel ORA_DISK_1: starting datafile conversion
input datafile file number=00003 name=/u01/app/oracle/product/tds12c/sysaux01.dbf
converted datafile=/u01/app/oracle/product/tds12c/convert/sysaux01.dbf
channel ORA_DISK_1: datafile conversion complete, elapsed time: 00:00:25
channel ORA_DISK_1: starting datafile conversion
input datafile file number=00004 name=/u01/app/oracle/product/tds12c/undotbs01.dbf
converted datafile=/u01/app/oracle/product/tds12c/convert/undotbs01.dbf
channel ORA_DISK_1: datafile conversion complete, elapsed time: 00:00:07
channel ORA_DISK_1: starting datafile conversion
input datafile file number=00006 name=/u01/app/oracle/product/tds12c/users01.dbf
converted datafile=/u01/app/oracle/product/tds12c/convert/users01.dbf
channel ORA_DISK_1: datafile conversion complete, elapsed time: 00:00:01
Edit init.ora file /u01/app/oracle/product/tds12c/12.1.0.2.0/dbs/init_00r5n9np_1_0.
ora. This PFILE will be used to create the database on the target platform
Run SQL script /u01/app/oracle/product/tds12c/convert/transportscript on the
target platform to create database
To recompile all PL/SQL modules, run utlirp.sql and utlrp.sql on the target platform
To change the internal database identifier, use DBNEWID Utility
Finished conversion at source
```

You can see the directory objects and users that exist in the password file in the previous output.

The following are the contents of the transport script:

```
-- The following commands will create a new control file and use it
-- to open the database.
-- Data used by Recovery Manager will be lost.
-- The contents of online logs will be lost and all backups will
-- be invalidated. Use this only if online logs are damaged.

-- After mounting the created controlfile, the following SQL
```

```
-- statement will place the database in the appropriate
-- protection mode:
--  ALTER DATABASE SET STANDBY DATABASE TO MAXIMIZE PERFORMANCE

STARTUP NOMOUNT PFILE='/u01/app/oracle/product/12.1.0.2.0/dbs/init_00r5n9np_1_0.ora'
CREATE CONTROLFILE REUSE SET DATABASE "SOL12" RESETLOGS  NOARCHIVELOG
    MAXLOGFILES 16
    MAXLOGMEMBERS 3
    MAXDATAFILES 100
    MAXINSTANCES 8
    MAXLOGHISTORY 292
LOGFILE
  GROUP 1 '/u01/app/oracle/product/12.1.0.2.0/dbs/arch_D-SOL12_id-4189992537_S-7_T-
1_A-911210012_03r5n9np'  SIZE 50M BLOCKSIZE 512,
  GROUP 2 '/u01/app/oracle/product/12.1.0.2.0/dbs/arch_D-SOL12_id-4189992537_S-8_T-
1_A-911210012_04r5n9np'  SIZE 50M BLOCKSIZE 512,
  GROUP 3 '/u01/app/oracle/product/12.1.0.2.0/dbs/arch_D-SOL12_id-4189992537_S-6_T-
1_A-911210012_05r5n9np'  SIZE 50M BLOCKSIZE 512
DATAFILE
  '/u01/app/oracle/product/tds12c/convert/system01.dbf',
  '/u01/app/oracle/product/tds12c/convert/sysaux01.dbf',
  '/u01/app/oracle/product/tds12c/convert/undotbs01.dbf',
  '/u01/app/oracle/product/tds12c/convert/users01.dbf'
CHARACTER SET UTF8
;
-- Database can now be opened zeroing the online logs.
ALTER DATABASE OPEN RESETLOGS UPGRADE;

-- Commands to add tempfiles to temporary tablespaces.
-- Online tempfiles have complete space information.
-- Other tempfiles may require adjustment.
ALTER TABLESPACE TEMP ADD TEMPFILE '/u01/app/oracle/product/12.1.0.2.0/dbs/data_D-
SOL12_I-4189992537_TS-TEMP_FNO-1_06r5n9np'
    SIZE 206569472  AUTOEXTEND ON NEXT 655360  MAXSIZE 32767M;
-- End of tempfile additions.
--

set echo off
prompt ~~~~~~~~~~~~~~~~~~~~~~~~~~~~~~~~~~~~~~~~~~~~~~~~~~~~~~~~~~~~~~~~~~~~~~~~~~~~~~~~
prompt * Your database has been created successfully!
prompt * There are many things to think about for the new database. Here
prompt * is a checklist to help you stay on track:
prompt * 1. You may want to redefine the location of the directory objects.
prompt * 2. You may want to change the internal database identifier (DBID)
prompt *    or the global database name for this database. Use the
prompt *    NEWDBID Utility (nid).
prompt ~~~~~~~~~~~~~~~~~~~~~~~~~~~~~~~~~~~~~~~~~~~~~~~~~~~~~~~~~~~~~~~~~~~~~~~~~~~~~~~~

SHUTDOWN IMMEDIATE
STARTUP UPGRADE PFILE='/u01/app/oracle/product/12.1.0.2.0/dbs/init_00r5n9np_1_0.ora'
@@ ?/rdbms/admin/utlirp.sql
SHUTDOWN IMMEDIATE
```

```
STARTUP PFILE='/u01/app/oracle/product/12.1.0.2.0/dbs/init_00r5n9np_1_0.ora'
-- The following step will recompile all PL/SQL modules.
-- It may take serveral hours to complete.
@@ ?/rdbms/admin/utlrp.sql
set feedback 6;
```

6) Copy the datafiles, transport script, and init parameter file to the target platform.

7) On the target server, modify the init file and start the database in nomount state.

```
SQL> startup nomount
ORACLE instance started.

Total System Global Area   629145600 bytes
Fixed Size                   3006784 bytes
Variable Size              281022144 bytes
Database Buffers           339738624 bytes
Redo Buffers                 5378048 bytes
```

8) From the transport script, collect the create control file statement and make the necessary changes to the datafile according to the target server.

```
SQL> CREATE CONTROLFILE REUSE SET DATABASE "SOL12" RESETLOGS  NOARCHIVELOG
    MAXLOGFILES 16
            MAXLOGMEMBERS 3
        MAXDATAFILES 100
        MAXINSTANCES 8
        MAXLOGHISTORY 292
    LOGFILE
    GROUP 1 '/u01/app/oracle/product/tds12c/sol12/redo01.log'  SIZE 50M BLOCKSIZE 512,
      GROUP 2 '/u01/app/oracle/product/tds12c/sol12/redo02.log'   SIZE 50M
BLOCKSIZE 512,
      GROUP 3 '/u01/app/oracle/product/tds12c/sol12/redo03.log'   SIZE 50M
BLOCKSIZE 512
    DATAFILE
      '/u01/app/oracle/product/tds12c/sol12/system01.dbf',
       '/u01/app/oracle/product/tds12c/sol12/sysaux01.dbf',
       '/u01/app/oracle/product/tds12c/sol12/undotbs01.dbf',
       '/u01/app/oracle/product/tds12c/sol12/users01.dbf'
CHARACTER SET UTF8
;
Control file created.
```

9) Open the database using the resetlogs option.

```
SQL> alter database open resetlogs;
Database altered.
```

10) Add the tempfile to the temporary tablespace.

```
SQL> ALTER TABLESPACE TEMP ADD TEMPFILE '/u01/app/oracle/product/tds12c/sol12/
temp01.dbf'
     SIZE 200m;  2
Tablespace altered.
```

11) Currently the database has been migrated successfully at the target server. Check for the directory objects. The location of those directories might require a change according to the target server. Drop and re-create those directories based on the target server.

In the previous example, the conversion is done at the primary. Let's try the same exercise with a conversion at the target server. Doing the conversion at the target will reduce the performance overhead at the source, and also this method will be useful if the same database is planned for migration to multiple target servers with the same endian format.

Until step 4, the steps are the same whether you do the conversion at the source or the target. Say you have completed step 4 and now the database is in read-only status. Execute the RMAN conversion script at the primary, as shown next. Specify ON TARGET PLATFORM to denote that the conversion will happen on the target server.

```
RMAN> CONVERT DATABASE ON TARGET PLATFORM
CONVERT SCRIPT '/u01/app/oracle/product/tds12c/convert/convertscript.rman'
2> 3> TRANSPORT SCRIPT '/u01/app/oracle/product/tds12c/convert/transportscript.sql'
4> new database 'sol12c'
5> FORMAT '/u01/app/oracle/product/tds12c/convert/%U';

Starting conversion at source
using target database control file instead of recovery catalog
allocated channel: ORA_DISK_1
channel ORA_DISK_1: SID=2 device type=DISK

External table SYS.OPATCH_XML_INV found in the database

Directory SYS.ORACLE_HOME found in the database
Directory SYS.ORACLE_BASE found in the database
Directory SYS.OPATCH_LOG_DIR found in the database
Directory SYS.OPATCH_SCRIPT_DIR found in the database
Directory SYS.OPATCH_INST_DIR found in the database
Directory SYS.DATA_PUMP_DIR found in the database
Directory SYS.XSDDIR found in the database
Directory SYS.ORACLE_OCM_CONFIG_DIR found in the database
Directory SYS.XMLDIR found in the database
Directory SYS.ORACLE_OCM_CONFIG_DIR2 found in the database
channel ORA_DISK_1: starting to check datafiles
input datafile file number=00001 name=/u01/app/oracle/product/tds12c/o1_mf_system_cmht7dkb_.
dbf
channel ORA_DISK_1: datafile checking complete, elapsed time: 00:00:00
channel ORA_DISK_1: starting to check datafiles
input datafile file number=00003 name=/u01/app/oracle/product/tds12c/o1_mf_sysaux_cmht5ojd_.
dbf
channel ORA_DISK_1: datafile checking complete, elapsed time: 00:00:00
```

```
channel ORA_DISK_1: starting to check datafiles
input datafile file number=00004 name=/u01/app/oracle/product/tds12c/o1_mf_undotbs1_
cmht94wr_.dbf
channel ORA_DISK_1: datafile checking complete, elapsed time: 00:00:00
channel ORA_DISK_1: starting to check datafiles
input datafile file number=00006 name=/u01/app/oracle/product/tds12c/o1_mf_users_cmht93rw_.
dbf
channel ORA_DISK_1: datafile checking complete, elapsed time: 00:00:00
Edit init.ora file /u01/app/oracle/product/tds12c/convert/init_00r5ngte_1_0.ora. This PFILE
will be used to create the database on the target platform
Run RMAN script /u01/app/oracle/product/tds12c/convert/convertscript.rman on target platform
to convert datafiles
Run SQL script /u01/app/oracle/product/tds12c/convert/transportscript.sql on the target
platform to create database
To recompile all PL/SQL modules, run utlirp.sql and utlrp.sql on the target platform
To change the internal database identifier, use DBNEWID Utility
```

The execution has created the init file, convertscript.rman, and transportscript.sql.

The convertscript.rman script is the conversion script to be executed at the target site.

```
STARTUP NOMOUNT PFILE = '/u01/app/oracle/product/tds12c/convert /init_00r5ngte_1_0.ora';
RUN {
  CONVERT
  FROM PLATFORM 'Linux x86 64-bit'
  PARALLELISM 1
DATAFILE '/u01/app/oracle/product/tds12c/o1_mf_system_cmht7dkb_.dbf' FORMAT '/u01/app/
oracle/product/tds12c/convert/data_D-ADG12C_I-4282403005_TS-SYSTEM_FNO-1_09r5ngte'
DATAFILE '/u01/app/oracle/product/tds12c/o1_mf_sysaux_cmht5ojd_.dbf' FORMAT '/u01/app/
oracle/product/tds12c/convert/data_D-ADG12C_I-4282403005_TS-SYSAUX_FNO-3_0ar5ngte'
DATAFILE '/u01/app/oracle/product/tds12c /o1_mf_undotbs1_cmht94wr_.dbf' FORMAT '/u01/app/
oracle/product/tds12c/convert/data_D-ADG12C_I-4282403005_TS-UNDOTBS1_FNO-4_0br5ngte'
DATAFILE '/u01/app/oracle/product/tds12c/o1_mf_users_cmht93rw_.dbf' FORMAT '/u01/app/oracle/
product/tds12c/convert/data_D-ADG12C_I-4282403005_TS-USERS_FNO-6_0cr5ngtf'
; }
```

transportscript.sql is the control file creation script and other execution instructions. Copy the datafiles, init file, convert script, and transport script to the target site.

Start the target database in nomount state using the copied pfile. Make the necessary changes in the pfile if required.

```
SQL> startup nomount
ORACLE instance started.

Total System Global Area  629145600 bytes
Fixed Size                  3006784 bytes
Variable Size             281022144 bytes
Database Buffers          339738624 bytes
Redo Buffers                5378048 bytes
```

Connect to the RMAN prompt and start converting the datafiles to the target platform. The datafiles are copied at /u01/app/oracle/product/sol12 on the target server.

```
RMAN> RUN {
  CONVERT
  FROM PLATFORM 'Linux x86 64-bit'
  PARALLELISM 1
 DATAFILE '/u01/app/oracle/product/sol12/o1_mf_system_cmht7dkb_.dbf' FORMAT '/u01/app/
oracle/product/sol12/convert/data_D-ADG12C_I-4282403005_TS-SYSTEM_FNO-1_09r5ngte'
DATAFILE '/u01/app/oracle/product/sol12/o1_mf_sysaux_cmht5ojd_.dbf' FORMAT '/u01/app/oracle/
product/sol12/convert/data_D-ADG12C_I-4282403005_TS-SYSAUX_FNO-3_0ar5ngte'
DATAFILE '/u01/app/oracle/product/sol12/o1_mf_undotbs1_cmht94wr_.dbf' FORMAT '/u01/app/
oracle/product/sol12/convert/data_D-ADG12C_I-4282403005_TS-UNDOTBS1_FNO-4_0br5ngte'
DATAFILE '/u01/app/oracle/product/sol12/o1_mf_users_cmht93rw_.dbf' FORMAT '/u01/app/oracle/
product/sol12/convert/data_D-ADG12C_I-4282403005_TS-USERS_FNO-6_0cr5ngtf'
 ; }

Starting conversion at target
using target database control file instead of recovery catalog
allocated channel: ORA_DISK_1
channel ORA_DISK_1: SID=13 device type=DISK
channel ORA_DISK_1: starting datafile conversion
input file name=/u01/app/oracle/product/sol12/o1_mf_system_cmht7dkb_.dbf
converted datafile=/u01/app/oracle/product/sol12/convert/data_D-ADG12C_I-4282403005_TS-
SYSTEM_FNO-1_09r5ngte
channel ORA_DISK_1: datafile conversion complete, elapsed time: 00:00:15
channel ORA_DISK_1: starting datafile conversion
input file name=/u01/app/oracle/product/sol12/o1_mf_sysaux_cmht5ojd_.dbf
converted datafile=/u01/app/oracle/product/sol12/convert/data_D-ADG12C_I-4282403005_TS-
SYSAUX_FNO-3_0ar5ngte
channel ORA_DISK_1: datafile conversion complete, elapsed time: 00:00:15
channel ORA_DISK_1: starting datafile conversion
input file name=/u01/app/oracle/product/sol12/o1_mf_undotbs1_cmht94wr_.dbf
converted datafile=/u01/app/oracle/product/sol12/convert/data_D-ADG12C_I-4282403005_TS-
UNDOTBS1_FNO-4_0br5ngte
channel ORA_DISK_1: datafile conversion complete, elapsed time: 00:00:01
channel ORA_DISK_1: starting datafile conversion
input file name=/u01/app/oracle/product/sol12/o1_mf_users_cmht93rw_.dbf
converted datafile=/u01/app/oracle/product/sol12/convert/data_D-ADG12C_I-4282403005_TS-
USERS_FNO-6_0cr5ngtf
channel ORA_DISK_1: datafile conversion complete, elapsed time: 00:00:01
```

The datafiles are converted and placed at /u01/app/oracle/product/sol12/convert.

The control file can be created using these datafiles:

```
SQL> CREATE CONTROLFILE REUSE SET DATABASE "sol12" RESETLOGS  ARCHIVELOG
  2      MAXLOGFILES 16
  3      MAXLOGMEMBERS 3
  4      MAXDATAFILES 100
  5      MAXINSTANCES 8
  6      MAXLOGHISTORY 292
  7  LOGFILE
  8    GROUP 1 '/u01/app/oracle/product/sol12/convert/redo01.log' SIZE 50M BLOCKSIZE 512,
  9    GROUP 2 '/u01/app/oracle/product/sol12/convert/redo02.log' SIZE 50M BLOCKSIZE 512,
 10    GROUP 3 '/u01/app/oracle/product/sol12/convert/redo03.log' SIZE 50M BLOCKSIZE 512
```

```
11  DATAFILE
12    '/u01/app/oracle/product/sol12/convert/data_D-ADG12C_I-4282403005_TS-SYSTEM_FNO-
1_09r5ngte',
13    '/u01/app/oracle/product/sol12/convert/data_D-ADG12C_I-4282403005_TS-SYSAUX_FNO-
3_0ar5ngte',
14    '/u01/app/oracle/product/sol12/convert/data_D-ADG12C_I-4282403005_TS-UNDOTBS1_FNO-
4_0br5ngte',
15    '/u01/app/oracle/product/sol12/convert/data_D-ADG12C_I-4282403005_TS-USERS_FNO-
6_0cr5ngtf'
16  CHARACTER SET WE8MSWIN1252
17  ;
```

Control file created.

Open the database using resetlogs.

```
SQL> alter database open resetlogs;
Database altered.
```

With 12*c*, a new feature was introduced to transfer data using RMAN backup sets. Along with the prerequisites shown earlier, you require the source and target databases to have the Oracle 12*c* version, and the compatible parameter value should be 12.0.0 or higher. Transferring as a backup set will avoid transferring unused blocks in a datafile. In the image copy, you transfer the whole datafile with the used and unused blocks; hence, the transfer will consume time.

Let's see an example.

- *Source platform*: Linux x86-64

- *Destination platform*: Solaris x86-64

- *Database version*: 12.1.0.2.0

Here are the steps:

1) Perform the prerequisite checks including endian format, external objects, and directories.

2) Open the source database in read-only mode.

3) Take an RMAN backup of the source database. In 12*c*, a backup can be taken as a backup set. You can do the conversion either at the source server or at the target server. FOR TRANSPORT is used along with the backup command to denote that conversion will happen at the target site. If conversion happens at the source, then TO PLATFORM will be used. Let's convert it at the target server in the first exercise.

```
RMAN> BACKUP
 FOR TRANSPORT
 FORMAT '/u01/app/oracle/oradata/linux12c/%U'
 database ;2> 3> 4>

Starting backup
using target database control file instead of recovery catalog
allocated channel: ORA_DISK_1
channel ORA_DISK_1: SID=1 device type=DISK
channel ORA_DISK_1: starting full datafile backup set
```

```
channel ORA_DISK_1: specifying datafile(s) in backup set
input datafile file number=00001 name=/u02/oradata/LINUX12C/datafile/o1_mf_system_cmm5whlx_.
dbf
input datafile file number=00003 name=/u02/oradata/LINUX12C/datafile/o1_mf_sysaux_cmm5ssy2_.
dbf
input datafile file number=00004 name=/u02/oradata/LINUX12C/datafile/o1_mf_undotbs1_
cmm5yw2g_.dbf
input datafile file number=00006 name=/u02/oradata/LINUX12C/datafile/o1_mf_users_cmm5ytxy_.
dbf
channel ORA_DISK_1: starting piece 1
channel ORA_DISK_1: finished piece 1
piece handle=/u01/app/oracle/oradata/linux12c/02r5npkp_1_1 tag=TAG20160516T111433
comment=NONE
channel ORA_DISK_1: backup set complete, elapsed time: 00:04:28
channel ORA_DISK_1: starting full datafile backup set
channel ORA_DISK_1: specifying datafile(s) in backup set
input datafile file number=00009 name=/u02/oradata/LINUX12C/32F3B6F135B31CD4E0530F02000AB
4C4/datafile/o1_mf_sysaux_cmm6nxmn_.dbf
input datafile file number=00008 name=/u02/oradata/LINUX12C/32F3B6F135B31CD4E0530F02000AB
4C4/datafile/o1_mf_system_cmm6nxh6_.dbf
input datafile file number=00010 name=/u02/oradata/LINUX12C/32F3B6F135B31CD4E0530F02000AB
4C4/datafile/o1_mf_users_cmm6qkrt_.dbf
channel ORA_DISK_1: starting piece 1
channel ORA_DISK_1: finished piece 1
piece handle=/u01/app/oracle/oradata/linux12c/03r5npt6_1_1 tag=TAG20160516T111433
comment=NONE
channel ORA_DISK_1: backup set complete, elapsed time: 00:01:15
channel ORA_DISK_1: starting full datafile backup set
channel ORA_DISK_1: specifying datafile(s) in backup set
input datafile file number=00007 name=/u02/oradata/LINUX12C/datafile/o1_mf_sysaux_cmm6oqvx_.
dbf
input datafile file number=00005 name=/u02/oradata/LINUX12C/datafile/o1_mf_system_cmm6oqw2_.
dbf
channel ORA_DISK_1: starting piece 1
channel ORA_DISK_1: finished piece 1
piece handle=/u01/app/oracle/oradata/linux12c/04r5npvh_1_1 tag=TAG20160516T111433
comment=NONE
channel ORA_DISK_1: backup set complete, elapsed time: 00:00:45
Finished backup
```

Here the source database is a multitenant database; hence, the backup of the container and pluggable database has been taken as the backup set.

Capture the control file creation script using the following:

```
SQL> alter database backup controlfile to trace;

Database altered.
```

Copy the backup set, init file, and control file creation script to the target server.

On the target server, start the database in nomount state using the copied init parameter file.

```
SQL> STARTUP NOMOUNT
ORACLE instance started.

Total System Global Area 1258291200 bytes
Fixed Size                   3003176 bytes
Variable Size              452988120 bytes
Database Buffers           788529152 bytes
Redo Buffers                13770752 bytes
SQL> exit
```

Connect to RMAN as the target database and restore the backup set along with conversion. This is a new feature of 12c.

```
RMAN> restore from platform 'Linux x86 64-bit'
2> foreign database to new
3> from backupset '/u01/app/oracle/oradata/LINUX12c/02r5npkp_1_1'
4> backupset '/u01/app/oracle/oradata/LINUX12c/03r5npt6_1_1'
5> backupset '/u01/app/oracle/oradata/LINUX12c/04r5npvh_1_1';

Starting restore
using target database control file instead of recovery catalog
allocated channel: ORA_DISK_1
channel ORA_DISK_1: SID=23 device type=DISK
channel ORA_DISK_1: starting datafile backup set restore
channel ORA_DISK_1: specifying datafile(s) to restore from backup set
channel ORA_DISK_1: restoring all foreign files in backup piece
channel ORA_DISK_1: reading from backup piece /u01/app/oracle/oradata/LINUX12c/02r5npkp_1_1
channel ORA_DISK_1: restoring foreign file 1 to /u01/app/oracle/oradata/LINUX12C/datafile/
o1_mf_system_cmmf2xom_.dbf
channel ORA_DISK_1: restoring foreign file 3 to /u01/app/oracle/oradata/LINUX12C/datafile/
o1_mf_sysaux_cmmf2xpq_.dbf
channel ORA_DISK_1: restoring foreign file 4 to /u01/app/oracle/oradata/LINUX12C/datafile/
o1_mf_undotbs1_cmmf2xpr_.dbf
channel ORA_DISK_1: restoring foreign file 6 to /u01/app/oracle/oradata/LINUX12C/datafile/
o1_mf_users_cmmf2xps_.dbf
channel ORA_DISK_1: foreign piece handle=/u01/app/oracle/oradata/LINUX12c/02r5npkp_1_1
channel ORA_DISK_1: restored backup piece 1
channel ORA_DISK_1: restore complete, elapsed time: 00:03:26
channel ORA_DISK_1: starting datafile backup set restore
channel ORA_DISK_1: specifying datafile(s) to restore from backup set
channel ORA_DISK_1: restoring all foreign files in backup piece
channel ORA_DISK_1: reading from backup piece /u01/app/oracle/oradata/LINUX12c/03r5npt6_1_1
channel ORA_DISK_1: restoring foreign file 9 to /u01/app/oracle/oradata/LINUX12C/datafile/
o1_mf_sysaux_cmmf9f62_.dbf
channel ORA_DISK_1: restoring foreign file 8 to /u01/app/oracle/oradata/LINUX12C/datafile/
o1_mf_system_cmmf9fpb_.dbf
channel ORA_DISK_1: restoring foreign file 10 to /u01/app/oracle/oradata/LINUX12C/datafile/
o1_mf_users_cmmf9fpo_.dbf
channel ORA_DISK_1: foreign piece handle=/u01/app/oracle/oradata/LINUX12c/03r5npt6_1_1
channel ORA_DISK_1: restored backup piece 1
channel ORA_DISK_1: restore complete, elapsed time: 00:02:08
channel ORA_DISK_1: starting datafile backup set restore
```

```
channel ORA_DISK_1: specifying datafile(s) to restore from backup set
channel ORA_DISK_1: restoring all foreign files in backup piece
channel ORA_DISK_1: reading from backup piece /u01/app/oracle/oradata/LINUX12c/04r5npvh_1_1
channel ORA_DISK_1: restoring foreign file 7 to /u01/app/oracle/oradata/LINUX12C/datafile/
o1_mf_sysaux_cmmfff5m_.dbf
channel ORA_DISK_1: restoring foreign file 5 to /u01/app/oracle/oradata/LINUX12C/datafile/
o1_mf_system_cmmfffpq_.dbf
channel ORA_DISK_1: foreign piece handle=/u01/app/oracle/oradata/LINUX12c/04r5npvh_1_1
channel ORA_DISK_1: restored backup piece 1
channel ORA_DISK_1: restore complete, elapsed time: 00:02:16
```

Create the control file using the copied control file creation script. Modify the datafile location according to the restore.

```
CREATE CONTROLFILE REUSE DATABASE "LINUX12C" RESETLOGS  NOARCHIVELOG
    MAXLOGFILES 16
    MAXLOGMEMBERS 3
    MAXDATAFILES 1024
    MAXINSTANCES 8
    MAXLOGHISTORY 292
LOGFILE
  GROUP 1 (
    '/u01/app/oracle/oradata/LINUX12C/redo01.log'
  ) SIZE 50M BLOCKSIZE 512,
  GROUP 2 (
    '/u01/app/oracle/oradata/LINUX12C/redo02.log'
  ) SIZE 50M BLOCKSIZE 512,
  GROUP 3 (
    '/u01/app/oracle/oradata/LINUX12C/redo03.log'
  ) SIZE 50M BLOCKSIZE 512
-- STANDBY LOGFILE
DATAFILE
  '/u01/app/oracle/oradata/LINUX12C/datafile/o1_mf_system_cmmf2xom_.dbf',
  '/u01/app/oracle/oradata/LINUX12C/datafile/o1_mf_sysaux_cmmf2xpq_.dbf',
  '/u01/app/oracle/oradata/LINUX12C/datafile/o1_mf_undotbs1_cmmf2xpr_.dbf',
  '/u01/app/oracle/oradata/LINUX12C/datafile/o1_mf_users_cmmf2xps_.dbf',
  '/u01/app/oracle/oradata/LINUX12C/datafile/o1_mf_sysaux_cmmf9f62_.dbf',
  '/u01/app/oracle/oradata/LINUX12C/datafile/o1_mf_system_cmmf9fpb_.dbf',
  '/u01/app/oracle/oradata/LINUX12C/datafile/o1_mf_users_cmmf9fpo_.dbf',
  '/u01/app/oracle/oradata/LINUX12C/datafile/o1_mf_sysaux_cmmfff5m_.dbf',
  '/u01/app/oracle/oradata/LINUX12C/datafile/o1_mf_system_cmmfffpq_.dbf'
CHARACTER SET WE8MSWIN1252
;
```

```
Control file created.
```

Open the database using the resetlogs option.

```
SQL> alter database open resetlogs;
```

```
Database altered.
```

You have seen how the conversion happens at the target site. Let's see the conversion at the source server.

1) Open the source database in read-only mode.

2) Execute the RMAN backup script with TO PLATFORM. This will take a backup with the converted datafile.

```
RMAN> BACKUP
TO PLATFORM 'Solaris Operating System (x86-64)'
 database ;
2> 3>
Starting backup
using target database control file instead of recovery catalog
allocated channel: ORA_DISK_1
channel ORA_DISK_1: SID=2 device type=DISK
channel ORA_DISK_1: starting full datafile backup set
channel ORA_DISK_1: specifying datafile(s) in backup set
input datafile file number=00001 name=/u01/app/oracle/oradata/LINUX12C/datafile/
o1_mf_system_cmmhf20h_.dbf
input datafile file number=00003 name=/u01/app/oracle/oradata/LINUX12C/datafile/
o1_mf_sysaux_cmmhcnpy_.dbf
input datafile file number=00004 name=/u01/app/oracle/oradata/LINUX12C/datafile/
o1_mf_undotbs1_cmmhgtcs_.dbf
input datafile file number=00006 name=/u01/app/oracle/oradata/LINUX12C/datafile/
o1_mf_users_cmmhgs76_.dbf
channel ORA_DISK_1: starting piece 1
channel ORA_DISK_1: finished piece 1
piece handle=/u01/app/oracle/product/12.1.0.2.0/dbs/01r5nv52_1_1
tag=TAG20160516T124834 comment=NONE
channel ORA_DISK_1: backup set complete, elapsed time: 00:00:35
channel ORA_DISK_1: starting full datafile backup set
channel ORA_DISK_1: specifying datafile(s) in backup set
input datafile file number=00009 name=/u01/app/oracle/oradata/LINUX12C/32F5EBB014
602EECE0535B08DC0A0321/datafile/o1_mf_sysaux_cmmhwwx3_.dbf
input datafile file number=00008 name=/u01/app/oracle/oradata/LINUX12C/32F5EBB014
602EECE0535B08DC0A0321/datafile/o1_mf_system_cmmhwwwj_.dbf
input datafile file number=00010 name=/u01/app/oracle/oradata/LINUX12C/32F5EBB014
602EECE0535B08DC0A0321/datafile/o1_mf_users_cmmhxlbb_.dbf
channel ORA_DISK_1: starting piece 1
channel ORA_DISK_1: finished piece 1
piece handle=/u01/app/oracle/product/12.1.0.2.0/dbs/02r5nv65_1_1
tag=TAG20160516T124834 comment=NONE
channel ORA_DISK_1: backup set complete, elapsed time: 00:00:25
channel ORA_DISK_1: starting full datafile backup set
channel ORA_DISK_1: specifying datafile(s) in backup set
input datafile file number=00007 name=/u01/app/oracle/oradata/LINUX12C/datafile/
o1_mf_sysaux_cmmhl6d3_.dbf
input datafile file number=00005 name=/u01/app/oracle/oradata/LINUX12C/datafile/
o1_mf_system_cmmhl6dc_.dbf
channel ORA_DISK_1: starting piece 1
channel ORA_DISK_1: finished piece 1
```

```
      piece handle=/u01/app/oracle/product/12.1.0.2.0/dbs/03r5nv6u_1_1
      tag=TAG20160516T124834 comment=NONE
      channel ORA_DISK_1: backup set complete, elapsed time: 00:00:15
```

3) Move the backup sets and init parameter file to the target server.

4) On the target server, start the database in nomount state.

```
      SQL> startup nomount
      ORACLE instance started.

      Total System Global Area 1.5234E+10 bytes
      Fixed Size                  3021416 bytes
      Variable Size            2147485080 bytes
      Database Buffers         1.3053E+10 bytes
      Redo Buffers               30531584 bytes
```

5) Restore the backup using RMAN.

```
      RMAN> RESTORE
      2> FOREIGN DATABASE TO NEW
      3> FROM BACKUPSET '/u01/app/oracle/oradata/linux12c/01r5nv52_1_1'
      4>     BACKUPSET '/u01/app/oracle/oradata/linux12c/02r5nv65_1_1'
      5>     BACKUPSET '/u01/app/oracle/oradata/linux12c/03r5nv6u_1_1';

      Starting restore
      using target database control file instead of recovery catalog
      allocated channel: ORA_DISK_1
      channel ORA_DISK_1: SID=242 device type=DISK

      channel ORA_DISK_1: starting datafile backup set restore
      channel ORA_DISK_1: specifying datafile(s) to restore from backup set
      channel ORA_DISK_1: restoring all foreign files in backup piece
      channel ORA_DISK_1: reading from backup piece /u01/app/oracle/oradata/
      linux12c/01r5nv52_1_1
      channel ORA_DISK_1: restoring foreign file 1 to /u01/app/oracle/oradata/LINUX12C/
      datafile/o1_mf_system_cmmnrkhb_.dbf
      channel ORA_DISK_1: restoring foreign file 3 to /u01/app/oracle/oradata/LINUX12C/
      datafile/o1_mf_sysaux_cmmnrkhr_.dbf
      channel ORA_DISK_1: restoring foreign file 4 to /u01/app/oracle/oradata/LINUX12C/
      datafile/o1_mf_undotbs1_cmmnrkj1_.dbf
      channel ORA_DISK_1: restoring foreign file 6 to /u01/app/oracle/oradata/LINUX12C/
      datafile/o1_mf_users_cmmnrkjj_.dbf
      channel ORA_DISK_1: foreign piece handle=/u01/app/oracle/oradata/
      linux12c/01r5nv52_1_1
      channel ORA_DISK_1: restored backup piece 1
      channel ORA_DISK_1: restore complete, elapsed time: 00:00:36
      channel ORA_DISK_1: starting datafile backup set restore
      channel ORA_DISK_1: specifying datafile(s) to restore from backup set
      channel ORA_DISK_1: restoring all foreign files in backup piece
```

```
channel ORA_DISK_1: reading from backup piece /u01/app/oracle/oradata/
linux12c/02r5nv65_1_1
channel ORA_DISK_1: restoring foreign file 9 to /u01/app/oracle/oradata/LINUX12C/
datafile/o1_mf_sysaux_cmmnsolj_.dbf
channel ORA_DISK_1: restoring foreign file 8 to /u01/app/oracle/oradata/LINUX12C/
datafile/o1_mf_system_cmmnsolv_.dbf
channel ORA_DISK_1: restoring foreign file 10 to /u01/app/oracle/oradata/
LINUX12C/datafile/o1_mf_users_cmmnsom6_.dbf
channel ORA_DISK_1: foreign piece handle=/u01/app/oracle/oradata/
linux12c/02r5nv65_1_1
channel ORA_DISK_1: restored backup piece 1
channel ORA_DISK_1: restore complete, elapsed time: 00:00:16
channel ORA_DISK_1: starting datafile backup set restore
channel ORA_DISK_1: specifying datafile(s) to restore from backup set
channel ORA_DISK_1: restoring all foreign files in backup piece
channel ORA_DISK_1: reading from backup piece /u01/app/oracle/oradata/
linux12c/03r5nv6u_1_1
channel ORA_DISK_1: restoring foreign file 7 to /u01/app/oracle/oradata/LINUX12C/
datafile/o1_mf_sysaux_cmmnt5mp_.dbf
channel ORA_DISK_1: restoring foreign file 5 to /u01/app/oracle/oradata/LINUX12C/
datafile/o1_mf_system_cmmnt5n2_.dbf
channel ORA_DISK_1: foreign piece handle=/u01/app/oracle/oradata/
linux12c/03r5nv6u_1_1
channel ORA_DISK_1: restored backup piece 1
channel ORA_DISK_1: restore complete, elapsed time: 00:00:16
```

6) Create the control file on the target server.

```
SQL> CREATE CONTROLFILE REUSE DATABASE "LINUX12C" RESETLOGS  ARCHIVELOG
    MAXLOGFILES 16
    MAXLOGMEMBERS 3
    MAXDATAFILES 1024
    MAXINSTANCES 8
    MAXLOGHISTORY 292
LOGFILE
  GROUP 1 (
    '/u01/app/oracle/oradata/LINUX12C/onlinelog/o1_mf_1_cmmhko00_.log'
  ) SIZE 50M BLOCKSIZE 512,
  GROUP 2 (
    '/u01/app/oracle/oradata/LINUX12C/onlinelog/o1_mf_2_cmmhkqj2_.log'
  ) SIZE 50M BLOCKSIZE 512,
  GROUP 3 (
    '/u01/app/oracle/oradata/LINUX12C/onlinelog/o1_mf_3_cmmhkt06_.log'
  ) SIZE 50M BLOCKSIZE 512
-- STANDBY LOGFILE
DATAFILE
  '/u01/app/oracle/oradata/LINUX12C/datafile/o1_mf_system_cmmnrkhb_.dbf',
  '/u01/app/oracle/oradata/LINUX12C/datafile/o1_mf_sysaux_cmmnrkhr_.dbf',
  '/u01/app/oracle/oradata/LINUX12C/datafile/o1_mf_undotbs1_cmmnrkj1_.dbf',
  /u01/app/oracle/oradata/LINUX12C/datafile/o1_mf_users_cmmnrkjj_.dbf',
  '/u01/app/oracle/oradata/LINUX12C/datafile/o1_mf_sysaux_cmmnsolj_.dbf',
```

```
        '/u01/app/oracle/oradata/LINUX12C/datafile/o1_mf_system_cmmnsolv_.dbf',
        '/u01/app/oracle/oradata/LINUX12C/datafile/o1_mf_users_cmmnsom6_.dbf',
        '/u01/app/oracle/oradata/LINUX12C/datafile/o1_mf_sysaux_cmmnt5mp_.dbf',
        '/u01/app/oracle/oradata/LINUX12C/datafile/o1_mf_system_cmmnt5n2_.dbf'
CHARACTER SET WE8MSWIN1252
;
Control file created.
```

7) Open the database using the `resetlogs` option.

```
SQL> alter database open resetlogs;
Database altered.
```

8) Create the temporary tablespace.

```
Sql> create temporary tablespace temp1;
Tablespace created.
```

Heterogeneous Standby Database

You saw how the Data Guard concept can be used for a database upgrade in Chapter 2. We discussed the transient logical standby method to upgrade the database with less downtime. There you considered that the databases are located in the same platform. But Data Guard has much more than that. It has limited support for heterogeneous standby databases. This means the primary and standby can be on different platforms. Using this heterogeneous concept, you can do a database migration though Data Guard.

In this section, we'll discuss how Data Guard can be used for a database migration. Suppose you want to move a database to a different platform. First you will be creating a standby database on a different platform, and then the redo data will get applied from the primary to the standby to make it sync. When you want to move to the migrated platform, the standby database can be activated as the primary database. There will be some downtime when activating the standby database, but the downtime is less than with the traditional export/import, Data Pump, and transport tablespace methods.

Note that the Data Guard setup will not support all platform combinations. There is a limitation on the supported heterogeneous platforms for Data Guard setup. The supported platforms can be verified through Oracle documentation or Oracle Support.

Let's discuss the migration steps with an example. Say that the current database is located on the Linux x86-64 platform and you want to migrate the database to the Solaris x86-64 platform. It has been confirmed with documentation that Data Guard will support this platform combination.

Primary platform: Linux x86-64	*Destination platform*: Solaris x86-64
Database version: 12.1.0.2.0	*Database version*: 12.1.0.2.0
Database name: adg12c	*Database name*: adg12c
	Unique name: adg12cs

1) Connect to the database and configure the `init` parameters for redo apply.

```
*.db_file_name_convert='/u01/app/oracle/oradata/adg12cs','/u01/app/oracle/
oradata/adg12c/datafile/'
```

```
*.log_file_name_convert='/u01/app/oracle/oradata/adg12cs','/u01/app/oracle/
oradata/adg12c/logfile/',
*.log_archive_config='dg_config=(adg12c,adg12cs)'
*.fal_server=adg12cs
*.fal_client=adg12c
*.log_archive_dest_2='service=adg12cs ASYNC NOAFFIRM delay=0 optional
compression=enable max_failure=0 max_connections=1 reopen=300 db_unique_
name=adg12cs net_timeout=30, valid_for=(online_logfile,all_roles)
```

2) On the target server, configure the init parameters for standby and start the database in nomount mode.

```
*.db_file_name_convert='/u01/app/oracle/oradata/ADG12C/datafile/','/u01/app/
oracle/oradata/adg12cs'
*.log_file_name_convert='/u01/app/oracle/oradata/ADG12C/datafile/','/u01/app/
oracle/oradata/adg12cs'
*.log_archive_config='dg_config=(adg12c,adg12cs)'
*.fal_server=adg12c
*.fal_client=adg12cs
```

3) Create the standby database on the remote server. It can be created either using the RMAN duplicate command or using backup restore. The RMAN active duplicate command (available since 11g R2) is easier because it will copy the datafiles to a remote location automatically, and also the standby control file will be created as part of the duplicate.

```
rman target sys/sys@adg12c auxiliary sys/sys@adg12cs

connected to target database: ADG12C (DBID=4282675890)
connected to auxiliary database: ADG12C (not mounted)
RMAN> duplicate target database for standby from active database;

Starting Duplicate Db
using target database control file instead of recovery catalog
allocated channel: ORA_AUX_DISK_1
channel ORA_AUX_DISK_1: SID=248 device type=DISK
.
.
Finished Duplicate Db at 18-MAY-16
```

4) Connect to the standby database server and check its details.

```
SQL> SELECT database_role role, name, db_unique_name, platform_id, open_mode,
log_mode, flashback_on, protection_mode, protection_level FROM v$database;
```

ROLE	NAME	DB_UNIQUE_NAME	PLATFORM_ID	OPEN_MODE
PROTECTION_MODE				
---------------	-------	--------------	-----------	---------
PHYSICAL STANDBY	ADG12C	adg12cs	20	READ ONLY
MAXIMUM				
PERFORMANCE				

269

5) Check the sync between the primary and standby databases.

```
SQL> SELECT al.thrd "Thread", almax "Last Seq Received", lhmax "Last Seq
Applied" FROM (select thread# thrd, MAX(sequence#) almax FROM v$archived_log
WHERE resetlogs_change#=(SELECT resetlogs_change# FROM v$database) GROUP BY
thread#) al, (SELECT thread# thrd, MAX(sequence#) lhmax FROM v$log_history WHERE
resetlogs_change#=(SELECT resetlogs_change# FROM v$database) GROUP BY thread#) lh
WHERE al.thrd = lh.thrd;
    Thread Last Seq Received Last Seq Applied
---------- ----------------- ----------------
         1                10               10
```

6) When the migration requires it, ensure the primary and standby are in sync.

```
SQL> SELECT THREAD#, LOW_SEQUENCE#, HIGH_SEQUENCE# FROM V$ARCHIVE_GAP;
no rows selected
```

If any archived logs are missing, then copy those to the standby and register the logs to the standby database.

7) Activate the standby database.

```
SQL> recover managed standby database cancel;
Media recovery complete.
SQL> alter database recover managed standby database finish;
Database altered.
SQL> ALTER DATABASE COMMIT TO SWITCHOVER TO PRIMARY WITH SESSION SHUTDOWN;
Database altered.
SQL> ALTER DATABASE OPEN;
Database altered.
```

8) Make changes in the TNS settings, which will divert the connections to the new migrated database.

Now the database has been migrated to a Solaris x86-64 bit server. In the previous example, you tried failover through SQL commands. You can try using the Data Guard Broker as well.

Once the Data Guard Broker is configured for the primary and standby servers, you can perform failover through the broker.

```
DGMGRL>  Failover to '<standby database name>';
```

Oracle Streams

Oracle Streams is one of the commonly used methods for data replication, but this product has been deprecated in favor of GoldenGate, which we discussed earlier in this chapter. You can use it to replicate the data to remote databases in different locations. The remote database can be on the same platform or on a different one. It could be with different database version also.

Streams has a capture process that captures database changes made to tables, schemas, or an entire database. Basically, these changes are recorded in a redo log. The capture process collects the changes from the redo log and creates a record that is called the *logical change record* (LCR). You can define rules to specify which changes have to be captured. The captured changes will be stored in a queue. The Streams feature propagates those changes from the source queue to the destination queue. The destination database will have a queue to receive the messages. There will be an apply process at the destination database that will dequeue the LCR from the destination queue and apply the changes to the destination database. That's how the replication happens via Streams. The replication can work in a single direction or bidirectionally.

You can make use of the Streams replication feature to migrate the database to different platforms. Let's discuss the steps with an example.

- *Source database name*: sol11203

- *Source platform*: Solaris Sparc 64-bit

- *Source database version*: 11.2.0.3.0

You want to migrate this database to the Linux x86-64 platform. For that, first you need to create the database in the destination platform.

- *Source database name*: Lin11203

- *Source platform*: Linux x8-64 bit

- Source database version: 11.2.0.3.0

Network connectivity should be present between the source and target databases. You have restored the required data in the destination database. In this case, the hr schema has to be migrated from the source to the target server. The hr schema has been exported and imported into the destination database. You configure the Streams feature to start replicating changes happening in the hr schema to the destination database.

1) Create an admin user for Streams in the source and target databases and provide the necessary privileges.

```
SQL> CREATE USER stradmin IDENTIFIED BY stradmin;
User created.
SQL> GRANT DBA TO stradmin;
Grant succeeded
SQL> BEGIN
DBMS_STREAMS_AUTH.GRANT_ADMIN_PRIVILEGE(
grantee => 'stradmin',
grant_privileges => true);
END;
PL/SQL procedure successfully completed.
```

2) You can check whether the Streams admin is created using the following:

```
SQL> select * from dba_streams_administrator;
USERNAME              LOCAL_PRIVILEGES          ACCESS_FROM_REMOTE
---------------       ----------------------    ------------------------
STRADMIN              YES                       YES
```

3) The following steps will be done as the STRADMIN user. Create a database link between the source and target under the stradmin user in both databases.

Source server:

```
SQL> create database link dest connect to stradmin identified by stradmin using
'Lin11203';
Database link created.
```

Target server:

```
SQL> create database link src connect to stradmin identified by stradmin using
'Sol11203';
Database link created.
```

4) Create supplementary logging for objects created in the hr schema in both the databases.

```
SQL> alter table test add supplemental log group supp_log_test(n);
Table altered.
```

Verify the creation using the following:

```
SQL> select log_group_name, table_name from dba_log_groups where owner='HR';
LOG_GROUP_NAME                    TABLE_NAME
------------------------------    ------------------------------
SUPP_LOG_TEST                     TEST
```

5) Create queues for the capture and apply processes at the source and target databases.

Source:

```
SQL> begin
dbms_streams_adm.set_up_queue(
queue_table => 'apply_srctab',
queue_name => 'apply_src',
queue_user => 'stradmin');
end;
/
PL/SQL procedure successfully completed.
SQL> begin
dbms_streams_adm.set_up_queue(
queue_table => 'capture_srctab',
queue_name => 'capture_src',
queue_user => 'stradmin');
end;
/
PL/SQL procedure successfully completed.
```

Target:

```
SQL> begin
dbms_streams_adm.set_up_queue(
queue_table => 'apply_desttab',
queue_name => 'apply_dest',
queue_user => 'stradmin');
end;
/
PL/SQL procedure successfully completed.
SQL> begin
dbms_streams_adm.set_up_queue(
queue_table => 'capture_desttab',
queue_name => 'capture_dest',
queue_user => 'stradmin');
end;
/
PL/SQL procedure successfully completed.
```

6) Configure the capture process on the source and target databases. This defines what to capture from the changes.

Source:

```
SQL> begin
dbms_streams_adm.add_schema_rules (
schema_name => 'hr',
streams_type => 'capture',
streams_name => 'captures_src',
queue_name => 'capture_src',
include_dml => true,
include_ddl => true,
inclusion_rule => true);
end;
/
PL/SQL procedure successfully completed.
```

This shows the DML and DDL changes that have to be captured.

Target:

```
SQL> begin
dbms_streams_adm.add_schema_rules (
schema_name => 'hr',
streams_type => 'capture',
streams_name => 'captures_dest',
queue_name => 'capture_dest',
include_dml => true,
include_ddl => true);
end;
/

PL/SQL procedure successfully completed.
```

7) Configure the apply process on the source and target databases.

Source:

```
SQL> begin
dbms_streams_adm.add_schema_rules (
schema_name => 'hr',
streams_type => 'apply',
streams_name => 'applys_src',
queue_name => 'apply_src',
include_dml => true,
include_ddl => true,
source_database => ' Lin11203');
end;
/
PL/SQL procedure successfully completed.
```

Target:

```
SQL> begin
dbms_streams_adm.add_schema_rules (
schema_name => 'hr',
streams_type => 'apply',
streams_name => 'applys_dest',
queue_name => 'apply_dest',
include_dml => true,
include_ddl => true,
source_database => 'Sol11203');
end;
/
PL/SQL procedure successfully completed.
```

8) Configure the propagation process on the source and target databases.

Source:

```
SQL> begin
  2  dbms_streams_adm.add_schema_propagation_rules (
  3  schema_name => 'hr',
  4  streams_name => 'prop_src_to_dest',
  5  source_queue_name => 'capture_src',
  6  destination_queue_name => 'apply_dest@dest',
  7  include_dml => true,
  8  include_ddl => true,
  9  source_database => 'Sol11203');
 10  end;
 11  /
```

Target:

```
SQL> begin
  2   dbms_streams_adm.add_schema_propagation_rules (
  3   schema_name => 'hr',
  4   streams_name => 'prop_dest_to_src',
  5   source_queue_name => 'capture_dest',
  6   destination_queue_name => 'apply_src@src',
  7   include_dml => true,
  8   include_ddl => true,
  9   source_database => 'Lin11203');
 10   end;
 11   /
PL/SQL procedure successfully completed.
```

9)   Set the initiation SCN by querying the target database SCN using a database link.
     This activity should be done at the source and target databases.

Source:

```
SQL> declare
 v_scn number;
 begin
 v_scn := dbms_flashback.get_system_change_number();
 dbms_apply_adm.set_schema_instantiation_scn@dest(
 source_schema_name => 'hr',
 source_database_name => 'Sol11203',
 instantiation_scn => v_scn,
 recursive => true);
 end;
  /
PL/SQL procedure successfully completed.
```

Target:

```
SQL> declare
 v_scn number;
 begin
 v_scn := dbms_flashback.get_system_change_number();
 dbms_apply_adm.set_schema_instantiation_scn@src(
 source_schema_name => 'hr',
 source_database_name => 'Lin11203',
 instantiation_scn => v_scn,
 recursive => true);
 end;  2   3   4   5   6   7   8   9   10
  /

PL/SQL procedure successfully completed.
```

10) Start the capture and apply process on the source and target databases.

Target:

```
SQL> begin
dbms_apply_adm.set_parameter (
apply_name => 'applys_dest',
parameter => 'disable_on_error',
value => 'N');
end;
/
PL/SQL procedure successfully completed.

SQL> exec dbms_apply_adm.start_apply (apply_name=> 'applys_dest');

PL/SQL procedure successfully completed.

SQL> exec dbms_capture_adm.start_capture (capture_name=>'captures_dest');

PL/SQL procedure successfully completed.
```

Source:

```
SQL> begin
dbms_apply_adm.set_parameter (
apply_name => 'applys_src',
parameter => 'disable_on_error',
value => 'N');
end;
/
PL/SQL procedure successfully completed.

SQL> exec dbms_apply_adm.start_apply (apply_name=> 'applys_src');

PL/SQL procedure successfully completed.

SQL>
SQL> exec dbms_capture_adm.start_capture (capture_name=>'captures_src');

PL/SQL procedure successfully completed.
```

11) Create some objects at the source or target database under the hr objects and see whether the objects replicate in the remote database.

Source:

```
SQL> select * from test;

         N
----------
         1
```

```
SQL> insert into test values(1);

1 row created.

SQL> commit;

Commit complete.
```

Target:

```
SQL>   select * from test;


         N
----------
         1
         1
```

Target:

```
SQL>   create table tablinux(n number);

Table created.
```

Source:

```
SQL> select * from tab;


TNAME                            TABTYPE  CLUSTERID
------------------------------   -------  ----------
TABLINUX                         TABLE
TEST                             TABLE
```

You can see that the changes happening in hr are replicated both ways. This means data is replicated from a Solaris Sparc 64-bit platform to a Linux x86-64 platform. Data is getting migrated to a different environment, and both the databases are in sync. When you decide to conclude the migration, you can shut down the source database and start using only the target database located in the Linux x86-64 server.

Summary

In this chapter, we discussed all the methods available to migrate Oracle Database to a new environment. You explored each method and its steps with examples. You will learn about upgrading in RAC, multitenant, and DG environments in the upcoming chapters.

CHAPTER 6

■ ■ ■

Migrating Oracle Database from Non-ASM to ASM Environments

You can migrate a container database (CDB) with pluggable databases (PDBs) from a traditional file system to Oracle's Automatic Storage Management (ASM) with less downtime by moving datafiles online, which is a new feature in Oracle Database 12*c* (Figure 6-1). You can also move non-CDBs from non-ASM to ASM environments. You will have some downtime while moving the control files from non-ASM to ASM environments, but it's minimal downtime compared to the traditional method. In previous versions of Oracle, you had to place the database in nomount state when moving the control files and place the database in nomount or mount when moving the datafiles (SYSTEM, SYSAUX, UNDO, and TEMP) from non-ASM to ASM environments. While moving application-related tablespaces from non-ASM to ASM environments, you have to make sure that those tablespaces are offline. The advantage of this method is that there is no need to shut down the database and there is no need to move datafiles offline. Because of this, you can at least eliminate some sort of downtime in mission-critical production environments.

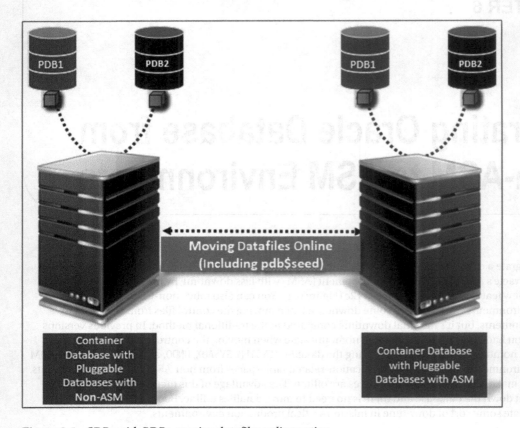

Figure 6-1. *CDBs with PDBs, moving datafiles online option*

These are the benefits of ASM:

- ASM was introduced in Oracle 10*g*. ASM acts like a volume manager and file system for Oracle Database files and supports a single instance as well as Real Application Clusters (RAC) configurations. ASM also plays a crucial role on the Oracle Exadata database machine. Oracle recommends ASM as a storage management solution for critical production database environments, and it provides alternate storage management to traditional volume managers, file systems, and raw devices. Oracle 12*c* has deprecated raw disk devices, so those on raw may want to move to ASM soon.

- ASM will stripe and mirror files across disks in an ASM disk group so that you can achieve high availability and balanced I/O.

- ASM provides an automatic "rebalance" for the disks.

- ASM can support large files.

- Oracle has introduced in 12*c* Flex ASM. Flex ASM reduces the per-node ASM instance in a cluster environment.

- In Oracle 12*c*, you have options while installing Grid Infrastructure (GI).

  a. You can configure a standard cluster.

- In Oracle 12*c*, if you want to convert from a configured standard cluster to Flex ASM, it's possible through the Automatic Storage Management Configuration Assistant (ASMCA), which has an option called Convert to Oracle Flex ASM.

In this chapter, we will walk you through three different scenarios:

- *Scenario 1*: Moving datafiles online from a non-ASM location to an ASM location using Oracle 12c's new option. This option also allows you to rename online datafiles, relocate online datafiles, and copy online datafiles.

- *Scenario 2*: Migrating an Oracle Database 12c CDB with PDBs from a non-ASM to ASM environment using Oracle Enterprise Manager Cloud Control 13c.

- *Scenario 3*: Migrating an Oracle Database 12c CDB with PDBs from a non-ASM to ASM environment using Recovery Manager (RMAN).

Scenario 1: Moving datafiles online from a non-ASM location to an ASM location

First we'll look at Oracle Database 12c's new option of moving datafiles online from a non-ASM location to an ASM location. Table 6-1 shows the setup information.

Table 6-1. *Locations of Datafiles, Redo Logs, and Control Files*

	Before Moving to ASM Oracle 12c (12.1.0.2.0)	After Moving to ASM Oracle 12c (12.1.0.2.0)
Used Method: **12c New Feature** **Move Datafile**	Container Database (cdb$root) SEED Database (pdb$root) Pluggable Databases (pdb1 & pdb2)	
Data File Locations	/u01/app/oracle/oradata/proddb/ /u01/app/oracle/oradata/proddb/pdbseed/ /u01/app/oracle/oradata/proddb/pdb1/ /u01/app/oracle/oradata/proddb/pdb2/	+DATA
Redo Log File Locations	/u01/app/oracle/oradata/proddb/	+DATA
Control Files	/u01/app/oracle/oradata/proddb/control01.ctl /u01/app/oracle/fast_recovery_area/proddb/control02.ctl	+DATA +FRA
SP file	/u01/app/oracle/product/12.1.0.2/dbhome_1/dbs/spfileproddb.ora	+DATA/PRODDB/spfilepro ddb.ora

Log in to the database instance and check the datafile locations of the CDB (proddb), seed database (pdb$seed), and PDBs (pdb1 and pdb2).

```
SQL> connect sys/oracle@proddb as sysdba
Connected.

SQL> show con_name
CON_NAME
-----------------
CDB$ROOT

SQL> show con_id
CON_ID
-----------------
```

1
```
SQL> select con_id, name, open_mode from v$pdbs;

CON_ID NAME           OPEN_MODE
------ -------------  ----------
     2 PDB$SEED       READ ONLY
     3 PDB1           MOUNTED
     4 PDB2           MOUNTED

SQL> alter pluggable database all open;
Pluggable database altered.
```

───

■ **Note**   Oracle 12*c* (12.1.0.2.0) has introduced an option called *faster PDB startups*.

───

This new clause is available with the ALTER PLUGGABLE DATABASE statement to preserve a PDB's open mode across CDB restarts. Here is the syntax:

```
alter pluggable database <pdb name> save|discard state
```

Note that the save state is the state of the PDB at the moment the save state command was issued, not the last state of the PDB before the CDB restart.

```
SQL> alter pluggable database pdb1 save state;
Pluggable database altered.

SQL> alter pluggable database pdb2 save state;
Pluggable database altered.

SQL> select con_id, name, open_mode from v$pdbs;

CON_ID     NAME                             OPEN_MODE
---------- ------------------------------   --------------------
         2 PDB$SEED                         READ ONLY
         3 PDB1                             READ WRITE
         4 PDB2                             READ WRITE
```

Check the locations of the datafiles, control files, and redo log groups for the CDB, seed database, and PDBs. The control files and redo log groups will be maintained at the container database level.

```
SQL> connect sys/oracle@192.168.56.100:1521/proddb as sysdba
Connected.

SQL> select file_name,tablespace_name from dba_data_files;

FILE_NAME                                    TABLESPACE_NAME
-------------------------------------------  ----------------
/u01/app/oracle/oradata/proddb/system01.dbf  SYSTEM
/u01/app/oracle/oradata/proddb/sysaux01.dbf  SYSAUX
/u01/app/oracle/oradata/proddb/undotbs01.dbf UNDOTBS1
/u01/app/oracle/oradata/proddb/users01.dbf   USERS
```

```
SQL> select file_name,tablespace_name from dba_temp_files;

FILE_NAME                                        TABLESPACE_NAME
----------------------------------------         ----------------
/u01/app/oracle/oradata/proddb/temp01.dbf        TEMP
```

In the same **way, you can check** the **datafile location for both pluggable databases** (pdb1 **and** pdb2). Connect to pdb1.

```
SQL> connect sys/oracle@192.168.56.100:1521/pdb1 as sysdba
Connected.

SQL> select file_name,tablespace_name from dba_data_files;
FILE_NAME                                        TABLESPACE_NAME
----------------------------------------------   ----------------
/u01/app/oracle/oradata/proddb/pdb1/system01.dbf      SYSTEM
/u01/app/oracle/oradata/proddb/pdb1/sysaux01.dbf      SYSAUX
/u01/app/oracle/oradata/proddb/pdb1/pdb1_users01.dbf  USERS

SQL> select file_name,tablespace_name from dba_temp_files;

FILE_NAME                                        TABLESPACE_NAME
----------------------------------------------   ----------------
/u01/app/oracle/oradata/proddb/pdb1/temp01.dbf        TEMP
```

Connect to pdb2.

```
SQL> connect sys/oracle@192.168.56.100:1521/pdb2 as sysdba
Connected.

SQL> select file_name,tablespace_name from dba_data_files;
FILE_NAME                                        TABLESPACE_NAME
----------------------------------------------   ----------------
/u01/app/oracle/oradata/proddb/pdb2/system01.dbf      SYSTEM
/u01/app/oracle/oradata/proddb/pdb2/sysaux01.dbf      SYSAUX
/u01/app/oracle/oradata/proddb/pdb2/pdb2_users01.dbf  USERS

SQL> select file_name,tablespace_name from dba_temp_files;

FILE_NAME                                        TABLESPACE_NAME
----------------------------------------------   ----------------
/u01/app/oracle/oradata/proddb/pdb2/temp01.dbf        TEMP
```

■ **Note** You can use one more option to find out the location of the datafiles and temp files of the container database (proddb), the seed database (pdb$seed), and the pluggable databases (pdb1 and pdb2) using the RMAN option report schema.

```
[oracle@db12cr2 ~]$ rman target /
Recovery Manager: Release 12.1.0.2.0 - Production on Tue Feb 23 16:27:57 2016
```

```
Copyright (c) 1982, 2014, Oracle and/or its affiliates.  All rights reserved.
connected to target database: PRODDB (DBID=644612420)

RMAN> report schema;

using target database control file instead of recovery catalog
Report of database schema for database with db_unique_name PRODDB

List of Permanent Datafiles
===========================

File Size(MB) Tablespace          RB segs Datafile Name
---- -------- ------------------- ------- ------------------------------------
1    770      SYSTEM              ***     /u01/app/oracle/oradata/proddb/system01.dbf
3    660      SYSAUX              ***     /u01/app/oracle/oradata/proddb/sysaux01.dbf
4    85       UNDOTBS1            ***     /u01/app/oracle/oradata/proddb/undotbs01.dbf
5    250      PDB$SEED:SYSTEM     ***     /u01/app/oracle/oradata/proddb/pdbseed/system01.
dbf
6    5        USERS               ***     /u01/app/oracle/oradata/proddb/users01.dbf
7    590      PDB$SEED:SYSAUX     ***     /u01/app/oracle/oradata/proddb/pdbseed/sysaux01.
dbf
8    260      PDB1:SYSTEM         ***     /u01/app/oracle/oradata/proddb/pdb1/system01.dbf
9    610      PDB1:SYSAUX         ***     /u01/app/oracle/oradata/proddb/pdb1/sysaux01.dbf
10   5        PDB1:USERS          ***     /u01/app/oracle/oradata/proddb/pdb1/pdb1_users01.
dbf
11   260      PDB2:SYSTEM         ***     /u01/app/oracle/oradata/proddb/pdb2/system01.dbf
12   610      PDB2:SYSAUX         ***     /u01/app/oracle/oradata/proddb/pdb2/sysaux01.dbf
13   5        PDB2:USERS          ***     /u01/app/oracle/oradata/proddb/pdb2/pdb2_users01.
dbf
```

Here is a list of the temporary files:

```
=========================
File Size(MB) Tablespace          Maxsize(MB) Tempfile Name
---- -------- ------------------- ----------- --------------------------------
1    60       TEMP                32767       /u01/app/oracle/oradata/proddb/temp01.dbf
2    20       PDB$SEED:TEMP       32767       /u01/app/oracle/oradata/proddb/pdbseed/
pdbseed_temp01.dbf
3    20       PDB1:TEMP           32767       /u01/app/oracle/oradata/proddb/pdb1/temp01.
dbf
4    20       PDB2:TEMP           32767       /u01/app/oracle/oradata/proddb/pdb2/temp01.
dbf
```

Connect to the container database (proddb) and move the datafiles from the file system location to the ASM location using the MOVE DATAFILE option.

```
SQL> show con_name


CON_NAME
------------------------------
CDB$ROOT
```

```
SQL> ALTER DATABASE MOVE DATAFILE '/u01/app/oracle/oradata/proddb/system01.dbf'
TO '+DATA';
Database altered.

SQL> ALTER DATABASE MOVE DATAFILE '/u01/app/oracle/oradata/proddb/sysaux01.dbf'
TO '+DATA';
Database altered.

SQL> ALTER DATABASE MOVE DATAFILE '/u01/app/oracle/oradata/proddb/undotbs01.dbf'
TO '+DATA';
Database altered.

SQL> ALTER DATABASE MOVE DATAFILE '/u01/app/oracle/oradata/proddb/users01.dbf'
TO '+DATA';
Database altered.
```

Connect to the seed database (pdb$seed) and move the datafiles from the file system location to the ASM location using the MOVE DATAFILE option.

```
SQL> alter session set container=PDB$SEED;
Session altered.

SQL> show con_name

CON_NAME
------------------------------
PDB$SEED

SQL> show con_id

CON_ID
------------------------------
2

SQL> ALTER DATABASE MOVE DATAFILE '/u01/app/oracle/oradata/proddb/pdbseed/system01.dbf' TO
'+DATA';
Database altered.

SQL> ALTER DATABASE MOVE DATAFILE '/u01/app/oracle/oradata/proddb/pdbseed/sysaux01.dbf' TO
'+DATA';
Database altered.
```

Connect to the pluggable database (pdb1) and move the datafiles from the file system location to the ASM location using the MOVE DATAFILE option.

```
SQL> alter session set container=pdb1;
Session altered.

SQL> show con_name

CON_NAME
------------------------------
```

PDB1

```
SQL> show con_id

CON_ID
------------------------------
3

SQL> ALTER DATABASE MOVE DATAFILE '/u01/app/oracle/oradata/proddb/pdb1/system01.dbf'
TO '+DATA';
Database altered.

SQL> ALTER DATABASE MOVE DATAFILE '/u01/app/oracle/oradata/proddb/pdb1/example01.dbf'
TO '+DATA';
Database altered.

SQL> ALTER DATABASE MOVE DATAFILE '/u01/app/oracle/oradata/proddb/pdb1/SAMPLE_SCHEMA_
users01.dbf' TO '+DATA';
Database altered.

SQL> ALTER DATABASE MOVE DATAFILE '/u01/app/oracle/oradata/proddb/pdb1/sysaux01.dbf'
TO '+DATA';
Database altered.
```

Connect to the pluggable database (pdb2) and move the datafiles from the file system location to the ASM location using the MOVE DATAFILE option.

```
SQL> alter session set container=pdb2;
Session altered.

SQL> show con_name

CON_NAME
-----------------
PDB2

SQL> show con_id
CON_ID
------------
4

SQL> ALTER DATABASE MOVE DATAFILE '/u01/app/oracle/oradata/proddb/pdb2/system01.dbf'
TO '+DATA';
Database altered.

SQL> ALTER DATABASE MOVE DATAFILE '/u01/app/oracle/oradata/proddb/pdb2/sysaux01.dbf'
TO '+DATA';
Database altered.

SQL> ALTER DATABASE MOVE DATAFILE '/u01/app/oracle/oradata/proddb/pdb2/pdb2_users01.dbf' TO
'+DATA';
Database altered.
```

286

Check the locations after moving all the datafiles. The redo log files, temp files, control files, and spfiles are still in the old location, so you have to move these file also (see Figure 6-2).

```
SQL> connect sys/oracle@192.168.56.100:1521/proddb as sysdba
Connected.

SQL> select name from v$datafile union all select name from v$tempfile union all
select member from v$logfile union all select name from v$controlfile;
```

```
NAME
--------------------------------------------------------------------------------
+DATA/PRODDB/DATAFILE/system.257.904583143
+DATA/PRODDB/DATAFILE/sysaux.258.904583165
+DATA/PRODDB/DATAFILE/undotbs1.259.904583183
+DATA/PRODDB/2C6B0EB411B055F8E0536438A8C0CB58/DATAFILE/system.261.904583277
+DATA/PRODDB/DATAFILE/users.260.904583189
+DATA/PRODDB/2C6B0EB411B055F8E0536438A8C0CB58/DATAFILE/sysaux.262.904583283
+DATA/PRODDB/2C6B191311735881E0536438A8C0CE33/DATAFILE/system.263.904583313
+DATA/PRODDB/2C6B191311735881E0536438A8C0CE33/DATAFILE/sysaux.266.904583349
+DATA/PRODDB/2C6B191311735881E0536438A8C0CE33/DATAFILE/users.265.904583347
+DATA/PRODDB/2C6B191311735881E0536438A8C0CE33/DATAFILE/example.264.904583319
+DATA/PRODDB/2C6B47049F9A5C03E0536438A8C0CE3E/DATAFILE/system.267.904583381
+DATA/PRODDB/2C6B47049F9A5C03E0536438A8C0CE3E/DATAFILE/sysaux.268.904583387
+DATA/PRODDB/2C6B47049F9A5C03E0536438A8C0CE3E/DATAFILE/users.269.904583409
/u01/app/oracle/oradata/proddb/temp01.dbf
/u01/app/oracle/oradata/proddb/pdbseed/pdbseed_temp012016-02-23_11-58-28-AM.dbf
/u01/app/oracle/oradata/proddb/pdb1/pdb1_temp012016-02-23_12-01-22-PM.dbf
/u01/app/oracle/oradata/proddb/pdb2/temp012016-02-23_11-58-28-AM.dbf
/u01/app/oracle/oradata/proddb/redo03.log
/u01/app/oracle/oradata/proddb/redo02.log
/u01/app/oracle/oradata/proddb/redo01.log
/u01/app/oracle/oradata/proddb/control01.ctl
/u01/app/oracle/fast_recovery_area/proddb/control02.ctl

22 rows selected.
```

Figure 6-2. Datafiles moved to ASM location for CDB and PDBs

```
SQL> show con_name

CON_NAME
----------------
CDB$ROOT

SQL> ALTER DATABASE MOVE DATAFILE '/u01/app/oracle/oradata/proddb/temp01.dbf' TO '+DATA';

    ALTER DATABASE MOVE DATAFILE '/u01/app/oracle/oradata/proddb/temp01.dbf' TO '+DATA'
    There is an error at line 1: ORA-01516, nonexistent log file, datafile, or temporary file "/u01/app/
oracle/oradata/proddb/temp01.dbf".
```

■ **Note** You can't move temp files to the ASM location directly. Drop and re-create the temp files of the container database, seed database (CDB$ROOT), and pluggable databases (pdb1 and pdb2).

```
SQL> alter session set container=CDB$ROOT;
Session altered.

SQL> show con_name
CON_NAME
-----------------
CDB$ROOT

SQL> alter tablespace temp add tempfile '+DATA';
Tablespace altered.

SQL> alter tablespace temp drop tempfile '/u01/app/oracle/oradata/proddb/temp01.dbf';
Tablespace altered.

SQL> alter session set container =pdb1;
Session altered.

SQL> show con_name
CON_NAME
-----------------
PDB1

SQL> alter tablespace temp add tempfile '+DATA';
Tablespace altered.

SQL> alter tablespace temp drop tempfile '/u01/app/oracle/oradata/proddb/pdb1/pdb1_
temp012016-02-23_12-01-22-PM.dbf';
Tablespace altered.

SQL> alter session set container =pdb2;
Session altered.

SQL> alter tablespace temp add tempfile '+DATA';
Tablespace altered.

SQL> alter tablespace temp drop tempfile '/u01/app/oracle/oradata/proddb/pdb2/temp012016-02-
23_11-58-28-AM.dbf';
Tablespace altered.
```

■ **Note**   To change the temp file location to ASM for the seed database (pdb$seed), connect to the container database (cdb$root) and change the parameter _oracle_script.

```
SQL> alter session set container=CDB$ROOT;
Session altered.

SQL> show con_name
CON_NAME
------------------
CDB$ROOT

SQL> alter session set "_oracle_script"=TRUE;
Session altered.

SQL> alter pluggable database pdb$seed close;
Pluggable database altered.

SQL> alter pluggable database pdb$seed open read write;
Pluggable database altered.

SQL> alter session set container=pdb$seed;
Session altered.

SQL> alter tablespace temp add tempfile '+DATA';
Tablespace altered.

SQL> alter tablespace TEMP drop tempfile '/u01/app/oracle/oradata/proddb/pdbseed/pdbseed_
temp012016-02-23_11-58-28-AM.dbf';
Tablespace altered.

SQL> alter session set container=CDB$ROOT;
Session altered.

SQL> alter pluggable database pdb$seed close;
Pluggable database altered.

SQL> alter pluggable database pdb$seed open read only;
Pluggable database altered.
```

After moving the temp files, check the locations of the control files and the spfile (see Figure 6-3).

```
SQL> connect sys/oracle@192.168.56.100:1521/proddb as sysdba
Connected.
```

```
NAME
----------------------------------------------------------------------------------
+DATA/PRODDB/DATAFILE/system.257.904583143
+DATA/PRODDB/DATAFILE/sysaux.258.904583165
+DATA/PRODDB/DATAFILE/undotbs1.259.904583183
+DATA/PRODDB/2C6B0EB411B055F8E0536438A8C0CB58/DATAFILE/system.261.904583277
+DATA/PRODDB/DATAFILE/users.260.904583189
+DATA/PRODDB/2C6B0EB411B055F8E0536438A8C0CB58/DATAFILE/sysaux.262.904583283
+DATA/PRODDB/2C6B191311735881E0536438A8C0CE33/DATAFILE/system.263.904583313
+DATA/PRODDB/2C6B191311735881E0536438A8C0CE33/DATAFILE/sysaux.266.904583349
+DATA/PRODDB/2C6B191311735881E0536438A8C0CE33/DATAFILE/users.265.904583347
+DATA/PRODDB/2C6B191311735881E0536438A8C0CE33/DATAFILE/example.264.904583319
+DATA/PRODDB/2C6B47049F9A5C03E0536438A8C0CE3E/DATAFILE/system.267.904583381
+DATA/PRODDB/2C6B47049F9A5C03E0536438A8C0CE3E/DATAFILE/sysaux.268.904583387
+DATA/PRODDB/2C6B47049F9A5C03E0536438A8C0CE3E/DATAFILE/users.269.904583409
+DATA/PRODDB/2C6B191311735881E0536438A8C0CE33/TEMPFILE/temp.271.904584517
+DATA/PRODDB/2C6B47049F9A5C03E0536438A8C0CE3E/TEMPFILE/temp.272.904584565
+DATA/PRODDB/2C6B0EB411B055F8E0536438A8C0CB58/TEMPFILE/temp.273.904584643
+DATA/PRODDB/TEMPFILE/temp.270.904584385
/u01/app/oracle/oradata/proddb/redo03.log
/u01/app/oracle/oradata/proddb/redo02.log
/u01/app/oracle/oradata/proddb/redo01.log
/u01/app/oracle/oradata/proddb/control01.ctl
/u01/app/oracle/fast_recovery_area/proddb/control02.ctl

22 rows selected.
```

Figure 6-3. Datafiles and temp files moved to the ASM location for the CDB and PDBs

```
SQL> show con_name
CON_NAME
----------------
CDB$ROOT

SQL> select member from v$logfile;
MEMBER
----------------------------------------------------------------
/u01/app/oracle/oradata/proddb/redo03.log
/u01/app/oracle/oradata/proddb/redo02.log
/u01/app/oracle/oradata/proddb/redo01.log

3 rows selected.
SQL> select group#, status from v$log;

GROUP#      STATUS
-------     -------------
1           CURRENT
2           INACTIVE
3           INACTIVE

3 rows selected.

SQL> alter database add logfile group 5;
Database altered.
```

```
SQL> alter database add logfile group 6;
Database altered.

SQL> alter database add logfile group 7;
Database altered.

SQL> select member from v$logfile;

MEMBER
--------------------------------------------------------------------------------
/u01/app/oracle/oradata/proddb/redo03.log
/u01/app/oracle/oradata/proddb/redo02.log
/u01/app/oracle/oradata/proddb/redo01.log
/u01/app/oracle/fast_recovery_area/PRODDB/onlinelog/o1_mf_5_cs6zymsc_.log
/u01/app/oracle/fast_recovery_area/PRODDB/onlinelog/o1_mf_6_cs6zysdf_.log
/u01/app/oracle/fast_recovery_area/PRODDB/onlinelog/o1_mf_7_cs6zyz27_.log

6 rows selected.

SQL> select group#, status from v$log;

    GROUP# STATUS
---------- ----------------
         1 INACTIVE
         2 INACTIVE
         3 INACTIVE
         5 CURRENT
         6 UNUSED
         7 UNUSED

6 rows selected.

SQL> alter database drop logfile group 1;
Database altered.

SQL> alter database drop logfile group 2;
Database altered.

SQL> alter database drop logfile group 3;
Database altered.

SQL> select group#, status from v$log;

    GROUP# STATUS
---------- ----------------
         5 CURRENT
         6 UNUSED
         7 UNUSED

SQL> alter system switch logfile;
```

```
System altered.

SQL> alter system switch logfile;
System altered.

SQL> select group#, status from v$log;

    GROUP# STATUS
---------- ----------------
         5 ACTIVE
         6 ACTIVE
         7 CURRENT

SQL>

SQL> select member from v$logfile;

MEMBER
--------------------------------------------------------------------------------
/u01/app/oracle/fast_recovery_area/PRODDB/onlinelog/o1_mf_5_cs6zymsc_.log
/u01/app/oracle/fast_recovery_area/PRODDB/onlinelog/o1_mf_6_cs6zysdf_.log
/u01/app/oracle/fast_recovery_area/PRODDB/onlinelog/o1_mf_7_cs6zyz27_.log

SQL>

SQL> shutdown immediate;
Database closed.
Database dismounted.
ORACLE instance shut down.

[oracle@db12cr2 ~]$ sqlplus /nolog
SQL*Plus: Release 12.1.0.2.0 Production on Tue Feb 23 17:36:09 2016
Copyright (c) 1982, 2014, Oracle.  All rights reserved.

SQL> connect sys/oracle as sysdba
Connected to an idle instance.

SQL> startup nomount;
ORACLE instance started.

Total System Global Area    3154116608    bytes
Fixed Size                     2929352    bytes
Variable Size                771755320    bytes
Database Buffers            2365587456    bytes
Redo Buffers                  13844480    bytes
SQL>exit
```

```
[oracle@db12cr2 ~]$ rman target /
Recovery Manager: Release 12.1.0.2.0 - Production on Tue Feb 23 17:37:15 2016
Copyright (c) 1982, 2014, Oracle and/or its affiliates.  All rights reserved.
connected to target database: PRODDB (not mounted)
```

Restore the control files to the +DATA and +FRA ASM disk groups from the non-ASM location.

```
RMAN> restore controlfile to '+DATA' from '/u01/app/oracle/oradata/proddb/control01.ctl';
Starting restore at 23-FEB-16
using target database control file instead of recovery catalog
allocated channel: ORA_DISK_1
channel ORA_DISK_1: SID=249 device type=DISK

channel ORA_DISK_1: copied control file copy
Finished restore at 23-FEB-16
```

Note that you will be multiplexing the control files with the help of the Flashback Recovery Area (+FRA).

```
RMAN> restore controlfile to '+FRA' from '/u01/app/oracle/fast_recovery_area/proddb/
control02.ctl';

Starting restore at 23-FEB-16
using channel ORA_DISK_1

channel ORA_DISK_1: copied control file copy
Finished restore at 23-FEB-16

RMAN> exit
Recovery Manager complete.

SQL> show parameter control_files
```

NAME	TYPE	VALUE
control_files	string	/u01/app/oracle/oradata/proddb/control01.ctl, /u01/app/oracle/fast_recovery_area/proddb/control02.ctl

---

■ **Note**   Find out the location of the control files from the ASM disk groups +DATA and +FRA using the ASMCMD command prompt.

```
[oracle@db12cr2 ~]$ . oraenv
ORACLE_SID = [proddb] ? +ASM
The Oracle base remains unchanged with value /u01/app/oracle
[oracle@db12cr2 ~]$ asmcmd

ASMCMD> cd DATA/PRODDB/CONTROLFILE

ASMCMD> pwd
```

```
+DATA/PRODDB/CONTROLFILE

ASMCMD> ls
current.277.904585141

ASMCMD> cd FRA/PRODDB/CONTROLFILE

ASMCMD> pwd
+FRA/PRODDB/CONTROLFILE

ASMCMD> ls
current.256.904585473

ASMCMD>exit
```

Switch to the database login from the ASMCMD command prompt.

```
SQL> alter system set control_files='+DATA/PRODDB/CONTROLFILE/current.277.904585141',
'+FRA/PRODDB/CONTROLFILE/current.256.904585473' scope=spfile;
System altered.

SQL> alter database open;
Database opened.
```

Now, check the locations of datafiles, temp files, redo log files, and control files, as shown in Figure 6-4.

```
NAME
---------------------------------------------------------------------------------
+DATA/PRODDB/DATAFILE/system.257.904583143
+DATA/PRODDB/DATAFILE/sysaux.258.904583165
+DATA/PRODDB/DATAFILE/undotbs1.259.904583183
+DATA/PRODDB/2C6B0EB411B055F8E0536438A8C0CB58/DATAFILE/system.261.904583277
+DATA/PRODDB/DATAFILE/users.260.904583189
+DATA/PRODDB/2C6B0EB411B055F8E0536438A8C0CB58/DATAFILE/sysaux.262.904583283
+DATA/PRODDB/2C6B191311735881E0536438A8C0CE33/DATAFILE/system.263.904583313
+DATA/PRODDB/2C6B191311735881E0536438A8C0CE33/DATAFILE/sysaux.266.904583349
+DATA/PRODDB/2C6B191311735881E0536438A8C0CE33/DATAFILE/users.265.904583347
+DATA/PRODDB/2C6B191311735881E0536438A8C0CE33/DATAFILE/example.264.904583319
+DATA/PRODDB/2C6B47049F9A5C03E0536438A8C0CE3E/DATAFILE/system.267.904583381

NAME
---------------------------------------------------------------------------------
+DATA/PRODDB/2C6B47049F9A5C03E0536438A8C0CE3E/DATAFILE/sysaux.268.904583387
+DATA/PRODDB/2C6B47049F9A5C03E0536438A8C0CE3E/DATAFILE/users.269.904583409
+DATA/PRODDB/2C6B191311735881E0536438A8C0CE33/TEMPFILE/temp.271.904584517
+DATA/PRODDB/2C6B47049F9A5C03E0536438A8C0CE3E/TEMPFILE/temp.272.904584565
+DATA/PRODDB/2C6B0EB411B055F8E0536438A8C0CB58/TEMPFILE/temp.273.904584643
+DATA/PRODDB/TEMPFILE/temp.270.904584385
+DATA/PRODDB/ONLINELOG/group_3.275.904584839
+DATA/PRODDB/ONLINELOG/group_2.274.904584813
+DATA/PRODDB/ONLINELOG/group_1.276.904584883
+DATA/PRODDB/CONTROLFILE/current.277.904585141
+FRA/PRODDB/CONTROLFILE/current.256.904585473

22 rows selected.
```

Figure 6-4. Datafiles, temp files, redo logs, and control files moved to the ASM location for the CDB and PDBs

```
SQL> shutdown immediate;
Database closed.
Database dismounted.
ORACLE instance shut down.

SQL> startup ;
ORACLE instance started.

Total System Global Area     3154116608   bytes
Fixed Size                      2929352   bytes
Variable Size                 771755320   bytes
Database Buffers             2365587456   bytes
Redo Buffers                   13844480   bytes
Database mounted.
Datbase Opened.

SQL> show parameter pfile

NAME           TYPE         VALUE
------------------------------------------------------------------------------
spfile         string       /u01/app/oracle/product/12.1.0.2/dbhome_1/dbs/spfileproddb.ora

[oracle@db12cr2 ~]$ rman target /
Recovery Manager: Release 12.1.0.2.0 - Production on Tue Feb 23 17:55:34 2016
Copyright (c) 1982, 2014, Oracle and/or its affiliates.  All rights reserved.
connected to target database: PRODDB (DBID=644612420, not open)

RMAN> run
{
BACKUP AS BACKUPSET SPFILE;
RESTORE SPFILE TO "+DATA/PRODDB/spfileproddb.ora";
}2> 3> 4> 5>

Starting backup at 23-FEB-16
using target database control file instead of recovery catalog
allocated channel: ORA_DISK_1
channel ORA_DISK_1: SID=252 device type=DISK
channel ORA_DISK_1: starting full datafile backup set
channel ORA_DISK_1: specifying datafile(s) in backup set
including current SPFILE in backup set
channel ORA_DISK_1: starting piece 1 at 23-FEB-16
channel ORA_DISK_1: finished piece 1 at 23-FEB-16
piece handle=/u01/app/oracle/fast_recovery_area/PRODDB/backupset/2016_02_23/o1_mf_nnsnf_
TAG20160223T175619_cdrmzctv_.bkp tag=TAG20160223T175619 comment=NONE
channel ORA_DISK_1: backup set complete, elapsed time: 00:00:01
Finished backup at 23-FEB-16

Starting Control File and SPFILE Autobackup at 23-FEB-16
piece handle=/u01/app/oracle/fast_recovery_area/PRODDB/autobackup/2016_02_23/o1_
mf_s_904585851_cdrmzf9f_.bkp comment=NONE
Finished Control File and SPFILE Autobackup at 23-FEB-16
```

```
Starting restore at 23-FEB-16
using channel ORA_DISK_1

channel ORA_DISK_1: starting datafile backup set restore
channel ORA_DISK_1: restoring SPFILE
output file name=+DATA/PRODDB/spfileproddb.ora
channel ORA_DISK_1: reading from backup piece /u01/app/oracle/fast_recovery_area/PRODDB/
autobackup/2016_02_23/o1_mf_s_904585851_cdrmzf9f_.bkp
channel ORA_DISK_1: piece handle=/u01/app/oracle/fast_recovery_area/PRODDB/
autobackup/2016_02_23/o1_mf_s_904585851_cdrmzf9f_.bkp tag=TAG20160223T175620
channel ORA_DISK_1: restored backup piece 1
channel ORA_DISK_1: restore complete, elapsed time: 00:00:01
Finished restore at 23-FEB-16

RMAN> exit
Recovery Manager complete.

SQL> show parameter pfile

NAME          TYPE         VALUE
------------- ------------ ---------------------------------------------------------------
Spfile        string       /u01/app/oracle/product/12.1.0.2/dbhome_1/dbs/spfileproddb.ora
```

Check the configuration of the database with srvctl command and change the location of the spfile for the database

```
[oracle@db12cr2 ~]$ srvctl modify database -db proddb -spfile '+DATA/PRODDB/spfileproddb.ora';

[oracle@db12cr2 ~]$ srvctl config database -db proddb
Database unique name: proddb
Database name: proddb
Oracle home: /u01/app/oracle/product/12.1.0.2/dbhome_1
Oracle user: oracle
Spfile: +DATA/PRODDB/spfileproddb.ora
Password file:
Domain:
Start options: open
Stop options: immediate
Database role: PRIMARY
Management policy: AUTOMATIC
Disk Groups: DATA,FRA
Services:
OSDBA group:
OSOPER group:
Database instance: proddb
```

```
SQL> select open_mode from v$database;
OPEN_MODE
------------------
MOUNTED

SQL> shutdown immediate;
ORA-01109: database not open
Database dismounted.
ORACLE instance shut down.

SQL> startup;
ORACLE instance started.

Total System Global Area    3154116608    bytes
Fixed Size                     2929352    bytes
Variable Size                771755320    bytes
Database Buffers            2365587456    bytes
Redo Buffers                  13844480    bytes
Database mounted.
Database Opened.

SQL> show parameter pfile
NAME                                       TYPE          VALUE
-----------------------------------------  -----------   -------------------------------
spfile                                     string        +DATA/PRODDB/spfileproddb.ora

SQL> alter database open;
Database altered.
```

Finally, you **have relocated** the **container database, seed database, and pluggable databases from a non-ASM location to an ASM location with minimal downtime.**

■ **Note**   You can also use RMAN to achieve the same functionality.

Scenario 2: Migrating an Oracle Database 12*c* CDB with PDBs from a non-ASM to ASM using EM 13*c*

Now let's look at how to migrate an Oracle Database 12*c* CDB with PDBs from a non-ASM location to an ASM location using Oracle Enterprise Manager (OEM) Cloud Control 13*c*. Table 6-2 shows the configured environment for the database server called db12cr2.

Table 6-2. *Home Directories for ORACLE_HOME, AGENT_HOME, and Container and Pluggable Database Information on Database Server*

Database Server	Home Directories Path
Oracle Home	ORACLE_HOME=/u01/app/oracle/product/12.1.0.2/db_1
Agent Home	/u01/app/oracle/agent12c/agent_inst
Agent Log Directory	/u01/app/oracle/agent12c/agent_inst/sysman/log
Agent Binaries	/u01/app/oracle/agent12c/agent_13.1.0.0.0
Agent Version & OMS Version	13.1.0.0.0
Container Database	Clouddb
Pluggable Databases	Pdb1 and pdb2
Database Host Name & IP address	Db12cr2 (192.168.56.100)

Table 6-3 shows the directories for Oracle Enterprise Manager Cloud Control 13*c*.

Table 6-3. *Home Directories for ORACLE_HOME, OMS_HOME, AGENT_HOME, and URLs for OEM Cloud Control and Admin Server*

Oracle Enterprise Manager Cloud Control 13c	Home Directories Path
Oracle Home	ORACLE_HOME=/u01/app/oracle/product/12.1.0.2/db_1
OMS Home	OMS_HOME=/u01/app/oracle/middleware
Agent Home	AGENT_HOME=/u01/app/oracle/agent/agent_13.1.0.0.0
Agent Binaries	/u01/app/oracle/agent12c/agent_13.1.0.0.0
OEM Cloud Control	https://em13c.localdomain:7802/em
Admin Server	https://em13c.localdomain:7102/console
Admin Server Port	7102
Database Host Name & IP address	Em13c.localdomain (192.168.56.200)

Install and configure Oracle Enterprise Manager Cloud Control 13c with a repository database called emrep using the **12.1.0.2.0_Database_Template_for_EM13_1_0_0_0_Linux_x64.zip** template. You can download it from Oracle.com.

Start the components of Oracle Enterprise Manager Cloud Control 13c by following these steps:

1. Start Oracle Database 12c (the repository database).

```
[oracle@em13c ~]$ . oraenv
ORACLE_SID = [cdb1] ? emrep
The Oracle base remains unchanged with value /u01/app/oracle

[oracle@em13c ~]$ sqlplus /nolog
SQL*Plus: Release 12.1.0.2.0 Production or Thu Feb 25 12:42:32 2016
Copyright (c) 1982, 2014, Oracle.  All rights reserved.

SQL> connect sys/oracle as sysdba
Connected to an idle instance.

SQL> startup;
ORACLE instance started.
Total System Global Area    3003121664    bytes
Fixed Size                     2928920    bytes
Variable Size                771755752    bytes
Database Buffers            2214592512    bytes
Redo Buffers                  13844480    bytes
Database mounted.
Database opened.
SQL>
```

2. Start Oracle Management Server (OMS).

```
[oracle@em13c ~]$ export OMS_HOME=/u01/app/oracle/middleware
[oracle@em13c ~]$ $OMS_HOME/bin/emctl start oms
Oracle Enterprise Manager Cloud Control 13c Release 1
Copyright (c) 1996, 2015 Oracle Corporation.  All rights reserved.
Starting Oracle Management Server...
WebTier Successfully Started
Oracle Management Server Successfully Started
Oracle Management Server is Up
JVMD Engine is Up
Starting BI Publisher Server ...
BI Publisher Server Successfully Started
BI Publisher Server is Up
[oracle@em13c ~]$
```

3. Start Oracle Agent (see Figure 6-5).

```
[oracle@em13c ~]$ export AGENT_HOME=/u01/app/oracle/agent/agent_13.1.0.0.0
[oracle@em13c ~]$ $AGENT_HOME/bin/emctl start agent
Oracle Enterprise Manager Cloud Control 13c Release 1
Copyright (c) 1996, 2015 Oracle Corporation.  All rights reserved.
Agent is already running
[oracle@em13c ~]$
Installed Agent in Oracle Database 12c (db12cr2) for converting database from NON
ASM to ASM through Oracle Enterprise Manager Cloud Control 13c. We can install
the agent from Cloud Control 13c Server (em13c.localdomain).
```

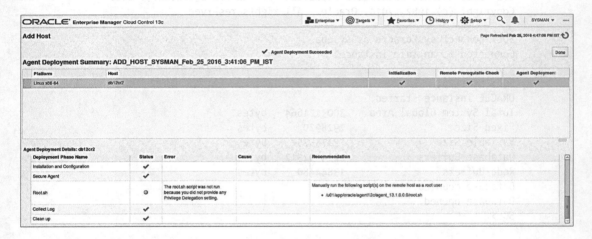

Figure 6-5. *Agent Deployment Summary page in Oracle Enterprise Manager Cloud Control 13c*

Check the Oracle Agent status from Oracle Database 12c (db12cr2), as shown in Figure 6-6.

```
[oracle@db12cr2 bin]$ pwd
/u01/app/oracle/agent12c/agent_13.1.0.0.0/bin
[oracle@db12cr2 bin]$ ./emctl status agent
Oracle Enterprise Manager Cloud Control 13c Release 1
Copyright (c) 1996, 2015 Oracle Corporation.  All rights reserved.
---------------------------------------------------------------
Agent Version            : 13.1.0.0.0
OMS Version              : 13.1.0.0.0
Protocol Version         : 12.1.0.1.0
Agent Home               : /u01/app/oracle/agent12c/agent_inst
Agent Log Directory      : /u01/app/oracle/agent12c/agent_inst/sysman/log
Agent Binaries           : /u01/app/oracle/agent12c/agent_13.1.0.0.0
Core JAR Location        : /u01/app/oracle/agent12c/agent_13.1.0.0.0/jlib
Agent Process ID         : 20199
Parent Process ID        : 20167
Agent URL                : https://db12cr2:3872/emd/main/
Local Agent URL in NAT   : https://db12cr2:3872/emd/main/
Repository URL           : https://em13c.localdomain:4903/empbs/upload
Started at               : 2016-02-25 16:50:28
Started by user          : oracle
Operating System         : Linux version 2.6.39-400.17.1.el6uek.x86_64 (amd64)
Number of Targets        : 2
Last Reload              : (none)
Last successful upload                       : 2016-02-25 16:54:32
Last attempted upload                        : 2016-02-25 16:54:32
Total Megabytes of XML files uploaded so far : 0.47
Number of XML files pending upload           : 0
Size of XML files pending upload(MB)         : 0
Available disk space on upload filesystem    : 63.44%
Collection Status                            : Collections enabled
Heartbeat Status                             : Ok
Last attempted heartbeat to OMS              : 2016-02-25 16:54:35
Last successful heartbeat to OMS             : 2016-02-25 16:54:35
Next scheduled heartbeat to OMS              : 2016-02-25 16:55:35

---------------------------------------------------------------
Agent is Running and Ready
[oracle@db12cr2 bin]$ []
```

Figure 6-6. *Agent status in Oracle Enterprise Manager Cloud Control 13c server*

You can register Oracle Database with Oracle Enterprise Manager Cloud Control 13*c* using the Database Configuration Assistant (DBCA) while creating the database, as shown in Figure 6-7.

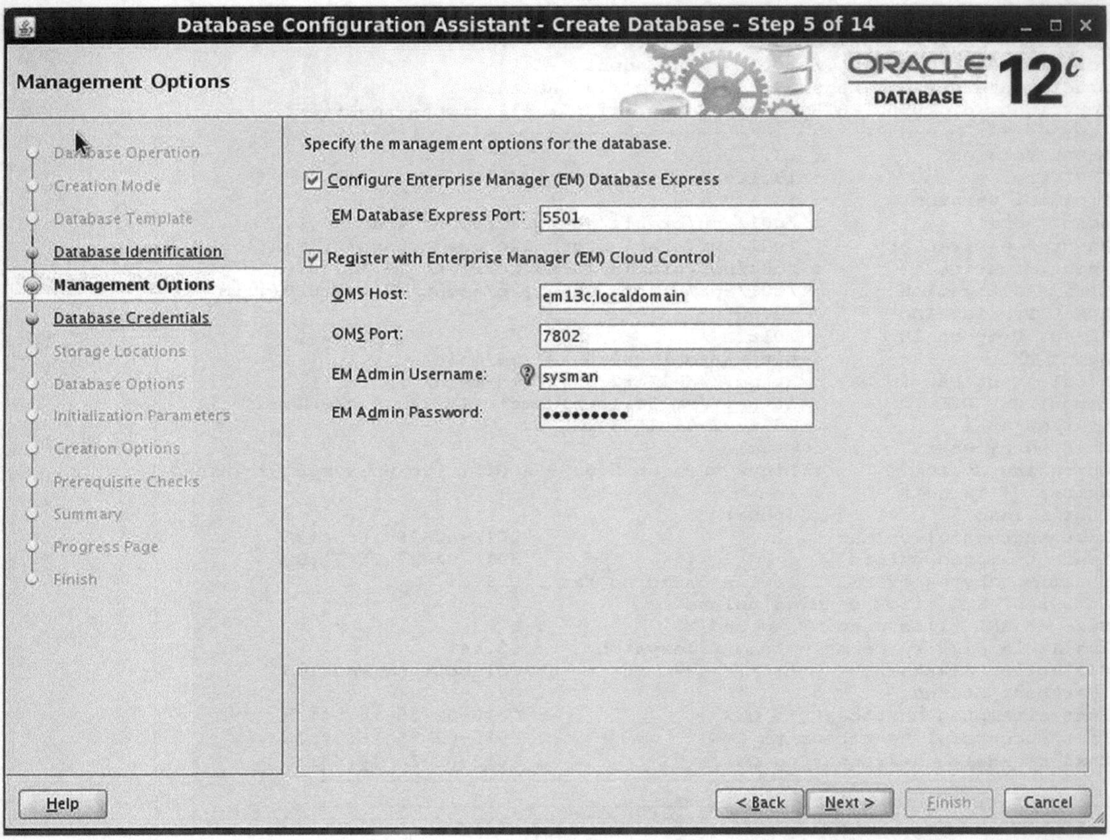

Figure 6-7. *EM database express port and registration information for OEM Cloud Control 13c in DBCA*

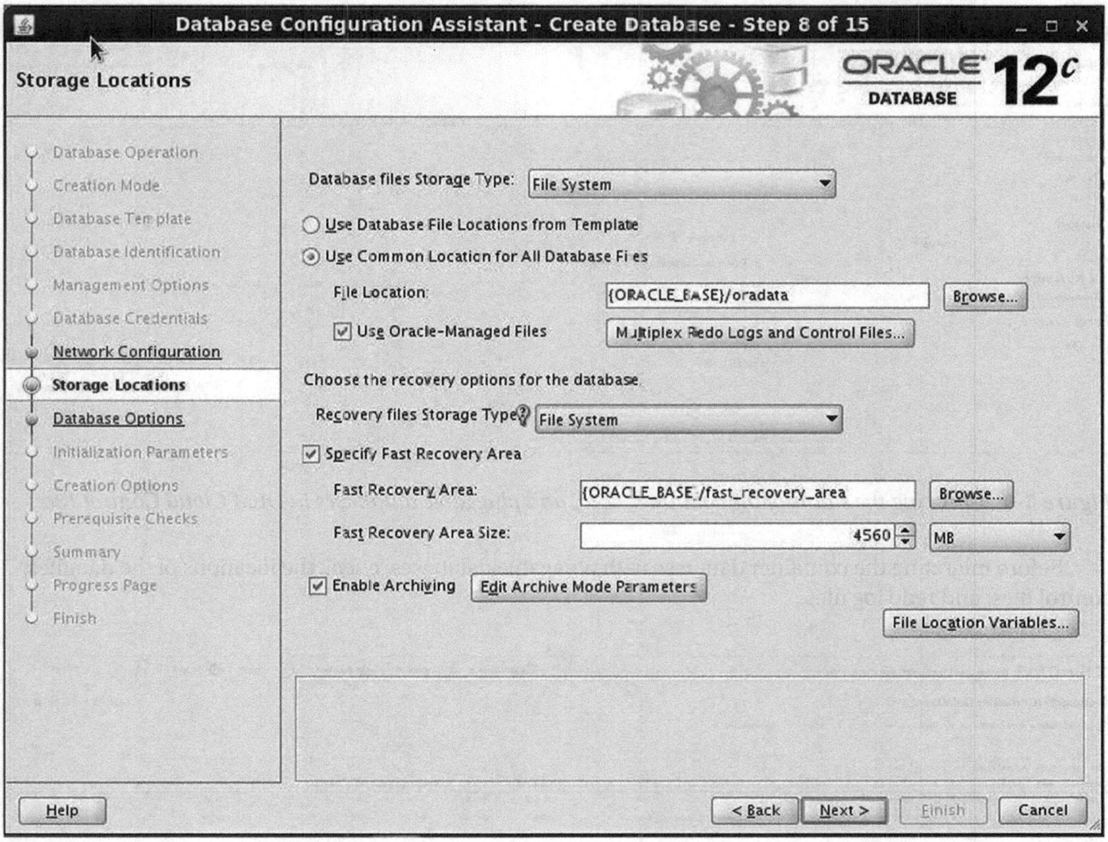

Figure 6-8. *Storage for datafiles, Fast Recovery Area, and archival options in DBCA*

After installing and configuring the agent in Oracle Database 12*c* (db12cr2), you can check the status of the container database (clouddb) along with two pluggable databases (pdb1 and pdb2) through Cloud Control 13*c* (em13c.localdomain).

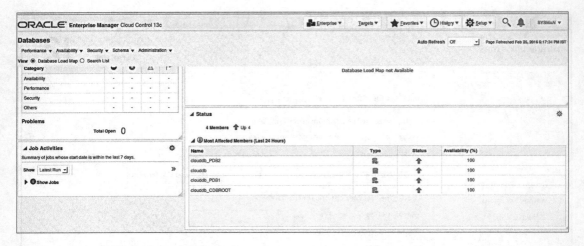

Figure 6-9. *Checking the status of the container, seed, and pluggable databases in OEM Cloud Control 13c*

Before migrating the container database with pluggable databases, check the locations of the datafiles, control files, and redo log files.

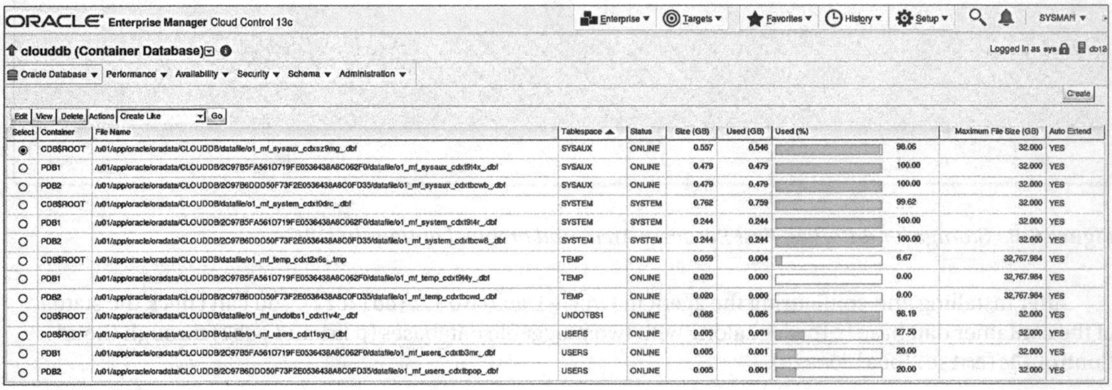

Figure 6-10. *Listing the location datafiles of the container, seed, and pluggable databases in OEM Cloud Control 13c*

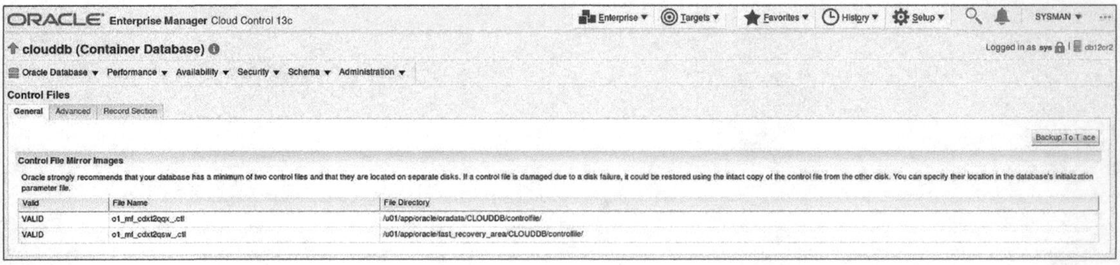

Figure 6-11. *Listing the locations of the control files of the container database in OEM Cloud Control 13c*

On the Administration tab, use the option Migrate to ASM in Cloud Control 13*c*.

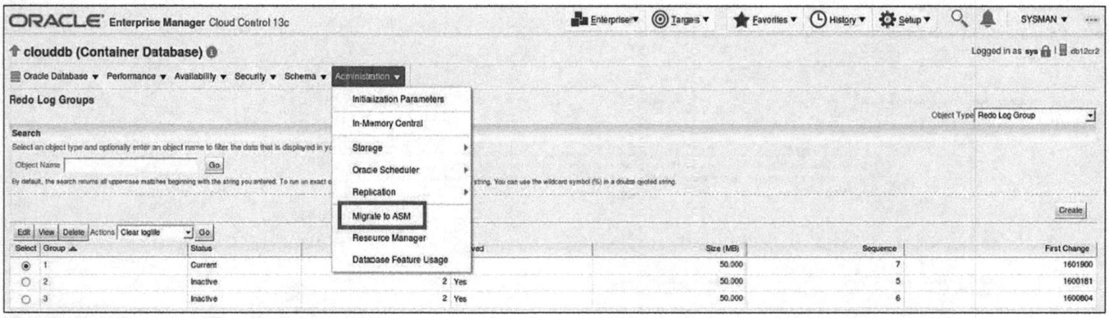

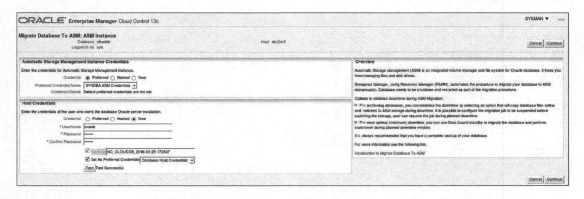

Figure 6-12. *Option to migrate the database from non-ASM to ASM environment in OEM Cloud Control 13c*

On the Migrate Database To ASM page, pass the ASM instance credentials and host credentials of the Oracle Database server (db12cr2).

Figure 6-13. *Using database credentials and host credentials option*

In Oracle Enterprise Manager Cloud Control 13*c*, you have two migration options before migrating to ASM.

- *Offline*: The database will be taken offline for the entire duration of the migration operation.

- *Minimum Downtime*: Copying the database files to the diskgroups is done online. The database will be taken offline only when switching to ASM storage.

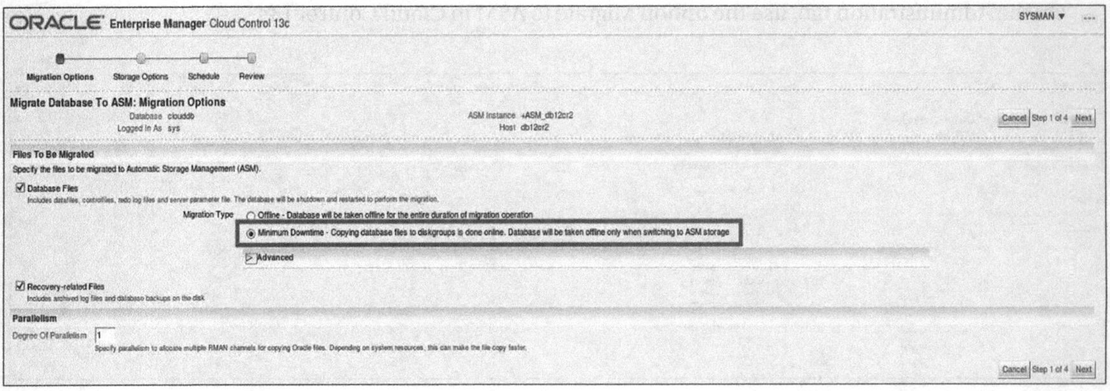

Figure 6-14. *Using the Minimum Downtime option*

In OEM Cloud Control 13*c*, you have an option called Migrate Database to ASM with storage options. There are two diskgroups: DATA and FRA.

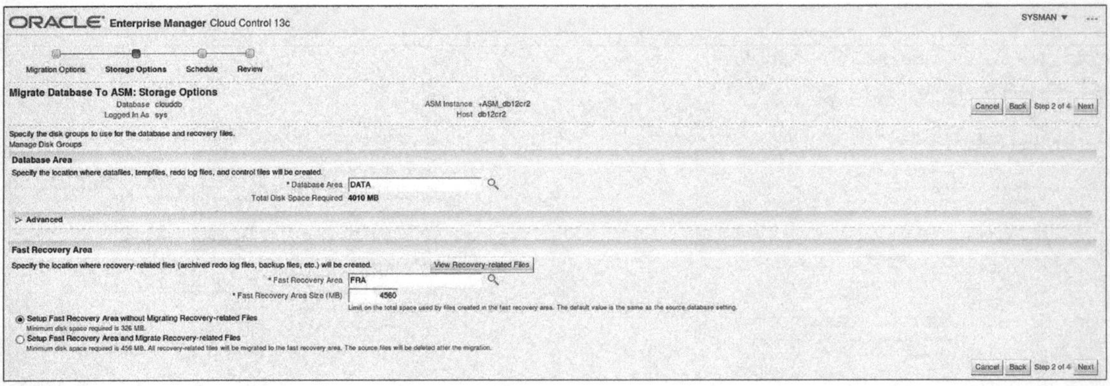

Figure 6-15. *Specifying the datafile and Fast Recovery Area locations*

In OEM Cloud Control 13*c*, you have the option to execute this schedule immediately or you can choose the date and time.

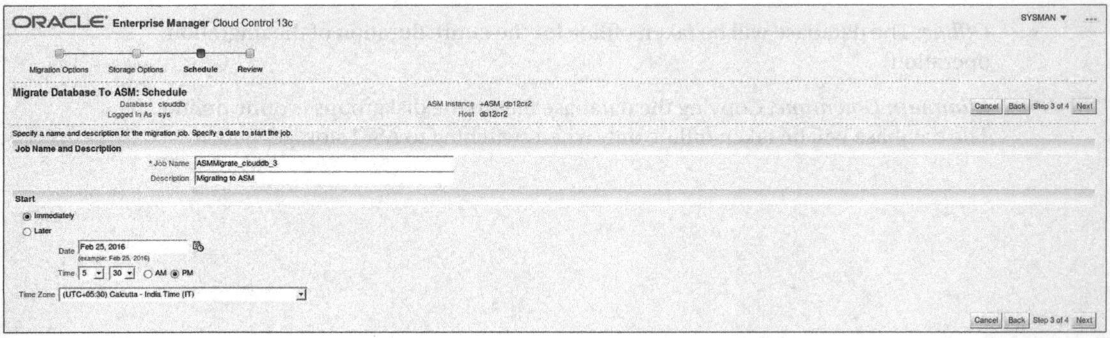

Figure 6-16. *Using the schedule option*

Review the job and submit it.

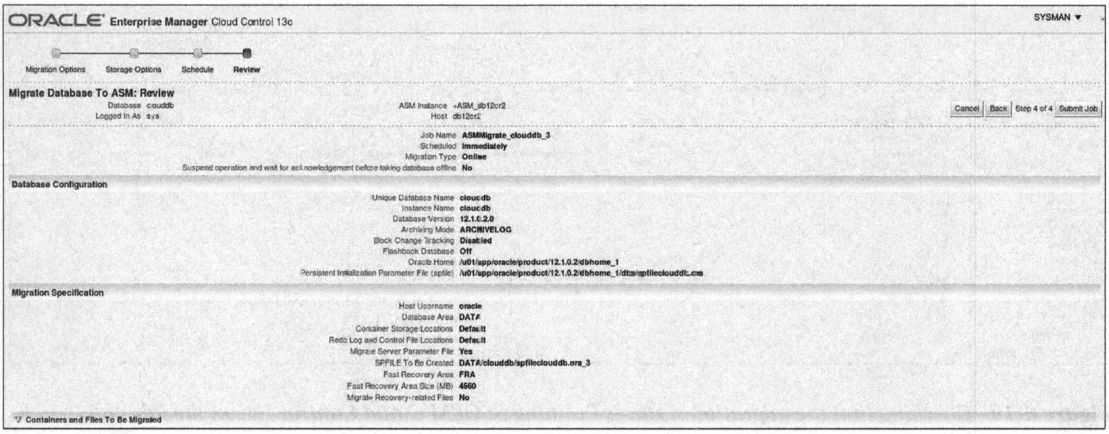

Figure 6-17. *Reviewing the summary*

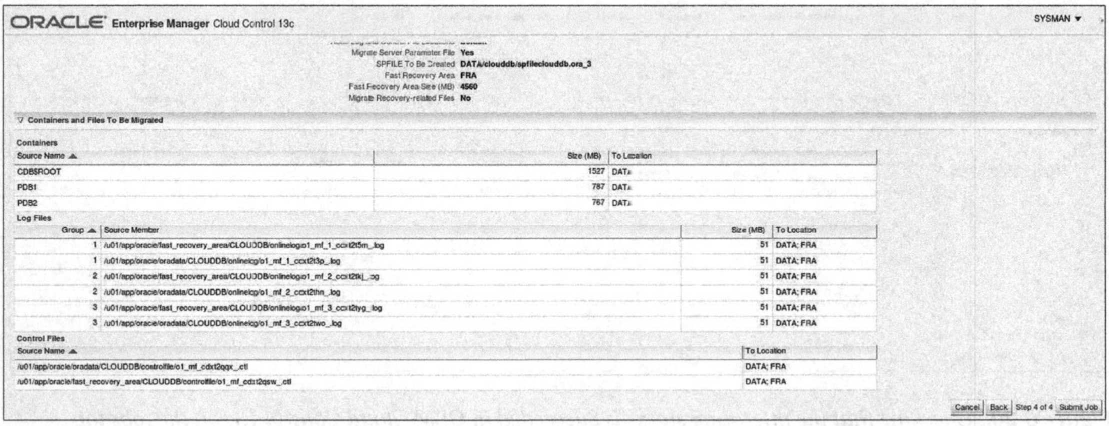

Figure 6-18. *ASM locations for datafiles and control files for the container and pluggable databases*

Check the status of the submitted job and the final status in Enterprise Manager Cloud Control 13*c* by selecting the Enterprise tab, clicking Job, and clicking the Activity option.

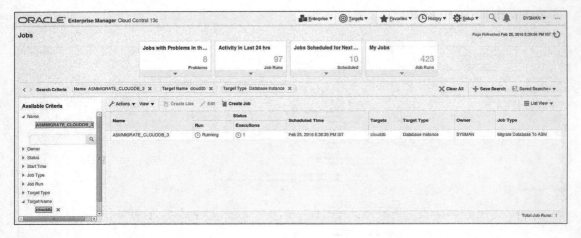

Figure 6-19. *Checking that the migration status is Running in OEM Cloud Control 13c on the Jobs tab*

Figure 6-20. *Checking that the migration status is Succeeded in OEM Cloud Control 13c on the Jobs tab*

Log in to the container database and check the updated locations of the datafiles, control files, and redo log files.

■ **Note**   OEM Cloud Control 13*c* can't convert the seed database (pdb$seed) to ASM.

```
SQL> connect sys/oracle@clouddb as sysdba
Connected.

SQL> select name from v$datafile union all
select name from v$tempfile union all
select member from v$logfile union all
select name from v$controlfile;
```

```
NAME
--------------------------------------------------------------------------------
+DATA/CLOUDDB/DATAFILE/system.271.904757925
+DATA/CLOUDDB/DATAFILE/sysaux.263.904757925
+DATA/CLOUDDB/DATAFILE/undotbs1.270.904757971
/u01/app/oracle/oradata/CLOUDDB/datafile/o1_mf_system_cdxt2zr5_.dbf
+DATA/CLOUDDB/DATAFILE/users.262.904757971
/u01/app/oracle/oradata/CLOUDDB/datafile/o1_mf_sysaux_cdxt2zqq_.dbf
+DATA/CLOUDDB/2C97B5FA561D719FE0536438A8C062F0/DATAFILE/system.274.904757955
+DATA/CLOUDDB/2C97B5FA561D719FE0536438A8C062F0/DATAFILE/sysaux.267.904757939
+DATA/CLOUDDB/2C97B5FA561D719FE0536438A8C062F0/DATAFILE/users.266.904757971
+DATA/CLOUDDB/2C97B6DDD50F73F2E0536438A8C0FD35/DATAFILE/system.275.904757957
+DATA/CLOUDDB/2C97B6DDD50F73F2E0536438A8C0FD35/DATAFILE/sysaux.276.904757939
+DATA/CLOUDDB/2C97B6DDD50F73F2E0536438A8C0FD35/DATAFILE/users.265.904757973
+DATA/CLOUDDB/TEMPFILE/temp.268.904758093
/u01/app/oracle/oradata/CLOUDDB/datafile/pdbseed_temp012016-02-25_05-11-47-PM.dbf
+DATA/CLOUDDB/2C97B5FA561D719FE0536438A8C062F0/TEMPFILE/temp.272.904758093
+DATA/CLOUDDB/2C97B6DDD50F73F2E0536438A8C0FD35/TEMPFILE/temp.278.904758093
+DATA/CLOUDDB/ONLINELOG/group_2.261.904758095
+FRA/CLOUDDB/ONLINELOG/group_2.267.904758097
+DATA/CLOUDDB/ONLINELOG/group_1.260.904758095
+FRA/CLOUDDB/ONLINELOG/group_1.266.904758095
+DATA/CLOUDDB/ONLINELOG/group_4.277.904758095
+FRA/CLOUDDB/ONLINELOG/group_4.265.904758095
+DATA/CLOUDDB/CONTROLFILE/current.269.904758037
+FRA/CLOUDDB/CONTROLFILE/current.264.904758037
```

You can check through RMAN using the report schema option.

```
[oracle@db12cr2 bin]$ . oraenv
ORACLE_SID = [oracle] ? clouddb
The Oracle base has been set to /u01/app/oracle
[oracle@db12cr2 bin]$ rman target /

Recovery Manager: Release 12.1.0.2.0 - Production on Thu Feb 25 17:48:39 2016

Copyright (c) 1982, 2014, Oracle and/or its affiliates.  All rights reserved.

connected to target database: CLOUDDB (DBID=3984498097)

RMAN> report schema;

using target database control file instead of recovery catalog
Report of database schema for database with db_unique_name CLOUDDB

List of Permanent Datafiles
===========================
File Size(MB) Tablespace        RB segs Datafile Name
---- -------- ----------------- ------- ------------------------
1    780      SYSTEM            YES     +DATA/CLOUDDB/DATAFILE/system.271.904757925
3    590      SYSAUX            NO      +DATA/CLOUDDB/DATAFILE/sysaux.263.904757925
4    90       UNDOTBS1          YES     +DATA/CLOUDDB/DATAFILE/undotbs1.270.904757971
5    250      PDB$SEED:SYSTEM   NO      /u01/app/oracle/oradata/CLOUDDB/datafile/o1_mf_system_cdxt2zr5_.dbf
6    5        USERS             NO      +DATA/CLOUDDB/DATAFILE/users.262.904757971
7    490      PDB$SEED:SYSAUX   NO      /u01/app/oracle/oradata/CLOUDDB/datafile/o1_mf_sysaux_cdxt2zqq_.dbf
8    250      PDB1:SYSTEM       NO      +DATA/CLOUDDB/2C97B5FA561D719FE0536438A8C062F0/DATAFILE/system.274.904757955
9    510      PDB1:SYSAUX       NO      +DATA/CLOUDDB/2C97B5FA561D719FE0536438A8C062F0/DATAFILE/sysaux.267.904757939
10   5        PDB1:USERS        NO      +DATA/CLOUDDB/2C97B5FA561D719FE0536438A8C062F0/DATAFILE/users.266.904757971
11   250      PDB2:SYSTEM       NO      +DATA/CLOUDDB/2C97B6DDD50F73F2E0536438A8C0FD35/DATAFILE/system.275.904757957
12   490      PDB2:SYSAUX       NO      +DATA/CLOUDDB/2C97B6DDD50F73F2E0536438A8C0FD35/DATAFILE/sysaux.276.904757939
13   5        PDB2:USERS        NO      +DATA/CLOUDDB/2C97B6DDD50F73F2E0536438A8C0FD35/DATAFILE/users.265.904757973

List of Temporary Files
=======================
File Size(MB) Tablespace      Maxsize(MB) Tempfile Name
---- -------- --------------- ----------- -------------------------
1    60       TEMP            32767       +DATA/CLOUDDB/TEMPFILE/temp.268.904758093
2    20       PDB$SEED:TEMP   32767       /u01/app/oracle/oradata/CLOUDDB/datafile/pdbseed_temp012016-02-25_05-11-47-PM.dbf
3    20       PDB1:TEMP       32767       +DATA/CLOUDDB/2C97B5FA561D719FE0536438A8C062F0/TEMPFILE/temp.272.904758093
4    20       PDB2:TEMP       32767       +DATA/CLOUDDB/2C97B6DDD50F73F2E0536438A8C0FD35/TEMPFILE/temp.278.904758093
```

Figure 6-21. *Checking the migration status through RMAN for the CDB and PDBs*

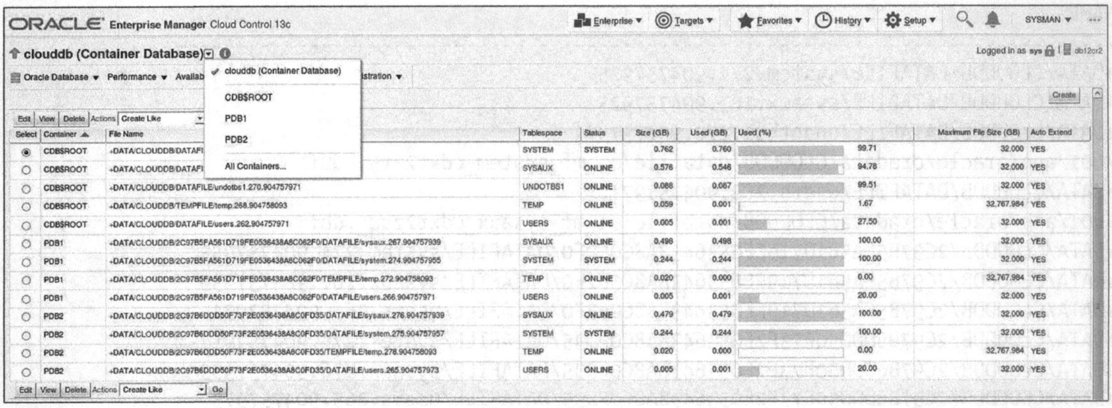

Figure 6-22. *Checking the completed migration status through OEM Cloud Control 13c for the CDB and PDBs*

Check the status of the CDB (clouddb) with two pluggable databases after relocating from a non-ASM location to an ASM location.

Scenario 3: Migrating an Oracle Database 12c CDB with PDBs from a non-ASM to ASM using RMAN

Let's now migrate the Oracle Database 12c CDB with PDBs from a non-ASM location to an ASM location using Recovery Manager.

This is the traditional way of converting from non-ASM to ASM. In Oracle 12c, this method will support a CDB with PDBs and also convert from non-ASM to ASM.

Log in to the primary container database (contdb) with the PDBs (pdb1 and pdb2).

```
[oracle@db12cr2 ~]$ sqlplus /nolog
SQL*Plus: Release 12.1.0.2.0 Production on Tue Mar 1 10:54:31 2016
Copyright (c) 1982, 2014, Oracle.  All rights reserved.

SQL> connect sys/oracle@contdb as sysdba
Connected.

SQL> alter pluggable database all open;
Pluggable database altered.

SQL> alter pluggable database pdb1 save state;
Pluggable database altered.

SQL> alter pluggable database pdb2 save state;
Pluggable database altered.
```

Log in as C##user1 in the container database (contdb) and check the table and rows for the table tab1 before converting from non-ASM to ASM in the primary container database (contdb) and the physical standby container database (contdbs).

```
SQL> connect c##user1/oracle@contdb
Connected.

SQL> select tname from tab;

TNAME
-----------
TAB1

SQL> select * from tab1;

NO     NAME
------ -------
1      ORACLE
```

Before converting the primary container database (contcb) with pluggable databases (pdb1 and pdb2) from non-ASM to ASM, check the status of the physical standby database (contdbs) with pluggable databases (pdb1 and pdb2).

```
SQL> connect sys/oracle@contdbs as sysdba
Connected.

SQL> select open_mode,database_role from v$database;

OPEN_MODE            DATABASE_ROLE
--------------       ----------------
MOUNTED              PHYSICAL STANDBY

SQL> alter database open read only;
Database altered.

SQL> connect c##user1/oracle@contdbs
Connected.

SQL> select tname from tab;

TNAME
------------
TAB1

SQL> select * from tab1;

NO     NAME
------ --------
1      ORACLE
```

Check the locations of the datafiles, control files, and temp files for the container database (contdb), seed database (pdb$seed), and pluggable databases (pdb1 and pdb2).

```
[oracle@db12cr2 ~]$ rman target /

Recovery Manager: Release 12.1.0.2.0 - Production on Tue Mar 1 13:35:58 2016

Copyright (c) 1982, 2014, Oracle and/or its affiliates.  All rights reserved.

connected to target database: CONTDB (DBID=1295430847)

RMAN> report schema;

using target database control file instead of recovery catalog
Report of database schema for database with db_unique_name CONTDB

List of Permanent Datafiles
===========================
File Size(MB) Tablespace          RB segs Datafile Name
---- -------- ------------------- ------- ------------------------
1    780      SYSTEM              YES     /u01/app/oracle/oradata/contdb/system01.dbf
3    600      SYSAUX              NO      /u01/app/oracle/oradata/contdb/sysaux01.dbf
4    90       UNDOTBS1            YES     /u01/app/oracle/oradata/contdb/undotbs01.dbf
5    250      PDB$SEED:SYSTEM     NO      /u01/app/oracle/oradata/contdb/pdbseed/system01.dbf
6    5        USERS               NO      /u01/app/oracle/oradata/contdb/users01.dbf
7    490      PDB$SEED:SYSAUX     NO      /u01/app/oracle/oradata/contdb/pdbseed/sysaux01.dbf
8    250      PDB1:SYSTEM         NO      /u01/app/oracle/oradata/contdb/pdb1/system01.dbf
9    520      PDB1:SYSAUX         NO      /u01/app/oracle/oradata/contdb/pdb1/sysaux01.dbf
10   5        PDB1:USERS          NO      /u01/app/oracle/oradata/contdb/pdb1/pdb1_users01.dbf
11   250      PDB2:SYSTEM         NO      /u01/app/oracle/oradata/contdb/pdb2/system01.dbf
12   520      PDB2:SYSAUX         NO      /u01/app/oracle/oradata/contdb/pdb2/sysaux01.dbf
13   5        PDB2:USERS          NO      /u01/app/oracle/oradata/contdb/pdb2/pdb2_users01.dbf

List of Temporary Files
=======================
File Size(MB) Tablespace          Maxsize(MB) Tempfile Name
---- -------- ------------------- ----------- --------------------
1    60       TEMP                32767       /u01/app/oracle/oradata/contdb/temp01.dbf
2    20       PDB$SEED:TEMP       32767       /u01/app/oracle/oradata/contdb/pdbseed/pdbseed_temp012016-02-29_05-41-49-PM.dbf
3    20       PDB1:TEMP           32767       /u01/app/oracle/oradata/contdb/pdb1/temp012016-02-29_05-41-49-PM.dbf
4    20       PDB2:TEMP           32767       /u01/app/oracle/oradata/contdb/pdb2/temp012016-02-29_05-41-49-PM.dbf
```

Figure 6-23. *Checking the locations of the datafiles and temp files of the container, seed, and pluggable databases through RMAN*

Use RMAN to do the following:

```
RMAN> backup as copy database format '+DATA';

Starting backup at 01-MAR-16
allocated channel: ORA_DISK_1
channel ORA_DISK_1: SID=275 device type=DISK
channel ORA_DISK_1: starting datafile copy
input datafile file number=00001 name=/u01/app/oracle/oradata/contdb/system01.dbf
output file name=+DATA/CONTDB/DATAFILE/system.293.905348225 tag=TAG20160301T133700 RECID=3
STAMP=905348232
channel ORA_DISK_1: datafile copy complete, elapsed time: 00:00:15
channel ORA_DISK_1: starting datafile copy
input datafile file number=00003 name=/u01/app/oracle/oradata/contdb/sysaux01.dbf
output file name=+DATA/CONTDB/DATAFILE/sysaux.292.905348235 tag=TAG20160301T133700 RECID=4
STAMP=905348243
channel ORA_DISK_1: datafile copy complete, elapsed time: 00:00:15
channel ORA_DISK_1: starting datafile copy
input datafile file number=00009 name=/u01/app/oracle/oradata/contdb/pdb1/sysaux01.dbf
output file
```

Here's the truncated output:

```
RMAN> shutdown immediate;
database closed
database dismounted
```

```
Oracle instance shut down

RMAN> startup mount;
connected to target database (not started)
Oracle instance started
database mounted

Total System Global Area    3154116608    bytes
Fixed Size                     2929352    bytes
Variable Size                771755320    bytes
Database Buffers            2365587456    bytes
Redo Buffers                 13844480    bytes
```

Switch the primary container database (contdb) from a non-ASM to ASM location using the following commands:

RMAN> switch database to copy;

```
datafile 1 switched to datafile copy "+DATA/CONTDB/DATAFILE/system.293.905348225"
datafile 3 switched to datafile copy "+DATA/CONTDB/DATAFILE/sysaux.292.905348235"
datafile 4 switched to datafile copy "+DATA/CONTDB/DATAFILE/undotbs1.295.905348301"
datafile 5 switched to datafile copy "+DATA/CONTDB/2CE88D4A926512A2E0536438A8C05421/
DATAFILE/system.290.905348281"
datafile 6 switched to datafile copy "+DATA/CONTDB/DATAFILE/users.291.905348305"
datafile 7 switched to datafile copy "+DATA/CONTDB/2CE88D4A926512A2E0536438A8C05421/
DATAFILE/sysaux.294.905348273"
datafile 8 switched to datafile copy "+DATA/CONTDB/2CE897FA0C0017CEE0536438A8C026AE/
DATAFILE/system.286.905348287"
datafile 9 switched to datafile copy "+DATA/CONTDB/2CE897FA0C0017CEE0536438A8C026AE/
DATAFILE/sysaux.285.905348251"
datafile 10 switched to datafile copy "+DATA/CONTDB/2CE897FA0C0017CEE0536438A8C026AE/
DATAFILE/users.287.905348305"
datafile 11 switched to datafile copy "+DATA/CONTDB/2CE898BEB6971B79E0536438A8C05C6F/
DATAFILE/system.317.905348295"
datafile 12 switched to datafile copy "+DATA/CONTDB/2CE898BEB6971B79E0536438A8C05C6F/
DATAFILE/sysaux.284.905348267"
datafile 13 switched to datafile copy "+DATA/CONTDB/2CE898BEB6971B79E0536438A8C05C6F/
DATAFILE/users.316.905348307"
```

RMAN> backup as copy current controlfile format '+DATA';
```
Starting backup at 01-MAR-16
allocated channel: ORA_DISK_1
channel ORA_DISK_1: SID=258 device type=DISK
channel ORA_DISK_1: starting datafile copy
copying current control file
output file name=+DATA/CONTDB/CONTROLFILE/backup.289.905348369 tag=TAG20160301T133928
RECID=27 STAMP=905348368
channel ORA_DISK_1: datafile copy complete, elapsed time: 00:00:01
Finished backup at 01-MAR-16

Starting Control File and SPFILE Autobackup at 01-MAR-16
```

```
piece handle=/u01/app/oracle/fast_recovery_area/CONTDB/autobackup/2016_03_01/o1_
mf_s_905348326_cfbmksks_.bkp comment=NONE
Finished Control File and SPFILE Autobackup at 01-MAR-16
```

RMAN> restore controlfile to '+DATA';

```
Starting restore at 01-MAR-16
using channel ORA_DISK_1

channel ORA_DISK_1: starting datafile backup set restore
channel ORA_DISK_1: restoring control file
output file name=+DATA
channel ORA_DISK_1: reading from backup piece /u01/app/oracle/fast_recovery_area/CONTDB/
autobackup/2016_03_01/o1_mf_s_905348326_cfbmksks_.bkp
channel ORA_DISK_1: piece handle=/u01/app/oracle/fast_recovery_area/CONTDB/
autobackup/2016_03_01/o1_mf_s_905348326_cfbmksks_.bkp tag=TAG20160301T133929
channel ORA_DISK_1: restored backup piece 1
channel ORA_DISK_1: restore complete, elapsed time: 00:00:01
Finished restore at 01-MAR-16
```

RMAN> shutdown immediate;
```
database dismounted
Oracle instance shut down
```

RMAN> startup nomount;
```
connected to target database (not started)
Oracle instance started
```

```
Total System Global Area      3154116608    bytes
Fixed Size                       2929352    bytes
Variable Size                  771755320    bytes
Database Buffers              2365587456    bytes
Redo Buffers                    13844480    bytes
```

Restore the control files from the non-ASM location to the ASM location using an RMAN prompt.

```
RMAN> restore controlfile to '+DATA' from '/u01/app/oracle/oradata/contdb/control01.ctl';
Starting restore at 01-MAR-16
using channel ORA_DISK_1
channel ORA_DISK_1: copied control file copy
Finished restore at 01-MAR-16
```

```
RMAN> restore controlfile to '+FRA' from '/u01/app/oracle/fast_recovery_area/contdb/
control02.ctl';
```

```
Starting restore at 01-MAR-16
using channel ORA_DISK_1
channel ORA_DISK_1: copied control file copy
Finished restore at 01-MAR-16
```

```
RMAN> exit
```

Log in to the ASMCMD prompt and check the current locations for the control files.

```
[oracle@db12cr2 ~]$ . oraenv
ORACLE_SID = [contdb] ? +ASM
The Oracle base remains unchanged with value /u01/app/oracle
[oracle@db12cr2 ~]$ asmcmd
```

+DATA Location:

```
ASMCMD> cd controlfile
ASMCMD> ls
Backup.289.905348369
current.288.905348429
current.315.905348731
ASMCMD> pwd
+DATA/contdb/controlfile
```

+FRA Location:

```
ASMCMD> cd controlfile
ASMCMD> ls
current.291.905348953
ASMCMD> pwd
+FRA/contdb/controlfile
```

```
SQL> show parameter control_files
```

NAME	TYPE	VALUE
control_files	string	

```
/u01/app/oracle/oradata/contd/control01.ctl,
/u01/app/oracle/fast_recovery_area/contdb/control02.ctl
```

```
SQL> alter system set control_files=
'+DATA/contdb/controlfile/current.315.905348731',
'+FRA/contdb/controlfile/current.291.905348953' scope=spfile;
```

```
System altered.
SQL> shutdown immediate;
ORA-01507: database not mounted
ORACLE instance shut down.
```

```
SQL> startup mount;
ORACLE instance started.
```

Total System Global Area	3154116608	bytes
Fixed Size	2929352	bytes
Variable Size	771755320	bytes
Database Buffers	2365587456	bytes
Redo Buffers	13844480	bytes

```
Database mounted.

SQL> show parameter control_files

NAME                           TYPE        VALUE
------------------------------ ----------- ------------------------------
control_files                  string
+DATA/contdb/controlfile/current.315.905348731,
+FRA/contdb/controlfile/current.291.905348953
SQL> exit
```

Restore the spfile to the ASM location using the RMAN prompt.

```
[oracle@db12cr2 ~]$ rman target /


Recovery Manager: Release 12.1.0.2.0 - Production on Tue Mar 1 13:53:59 2016
Copyright (c) 1982, 2014, Oracle and/or its affiliates.  All rights reserved.
connected to target database: CONTDB (DBID=1295430847, not open)


RMAN> run
{
BACKUP AS BACKUPSET SPFILE;
RESTORE SPFILE TO "+DATA/CONTDB/spfileccontdb.ora";
}

Starting backup at 01-MAR-16
using target database control file instead of recovery catalog
allocated channel: ORA_DISK_1
channel ORA_DISK_1: SID=257 device type=DISK
channel ORA_DISK_1: starting full datafile backup set
channel ORA_DISK_1: specifying datafile(s) in backup set
including current SPFILE in backup set
channel ORA_DISK_1: starting piece 1 at 01-MAR-16
channel ORA_DISK_1: finished piece 1 at 01-MAR-16
piece handle=/u01/app/oracle/fast_recovery_area/CONTDB/backupset/2016_03_01/o1_mf_nnsnf_
TAG20160301T135445_cfbngfqf_.bkp tag=TAG20160301T135445 comment=NONE
channel ORA_DISK_1: backup set complete, elapsed time: 00:00:01
Finished backup at 01-MAR-16

Starting Control File and SPFILE Autobackup at 01-MAR-16
piece handle=/u01/app/oracle/fast_recovery_area/CONTDB/autobackup/2016_03_01/o1_
mf_s_905348326_cfbngh3s_.bkp comment=NONE
Finished Control File and SPFILE Autobackup at 01-MAR-16
```

Here's the truncated output:

```
RMAN> recover database;
Starting recover at 01-MAR-16
using channel ORA_DISK_1
starting media recovery
```

```
media recovery complete, elapsed time: 00:00:01
Finished recover at 01-MAR-16

RMAN> alter database open;
Statement processed

RMAN> exit

SQL> connect sys/oracle@contdb as sysdba
Connected.

SQL> show con_name

CON_NAME
-----------------
CDB$ROOT
```

Convert the temporary tablespace and redo log groups from the non-ASM to ASM location.

■ **Note**   Similarly, you can convert the standby redo log groups from non-ASM to ASM.

```
SQL> alter tablespace TEMP add tempfile '+DATA';
Tablespace altered.

SQL> alter tablespace TEMP drop tempfile '/u01/app/oracle/oradata/contdb/temp01.dbf';
Tablespace altered.

SQL> alter session set container=PDB1;
Session altered.
SQL> alter tablespace TEMP add tempfile '+DATA';
Tablespace altered.

SQL> alter tablespace TEMP drop tempfile '/u01/app/oracle/oradata/contdb/pdb1/temp012016-02-
29_05-41-49-PM.dbf';
Tablespace altered.
SQL> alter session set container=PDB2;
Session altered.

SQL> alter tablespace TEMP add tempfile '+DATA';
Tablespace altered.

SQL> alter tablespace TEMP drop tempfile '/u01/app/oracle/oradata/contdb/pdb2/temp012016-02-
29_05-41-49-PM.dbf';
Tablespace altered.

SQL> alter session set container=CDB$ROOT;
Session altered.

SQL> show con_name
```

```
CON_NAME
----------------
CDB$ROOT

SQL> alter session set "_oracle_script"=TRUE;
Session altered.

SQL> alter pluggable database pdb$seed close;
Pluggable database altered.

SQL> alter pluggable database pdb$seed open read write;
Pluggable database altered.

SQL> alter session set container=pdb$seed;
Session altered.

SQL> alter tablespace temp add tempfile '+DATA';
Tablespace altered.

SQL> alter tablespace TEMP drop tempfile '/u01/app/oracle/oradata/contdb/pdbseed/pdbseed_
temp012016-02-29_05-41-49-PM.dbf';
Tablespace altered.

SQL> alter session set container=CDB$ROOT;
Session altered.

SQL> alter pluggable database pdb$seed close;
Pluggable database altered.

SQL> alter pluggable database pdb$seed open read only;
Pluggable database altered.

SQL> select group#, status from v$log;
GROUP#    STATUS
-------   ---------
1         INACTIVE
2         INACTIVE
3         CURRENT

SQL> alter database drop logfile group 1;
Database altered.

SQL> alter database add logfile group 1 '+DATA';
Database altered.

SQL> select group#, status from v$log;

GROUP#    STATUS
-------   ---------
   1      UNUSED
   2      INACTIVE
```

```
    3       CURRENT
```

```
SQL> alter database drop logfile group 2;
Database altered.
```

```
SQL> alter database add logfile group 2 '+DATA';
Database altered.
```

```
SQL> select group#, status from v$log;
```

```
GROUP#      STATUS
-------     --------
    1       INACTIVE
    2       CURRENT
    3       INACTIVE
```

```
SQL> alter database drop logfile group 3;
Database altered.
```

```
SQL> alter database add logfile group 3 '+DATA';
Database altered.
```

```
RMAN> report schema;

using target database control file instead of recovery catalog
Report of database schema for database with db_unique_name CONTDB

List of Permanent Datafiles
===========================
File Size(MB) Tablespace         RB segs Datafile Name
---- -------- ------------------ ------- --------------------------
1    780      SYSTEM             YES     +DATA/CONTDB/DATAFILE/system.293.905348225
3    610      SYSAUX             NO      +DATA/CONTDB/DATAFILE/sysaux.292.905348235
4    90       UNDOTBS1           YES     +DATA/CONTDB/DATAFILE/undotbs1.295.905348301
5    250      PDB$SEED:SYSTEM    NO      +DATA/CONTDB/2CE88DAA926512A2E0536438A8C05421/DATAFILE/system.290.905348281
6    5        USERS              NO      +DATA/CONTDB/DATAFILE/users.291.905348305
7    490      PDB$SEED:SYSAUX    NO      +DATA/CONTDB/2CE88DAA926512A2E0536438A8C05421/DATAFILE/sysaux.294.905348273
8    250      PDB1:SYSTEM        NO      +DATA/CONTDB/2CE897FA0C0017CEE0536438A8C026AE/DATAFILE/system.286.905348287
9    520      PDB1:SYSAUX        NO      +DATA/CONTDB/2CE897FA0C0017CEE0536438A8C026AE/DATAFILE/sysaux.285.905348251
10   5        PDB1:USERS         NO      +DATA/CONTDB/2CE897FA0C0017CEE0536438A8C026AE/DATAFILE/users.287.905348305
11   250      PDB2:SYSTEM        NO      +DATA/CONTDB/2CE898BEB6971B79E0536438A8C05C6F/DATAFILE/system.317.905348295
12   520      PDB2:SYSAUX        NO      +DATA/CONTDB/2CE898BEB6971B79E0536438A8C05C6F/DATAFILE/sysaux.284.905348267
13   5        PDB2:USERS         NO      +DATA/CONTDB/2CE898BEB6971B79E0536438A8C05C6F/DATAFILE/users.316.905348307

List of Temporary Files
=======================
File Size(MB) Tablespace         Maxsize(MB) Tempfile Name
---- -------- ------------------ ----------- --------------------------
5    100      TEMP               32767       +DATA/CONTDB/TEMPFILE/temp.309.905349487
6    100      PDB1:TEMP          32767       +DATA/CONTDB/2CE897FA0C0017CEE0536438A8C026AE/TEMPFILE/temp.308.905349619
7    100      PDB2:TEMP          32767       +DATA/CONTDB/2CE898BE36971B79E0536438A8C05C6F/TEMPFILE/temp.307.905349645
8    100      PDB$SEED:TEMP      32767       +DATA/CONTDB/2CE88DAA326512A2E0536438A8C05421/TEMPFILE/temp.306.905349755

RMAN> exit
```

Figure 6-24. *Checking the locations of the datafiles and temp files of the container, seed, and pluggable databases through RMAN in the ASM location*

```
SQL> connect sys/oracle@contdb as sysdba
Connected.
```

```
SQL> select name from v$datafile union all
select name from v$tempfile union all
select member from v$logfile union all
select name from v$controlfile;
```

```
NAME
-------------------------------------------------------------------------------------------
-----------------------------------
+DATA/CONTDB/DATAFILE/system.293.905348225
+DATA/CONTDB/DATAFILE/sysaux.292.905348235
+DATA/CONTDB/DATAFILE/undotbs1.295.905348301
+DATA/CONTDB/2CE88DAA926512A2E0536438A8C05421/DATAFILE/system.290.905348281
+DATA/CONTDB/DATAFILE/users.291.905348305
+DATA/CONTDB/2CE88DAA926512A2E0536438A8C05421/DATAFILE/sysaux.294.905348273
+DATA/CONTDB/2CE897FA0C0017CEE0536438A8C026AE/DATAFILE/system.286.905348287
+DATA/CONTDB/2CE897FA0C0017CEE0536438A8C026AE/DATAFILE/sysaux.285.905348251
+DATA/CONTDB/2CE897FA0C0017CEE0536438A8C026AE/DATAFILE/users.287.905348305
+DATA/CONTDB/2CE898BEB6971B79E0536438A8C05C6F/DATAFILE/system.317.905348295
+DATA/CONTDB/2CE898BEB6971B79E0536438A8C05C6F/DATAFILE/sysaux.284.905348267
+DATA/CONTDB/2CE898BEB6971B79E0536438A8C05C6F/DATAFILE/users.316.905348307
+DATA/CONTDB/2CE897FA0C0017CEE0536438A8C026AE/TEMPFILE/temp.308.905349619
+DATA/CONTDB/2CE898BEB6971B79E0536438A8C05C6F/TEMPFILE/temp.307.905349645
+DATA/CONTDB/2CE88DAA926512A2E0536438A8C05421/TEMPFILE/temp.306.905349755
+DATA/CONTDB/TEMPFILE/temp.309.905349487
+DATA/CONTDB/ONLINELOG/group_3.302.905350245
+DATA/CONTDB/ONLINELOG/group_2.304.905350125
+DATA/CONTDB/ONLINELOG/group_1.305.905350087
+DATA/contdb/controlfile/current.315.905348731
+FRA/contdb/controlfile/current.291.905348953

25 rows selected.
```

Now, the primary container database (contdb) has been relocated to ASM, but still the physical standby container database (contdbs) is in a non-ASM location. Create a new tablespace called example in the primary container database (contdb) and check whether it is applied to the physical standby container database (contdbs).

```
SQL> create tablespace example datafile '+DATA' size 10M autoextend on maxsize unlimited
  2  segment space management auto
  3  extent management local;

Tablespace created.

SQL> select tablespace_name from dba_tablespaces;

TABLESPACE_NAME
-----------------------------
SYSTEM
SYSAUX
UNDOTBS1
TEMP
USERS
EXAMPLE

6 rows selected.
```

Log in after converting the primary container database (contdb) with pluggable databases (pdb1 and pdb2) from non-ASM to ASM and check the data replication status of the physical standby container database (contdbs) with pluggable databases (pdb1 and pdb2).

■ **Note**   Create the new tablespace called example in the primary container database (contdb) in ASM and replicate the same tablespace in the physical standby container database (contdbs) in the non-ASM location.

```
SQL> connect sys/oracle@contdbs as sysdba
Connected.
SQL> select open_mode,database_role from V$database;

OPEN_MODE                 DATABASE_ROLE
--------------------      -----------------
READ ONLY                 PHYSICAL STANDBY

SQL> select tablespace_name from dba_tablespaces;

TABLESPACE_NAME
------------------------------
SYSTEM
SYSAUX
UNDOTBS1
TEMP
USERS
EXAMPLE

6 rows selected.

SQL> []
```

Figure 6-25. *Checking the newly created tablespace (example) in the physical standby database*

Note that the physical standby database is in Active Data Guard (ADG) status (the status can be opened either in read-only mode or in managed recovery).

Now you can move the online datafiles while in managed recovery mode. In other words, the physical standby database is in Active Data Guard (ADG) status. Use the following command:

```
SQL> alter database move datafile <File#> to '<Destination>' [keep];
```

Summary

You have moved datafiles on a traditional file system to Automatic Storage Management via several options, including Oracle 12*c*'s new feature, Oracle Enterprise Manager Cloud Control 13*c*, and Recovery Manager.

CHAPTER 7

■ ■ ■

Oracle GI and Oracle 12c Database Upgrades in RAC Environments

You can upgrade Oracle Grid Infrastructure (GI) with either of these methods:

- *Rolling upgrade*: This involves upgrading individual cluster nodes in a cluster environment without stopping Oracle GI on other nodes in the cluster.

- *Nonrolling upgrade*: This involves bringing down all the nodes except one. A complete cluster outage occurs while the root script stops the old Oracle Clusterware stack and starts the new Oracle Clusterware stack on the node where you initiate the upgrade. Once the Oracle GI upgrade is completed, the new Oracle Clusterware is started on all the cluster nodes.

The following are the prerequisites for Oracle Grid Infrastructure:

- Operating system (OS) certification for Oracle 12c R1 (12.1.0.2.0)

- OS kernel and packages

- Oracle 12c R1 base location

- Oracle Grid Infrastructure home location

- Unset the environment variables (ORACLE_BASE, ORACLE_HOME, GI_HOME, and TNS_ADMIN)

- Additional space is required for the mount point (/u01). At least 8 GB of space for Oracle GI is needed for a cluster home, and Oracle recommends 100 GB to allow additional space for patches and 10 GB of additional space in the Oracle base directory of the GI owner for diagnostic collections generated by Trace File Analyzer (TFA) Collector. Check the space for the mount point (/tmp). You need at least 1 GB allocated to /tmpBackup for the Oracle Cluster Registry (OCR), Cluster, and Oracle Homes.

- Check the space for the mount point (/tmp). You need at least 1 GB allocated to /tmp.

- Back up the OCR, Cluster, and Oracle Homes.

  Note: Oracle Database 12c deprecated raw devices. Upgrading to Oracle Database 12c Grid Infrastructure makes sure that the OCR and Voting Disk (VD) is not on a raw device or block device. Oracle Database 11g started supporting OCR and VD on ASM storage and on a file system.

  - If it is on a raw device or block device, relocate OCR and VD to ASM and you can upgrade to Oracle Database 12c GI.

© Y V Ravikumar, K M Krishnakumar and Nassyam Basha 2017

N. Basha et al., *Oracle Database Upgrade and Migration Methods*, DOI 10.1007/978-1-4842-2328-4_7

- If it is on a raw device or block device, relocate OCR and VD to the Network File System (NFS)/Cluster File System (CFS) and you can upgrade to Oracle Database 12c GI.

- Finally, check the following before and after the Oracle Grid Infrastructure upgrade; both should be the same:

  ```
  $ crsctl query crs activeversion
  $ crsctl query crs softwareversion
  ```

- Check the space availability in the disk groups (+DATA, +FRA, and so on). For the Flash Recovery Area (FRA), you need a minimum of 10240 MB space when you are upgrading Oracle Database.

- Oracle Standard Cluster can't be directly upgraded to Oracle 12c Flex ASM. There is an option in the ASMCA in Oracle 12c to convert to Flex ASM.

- OCR and VD must be placed in ASM disk groups rather than on raw devices. This is a requirement for Grid Infrastructure 12c.

- Install/upgrade Oracle GI first.

- Oracle recommends that the installation/upgrade of Oracle GI should be in a different path than the ORACLE_BASE. See Table 7-1 for more information.

Table 7-1. *Status of GI and Database Before and After the Upgrade Process, with Versions*

Source Database (RAC)		Target Database (RAC)
BEFORE UPGRADE:		**AFTER UPGRADE:**
Oracle 11g Grid Infrastructure (11.2.0.3.0) (/u01/app/11.2.0/grid)	Rolling Upgrade ➤	Oracle 12c Grid Infrastructure (12.1.0.2.0) (/u01/app/12.1.0.2/grid)
BEFORE UPGRADE:		**AFTER UPGRADE:**
Oracle Database 11g (11.2.0.3.0) (/u01/app/oracle/product/11.2.0/dbhome_1)		Oracle Database 12c (12.1.0.2.0) (/u01/app/oracle/product/12.1.0.2/dbhome_1)

Run the CVU Pre-upgrade Check Tool

Execute runcluvfy.sh in the unzipped GI software location as a grid user to confirm whether the environment is suitable for upgrading.

> *Usage*: runcluvfy.sh stage -pre crsinst -upgrade [-n] [-rolling] -src_crshome -dest_crshome -dest_version [-fixup [-fixupdir]] [-verbose]

> *Example*: To upgrade a two-node Oracle Clusterware setup in /u01/ app/**11.2.0.3.0** to 12.1.0.2.0 in /u01/app/grid in a rolling fashion, execute the following (see Figure 7-1):

```
$ runcluvfy.sh stage -pre crsinst -upgrade -n rac1,rac2 -rolling -src_crshome /u01/
app/11.2.0/grid -dest_crshome /u01/app/12.1.0.2/grid -dest_version 12.1.0.2.0 -fixup
-fixupdir /tmp -verbose
```

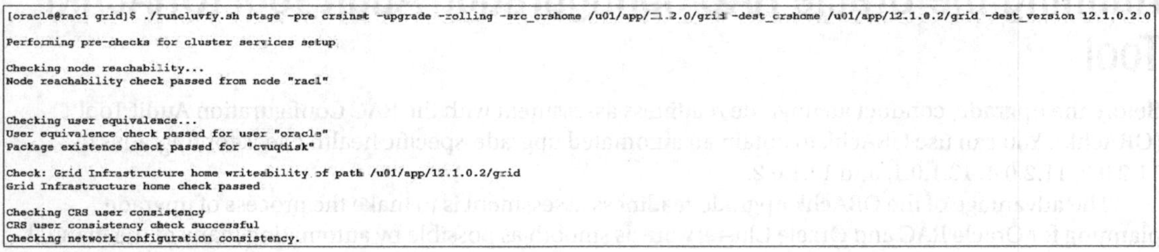

```
[oracle@rac1 grid]$ ./runcluvfy.sh stage -pre crsinst -upgrade -rolling -src_crshome /u01/app/11.2.0/grid -dest_crshome /u01/app/12.1.0.2/grid -dest_version 12.1.0.2.0

Performing pre-checks for cluster services setup

Checking node reachability...
Node reachability check passed from node "rac1"

Checking user equivalence...
User equivalence check passed for user "oracle"
Package existence check passed for "cvuqdisk"

Check: Grid Infrastructure home writeability of path /u01/app/12.1.0.2/grid
Grid Infrastructure home check passed

Checking CRS user consistency
CRS user consistency check successful
Checking network configuration consistency.
```

***Figure 7-1.** Checking node reachability, CRS consistency, the network, and so on, from cluster nodes using the cluvfy command*

```
 [oracle@rac1 grid]$ ./runcluvfy.sh stage -pre crsinst -upgrade -n rac1,rac2 -rolling -src_
crshome /u01/app/11.2.0/grid -dest_crshome /u01/app/12.1.0.2/grid -dest_version 12.1.0.2.0
-fixup -fixupdir /tmp -verbose

Performing pre-checks for cluster services setup

Checking node reachability...

Check: Node reachability from node "rac1"
  Destination Node                      Reachable?
  ------------------------------------  ------------------------
  rac2                                  yes
  rac1                                  yes
Result: Node reachability check passed from node "rac1"

Checking user equivalence...

Check: User equivalence for user "oracle"
  Node Name                             Status
  ------------------------------------  ------------------------
  rac2                                  passed
  rac1                                  passed
Result: User equivalence check passed for user "oracle"

Checking CRS user consistency
Result: CRS user consistency check successful

Checking node connectivity...

Checking hosts config file...
  Node Name                             Status
  ------------------------------------  ------------------------
  rac2                                  passed
  rac1                                  passed

Verification of the hosts config file successful
```

Note: The output has been truncated for better readability.

Running the Oracle RAC Configuration Audit Tool (ORAchk) Tool

Before the upgrade, conduct an upgrade readiness assessment with the RAC Configuration Audit Tool (ORAchk). You can use ORAchk to obtain an automated upgrade-specific health check for upgrades to 11.2.0.3, 11.2.0.4, 12.1.0.1, and 12.1.0.2.

The advantage of the ORAchk upgrade readiness assessment is to make the process of upgrade planning for Oracle RAC and Oracle Clusterware as smooth as possible by automating many of the manual pre- and post-checks.

Oracle recommends that you download and run the latest version of ORAchk from My Oracle Support. For information about downloading, configuring, and running the ORAchk tool, refer to My Oracle Support Note 1457357.1.

Review the HTML report generated by the ORAchk tool before executing the upgrade and implement the recommended changes as necessary.

Once you have successfully upgraded (GI and/or the RDBMS), execute ORAchk in post-upgrade mode and follow the onscreen prompts.

Execution Steps for ORAchk

Unzip the orachk.zip kit. Validate that the permissions for orachk are 755 (-rwxr-xr-x).

If the permissions are not currently set to 755, set the permissions on orachk as follows:

```
[oracle@rac1 ~]$ unzip orachk.zip
[oracle@rac1 ~]$ chmod -R 755 orachk.zip
[oracle@rac1 ~]$ ./orachk -u.-o pre
```

Enter the upgrade target version (valid versions are 11.2.0.3.0, 11.2.0.4.0, 12.1.0.1.0 and 12.1.0.2.0.

The CRS stack is running, and CRS_HOME is not set. Do you want to set CRS_HOME to /u01/app/11.2.0/ grid? Answer yes or no.

Checking ssh user equivalency settings on all nodes in cluster Node rac2 is configured for ssh user equivalency for oracle user Searching for running databases . . . . .

- Download/execute newest pre-upgrade scripts; see MOS Note 884522.1.

  - preupgrd.sql and utluppkg.sql
  - You can find files in Oracle 12c's ?/rdbms/admin as well.

---------- Output Truncated---

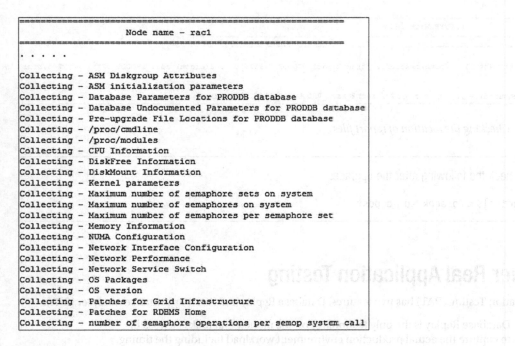

```
================================================================
                      Node name - rac1
================================================================

. . . . .

Collecting - ASM Diskgroup Attributes
Collecting - ASM initialization parameters
Collecting - Database Parameters for PRODDB database
Collecting - Database Undocumented Parameters for PRODDB database
Collecting - Pre-upgrade File Locations for PRODDB database
Collecting - /proc/cmdline
Collecting - /proc/modules
Collecting - CPU Information
Collecting - DiskFree Information
Collecting - DiskMount Information
Collecting - Kernel parameters
Collecting - Maximum number of semaphore sets on system
Collecting - Maximum number of semaphores on system
Collecting - Maximum number of semaphores per semaphore set
Collecting - Memory Information
Collecting - NUMA Configuration
Collecting - Network Interface Configuration
Collecting - Network Performance
Collecting - Network Service Switch
Collecting - OS Packages
Collecting - OS version
Collecting - Patches for Grid Infrastructure
Collecting - Patches for RDBMS Home
Collecting - number of semaphore operations per semop system call
```

Figure 7-2. *Collecting system information from node 1 (rac1)*

```
================================================================
                      Node name - rac2
================================================================

. . . . .

Collecting - /proc/cmdline
Collecting - /proc/modules
Collecting - CPU Information
Collecting - DiskFree Information
Collecting - DiskMount Information
Collecting - Kernel parameters
Collecting - Maximum number of semaphore sets on system
Collecting - Maximum number of semaphores on system
Collecting - Maximum number of semaphores per semaphore set
Collecting - Memory Information
Collecting - NUMA Configuration
Collecting - Network Interface Configuration
Collecting - Network Performance
Collecting - Network Service Switch
Collecting - OS Packages
Collecting - OS version
Collecting - Patches for Grid Infrastructure
Collecting - Patches for RDBMS Home
Collecting - number of semaphore operations per semop system call
```

Figure 7-3. *Collecting system information from node 2 (rac2)*

```
                    CLUSTERWIDE CHECKS
-------------------------------------------------------------------------
-------------------------------------------------------------------------
Detailed report (html) - /home/oracle/12c/orachk_rac1_PRODDB_021516_082308/orachk_rac1_PRODDB_021516_082308.html

UPLOAD(if required) - /home/oracle/12c/orachk_rac1_PRODDB_021516_082308.zip
```

Figure 7-4. *Checking the location of report files*

■ **Note**   Check the following after the upgrade:

[oracle@rac1 ~]$ ./orachk -u -o post

Consider Real Application Testing

Real Application Testing (RAT) has two features, Database Replay and SQL Performance Analyzer (SPA).

- Database Replay is the only technology on the market that makes it possible to capture the actual production environment workload including the timing, concurrency, and dependency information with negligible performance overhead and with minimal time and effort. Database Replay allows the captured workload to be replayed on a test system to assess the impact of change in terms of timing, concurrency, and dependency information.

- SQL Performance Analyzer allows fine-grained impact analysis of a database environment change on SQL execution plan changes and performance.

Performing a Rolling Upgrade Using Oracle GI

Create the Grid Infrastructure directory in /u01/app and change the owner privileges to oracle: install in both RAC nodes, as shown in Figures 7-5 through 7-x.

```
[root@rac1 ~]# cd /u01/app/
[root@rac1 app]# mkdir -p 12.1.0.2/grid
[root@rac1 ~]# chown -R oracle:oinstall /u01/app/12.1.0.2/grid/
[root@rac1 ~]# chmod -R 777 /u01/app/12.1.0.2/grid/
[root@rac2 ~]# cd /u01/app/
[root@rac2 app]# mkdir -p 12.1.0.2/grid
[root@rac2 ~]# chown -R oracle:oinstall /u01/app/12.1.0.2/grid/
[root@rac2 ~]# chmod -R 777 /u01/app/12.1.0.2/grid/
Execute ./runInstaller of Grid Infrastructure from RAC node1
```

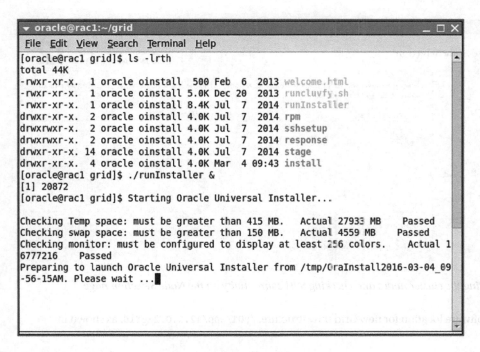

Figure 7-5. *Executed /runInstaller from Oracle GI location*

Select the option Upgrade Oracle Grid Infrastructure or Oracle Automatic Storage Management on the Installation Option page, as shown in Figure 7-6.

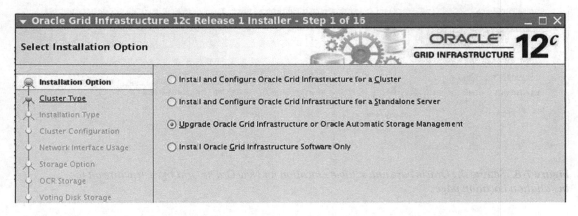

Figure 7-6. *Selecting the option Upgrade Oracle Grid Infrastructure or Oracle Automatic Storage Management*

Verify that you will be selecting all the nodes in the cluster, as shown in Figure 7-7. Currently you have a two-node cluster, and OUI will validate ssh before installation continues.

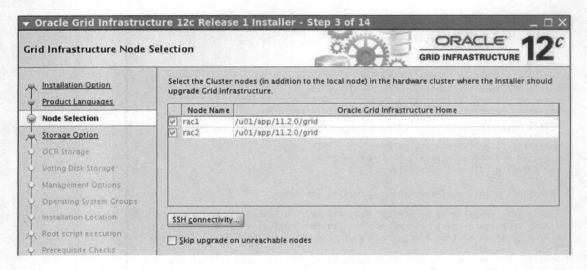

Figure 7-7. *Selecting the cluster nodes and checking SSH connectivity on the Node Selection page*

Specify the software location for new Grid Infrastructure, /u01/app/12.1.0.2/grid, as shown in Figure 7-8.

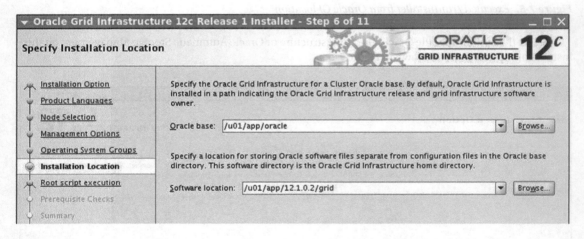

Figure 7-8. *Setting the Oracle base and software location for New Oracle Grid Infrastructure on the Installation Location page*

Before starting the install, check the summary, including the disk space, selected nodes in the cluster, and so on, as shown in Figure 7-9.

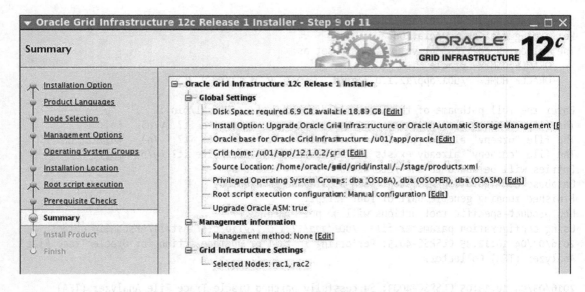

Figure 7-9. *Summary for New Oracle Grid Infrastructure 12c Release 1 installer with selected nodes and global settings*

Execute the script rootupgrade.sh serially from /u01/app/12.1.0.2/grid/rootupgrade.sh in the rac1 and rac2 nodes, as shown in Figure 7-10.

Note: Make sure you do not run rootupgrade.sh on rac2 until it has successfully completed on rac1.

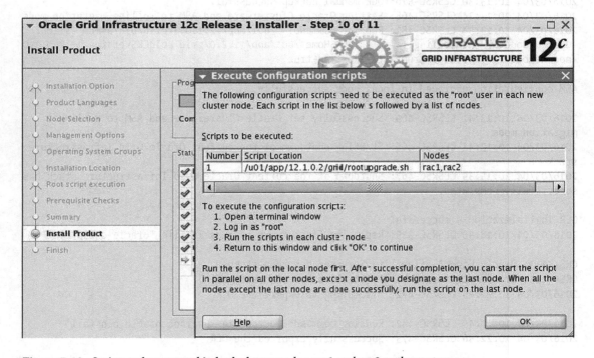

Figure 7-10. *Scripts to be executed in both cluster nodes: rac1 and rac2 as the root user*

```
[root@rac1 app]# sh /u01/app/12.1.0.2/grid/rootupgrade.sh
Performing root user operation.
The following environment variables are set as:
    ORACLE_OWNER= oracle
    ORACLE_HOME=  /u01/app/12.1.0.2/grid

Enter the full pathname of the local bin directory: [/usr/local/bin]:
The file "dbhome" already exists in /usr/local/bin.  Overwrite it? (y/n)   [n]:
The file "oraenv" already exists in /usr/local/bin.  Overwrite it? (y/n)   [n]:
The file "coraenv" already exists in /usr/local/bin.  Overwrite it? (y/n)   [n]:
Entries will be added to the /etc/oratab file as needed by
Database Configuration Assistant when a database is created
Finished running generic part of root script.
Now product-specific root actions will be performed.
Using configuration parameter file: /u01/app/12.1.0.2/grid/crs/install/crsconfig_params
2016/03/04 10:12:35 CLSRSC-4015: Performing install or upgrade action for Oracle Trace File
Analyzer (TFA) Collector.

2016/03/04 10:13:05 CLSRSC-4003: Successfully patched Oracle Trace File Analyzer (TFA)
Collector.
2016/03/04 10:13:07 CLSRSC-464: Starting retrieval of the cluster configuration data
2016/03/04 10:13:16 CLSRSC-465: Retrieval of the cluster configuration data has successfully
completed.
2016/03/04 10:13:16 CLSRSC-363: User ignored prerequisites during installation
2016/03/04 10:13:28 CLSRSC-515: Starting OCR manual backup.
2016/03/04 10:13:30 CLSRSC-516: OCR manual backup successful.
2016/03/04 10:13:34 CLSRSC-468: Setting Oracle Clusterware and ASM to rolling migration mode
2016/03/04 10:13:34 CLSRSC-482: Running command: '/u01/app/12.1.0.2/grid/bin/asmca -silent
-upgradeNodeASM -nonRolling false -oldCRSHome /u01/app/11.2.0/grid -oldCRSVersion 11.2.0.3.0
-nodeNumber 1 -firstNode true -startRolling true'

ASM configuration upgraded in local node successfully.

2016/03/04 10:13:41 CLSRSC-469: Successfully set Oracle Clusterware and ASM to rolling
migration mode
2016/03/04 10:13:41 CLSRSC-466: Starting shutdown of the current Oracle Grid Infrastructure
stack
2016/03/04 10:15:39 CLSRSC-467: Shutdown of the current Oracle Grid Infrastructure stack has
successfully completed.

OLR initialization - successful
2016/03/04 10:18:35 CLSRSC-329: Replacing Clusterware entries in file 'oracle-ohasd.conf'

CRS-4133: Oracle High Availability Services has been stopped.
CRS-4123: Oracle High Availability Services has been started.
2016/03/04 10:22:45 CLSRSC-472: Attempting to export the OCR

2016/03/04 10:22:45 CLSRSC-482: Running command: 'ocrconfig -upgrade oracle oinstall'
2016/03/04 10:22:56 CLSRSC-473: Successfully exported the OCR

2016/03/04 10:23:01 CLSRSC-486:
 At this stage of upgrade, the OCR has changed.
```

Any attempt to downgrade the cluster after this point will require a complete cluster outage to restore the OCR.

2016/03/04 10:23:01 CLSRSC-541:

> To downgrade the cluster, follow these steps:

> 1. Downgrade all the nodes that have been upgraded.

2016/03/04 10:23:01 CLSRSC-542:

> 2. Before downgrading the last node, the Grid Infrastructure stack on all other cluster nodes must be down.

2016/03/04 10:23:01 CLSRSC-543:

> 3. Run the downgrade command on the node rac1 with the -lastnode option to restore the global configuration data.

2016/03/04 10:23:32 CLSRSC-343: Successfully started Oracle Clusterware stack

```
clscfg: EXISTING configuration version 5 detected.
clscfg: version 5 is 11g Release 2.
Successfully taken the backup of node specific configuration in OCR.
Successfully accumulated necessary OCR keys.
Creating OCR keys for user 'root', privgrp 'root'..
Operation successful.
2016/03/04 10:23:57 CLSRSC-474: Initiating upgrade of resource types
2016/03/04 10:24:18 CLSRSC-482: Running command: 'upgrade model  -s 11.2.0.3.0 -d 12.1.0.2.0
-p first'
2016/03/04 10:24:18 CLSRSC-475: Upgrade of resource types successfully initiated.
2016/03/04 10:24:24 CLSRSC-325: Configure Oracle Grid Infrastructure for a Cluster ...
succeeded
```

■ **Note**   It is now safe to execute the script in rac2.

```
[root@rac2 ~]# sh /u01/app/12.1.0.2/grid/rootupgrade.sh
Performing root user operation.
The following environment variables are set as:
    ORACLE_OWNER= oracle
    ORACLE_HOME=  /u01/app/12.1.0.2/grid
Enter the full pathname of the local bin directory: [/usr/local/bin]:
The file "dbhome" already exists in /usr/local/bin. Overwrite it? (y/n)
[n]:
The file "oraenv" already exists in /usr/local/bin. Overwrite it? (y/n)
[n]:
The file "coraenv" already exists in /usr/local/bin.  Overwrite it? (y/n)
[n]:
```

Entries will be added to the /etc/oratab file as needed by
Database Configuration Assistant when a database is created
Finished running generic part of root script.
Now product-specific root actions will be performed.
Using configuration parameter file: /u01/app/12.1.0.2/grid/crs/install/crsconfig_params
2016/07/20 22:05:58 CLSRSC-4015: Performing install or upgrade action for Oracle Trace File
Analyzer (TFA) Collector.
2016/07/20 22:06:26 CLSRSC-4003: Successfully patched Oracle Trace File Analyzer (TFA)
Collector.
2016/07/20 22:06:27 CLSRSC-464: Starting retrieval of the cluster configuration data
2016/07/20 22:06:32 CLSRSC-465: Retrieval of the cluster configuration data has successfully
completed.
2016/07/20 22:06:32 CLSRSC-363: User ignored prerequisites during installation
ASM configuration upgraded in local node successfully.
2016/07/20 22:06:44 CLSRSC-466: Starting shutdown of the current Oracle Grid Infrastructure
stack
2016/07/20 22:08:48 CLSRSC-467: Shutdown of the current Oracle Grid Infrastructure stack has
successfully completed.
OLR initialization - successful
2016/07/20 22:09:15 CLSRSC-329: Replacing Clusterware entries in file 'oracle-ohasd.conf'
CRS-4133: Oracle High Availability Services has been stopped.
CRS-4123: Oracle High Availability Services has been started.
2016/07/20 22:12:24 CLSRSC-343: Successfully started Oracle Clusterware stack
        clscfg: EXISTING configuration version 5 detected.
clscfg: version 5 is 12c Release 1.
Successfully taken the backup of node specific configuration in OCR.
Successfully accumulated necessary OCR keys.
Creating OCR keys for user 'root', privgrp 'root'..
Operation successful.
Start upgrade invoked..
2016/07/20 22:12:36 CLSRSC-478: Setting Oracle Clusterware active version on the last node
to be upgraded
2016/07/20 22:12:36 CLSRSC-482: Running command: '/u01/app/12.1.0.2/grid/bin/crsctl set crs
activeversion'
Started to upgrade the Oracle Clusterware. This operation may take a few minutes.
Started to upgrade the OCR.
Started to upgrade the CSS.
The CSS was successfully upgraded.
Started to upgrade the CRS.
The CRS was successfully upgraded.
Successfully upgraded the Oracle Clusterware.
Oracle Clusterware operating version was successfully set to 12.1.0.2.0
2016/07/20 22:14:13 CLSRSC-479: Successfully set Oracle Clusterware active version
2016/07/20 22:14:17 CLSRSC-476: Finishing upgrade of resource types
2016/07/20 22:14:30 CLSRSC-482: Running command: 'upgrade model -s 11.2.0.3.0 -d 12.1.0.2.0
-p last'
2016/07/20 22:14:30 CLSRSC-477: Successfully completed upgrade of resource types
2016/07/20 22:15:00 CLSRSC-325: Configure Oracle Grid Infrastructure for a Cluster ...
succeeded

Once rootupgrade.sh has completed on all nodes, it is now time to click the OK button to proceed. The OUI will then run the required upgrade assistants.

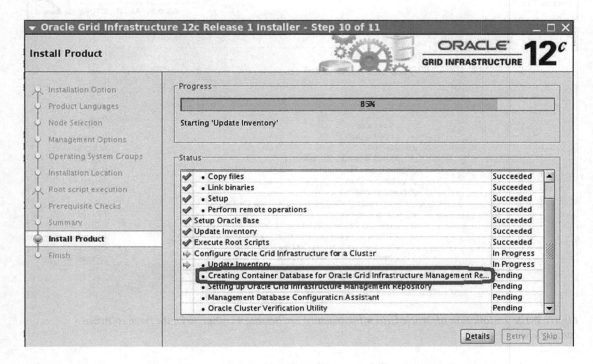

Figure 7-11. *Starting the Oracle Grid Infrastructure 12c Release 1 installation with the GIMR option*

■ **Note** The Oracle Grid Infrastructure Management Repository has been made mandatory in Oracle 12*c* (12.1.0.2.0). In previous versions, it will prompt as a separate option, called Configure Grid Infrastructure Management Repository (GIMR), with a Yes or No option.

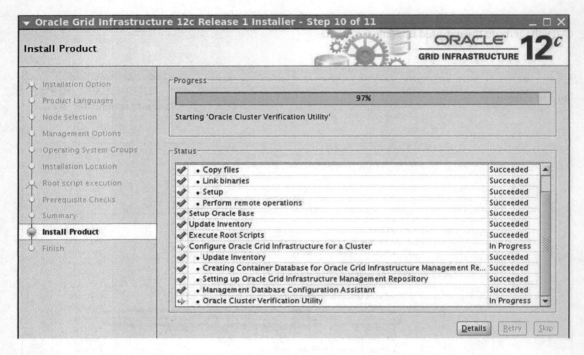

Figure 7-12. *Installation of Oracle Grid Infrastructure 12c Release 1 completed with these software components*

Note that you can run upgrade validations in the following ways:

- Run Oracle Universal Installer, and allow the Cluster Verification Utility (CVU) validation built into OUI to perform system checks and generate fixup scripts as part of the upgrade process.

- Run the Cluster Verification Utility (CUV) manual script to perform system checks and generate fixup scripts as part of the upgrade process.

```
[oracle@rac1 ~]$ . oraenv
ORACLE_SID = [+ASM1] ?
The Oracle base remains unchanged with value /u01/app/oracle
[oracle@rac1 ~]$ crs_stat -t
Name           Type          Target    State     Host
------------------------------------------------------------
ora.DATA.dg    ora....up.type ONLINE    ONLINE    rac1
ora.FRA.dg     ora....up.type ONLINE    ONLINE    rac1
ora....ER.lsnr ora....er.type ONLINE    ONLINE    rac1
ora....N1.lsnr ora....er.type ONLINE    ONLINE    rac2
ora....N2.lsnr ora....er.type ONLINE    ONLINE    rac1
ora....N3.lsnr ora....er.type ONLINE    ONLINE    rac1
ora.MGMTLSNR   ora....nr.type ONLINE    ONLINE    rac1
ora.asm        ora.asm.type   ONLINE    ONLINE    rac1
ora.cvu        ora.cvu.type   ONLINE    ONLINE    rac2
ora.mgmtdb     ora....db.type ONLINE    ONLINE    rac1
ora....network ora....rk.type ONLINE    ONLINE    rac1
ora.oc4j       ora.oc4j.type  ONLINE    ONLINE    rac2
ora.ons        ora.ons.type   ONLINE    ONLINE    rac1
ora.proddb.db  ora....se.type ONLINE    ONLINE    rac1
ora....SM1.asm application    ONLINE    ONLINE    rac1
ora....C1.lsnr application    ONLINE    ONLINE    rac1
ora.rac1.ons   application    ONLINE    ONLINE    rac1
ora.rac1.vip   ora....t1.type ONLINE    ONLINE    rac1
ora....SM2.asm application    ONLINE    ONLINE    rac2
ora....C2.lsnr application    ONLINE    ONLINE    rac2
ora.rac2.ons   application    ONLINE    ONLINE    rac2
ora.rac2.vip   ora....t1.type ONLINE    ONLINE    rac2
ora.scan1.vip  ora....ip.type ONLINE    ONLINE    rac2
ora.scan2.vip  ora....ip.type ONLINE    ONLINE    rac1
ora.scan3.vip  ora....ip.type ONLINE    ONLINE    rac1
[oracle@rac1 ~]$ crsctl query crs activeversion
Oracle Clusterware active version on the cluster is [12.1.0.2.0]
[oracle@rac1 ~]$ []
```

Figure 7-13. *Checking the complete stack of processes for cluster nodes*

```
[oracle@rac1 ~]$ . oraenv
ORACLE_SID = [proddb] ? +ASM1
The Oracle base remains unchanged with value /u01/app/oracle

[oracle@rac1 ~]$ crsctl query crs releaseversion
Oracle High Availability Services release version on the local node is [12.1.0.2.0]

[oracle@rac1 ~]$ crsctl check crs
CRS-4638: Oracle High Availability Services is online
CRS-4537: Cluster Ready Services is online
CRS-4529: Cluster Synchronization Services is online
CRS-4533: Event Manager is online

[oracle@rac2 ~]$ . oraenv
ORACLE_SID = [oracle] ? +ASM2
The Oracle base has been set to /u01/app/oracle

[oracle@rac2 ~]$  crsctl query crs releaseversion
Oracle High Availability Services release version on the local node is [12.1.0.2.0]

[oracle@rac2 ~]$ crsctl check crs
CRS-4638: Oracle High Availability Services is online
CRS-4537: Cluster Ready Services is online
CRS-4529: Cluster Synchronization Services is online
CRS-4533: Event Manager is online
```

After upgrading Oracle Grid Infrastructure from Oracle 11*g* (11.2.0.3.0) to Oracle 12*c* (12.1.0.2.0), check the status of the RAC instances (rac1 and rac2).

```
[oracle@rac1 ~]$ . oraenv
ORACLE_SID = [proddb] ? proddb
The Oracle base remains unchanged with value /u01/app/oracle
[oracle@rac1 ~]$ sqlplus /nolog

SQL*Plus: Release 11.2.0.3.0 Production on Mon Jun 27 02:35:21 2016

Copyright (c) 1982, 2011, Oracle.  All rights reserved.

SQL> connect sys/oracle@proddb as sysdba
Connected.
SQL> select instance_name,instance_number,status from gv$instance;

INSTANCE_NAME    INSTANCE_NUMBER STATUS
---------------- --------------- ------------
proddb2                        2 OPEN
proddb1                        1 OPEN
```

Note: While upgrading Oracle Grid Infrastructure from Oracle 11*g* (11.2.0.3.0) to Oracle 12*c* (12.1.0.2.0), keep checking the status of the RAC database instances (rac1 and rac2). In Oracle 12*c*, the Oracle GI rolling upgrade involves upgrading individual nodes in cluster nodes without stopping Oracle GI on other nodes in the cluster. So, you can check this functionality while doing a rolling upgrade.

```
[oracle@rac2 ~]$ ps -ef | grep pmon
oracle     3765     1  0 12:37 ?        00:00:01 asm_pmon_+ASM2
oracle     4206     1  0 12:39 ?        00:00:01 ora_pmon_proddb2
oracle    20718 16613  0 14:03 pts/1    00:00:00 grep pmon
[oracle@rac2 ~]$ ps -ef | grep pmon
oracle     3765     1  0 12:37 ?        00:00:01 asm_pmon_+ASM2
oracle     4206     1  0 12:39 ?        00:00:01 ora_pmon_proddb2
oracle    20772 16613  0 14:03 pts/1    00:00:00 grep pmon
[oracle@rac2 ~]$ ps -ef | grep pmon
oracle     3765     1  0 12:37 ?        00:00:01 asm_pmon_+ASM2
oracle    21990 16613  0 14:03 pts/1    00:00:00 grep pmon
[oracle@rac2 ~]$ ps -ef | grep pmon
oracle     3765     1  0 12:37 ?        00:00:01 asm_pmon_+ASM2
oracle    22008 16613  0 14:03 pts/1    00:00:00 grep pmon
[oracle@rac2 ~]$ ps -ef | grep pmon
oracle     3765     1  0 12:37 ?        00:00:01 asm_pmon_+ASM2
oracle    22022 16613  0 14:03 pts/1    00:00:00 grep pmon
[oracle@rac2 ~]$ ps -ef | grep pmon
oracle     3765     1  0 12:37 ?        00:00:01 asm_pmon_+ASM2
oracle    22056 16613  0 14:03 pts/1    00:00:00 grep pmon
[oracle@rac2 ~]$ ps -ef | grep pmon
oracle     3765     1  0 12:37 ?        00:00:01 asm_pmon_+ASM2
oracle    22071 16613  0 14:03 pts/1    00:00:00 grep pmon
[oracle@rac2 ~]$ ssh rac1
Last login: Mon Feb 15 12:40:40 2016 from 192.168.56.1
[oracle@rac1 ~]$ ps -ef | grep pmon
oracle      916     1  0 14:00 ?        00:00:00 ora_pmon_proddb1
oracle     3079  3015  0 14:03 pts/2    00:00:00 grep pmon
oracle    32592     1  0 14:00 ?        00:00:00 asm_pmon_+ASM1
[oracle@rac1 ~]$ ps -ef | grep pmon
oracle      916     1  0 14:00 ?        00:00:00 ora_pmon_proddb1
oracle     3190  3015  0 14:03 pts/2    00:00:00 grep pmon
oracle    32592     1  0 14:00 ?        00:00:00 asm_pmon_+ASM1
[oracle@rac1 ~]$ []
```

Figure 7-14. Checking ASM and database instances while installing in rac1 and rac2 nodes

```
[oracle@rac1 ~]$ ps -ef | grep pmon
oracle      916     1  0 14:00 ?        00:00:00 ora_pmon_proddb1
oracle    18623     1  0 14:22 ?        00:00:00 mdb_pmon_-MGMTDB
oracle    30049  4967  0 14:31 pts/1    00:00:00 grep pmon
oracle    32592     1  0 14:00 ?        00:00:00 asm_pmon_+ASM1
[oracle@rac1 ~]$ ssh rac2
Last login: Mon Feb 15 14:26:19 2016 from rac2.mlg.oracle.com
[oracle@rac2 ~]$ ps -ef | grep pmon
oracle     4293  4259  0 14:31 pts/2    00:00:00 grep pmon
oracle    14784     1  0 14:08 ?        00:00:00 asm_pmon_+ASM2
oracle    15365     1  0 14:08 ?        00:00:00 ora_pmon_proddb2
[oracle@rac2 ~]$ []
```

Figure 7-15. Checking ASM and database instances while installing in rac1 and rac2 nodes, continued

■ **Note** After upgrading, you will notice that MGMTDB is up and running. In Oracle 12*c* (12.1.0.2.0), it is mandatory, so do not delete it.

The Grid Infrastructure Management Repository (GIMR) will take approximately 750 MB per day per node. By default, the retention period is three days.

- If you want to change the retention on Oracle 12*c* (12.1.0.1), use this:

```
$CRS_HOME/bin/oclumon manage -repos changeretentiontime 260000
```

- If you want to change the retention on Oracle 12*c* (12.1.0.2), use this:

```
$CRS_HOME/bin/oclumon manage -repos checkretentiontime 260000
```

During the installation of Oracle Grid Infrastructure (12.1.0.1.0), you had the option to select Yes/No to install the GIMR database MGMTDB, as shown in Figure 7-16.

```
[oracle@rac1 ~]$ crs_stat -t
Name            Type            Target    State     Host
--------------------------------------------------------------
ora.DATA.dg     ora....up.type  ONLINE    ONLINE    rac1
ora.FRA.dg      ora....up.type  ONLINE    ONLINE    rac1
ora....ER.lsnr  ora....er.type  ONLINE    ONLINE    rac1
ora....N1.lsnr  ora....er.type  ONLINE    ONLINE    rac2
ora....N2.lsnr  ora....er.type  ONLINE    ONLINE    rac1
ora....N3.lsnr  ora....er.type  ONLINE    ONLINE    rac1
ora.MGMTLSNR    ora....nr.type  ONLINE    ONLINE    rac1
ora.asm         ora.asm.type    ONLINE    ONLINE    rac1
ora.cvu         ora.cvu.type    ONLINE    ONLINE    rac2
ora.mgmtdb      ora....db.type  ONLINE    ONLINE    rac1
```

Figure 7-16. *Check the status of MGMTDB with the associated listener using the cluster status command*

■ **Note** MGMTDB is a single-instance database. It is up and running in only one node in the cluster environment. MGMTDB is managed by Oracle Clusterware in Oracle Database 12*c*, and if the node is down, the database will be automatically failed over to another node in the cluster.

In Oracle 12*c* (12.1.0.2.0), the GIMR database MGMTDB has become mandatory.

The GIMR is automatically installed with Oracle Grid Infrastructure 12*c* (12.1.0.2).

The GIMR enables such features as the Cluster Health Monitor, Oracle Database quality of service (QoS) Management, and rapid home provisioning.

```
[oracle@rac1 ~]$ ps -ef | grep pmon
oracle      916      1   0 14:00 ?         00:00:00 ora_pmon_proddb1
oracle    18623      1   0 14:22 ?         00:00:00 mdb_pmon_-MGMTDB
oracle    30049   4967   0 14:31 pts/1     00:00:00 grep pmon
oracle    32592      1   0 14:00 ?         00:00:00 asm_pmon_+ASM1
[oracle@rac1 ~]$ ssh rac2
Last login: Mon Feb 15 14:26:19 2016 from rac2.mlg.oracle.com
[oracle@rac2 ~]$ ps -ef | grep pmon
oracle     4293   4259   0 14:31 pts/2     00:00:00 grep pmon
oracle    14784      1   0 14:08 ?         00:00:00 asm_pmon_+ASM2
oracle    15365      1   0 14:08 ?         00:00:00 ora_pmon_proddb2
[oracle@rac2 ~]$ []
```

Figure 7-17. *Checking the ASM and database status in cluster nodes after the rolling method*

You have completed the Oracle GRID Infrastructure upgrade using the rolling method. Now you can upgrade Oracle Database from 11.2.0.3.0 to 12.1.0.2.0 using an existing database method.

Scenario 1: Upgrading Oracle 11*g* RAC (11.2.0.3.0) to Oracle 12*c* RAC (12.1.0.2.0)

Let's look at how to upgrade an Oracle 11*g* RAC database (11.2.0.3.0) to an Oracle 12c RAC database (12.1.0.2.0). Oracle Clusterware and ASM are upgraded to an Oracle 12c database (12.1.0.2.0), but Oracle Database is still 11*g* (11.2.0.3.0). So, Clusterware and ASM version 12.1.0.2.0 will support Oracle 11*g* (11.2).

Execute **runInstaller** from the Oracle 12*c* database (12.1.0.2.0) software binaries and select the option "Upgrade an existing database" from the install options, as shown in Figure 7-18. This option will create a new Oracle Home directory automatically in both nodes, and it will install the Oracle 12*c* database binaries in both nodes.

Note: You can also use the alternate option "Install database software only" and use the Database Upgrade Assistant (DBUA) to upgrade the database to a newer version.

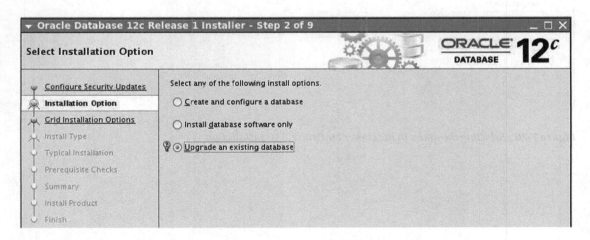

Figure 7-18. *Selecting the option "Upgrade an existing database" from the installation options*

Based on your environment, you can select an option on the next screen, as shown in Figure 7-19. Here we are selecting the option "Oracle Real Application Clusters database installation."

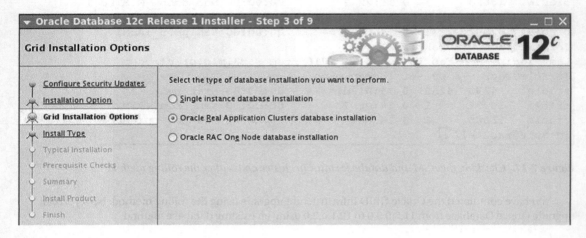

Figure 7-19. *Selecting the option "Oracle Real Application Clusters database installation"*

Verify that you will be selecting all the nodes in the cluster. Currently you have a two-node cluster, as shown in Figure 7-20.

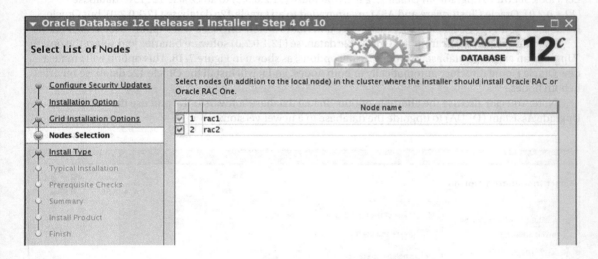

Figure 7-20. *Selecting the nodes in the cluster for Oracle RAC installation*

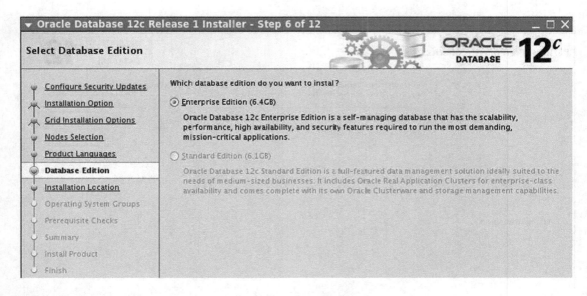

Figure 7-21. *Selecting Enterprise Edition (6.4 GB) for this installation*

Specify the software location for the new Oracle 12*c* database home: /u01/app/oracle/
product/12.1.0.2/dbhome_1, as shown in Figure 7-22.

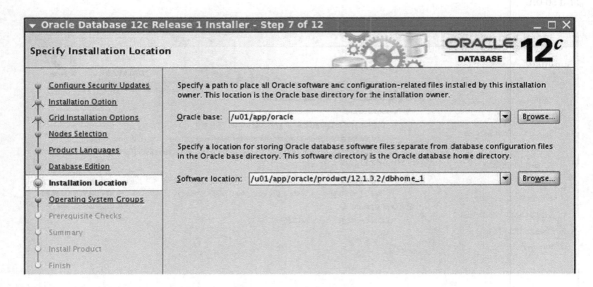

Figure 7-22. *Specifying the locations for Oracle base and software*

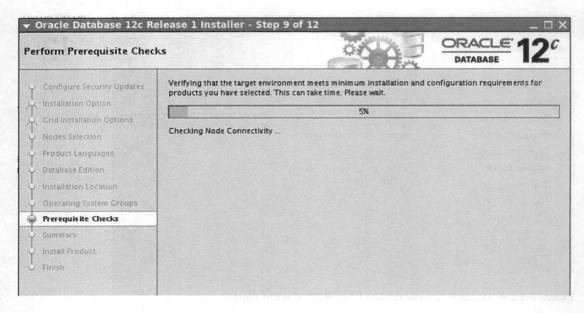

Figure 7-23. Performing prerequisite checks in cluster nodes

Before clicking Install, check the summary including the disk space, the selected nodes in the cluster, and so on.

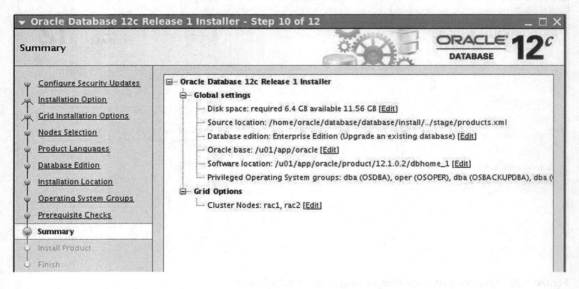

Figure 7-24. Checking the summary of global settings and grid options

Execute the root.sh script serially from /u01/app/oracle/product/12.1.0.2/dbhome_1/root.sh in the rac1 and rac2 nodes as a root user, as shown in Figure 7-25.

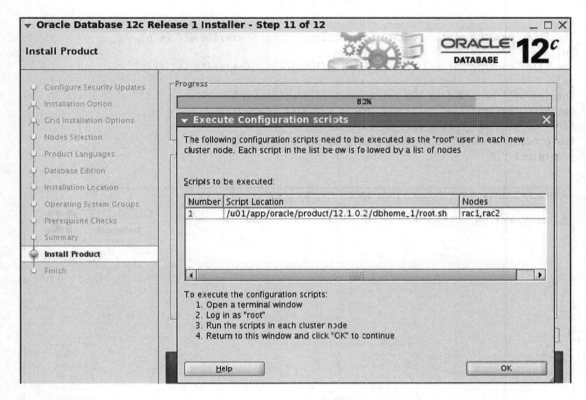

Figure 7-25. *Executing the script root.sh from the cluster nodes (rac1 and rac2 for ORACLE_HOME)*

```
[root@rac1 ~]# sh /u01/app/oracle/product/12.0.1.2/dbhome_1/root.sh
Performing root user operation.
The following environment variables are set as:
    ORACLE_OWNER= oracle
    ORACLE_HOME=  /u01/app/oracle/product/12.0.1.2/dbhome_1
Enter the full pathname of the local bin directory: [/usr/local/bin]:
The file "dbhome" already exists in /usr/local/bin.  Overwrite it? (y/n)
[n]:
The file "oraenv" already exists in /usr/local/bin.  Overwrite it? (y/n)
[n]:
The file "coraenv" already exists in /usr/local/bin.  Overwrite it? (y/n)
[n]:
Entries will be added to the /etc/oratab file as needed by
Database Configuration Assistant when a database is created
Finished running generic part of root script.
Now product-specific root actions will be performed.
[root@rac2 ~]# sh /u01/app/oracle/product/12.0.1.2/dbhome_1/root.sh
Performing root user operation.
The following environment variables are set as:
    ORACLE_OWNER= oracle
    ORACLE_HOME=  /u01/app/oracle/product/12.0.1.2/dbhome_1
Enter the full pathname of the local bin directory: [/usr/local/bin]:
The file "dbhome" already exists in /usr/local/bin.  Overwrite it? (y/n)
```

```
[n]:
The file "oraenv" already exists in /usr/local/bin.  Overwrite it? (y/n)
[n]:
The file "coraenv" already exists in /usr/local/bin.  Overwrite it? (y/n)
[n]:
Entries will be added to the /etc/oratab file as needed by
Database Configuration Assistant when a database is created
Finished running generic part of root script.
Now product-specific root actions will be performed.
[root@rac2 ~]#
```

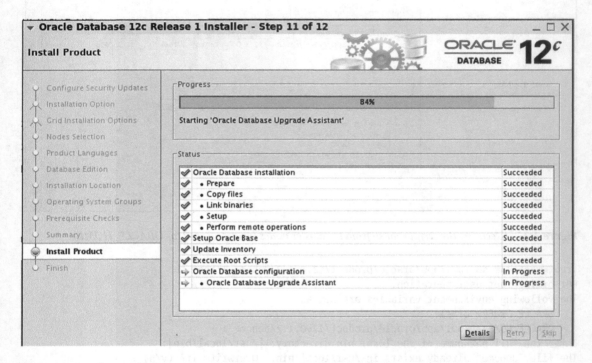

Figure 7-26. *The installation automatically starts the Oracle Database Upgrade Assistant (DBUA)*

After installing the Oracle 12*c* binaries in both the nodes shown in Figure 7-xx, the tool will automatically invoke the Database Upgrade Assistant (DBUA) options. Select the option Upgrade Oracle Database, as shown in Figure 7-27.

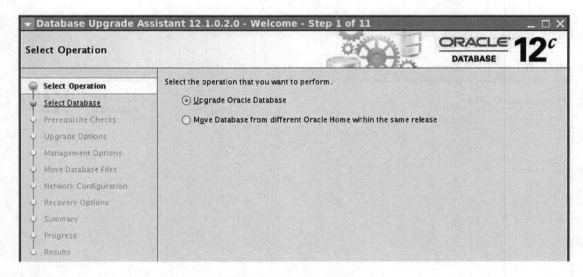

Figure 7-27. Selecting the option Upgrade Oracle Database from DBUA

This screen will show the following information, as shown in Figure 7-28:

- Source database Oracle Home

- Source database version

- Source database (name/SID)

- Source database status

- Source database type

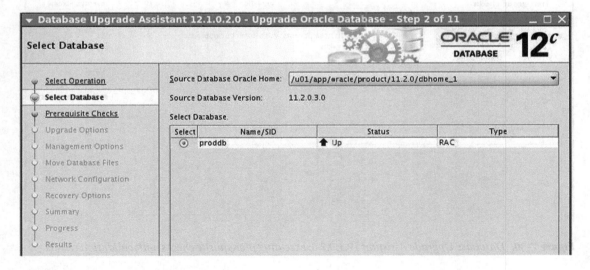

Figure 7-28. Selecting the required source database to upgrade with ORACLE_HOME and database version

The Database Upgrade Assistant (12.1.0.2.0) will automatically invoke the option Run Pre Upgrade Utility, as shown in Figure 7-xx.

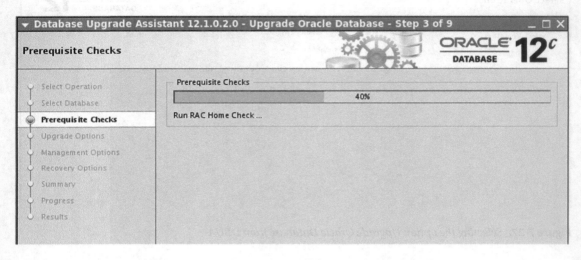

Figure 7-29. *Database Upgrade Assistant 12.1.0.2.0, executing prerequisite checks*

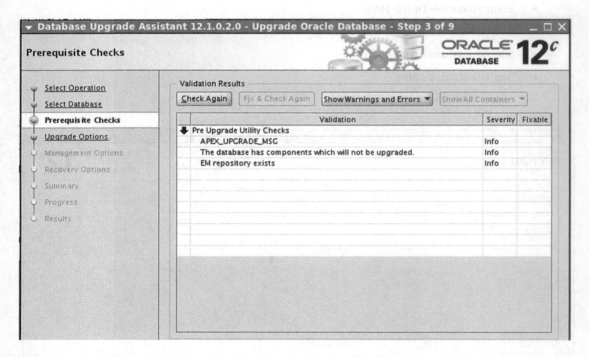

Figure 7-30. *Database Upgrade Assistant 12.1.0.2.0, executing prerequisite checks with validation results*

Run the database upgrade in parallel by selecting the option Select Upgrade Parallelism.

- Upgrade parallelism is a new feature introduced in Oracle 12c R1 where you can execute upgrade scripts and processes can run in parallel.

- Parallelism was introduced to take full advantage of the CPU capacity so that you can reduce the upgrade time in mission-critical environments.

- Parallelism will break down each SQL file into stand-alone components so that each one will have to execute separately.

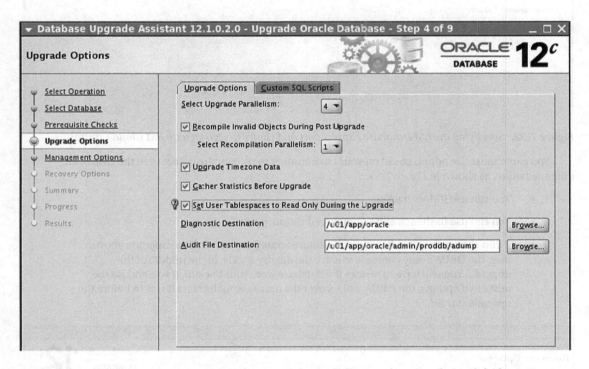

Figure 7-31. *Specifying upgrade options: Select Upgrade Parallelism and Recompile Invalid Objects During Post Upgrade*

You can configure EM Database Express Port, and you can also specify the Register with Enterprise Manager (EM) Cloud Control settings with the fields OMS Host, OMS Port, EM Admin Username, EM Admin Password, and DBSNMP User Password.

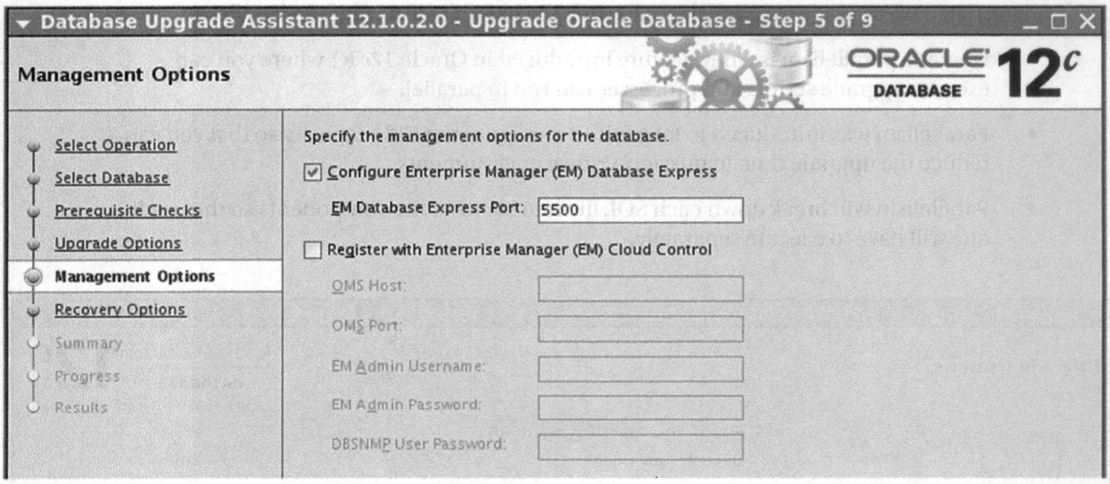

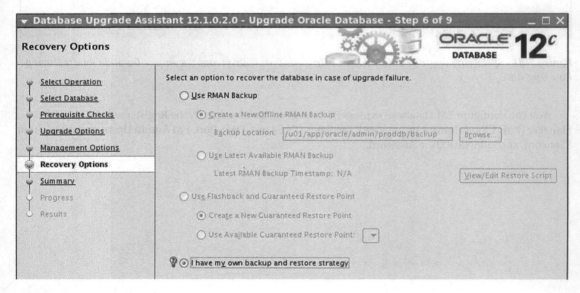

Figure 7-32. *Specifying the EM Database Express port and choice to register with EM Cloud Control*

You can choose the option based on your environment to recover the database in the case of an upgrade failure, as shown in Figure 7-33.

- You can use RMAN backup.

- You can use flashback and a guaranteed restore point.

- If you choose the Own Backup and Restore Strategy option and the upgrade aborts, then the DBUA's only choice is to leave the database as is, in the middle of the upgrade. You will have to restore the database from your backup. If you choose the other two options, the DBUA will recover the database to the state it was in before the upgrade started.

Figure 7-33. *Specifying to recover the database in case of upgrade failure*

Check the summary for the following information:

- Source database name, release, and Oracle Home
- Target database name, release, and Oracle Home
- Instance name, node name, and node status
- Pre-upgrade checks
- Initialization parameter changes
- Time zone upgrade
- Enterprise Manager

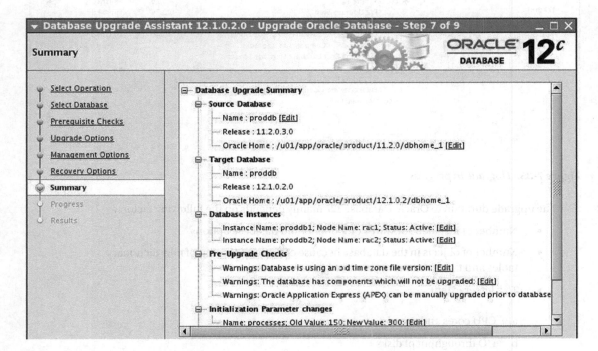

Figure 7-34. *Database upgrade summary including source database and target database*

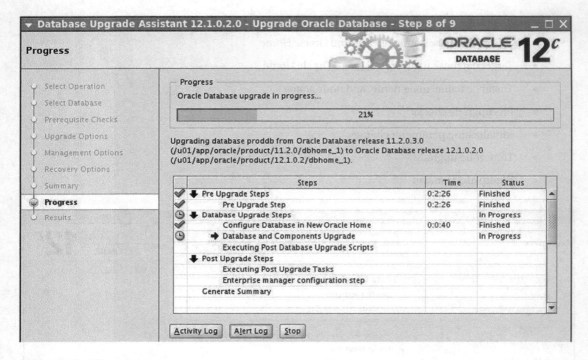

Figure 7-35. *Upgrade in progress*

The upgrade duration to Oracle Database 12*c* mainly depends on the following factors:

- Number of installed software components and database options

- Number of objects in the database because of the high amount of new dictionary tables and the restructuring of some base system tables

- To a lesser extent:

    a. CPU cores and speed

    b. I/O throughput of disks

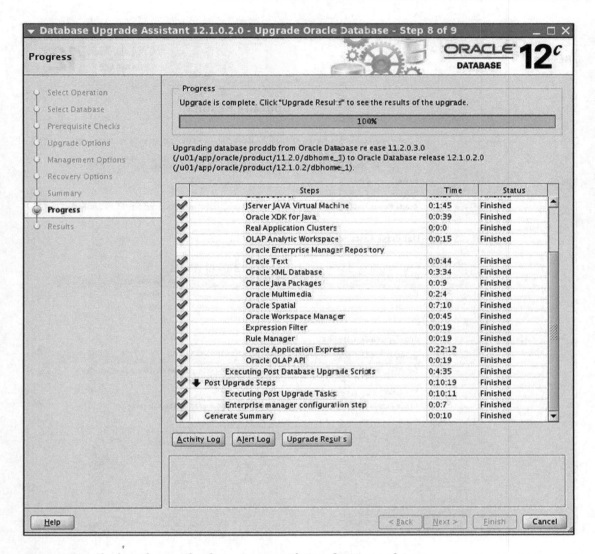

Figure 7-36. *Checking the completed components with time duration and status*

Click the Upgrade Results button before you go further. Check the following (see Figure 7-37): the source database's release and home and the upgraded target database's release and home.

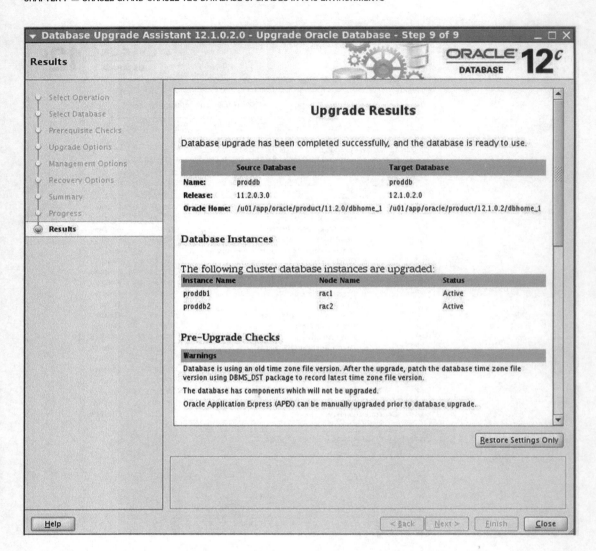

Figure 7-37. *Checking the upgrade results with version for source database and target database with instances*

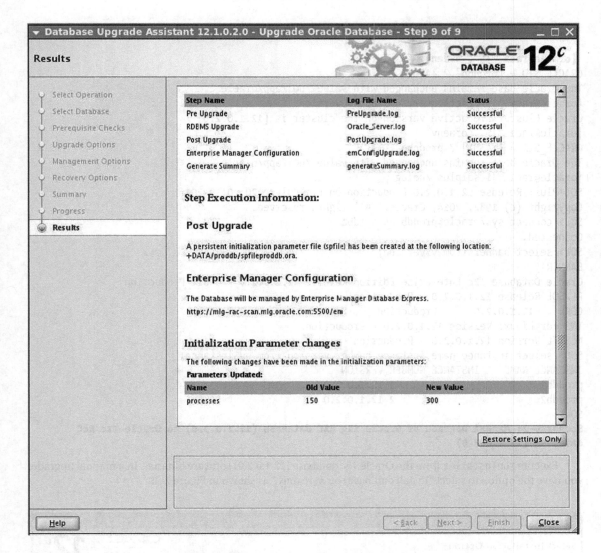

Figure 7-38. *Checking the script status with the initialization parameter changes*

After upgrading, check the CRS version and the Oracle database version.

```
[oracle@rac1 ~]$ . oraenv
ORACLE_SID = [proddb] ? +ASM1
The Oracle base remains unchanged with value /u01/app/oracle
[oracle@rac1 ~]$ crsctl query crs activeversion
Oracle Clusterware active version on the cluster is [12.1.0.2.0]
[oracle@rac1 ~]$ . oraenv
ORACLE_SID = [+ASM1] ? proddb
The Oracle base remains unchanged with value /u01/app/oracle
[oracle@rac1 ~]$ sqlplus /nolog
SQL*Plus: Release 12.1.0.2.0 Production on Fri Jul 22 20:20:53 2016
Copyright (c) 1982, 2014, Oracle.  All rights reserved.
SQL> connect sys/oracle@proddb as sysdba
Connected.
SQL> select banner from v$version;
BANNER
Oracle Database 12c Enterprise Edition Release 12.1.0.2.0 - 64bit Production
PL/SQL Release 12.1.0.2.0 - Production
CORE    12.1.0.2.0       Production
TNS for Linux: Version 12.1.0.2.0 - Production
NLSRTL Version 12.1.0.2.0 - Production
SQL> select instance_name,instance_number,version from gv$instance;
INSTANCE_NAME    INSTANCE_NUMBER VERSION
proddb1                        1 12.1.0.2.0
proddb2                        2 12.1.0.2.0
SQL>
```

Scenario-2: Manual upgrade of Oracle 11g RAC database (11.2.0.3.0) to Oracle 12c RAC database (12.1.0.2.0)

Execute runInstaller from the Oracle 12c database (12.1.0.2.0) software binaries. In a manual upgrade, you have the option to select "Install database software only," as shown in Figure 7-39.

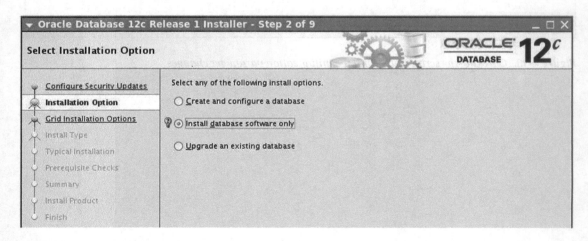

Figure 7-39. *Selecting "Install database software only"*

Next, select the option "Oracle Real Application Clusters database installation," as shown in Figure 7-40.

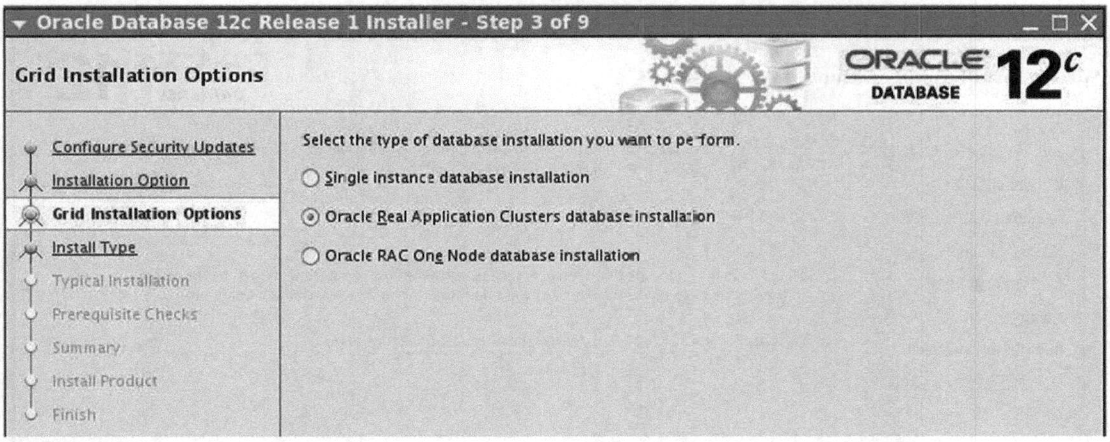

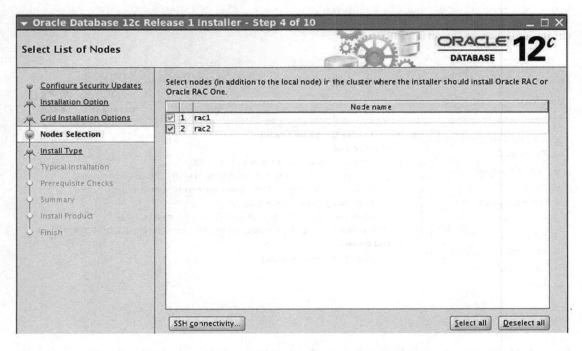

Figure 7-40. *Selecting the option "Oracle Real Application Clusters database installation"*

Verify that you will be selecting all the nodes in the cluster. Currently you have a two-node cluster, as shown in Figure 7-41.

Figure 7-41. *Selecting the cluster nodes rac1 and rac2 on the Nodes Selection page*

Specify the software location for the new Oracle 12*c* database Home: /u01/app/oracle/product/12.1.0.2/dbhome_1, as shown in Figure 7-42.

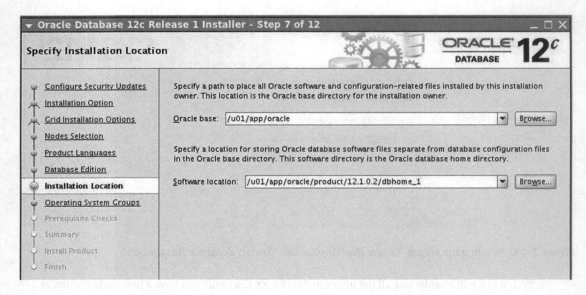

Figure 7-42. *Selecting the installation location for the Oracle base and the software location*

Before clicking the Install option, check the summary such as the disk space, selected nodes in the cluster, and so on, as shown in Figure 7-43.

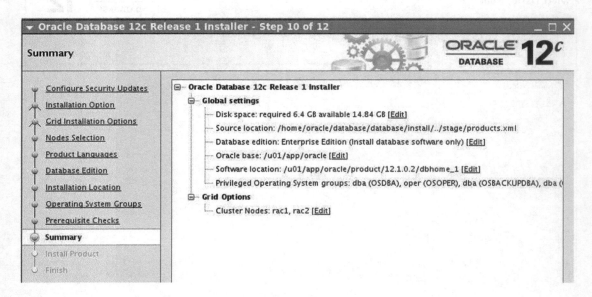

Figure 7-43. *Checking the global settings" and grid options for the cluster nodes (rac1 and rac2)*

Execute the script root.sh from /u01/app/oracle/product/12.1.0.2/dbhome_1/root.sh in the rac1 and rac2 nodes as a root user, as shown in Figure 7-44.

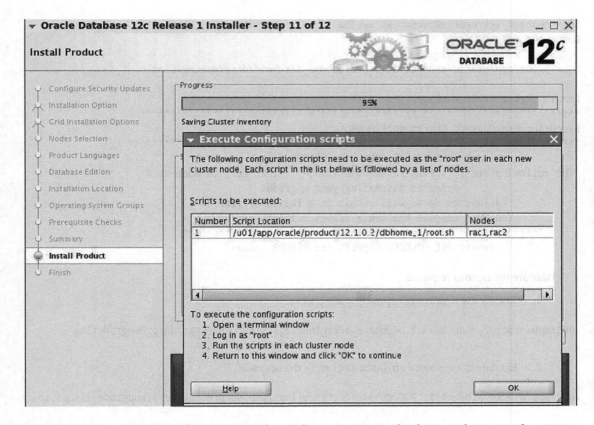

Figure 7-44. *Executing the configuration script's root.sh as a root user in the cluster nodes rac1 and rac2*

Execute the following scripts:

```
[root@rac1 ~]# sh /u01/app/oracle/product/12.1.0.2/dbhome_1/root.sh
[root@rac2 ~]# sh /u01/app/oracle/product/12.1.0.2/dbhome_1/root.sh
```

■ **Note**   Execute the pre-upgrade script from the Oracle 12*c* ?/rdbms/admin location or download the following scripts from MOS Note 884522.1.

Log in to the RAC database and execute the script preupgrd.sql. Check the section "ACTIONS REQUIRED." Execute the preupgrd.sql file of Oracle 12*c* after logging in to the Oracle 11*g* database.

```
[oracle@rac1 ~]$ . oraenv
ORACLE_SID = [oracle] ? proddb
The Oracle base has been set to /u01/app/oracle

[oracle@rac1 ~]$ sqlplus /nolog
SQL*Plus: Release 11.2.0.3.0 Production on Fri Feb 19 10:33:56 2016
Copyright (c) 1982, 2011, Oracle.  All rights reserved.
```

```
SQL> connect sys/oracle@proddb as sysdba
Connected.

SQL> @/u01/app/oracle/product/12.1.0.2/dbhome_1/rdbms/admin/preupgrd.sql

Loading Pre-Upgrade Package...
**************************************************************************
Executing Pre-Upgrade Checks in PRODDB...
**************************************************************************
                   ====>> ERRORS FOUND for PRODDB <<====
  The following are *** ERROR LEVEL CONDITIONS *** that must be addressed
                     prior to attempting your upgrade.
             Failure to do so will result in a failed upgrade.
            You MUST resolve the above errors prior to upgrade
        ************************************************************
              ====>> PRE-UPGRADE RESULTS for PRODDB <<====
```

Here are the actions required:

1. Review the results of the pre-upgrade checks.

/u01/app/oracle/product/11.2.0/dbhome_1/cfgtoollogs/proddb/preupgrade/preupgrade.log

2. Execute in the source environment before the upgrade.

/u01/app/oracle/product/11.2.0/dbhome_1/cfgtoollogs/proddb/preupgrade/preupgrade_fixups.sql

3. Execute in the new environment after the upgrade.

/u01/app/oracle/product/11.2.0/dbhome_1/cfgtoollogs/proddb/preupgrade/postupgrade_fixups.sql

```
**************************************************************************
Pre-Upgrade Checks in PRODDB Completed.
**************************************************************************
```

```
[oracle@rac1 ~]$ cd /u01/app/oracle/product/11.2.0/dbhome_1/cfgtoollogs/proddb/preupgrade/
[oracle@rac1 preupgrade]$ ls -lrth
total 16K
-rw-r--r--. 1 oracle dba 7.7K Feb 19 10:52 preupgrade.log
-rw-r--r--. 1 oracle dba 3.5K Feb 19 10:52 preupgrade_fixups.sql
-rw-r--r--. 1 oracle dba 2.6K Feb 19 10:52 postupgrade_fixups.sql
```

Figure 7-45. Showing "pre-upgrade" script locations with files

■ **Note** Take a look preupgrade.log for the following information:

- Update parameters
- Renamed parameters

- Obsolete/deprecated parameters
- Component list
- Tablespaces
- Pre-upgrade checks
- Pre-upgrade recommendations
  - Dictionary statistics
- Post-upgrade recommendations
  - Fixed object statistics

```
[oracle@rac1 preupgrade]$

[oracle@rac2 preupgrade]$ cat preupgrade.log
Oracle Database Pre-Upgrade Information Tool 03-04-2016 11:34:09
Script Version: 12.1.0.2.0 Build: 006
****************************************************************************
 Database Name:  PRODDB
 Container Name: Not Applicable in Pre-12.1 database
  Container ID:  Not Applicable in Pre-12.1 database
       Version:  11.2.0.3.0
    Compatible:  11.2.0.0.0
     Blocksize:  8192
      Platform:  Linux x86 64-bit
 Timezone file: V14
****************************************************************************
                      [Update parameters]
         [Update Oracle Database 11.2.0.3.0 init.ora or spfile]

--> If Target Oracle is 32-bit, refer here for Update Parameters:
WARNING: --> "processes" needs to be increased to at least 300

--> If Target Oracle is 64-bit, refer here for Update Parameters:
WARNING: --> "processes" needs to be increased to at least 300
****************************************************************************
****************************************************************************
                      [Renamed Parameters]
                [No Renamed Parameters in use]
****************************************************************************
****************************************************************************
               [Obsolete/Deprecated Parameters]
        [No Obsolete or Desupported Parameters in use]
****************************************************************************
                       [Component List]
****************************************************************************
--> Oracle Catalog Views            [upgrade]  VALID
--> Oracle Packages and Types       [upgrade]  VALID
--> JServer JAVA Virtual Machine    [upgrade]  VALID
--> Oracle XDK for Java             [upgrade]  VALID
```

```
--> Real Application Clusters           [upgrade]   VALID
--> Oracle Workspace Manager            [upgrade]   VALID
--> OLAP Analytic Workspace             [upgrade]   VALID
--> Oracle Enterprise Manager Repository [upgrade]  VALID
--> Oracle Text                         [upgrade]   VALID
--> Oracle XML Database                 [upgrade]   VALID
--> Oracle Java Packages                [upgrade]   VALID
--> Oracle Multimedia                   [upgrade]   VALID
--> Oracle Spatial                      [upgrade]   VALID
--> Expression Filter                   [upgrade]   VALID
--> Rule Manager                        [upgrade]   VALID
--> Oracle Application Express          [upgrade]   VALID
--> Oracle OLAP API                     [upgrade]   VALID
*************************************************************************
                          [Tablespaces]
*************************************************************************
--> SYSTEM tablespace is adequate for the upgrade.
      minimum required size: 1211 MB
--> SYSAUX tablespace is adequate for the upgrade.
      minimum required size: 1476 MB
--> TEMP tablespace is adequate for the upgrade.
      minimum required size: 60 MB
--> UNDOTBS2 tablespace is adequate for the upgrade.
      minimum required size: 400 MB


                  [No adjustments recommended]


*************************************************************************
*************************************************************************
                       [Pre-Upgrade Checks]
*************************************************************************
WARNING: --> Process Count may be too low

    Database has a maximum process count of 150 which is lower than the
    default value of 300 for this release.
    You should update your processes value prior to the upgrade
    to a value of at least 300.
    For example:
        ALTER SYSTEM SET PROCESSES=300 SCOPE=SPFILE
    or update your init.ora file.

WARNING: --> Enterprise Manager Database Control repository found in the database

    In Oracle Database 12c, Database Control is removed during
    the upgrade. To save time during the Upgrade, this action
    can be done prior to upgrading using the following steps after
    copying rdbms/admin/emremove.sql from the new Oracle home
  - Stop EM Database Control:
   $> emctl stop dbconsole

  - Connect to the Database using the SYS account AS SYSDBA:
```

```
    SET ECHO ON;
    SET SERVEROUTPUT ON;
    @emremove.sql
      Without the set echo and serveroutput commands you will not
      be able to follow the progress of the script.

INFORMATION: --> OLAP Catalog(AMD) exists in database

      Starting with Oracle Database 12c, OLAP Catalog component is desupported.
      If you are not using the OLAP Catalog component and want
      to remove it, then execute the
      ORACLE_HOME/olap/admin/catnoamd.sql script before or
      after the upgrade.

INFORMATION: --> Older Timezone in use

      Database is using a time zone file older than version 18.
      After the upgrade, it is recommended that DBMS_DST package
      be used to upgrade the 11.2.0.3.0 database time zone version
      to the latest version which comes with the new release.
      Please refer to My Oracle Support note number 977512.1 for details.

INFORMATION: --> There are existing Oracle components that will NOT be
      upgraded by the database upgrade script.  Typically, such components
      have their own upgrade scripts, are deprecated, or obsolete.
      Those components are:  OLAP Catalog,OWB

INFORMATION: --> Oracle Application Express (APEX) can be
      manually upgraded prior to database upgrade

      APEX is currently at version 3.2.1.00.12 and will need to be
      upgraded to APEX version 4.2.5 in the new release.
      Note 1: To reduce database upgrade time, APEX can be manually
              upgraded outside of and prior to database upgrade.
      Note 2: See MOS Note 1088970.1 for information on APEX
              installation upgrades.

**************************************************************************
                      [Pre-Upgrade Recommendations]
**************************************************************************

                  ******************************************
                  ********* Dictionary Statistics *********
                  ******************************************

Please gather dictionary statistics 24 hours prior to
upgrading the database.
To gather dictionary statistics execute the following command
while connected as SYSDBA:
    EXECUTE dbms_stats.gather_dictionary_stats;

^^^ MANUAL ACTION SUGGESTED ^^^
```

```
*********************************************************************
                    [Post-Upgrade Recommendations]
*********************************************************************

               ******************************************
               ******** Fixed Object Statistics ********
               ******************************************

Please create stats on fixed objects two weeks
after the upgrade using the command:
   EXECUTE DBMS_STATS.GATHER_FIXED_OBJECTS_STATS;

^^^ MANUAL ACTION SUGGESTED ^^^

*********************************************************************
               ***********   Summary   ***********

0 ERRORS exist in your database.
2 WARNINGS that Oracle suggests are addressed to improve database performance.
4 INFORMATIONAL messages that should be reviewed prior to your upgrade.

After your database is upgraded and open in normal mode you must run
rdbms/admin/catuppst.sql which executes several required tasks and completes
the upgrade process.

You should follow that with the execution of rdbms/admin/utlrp.sql, and a
comparison of invalid objects before and after the upgrade using
rdbms/admin/utluiobj.sql

If needed you may want to upgrade your timezone data using the process
described in My Oracle Support note 1509653.1
               ***********************************
[oracle@rac2 preupgrade]$
```

Change the Processes parameter value from 150 to 300 as suggested by the preupgrd.sql script and change the cluster_database parameter value from TRUE to FALSE.

■ **Note** When you execute preupgrd.sql, note the instance number so that you can find the following logs in that instance directories.

- preupgrade.log
- preupgrade_fixups.sql
- postupgrade_fixups.sql

```
SQL> select instance_name,instance_number from v$instance;

instance_name    instance_number
--------------   ---------------------
proddb1          1
```

```
SQL> show parameter processes

NAME                                 TYPE        VALUE
------------------------------------ ---------   ------
processes                            integer     150

SQL> ALTER SYSTEM SET PROCESSES=300 SCOPE=SPFILE SID='*';
SQL> @/u01/app/oracle/product/11.2.0/dbhome_1/olap/admin/catnoamd.sql
SQL> @/u01/app/oracle/cfgtoollogs/proddb/preupgrade/preupgrade_fixups.sql

Pre-Upgrade Fixup Script Generated on 2016-03-04 11:34:08  Version: 12.1.0.2 Build: 006
Beginning Pre-Upgrade Fixups...
Executing in container PRODDB

**********************************************************************
Check Tag:      DEFAULT_PROCESS_COUNT
Check Summary: Verify min process count is not too low
Fix Summary:    Review and increase if needed, your PROCESSES value.
**********************************************************************
Fixup Returned Information:
WARNING: --> Process Count may be too low

    Database has a maximum process count of 150 which is lower than the
    default value of 300 for this release.
    You should update your processes value prior to the upgrade
    to a value of at least 300.
    For example:
       ALTER SYSTEM SET PROCESSES=300 SCOPE=SPFILE
    or update your init.ora file.
**********************************************************************


**********************************************************************
Check Tag:      EM_PRESENT
Check Summary: Check if Enterprise Manager is present
Fix Summary:    Execute emremove.sql prior to upgrade.
**********************************************************************
Fixup Returned Information:
WARNING: --> Enterprise Manager Database Control repository found in the database

    In Oracle Database 12c, Database Control is removed during
    the upgrade. To save time during the Upgrade, this action
    can be done prior to upgrading using the following steps after
    copying rdbms/admin/emremove.sql from the new Oracle home
  - Stop EM Database Control:
   $> emctl stop dbconsole

  - Connect to the Database using the SYS account AS SYSDBA:

SET ECHO ON;
SET SERVEROUTPUT ON;
@emremove.sql
```

```
        Without the set echo and serveroutput commands you will not
        be able to follow the progress of the script.
**********************************************************************


**********************************************************************
Check Tag:      AMD_EXISTS
Check Summary: Check to see if AMD is present in the database
Fix Summary:    Manually execute ORACLE_HOME/oraolap/admin/catnoamd.sql script to remove
OLAP.
**********************************************************************
Fixup Returned Information:
INFORMATION: --> OLAP Catalog(AMD) exists in database

        Starting with Oracle Database 12c, OLAP Catalog component is desupported.
        If you are not using the OLAP Catalog component and want
        to remove it, then execute the
        ORACLE_HOME/olap/admin/catnoamd.sql script before or
        after the upgrade.
**********************************************************************


**********************************************************************
Check Tag:      APEX_UPGRADE_MSG
Check Summary: Check that APEX will need to be upgraded.
Fix Summary:    Oracle Application Express can be manually upgraded prior to database
upgrade.
**********************************************************************
Fixup Returned Information:
INFORMATION: --> Oracle Application Express (APEX) can be
        manually upgraded prior to database upgrade

        APEX is currently at version 3.2.1.00.12 and will need to be
        upgraded to APEX version 4.2.5 in the new release.
        Note 1: To reduce database upgrade time, APEX can be manually
                upgraded outside of and prior to database upgrade.
        Note 2: See MOS Note 1088970.1 for information on APEX
                installation upgrades.
**********************************************************************


**********************************************************************
                       [Pre-Upgrade Recommendations]
**********************************************************************

                    ****************************************
                    ********* Dictionary Statistics *********
                    ****************************************

Please gather dictionary statistics 24 hours prior to
upgrading the database.
To gather dictionary statistics execute the following command
while connected as SYSDBA:
    EXECUTE dbms_stats.gather_dictionary_stats;
```

```
^^^ MANUAL ACTION SUGGESTED ^^^

        **************************************************
        ************* Fixup Summary ************

 4 fixup routines generated INFORMATIONAL messages that should be reviewed.

SQL> EXECUTE dbms_stats.gather_dictionary_stats;
SQL> alter system set cluster_database=false scope=spfile sid='*';
System altered.

[oracle@rac1 ~]$ srvctl stop database -d proddb

[oracle@rac1 ~]$ srvctl status database -d proddb
Instance proddb1 is not running on node rac1
Instance proddb2 is not running on node rac2
[oracle@rac1 ~]$

[oracle@rac1 ~]$ . oraenv
ORACLE_SID = [+ASM1] ? proddb1
ORACLE_HOME = [/home/oracle] ? /u01/app/oracle/product/11.2.0/dbhome_1
The Oracle base remains unchanged with value /u01/app/oracle

[oracle@rac1 ~]$ sqlplus /nolog
SQL*Plus: Release 11.2.0.3.0 Production on Fri Mar 4 11:52:49 2016
Copyright (c) 1982, 2011, Oracle.  All rights reserved.

SQL> connect sys/oracle as sysdba
Connected to an idle instance.

SQL> startup;

SQL> show parameter pfile

NAME                                 TYPE        VALUE
------------------------------------ --------    -------
spfile                               string      +DATA/proddb/spfileproddb.ora

SQL> show parameter processes

NAME                                 TYPE        VALUE
------------------------------------ --------    ----------
processes                            integer     300

SQL> show parameter cluster_database

NAME                                 TYPE        VALUE
------------------------------------ --------    -----------
cluster_database                     boolean     FALSE

SQL> create pfile='/home/oracle/initproddb1.ora' from spfile;
```

File created.

```
[oracle@rac1 ~]$ srvctl stop database -d proddb
```

■ **Note**   Copy the pfile to the Oracle 12*c* database home location.

```
[oracle@rac1 dbs]$ cp initproddb1.ora /u01/app/oracle/product/12.1.0.2/dbhome_1/dbs/

[oracle@rac1 ~]$ export ORACLE_HOME=/u01/app/oracle/product/12.1.0.2/dbhome_1
[oracle@rac1 ~]$ export PATH=$ORACLE_HOME/bin:$PATH
[oracle@rac1 ~]$ export ORACLE_BASE=/u01/app/oracle
```

Note: Make sure the following environment variables point to the Oracle 12*c* Release 1 (12.1.0.2) directories based on the operating system.

- ORACLE_BASE
- ORACLE_HOME
- PATH
- LD_LIBRARY_PATH
- SHLIB_PATH

```
[oracle@rac1 ~]$ sqlplus /nolog
SQL*Plus: Release 12.1.0.2.0 Production on Fri Feb 19 11:52:42 2016
Copyright (c) 1982, 2014, Oracle.  All rights reserved.

SQL> connect sys/oracle as sysdba
Connected to an idle instance.
```

■ **Note**   Start up the Oracle 12*c* database instance through the pfile using the option UPGRADE.

```
SQL> startup upgrade
ORACLE instance started.
Total System Global Area   1056964608    bytes
Fixed Size                    2932432    bytes
Variable Size               373293360    bytes
Database Buffers            675282944    bytes
Redo Buffers                  5455872    bytes
Database mounted.
Database opened.
```

Scenario 2: Manual upgrade of Oracle 11*g* RAC (11.2.0.3.0) to Oracle 12*c* RAC (12.1.0.2.0)

Here's information about the new parallel upgrade script:

- The script `catctl.pl` runs the database upgrade in parallel. It will drastically reduce downtime in critical production environments due to planned maintenance.

- The benefit of `catctl.pl` is that it loads the data dictionary and components in parallel to minimize the overall upgrade time in critical production environments.

- The following command uses the option –n to denote the number of processes to use for parallel operations.

- The upgrade script (`catctl.pl`) can contain the following options:

    - -u for username

    - -d for the directory containing the files to be run

    - -y for display phases only

    - -p for the restart phase

    - -s for the SQL script to initialize sessions

```
[oracle@rac1 admin]$ $ORACLE_HOME/perl/bin/perl catctl.pl -n  6 catupgrd.sql
```

```
[oracle@rac1 admin]$ $ORACLE_HOME/perl/bin/perl catctl.pl -n  6 catupgrd.sql

Argument list for [catctl.pl]
SQL Process Count           n = 6
SQL PDB Process Count       N = 0
Input Directory             d = 0
Phase Logging Table         t = 0
Log Dir                     l = 0
Script                      s = 0
Serial Run                  S = 0
Upgrade Mode active         M = 0
Start Phase                 p = 0
End Phase                   P = 0
Log Id                      i = 0
Run in                      c = 0
Do not run in               C = 0
Echo OFF                    e = 1
No Post Upgrade             x = 0
Reverse Order               r = 0
Open Mode Normal            o = 0
Debug catcon.pm             z = 0
Debug catctl.pl             Z = 0
Display Phases              y = 0
Child Process               I = 0

catctl.pl version: 12.1.0.2.0
Oracle Base          = /u01/app/oracle

Analyzing file catupgrd.sql
Log files in /u01/app/oracle/product/12.1.0.2/dbhome_1/rdbms/admin
catcon: ALL catcon-related output will be written to catupgrd_catcon_3792.lst
catcon: See catupgrd*.log files for output generated by scripts
catcon: See catupgrd_*.lst files for spool files, if any
Number of Cpus       = 2
SQL Process Count    = 6

-------------------------------------------------------
Phases [0-73]
Serial   Phase #: 0 Files: 1     Time: 179s
Serial   Phase #: 1 Files: 5     Time: 54s
Restart  Phase #: 2 Files: 1     Time: 0s
```

Figure 7-46. *Showing the status of catupgrd.sql script with time*

Note: ---------------------- output truncated --------------
You can check the total time taken for the 73 phases with each phase time in seconds, as shown in Figure 7-47.

```
Serial    Phase #:70 Files: 1       Time: 209s
Serial    Phase #:71 Files: 1       Time: 0s
Serial    Phase #:72 Files: 1       Time: 0s
Serial    Phase #:73 Files: 1       Time: 28s

Grand Total Time: 3778s

LOG FILES: (catupgrd*.log)

Upgrade Summary Report Located in:
/u01/app/oracle/product/12.1.0.2/dbhome_1/cfgtoollogs/proddb/upgrade/upg_summary.log

Grand Total Upgrade Time:    [0d:1h:2m:58s]
[oracle@rac1 admin]$ []
```

Figure 7-47. *Showing the output of catupgrd.log script with time*

■ **Note**   The `catctl.pl` script will create multiple log files depending on the degree of parallelism selected. Here we have used a degree of parallelism of 4.

- The log files are in `/u01/app/oracle/product/12.1.0.2/dbhome_1/rdbms/admin`, as shown in Figure 7-48.

- All `catcon`-related output will be written to `catupgrd_catcon_10998.lst`.

```
[oracle@rac1 ~]$ cd /u01/app/oracle/product/12.1.0.2/dbhome_1/rdbms/admin
[oracle@rac1 admin]$ ls -lrth catupgrd*.log
-rw-r--r--. 1 oracle oinstall  221 Mar  4 12:00 catupgrd1.log
-rw-r--r--. 1 oracle oinstall  221 Mar  4 12:00 catupgrd3.log
-rw-r--r--. 1 oracle oinstall  221 Mar  4 12:00 catupgrd4.log
-rw-r--r--. 1 oracle oinstall  221 Mar  4 12:00 catupgrd5.log
-rw-r--r--. 1 oracle oinstall  221 Mar  4 12:00 catupgrd2.log
-rw-r--r--. 1 oracle oinstall 933K Mar  4 12:01 catupgrd0.log
[oracle@rac1 admin]$ ls -lrth catupgrd*.lst
-rw-r--r--. 1 oracle oinstall  348 Mar  4 12:00 catupgrd_catcon_10998.lst
```

Figure 7-48. *Showing the log files of catupgrd.sql script in the ORACLE_HOME/rdbms/admin directory*

Execute the following in the new environment after the upgrade, as shown in Figure 7-49:

```
SQL> @/u01/app/oracle/cfgtoollogs/proddb/preupgrade/postupgrade_fixups.sql
Upgrade status check: utlu121s.sql
```

```
[oracle@rac1 ~]$ export ORACLE_HOME=/u01/app/oracle/product/12.1.0.2/dbhome_1
[oracle@rac1 ~]$ export PATH=$ORACLE_HOME/bin:$PATH
[oracle@rac1 ~]$ export ORACLE_BASE=/u01/app/oracle
[oracle@rac1 ~]$ export ORACLE_SID=proddb1
[oracle@rac1 ~]$ sqlplus /nolog

SQL*Plus: Release 12.1.0.2.0 Production on Fri Feb 19 13:22:15 2016

Copyright (c) 1982, 2014, Oracle.  All rights reserved.

SQL> connect sys/oracle as sysdba
Connected to an idle instance.
SQL> startup;
ORACLE instance started.

Total System Global Area 1056964608 bytes
Fixed Size                  2932432 bytes
Variable Size             373293360 bytes
Database Buffers          675282944 bytes
Redo Buffers                5455872 bytes
Database mounted.
Database opened.
SQL> @?/rdbms/admin/utlu121s.sql

PL/SQL procedure successfully completed.
```

Figure 7-49. *Showing the status of the database instance and executing utlu121s.sql*

```
------------------------- output truncated----------------------------------
```
Upgrade Summary Report Located in:

```
/u01/app/oracle/product/12.1.0.2/dbhome_1/cfgtoollogs/proddb/upgrade/upg_summary.log
```

```
Oracle Database 12.1 Post-Upgrade Status Tool          02-19-2016 13:25:21

Component                              Current          Version   Elapsed Time
Name                                   Status           Number    HH:MM:SS

Oracle Server                          UPGRADED         12.1.0.2.0  00:12:41
JServer JAVA Virtual Machine           VALID            12.1.0.2.0  00:03:54
Oracle Real Application Clusters       VALID            12.1.0.2.0  00:00:01
Oracle Workspace Manager               VALID            12.1.0.2.0  00:00:51
OLAP Analytic Workspace                VALID            12.1.0.2.0  00:00:35
Oracle OLAP API                        VALID            12.1.0.2.0  00:00:18
Oracle XDK                             VALID            12.1.0.2.0  00:00:44
Oracle Text                            VALID            12.1.0.2.0  00:01:12
Oracle XML Database                    VALID            12.1.0.2.0  00:04:03
Oracle Database Java Packages          VALID            12.1.0.2.0  00:00:20
Oracle Multimedia                      VALID            12.1.0.2.0  00:02:22
Spatial                                UPGRADED         12.1.0.2.0  00:08:32
Oracle Application Express             VALID            4.2.5.00.08 00:20:06
Final Actions                                                       00:01:30
Post Upgrade                                                        00:03:19

Total Upgrade Time: 01:01:04

PL/SQL procedure successfully completed.
```

Figure 7-50. Showing the status of components with a status of VALID and the version number

Figure 7-51 shows the locations of the log files after `catctl.sql` has completed.

```
[oracle@rac1 ~]$ cd /u01/app/oracle/product/12.1.0.2/dbhome_1/rdbms/admin
[oracle@rac1 admin]$ ls -lrth catupgrd*.log
-rw-r--r--. 1 oracle oinstall  396 Mar  4 12:51 catupgrd_datapatch_upgrade.log
-rw-r--r--. 1 oracle oinstall  396 Mar  4 12:53 catupgrd_datapatch_normal.log
-rw-r--r--. 1 oracle oinstall 3.8M Mar  4 12:56 catupgrd1.log
-rw-r--r--. 1 oracle oinstall 3.3M Mar  4 12:56 catupgrd2.log
-rw-r--r--. 1 oracle oinstall 4.2M Mar  4 12:56 catupgrd3.log
-rw-r--r--. 1 oracle oinstall 4.3M Mar  4 12:56 catupgrd4.log
-rw-r--r--. 1 oracle oinstall 2.9M Mar  4 12:56 catupgrd5.log
-rw-r--r--. 1 oracle oinstall 337M Mar  4 12:56 catupgrd0.log
[oracle@rac1 admin]$ []
```

Figure 7-51. Showing the locations of log files of the script catupgrd.sql

The post-upgrade script `catuppst.sql` performs the remaining upgrade actions that do not require that the database be open in upgrade mode, as shown in Figure 7-52. It automatically applies the latest PSU.

```
SQL> @?/rdbms/admin/catuppst.sql
SQL> Rem
SQL> Rem $Header: rdbms/admin/catuppst.sql /st_rdbms_12.1/1 2014/06/11 20:58:01 surman Exp $
SQL> Rem
SQL> Rem catuppst.sql
SQL> Rem
SQL> Rem Copyright (c) 2006, 2014, Oracle and/or its affiliates.
SQL> Rem All rights reserved.
SQL> Rem
SQL> Rem      NAME
SQL> Rem              catuppst.sql - CATalog UPgrade PoST-upgrade actions
```

Figure 7-52. *Showing the status of execution of the script catuppst.sql*

This script utlrp.sql recompiles the invalid objects in the database, as shown in Figure 7-53.

```
SQL> @?/rdbms/admin/utlrp.sql
SQL> Rem
SQL> Rem $Header: utlrp.sql 24-jul-2003.10:06:51 gviswana Exp $
SQL> Rem
SQL> Rem utlrp.sql
SQL> Rem
SQL> Rem Copyright (c) 1998, 2003, Oracle Corporation.  All rights reserved.
SQL> Rem
SQL> Rem      NAME
SQL> Rem              utlrp.sql - Recompile invalid objects
SQL> Rem
```

Figure 7-53. *Showing the status of execution of the script utlrp.sql*

Check the time zone, as shown in Figure 7-54.

```
SQL> select version from v$timezone_file;

   VERSION
----------
        14
```

Figure 7-54. *Showing the output of v$timezone_file*

Note that you can download the DBMS_DST_scriptsV1.9.zip file from MOS Note 1585343.1 and unzip it. It contains these four files, as shown in Figure 7-55:

- upg_tzv_check.sql

- upg_tzv_apply.sql

- countstatsTSTZ.sql

- countstarTSTZ.sql

```
[oracle@rac1 ~]$ ls -lrth DB*
-rwxrwxrwx. 1 oracle oinstall 16K Feb 19 13:49 DBMS_DST_scriptsV1.9.zip
[oracle@rac1 ~]$ unzip DBMS_DST_scriptsV1.9.zip
Archive:  DBMS_DST_scriptsV1.9.zip
   creating: DBMS_DST_scriptsV1.9/
  inflating: DBMS_DST_scriptsV1.9/countstarTSTZ.sql
  inflating: DBMS_DST_scriptsV1.9/countstatsTSTZ.sql
  inflating: DBMS_DST_scriptsV1.9/upg_tzv_apply.sql
  inflating: DBMS_DST_scriptsV1.9/upg_tzv_check.sql
[oracle@rac1 ~]$ exit
```

Figure 7-55. *Showing the output of the DBMS_DST scripts with SQL files*

Execute the SQL statements one by one to update the time zone, as shown in Figure 7-56.

```
SQL> @/home/oracle/DBMS_DST_scriptsV1.9/countstarTSTZ.sql
SQL> @/home/oracle/DBMS_DST_scriptsV1.9/countstatsTSTZ.sql
SQL> @/home/oracle/DBMS_DST_scriptsV1.9/upg_tzv_check.sql
SQL> @/home/oracle/DBMS_DST_scriptsV1.9/upg_tzv_apply.sql
```

```
SQL> @/home/oracle/DBMS_DST_scriptsV1.9/upg_tzv_apply.sql
INFO: If an ERROR occurs the script will EXIT sqlplus.
INFO: The database RDBMS DST version will be updated to DSTv18 .
WARNING: This script will restart the database 2 times
WARNING: WITHOUT asking ANY confirmation.
WARNING: Hit control-c NOW if this is not intended.
INFO: Restarting the database in UPGRADE mode to start the DST upgrade.
Database closed.
Database dismounted.
ORACLE instance shut down.
ORACLE instance started.

Total System Global Area 1056964608 bytes
Fixed Size                   2932432 bytes
Variable Size              373293360 bytes
Database Buffers           675282944 bytes
Redo Buffers                 5455872 bytes
Database mounted.
Database opened.
INFO: Starting the RDBMS DST upgrade.
INFO: Upgrading all SYS owned TSTZ data.
INFO: It might take time before any further output is seen ...
An upgrade window has been successfully started.
INFO: Restarting the database in NORMAL mode to upgrade non-SYS TSTZ data.
Database closed.
Database dismounted.
ORACLE instance shut down.
ORACLE instance started.

Total System Global Area 1056964608 bytes
Fixed Size                   2932432 bytes
Variable Size              373293360 bytes
Database Buffers           675282944 bytes
Redo Buffers                 5455872 bytes
Database mounted.
Database opened.
```

Figure 7-56. Showing the output of the upg_tzv_apply.sql instance

---

■ **Note**   The previous script will restart the database a couple of times.

After manually upgrading a database, the srvctl commands fail with errors similar to the following:

```
[oracle@rac1 ~]$ srvctl start database -d proddb
```

PRCD-1229 means an attempt to access the configuration of the database proddb was rejected because its version, 11.2.0.3.0, differs from the program version of 12.1.0.2.0. Instead, run the program from /u01/app/oracle/product/11.2.0/dbhome_1.

Oracle Clusterware keys for the database still refer to the old ORACLE_HOME.

Upgrade the Oracle Clusterware keys for the database by running the srvctl upgrade database command.

Run srvctl from the new release ORACLE_HOME to upgrade the database keys.

Here's an example:

```
./srvctl upgrade database -d proddb -o /u01/app/oracle/product/12.1.0.2/dbhome_1/
```

Check the database status with the following:

```
[oracle@rac1 ~]$ cd /u01/app/12.1.0.2/grid/bin
[oracle@rac1 bin]$ ./srvctl upgrade database -d proddb -o /u01/app/oracle/product/12.1.0.2/
dbhome_1/

[oracle@rac1 bin]$ ./srvctl modify database -db proddb -spfile '+DATA/PRODDB/spfileproddb.
ora';

[oracle@rac1 bin]$ . oraenv
ORACLE_SID = [proddb1] ? proddb1
ORACLE_HOME = [/home/oracle] ? /u01/app/oracle/product/12.1.0.2/dbhome_1/
The Oracle base remains unchanged with value /u01/app/oracle

[oracle@rac1 bin]$ sqlplus /nolog
SQL*Plus: Release 12.1.0.2.0 Production on Fri Mar 4 13:41:22 2016
Copyright (c) 1982, 2014, Oracle.  All rights reserved.

SQL> connect sys/oracle as sysdba
Connected.

SQL> shutdown immediate;
Database closed.
Database dismounted.
ORACLE instance shut down.
[oracle@rac1 bin]$ srvctl start database -d proddb
```

Check the database status from instance1.

```
 [oracle@rac1 ~]$ . oraenv
ORACLE_SID = [proddb1] ? proddb
The Oracle base remains unchanged with value /u01/app/oracle
[oracle@rac1 ~]$ srvctl status database -d proddb
```

```
Instance proddb1 is running on node rac1
Instance proddb2 is running on node rac2
[oracle@rac1 ~]$
```

Check the database status from instance2.

```
[oracle@rac2 ~]$ . oraenv
ORACLE_SID = [proddb2] ? proddb
The Oracle base remains unchanged with value /u01/app/oracle
[oracle@rac2 ~]$ srvctl status database -d proddb
Instance proddb1 is running on node rac1
Instance proddb2 is running on node rac2
[oracle@rac2 ~]$Check Oracle GI Version, Oracle Database Version and output of crs_stat
```

```
[oracle@rac1 ~]$ . oraenv
ORACLE_SID = [proddb] ? proddb
The Oracle base remains unchanged with value /u01/app/oracle
[oracle@rac1 ~]$ sqlplus /nolog

SQL*Plus: Release 12.1.0.2.0 Production on Fri Mar 4 13:59:47 2016

Copyright (c) 1982, 2014, Oracle.  All rights reserved.

SQL> exit
[oracle@rac1 ~]$ . oraenv
ORACLE_SID = [proddb] ? +ASM1
The Oracle base remains unchanged with value /u01/app/oracle
[oracle@rac1 ~]$ sqlplus / as sysasm

SQL*Plus: Release 12.1.0.2.0 Production on Fri Mar 4 13:59:55 2016

Copyright (c) 1982, 2014, Oracle.  All rights reserved.


Connected to:
Oracle Database 12c Enterprise Edition Release 12.1.0.2.0 - 64bit Production
With the Real Application Clusters and Automatic Storage Management options

SQL> exit
Disconnected from Oracle Database 12c Enterprise Edition Release 12.1.0.2.0 - 64bit Production
With the Real Application Clusters and Automatic Storage Management options
[oracle@rac1 ~]$ crs_stat -t
Name           Type          Target     State      Host
------------------------------------------------------------
ora.DATA.dg    ora....up.type ONLINE     ONLINE     rac1
ora.FRA.dg     ora....up.type ONLINE     ONLINE     rac1
ora....ER.lsnr ora....er.type ONLINE     ONLINE     rac1
ora....N1.lsnr ora....er.type ONLINE     ONLINE     rac2
ora....N2.lsnr ora....er.type ONLINE     ONLINE     rac1
ora....N3.lsnr ora....er.type ONLINE     ONLINE     rac1
ora.MGMTLSNR   ora....nr.type ONLINE     ONLINE     rac1
ora.asm        ora.asm.type   ONLINE     ONLINE     rac1
ora.cvu        ora.cvu.type   ONLINE     ONLINE     rac2
ora.mgmtdb     ora....db.type ONLINE     ONLINE     rac1
ora....network ora....rk.type ONLINE     ONLINE     rac1
ora.oc4j       ora.oc4j.type  ONLINE     ONLINE     rac2
ora.ons        ora.ons.type   ONLINE     ONLINE     rac1
ora.proddb.db  ora....se.type ONLINE     ONLINE     rac1
ora....SM1.asm application    ONLINE     ONLINE     rac1
ora....C1.lsnr application    ONLINE     ONLINE     rac1
ora.rac1.ons   application    ONLINE     ONLINE     rac1
ora.rac1.vip   ora....t1.type ONLINE     ONLINE     rac1
ora....SM2.asm application    ONLINE     ONLINE     rac2
ora....C2.lsnr application    ONLINE     ONLINE     rac2
ora.rac2.ons   application    ONLINE     ONLINE     rac2
ora.rac2.vip   ora....t1.type ONLINE     ONLINE     rac2
ora.scan1.vip  ora....ip.type ONLINE     ONLINE     rac2
ora.scan2.vip  ora....ip.type ONLINE     ONLINE     rac1
ora.scan3.vip  ora....ip.type ONLINE     ONLINE     rac1
```

Figure 7-57. Showing the output complete stack to cluster components with database instances

Scenario 3 Upgrading of Oracle 11*g* RAC (11.2.0.3.0) to Oracle 12*c* RAC (12.1.0.2.0) with GI and Database using EMCC 13c

We'll walk you through upgrading an Oracle 11*g* RAC database (11.2.0.3.0) to an Oracle 12*c* RAC database (12.1.0.2.0) with Grid Infrastructure and database using Oracle Enterprise Manager Cloud Control 13*c*. Figure 7-58 shows the configured environment.

Database Server	Home Directories Path
Oracle Home	/u01/app/oracle/product/11.2.0/db_1
Grid Home	/u01/app/11.2.0/grid
Agent Home	/u01/app/oracle/agent/agent_inst
Agent Log Directory	/u01/app/oracle/agent/agent_inst/sysman/log
Agent Binaries	/u01/app/oracle/agent/agent_13.1.0.0.0
Agent Version & OMS Version	13.1.0.0.0
RAC Database	proddb (proddb1 & proddb2)
Host Names & IP addresses of RAC Instance	rac1.mlg.oracle.com (192.168.56.21) rac2.mlg.oracle.com (192.168.56.22)

Figure 7-58. *Locations of ORACLE_HOME, GRID_HOME, and AGENT_HOME on the database server*

Oracle Enterprise Manager Cloud Control 13c	Home Directories and Path
Oracle Home	/u01/app/oracle/product/12.1.0.2/db_1
OMS Home	/u01/app/oracle/middleware
Agent Home	/u01/app/oracle/agent/agent_inst
Agent Binaries	/u01/app/oracle/agent/agent_13.1.0.0.0
OEM Cloud Control	https://em13c.localdomain:7802/em
Host Name & IP address	em13c.localdomain (192.168.56.200)

Figure 7-59. *Locations of ORACLE_HOME, GRID_HOME, and AGENT_HOME on Oracle Enterprise Manager Cloud Control*

There's one more method for upgrading GI and Oracle Database from an older version to a later version. You can use the option Upgrade Oracle Home and Database in Enterprise Manager Cloud Control 13*c*.

Click Targets and then click Cluster Database after logging in to the Enterprise Manager Cloud Control 13*c*.

Go to the option Provisioning and select the suboption Upgrade Oracle Home & Database, as shown in Figure 7-60.

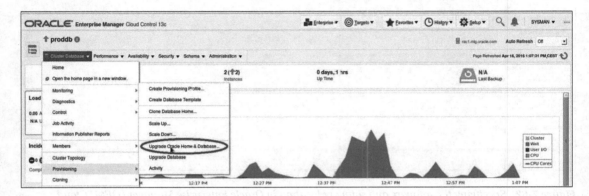

Figure 7-60. *The Upgrade Oracle Home & Database option under Cluster Database in Oracle Enterprise Manager Cloud Control*

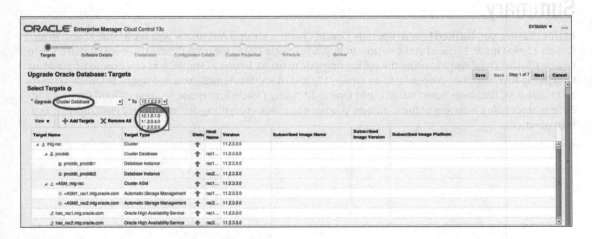

Figure 7-61. *Upgrading the cluster database to list of available Oracle Database versions in Oracle Enterprise Manager Cloud Control*

Select Grid Infrastructure Software from Software Library to create a new Oracle Home, as shown in Figure 7-62. Here you have the following options:

- Software may be stored as a gold image
- Zipped-up installation media in the software library

Figure 7-62. *Specifying the software and software location in Oracle Enterprise Manager (OEM) Cloud Control*

Summary

In this chapter, you learned how to upgrade Oracle Clusterware and Automatic Storage Management from Oracle 11*g* to Oracle 12*c*, and you saw how to upgrade Oracle Database from Oracle Cluster Database 11*g* to Oracle Cluster Database 12*c* using the rolling upgrade method. In one example, you saw how to upgrade an Oracle 11*g* RAC database manually to an Oracle 12*c* RAC database. Finally, you can upgrade Oracle GI and an Oracle RAC database from Oracle 11*g* to Oracle 12*c* using Oracle Enterprise Manager Cloud Control 13*c*. Before proceeding with any of the methods, you have to check everything out in your test environment as a best practice.

CHAPTER 8

■ ■ ■

Database Upgrades in Data Guard Environments

In today's world, high availability is the utmost priority for critical production databases, and there are various high availability solutions available from Oracle using Data Guard and GoldenGate, as well as other vendors. The best high availability solution is considered to be Data Guard because the standby database will work the same as the primary database, because it can be configured with the same parameters, and because it can assign the same memory to use the standby as the production database in case of any disasters at the primary site. Again, with Data Guard, there is no need to have only a physical standby; you can also have logical standby or snapshot standby databases according to the business demand.

Usually you will continue to upgrade your databases when new versions are available depending on the support for older versions or whether there are any bugs in the current release. Additionally, when the primary database is the physical standby database in a high availability solution, then you need to upgrade the standby database as well. This chapter explains all about upgrading the databases of the Data Guard environment.

Prior to 11g, you have only one upgrade method. You install the software on both the primary and standby sites, and then you upgrade the primary first and start MRP on the standby so that the redo changes will be applied on the standby. However, in this method, downtime is expected until you completely upgrade the primary database, and in general, the main requirements of production databases are minimal downtime, maximum availability, and the protection of databases. Therefore, the traditional upgrade method is not the best for high availability.

With 11g, Oracle introduced rolling database upgrades with the transient logical standby. Using this method, you can achieve less than one minute of downtime to upgrade the primary and standby databases, but the challenging part is that the upgrade procedure is lengthy, with about 40 steps. This method can be used from 10g R2 to 11g R1 or above. If you compare the traditional upgrade method to the rolling upgrade, you can reduce the downtime by about 96 percent with the rolling method. So, you get the advantage of minimal downtime, but the downside is that the process is complex. No matter which upgrade method you choose, practice in a test environment before upgrading in production.

Now let's move to the topic of upgrading a 12c multitenant environment. As you know, there are 500+ features in 12c. There are many new features in Data Guard as well. With respect to Data Guard upgrades, one new feature is the DBMS_ROLLING method, which makes upgrading Data Guard easy. It has just five major steps. It's a great feature to achieve minimal downtime with less effort. This method is applicable only for 12c release 1 or higher but not applicable for upgrading from 11g R2 to 12c.

In this chapter, we will walk you through two examples of upgrading the Data Guard environment to 12c.

- Traditional method to upgrade Data Guard from 11.2.0.4 to 12.1.0.1

- The DBMS_ROLLING method to upgrade Data Guard from 12.1.0.1 to 12.1.0.2

© Y V Ravikumar, K M Krishnakumar and Nassyam Basha 2017
N. Basha et al., *Oracle Database Upgrade and Migration Methods*, DOI 10.1007/978-1-4842-2328-4_8

Upgrading Data Guard from 11.2.0.4 to 12.1.0.2

In this section, consider that you have a Data Guard configuration on an RDBMS 11.2.0.4 and you are upgrading to 12.1.0.1 using the DBUA with the regular method instead of using rolling upgrades.

- *Source database version*: 11.2.0.4.0

- *Primary database name*: ORC1, db_unique_name=ORC1P

- *Standby database name*: ORC1, db_unique_name=ORC1S

You can review the overall configuration of Data Guard and also the standby details of the transport lag and apply a lag with the Data Guard Broker.

```
DGMGRL> show configuration

Configuration - upgha

  Protection Mode: MaxPerformance
  Databases:
    orc1p - Primary database
    orc1s - Physical standby database

Fast-Start Failover: DISABLED

Configuration Status:
SUCCESS

DGMGRL> show database orc1s

Database - orc1s

  Role:               PHYSICAL STANDBY
  Intended State:     APPLY-ON
  Transport Lag:      0 seconds (computed 0 seconds ago)
  Apply Lag:          0 seconds (computed 0 seconds ago)
  Apply Rate:         0 Byte/s
  Real Time Query:    OFF
  Instance(s):
    ORC1
Database Status:
SUCCESS
```

Pre-upgrade Steps

In this method, you are not upgrading the existing home. Instead, you are installing the new Oracle 12.1.0.1 software again in both the primary and standby servers. So, assume that 12.1.0.1 is installed already on both the primary and standby servers and then go ahead and perform the pre-upgrade steps, the actual upgrade steps, and the post-upgrade steps.

The next part is to run the pre-upgrade script provided by Oracle within the Oracle Homes on the primary database. This example's Data Guard configuration is on 11.2.0.4, but to upgrade, you must use the pre-upgrade script of the target RDBMS software (in other words, 12.1.0.1). You will see how to take care of this in the following script:

```
[oracle@ORA-U1 dbhome_1]$ cd /u01/app/oracle/product/12.1.0/dbhome_1/rdbms/admin/
[oracle@ORA-U1 admin]$ ls -ltr preu*
-rw-r--r--. 1 oracle oinstall 5231 Apr  2  2013 preupgrd.sql
[oracle@ORA-U1 admin]$ sqlplus / as sysdba

SQL*Plus: Release 11.2.0.4.0 Production on Sun May 22 12:53:27 2016

Copyright (c) 1982, 2013, Oracle.  All rights reserved.

Connected to:
Oracle Database 11g Enterprise Edition Release 11.2.0.4.0 - 64bit Production
With the Partitioning, OLAP, Data Mining and Real Application Testing options

SQL> @preupgrd.sql
Loading Pre-Upgrade Package...
Executing Pre-Upgrade Checks...
Pre-Upgrade Checks Complete.
       ************************************************************

Results of the checks are located at:
 /u01/app/oracle/cfgtoollogs/ORC1P/preupgrade/preupgrade.log

Pre-Upgrade Fixup Script (run in source database environment):
 /u01/app/oracle/cfgtoollogs/ORC1P/preupgrade/preupgrade_fixups.sql

Post-Upgrade Fixup Script (run shortly after upgrade):
 /u01/app/oracle/cfgtoollogs/ORC1P/preupgrade/postupgrade_fixups.sql


       ************************************************************

       Fixup scripts must be reviewed prior to being executed.

       ************************************************************


       ************************************************************
             ====>> USER ACTION REQUIRED  <<====
       ************************************************************

The following are *** ERROR LEVEL CONDITIONS *** that must be addressed
                prior to attempting your upgrade.
       Failure to do so will result in a failed upgrade.

       You MUST resolve the above errors prior to upgrade

       ************************************************************
```

You already saw these steps in prior chapters, and we hope you have a clear idea of how this script works. However, we will review them since we are dealing with Data Guard in this chapter. In fact, there are no special steps you have to execute from Data Guard, because a physical standby is considered an image copy of the primary database, and in the case of the logical standby, you have to run from both databases.

So, with this script, you have to execute only on the primary database. On top of that, the script contains various PL/SQL packages, which you cannot run on standby read-only databases.

Let's go back to the previous script you executed. This script will not give all the results, but it diverts the output into the log file/u01/app/oracle/cfgtoollogs/ORC1P/preupgrade/preupgrade.log, where you can check the things that need to be fixed manually or by using the fixup script shown in the next section. Please note this fixup script cannot fix everything. The fixup script, /u01/app/oracle/cfgtoollogs/ORC1P/preupgrade/preupgrade_fixups.sql, will be available in the pre-upgrade script output.

Review of the Pre-upgrade Log

You have already run the pre-upgrade script, and the following is the log generated by the script to review and fix the tasks that can be done manually:

```
[oracle@ORA-U1 admin]$ cat /u01/app/oracle/cfgtoollogs/ORC1P/preupgrade/preupgrade.log
Oracle Database Pre-Upgrade Information Tool 05-22-2016 12:53:39
Script Version: 12.1.0.1.0 Build: 006
**********************************************************************
    Database Name:  ORC1
          Version:  11.2.0.4.0
       Compatible:  11.2.0.4.0
        Blocksize:  8192
         Platform:  Linux x86 64-bit
    Timezone file:  V14
**********************************************************************
                         [Renamed Parameters]
                    [No Renamed Parameters in use]
**********************************************************************
**********************************************************************
                    [Obsolete/Deprecated Parameters]
             [No Obsolete or Desupported Parameters in use]
**********************************************************************
                            [Component List]
**********************************************************************
--> Oracle Catalog Views              [upgrade]  VALID
--> Oracle Packages and Types         [upgrade]  VALID
--> JServer JAVA Virtual Machine      [upgrade]  VALID
--> Oracle XDK for Java               [upgrade]  VALID
--> Oracle Workspace Manager          [upgrade]  VALID
--> OLAP Analytic Workspace           [upgrade]  VALID
--> Oracle Enterprise Manager Repository  [upgrade]  VALID
--> Oracle Text                       [upgrade]  VALID
--> Oracle XML Database               [upgrade]  VALID
--> Oracle Java Packages              [upgrade]  VALID
--> Oracle Multimedia                 [upgrade]  VALID
--> Oracle Spatial                    [upgrade]  VALID
--> Expression Filter                 [upgrade]  VALID
--> Rule Manager                      [upgrade]  VALID
--> Oracle Application Express        [upgrade]  VALID
--> Oracle OLAP API                   [upgrade]  VALID
**********************************************************************
                            [Tablespaces]
**********************************************************************
```

```
--> SYSTEM tablespace is adequate for the upgrade.
    minimum required size: 1261 MB
--> SYSAUX tablespace is adequate for the upgrade.
    minimum required size: 1435 MB
--> UNDOTBS1 tablespace is adequate for the upgrade.
    minimum required size: 400 MB
--> TEMP tablespace is adequate for the upgrade.
    minimum required size: 60 MB
--> EXAMPLE tablespace is adequate for the upgrade.
    minimum required size: 309 MB

                    [No adjustments recommended]


**********************************************************************
**********************************************************************
                        [Pre-Upgrade Checks]
**********************************************************************
WARNING: --> Process Count may be too low

    Database has a maximum process count of 150 which is lower than the
    default value of 300 for this release.
    You should update your processes value prior to the upgrade
    to a value of at least 300.
    For example:
        ALTER SYSTEM SET PROCESSES=300 SCOPE=SPFILE
    or update your init.ora file.

WARNING: --> Enterprise Manager Database Control repository found in the database

    In Oracle Database 12c, Database Control is removed during
    the upgrade. To save time during the Upgrade, this action
    can be done prior to upgrading using the following steps after
    copying rdbms/admin/emremove.sql from the new Oracle home
    - Stop EM Database Control:
    $> emctl stop dbconsole

    - Connect to the Database using the SYS account AS SYSDBA:

    SET ECHO ON;
    SET SERVEROUTPUT ON;
    @emremove.sql
    Without the set echo and serveroutput commands you will not
    be able to follow the progress of the script.

WARNING: --> Standby database not synced

    Sync standby database prior to upgrade.
    Your standby databases should be synched prior to upgrading.

WARNING: --> Existing DBMS_LDAP dependent objects
```

Database contains schemas with objects dependent on DBMS_LDAP package.
Refer to the Upgrade Guide for instructions to configure Network ACLs.
USER APEX_030200 has dependent objects.

WARNING: --> Database contains INVALID objects prior to upgrade

The list of invalid SYS/SYSTEM objects was written to
registry$sys_inv_objs.
The list of non-SYS/SYSTEM objects was written to
registry$nonsys_inv_objs unless there were over 5000.
Use utluiobj.sql after the upgrade to identify any new invalid
objects due to the upgrade.

INFORMATION: --> OLAP Catalog(AMD) exists in database

Starting with Oracle Database 12c, OLAP is desupported.
If you are not using the OLAP Catalog component and want
to remove it, then execute the
ORACLE_HOME/oraolap/admin/catnoamd.sql script before or
after the upgrade.

INFORMATION: --> Older Timezone in use

Database is using a time zone file older than version 18.
After the upgrade, it is recommended that DBMS_DST package
be used to upgrade the 11.2.0.4.0 database time zone version
to the latest version which comes with the new release.
Please refer to My Oracle Support note number 977512.1 for details.

```
**********************************************************************
                  [Pre-Upgrade Recommendations]
**********************************************************************

            ***************************************
            ********* Dictionary Statistics *********
            ***************************************
```

Please gather dictionary statistics 24 hours prior to
upgrading the database.
To gather dictionary statistics execute the following command
while connected as SYSDBA:
    EXECUTE dbms_stats.gather_dictionary_stats;

^^^ MANUAL ACTION SUGGESTED ^^^

```
**********************************************************************
                  [Post-Upgrade Recommendations]
**********************************************************************

            ***************************************
            ********* Fixed Object Statistics *********
            ***************************************
```

```
Please create stats on fixed objects two weeks
after the upgrade using the command:
   EXECUTE DBMS_STATS.GATHER_FIXED_OBJECTS_STATS;

^^^ MANUAL ACTION SUGGESTED ^^^

**********************************************************************
                  ***********  Summary  ***********

0 ERRORS exist in your database.
5 WARNINGS that Oracle suggests are addressed to improve database performance.
2 INFORMATIONAL messages that should be reviewed prior to your upgrade.

After your database is upgraded and open in normal mode you must run
rdbms/admin/catuppst.sql which executes several required tasks and completes
the upgrade process.

You should follow that with the execution of rdbms/admin/utlrp.sql, and a
comparison of invalid objects before and after the upgrade using
rdbms/admin/utluiobj.sql

If needed you may want to upgrade your timezone data using the process
described in My Oracle Support note 977512.1
                  **********************************
[oracle@ORA-U1 admin]$
```

The log file is readable. If you review the many components, you'll see a few of them need to be fixed, and a few of them can be considered optional. Even when they're optional, it is highly recommended to fix/implement them before the upgrade.

In the following steps, you will fix the pending tasks one by one. The commands are already available in the log file, so there's no need to perform anything manually.

1. Here is the process limit:

    ```
    SQL> ALTER SYSTEM SET PROCESSES=300 SCOPE=SPFILE;

    System altered.

    SQL>
    ```

2. Remove the EM repository.

    ```
    SQL>
       SET ECHO ON;
       SET SERVEROUTPUT ON;
       @emremove.sqlSQL> SQL> SQL>
    SQL> Rem
    SQL> Rem $Header: rdbms/admin/emremove.sql /main/2 2012/07/27 01:19:53
    spramani Exp $
    SQL> Rem
    SQL> Rem emremove.sql
    ```

3. The standby database is not synced.

   a. Ensure the standby is able to receive archive logs whenever the log switch or any commit is performed.

   ```
   Sun May 22 13:25:16 2016
   Media Recovery Waiting for thread 1 sequence 39 (in transit)
   Recovery of Online Redo Log: Thread 1 Group 4 Seq 39 Reading mem 0
     Mem# 0: /u01/app/oracle/fast_recovery_area/ORC1S/onlinelog/o1_mf_4_
   cn206368_.log
   Sun May 22 13:25:17 2016
   ```

4. Compile the invalid objects.

   ```
   SQL> @?/rdbms/admin/utlrp.sql
   SQL> Rem
   SQL> Rem $Header: utlrp.sql 24-jul-2003.10:06:51 gviswana Exp $

   SQL> select count(*),object_type from dba_objects
   where status='INVALID' group by object_type;

   no rows selected

   SQL>
   ```

5. The OLAP catalog (AMD) exists; it is deprecated in 12*c*.

   a. As it is deprecated, it is recommended you remove the component prior to the upgrade.

   ```
   SQL> @/u01/app/oracle/product/11.2.0/dbhome_1/olap/admin/catnoamd.sql

   Synonym dropped.

   Synonym dropped.
   . . .
   . .
   .
   PL/SQL procedure successfully completed.

   1 row deleted.

   SQL>
   ```

6. Gather the dictionary statistics.

   ```
   SQL> EXECUTE dbms_stats.gather_dictionary_stats;

   PL/SQL procedure successfully completed.

   Elapsed: 00:00:19.22
   SQL>
   ```

Finally, after the changes, perform a database bounce like you performed when you changed a few static parameters.

```
SQL> shutdown immediate;
Database closed.
Database dismounted.
ORACLE instance shut down.
SQL> startup
ORACLE instance started.

Total System Global Area   626327552 bytes
Fixed Size                   2255832 bytes
Variable Size              515900456 bytes
Database Buffers           100663296 bytes
Redo Buffers                 7507968 bytes
Database mounted.
Database opened.
```

So far, you have completed all the tasks related to the pre-upgrade and have a few things pending that you have to perform after the upgrade. They are as follows:

1. Run the post-upgrade fixup script shortly after the upgrade.

   /u01/app/oracle/cfgtoollogs/ORC1P/preupgrade/postupgrade_fixups.sql

2. There is an older time zone in use. Select the relevant option while the DBUA is running.

3. Gather the dictionary statistics.

Upgrade the Data Guard Environment

You should have a proper plan in place for whether you want to start the upgrade of the primary database first or the standby database first, and you should know the steps to be performed, especially in the case of Data Guard. In fact, upgrading Data Guard is not complicated and does not have many steps to perform in the case of a traditional upgrade. You will see where to start and how to perform the upgrade in this section.

1. Disable the broker configuration from both the primary and standby databases.

   ```
   SQL> alter system set dg_broker_start=false scope=both;

   System altered.

   SQL>
   ```

2. Cancel MRP on the standby database and defer the standby destination from the primary database.

   ```
   SQL> alter database recover managed standby database cancel;

   Database altered.
   ```

```
SQL> !ps -ef|grep mrp
oracle   13240 13238  0 16:09 pts/4   00:00:00 /bin/bash -c ps -ef|grep mrp
oracle   13242 13240  0 16:09 pts/4   00:00:00 grep mrp

SQL> alter system set log_archive_dest_state_2='defer' scope=both;

System altered.
```

3. Shut down the standby database and listener of the standby database from the
    11g R2 home.

```
SQL> shutdown immediate;
ORA-01109: database not open

Database dismounted.
ORACLE instance shut down.
```

4. Copy the spfile and password file and add network parameters from 11.2.0.4 into
    the new 12c R1 home of the standby database.

```
[oracle@ORA-U2 dbs]$ cd /u01/app/oracle/product/11.2.0/dbhome_1/dbs
[oracle@ORA-U2 dbs]$ ls -ltr
total 56
-rw-r--r--. 1 oracle oinstall  2851 May 15  2009 init.ora
-rw-r--r--. 1 oracle oinstall   613 May 22 12:13 initORC1.ora
-rw-r-----. 1 oracle oinstall  1536 May 22 12:21 orapwORC1
-rw-r-----. 1 oracle oinstall    24 May 22 12:22 lkORC1
-rw-r-----. 1 oracle oinstall    24 May 22 12:24 lkORC1S
-rw-r-----. 1 oracle oinstall  8192 May 22 12:44 dr1ORC1S.dat
-rw-r-----. 1 oracle oinstall 20480 May 22 12:44 dr2ORC1S.dat
-rw-r-----. 1 oracle oinstall  3584 May 22 12:44 spfileORC1.ora
-rw-rw----. 1 oracle oinstall  1544 May 22 16:10 hc_ORC1.dat
[oracle@ORA-U2 dbs]$ cp *ORC1S* /u01/app/oracle/product/12.1.0/dbhome_1/dbs/
[oracle@ORA-U2 dbs]$ scp spfileORC1.ora /u01/app/oracle/product/12.1.0/dbhome_1/
dbs/
[oracle@ORA-U2 dbs]$
```

5. Start the standby instance in mount state using the 12c Oracle Home. Before that,
    add the new 12c Home exported into the /etc/oratab file so that the instance
    can be easily accessible.

```
[oracle@ORA-U2 dbs]$ . oraenv
ORACLE_SID = [orcl] ? ORC1
The Oracle base remains unchanged with value /u01/app/oracle
[oracle@ORA-U2 dbs]$
[oracle@ORA-U2 ~]$ sqlplus / as sysdba

SQL*Plus: Release 12.1.0.1.0 Production on Sun May 22 16:16:45 2016

Copyright (c) 1982, 2013, Oracle.  All rights reserved.
```

```
Connected to an idle instance.

SQL> startup mount
ORACLE instance started.

Total System Global Area  626327552 bytes
Fixed Size                  2291472 bytes
Variable Size             440404208 bytes
Database Buffers          176160768 bytes
Redo Buffers                7471104 bytes
Database mounted.
SQL>
```

6. Configure the listener with the 12c Home and start the new listener from the standby server.

```
[oracle@ORA-U2 admin]$ cp *ora /u01/app/oracle/product/12.1.0/dbhome_1/network/
admin/
[oracle@ORA-U2 admin]$ cd /u01/app/oracle/product/12.1.0/dbhome_1/network/admin/
[oracle@ORA-U2 admin]$ vi listener.ora
[oracle@ORA-U2 admin]$ cat listener.ora
SID_LIST_LISTENER12C =
  (SID_LIST =
    (SID_DESC =
      (GLOBAL_DBNAME = ORC1)
      (ORACLE_HOME = /u01/app/oracle/product/12.1.0/dbhome_1)
      (SID_NAME = ORC1)
    )
  )

LISTENER12C =
  (DESCRIPTION =
    (ADDRESS = (PROTOCOL = TCP)(HOST = 192.168.0.120)(PORT = 1521))
  )

[oracle@ORA-U2 ~]$ lsnrctl start LISTENER12C

LSNRCTL for Linux: Version 12.1.0.1.0 - Production on 23-MAY-2016 05:14:04

Copyright (c) 1991, 2013, Oracle.  All rights reserved.

Starting /u01/app/oracle/product/12.1.0/dbhome_1/bin/tnslsnr: please wait...

TNSLSNR for Linux: Version 12.1.0.1.0 - Production
System parameter file is /u01/app/oracle/product/12.1.0/dbhome_1/network/admin/
listener.ora
Log messages written to /u01/app/oracle/diag/tnslsnr/ORA-U2/listener12c/alert/
log.xml
Listening on: (DESCRIPTION=(ADDRESS=(PROTOCOL=tcp)(HOST=192.168.0.120)
(PORT=1521)))
```

```
Connecting to (DESCRIPTION=(ADDRESS=(PROTOCOL=TCP)(HOST=192.168.0.120)
(PORT=1521)))
STATUS of the LISTENER
------------------------
Alias                     LISTENER12C
Version                   TNSLSNR for Linux: Version 12.1.0.1.0 - Production
Start Date                23-MAY-2016 05:14:04
Uptime                    0 days 0 hr. 0 min. 0 sec
Trace Level               off
Security                  ON: Local OS Authentication
SNMP                      OFF
Listener Parameter File   /u01/app/oracle/product/12.1.0/dbhome_1/network/admin/
listener.ora
Listener Log File         /u01/app/oracle/diag/tnslsnr/ORA-U2/listener12c/alert/
log.xml
Listening Endpoints Summary...
  (DESCRIPTION=(ADDRESS=(PROTOCOL=tcp)(HOST=192.168.0.120)(PORT=1521)))
Services Summary...
Service "ORC1" has 1 instance(s).
  Instance "ORC1", status UNKNOWN, has 1 handler(s) for this service...
The command completed successfully
[oracle@ORA-U2 ~]$

[oracle@ORA-U2 admin]$
```

7. Update the LOCAL_LISTENER from the standby database.

```
[oracle@ORA-U2 admin]$ tail -6 tnsnames.ora

LISTENER12C =
  (DESCRIPTION =
    (ADDRESS = (PROTOCOL = TCP)(HOST = 192.168.0.120)(PORT = 1521))
  )

[oracle@ORA-U2 admin]$ sqlplus / as sysdba

SQL*Plus: Release 12.1.0.1.0 Production on Mon May 23 05:16:14 2016

Copyright (c) 1982, 2013, Oracle.  All rights reserved.

Connected to:
Oracle Database 12c Enterprise Edition Release 12.1.0.1.0 - 64bit Production
With the Partitioning, OLAP, Advanced Analytics and Real Application Testing
options

SQL> alter system set local_listener=LISTENER12C scope=both;

System altered.

SQL>
```

8. Disable crontab jobs, if any, from the primary and standby databases.

9. Ensure that you have a full database backup of the primary database.

   – There's no need to perform a backup of the 11*g* R2 home because you are not touching it any way.

10. If FRA is in use on the primary, then increase the value to the maximum available from the mount point until the upgrade is successful. If the utilization is reaching a threshold, then perform maintenance tasks to clean up the archive logs.

Now it's time to start the DBUA to upgrade the primary database. Do not forget to disable the Data Guard Broker until the upgrade process is completed. You will start the DBUA from the new 12*c* home and select the option Upgrade Oracle Database, as shown in Figure 8-1.

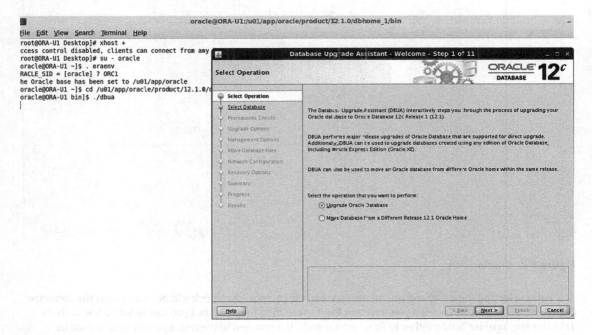

Figure 8-1. *Caption here*

DBUA shows you the source Oracle Home to select so that the DBUA can get the details of the database to upgrade. As your primary database is running from 11*g* R2, select the appropriate Oracle Home. As soon as you select the Oracle Home, it shows all of the databases running under the Oracle Home. Select the database name ORC1, as shown in Figure 8-2.

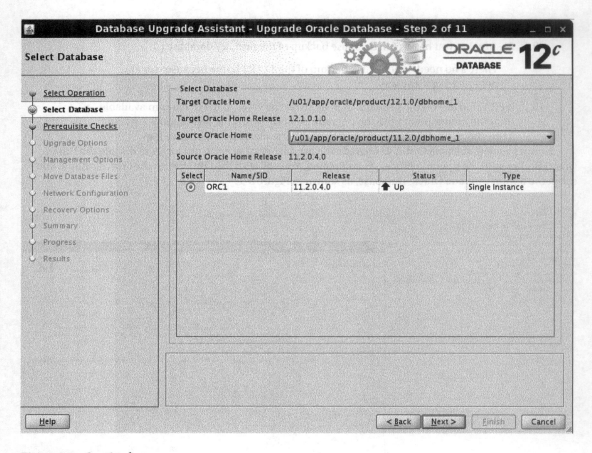

Figure 8-2. *Caption here*

After selecting the database, on the next screen, the prerequisite check will be run against the database ORC1. You will see some issues if you have not fixed something properly, but you can ignore a few of them. Take the appropriate action either to fix or ignore and then proceed to the next operation, as shown in Figure 8-3.

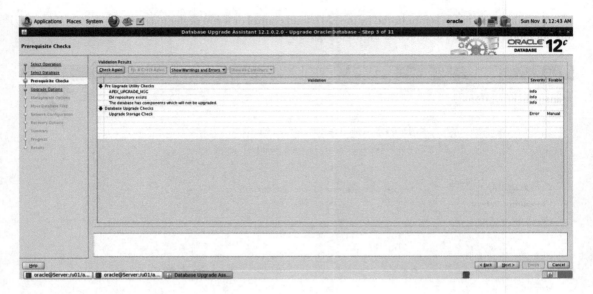

Figure 8-3. *Caption here*

This operation will give you several options such as to select the parallelism you prefer to run the upgrade, recompiling options after upgrade, and so on. You can select whichever is appropriate, as shown in Figure 8-4, and then proceed to the next operation.

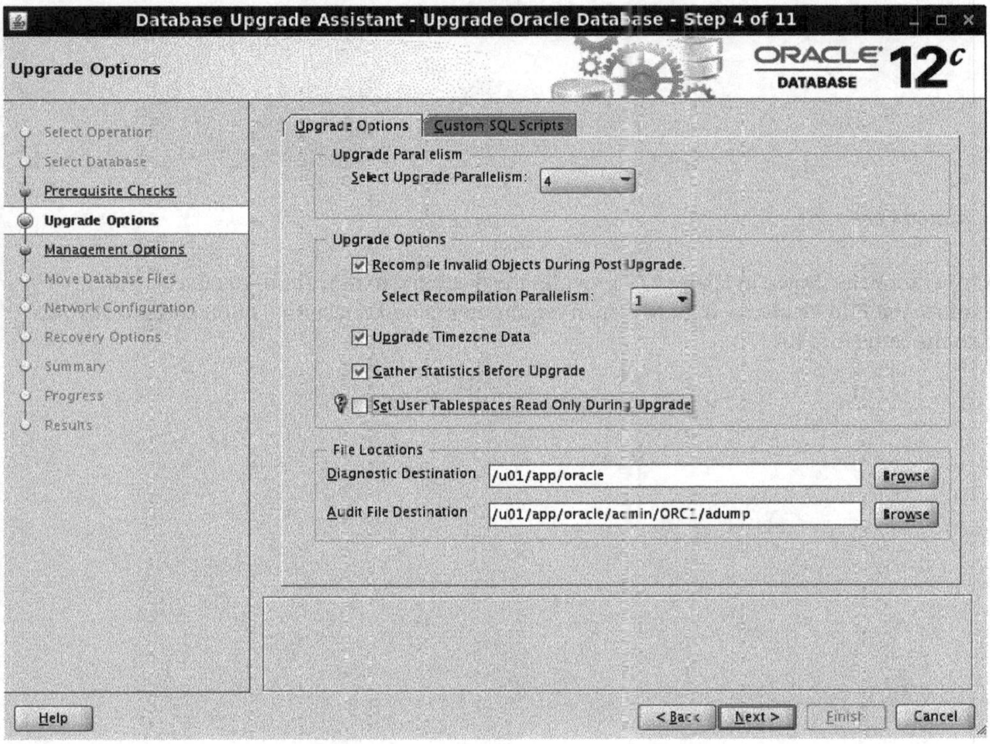

Figure 8-4. *Caption here*

If the database target is monitored by the EM/cloud control or if you prefer to configure the EM Express, this operation allows you to select, as shown in Figure 8-5.

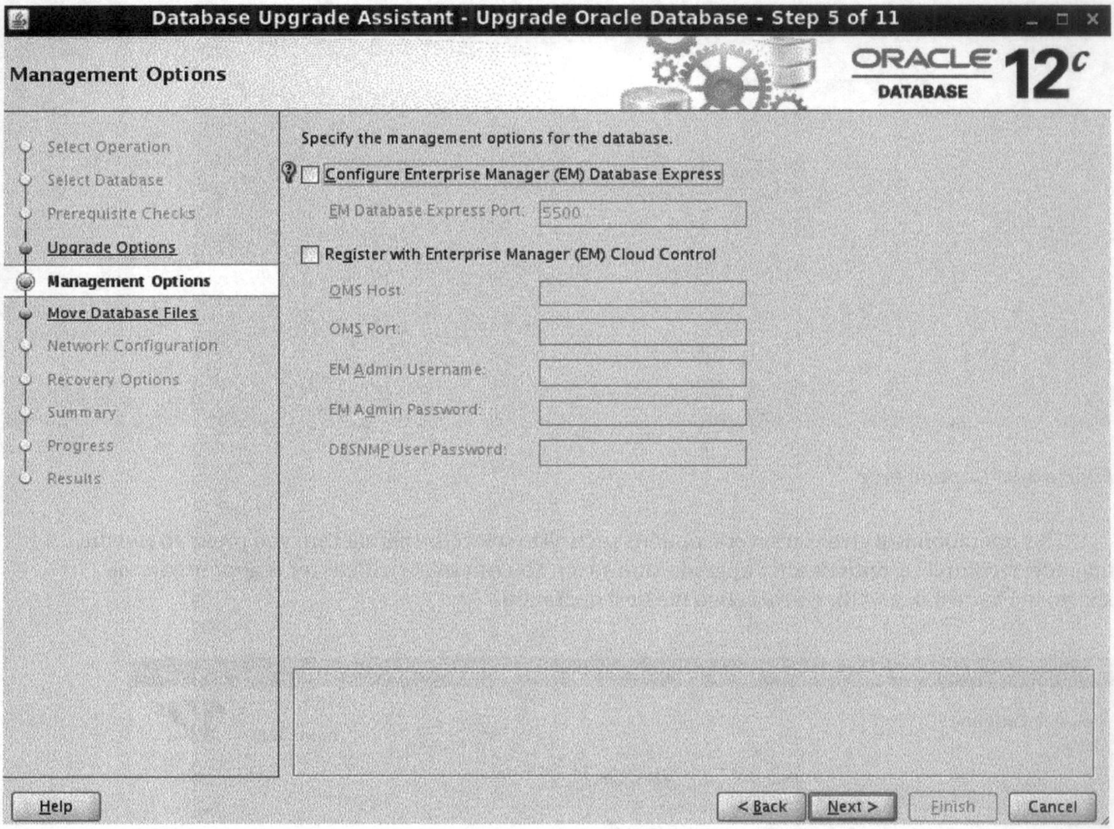

Figure 8-5. *Caption here*

The next operation, as shown in Figure 8-6, provides the flexibility to move your database to another location or to move the FRA locations. If there is such requirement, then select the option and provide the file location; do the same for FRA.

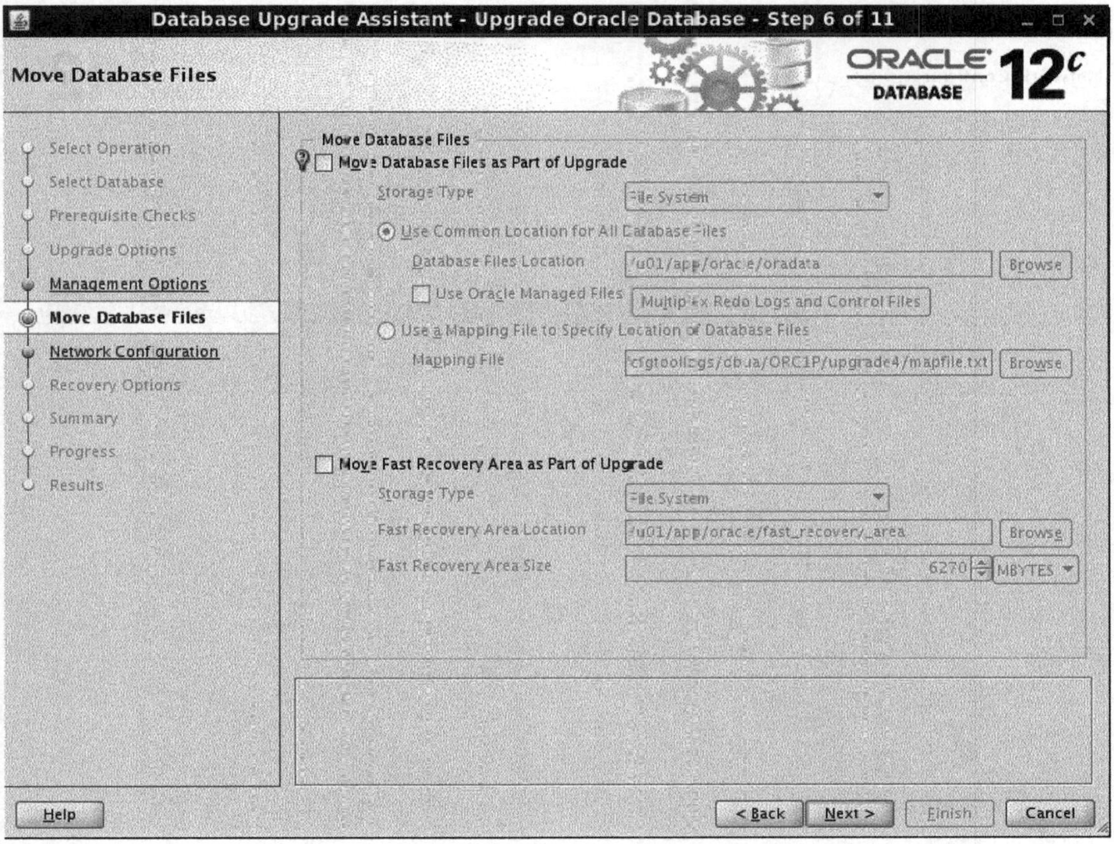

Figure 8-6. *Caption here*

The next step is to select the listener or create a new listener. In many cases, after upgrading to a new Oracle version, then you should always prefer the listener from the new Oracle Home, as shown in Figure 8-7. Before this, you have to add the following listener contents into $ORACLE_HOME/network/admin/listener.ora:

```
[oracle@ORA-U1 admin]$ cat listener.ora
SID_LIST_LISTENER_12c =
  (SID_LIST =
    (SID_DESC =
      (GLOBAL_DBNAME = ORC1)
      (ORACLE_HOME = /u01/app/oracle/product/12.1.0/dbhome_1)
      (SID_NAME = ORC1)
    )
  )
LISTENER_12c =
  (DESCRIPTION =
    (ADDRESS = (PROTOCOL = TCP)(HOST = 192.168.0.110)(PORT = 1521))
  )
ADR_BASE_LISTENER = /u01/app/oracle
[oracle@ORA-U1 admin]$
```

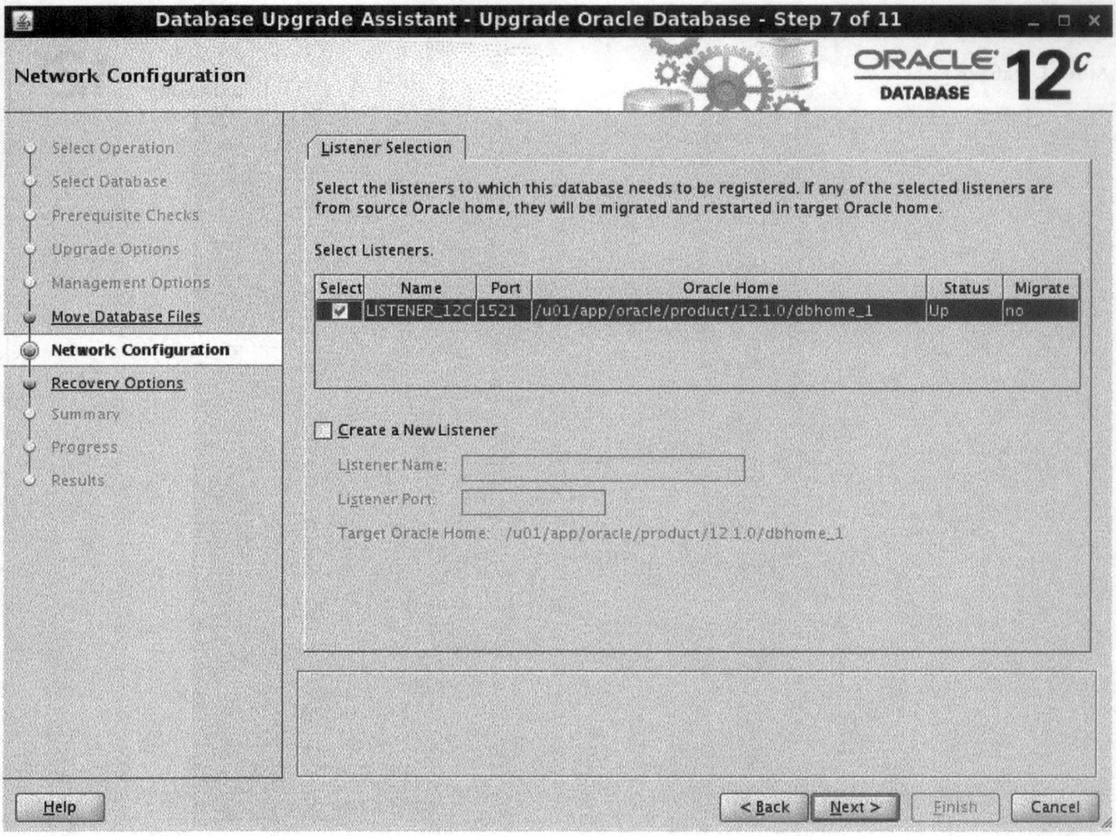

Figure 8-7. *Caption here*

The next screen allows you to configure the RMAN backup strategy. If you want to set up your RMAN backup, then select the appropriate option, as shown in Figure 8-8.

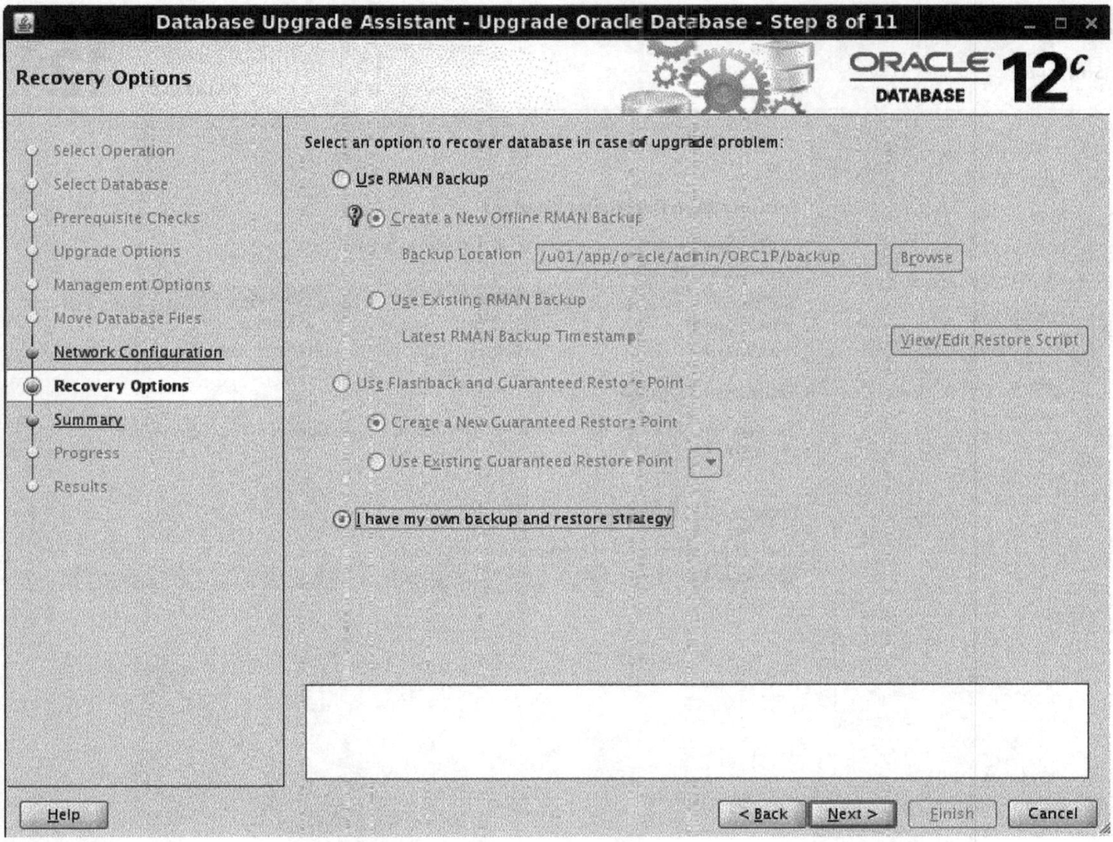

Figure 8-8. *Caption here*

Now you are at the final steps to check the overall summary of the upgrade configuration and the various options you selected as part of the upgrade. If the summary is not as expected, then at any time you can go back and change the options accordingly, as shown in Figure 8-9.

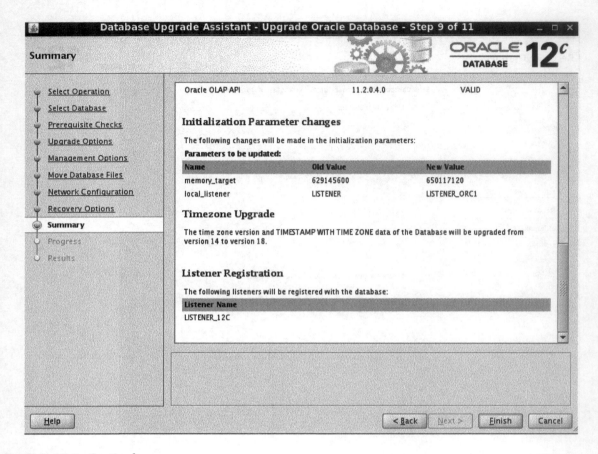

Figure 8-9. *Caption here*

As soon as you click Finish, you can relax until the upgrade completes successfully or fails, as shown in Figure 8-10.

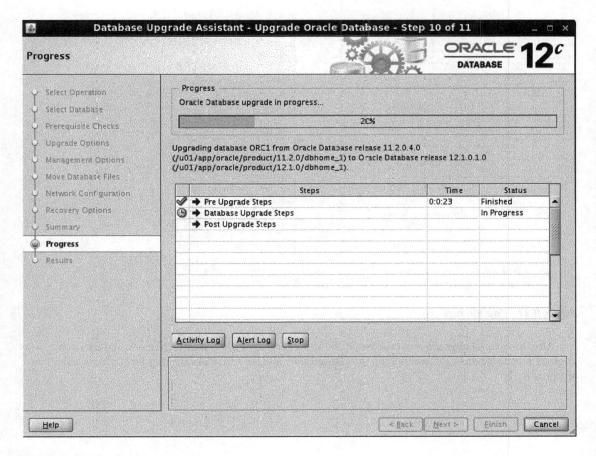

Figure 8-10. *Caption here*

Considering you already learned in the earlier chapters about the changes in the 12c upgrade options, the DBUA provides a great advantage because it tracks the alert logs or upgrade logs in one place in GUI mode, as shown in Figure 8-11.

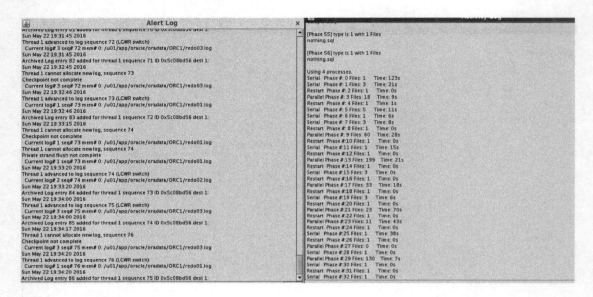

Figure 8-11. *Caption here*

After the overall upgrade is completed, it will show a status of 100 percent. Then you can check the upgrade results for more information on the elapsed time and the status of each upgrade process, as shown in Figure 8-12.

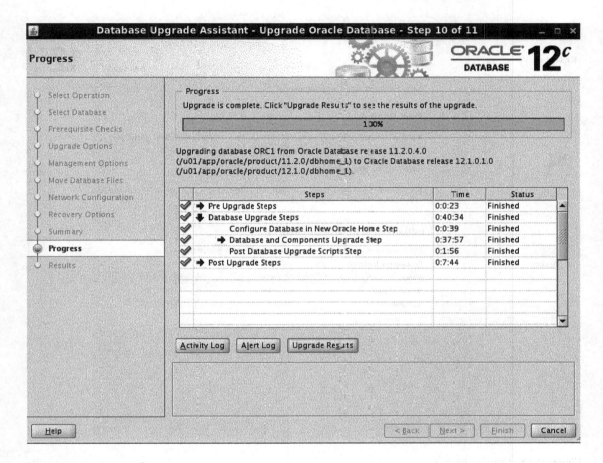

Figure 8-12. *Caption here*

In the overall results of upgrade, please carefully read the changes that have been made, as shown in Figure 8-13.

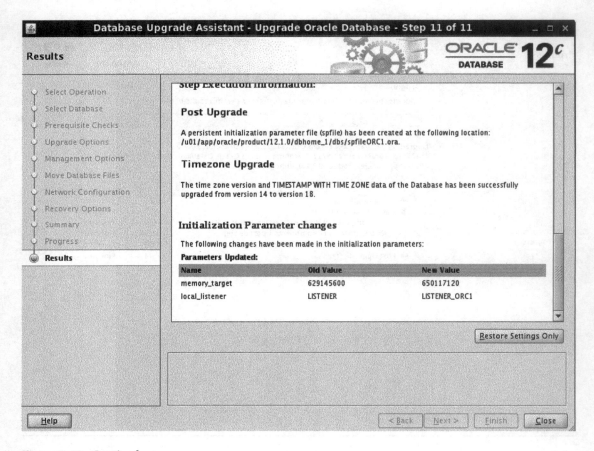

Figure 8-13. *Caption here*

As you can see in Figure 8-13, the actual listener you set is LISTENER_12c, but local_listener was modified to LISTENER_ORC1. If you prefer to change this, you can do so at any time. There's no need to worry because the DBUA can also update the tnsnames.ora file with new entries.

```
LISTENER_ORC1 =
  (ADDRESS = (PROTOCOL = TCP)(HOST = 192.168.0.110)(PORT = 1521))
```

Now you can safely close the DBUA and proceed to wrap up the final steps and sync the standby with the primary.

■ **Tip**　In this example we encountered a bug while running prerequisite checks. The process hangs at 0 percent and runs forever because of a few errors in the upgrade trace logs such as DatabaseQueryManager. getHost:200. This has been identified as bug 22858130. This issue is actually fixed in 12.2, and there is a workaround to download and copy the latest versions of the files rconfig.jar and assistantsCommon.jar into $ORACLE_HOME/assistants/jlib/.

Post-upgrade Tasks

Before proceeding with the post-upgrade tasks, you need to cross-check the primary database environment and gather statistics from the database.

1. Check the registry components' status.

    ```
    SQL> select comp_name,version,status from dba_registry;

    COMP_NAME                             VERSION         STATUS
    ------------------------------------- --------------- -----------
    Oracle Application Express            4.2.0.00.27     VALID
    OWB                                   11.2.0.4.0      VALID
    Spatial                               12.1.0.1.0      VALID
    Oracle Multimedia                     12.1.0.1.0      VALID
    Oracle XML Database                   12.1.0.1.0      VALID
    Oracle Text                           12.1.0.1.0      VALID
    Oracle Workspace Manager              12.1.0.1.0      VALID
    Oracle Database Catalog Views         12.1.0.1.0      VALID
    Oracle Database Packages and Types    12.1.0.1.0      VALID
    JServer JAVA Virtual Machine          12.1.0.1.0      VALID
    Oracle XDK                            12.1.0.1.0      VALID
    Oracle Database Java Packages         12.1.0.1.0      VALID
    OLAP Analytic Workspace               12.1.0.1.0      VALID
    Oracle OLAP API                       12.1.0.1.0      VALID

    14 rows selected.
    ```

2. Check for invalid objects.

    ```
    SQL> select object_type,count(*) from dba_objects where status='INVALID'
    group by object_type;

    no rows selected
    ```

3. Perform the gather dictionary statistics process after the upgrade.

    ```
    SQL> EXECUTE dbms_stats.gather_dictionary_stats;

    PL/SQL procedure successfully completed.

    Elapsed: 00:01:17.11
    ```

4. Run the post-upgrade fix script.

    ```
    SQL> @/u01/app/oracle/cfgtoollogs/ORC1P/preupgrade/postupgrade_fixups.sql
    Post Upgrade Fixup Script Generated on 2016-05-22 12:53:38
    Version: 12.1.0.1 Build: 006
    Beginning Post-Upgrade Fixups...

    PL/SQL procedure successfully completed.
    ```

```
Elapsed: 00:00:00.01

PL/SQL procedure successfully completed.

Elapsed: 00:00:01.56

**********************************************************************
Check Tag:     INVALID_OBJECTS_EXIST
Check Summary: Check for invalid objects
Fix Summary:   Invalid objects are displayed and must be reviewed.
**********************************************************************
Fixup Returned Information:
WARNING: --> Database contains INVALID objects prior to upgrade

    The list of invalid SYS/SYSTEM objects was written to
    registry$sys_inv_objs.
    The list of non-SYS/SYSTEM objects was written to
    registry$nonsys_inv_objs unless there were over 5000.
    Use utluiobj.sql after the upgrade to identify any new invalid
    objects due to the upgrade.
**********************************************************************

PL/SQL procedure successfully completed.

Elapsed: 00:00:00.01

**********************************************************************
Check Tag:     OLD_TIME_ZONES_EXIST
Check Summary: Check for use of older timezone data file
Fix Summary:   Update the timezone using the DBMS_DST package after upgrade is
complete.
**********************************************************************
Fixup Returned Information:
INFORMATION: --> Older Timezone in use

    Database is using a time zone file older than version 18.
    After the upgrade, it is recommended that DBMS_DST package
    be used to upgrade the 12.1.0.1.0 database time zone version
    to the latest version which comes with the new release.
    Please refer to My Oracle Support note number 977512.1 for details.
**********************************************************************

PL/SQL procedure successfully completed.

Elapsed: 00:00:00.00
**********************************************************************
                    [Post-Upgrade Recommendations]
**********************************************************************

PL/SQL procedure successfully completed.
```

```
Elapsed: 00:00:00.00
                *******************************************
                ******** Fixed Object Statistics ********
                *******************************************

Please create stats on fixed objects two weeks
after the upgrade using the command:
    EXECUTE DBMS_STATS.GATHER_FIXED_OBJECTS_STATS;

^^^ MANUAL ACTION SUGGESTED ^^^

PL/SQL procedure successfully completed.

Elapsed: 00:00:00.00

            ****************************************************
            ************* Fixup Summary *************

 2 fixup routines generated INFORMATIONAL messages that should be reviewed.

PL/SQL procedure successfully completed.

Elapsed: 00:00:00.00
*************** Post Upgrade Fixup Script Complete ********************

PL/SQL procedure successfully completed.

Elapsed: 00:00:00.00
```

5. Check the time zone file version. You have opted to update the time zone file
    version from the DBUA. This can be done even in the manual method using MOS
    Note 977512.1.

    ```
    SQL> select * from v$timezone_file;

    FILENAME               VERSION     CON_ID
    -------------------- ---------- ----------
    timezlrg_18.dat             18          0
    ```

6. The standby database already has been mounted. Now you will start the MRP.
    Please note that the Data Guard Broker will be enabled after the complete sync
    between the primary and standby databases.

    ```
    SQL> alter database recover managed standby database disconnect from session;

    Database altered.
    ```

7. Enable the redo transport from the primary database.

    ```
    SQL> alter system set log_archive_dest_state_2='enable' scope=both;

    System altered.
    ```

8. You started MRP on the standby and also enabled redo transport. After that, the archives started receiving the standby database and applied everything as per the alert log of the standby database.

9. When the recovery is in progress, internally the standby is upgrading with the archives generated by the primary upgrade.

    ```
    Mon May 23 05:28:06 2016
    Media Recovery Log /u01/app/oracle/fast_recovery_area/ORC1S/
    archivelog/2016_05_23/o1_mf_1_161_cn3twscv_.arc
    Mon May 23 05:28:07 2016
    Media Recovery Log /u01/app/oracle/fast_recovery_area/ORC1S/
    archivelog/2016_05_23/o1_mf_1_162_cn3twsy3_.arc
    Mon May 23 05:28:09 2016
    Media Recovery Log /u01/app/oracle/fast_recovery_area/ORC1S/
    archivelog/2016_05_23/o1_mf_1_163_cn3twsxs_.arc
    Mon May 23 05:28:11 2016
    Media Recovery Log /u01/app/oracle/fast_recovery_area/ORC1S/
    archivelog/2016_05_23/o1_mf_1_164_cn3twvws_.arc
    Mon May 23 05:28:13 2016
    Media Recovery Log /u01/app/oracle/fast_recovery_area/ORC1S/
    archivelog/2016_05_23/o1_mf_1_165_cn3twwwg_.arc
    Mon May 23 05:28:13 2016
    Media Recovery Log /u01/app/oracle/fast_recovery_area/ORC1S/
    archivelog/2016_05_23/o1_mf_1_166_cn3ttnp9_.arc
    Media Recovery Waiting for thread 1 sequence 167
    Mon May 23 05:30:53 2016
    RFS[7]: Assigned to RFS process (PID:5787)
    RFS[7]: Selected log 4 for thread 1 sequence 167 dbid 1544101206 branch 912228376
    Mon May 23 05:30:53 2016
    Archived Log entry 144 added for thread 1 sequence 167 ID 0x5c08bd56 dest 1:
    Mon May 23 05:30:53 2016
    Media Recovery Log /u01/app/oracle/fast_recovery_area/ORC1S/
    archivelog/2016_05_23/o1_mf_1_167_cn3v6fow_.arc
    Media Recovery Waiting for thread 1 sequence 168
    Mon May 23 05:35:53 2016
    Primary database is in MAXIMUM PERFORMANCE mode
    RFS[8]: Assigned to RFS process (PID:5799)
    RFS[8]: Selected log 4 for thread 1 sequence 168 dbid 1544101206 branch 912228376
    Mon May 23 05:35:54 2016
    Recovery of Online Redo Log: Thread 1 Group 4 Seq 168 Reading mem 0
      Mem# 0: /u01/app/oracle/fast_recovery_area/ORC1S/onlinelog/o1_mf_4_cn206368_.log
    ```

10. Now you will enable the Data Guard Broker from both the primary and standby databases.

```
SQL> alter system set dg_broker_start=true scope=both;

System altered.

DGMGRL> show configuration

Configuration - upgha

  Protection Mode: MaxPerformance
  Databases:
  orc1p - Primary database
    orc1s - Physical standby database

Fast-Start Failover: DISABLED

Configuration Status:
SUCCESS

DGMGRL> show database orc1s

Database - orc1s

  Role:               PHYSICAL STANDBY
  Intended State:     APPLY-ON
  Transport Lag:      0 seconds (computed 1 second ago)
  Apply Lag:          0 seconds (computed 1 second ago)
  Apply Rate:         14.95 MByte/s
  Real Time Query:    OFF
  Instance(s):
    ORC1

Database Status:
SUCCESS
```

From the previous output, you can see that the standby is completely synced with the primary database.

11. Verify the standby database registry components' status.

```
SQL> alter database open read only;

Database altered.

SQL> select comp_name,version,status from dba_registry;
```

```
COMP_NAME                              VERSION          STATUS
-----------------------------------    ---------------  -----------
Oracle Application Express             4.2.0.00.27      VALID
OWB                                    11.2.0.4.0       VALID
Spatial                                12.1.0.1.0       VALID
Oracle Multimedia                      12.1.0.1.0       VALID
Oracle XML Database                    12.1.0.1.0       VALID
Oracle Text                            12.1.0.1.0       VALID
Oracle Workspace Manager               12.1.0.1.0       VALID
Oracle Database Catalog Views          12.1.0.1.0       VALID
Oracle Database Packages and Types     12.1.0.1.0       VALID
JServer JAVA Virtual Machine           12.1.0.1.0       VALID
Oracle XDK                             12.1.0.1.0       VALID
Oracle Database Java Packages          12.1.0.1.0       VALID
OLAP Analytic Workspace                12.1.0.1.0       VALID
Oracle OLAP API                        12.1.0.1.0       VALID

14 rows selected.
```

Summary

You saw how to upgrade a Data Guard environment from 11.2.0.4 to 12.1.0.1 using the traditional method with step-by-step executions including images. You also got a few tips about the process. Please note that the upgrade process was not divided into two for the primary and standby databases, because a few steps need to be performed in parallel.

Rolling Database Upgrades Using DBMS_ROLLING in 12*c*

In the previous upgrade section, you used the traditional method to upgrade the Data Guard environment. After the traditional method, a few advanced methods were introduced by Oracle, namely, rolling upgrades in 11*g* and rolling upgrades using DBMS_ROLLING in 12*c*. These two techniques do the same job; the main difference is that it's simplified in 12*c*. Before moving forward to the 12*c* method, you will see a comparison between rolling upgrades in 11*g* and the DBMS_ROLLING method in 12*c*.

Rolling Upgrades in 11*g* vs. DBMS_ROLLING in 12*c*

The rolling upgrade of the 11*g* method provides minimal downtime, but many manual steps are involved, and you have to perform these operations from both sites. For example, if there is more than one standby databases as part of the configuration, then the process is more complex for sure. Overall, there are 41 steps involved to do rolling upgrades; the following are a few of the high-level steps:

1. Disable Broker.

2. Create a guaranteed restore point on the primary and the standby.

3. Convert the standby to a transient logical standby.

4. Create a second guaranteed restore point.

5. Upgrade the transient logical standby.

6. Switch to the primary.

7. Flash back the original primary.

8. Mount the primary from the new home and convert it to a physical standby.

9. Start the switchover on the primary.

10. Complete the switchover on the standby.

11. Restart the old primary as the standby.

12. Drop the restore points.

This is going to be hectic upgrade with a lot of maintenance window time, and the DBA should be involved the entire time.

Because 12c has a similar architecture, Oracle introduced the DBMS_ROLLING technique in 12c under the active Data Guard feature. This technique is straightforward and can be finished with five to six steps after proper planning. Even though you have many databases as part of the configuration, you can easily classify them, and accordingly the upgrade can be performed with minimal downtime.

DBMS_ROLLING: 12c

Today you are looking for the best upgrade methods to provide a quick upgrade that is safe, less complex, and straightforward. Since Oracle 12c there is a new method to upgrade the Data Guard environment with minimal downtime. This method can be used from 12.1.0.1 and higher and is not available in 11g. In this section, the example is using DBMS_ROLLING to upgrade from 12.1.0.1 to 12.1.0.2.

As discussed earlier, this method works the same as the traditional rolling upgrade, but it has been automated with the PL/SQL packages of DBMS_ROLLING so that you can complete the whole upgrade process in five to six steps. Sometimes it's hard to track the process of an upgrade, but in this method, the plan shows each step where exactly it is running and what the status is, with various views related to DBMS_ROLLING.

DBMS_ROLLING is a smart method to use. It designates the databases and assigns roles internally to ensure the upgrade procedure is smooth. For example, if you have one primary database, two physical standby databases, and one logical standby database in a single Data Guard configuration, it is challenging to manage the upgrade. But you can let DBMS_ROLLING categorize the roles.

For example, let's say your West site has two physical standby databases, and your East site has two primary databases, one physical database, and one logical standby database. For better understanding, Figure 8-14 shows a high-level view of how the databases will be named internally with DBMS_ROLLING.

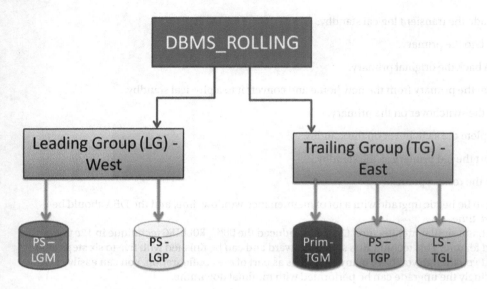

Figure 8-14. *Caption here*

It is crucial to understand what the roles are prior to the upgrade. The nearest physical standby database is always considered the leading group master because you are going to upgrade the physical standby database when it is converted to a logical standby database. The actual primary is considered the trailing group master, and hence it falls under the trailing group as you are going to perform the upgrade after the standby database. If any additional databases are in the configuration, then you consider them as the leading group physical or leading group logical. The thumb rule is that you should not include the logical standby in the leading group.

Here are what the abbreviations in Figure 8-14 mean:

Leading group (LG)

- Leading group master (LGM)

- Leading group physical (LGP) standby

Trailing group (TG)

- Trailing group master (TGM)

- Trailing group physical (TGP) standby database

- Trailing group logical (TGL) standby database

Now let's move to the practice of DBMS_ROLLING. In this Data Guard setup, you have the primary database (NYDB) and only one physical standby database (INDDB), so simply you can consider as leading group master and trailing group master as you don't have any more databases in the configuration.

1. Initialize the upgrade from the standby database.

    In this initial step you are going to inform DBMS_ROLLING that the leading group master/future primary will be the physical standby database.

    ```
    SQL> select db_unique_name,database_role from v$database;
    ```

```
DB_UNIQUE_NAME                      DATABASE_ROLE
------------------------------ ----------------
inddb                              PHYSICAL STANDBY

SQL> exec dbms_rolling.init_plan('inddb');

PL/SQL procedure successfully completed.

SQL> select revision,status,phase,future_primary,init_time from dba_rolling_
status;

  REVISION STATUS        PHASE          FUTURE_PRIMARY        INIT_TIME
---------- ------------ -------------- -------------------- ----------------------
---------
         O READY         BUILD PENDING  incdb                 17-JUN-16
01.22.53.558327 PM

SQL> select * from dba_rolling_parameters where scope is not null;

SCOPE      TYPE    NAME                           DESCRIPTION
CURVAL     LSTVAL  DEFVAL         MINVAL          MAXVAL
---------- ------- ------------------------------ -----------------------------
------ ---------- ---------- ---------- -------------- --------------
inddb      USER    INVOLVEMENT                    Involvement level
FULL               FULL
inddb      USER    MEMBER                         Group to which the database
is a me TRAILING               TRAILING
                                                  mber

nydb       USER    INVOLVEMENT                    Involvement level
FULL               FULL
nydb       USER    MEMBER                         Group to which the database
is a me NONE                   NONE
                                                  mber
```

In this upgrade process, you can track DBA_ROLLING_DATABASES in a single view called DBA_ROLLING_STATUS, and also there are various other views related to DBMS_ROLLING, such as DBA_ROLLING_EVENTS and so on.

2. Change the upgrade parameter values.

This step helps you to change any parameters related to the upgrade, such as changing the values for parameters such as SWITCH_LGM_LAG_TIME, SWITCH_LGM_LAG_WAIT, ACTIVE_SESSIONS_TIMEOUT, and so on.

```
SQL> exec dbms_rolling.set_parameter(name=> 'ACTIVE_SESSIONS_TIMEOUT', value =>
2000);

PL/SQL procedure successfully completed.
SQL> select scope, name, curval from dba_rolling_parameters where name='ACTIVE_
SESSIONS_TIMEOUT';
```

```
SCOPE       NAME                            CURVAL
----------  ------------------------------  ----------
            ACTIVE_SESSIONS_TIMEOUT         2000
```

3. Build the upgrade plan.

   This step is the crucial one in designing the upgrade plan; it lists all the steps
   to be performed in the primary and standby databases in ordered format and
   populates the view DBA_ROLLING_PLAN. To execute this step, the standby database
   should be in MOUNT status.

   ```
   SQL> exec dbms_rolling.build_plan;

   PL/SQL procedure successfully completed.

   SQL> select revision, status, phase from dba_rolling_status;

      REVISION STATUS        PHASE
   ---------- ------------- ---------------
            1 READY         START PENDING

   SQL> select dbun,role,open_mode,engine_status,update_progress from dba_rolling_
   databases;

   DBUN        ROLE      OPEN_MODE        ENGINE_STATUS   UPDATE_PROG
   ----------  --------  ---------------  --------------- -----------
   nydb        PRIMARY   OPEN READ WRITE  NOT APPLICABLE  NOT STARTED
   inddb       PHYSICAL  MOUNTED          STOPPED         NOT STARTED
   ```

   Now you can see the detailed plan from DBA_ROLLING_PLAN, which gives all the
   information related to all the stages including the current status, as shown in
   Figure 8-15.

```
SQL> ;
  1* select instid,source,target,phase,status,progress,description from dba_rolling_plan
SQL> /

  INSTID SOURCE    TARGET    PHASE     STATUS   PROGRESS  DESCRIPTION
-------- --------- --------- --------- -------- --------- -------------------------------------------------
       1 nydb      nydb      START     PENDING  PENDING   Verify database is a primary
       2 nydb      nydb      START     PENDING  PENDING   Verify MAXIMUM PROTECTION is disabled
       3 nydb      inddb     START     PENDING  PENDING   Verify database is a physical standby
       4 nydb      inddb     START     PENDING  PENDING   Verify physical standby is mounted
       5 nydb      nydb      START     PENDING  PENDING   Verify server parameter file exists and is modifiable
       6 nydb      inddb     START     PENDING  PENDING   Verify server parameter file exists and is modifiable
       7 nydb      nydb      START     PENDING  PENDING   Verify Data Guard Broker configuration is disabled
       8 nydb      inddb     START     PENDING  PENDING   Verify Data Guard Broker configuration is disabled
       9 nydb      nydb      START     PENDING  PENDING   Verify flashback database is enabled
      10 nydb      nydb      START     PENDING  PENDING   Verify available flashback restore points
      11 nydb      inddb     START     PENDING  PENDING   Verify flashback database is enabled
      12 nydb      inddb     START     PENDING  PENDING   Verify available flashback restore points
      13 nydb      inddb     START     PENDING  PENDING   Stop media recovery
      14 nydb      inddb     START     PENDING  PENDING   Drop guaranteed restore point DBMSRU_INITIAL
      15 nydb      inddb     START     PENDING  PENDING   Create guaranteed restore point DBMSRU_INITIAL
      16 nydb      nydb      START     PENDING  PENDING   Drop guaranteed restore point DBMSRU_INITIAL
      17 nydb      nydb      START     PENDING  PENDING   Create guaranteed restore point DBMSRU_INITIAL
      18 nydb      inddb     START     PENDING  PENDING   Start media recovery
      19 nydb      inddb     START     PENDING  PENDING   Verify media recovery is running
      20 nydb      nydb      START     PENDING  PENDING   Verify user_dump_dest has been specified
      21 nydb      nydb      START     PENDING  PENDING   Backup control file to rolling_change_backup.f
      22 nydb      inddb     START     PENDING  PENDING   Verify user_dump_dest has been specified
      23 nydb      inddb     START     PENDING  PENDING   Backup control file to rolling_change_backup.f
      24 nydb      nydb      START     PENDING  PENDING   Get current redo branch of the primary database
      25 nydb      inddb     START     PENDING  PENDING   Wait until recovery is active on the primary's redo branch
      26 nydb      inddb     START     PENDING  PENDING   Stop media recovery
      27 nydb      nydb      START     PENDING  PENDING   Execute dbms_logstdby.build
      28 nydb      inddb     START     PENDING  PENDING   Convert into a transient logical standby
      29 nydb      inddb     START     PENDING  PENDING   Open database
      30 nydb      inddb     START     PENDING  PENDING   Configure logical standby parameters
      31 nydb      inddb     START     PENDING  PENDING   Start logical standby apply
      32 nydb      inddb     START     PENDING  PENDING   Get redo branch of transient logical standby
      33 nydb      inddb     START     PENDING  PENDING   Get reset scn of transient logical redo branch
      34 nydb      inddb     START     PENDING  PENDING   Enable compatibility advance despite presence of GRPs
      35 nydb      nydb      START     PENDING  PENDING   Log pre-switchover instructions to events table
      36 nydb      inddb     START     PENDING  PENDING   Record start of user upgrade of inddb
      37 nydb      inddb     SWITCH    PENDING  PENDING   Verify database is in OPENRW mode
      38 nydb      inddb     SWITCH    PENDING  PENDING   Record completion of user upgrade of inddb
      39 nydb      inddb     SWITCH    PENDING  PENDING   Scan LADs for presence of nydb destination
      40 nydb      inddb     SWITCH    PENDING  PENDING   Test if nydb is reachable using configured TNS service
      41 nydb      nydb      SWITCH    PENDING  PENDING   Enable log file archival to inddb
      42 nydb      inddb     SWITCH    PENDING  PENDING   Start logical standby apply
      43 nydb      inddb     SWITCH    PENDING  PENDING   Wait until apply lag has fallen below 600 seconds
      44 nydb      nydb      SWITCH    PENDING  PENDING   Log post-switchover instructions to events table
      45 nydb      nydb      SWITCH    PENDING  PENDING   Switch database to a logical standby
      46 nydb      inddb     SWITCH    PENDING  PENDING   Wait until end-of-redo has been applied
      47 nydb      inddb     SWITCH    PENDING  PENDING   Switch database to a primary
      48 nydb      nydb      SWITCH    PENDING  PENDING   Enable compatibility advance despite presence of GRPs
      49 nydb      nydb      SWITCH    PENDING  PENDING   Synchronize plan with new primary
      50 inddb     nydb      FINISH    PENDING  PENDING   Verify only a single instance is active
      51 inddb     nydb      FINISH    PENDING  PENDING   Verify database is mounted
      52 inddb     nydb      FINISH    PENDING  PENDING   Flashback database
      53 inddb     nydb      FINISH    PENDING  PENDING   Convert into a physical standby
      54 inddb     inddb     FINISH    PENDING  PENDING   Verify database is open
      55 inddb     inddb     FINISH    PENDING  PENDING   Save the DBID of the new primary
      56 inddb     inddb     FINISH    PENDING  PENDING   Save the logminer session start scn
      57 inddb     nydb      FINISH    PENDING  PENDING   Wait until transient logical redo branch has been registered
      58 inddb     nydb      FINISH    PENDING  PENDING   Start media recovery
      59 inddb     nydb      FINISH    PENDING  PENDING   Wait until apply/recovery has started on the transient branch
      60 inddb     nydb      FINISH    PENDING  PENDING   Wait until upgrade redo has been fully recovered
      61 inddb     nydb      FINISH    PENDING  PENDING   Prevent compatibility advance if GRPs are present
      62 inddb     inddb     FINISH    PENDING  PENDING   Prevent compatibility advance if GRPs are present
      63 inddb     nydb      FINISH    PENDING  PENDING   Drop guaranteed restore point DBMSRU_INITIAL
      64 inddb     inddb     FINISH    PENDING  PENDING   Drop guaranteed restore point DBMSRU_INITIAL

64 rows selected.
```

Figure 8-15. *Caption here*

4. Complete the verify steps.

   Based on this upgrade plan, you have to complete a few initial verify steps, such
   as ensuring that instances are using the spfile, enabling flashback, and building
   the log miner dictionary for the logical standby database. There is no risk
   because all the steps are already in the plan for what to do.

```
SQL> select db_unique_name,database_role from v$database;

DB_UNIQUE_NAME                  DATABASE_ROLE
------------------------------- ----------------
nydb                            PRIMARY

SQL> select db_unique_name,database_role,protection_mode,open_mode from
v$database;

DB_UNIQUE_NAME                  DATABASE_ROLE    PROTECTION_MODE      OPEN_MODE
------------------------------- ---------------- -------------------- ------------
--------
inddb                           PHYSICAL STANDBY MAXIMUM PERFORMANCE  MOUNTED

SQL> show parameter spfile

NAME                                 TYPE        VALUE
------------------------------------ ----------- -------------------------------
spfile                               string      /u01/app/oracle/product/12.1.0
                                                 /dbhome_1/dbs/spfileadbp.ora

SQL> show parameter spfile

NAME                                 TYPE        VALUE
------------------------------------ ----------- -------------------------------
spfile                               string      /u01/app/oracle/product/12.1.0
                                                 /dbhome_1/dbs/spfileadbs.ora
DGMGRL> disable configuration
Disabled.
DGMGRL> show configuration

Configuration - apha

  Protection Mode: MaxPerformance
  Databases:
  nydb  - Primary database
    inddb - Physical standby database

Fast-Start Failover: DISABLED

Configuration Status:
DISABLED

SQL> select flashback_on from v$database;

FLASHBACK_ON
-------------------
NO

SQL> alter database flashback on;

Database altered.
```

```
SQL>
SQL> select flashback_on,database_role from v$database;

FLASHBACK_ON        DATABASE_ROLE
------------------  ----------------
NO                  PHYSICAL STANDBY

SQL> alter database flashback on;

Database altered.

From primary database perform below steps

SQL> alter pluggable database all open;

Pluggable database altered.

SQL> Execute dbms_logstdby.build

PL/SQL procedure successfully completed.
```

Ensure that the standby is completely in sync with the primary database after all the changes.

5. Perform the upgrade.

   a. Start the plan.

   This step basically allows you to upgrade the leading group master, which means DBMS_ROLLING converts the physical standby database to a logical standby database.

   ```
   SQL>  exec dbms_rolling.start_plan();

   PL/SQL procedure successfully completed.

   SQL> select revision, status, phase from dba_rolling_status;

      REVISION STATUS       PHASE
   ---------- ------------ ---------------
            1 READY        SWITCH PENDING

   SQL> select dbun, role, engine_status,update_progress from dba_rolling_
   databases;

   DBUN       ROLE     ENGINE_STATUS   UPDATE_PROG
   ---------- -------- --------------- -----------
   nydb       PRIMARY  NOT APPLICABLE  NOT STARTED
   inddb      LOGICAL  RUNNING         NOT STARTED
   ```

```
SQL> select database_role from v$database;

DATABASE_ROLE
----------------
LOGICAL STANDBY
```

After this step is completed, you can proceed with upgrading the logical standby. As you will see next, that database role has changed.

a.   Run the pre-upgrade script.

Here you will perform a manual upgrade and do all the steps already discussed in earlier chapters.

```
[oracle@ORA-U1 ~]$ cd /u01/app/oracle/product/12.1.0.2/dbhome_1/rdbms/admin/
SQL> @preupgrd.sql
SQL> @preupgrd.sql

Loading Pre-Upgrade Package...

*************************************************************************
Executing Pre-Upgrade Checks in CDB$ROOT...
*************************************************************************


            *************************************************************

                   ====>> ERRORS FOUND for CDB$ROOT <<====

     The following are *** ERROR LEVEL CONDITIONS *** that must be addressed
                      prior to attempting your upgrade.
                 Failure to do so will result in a failed upgrade.


     1) Check Tag:    FILES_NEED_RECOVERY
        Check Summary: Check for any pending file recoveries
        Fixup Summary:
        "Recover or repair these files prior to upgrade."
        +++ Source Database Manual Action Required +++


                 You MUST resolve the above error prior to upgrade

            *************************************************************

            *************************************************************


                  ====>> PRE-UPGRADE RESULTS for CDB$ROOT <<====

ACTIONS REQUIRED:

1. Review results of the pre-upgrade checks:
 /u01/app/oracle/cfgtoollogs/inddb/preupgrade/preupgrade.log
```

2. Execute in the SOURCE environment BEFORE upgrade:
/u01/app/oracle/cfgtoollogs/inddb/preupgrade/preupgrade_fixups.sql

3. Execute in the NEW environment AFTER upgrade:
/u01/app/oracle/cfgtoollogs/inddb/preupgrade/postupgrade_fixups.sql

```
**************************************************************


**********************************************************************************
Pre-Upgrade Checks in CDB$ROOT Completed.
**********************************************************************************


**********************************************************************************
**********************************************************************************
SQL>
```

b. Check the log file of the pre-upgrade script, run the actions to be performed manually, and run the fixup script of the pre-upgrade.

c. Copy the spfile, password file, and network files to the new Oracle Home of 12.1.0.2.

d. Start the logical standby database in upgrade mode.

```
[oracle@ORA-U1 admin]$ sqlplus / as sysdba

SQL*Plus: Release 12.1.0.2.0 Production on Sun Jun 5 17:11:18 2016

Copyright (c) 1982, 2014, Oracle.  All rights reserved.

Connected to an idle instance.

SQL> startup mount
ORACLE instance started.

Total System Global Area  683671552 bytes
Fixed Size                  2928152 bytes
Variable Size             549454312 bytes
Database Buffers          125829120 bytes
Redo Buffers                5459968 bytes
Database mounted.
SQL>

SQL> alter database open upgrade;

Database altered.

SQL> alter pluggable database all open upgrade;

Pluggable database altered.
```

e. Run the upgrade using the catctl.pl script.

```
[oracle@ORA-U1 admin]$ cd /u01/app/oracle/product/12.1.0.2/dbhome_1/rdbms/
admin/
[oracle@ORA-U1 admin]$ /u01/app/oracle/product/12.1.0.2/dbhome_1/perl/bin/
perl catctl.pl -n 5 catupgrd.sql

Argument list for [catctl.pl]
SQL Process Count        n = 5
SQL PDB Process Count    N = 0
Input Directory          d = 0
Phase Logging Table      t = 0
Log Dir                  l = 0
Script                   s = 0
Serial Run               S = 0
Upgrade Mode active      M = 0
Start Phase              p = 0
End Phase                P = 0
Log Id                   i = 0
Run in                   c = 0
Do not run in            C = 0
Echo OFF                 e = 1
No Post Upgrade          x = 0
Reverse Order            r = 0
Open Mode Normal         o = 0
Debug catcon.pm          z = 0
Debug catctl.pl          Z = 0
Display Phases           y = 0
Child Process            I = 0

catctl.pl version: 12.1.0.2.0
Oracle Base            = /u01/app/oracle

Analyzing file catupgrd.sql
Log files in /u01/app/oracle/product/12.1.0.2/dbhome_1/rdbms/admin
catcon: ALL catcon-related output will be written to catupgrd_catcon_20818.
lst
catcon: See catupgrd*.log files for output generated by scripts
catcon: See catupgrd_*.lst files for spool files, if any
Number of Cpus         = 2
Parallel PDB Upgrades = 2
SQL PDB Process Count = 2
SQL Process Count      = 5

[CONTAINER NAMES]

CDB$ROOT
PDB$SEED
APDB
PDB Inclusion:[PDB$SEED APDB] Exclusion:[]
```

```
-------------------------------------------------------
Phases [0-73]
Container Lists Inclusion:[CDB$ROOT] Exclusion:[]
Serial   Phase #: 0 Files: 1
. . .
. .
.
Upgrade Summary Report Located in:
/u01/app/oracle/product/12.1.0.2/dbhome_1/cfgtoollogs/inddb/upgrade/upg_
summary.                                                log

Total Upgrade Time:          [0d:0h:13m:10s]
returned from sqlpatch
    Time: 5s    PDB$SEED
Serial   Phase #:70 Files: 1    Time: 132s  PDB$SEED
Serial   Phase #:71 Files: 1    Time: 0s    PDB$SEED
Serial   Phase #:72 Files: 1    Time: 4s    PDB$SEED
Serial   Phase #:73 Files: 1    Time: 0s    PDB$SEED

Grand Total Time: 927s PDB$SEED

LOG FILES: (catupgrdpdb_seed*.log)

Upgrade Summary Report Located in:
/u01/app/oracle/product/12.1.0.2/dbhome_1/cfgtoollogs/inddb/upgrade/upg_
summary.                                                log

Total Upgrade Time:          [0d:0h:15m:27s]

    Time: 448s For CDB$ROOT
    Time: 931s For PDB(s)

Grand Total Time: 1379s

LOG FILES: (catupgrd*.log)

Upgrade Summary Report Located in:
/u01/app/oracle/product/12.1.0.2/dbhome_1/cfgtoollogs/inddb/upgrade/upg_
summary.                                                log

Grand Total Upgrade Time:     [0d:0h:22m:59s]
[oracle@ORA-U1 admin]$
```

f. Run the post-upgrade fixup script that is generated at the pre-upgrade
    script.

```
SQL> @ /u01/app/oracle/cfgtoollogs/inddb/preupgrade/postupgrade_fixups.sql
Post Upgrade Fixup Script Generated on 2016-06-05 16:59:02  Version: 12.1.0.2
Build: 006
Beginning Post-Upgrade Fixups...
```

```
**********************************************************************
                    [Post-Upgrade Recommendations]
**********************************************************************

              *******************************************
              ******** Fixed Object Statistics ********
              *******************************************
```

Please create stats on fixed objects two weeks
after the upgrade using the command:
```
   EXECUTE DBMS_STATS.GATHER_FIXED_OBJECTS_STATS;
```

^^^ MANUAL ACTION SUGGESTED ^^^

```
              ****************************************************
              ************** Fixup Summary ***********
```

No fixup routines were executed.

```
              ****************************************************
************** Post Upgrade Fixup Script Complete ********************
```

PL/SQL procedure successfully completed.

g. Run the utlrp.sql script to validate the objects.

```
SQL> @?/rdbms/admin/utlrp.sql


TIMESTAMP
--------------------------------COMP_TIMESTAMP UTLRP_BGN  2016-06-06 08:27:11
. . .
 . .
.
...Database user "SYS", database schema "APEX_040200", user# "98" 08:27:42
...Compiled 0 out of 3014 objects considered, 0 failed compilation 08:27:43
...271 packages
...263 package bodies
...452 tables
...11 functions
...16 procedures
...3 sequences
...457 triggers
...1320 indexes
...211 views
...0 libraries
...6 types
...0 type bodies
...0 operators
...0 index types
...Begin key object existence check 08:27:43
```

```
...Completed key object existence check 08:27:43
...Setting DBMS Registry 08:27:43
...Setting DBMS Registry Complete 08:27:43
...Exiting validate 08:27:43

PL/SQL procedure successfully completed.

Check the registry components are in Valid status or not.
SQL> select comp_name,version,status from dba_registry;

COMP_NAME                          VERSION
STATUS
--------------------------------   ----------------------   -----------
Oracle Database Vault              12.1.0.2.0               VALID
Oracle Application Express         4.2.5.00.08              VALID
Oracle Label Security              12.1.0.2.0               VALID
Spatial                            12.1.0.2.0               VALID
Oracle Multimedia                  12.1.0.2.0               VALID
Oracle Text                        12.1.0.2.0               VALID
Oracle Workspace Manager           12.1.0.2.0               VALID
Oracle XML Database                12.1.0.2.0               VALID
Oracle Database Catalog Views      12.1.0.2.0               VALID
Oracle Database Packages and Types 12.1.0.2.0               VALID
JServer JAVA Virtual Machine       12.1.0.2.0               VALID
Oracle XDK                         12.1.0.2.0               VALID
Oracle Database Java Packages      12.1.0.2.0               VALID
OLAP Analytic Workspace            12.1.0.2.0               VALID
Oracle OLAP API                    12.1.0.2.0               VALID
Oracle Real Application Clusters   12.1.0.2.0
OPTION OFF

16 rows selected.
```

After the upgrade completes, ensure the logical standby is in sync with the primary database. Once the standby is in sync, then you can proceed with the next steps.

■ **Tip** In most cases, there will be no redo transport configured from the standby to the primary. To perform the switchover, there should be a two-way redo transport that you have to configure.

---

6. Switch the roles.

   Execute the switchover step from the logical standby database after checking that the redo transport is configured. In this step, there could be reason to fail the statement, but actually the switchover succeeds. This is because of the synchronization problem between the primary and logical standby databases.

   ```
   SQL> select database_role from v$database;

   DATABASE_ROLE
   ```

```
----------------
LOGICAL STANDBY

SQL> execute dbms_rolling.switchover;

PL/SQL procedure successfully completed.

SQL>  select database_role from v$database;

DATABASE_ROLE
----------------
PRIMARY
```

As you can see, the database role was changed successfully with the switchover.

```
SQL> col dbun for a10
SQL> select dbun, role, engine_status,update_progress from dba_rolling_databases;

DBUN        ROLE      ENGINE_STATUS   UPDATE_PROG
----------  --------  --------------  -----------
nydb        LOGICAL   STOPPED         NOT STARTED
inddb       PRIMARY   NOT APPLICABLE  STARTED

SQL>
```

7. Convert from the logical standby database to the physical standby database.

   This step can be considered the final step in the DBMS_ROLLING upgrade procedure; it converts the logical standby database to the physical standby database. This step should be performed after starting the former primary database (logical standby database) from the new Oracle Home 12.1.0.2.

   a. Copy the spfile, password file, and network files to the new 12.1.0.2 home.

   b. Initiate the finish plan.

```
SQL> execute dbms_rolling.finish_plan;

PL/SQL procedure successfully completed.

SQL>
```

Summary

In this chapter, you learned about the various methods available to upgrade your Data Guard environment. You also saw a comparison between the upgrade methods so that you can choose the best method to upgrade with minimal downtime with the advanced features of 12c.

Specifically, we discussed the traditional method upgrade and the DBMS_ROLLING method. We skipped the rolling upgrade, which was introduced in 11g, because this method uses the same technique as DBMS_ROLLING in 12c.

CHAPTER 9

■ ■ ■

Database Upgrades in EBS Environments

Oracle E-Business Suite (EBS) is a rich set of business applications that includes Oracle Financials, supply-chain management, order management, a human resource management system (HRMS), and so on. Many industries are using the E-Business Suite application to manage their day-to-day business. The E-Business Suite application uses Oracle Database as the back end. Its first version was introduced in 1987. Like the database software, Oracle EBS has seen improvements during its journey. Each EBS software version has an interoperability matrix for Oracle Database. In fact, when the EBS software is getting upgraded, then its associated database also might require an upgrade based on the interoperability between the EBS application and the database. Database upgrades in EBS environments require additional steps compared to the normal database upgrade process covered in previous chapters; that's why we're covering it in a separate chapter here. In this chapter, we'll discuss the things that you have to consider when performing an EBS database upgrade, and we'll show its upgrade steps in detail with an example.

Prerequisite Steps

We already discussed the database pre-upgrade checklist in Chapter 2. Those upgrade prerequisite checks are applicable to EBS databases also. This means all database components should be in a valid state and there should not be any invalid database objects with the SYS or SYSTEM schema. In addition to that, the pre-upgrade script should have been executed on the source database to confirm that there are no errors or warnings in the pre-upgrade script output.

In addition to these usual upgrade prerequisites, there are additional prerequisites required for databases in EBS environments. We will discuss those prerequisites in this section. These additional prerequisites may differ for each EBS version. The prerequisites for each EBS version have been documented by Oracle as interoperability notes for each EBS version, as shown in Table 9-1.

© Y V Ravikumar, K M Krishnakumar and Nassyam Basha 2017
N. Basha et al., *Oracle Database Upgrade and Migration Methods*, DOI 10.1007/978-1-4842-2328-4_9

Table 9-1. *EBS Interoperability with Different Database Versions*

EBS Version	Database Version	My Oracle Support Interoperability Note
12.0, 12.1	11*g* R2	1058763.1
12.0, 12.1	12.1.0.2.0	1524398.1
12.0, 12.1	12.1.0.1.0	1930134.1
12.2	11*g* R2	1623879.1
12.2	12.1.0.1.0	1959604.1
12.2	12.1.0.2.0	1926201.1

Pre-upgrade steps

The following are the pre-upgrade steps for EBS databases:

1) As the first step, take a backup of the database. The backup can be a cold backup or hot backup or RMAN backup. The backup should be consistent to restore the database to a valid state.

2) Install the target database version at the new location. The target database version should have been certified with the EBS version. Ensure that the Oracle software is installed properly and there are no binary linking issues.

3) Install the Oracle examples on the target Oracle database home.

4) As part of the prerequisites, you need to install some patches on the EBS home and on the target Oracle database home. The patch list is based on EBS and the database version. You can get the list of patches from the interoperability notes. The EBS home requires the interoperability patches and other sets of patches to prepare for the database upgrade. The database home requires patches to proactively fix bugs identified in the target version.

5) Create the `nls/data/9idata` directory in the Oracle Home on the database server node. This can be created by executing `cr9idata.pl`. This script copies the NLB files into the `9idata` directory in case you need to revert to the `9i` locale behavior. NLB files are binary files that contain the settings for a specific language, character set, or territory.

6) Drop the table `sys.enabled$indexes` in the source database if it exists. This table will be automatically created while executing `catupgrd.sql`. This table has a list of function-based indexes that are not disabled currently. This list will be used by `utlrp.sql` to enable indexes that might have been disabled during upgrade.

7) Execute the pre-upgrade scripts on the source database. Ensure the prerequisite output doesn't have any errors or warnings.

Upgrade Steps

Once the pre-upgrade steps are successful, you can proceed to a database upgrade.

1) Disable Data Vault if it is enabled.

2) Remove the MGDSYS schema. This schema holds database objects for the "identity code package" functionality. This functionality offers tools and techniques to store, retrieve, encode, decode, and translate between various product or identity codes, including the Electronic Product Code (EPC), in an Oracle database.

3) Upgrade the database to the higher version. The upgrade can be done through any of the upgrade methods. (All database upgrade methods were discussed in Chapter 2.)

4) Perform the post-patch instructions. Some patches require execution steps at a database level. This can be done once the database is upgraded. For 12c, the database datapatch utility can be executed to complete the post-patch steps.

Post-upgrade Steps

The following steps are the post-upgrade steps:

1) Start the new listener in the target Oracle Home.

2) Execute adgrants.sql as the sysdba user. This script is available in the $APPL_TOP/admin directory. This script grants the necessary privileges to the user passed as the argument. The application user has defined the $APPL_TOP environment variable.

3) Grant the create procedure privilege to the CTXSYS schema. This can be done by executing adctxprv.sql as the apps user. In 10g, the CTSYS user doesn't have the create procedure privilege, and hence this script execution is necessary. Also, provide the file_access_role privilege to the public.

4) Validate the workflow ruleset. This can be done by connecting to the database as the apps user and executing wfaqupfix.sql. This script is a workaround to fix the AQ rulesets that become invalid during the upgrade.

5) Gather the SYS schema statistics. For that, execute $APPL_TOP/admin/adstats.sql as the sys user.

6) Create the context file at the new Oracle Home by executing $ORACLE_HOME/appsutil/bin/adbldxml.pl.

7) Execute autoconfig.sh available in the $ORACLE_HOME/appsutil/bin directory. This will update the new Oracle Home settings on all the required configuration files at the database and app levels. Hence, this script should be executed at the database home and apps home. This will take the context file as input, which was created in the previous step.

8) Create the MGDSYS schema in case the database is upgraded from a prior version to 12c.

9) Do a database time zone version upgrade.

Example

We'll now walk you through the EBS database upgrade process with an example.

- *EBS version*: 12.1.3

- *Database version* : 11.2.0.3.0

- *Target database version*: 12.1.0.2.0

- *Oracle database user*: oramgr

- *Oracle apps user*: applmgr

As a first step, install the 12.1.0.2.0 database version at a different location. Invoke the 12.1.0.2.0 install (runInstaller/setup.exe); this will show the Configure Security Updates page, as shown in Figure 9-1.

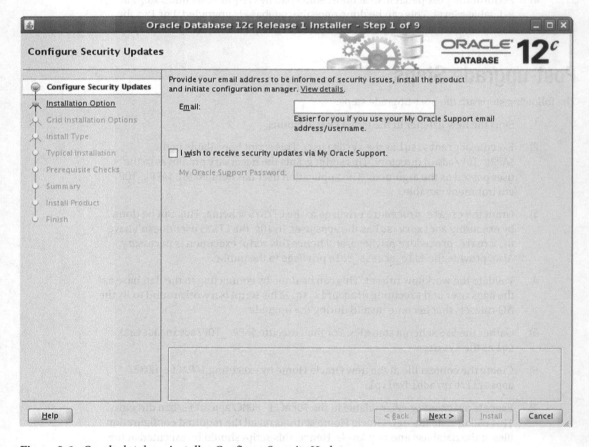

Figure 9-1. *Oracle database installer, Configure Security Updates page*

Based on the preferred security updates, you can choose or ignore this option. On the next page, choose the "Install database software only" option (Figure 9-2). This will install the 12.1.0.2.0 software binary at the mentioned location. Note that you should not choose "Upgrade an existing database" because you need to install the prerequisite patches on the 12.1.0.2.0 home before the database upgrade.

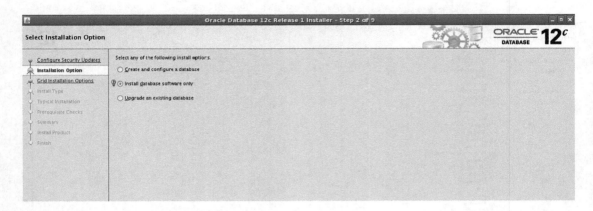

Figure 9-2. *Oracle database installation options*

Choose the type of instance required to install. (In Figure 9-3 we have chosen a single-instance installation.)

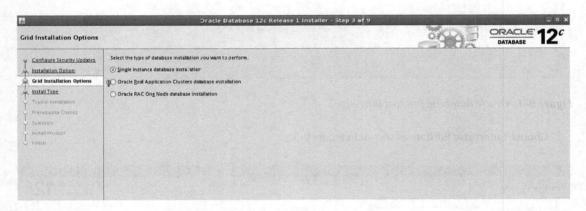

Figure 9-3. *Oracle Grid Installation Options page*

Choose the appropriate language (Figure 9-4).

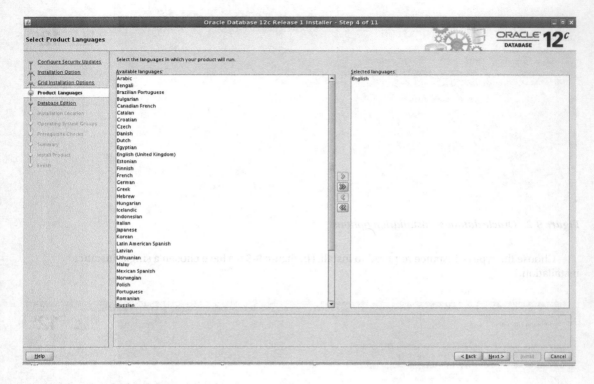

Figure 9-4. *Oracle database product language*

Choose Enterprise Edition, as shown in Figure 9-5.

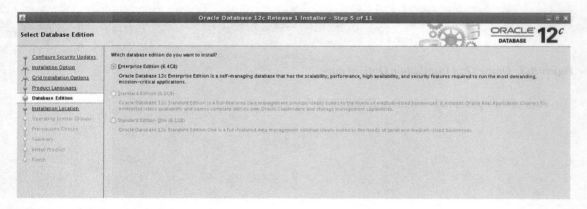

Figure 9-5. *Oracle database edition*

Set the Oracle base and Oracle database software installation locations, as shown in Figure 9-6.

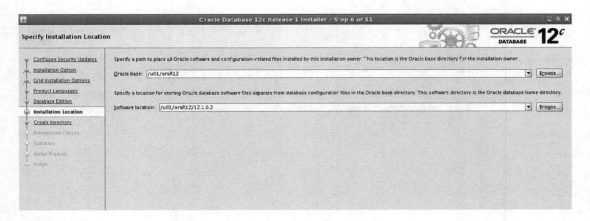

Figure 9-6. *Oracle database installation locations*

Specify the Oracle inventory location for the software installation (Figure 9-7).

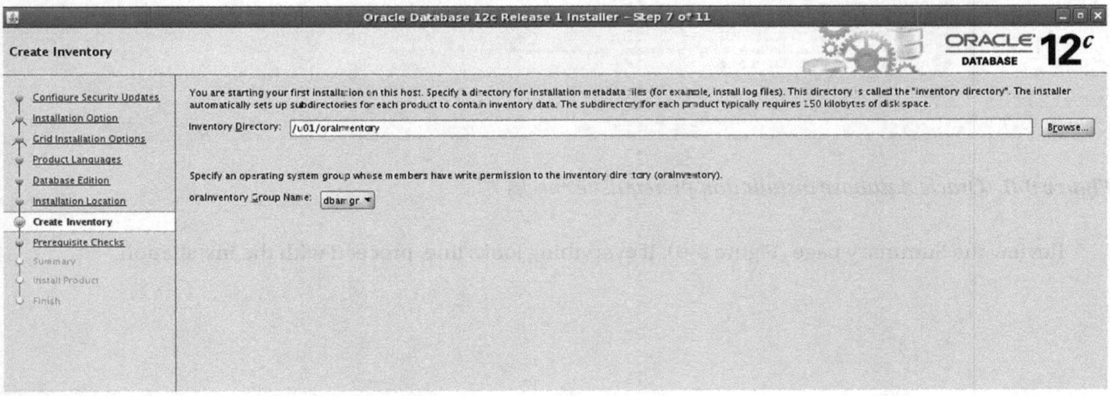

Figure 9-7. *Oracle database inventory details*

After collecting the inventory details, the installer performs the prerequisite checks for the database installation (Figure 9-8).

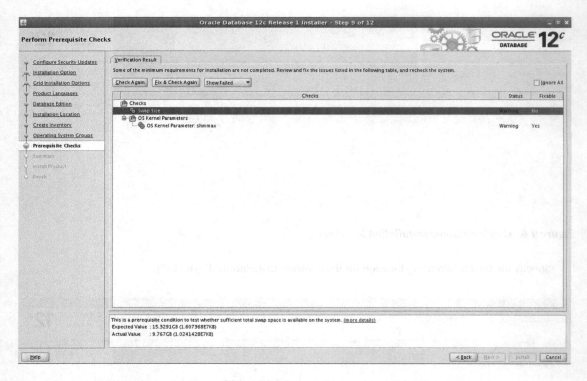

Figure 9-8. *Oracle database installation prerequisite checks*

Review the Summary page (Figure 9-9). If everything looks fine, proceed with the installation.

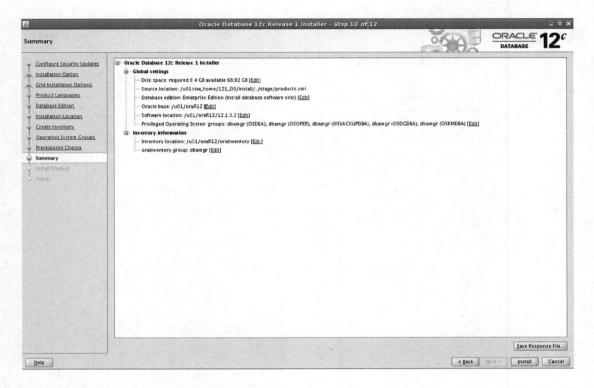

Figure 9-9. *Oracle database installation, Summary page*

Once the 12.1.0.2.0 database installation has completed, successfully install the 12.1.0.2.0 examples on top of the 12.1.0.2.0 database home. Invoke runInstaller or setup.exe in the Oracle database examples 12*c* software. Choose the database home as the software installation location, as shown in Figure 9-10.

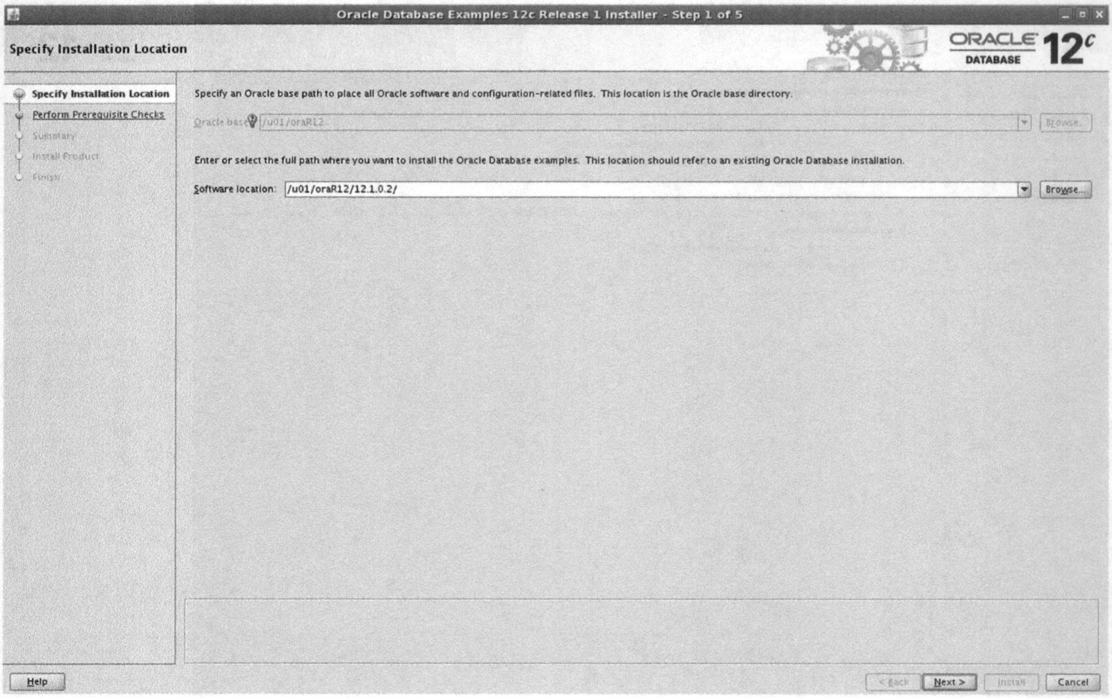

Figure 9-10. *Oracle examples installation location*

Ensure the installation prerequisites are successful. If the warnings are ignorable, choose the Ignore All check box (Figure 9-11).

Figure 9-11. *Oracle examples prerequisite check page*

Review the Summary page (Figure 9-12). If the listed settings are fine, proceed with the installation.

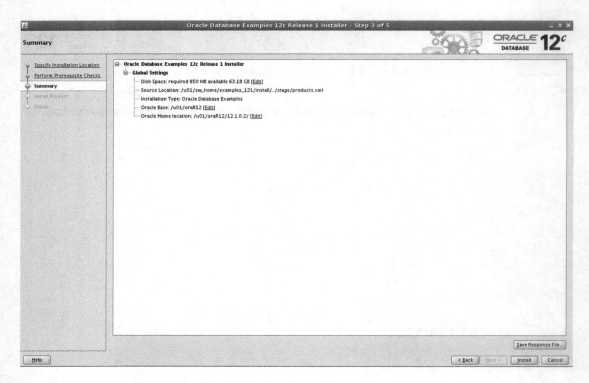

Figure 9-12. *Oracle examples installation, Summary page*

When you click the Install button, the installation progress starts, as shown in Figure 9-13.

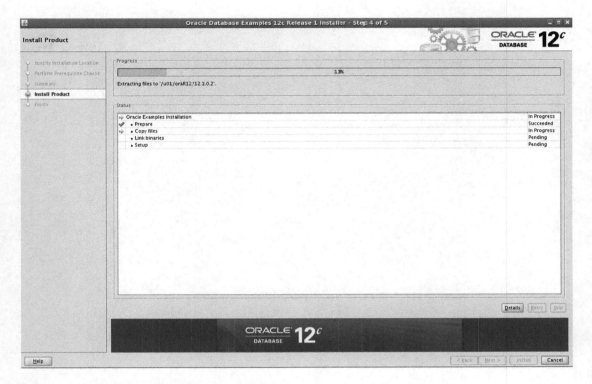

Figure 9-13. *Oracle examples installation progress*

Once the installation has completed successfully, you will see the Finish screen, as shown in Figure 9-14.

Figure 9-14. Oracle examples installation completion

The 12*c* Oracle database examples installation is complete.

Apply the Prerequisite Patches to the Apps Home

You can get details of the prerequisite patches for EBS through the interoperability notes or by contacting Oracle Support. For EBS 12.1.3 version, the following are the prerequisite patches, as mentioned in note 1524398.1:

```
Patch 8796558
Patch 12923944
Patch 13473483
Patch 16289505
Patch 18843706
```

You can apply these patches through the adpatch utility.

Apply the Prerequisite Patches to the Database Home

The Oracle EBS database requires prerequisite patches before the upgrade. The patch list can be collected from Oracle Support or the interoperability notes. The required patches to apply on the 12.1.0.2.0 version are as follows:

```
Patch 6880880 - the latest OPatch version for 12.1.C.
Patch 19382851 - ORA-1031 DURING MVIEW CREATION/REFRESH
Patch 19393542 - TIMESTAMP MISMATCHES ON RULE SET & EVALUATION CONTEXT
Patch 19627012 - APPSST12102 : ORA-7445 [KD9IR2TCOMPUTETREESERCS()+160] DURING IMPDP
Patch 19649152 - ORA-600 [KTURRUR_0] RUNNING OPM LOT COST PROCESSOR IN FDPSTP
Patch 20204035 - MERGE REQUEST ON TOP OF 12.1.0.2.0 FOR BUGS 15894842 20123899
```

In this patch list, first apply patch 6880880. This will update the Opatch tool to the latest version. Using the Opatch utility, you can apply these patches in the database 12.1.0.2.0 home. Chapter 12 has information about the Opatch tool, the patch prerequisites, and the patch apply steps.

Shut Down the Application Process

On the application server nodes, shut down all the server process and services. The application will be unavailable to users starting at this stage.

Execute cr9idata.pl

This is a Perl script and should be executed by the Perl utility. The Oracle database software provides the Perl utility inside the Oracle Home, which can be used to execute Perl scripts. Use the 12*c* database software Perl utility to execute cr9idata.pl.

```
$ perl /u01/oraR12/12.1.0.2/nls/data/old/cr9idata.pl
Creating directory /u01/oraR12/12.1.0.2/nls/data/9icata ...
Copying files to /u01/oraR12/12.1.0.2/nls/data/9idata...
Copy finished.
Please reset environment variable ORA_NLS10 to /u01/oraR12/12.1.0.2/nls/data/9idata!
```

Drop the sys.enabled$indexes Table

Connect to the source database as the sys user. If the enabled$indexes table exists, then drop it.

```
SQL> desc enabled$indexes
ERROR:
ORA-04043: object enabled$indexes does not exist
```

Execute the Pre-upgrade Scripts

Execute the pre-upgrade script to validate the database before the upgrade. Verify the pre-upgrade output for errors and warnings. Chapter 2 explains how to diagnose the pre-upgrade script output.

```
SQL> @/u01/oraR12/12.1.0.2/rdbms/admin/preupgrd.sql

Loading Pre-Upgrade Package...
```

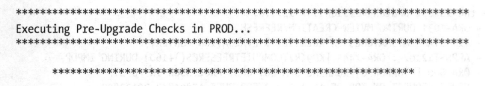

```
******************************************************************************
Executing Pre-Upgrade Checks in PROD...
******************************************************************************

        ************************************************************
```

```
                ====>> ERRORS FOUND for PROD <<====
```

```
   The following are *** ERROR LEVEL CONDITIONS *** that must be addressed
                      prior to attempting your upgrade.
              Failure to do so will result in a failed upgrade.
```

Check the Database Components' Status

Check the database components' status with the following:

```
SQL> select comp_name, status, version from dba_registry;
OLAP Catalog                            VALID       11.2.0.3.0
Oracle Data Mining                      VALID       11.2.0.3.0
Oracle XML Database                     VALID       11.2.0.3.0
Oracle Text                             VALID       11.2.0.3.0
Spatial                                 VALID       11.2.0.3.0
Oracle Multimedia                       VALID       11.2.0.3.0
Oracle Database Catalog Views           VALID       11.2.0.3.0
Oracle Database Packages and Types      VALID       11.2.0.3.0
JServer JAVA Virtual Machine            VALID       11.2.0.3.0
Oracle Database Java Packages           VALID       11.2.0.3.0
Oracle XDK                              VALID       11.2.0.3.0
OLAP Analytic Workspace                 VALID       11.2.0.3.0
Oracle OLAP API                         VALID       11.2.0.3.0
```

Check the Invalid SYS/SYSTEM Schema Objects

The SYS and SYSTEM schema objects are part of the Oracle database dictionary. Ensure there are no invalid objects in the SYS and SYSTEM schemas.

```
SQL> select owner, object_name,  status from dba_objects where owner in ('SYS','SYSTEM') and
status!='VALID';
No rows selected
```

Drop the MGDSYS Schema

If the database is getting upgraded from versions prior to 12c, then this step is necessary. The MGDSYS user can be dropped by executing $ORACLE_HOME/md/admin/catnomgdidcode.sql as the sysdba user.

```
Sql> connect sys/<password> as sysdba
SQL> @?/md/admin/catnomgdidcode.sql
SQL> select username from dba_users where username like '%MGD%';
No rows selected
```

Upgrade the Database to the 12c Version

The database can be upgraded using any of the upgrade methods. (The methods are discussed in Chapter 2.) Make sure to follow database upgrade best practices to ensure the database upgrade is effective, as discussed in detail in Chapter 1. In this example, we are showing the process for a stand-alone database. For the RAC database, the upgrade steps are explained in Chapter 7.

Here are the steps for using the manual upgrade method to upgrade the database:

1) Shut down the 11.2.0.3.0 database.

```
Sql> shutdown immediate
Database closed
Instance shutdown
```

2) Copy the init parameter file to 12c and make any necessary changes.

3) Create a password file at the 12c Oracle Home.

4) Modify the environment variables ORACLE_HOME, PATH, and LD_LIBRARY_PATH to point to the 12c home.

5) Start the database in upgrade mode using the 12c Oracle Home.

```
SQL> startup upgrade
ORACLE instance started.
Total System Global Area 1073741824 bytes
Fixed Size                   2932632 bytes
Variable Size              436207720 bytes
Database Buffers           620756992 bytes
Redo Buffers                13844480 bytes
Database mounted.
Database opened.
```

6) Execute the upgrade scripts.

In Oracle 12c, the database can be upgraded in parallel using the Perl script catctl.pl. You can specify the number of parallelism along with the catupgrd.sql execution.

```
$ $ORACLE_HOME/perl/bin/perl catctl.pl  -n 4 -l /tmp catupgrd.sql
```

Here you can execute catctl.pl using the Perl utility available in $ORACLE_HOME. Note that –l denotes the log location, and the number of parallelism (-n) is 4.

After catupgrd.sql, execute utlrp.sql to compile any invalid objects.

```
SQL> @?/rdbms/admin/utlrp.sql
```

7) Check the database component version and status.

```
SQL> select comp_name, status, version from dba_registry;
OLAP Catalog                            VALID       12.1.0.2.0
Oracle Data Mining                      VALID       12.1.0.2.0
Oracle XML Database                     VALID       12.1.0.2.0
Oracle Text                             VALID       12.1.0.2.0
```

```
    Spatial                              VALID      12.1.0.2.0
    Oracle Multimedia                    VALID      12.1.0.2.0
    Oracle Database Catalog Views        VALID      12.1.0.2.0
    Oracle Database Packages and Types   VALID      12.1.0.2.0
    JServer JAVA Virtual Machine         VALID      12.1.0.2.0
    Oracle Database Java Packages        VALID      12.1.0.2.0
    Oracle XDK                           VALID      12.1.0.2.0
    OLAP Analytic Workspace              VALID      12.1.0.2.0
    Oracle OLAP API                      VALID      12.1.0.2.0
```

Post-upgrade Steps for an EBS Database Upgrade

Here are the post-upgrade steps for an EBS database upgrade:

1) Start the listener from a new Oracle Home.

    ```
    $lsnrctl start
    ```

2) Execute adgrants.sql as the sysdba user. This script is available in the $APPL_
    TOP/admin directory. This script grants the necessary privilege to the user passed
    as the argument. APPS is the schema configured at the database level for the
    application. This script is available on the application server; you can copy this
    script to the database server and execute it.

    ```
    SQL> @adgrants.sql <APPS schema name>
    SQL> @adgrants.sql APPS
    Connected.

    ---------------------------------------------------
    --- adgrants.sql started at 2016-05-29 20:13:46 ---

    Creating PL/SQL profiler objects.

    ---------------------------------------------------
    --- profload.sql started at 2016-05-29 20:13:46 ---

    Session altered.
    Package created.
    Grant succeeded.
    Synonym created.
    .
    .
    .

    End of Creating PL/SQL Package AD_ZD_SYS.
    PL/SQL procedure successfully completed.
    Commit complete.
    ```

3) Grant the create procedure privilege to the CTXSYS schema. This can be done by executing $AD_TOP/patch/115/wsql/adctxprv.sql as the apps user. In 10*g* the CTSYS user doesn't have the create procedure privilege, and hence this script execution is necessary. You can copy this script to the database server and execute it.

```
Sql> connect apps/<password>
Sql> @adctxprv.sql <password of system account> CTXSYS

SQL> @?/apps/adctxprv.sql Manager CTXSYS

Connecting to SYSTEM
Connected.

PL/SQL procedure successfully completed.

Commit complete.
```

Set file_access_role to public. To change file_access_role, you need to connect the database as the sysdba user and execute the following:

```
SQL> exec ctxsys.ctx_adm.set_parameter('file_access_role','public');

PL/SQL procedure successfully completed.
```

4) Validate the workflow ruleset. This can be done by connecting to the database as the apps user and executing wfaqupfix.sql. This script is a workaround to fix invalid AQ rulesets that become invalid during the upgrade.

```
Sql> wfaqupfix.sql <APPSSYS user>  <APPS user>

SQL> @?/apps/wfaqupfix.sql APPS APPS

PL/SQL procedure successfully completed.

Commit complete.
```

5) Gather statistics for the sys user. This can be done by executing adstats.sql, which is available in the $APPL_TOP/admin folder. Copy this file to the database server and execute it as the sys user. This has to run in restricted mode. Hence, before executing the script, enable the restricted session.

```
Sql> connect sys/<password> as sysdba
SQL> alter system enable restricted session;
System altered.
SQL> @adstats.sql

Sql> > alter system disable restricted session;
```

6) Create a new MGDSYS user as this database is upgraded from the 11.2.0.3.0 version. Execute $ORACLE_HOME/rdbms/admin/catmgd.sql as the sysdba user to create the MGDSYS user with the required privileges.

```
SQL> @?/rdbms/admin/catmgd.sql
.. Creating MGDSYS schema

User created.

.. Granting permissions to MGDSYS

Grant succeeded.
Grant succeeded.
Grant succeeded.
```

7) Create the context file by executing the $ORACLE_HOME/appsutil//bin/ adbldxml.pl file. Here ORACLE_HOME refers to the database Oracle installation directory. The context file will have information about the hostname and listener port information. Re-creating the context file will modify the entries according to the 12*c* Oracle Home.

```
$ perl adbldxml.pl

Starting context file generation for db tier..
Using JVM from /u01/oraR12/12.1.0.2//jdk/jre/bin/java to execute java programs..
APPS Password:
  .
  .
Enter Port of Database server: 1521

Enter SID of Database server: <DBNAME>
  .
  .
The context file has been created at:
/u01/oraR12/12.1.0.2/appsutil/prod_erpnode3.xml
```

8) Execute autoconfig.sh available in the $ORACLE_HOME/appsutil/bin directory. This will update the new Oracle Home settings on all the required configuration files at the database and app levels.

```
$ sh adconfig.sh
Enter the full path to the Context file: /u01/oraR12/12.1.0.2/appsutil/prod_
erpnode3.xml
Enter the APPS user password:
  .
  .
Context Value Management will now update the Context file
        Updating Context file...COMPLETED
        Attempting upload of Context file and templates to database...COMPLETED
Updating rdbms version in Context file to <dbname>
```

```
Updating rdbms type in Context file to 64 bits
Configuring templates from ORACLE_HOME ...
AutoConfig completed successfully.
```

Summary

This chapter explained the upgrade steps for an E-Business Suite database. You learned about the prerequisites, upgrade steps, and post-upgrade steps to configure the E-Business Suite application with the upgraded database.

CHAPTER 10

■■■

Multitenant Database Upgrades

A company can have more than one database for different purposes. For example, there might be databases for HR, finance, and facilities. Each database has its own background process and memory allocation. When you have more than one database on the same server, each database should be allotted its own required resources. You cannot guarantee that at any point in time all the allotted resources are 100 percent utilized by each database on the ported server. At times, the database might not require all the allotted resources when it is load-free. In that case, the allotted resource remains unutilized.

To overcome these issues and to achieve better consolidation, the Oracle 12c database has introduced a new concept called the Oracle *multitenant architecture*. This multitenant architecture simplifies consolidation, provisioning, upgrading, patching, and more. The databases will be consolidated under one master database that is called the *root* database.

This is similar to the differences between a house and an apartment complex (see Figure 10-1). In the house, all the facilities are allotted to that particular house whether they are used or not. In the apartment complex, common facilities are shared by all residents of the different apartments. Here the resources are utilized effectively.

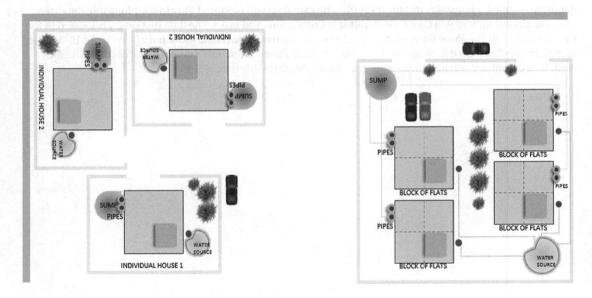

***Figure 10-1.** Example of multitenant architecture*

© Y V Ravikumar, K M Krishnakumar and Nassyam Basha 2017

N. Basha et al., *Oracle Database Upgrade and Migration Methods*, DOI 10.1007/978-1-4842-2328-4_10

Multitenant Architecture

A multitenant architecture consolidates all the databases under a single root database (see Figure 10-2). The background process and memory will be shared by all databases. Here resource usage is optimized.

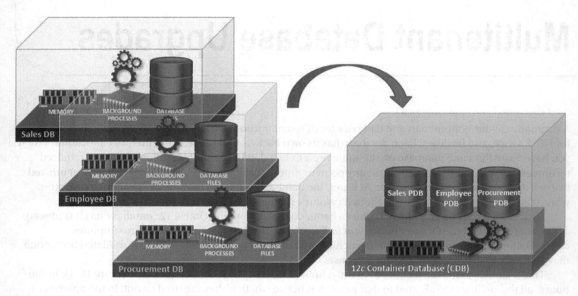

Figure 10-2. *Oracle Database multitenant architecture*

With a multitenant architecture, the root database is called the *container database* (CDB), and each user database is called a *pluggable database* (PDB). The user data will be stored only in the pluggable database. The container database will take care of root-level allocations and tasks. The data dictionary is located in the root container. At the same time, each pluggable database has its own data dictionary (see Figure 10-3). The dictionary available on the pluggable database will have information only about its own objects. The root container dictionary will have information about all the pluggable databases.

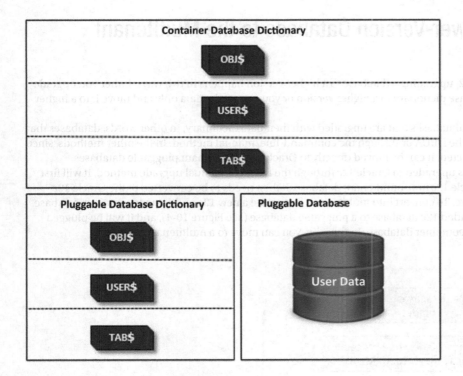

Figure 10-3. *Multitenant database dictionary*

The container database and pluggable database will be at the same database version, and the pluggable database will have its own admin user.

Kindly note that for the upcoming Oracle version 12.2, the non-multitenant architecture is deprecated. This means there won't be any new features or enhancements for the non-multitenant model in the future. So, it is advisable to move to a multitenant architecture when upgrading to higher Oracle 12*c* versions. If your database is not licensed for the multitenant option, you will be able to stand up a database with one CBD and only one PDB. If you want more than one PDB in the database, you will need to pay for the extra option.

In a multitenant architecture, the database can be upgraded in two ways: the entire container database with pluggable databases can be upgraded to a higher version, or just particular pluggable databases can be upgraded to higher versions. You do this by migrating the pluggable database to a higher-version container database, followed by the upgrade steps.

Now, you might be wondering as Oracle 12*c* has this multitenant feature. When you upgrade a lower-version database to Oracle 12*c*, is it possible to directly upgrade the lower-version database to the Oracle 12*c* multitenant architecture? The answer is no. You cannot directly upgrade (meaning do a whole-database upgrade along with database dictionary) the lower-version database to an Oracle 12*c* pluggable database. The database architecture is different. You need to first upgrade to an Oracle 12*c* non-multitenant database and then convert it to a pluggable database.

Before getting to the multitenant database upgrade, we'll first show how to convert the lower-version stand-alone database to an Oracle 12*c* multitenant architecture.

Move the Lower-Version Database to the Multitenant Architecture

As you saw in Chapter 2, upgrading a database to a higher version happens in two ways. Either you upgrade the data and the database dictionary to a higher version or you extract the data only and move it to a higher version.

Here we'll discuss databases that are upgraded with their data dictionary, in other words, databases that are upgraded through the DBUA or through the command-line/manual method. In the other methods, since the data is getting extracted, it can be moved directly to Oracle 12*c* multitenant pluggable databases.

When a database is upgraded to Oracle 12*c* through the DBUA or manual upgrade method, it will first be upgraded to an Oracle 12*c* non-multitenant database. It then needs to be converted to the Oracle 12*c* multitenant architecture. To convert into multitenant, first create a new 12*c* multitenant container database. Then convert the upgraded 12c database to a pluggable database (see Figure 10-4), and it will be plugged into the newly created container database. In this way, you can move to a multitenant model.

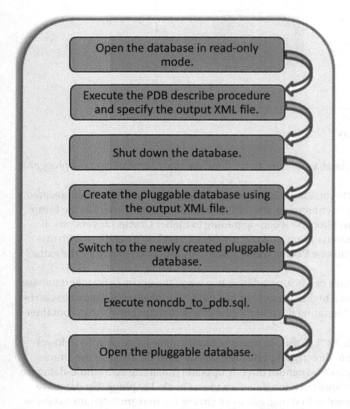

Figure 10-4. *Converting a non-CDB to a pluggable database*

Here are steps in detail:

1) Say the database has been upgraded to Oracle 12c and is a regular Oracle 12c database. It can be identified through SQL queries. You want to get this database into a multitenant architecture.

```
SQL> select NAME, DECODE(CDB, 'YES', 'Multitenant Option enabled', 'Regular 12c
Database ') "Multitenant Option" , OPEN_MODE, CON_ID from V$DATABASE;


NAME          Multitenant Option      OPEN_MODE        CON_ID
---------     --------------------    ---------------  ----------
NOCDB11G      Regular 12c Database    READ WRITE         0
```

2) Shut down the database and open it in read-only mode.

```
SQL> shutdown immediate;
Database closed.
Database dismounted.
ORACLE instance shut down.

SQL> startup open read only
ORACLE instance started.
Total System Global Area 1593835520 bytes
Fixed Size                   2924880 bytes
Variable Size             1023413936 bytes
Database Buffers           553648128 bytes
Redo Buffers                13848576 bytes
Database mounted.
Database opened.
```

3) Execute a PDB describe procedure and specify the output XML file.

```
SQL> BEGIN
DBMS_PDB.DESCRIBE(pdb_descr_file => '/tmp/12cNoCDB.xml');
END;
/
PL/SQL procedure successfully completed.
```

This 12cNoCDB.xml file will have information about each tablespace of this database. A small piece of 12cNoCDB.xml is shown here:

```
<tablespace>
  <name>TEMP</name>
  <type>1</type>
  <tsn>3</tsn>
  <status>1</status>
  <issft>0</issft>
  <bmunitsize>128</bmunitsize>
  <file>
```

```
            <path>/u01/app/oracle/oradata/nocdb11g/temp01.dbf</path>
            <afn>1</afn>
            <rfn>1</rfn>
            <createscnbas>995623</createscnbas>
            <createscnwrp>0</createscnwrp>
            <status>1</status>
            <fileblocks>2560</fileblocks>
            <blocksize>8192</blocksize>
            <vsn>186646528</vsn>
            <autoext>1</autoext>
            <maxsize>4194302</maxsize>
            <incsize>80</incsize>
        </file>
```

Also, it will have information about the database components and their version.

4)   Shut down the database.

```
SQL> shutdown immediate
Database closed.
Database dismounted.
ORACLE instance shut down
```

5)   Now start the newly created Oracle 12*c* container database.

```
[oracle@oel58 ~]$ . oraenv
ORACLE_SID = [CDB12C] ? CDB12C
The Oracle base remains unchanged with value /u01/app/oracle

[oracle@oel58 ~]$ sqlplus /nolog

SQL*Plus: Release 12.1.0.2.0 Production
Copyright (c) 1982, 2014, Oracle.  All rights reserved.

SQL> connect sys/oracle as sysdba
Connected.

SQL> startup
ORACLE instance started.
Total System Global Area 1459617792 bytes
Fixed Size                  2924496 bytes
Variable Size             922746928 bytes
Database Buffers          520093696 bytes
Redo Buffers               13852672 bytes
Database mounted.
Database opened.
```

```
SQL> select NAME, DECODE(CDB, 'YES', 'Multitenant Option enabled', 'Regular 12c
Database ') "Multitenant Option" , OPEN_MODE, CON_ID from V$DATABASE;

NAME        Multitenant Option          OPEN_MODE        CON_ID
---------   ------------------------    --------------   ----------
CDB12C      Multitenant Option enabled READ WRITE        0

SQL> show pdbs

    CON_ID CON_NAME                         OPEN MODE  RESTRICTED
---------- ------------------------------- ---------- ----------
         2 PDB$SEED                         READ ONLY  NO
         3 PDB12C                           MOUNTED
```

Currently the CDB has one PDB called PDB12c. Now you will add NOCDB12c as a pluggable database to this container database.

6) Create a pluggable database using the output /tmp/12cNoCDB.xml.

```
SQL> CREATE PLUGGABLE DATABASE newpdb12c
USING '/tmp/12cNoCDB.xml' nocopy TEMPFILE REUSE;

Pluggable database created.
```

7) The database name can be changed while creating a pluggable database. Here we have changed the database name to newpdb12c.

- nocopy denotes the use of the existing datafiles for the pluggable database.

- TEMPFILE REUSE means the existing temp file can be reused.

```
SQL> show pdbs

    CON_ID CON_NAME                         OPEN MODE  RESTRICTED
---------- ------------------------------- ---------- ----------
         2 PDB$SEED                         READ ONLY  NO
         3 PDB12C                           MOUNTED
         4 NEWPDB12C                        MOUNTED
```

8) Switch to the newly created pluggable database.

```
SQL> alter session set container= NEWPDB12C;
Session altered.
```

9) Execute noncdb_to_pdb.sql to convert the database to a pluggable database by modifying and deleting the unnecessary metadata.

```
Sql> @?/rdbms/admin/noncdb_to_pdb.sql
```

10) Shut down and start the pluggable database.

```
SQL> alter pluggable database close;
Pluggable database altered.

SQL> alter pluggable database open;
Pluggable database altered.

SQL> select name, open_mode from v$pdbs;

NAME                            OPEN_MODE
------------------------------- ----------
NEWPDB12C                       READ WRITE
```

Container Database Upgrade

In this section, we will discuss how to upgrade a container database and all its associated pluggable databases. This multitenant database upgrade is a little different from a stand-alone database. Currently Oracle 12*c* has versions 12.1.0.1.0 and 12.1.0.2.0. We will cover upgrading an Oracle 12*c* database version 12.1.0.1.0 container and its pluggable database to an Oracle 12*c* database version 12.1.0.2.0.

For a stand-alone database upgrade, you need to perform pre-upgrade checks for the container and pluggable databases. You can connect each database separately and execute the pre-upgrade script preupgrade.sql or you can use the Perl script catcon.pl (a container-aware Perl script), which will execute the pre-upgrade script on the container database and all its pluggable databases. This Perl script is available in the Oracle 12*c* home directory. It should be invoked by the Oracle Home owner.

```
Catcon.pl usage
catcon   [-u username[/password]] [-U username[/password]]
         [-d directory] [-l directory]
         [{-c|-C} container] [-p degree-of-parallelism]
         [-z EZConnect strings]
         [-e] [-s]
         [-E { ON | errorlogging-table-other-than-SPERRORLOG}]
         [-I]
         [-g]
         [-f]
         [-r]
         -b log-file-name-base
         --
       { sqlplus-script [arguments] | --x<SQL-statement> } ...
```

Here are the mandatory arguments:

```
-b log-file-name-base : Execution creates log files start with value of this argument
- sqlplus-script - sql script to be executed
```

Or here:

```
SQL-statement - sql statement to execute
```

The following are other commonly used optional parameters:

-u: This specifies user login credentials to execute user-supplied SQL scripts or SQL statements.

-U: This specifies user login credentials to execute Oracle internal tasks.

Both the options by default connect as / as syscba.

-c: This specifies containers in which the given SQL has to be executed.

-C: This specifies containers in which the given SQL should not be executed.

-d: This specifies the directory that contains the SQL to run.

-p: This specifies the expected degree of parallelism.

-e: This turns echo on while executing the script.

-E: This specifies that error details will be logged into the table.

-g: This is for generating debugging information.

Let's understand catcon.pl by looking at the pre-upgrade script execution.

```
$/u01/app/oracle/product/12.1.0/perl/bin/perl catcon.pl -d /u01/app/oracle/backup -b
catpreupgrd_log -l /u01/app/oracle/backup preupgrd.sql
catcon: ALL catcon-related output will be written to /u01/app/oracle/backup/catpreupgrd_log_
catcon_4621.lst
catcon: See /u01/app/oracle/backup/catpreupgrd_log*.log files for output generated by
scripts
catcon: See /u01/app/oracle/backup/catpreupgrd_log_*.lst files for spool files, if any
catcon.pl: completed successfully
```

In the previous example, catcon.pl is executed through the Perl binary available at the destination Oracle Home.

-d denotes where preupgrd.sql and utluppkg.sql is placed

-l denotes the location where log has to be placed

-b denotes the base name used for log file

The sql script passed to catcon.pl is preupgrd.sql

The output-generated files are as follows:

```
-rw-r--r--. 1 oracle oinstall      42 catpreupgrd_log_catcon_4548.done
-rw-r--r--. 1 oracle oinstall      42 catpreupgrd_log_catcon_4547.done
-rw-r--r--. 1 oracle oinstall     408 catpreupgrd_log_catcon_4621.lst
-rw-r--r--. 1 oracle oinstall    5991 catpreupgrd_log0.log
-rw-r--r--. 1 oracle oinstall    3244 catpreupgrd_log1.log
```

You should notice that the generated log files have the base names specified in the command along with the -b option. Files with the extension .done show the SQL*Plus version details, and the .lst file shows the output of execution.

The preupgrade.log file is stored at $ORACLE_BASE/cfgtoollogs/<container_db_name>/preupgrade. The log has been created for the CDB and PDB and has the output of preupgrd.sql execution in the respective containers. In this example, it is stored in the /u02/app/oracle/cfgtoollogs/cdb121/ Preupgrade folder. This folder contains the log and fixup scripts for the container database. The PDB's pre-upgrade log and fixup scripts are stored in the pdbfiles folder.

```
$ ls -lrt
-rw-r--r--. 1 oracle oinstall 15376  preupgrade.log
-rw-r--r--. 1 oracle oinstall  7346  preupgrade_fixups.sql
-rw-r--r--. 1 oracle oinstall  5557  postupgrade_fixups.sql
drwxr-xr-x. 2 oracle oinstall  4096  pdbfiles

$ ls -lrt pdbfiles/
-rw-r--r--. 1 oracle oinstall 5124  preupgrade.PDB121.log
-rw-r--r--. 1 oracle oinstall 2446  preupgrade_fixups.PDB121.sql
-rw-r--r--. 1 oracle oinstall 1851  postupgrade_fixups.PDB121.sql
-rw-r--r--. 1 oracle oinstall 5126  preupgrade.PDB$SEED.log
-rw-r--r--. 1 oracle oinstall 2450  preupgrade_fixups.PDB$SEED.sql
-rw-r--r--. 1 oracle oinstall 1853  postupgrade_fixups.PDB$SEED.sql
```

This container database has one pluggable database called pdb121, and this PDB and pdb$seed pre-upgrade log and fixup scripts are generated in the pdbfiles folder.

Since you haven't specified the container details with the -c option, catcon.pl has executed the given script preupgrd.sql in the container database, the PDB seed database, and pdb121. If any pluggable database is not open, then an error will be thrown.

```
$ /u01/app/oracle/product/12.1.0/perl/bin/perl catcon.pl -d /u01/app/oracle/ -b catpreupgrd_
log -l /u01/app/oracle/backup preupgrd.sql
catcon: ALL catcon-related output will be written to /u01/app/oracle/backup/catpreupgrd_log_
catcon_4431.lst
catcon: See /u01/app/oracle/backup/catpreupgrd_log*.log files for output generated by
scripts
catcon: See /u01/app/oracle/backup/catpreupgrd_log_*.lst files for spool files, if any
validate_con_names: PDB121 is not open
catconInit: Unexpected error returned by validate_con_names
Unexpected error encountered in catconInit; exiting
```

In the previous execution, catcon.pl has tried to execute preupgrd.sql in the container, and all the pluggable databases including pdb121 which is in closed state; therefore, execution has been terminated.

If you want to execute preupgrd.sql only in the container database (not on the pluggable databases), you need to invoke it as follows to avoid the previous errors:

```
$ /u01/app/oracle/product/12.1.0/perl/bin/perl catcon.pl -C PDB121 -d /u01/app/oracle/backup
-b catpreupgrd_log -l /u01/app/oracle/backup preupgrd.sql
catcon: ALL catcon-related output will be written to /u01/app/oracle/backup/catpreupgrd_log_
catcon_5809.lst
catcon: See /u01/app/oracle/backup/catpreupgrd_log*.log files for output generated by
scripts
catcon: See /u01/app/oracle/backup/catpreupgrd_log_*.lst files for spool files, if any
catcon.pl: completed successfully
```

You have avoided script execution for the PDB using the -C exclude option. It has executed the pre-upgrade script only in the container and pdb$seed databases.

```
$ ls -lrt /u02/cfgtoollogs/cdb121/preupgrade
total 28
-rw-r--r--. 1 oracle oinstall 10252  preupgrade.log
-rw-r--r--. 1 oracle oinstall  4900  preupgrade_fixups.sql
-rw-r--r--. 1 oracle oinstall  3706  postupgrade_fixups.sql
drwxr-xr-x. 2 oracle oinstall  4096  pdbfiles

$ ls -lrt /u02/cfgtoollogs/cdb121/preupgrade/pdbfiles/
total 16
-rw-r--r--. 1 oracle oinstall 5126  preupgrade.PDB$SEED.log
-rw-r--r--. 1 oracle oinstall 2450  preupgrade_fixups.PDBSSEED.sql
-rw-r--r--. 1 oracle oinstall 1853  postupgrade_fixups.PDB$SEED.sql
```

To avoid execution at the pdb$seed database as well, execute catcon.pl as follows:

```
$ /u01/app/oracle/product/12.1.0/perl/bin/perl catcon.pl -C 'PDB$SEED PDB121' -d /u01/app/
oracle/backup -b catpreupgrd_log -l /u01/app/oracle/backup preupgrd.sql
catcon: ALL catcon-related output will be written to /u01/app/oracle/backup/catpreupgrd_log_
catcon_6349.lst
catcon: See /u01/app/oracle/backup/catpreupgrd_log*.log files for output generated by
scripts
catcon: See /u01/app/oracle/backup/catpreupgrd_log_*.lst files for spool files, if any
catcon.pl: completed successfully
```

Suppose you want to compile invalid objects in all container and pluggable databases. In that case, you invoke catcon.pl as follows:

```
$ /u01/app/oracle/product/12.1.0/perl/bin/perl catcon.pl  -d /u01/app/oracle/backup -b
catpreupgrd_log -l /u01/app/oracle/backup utlrp.sql
catcon: ALL catcon-related output will be written to /u01/app/oracle/backup/catpreupgrd_log_
catcon_12095.lst
catcon: See /u01/app/oracle/backup/catpreupgrd_log*.log files for output generated by
scripts
catcon: See /u01/app/oracle/backup/catpreupgrd_log_*.lst files for spool files, if any
catcon.pl: completed successfully
```

This shows catcon.pl can be used to execute any SQL script in the container database.

Before upgrading the container database, you have to execute the pre-upgrade script using catcon.pl. The pre-upgrade checklists are the same as for a stand-alone database.

While upgrading the container database, all the associated pluggable databases get upgraded to a higher version. Hence, you need to execute the pre-upgrade scripts at the container database and pluggable databases and ensure that all databases are in good shape for the upgrade.

The container database can be upgraded via two methods: using the DBUA and using the manual method.

Database Upgrade Assistant

Database Upgrade Assistant (DBUA) execution is the same as with a stand-alone database. There are some additions for a multitenant database. The DBUA will show the container and all its pluggable databases; you cannot skip any pluggable database during the upgrade.

The initial DBUA screen looks like Figure 10-5. Choose the Upgrade Oracle Database option.

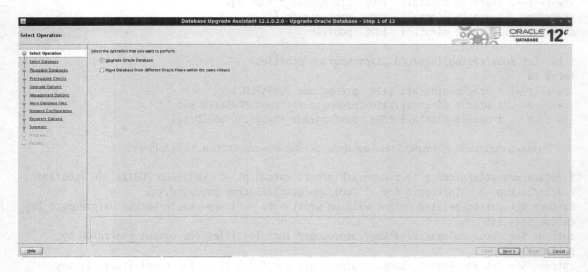

Figure 10-5. *DBUA initial screen*

The next page lists the container databases available on the server, as shown in Figure 10-6.

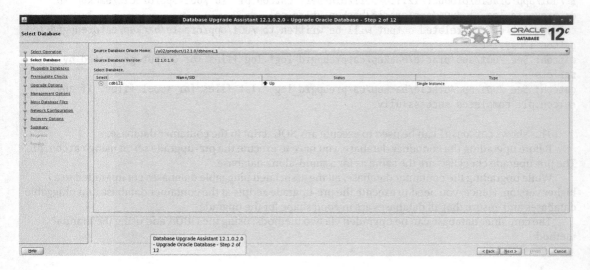

Figure 10-6. *DBUA, database selection*

All the associated pluggable databases of the chosen container database will be listed on the next page, as shown in Figure 10-7. If the pluggable database is in mount state, it will be opened in read-write mode.

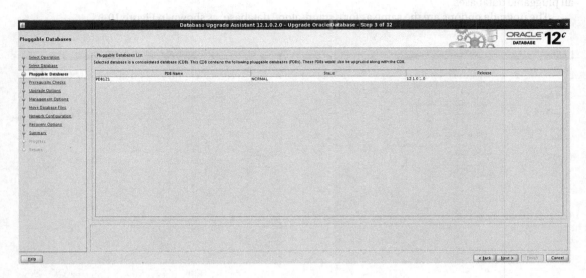

Figure 10-7. *DBUA, PDB list*

In the next step, as shown in Figure 10-8, the DBUA executes the pre-upgrade script in the container and all its pluggable databases.

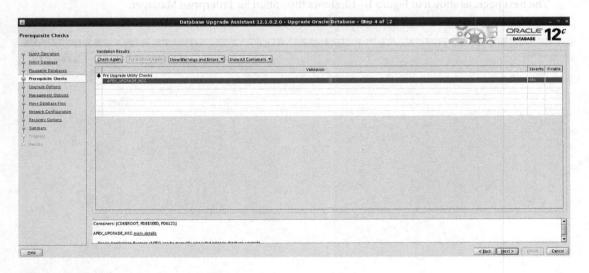

Figure 10-8. *DBUA, pre-upgrade results*

Internally, the DBUA option calls `catcon.pl` to execute the pre-upgrade scripts in all databases. The pre-upgrade results are shown at the bottom of the screen. It will look like Figure 10-8 for the container and all pluggable databases.

The upgrade options are the same as for a stand-alone database, as shown in Figure 10-9.

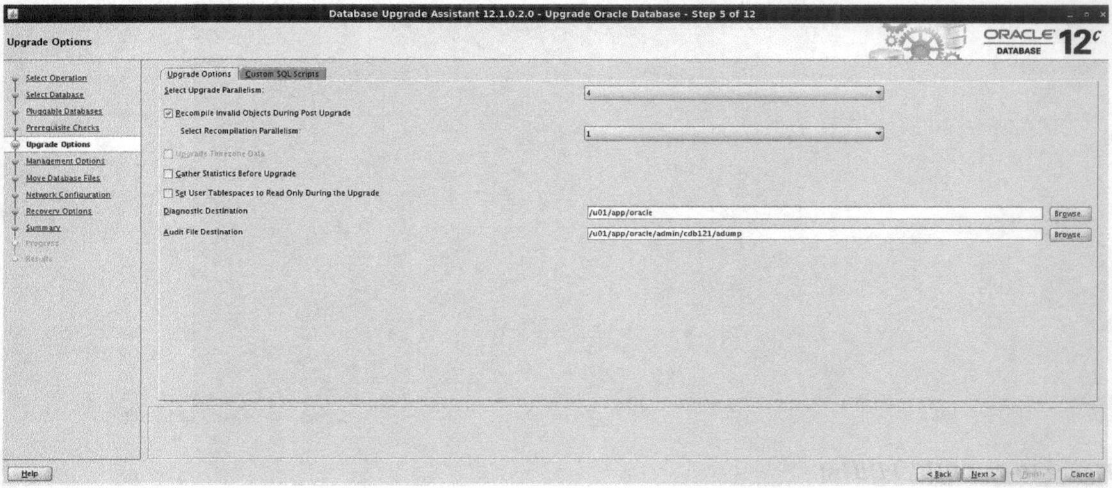

Figure 10-9. *DBUA, upgrade options*

The next page, as shown in Figure 10-10, shows the option for Enterprise Manager.

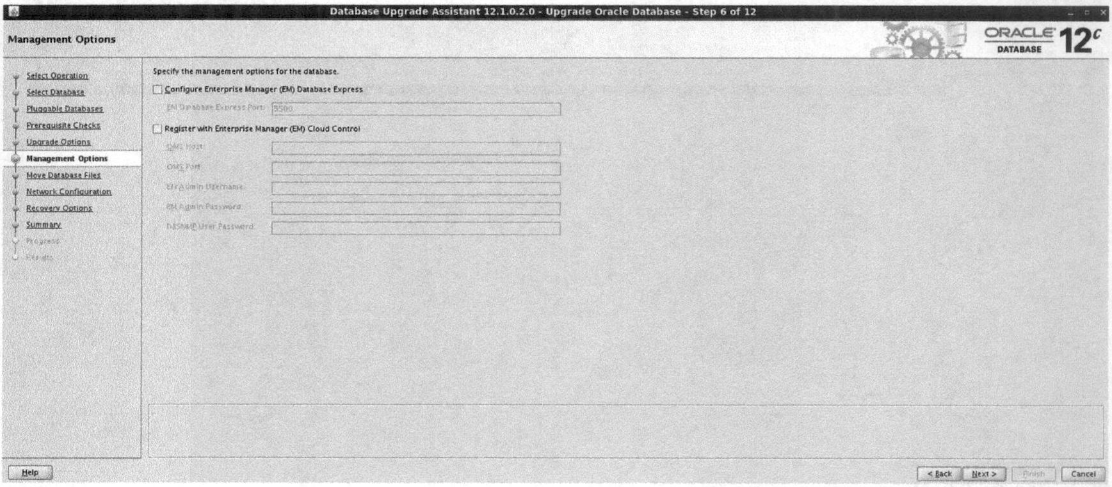

Figure 10-10. *DBUA, management options*

The Move Database Files as Part of Upgrade option is the same as the stand-alone database, as shown in Figure 10-11. The move option will move the CDB and PDB datafiles to the new location.

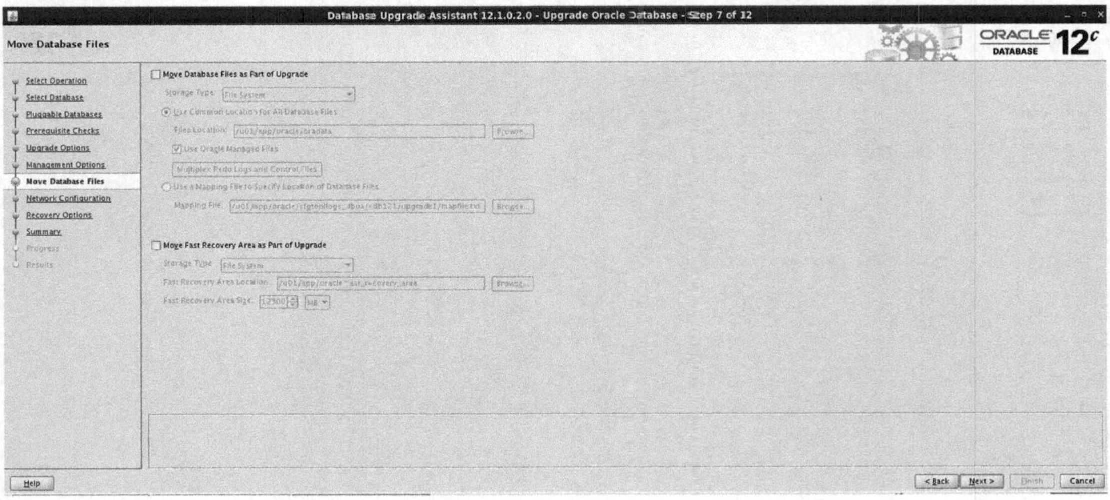

Figure 10-11. *DBUA, moving datafile options*

This page in Figure 10-12 explores options for the listener configuration.

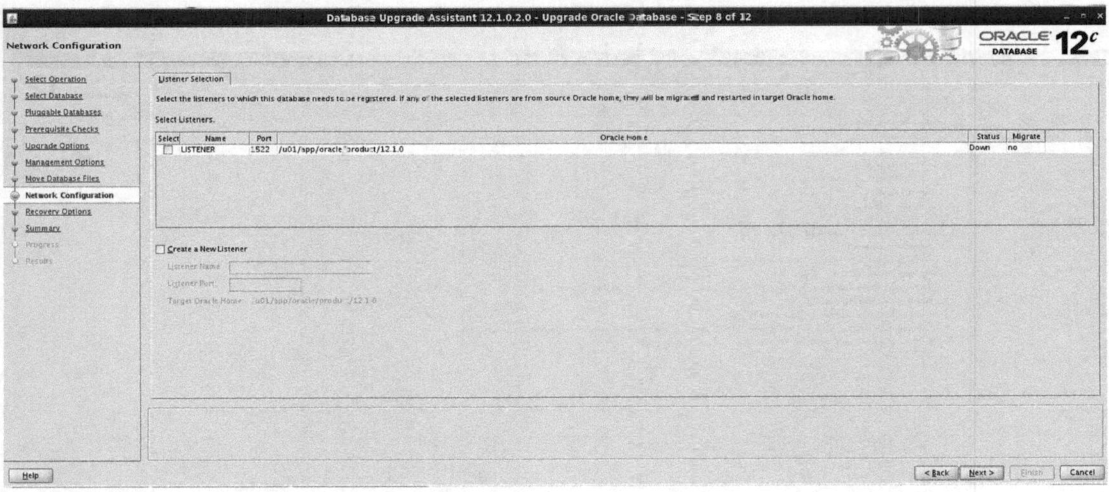

Figure 10-12. *DBUA, network configuration*

461

RMAN will take a backup of the container database and all the pluggable databases, as shown in Figure 10-13.

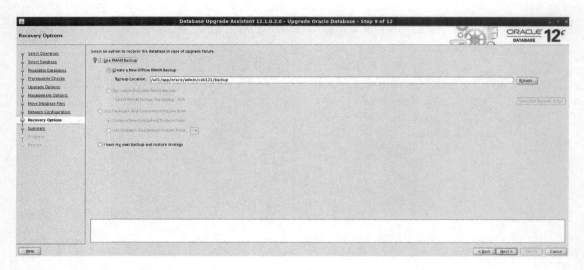

Figure 10-13. *DBUA, recovery options*

The summary page, as shown in Figure 10-14, details the container and pluggable databases that are getting upgraded.

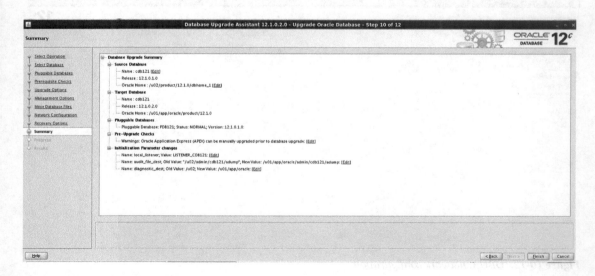

Figure 10-14. *DBUA, upgrade summary*

The upgrade process will first upgrade the container databases. Once it completes the post-upgrade steps for the container database, it will move to upgrading each pluggable database. The database upgrade will complete after executing the post-upgrade steps of all the pluggable databases, as shown in Figure 10-15.

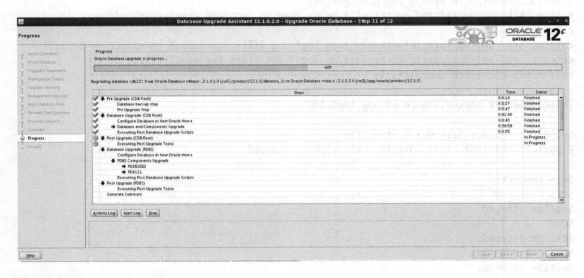

Figure 10-15. *DBUA, upgrade progress*

Manual Database Upgrade or Command-Line Upgrade

You can also use a command-line upgrade to upgrade the container and pluggable databases. Here you will perform the upgrade steps manually in the prescribed order. You have to make sure that each step has completed successfully before proceeding to the next step. You have already seen the necessity and benefits of the manual upgrade method in Chapter 2. In this section, we will cover the steps for upgrading the container and all its pluggable databases. In this method, the data dictionary of the container and all pluggable databases will get upgraded to the higher-database version.

First you start the container database and all of its pluggable databases and then you execute the pre-upgrade script.

```
$ /u01/app/oracle/product/12.1.0/perl/bin/perl catcon.pl -d /u01/app/oracle/backup -b
catpreupgrd_log -l /u01/app/oracle/backup preupgrd.sql
-d denotes has the location of scripts preupgrd.sql and utluppkg.sql
-l denotes the location where log has to be placed
-b denotes the base name used for log file
```

The SQL script passed to catcon.pl is preupgrd.sql.

This script will be executed at the container database and pluggable databases. Its output will be stored in the log directory /u01/app/oracle/backup.

The pre-upgrade results and fixup scripts are stored in the $ORACLE_BASE/cfgtoollogs/<ORACLE_SID>/ preupgrade folder.

The pluggable database pre-upgrade results are stored in the pdbfiles folder.

The sample output of the pre-upgrade script (preupgrade.log) is as follows:

```
$ /u02/product/12.1.0/dbhome_1/perl/bin/perl catcon.pl -d /u01/app/oracle/backup -l /u01/
app/oracle/backup -b preupg_log preupgrd.sql
catcon: ALL catcon-related output will be written to /u01/app/oracle/backup/preupg_log_
catcon_3536.lst
catcon: See /u01/app/oracle/backup/preupg_log*.log files for output generated by scripts
catcon: See /u01/app/oracle/backup/preupg_log_*.lst files for spool files, if any
catcon.pl: completed successfully

[oracle@Server backup]$ more preupg_log0.log

SQL*Plus: Release 12.1.0.1.0 Production
Copyright (c) 1982, 2013, Oracle.  All rights reserved.

SQL> Connected.
SQL>   2
Session altered.
SQL>   2
Session altered.
SQL>   2
Session altered.
SQL>   2
Session altered.
SQL> SQL>
SQL>   2
Session altered.
SQL>
NOW_CONNECTED_TO
------------------------------------------------------------------------------
==== Current Container = CDB$ROOT Id = 1 ====
SQL>
NOW_CONNECTED_TO
------------------------------------------------------------------------------
==== Current Container = CDB$ROOT Id = 1 ====
SQL>   2
Session altered.
SQL> SQL> SQL> SQL> SQL> SQL> SQL> SQL> SQL> SQL> SQL> SQL> SQL> SQL> SQL> SQL> SQL>
SQL> SQL>   2
CATCONSECTION
--------------------------
==== CATCON EXEC ROOT ====
SQL>
BEGIN_RUNNING
------------------------------------------------------------------------------
==== @/u01/app/oracle/backup/preupgrd.sql Container:CDB$ROOT Id:1 Proc:0 ====
SQL>
```

```
BEGIN_RUNNING
--------------------------------------------------------------------------------
==== @/u01/app/oracle/backup/preupgrd.sql Container:CDB$ROOT Id:1 Proc:0 ====
SQL>   2
Session altered.
SQL>   2
Session altered.
SQL>
Loading Pre-Upgrade Package...
*****************************************************************************
Executing Pre-Upgrade Checks in CDB$ROOT...
*****************************************************************************

        *****************************************************************
                    ====>> ERRORS FOUND for CDB$ROOT <<====
    The following are *** ERROR LEVEL CONDITIONS *** that must be addressed
                       prior to attempting your upgrade.
                 Failure to do so will result in a failed upgrade.
                 You MUST resolve the above errors prior to upgrade
        *****************************************************************
        *****************************************************************

                ====>> PRE-UPGRADE RESULTS for CDB$ROOT <<====
ACTIONS REQUIRED:
1. Review results of the pre-upgrade checks:
 /u02/cfgtoollogs/cdb121/preupgrade/preupgrade.log
2. Execute in the SOURCE environment BEFORE upgrade:
 /u02/cfgtoollogs/cdb121/preupgrade/preupgrade_fixups.sql
3. Execute in the NEW environment AFTER upgrade:
 /u02/cfgtoollogs/cdb121/preupgrade/postupgrade_fixups.sql
        *****************************************************************
*****************************************************************************
Pre-Upgrade Checks in CDB$ROOT Completed.
*****************************************************************************
*****************************************************************************
*****************************************************************************
SQL> ==== @/u01/app/oracle/backup/preupgrd.sql Container:CDB$ROOT Id:1 Proc:0 ====
SQL> ==== @/u01/app/oracle/backup/preupgrd.sql Container:CDB$ROOT Id:1 Proc:0 ====
SQL> SQL>
SQL>   2 SQL> SQL>
SQL>   2  SQL> SQL> SQL> SQL> SQL> SQL> SQL> SQL> SQL> SQL> SQL> SQL> SQL> SQL> SQL>
SQL> SQL> SQL> SQL>    2
Session altered.
SQL>
NOW_CONNECTED_TO
--------------------------------------------------------------------------------
==== Current Container = PDB$SEED Id = 2 ====
SQL>
NOW_CONNECTED_TO
--------------------------------------------------------------------------------
==== Current Container = PDB$SEED Id = 2 ====
SQL>   2
```

```
CATCONSECTION
------------------------------------
==== CATCON EXEC IN CONTAINERS ====
SQL>
BEGIN_RUNNING
----------------------------------------------------------------------
==== @/u01/app/oracle/backup/preupgrd.sql Container:PDB$SEED Id:2 Proc:0 ====
SQL>
BEGIN_RUNNING
----------------------------------------------------------------------
==== @/u01/app/oracle/backup/preupgrd.sql Container:PDB$SEED Id:2 Proc:0 ====
SQL>    2
Session altered.
SQL>    2
Session altered.
SQL>
Loading Pre-Upgrade Package...
**********************************************************************Executing Pre-Upgrade
Checks in PDB$SEED...
**********************************************************************

 ====>> ERRORS FOUND for PDB$SEED <<====
 The following are *** ERROR LEVEL CONDITIONS *** that must be addressed
                  prior to attempting your upgrade.
       Failure to do so will result in a failed upgrade.
       You MUST resolve the above errors prior to upgrade


       **************************************************************
       **************************************************************
          ====>> PRE-UPGRADE RESULTS for PDB$SEED <<====
ACTIONS REQUIRED:
1. Review results of the pre-upgrade checks:
 /u02/cfgtoollogs/cdb121/preupgrade/preupgrade.log
2. Execute in the SOURCE environment BEFORE upgrade:
 /u02/cfgtoollogs/cdb121/preupgrade/preupgrade_fixups.sql
3. Execute in the NEW environment AFTER upgrade:
 /u02/cfgtoollogs/cdb121/preupgrade/postupgrade_fixups.sql
       **************************************************************
**********************************************************************
Pre-Upgrade Checks in PDB$SEED Completed.
**********************************************************************
SQL> ==== @/u01/app/oracle/backup/preupgrd.sql Container:PDB$SEED Id:2  Proc:0 ====
SQL> ==== @/u01/app/oracle/backup/preupgrd.sql Container:PDB$SEED Id:2  Proc:0 ====
SQL> SQL>
SQL>    2  SQL> SQL>
SQL> ========== PROCESS ENDED ==========
SQL> Disconnected from Oracle Database 12c Enterprise Edition Release 12.1.0.1.0 - 64bit
Production
With the Partitioning, OLAP, Advanced Analytics and Real Application Testing options

$ more /u01/app/oracle/backup/preupg_log1.log
SQL*Plus: Release 12.1.0.1.0 Production
```

```
Copyright (c) 1982, 2013, Oracle.  All rights reserved.
SQL> Connected.
SQL>   2
Session altered.
SQL>   2
Session altered.
SQL>   2
Session altered.
SQL>   2
Session altered.
SQL> SQL>
SQL>   2
Session altered.
SQL> SQL> SQL> SQL> SQL> SQL> SQL> SQL> SQL> SQL> SQL> SQL> SQL> SQL> SQL> SQL> SQL> SQL>
SQL> SQL>   2
Session altered.
SQL>
NOW_CONNECTED_TO
--------------------------------------------------------------------------------
==== Current Container = PDB121 Id = 3 ====
SQL>
NOW_CONNECTED_TO
--------------------------------------------------------------------------------
==== Current Container = PDB121 Id = 3 ====
SQL>   2
CATCONSECTION
----------------------------------------
==== CATCON EXEC IN CONTAINERS ====
SQL>
BEGIN_RUNNING
--------------------------------------------------------------------------------
==== @/u01/app/oracle/backup/preupgrd.sql Container:PDB121 Id:3 Proc:1 ====
SQL>
BEGIN_RUNNING
--------------------------------------------------------------------------------
==== @/u01/app/oracle/backup/preupgrd.sql Container:PDB121 Id:3 Proc:1 ====
SQL>   2
Session altered.
SQL>   2
Session altered.
SQL>
Loading Pre-Upgrade Package...
********************************************************************************
Executing Pre-Upgrade Checks in PDB121...
********************************************************************************
    ************************************************************
```

```
              ====>> ERRORS FOUND for PDB121 <<====
The following are *** ERROR LEVEL CONDITIONS *** that must be addressed
                  prior to attempting your upgrade.
          Failure to do so will result in a failed upgrade.
          You MUST resolve the above errors prior to upgrade
       ************************************************************
       ************************************************************
              ====>> PRE-UPGRADE RESULTS for PDB121 <<====
ACTIONS REQUIRED:
1. Review results of the pre-upgrade checks:
 /u02/cfgtoollogs/cdb121/preupgrade/preupgrade.log
2. Execute in the SOURCE environment BEFORE upgrade:
 /u02/cfgtoollogs/cdb121/preupgrade/preupgrade_fixups.sql
3. Execute in the NEW environment AFTER upgrade:
 /u02/cfgtoollogs/cdb121/preupgrade/postupgrade_fixups.sql
       ************************************************************
*******************************************************************************
Pre-Upgrade Checks in PDB121 Completed.
*******************************************************************************
*******************************************************************************
*******************************************************************************
SQL> ==== @/u01/app/oracle/backup/preupgrd.sql Container:PDB121 Id:3 Proc:1 ====
```

First execute the pre-upgrade script in the container database and then in the seed database followed by the pluggable databases. The pre-upgrade output will be the same as the stand-alone database. The output should be clean; it should not have any error or warnings. The prerequisite steps before the upgrade are same as the stand-alone ones (discussed in Chapter 2).

As the first upgrade step, take a backup of the entire container database. The backup could be a cold backup or a traditional hot backup or an RMAN backup. The backup should be capable enough to restore the database to a valid state. This means the backup should contain valid datafiles and the necessary archived logs for recovery.

```
RMAN> backup database plus archivelog;
```

Upgrade Steps

Once you confirm that the database is ready for the upgrade, shut down the database and start it in upgrade mode using the higher-version database binaries. In this example, you use the 12.1.0.2.0 binaries to start the database in upgrade mode.

```
SQL> shutdown immediate;
Database closed.
Database dismounted.
ORACLE instance shut down.
```

Set the environment variables to a higher database version home. Edit the /etc/oratab file and change the Oracle Home of the database to the higher 12c version (12.1.0.2.0).

Create a new password file for the container database or copy it from the source Oracle Home. If the platform is Windows, create a new service for the database to be upgraded.

Copy the init parameter file to the new 12c Oracle Home.

Start the database in upgrade mode.

```
SQL> startup upgrade
ORACLE instance started.

Total System Global Area 1660944384 bytes
Fixed Size                    2925072 bytes
Variable Size              1056968176 bytes
Database Buffers            587202560 bytes
Redo Buffers                13848576 bytes
Database mounted.
Database opened
```

Right now only the container database is opened in upgrade mode. Start the pluggable databases in upgrade mode as they also need to be upgraded.

```
SQL> show pdbs

    CON_ID CON_NAME                        OPEN MODE  RESTRICTED
---------- ------------------------------ ---------- ----------
         2 PDB$SEED                        MIGRATE    YES
         3 PDB121                          MOUNTED

SQL> alter pluggable database all open upgrade;
Pluggable database altered.

SQL> show pdbs

    CON_ID CON_NAME                        OPEN MODE  RESTRICTED
---------- ------------------------------ ---------- ----------
         2 PDB$SEED                        MIGRATE    YES
         3 PDB121                          MIGRATE    YES
```

You can see now that the pluggable database is started in upgrade mode.

Exit SQL*Plus and invoke catctl.pl to run the catupgrd.sql script.

The script Catctl.pl has the options –c and –C like you have for catcon.pl to execute catupgrd.sql in a particular PDB. Here you are upgrading the container and all the pluggable databases, and hence you won't use those options.

```
$ /u01/app/oracle/product/12.1.0/perl/bin/perl catctl.pl -n 4 -N 4 -l /u01/app/oracle/backup
catupgrd.sql

Argument list for [catctl.pl]
SQL Process Count       n = 4
SQL PDB Process Count   N = 4
Input Directory         d = 0
Phase Logging Table     t = 0
Log Dir                 l = /u01/app/oracle/backup
Script                  s = 0
Serial Run              S = 0
Upgrade Mode active     M = 0
```

```
Start Phase          p = 0
End Phase            P = 0
Log Id               i = 0
Run in               c = 0
Do not run in        C = 0
Echo OFF             e = 1
No Post Upgrade      x = 0
Reverse Order        r = 0
Open Mode Normal     o = 0
Debug catcon.pm      z = 0
Debug catctl.pl      Z = 0
Display Phases       y = 0
Child Process        I = 0

catctl.pl version: 12.1.0.2.0
Oracle Base            = /u01/app/oracle

Analyzing file catupgrd.sql
Log files in /u01/app/oracle/backup
catcon: ALL catcon-related output will be written to /u01/app/oracle/backup/catupgrd_
catcon_14419.lst
catcon: See /u01/app/oracle/backup/catupgrd*.log files for output generated by scripts
catcon: See /u01/app/oracle/backup/catupgrd_*.lst files for spool files, if any
Number of Cpus         = 1
Parallel PDB Upgrades = 2
SQL PDB Process Count = 4
SQL Process Count      = 4

[CONTAINER NAMES]

CDB$ROOT
PDB$SEED
PDB121
PDB Inclusion:[PDB$SEED PDB121] Exclusion:[]

------------------------------------------------------------
Phases [0-73]         Start Time:[2016_03_15 16:34:27]
Container Lists Inclusion:[CDB$ROOT] Exclusion:[NONE]
------------------------------------------------------------
Serial   Phase #: 0    CDB$ROOT Files: 1
-rw-r-----. 1 oracle oinstall      365 Mar 13 13:52 catupgrd40.736783148345665.sql
[oracle@Server admin]$ /u01/app/oracle/product/12.1.0/perl/bin/perl catctl.pl -n 4 -N 4 -l /
u01/app/oracle/backup catupgrd.sql

Argument list for [catctl.pl]
SQL Process Count      n = 4
SQL PDB Process Count N = 4
Input Directory        d = 0
Phase Logging Table    t = 0
Log Dir                l = /u01/app/oracle/backup
Script                 s = 0
```

```
Serial Run              S = 0
Upgrade Mode active     M = 0
Start Phase             p = 0
End Phase               P = 0
Log Id                  i = 0
Run in                  c = 0
Do not run in           C = 0
Echo OFF                e = 1
No Post Upgrade         x = 0
Reverse Order           r = 0
Open Mode Normal        o = 0
Debug catcon.pm         z = 0
Debug catctl.pl         Z = 0
Display Phases          y = 0
Child Process           I = 0

catctl.pl version: 12.1.0.2.0
Oracle Base       = /u01/app/oracle

Analyzing file catupgrd.sql
Log files in /u01/app/oracle/backup
catcon: ALL catcon-related output will be written to /u01/app/oracle/backup/catupgrd_
catcon_14419.lst
catcon: See /u01/app/oracle/backup/catupgrd*.log files for output generated by scripts
catcon: See /u01/app/oracle/backup/catupgrd_*.lst files for spool files, if any
Number of Cpus        = 1
Parallel PDB Upgrades = 2
SQL PDB Process Count = 4
SQL Process Count     = 4

[CONTAINER NAMES]

CDB$ROOT
PDB$SEED
PDB121
PDB Inclusion:[PDB$SEED PDB121] Exclusion:[]

-------------------------------------------------------
Phases [0-73]         Start Time:[2016_03_15 16:34:27]
Container Lists Inclusion:[CDB$ROOT] Exclusion:[NONE]
-------------------------------------------------------
Serial   Phase #: 0   CDB$ROOT Files: 1    Time: 20s
Serial   Phase #: 1   CDB$ROOT Files: 5    Time: 85s
Restart  Phase #: 2   CDB$ROOT Files: 1    Time: 0s
Parallel Phase #: 3   CDB$ROOT Files: 18   Time: 27s
Restart  Phase #: 4   CDB$ROOT Files: 1    Time: 0s
Serial   Phase #: 5   CDB$ROOT Files: 5    Time: 30s
Serial   Phase #: 6   CDB$ROOT Files: 1    Time: 17s
Serial   Phase #: 7   CDB$ROOT Files: 4    Time: 10s
Restart  Phase #: 8   CDB$ROOT Files: 1    Time: 0s
Parallel Phase #: 9   CDB$ROOT Files: 62   Time: 95s
```

```
Restart  Phase #:10   CDB$ROOT Files: 1     Time: 0s
Serial   Phase #:11   CDB$ROOT Files: 1     Time: 23s
Restart  Phase #:12   CDB$ROOT Files: 1     Time: 0s
Parallel Phase #:13   CDB$ROOT Files: 91    Time: 12s
Restart  Phase #:14   CDB$ROOT Files: 1     Time: 0s
Parallel Phase #:15   CDB$ROOT Files: 111   Time: 33s
Restart  Phase #:16   CDB$ROOT Files: 1     Time: 0s
Serial   Phase #:17   CDB$ROOT Files: 3     Time: 2s
Restart  Phase #:18   CDB$ROOT Files: 1     Time: 0s
Parallel Phase #:19   CDB$ROOT Files: 32    Time: 50s
Restart  Phase #:20   CDB$ROOT Files: 1     Time: 0s
Serial   Phase #:21   CDB$ROOT Files: 3     Time: 11s
Restart  Phase #:22   CDB$ROOT Files: 1     Time: 1s
Parallel Phase #:23   CDB$ROOT Files: 23    Time: 121s
Restart  Phase #:24   CDB$ROOT Files: 1     Time: 0s
Parallel Phase #:25   CDB$ROOT Files: 11    Time: 68s
Restart  Phase #:26   CDB$ROOT Files: 1     Time: 0s
Serial   Phase #:27   CDB$ROOT Files: 1     Time: 0s
Restart  Phase #:28   CDB$ROOT Files: 1     Time: 0s
Serial   Phase #:30   CDB$ROOT Files: 1     Time: 0s
Serial   Phase #:31   CDB$ROOT Files: 257   Time: 26s
Serial   Phase #:32   CDB$ROOT Files: 1     Time: 0s
Restart  Phase #:33   CDB$ROOT Files: 1     Time: 0s
Serial   Phase #:34   CDB$ROOT Files: 1     Time: 3s
Restart  Phase #:35   CDB$ROOT Files: 1     Time: 0s
Restart  Phase #:36   CDB$ROOT Files: 1     Time: 1s
Serial   Phase #:37   CDB$ROOT Files: 4     Time: 50s
Restart  Phase #:38   CDB$ROOT Files: 1     Time: 0s
Parallel Phase #:39   CDB$ROOT Files: 13    Time: 72s
Restart  Phase #:40   CDB$ROOT Files: 1     Time: 0s
Parallel Phase #:41   CDB$ROOT Files: 10    Time: 13s
Restart  Phase #:42   CDB$ROOT Files: 1     Time: 1s
Serial   Phase #:43   CDB$ROOT Files: 1     Time: 7s
Restart  Phase #:44   CDB$ROOT Files: 1     Time: 0s
Serial   Phase #:45   CDB$ROOT Files: 1     Time: 2s
Serial   Phase #:46   CDB$ROOT Files: 1     Time: 1s
Restart  Phase #:47   CDB$ROOT Files: 1     Time: 0s
Serial   Phase #:48   CDB$ROOT Files: 1     Time: 217s
Restart  Phase #:49   CDB$ROOT Files: 1     Time: 0s
Serial   Phase #:50   CDB$ROOT Files: 1     Time: 49s
Restart  Phase #:51   CDB$ROOT Files: 1     Time: 0s
Serial   Phase #:52   CDB$ROOT Files: 1     Time: 60s
Restart  Phase #:53   CDB$ROOT Files: 1     Time: 0s
Serial   Phase #:54   CDB$ROOT Files: 1     Time: 76s
Restart  Phase #:55   CDB$ROOT Files: 1     Time: 0s
Serial   Phase #:56   CDB$ROOT Files: 1     Time: 91s
Restart  Phase #:57   CDB$ROOT Files: 1     Time: 0s
Serial   Phase #:58   CDB$ROOT Files: 1     Time: 146s
Restart  Phase #:59   CDB$ROOT Files: 1     Time: 0s
Serial   Phase #:60   CDB$ROOT Files: 1     Time: 211s
Restart  Phase #:61   CDB$ROOT Files: 1     Time: 0s
```

```
Serial    Phase #:62    CDB$ROOT Files: 1      Time: 2332s
Restart   Phase #:63    CDB$ROOT Files: 1      Time: 0s
Serial    Phase #:64    CDB$ROOT Files: 1      Time: 0s
Serial    Phase #:65    CDB$ROOT Files: 1 Calling sqlpatch with LD_LIBRARY_PATH=/u01/app/
oracle/product/12.1.0/lib; export LD_LIBRARY_PATH; LIBPATH=/u01/app/oracle/product/12.1.0/
lib; export LIBPATH; LD_LIBRARY_PATH_64=/u01/app/oracle/product/12.1.0/lib; export LD_
LIBRARY_PATH_64; DYLD_LIBRARY_PATH=/u01/app/oracle/product/12.1.0/lib; export DYLD_LIBRARY_
PATH; /u01/app/oracle/product/12.1.0/perl/bin/perl -I /u01/app/oracle/product/12.1.0/
rdbms/admin -I /u01/app/oracle/product/12.1.0/rdbms/admin/../../sqlpatch /u01/app/oracle/
product/12.1.0/rdbms/admin/../../sqlpatch/sqlpatch.pl -verbose -upgrade_mode_only -pdbs
'CDB$ROOT' > /u01/app/oracle/backup/catupgrd_datapatch_upgrade.log 2> /u01/app/oracle/
backup/catupgrd_datapatch_upgrade.err
returned from sqlpatch    Time: 43s
Serial    Phase #:66    CDB$ROOT Files: 1      Time: 3s
Serial    Phase #:68    CDB$ROOT Files: 1      Time: 1s
Serial    Phase #:69    CDB$ROOT Files: 1 Calling sqlpatch with LD_LIBRARY_PATH=/u01/app/
oracle/product/12.1.0/lib; export LD_LIBRARY_PATH; LIBPATH=/u01/app/oracle/product/12.1.0/
lib; export LIBPATH; LD_LIBRARY_PATH_64=/u01/app/oracle/product/12.1.0/lib; export LD_
LIBRARY_PATH_64; DYLD_LIBRARY_PATH=/u01/app/oracle/product/12.1.0/lib; export DYLD_LIBRARY_
PATH; /u01/app/oracle/product/12.1.0/perl/bin/perl -I /u01/app/oracle/product/12.1.0/
rdbms/admin -I /u01/app/oracle/product/12.1.0/rdbms/admin/../../sqlpatch /u01/app/oracle/
product/12.1.0/rdbms/admin/../../sqlpatch/sqlpatch.pl -verbose -pdbs 'CDB$ROOT' > /u01/app/
oracle/backup/catupgrd_datapatch_normal.log 2> /u01/app/oracle/backup/catupgrd_datapatch_
normal.err
returned from sqlpatch
    Time: 113s
Serial    Phase #:70    CDB$ROOT Files: 1      Time: 9s
Serial    Phase #:71    CDB$ROOT Files: 1      Time: 0s
Serial    Phase #:72    CDB$ROOT Files: 1      Time: 1s
Serial    Phase #:73    CDB$ROOT Files: 1      Time: 0s

------------------------------------------------------
Phases [0-73]          End Time:[2016_03_15 17:53:20]
Container Lists Inclusion:[CDB$ROOT] Exclusion:[NONE]
------------------------------------------------------

Start processing of PDB$SEED
[/u01/app/oracle/product/12.1.0/perl/bin/perl catctl.pl -n 4 -N 4 -l /u01/app/oracle/backup
-I -i pdb_seed -c 'PDB$SEED' catupgrd.sql]

Start processing of PDB121
[/u01/app/oracle/product/12.1.0/perl/bin/perl catctl.pl -n 4 -N 4 -l /u01/app/oracle/backup
-I -i pdb121 -c 'PDB121' catupgrd.sql]

Argument list for [catctl.pl]

Argument list for [catctl.pl]
SQL Process Count      n = 4
SQL PDB Process Count N = 4
Input Directory        d = 0
Phase Logging Table    t = 0
```

```
Log Dir                 l = /u01/app/oracle/backup
Script                  s = 0
Serial Run              S = 0
Upgrade Mode active     M = 0
Start Phase             p = 0
End Phase               P = 0
Log Id                  i = pdb121
Run in                  c = PDB121
Do not run in           C = 0
Echo OFF                e = 1
No Post Upgrade         x = 0
Reverse Order           r = 0
Open Mode Normal        o = 0
Debug catcon.pm         z = 0
Debug catctl.pl         Z = 0
Display Phases          y = 0
Child Process           I = 1

catctl.pl version: 12.1.0.2.0
Oracle Base             = /u01/app/oracle

Analyzing file catupgrd.sql
Log files in /u01/app/oracle/backup
SQL Process Count       n = 4
SQL PDB Process Count   N = 4
Input Directory         d = 0
Phase Logging Table     t = 0
Log Dir                 l = /u01/app/oracle/backup
Script                  s = 0
Serial Run              S = 0
Upgrade Mode active     M = 0
Start Phase             p = 0
End Phase               P = 0
Log Id                  i = pdb_seed
Run in                  c = PDB$SEED
Do not run in           C = 0
Echo OFF                e = 1
No Post Upgrade         x = 0
Reverse Order           r = 0
Open Mode Normal        o = 0
Debug catcon.pm         z = 0
Debug catctl.pl         Z = 0
Display Phases          y = 0
Child Process           I = 1

catctl.pl version: 12.1.0.2.0
Oracle Base             = /u01/app/oracle

Analyzing file catupgrd.sql
Log files in /u01/app/oracle/backup
```

```
catcon: ALL catcon-related output will be written tc /u01/app/oracle/backup/catupgrdpdb_
seed_catcon_19748.lst
catcon: ALL catcon-related output will be written tc /u01/app/oracle/backup/catupgrdpdb121_
catcon_19750.lst
catcon: See /u01/app/oracle/backup/catupgrdpdb121*.log files for output generated by scripts
catcon: See /u01/app/oracle/backup/catupgrdpdb121_*.lst files for spool files, if any
catcon: See /u01/app/oracle/backup/catupgrdpdb_seed*.log files for output generated by
scripts
catcon: See /u01/app/oracle/backup/catupgrdpdb_seed_*.lst files for spool files, if any
Number of Cpus       = 1
SQL PDB Process Count = 4
SQL Process Count     = 4

[CONTAINER NAMES]

CDB$ROOT
PDB$SEED
PDB121
Number of Cpus       = 1
SQL PDB Process Count = 4
SQL Process Count     = 4

[CONTAINER NAMES]

CDB$ROOT
PDB$SEED
PDB121
PDB Inclusion:[PDB$SEED] Exclusion:[]
PDB Inclusion:[PDB121] Exclusion:[]

-----------------------------------------------------
Phases [0-73]          Start Time:[2016_03_15 17:53:33]
Container Lists Inclusion:[PDB$SEED] Exclusion:[NONE]
-----------------------------------------------------
Serial   Phase #: 0   PDB$SEED Files: 1
-----------------------------------------------------
Phases [0-73]          Start Time:[2016_03_15 17:53:33]
Container Lists Inclusion:[PDB121] Exclusion:[NONE]
-----------------------------------------------------
Serial   Phase #: 0   PDB121 Files: 1     Time: 36s
Serial   Phase #: 1   PDB121 Files: 5     Time: 36s
Serial   Phase #: 1   PDB$SEED Files: 5   Time: 91s
Restart  Phase #: 2   PDB$SEED Files: 1   Time: 91s
Restart  Phase #: 2   PDB121 Files: 1     Time: 0s
Parallel Phase #: 3   PDB$SEED Files: 18  Time: 0s
Parallel Phase #: 3   PDB121 Files: 18    Time: 43s
Restart  Phase #: 4   PDB121 Files: 1     Time: 43s
Restart  Phase #: 4   PDB$SEED Files: 1   Time: 1s
Serial   Phase #: 5   PDB121 Files: 5     Time: 1s
Serial   Phase #: 5   PDB$SEED Files: 5   Time: 33s
Serial   Phase #: 6   PDB121 Files: 1     Time: 33s
```

```
Serial    Phase #: 6    PDB$SEED Files: 1      Time: 22s
Serial    Phase #: 7    PDB$SEED Files: 4      Time: 22s
Serial    Phase #: 7    PDB121 Files: 4        Time: 13s
Restart   Phase #: 8    PDB121 Files: 1        Time: 13s
Restart   Phase #: 8    PDB$SEED Files: 1      Time: 0s
Parallel  Phase #: 9    PDB121 Files: 62       Time: 0s
Parallel  Phase #: 9    PDB$SEED Files: 62     Time: 278s
Restart   Phase #:10    PDB$SEED Files: 1      Time: 278s
Restart   Phase #:10    PDB121 Files: 1        Time: 0s
Serial    Phase #:11    PDB$SEED Files: 1      Time: 0s
Serial    Phase #:11    PDB121 Files: 1        Time: 71s
Restart   Phase #:12    PDB$SEED Files: 1      Time: 71s
Restart   Phase #:12    PDB121 Files: 1        Time: 0s
Parallel  Phase #:13    PDB$SEED Files: 91     Time: 0s
Parallel  Phase #:13    PDB121 Files: 91       Time: 15s
Restart   Phase #:14    PDB$SEED Files: 1      Time: 15s
Restart   Phase #:14    PDB121 Files: 1        Time: 0s
Parallel  Phase #:15    PDB$SEED Files: 111    Time: 0s
Parallel  Phase #:15    PDB121 Files: 111      Time: 33s
Restart   Phase #:16    PDB$SEED Files: 1      Time: 1s
Serial    Phase #:17    PDB$SEED Files: 3      Time: 2s
Restart   Phase #:18    PDB$SEED Files: 1      Time: 0s
Parallel  Phase #:19    PDB$SEED Files: 32     Time: 74s
Restart   Phase #:16    PDB121 Files: 1        Time: 0s
Serial    Phase #:17    PDB121 Files: 3        Time: 5s
Restart   Phase #:18    PDB121 Files: 1        Time: 0s
Parallel  Phase #:19    PDB121 Files: 32       Time: 97s
Restart   Phase #:20    PDB$SEED Files: 1      Time: 0s
Serial    Phase #:21    PDB$SEED Files: 3      Time: 63s
Restart   Phase #:20    PDB121 Files: 1        Time: 0s
Serial    Phase #:21    PDB121 Files: 3        Time: 17s
Restart   Phase #:22    PDB$SEED Files: 1      Time: 0s
Parallel  Phase #:23    PDB$SEED Files: 23     Time: 14s
Restart   Phase #:22    PDB121 Files: 1        Time: 1s
Parallel  Phase #:23    PDB121 Files: 23       Time: 437s
Restart   Phase #:24    PDB$SEED Files: 1      Time: 430s
Restart   Phase #:24    PDB121 Files: 1        Time: 0s
Parallel  Phase #:25    PDB$SEED Files: 11     Time: 0s
Parallel  Phase #:25    PDB121 Files: 11       Time: 33s
Restart   Phase #:26    PDB121 Files: 1        Time: 0s
Serial    Phase #:27    PDB121 Files: 1        Time: 0s
Restart   Phase #:28    PDB121 Files: 1        Time: 1s
Serial    Phase #:30    PDB121 Files: 1        Time: 0s
Serial    Phase #:31    PDB121 Files: 257      Time: 85s
Restart   Phase #:26    PDB$SEED Files: 1      Time: 1s
Serial    Phase #:27    PDB$SEED Files: 1      Time: 0s
Restart   Phase #:28    PDB$SEED Files: 1      Time: 0s
Serial    Phase #:30    PDB$SEED Files: 1      Time: 0s
Serial    Phase #:31    PDB$SEED Files: 257    Time: 116s
Serial    Phase #:32    PDB121 Files: 1        Time: 0s
Restart   Phase #:33    PDB121 Files: 1        Time: 64s
```

```
Serial   Phase #:32   PDB$SEED Files: 1      Time: 0s
Restart  Phase #:33   PDB$SEED Files: 1      Time: 1s
Serial   Phase #:34   PDB121 Files: 1        Time: 1s
Serial   Phase #:34   PDB$SEED Files: 1      Time: 3s
Restart  Phase #:35   PDB$SEED Files: 1      Time: 3s
Restart  Phase #:35   PDB121 Files: 1        Time: 1s
Restart  Phase #:36   PDB121 Files: 1        Time: 1s
Restart  Phase #:36   PDB$SEED Files: 1      Time: 0s
Serial   Phase #:37   PDB121 Files: 4        Time: 0s
Serial   Phase #:37   PDB$SEED Files: 4      Time: 102s
Restart  Phase #:38   PDB121 Files: 1        Time: 0s
Parallel Phase #:39   PDB121 Files: 13       Time: 116s
Restart  Phase #:38   PDB$SEED Files: 1      Time: 0s
Parallel Phase #:39   PDB$SEED Files: 13     Time: 129s
Restart  Phase #:40   PDB121 Files: 1        Time: 1s
Parallel Phase #:41   PDB121 Files: 10       Time: 56s
Restart  Phase #:42   PDB121 Files: 1        Time: 1s
Serial   Phase #:43   PDB121 Files: 1        Time: 29s
Restart  Phase #:44   PDB121 Files: 1        Time: 0s
Serial   Phase #:45   PDB121 Files: 1        Time: 3s
Serial   Phase #:46   PDB121 Files: 1
   Time: 233s
Restart  Phase #:40   PDB$SEED Files: 1      Time: 0s
Parallel Phase #:41   PDB$SEED Files: 10     Time: 9s
Restart  Phase #:42   PDB$SEED Files: 1      Time: 1s
Serial   Phase #:43   PDB$SEED Files: 1      Time: 6s
Restart  Phase #:44   PDB$SEED Files: 1      Time: 0s
Serial   Phase #:45   PDB$SEED Files: 1      Time: 3s
Serial   Phase #:46   PDB$SEED Files: 1      Time: 0s
Restart  Phase #:47   PDB$SEED Files: 1      Time: 0s
Serial   Phase #:48   PDB$SEED Files: 1      Time: 169s
Restart  Phase #:49   PDB$SEED Files: 1      Time: 1s
Serial   Phase #:50   PDB$SEED Files: 1      Time: 47s
Restart  Phase #:51   PDB$SEED Files: 1      Time: 0s
Serial   Phase #:52   PDB$SEED Files: 1      Time: 64s
Restart  Phase #:53   PDB$SEED Files: 1      Time: 0s
Serial   Phase #:54   PDB$SEED Files: 1      Time: 108s
Restart  Phase #:55   PDB$SEED Files: 1      Time: 0s
Serial   Phase #:56   PDB$SEED Files: 1      Time: 139s
Restart  Phase #:57   PDB$SEED Files: 1      Time: 0s
Serial   Phase #:58   PDB$SEED Files: 1      Time: 100s
Restart  Phase #:59   PDB$SEED Files: 1      Time: 0s
Serial   Phase #:60   PDB$SEED Files: 1      Time: 113s
Restart  Phase #:61   PDB$SEED Files: 1      Time: 0s
Serial   Phase #:62   PDB$SEED Files: 1      Time: 204s
Restart  Phase #:63   PDB$SEED Files: 1      Time: 0s
Serial   Phase #:64   PDB$SEED Files: 1      Time: 1s
Serial   Phase #:65   PDB$SEED Files: 1 Calling sqlpatch with LD_LIBRARY_PATH=/u01/app/
oracle/product/12.1.0/lib; export LD_LIBRARY_PATH; LIBPATH=/u01/app/oracle/product/12.1.0/
lib; export LIBPATH; LD_LIBRARY_PATH_64=/u01/app/oracle/product/12.1.0/lib; export LD_
LIBRARY_PATH_64; DYLD_LIBRARY_PATH=/u01/app/oracle/product/12.1.0/lib; export DYLD_LIBRARY_
```

```
PATH; /u01/app/oracle/product/12.1.0/perl/bin/perl -I /u01/app/oracle/product/12.1.0/
rdbms/admin -I /u01/app/oracle/product/12.1.0/rdbms/admin/../../sqlpatch /u01/app/oracle/
product/12.1.0/rdbms/admin/../../sqlpatch/sqlpatch.pl -verbose -upgrade_mode_only -pdbs
'PDB$SEED' > /u01/app/oracle/backup/catupgrdpdb_seed_datapatch_upgrade.log 2> /u01/app/
oracle/backup/catupgrdpdb_seed_datapatch_upgrade.err
returned from sqlpatch
    Time: 78s
Serial   Phase #:66   PDB$SEED Files: 1    Time: 4s
Serial   Phase #:68   PDB$SEED Files: 1    Time: 12s
Serial   Phase #:69   PDB$SEED Files: 1 Calling sqlpatch with LD_LIBRARY_PATH=/u01/app/
oracle/product/12.1.0/lib; export LD_LIBRARY_PATH; LIBPATH=/u01/app/oracle/product/12.1.0/
lib; export LIBPATH; LD_LIBRARY_PATH_64=/u01/app/oracle/product/12.1.0/lib; export LD_
LIBRARY_PATH_64; DYLD_LIBRARY_PATH=/u01/app/oracle/product/12.1.0/lib; export DYLD_LIBRARY_
PATH; /u01/app/oracle/product/12.1.0/perl/bin/perl -I /u01/app/oracle/product/12.1.0/
rdbms/admin -I /u01/app/oracle/product/12.1.0/rdbms/admin/../../sqlpatch /u01/app/oracle/
product/12.1.0/rdbms/admin/../../sqlpatch/sqlpatch.pl -verbose -pdbs 'PDB$SEED' > /u01/app/
oracle/backup/catupgrdpdb_seed_datapatch_normal.log 2> /u01/app/oracle/backup/catupgrdpdb_
seed_datapatch_normal.err
returned from sqlpatch
    Time: 76s
Serial   Phase #:70   PDB$SEED Files: 1    Time: 198s
Serial   Phase #:71   PDB$SEED Files: 1    Time: 1s
Serial   Phase #:72   PDB$SEED Files: 1    Time: 6s
Serial   Phase #:73   PDB$SEED Files: 1    Time: 0s

-------------------------------------------------------
Phases [0-73]         End Time:[2016_03_15 18:44:07]
Container Lists Inclusion:[PDB$SEED] Exclusion:[NONE]
-------------------------------------------------------

Grand Total Time: 3038s PDB$SEED

LOG FILES: (catupgrdpdb_seed*.log)

Upgrade Summary Report Located in:
/u01/app/oracle/product/12.1.0/cfgtoollogs/cdb121/upgrade/upg_summary.log

Total Upgrade Time:          [0d:0h:50m:38s]

    Time: 4733s For CDB$ROOT
    Time: 3054s For PDB(s)

Grand Total Time: 7787s

LOG FILES: (catupgrd*.log)

Upgrade Summary Report Located in:
/u01/app/oracle/product/12.1.0/cfgtoollogs/cdb121/upgrade/upg_summary.log

Grand Total Upgrade Time:    [0d:2h:9m:47s]
```

First it executes `catupgrd.sql` in the container database, then in PDB$SEED, and finally in all the pluggable databases. In each database, `catupgrd.sql` execution goes in phases as the upgrade happens in the noncontainer databases.

If `catupgrd.sql` execution fails in the container database or any pluggable database, then execution can be invoked from a particular phase in a particular database.

Post-upgrade Tasks

Execute the post-upgrade fixups generated for the container and pluggable databases. The fixup scripts are generated separately for the container and each pluggable database. So, they need to be executed in the appropriate databases.

While executing the fixup scripts, it will check for the current container name. If it is found to be different, then it will terminate without executing it.

For example, the following is the post-upgrade script of pluggable database PDB12101:

```
execute immediate   'select dbms_preup.get_con_name from sys.dual' into con_name;
 IF con_name = 'PDB12101' THEN
 BEGIN
dbms_output.put_line ('Post Upgrade Fixup Script Generated on 2016-03-31 07:41:26  Version:
12.1.0.2 Build: 008');
dbms_output.put_line ('Beginning Post-Upgrade Fixups...');
END;
```

If this script is executed in another container, then it will not get executed. So, the pre-upgrade and post-upgrade fixup scripts cannot be executed through `catcon.pl`. They have to be executed individually.

Check the database component version and its status from `dba_registry` at the container and each pluggable database.

The following are other generic post-upgrade checks:

1) Edit /etc/oratab and modify Oracle Home for the upgraded databases.

2) If the database belongs to an RAC environment, change the `cluster_database` parameter value to `true`.

3) If there is a plan to change the compatible parameter value to the higher upgraded version, change it. Remember, this change cannot be rolled back. Hence, before making the change, perform the necessary testing with the application.

Pluggable Database Upgrade

In a multitenant architecture, an individual pluggable database can be upgraded to a higher version. This is one of the main features of a multitenant architecture. Suppose a container database has multiple pluggable databases and there is an upgrade requirement for a specific pluggable database. In that case, you can easily detach and attach that particular pluggable database to a higher-version container database and execute the upgrade scripts only for that particular pluggable database. The same applies to patching. Suppose a pluggable database requires a bug fix patch that is not required by the other pluggable databases. In that case, create a new container and apply the patch. Detach the pluggable database from the old container database and plug it into the patched container database. By doing so, the other pluggable databases will remain unaffected.

In this chapter, we'll talk about upgrading pluggable databases on the same platform. In Chapter 11, we will discuss migration and how to upgrade pluggable databases across platforms.

Figure 10-16 shows the flow of upgrade steps.

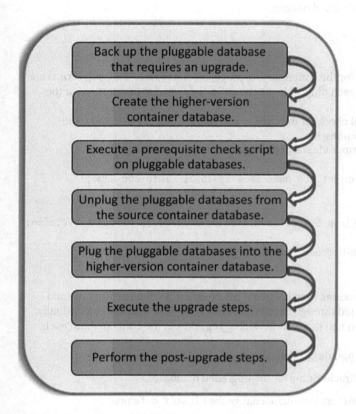

Figure 10-16. *Pluggable database upgrade steps*

1. Back up the pluggable database.

    As a first step, take a backup of the pluggable databases chosen for the upgrade. The backup can be a cold backup or a traditional hot backup or an RMAN backup. Here we will discuss how to do a database backup through RMAN.

    We'll discuss the upgrade exercise using an example. The source database pluggable version is Oracle 12*c* version 12.1.0.1.0, and it needs to be upgraded to Oracle 12*c* version 12.1.0.2.0.

```
SQL> show pdbs

    CON_ID CON_NAME                      OPEN MODE  RESTRICTED
---------- ------------------------------ ---------- ----------
         2 PDB$SEED                      READ ONLY  NO
         3 PDB12101                      READ WRITE NO
```

```
RMAN> backup pluggable database pdb12101 plus archivelog tag 'before_upgrade';

Starting backup at <date>
current log archived
using channel ORA_DISK_1
channel ORA_DISK_1: starting archived log backup set
channel ORA_DISK_1: specifying archived log(s) in backup set
input archived log thread=1 sequence=11 RECID=1 STAMP=907573275
input archived log thread=1 sequence=12 RECID=2 STAMP=907573356
input archived log thread=1 sequence=13 RECID=3 STAMP=907573423
input archived log thread=1 sequence=14 RECID=4 STAMP=907573567
channel ORA_DISK_1: starting piece 1 at <date>
channel ORA_DISK_1: finished piece 1 at <date>
piece handle=/u01/app/oracle/fast_recovery_area/CDB12101/backupset/<date> /o1_mf_annnn_
BEFORE_UPGRADE_chh0fhvr_.bkp tag=BEFORE_UPGRADE comment=NONE
channel ORA_DISK_1: backup set complete, elapsed time: 00:00:07
Finished backup at <date>
Starting backup at <date>
using channel ORA_DISK_1
channel ORA_DISK_1: starting full datafile backup set
channel ORA_DISK_1: specifying datafile(s) in backup set
input datafile file number=00009 name=/u01/app/oracle/oradata/CDB12101/2EBB328E7A451883E0530
F02000AE9E5/datafile/o1_mf_sysaux_ch5ln34v_.dbf
input datafile file number=00008 name=/u01/app/oracle/oradata/CDB12101/2EBB328E7A451883E0530
F02000AE9E5/datafile/o1_mf_system_ch5ln35w_.dbf
input datafile file number=00010 name=/u01/app/oracle/oradata/CDB12101/2EBB328E7A451883E0530
F02000AE9E5/datafile/o1_mf_users_ch5looql_.dbf
channel ORA_DISK_1: starting piece 1 at <date>
channel ORA_DISK_1: finished piece 1 at <date>
piece handle=/u01/app/oracle/fast_recovery_area/CDB12101/2EBB328E7A451883E0530F02000AE
9E5/backupset/<date>/o1_mf_nnndf_TAG20160327T074615_chh0fqr1_.bkp tag=TAG20160327T074615
comment=NONE
channel ORA_DISK_1: backup set complete, elapsed time: 00:00:45
Finished backup at <date>

Starting backup at <date>
current log archived
using channel ORA_DISK_1
channel ORA_DISK_1: starting archived log backup set
channel ORA_DISK_1: specifying archived log(s) in backup set
input archived log thread=1 sequence=15 RECID=5 STAMP=907573621
channel ORA_DISK_1: starting piece 1 at <date>
channel ORA_DISK_1: finished piece 1 at <date>
piece handle=/u01/app/oracle/fast_recovery_area/CDB12101/backupset/<date> /o1_mf_annnn_
BEFORE_UPGRADE_chh0h61q_.bkp tag=BEFORE_UPGRADE comment=NONE
channel ORA_DISK_1: backup set complete, elapsed time: 00:00:01
Finished backup at <date>

Starting Control File and SPFILE Autobackup at <date>
piece handle=/u01/app/oracle/fast_recovery_area/CDB12101/autobackup/<date> /o1_
mf_s_907573623_chh0h8ld_.bkp comment=NONE
```

481

```
Finished Control File and SPFILE Autobackup at <date>
```

2. Create the higher-version CDB.

   Install the higher-database version at the new location. The owner can be the same owner or a different owner. In this example, the higher-database version 12.1.0.2.0 has been installed at the /u01/app/oracle/product/12.1.0 location, and a container database has been created in the higher version.

3. Execute the pre-upgrade script at the chosen pluggable databases.

   Before proceeding with the upgrade, you need to make sure that the pluggable databases are in the right shape. This can be done by verifying the pre-upgrade script output. Execute the higher-version pre-upgrade script in the pluggable databases. First install the higher database version in a different location. The pre-upgrade script will be located at the higher-version ORACLE_HOME/rdbms/admin directory.

   Using the catcon.pl pre-upgrade script, preupgrd.sql can be executed in specific pluggable databases.

```
cd $ORACLE_HOME/rdbms/admin

$ORACLE_HOME/perl/bin/perl catcon.pl -d <directory location of preupgrade scripts> -l <log
location of preupgrade script> -c <PDB_Name> -b <preupgrade_log_base_name> preupgrd.sql

[oracle@Server admin]$ /u02/product/12.1.0/dbhome_1/perl/bin/perl catcon.pl -d /u01/app/
oracle/pre_scripts -l /u01/app/oracle/pre_scripts -b pre_upgrade -c PDB12101 preupgrd.sql
```

In the previous example, the pre-upgrade scripts preupgrd.sql and utluppkg.sql from the higher-version Oracle Home are copied to the /u01/app/oracle/pre_scripts folder, and this location has been specified using the -d option. The pre-upgrade execution log location is specified with the -l option.

The pluggable databases for pre-upgrade are chosen using the -c option. The pre-upgrade script output is stored in $ORACLE_BASE/cfgtoollogs/<Database_name>/preupgrade/preupgrade.log.

The pre-upgrade output is the same as the stand-alone database's pre-upgrade output. It will validate database components, init parameters, and recommendations.

Once you have confirmed the pre-upgrade is clean, you can proceed to the next step. As a general upgrade practice, you should do the steps shown in Figure 10-17.

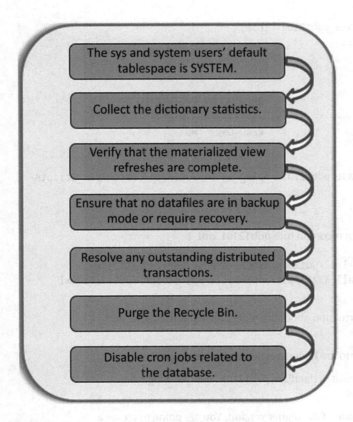

The sys and system users' default tablespace is SYSTEM.

Collect the dictionary statistics.

Verify that the materialized view refreshes are complete.

Ensure that no datafiles are in backup mode or require recovery.

Resolve any outstanding distributed transactions.

Purge the Recycle Bin.

Disable cron jobs related to the database.

Figure 10-17. Pluggable database pre-upgrade steps

■ **Note**   While upgrading, the database should be free from user accesses.

---

4. Unplug the pluggable databases from the source container database.

    The chosen pluggable database needs to be unplugged from the source Oracle
    Home container database.

    ```
    SQL> alter session set container=CDB$ROOT;
    Session altered.

    SQL> show pdbs

        CON_ID CON_NAME                       OPEN MODE  RESTRICTED
    ---------- ------------------------------ ---------- ----------
             2 PDB$SEED                       READ ONLY  NO
             3 PDB12101                       READ WRITE NO
    ```

    Before unplugging database it should be closed.

```
SQL> alter pluggable database pdb12101 close;
Pluggable database altered.

SQL> show pdbs

    CON_ID CON_NAME                        OPEN MODE  RESTRICTED
---------- ------------------------------ ---------- ----------
         2 PDB$SEED                        READ ONLY  NO
         3 PDB12101                        MOUNTED

SQL> alter pluggable database pdb12101 unplug into '/u01/app/oracle/pre_scripts/
pdb12101.xml';
Pluggable database altered.
```

PDB definition would have been recorded into pdb12101.xml

```
[oracle@Server admin]$ ls -lrt /u01/app/oracle/pre_scripts/pdb12101.xml
-rw-r--r--. 1 oracle oinstall 4236 /u01/app/oracle/pre_scripts/pdb12101.xml
```

This XML output will have information about the pluggable database name and each datafile with its location.

5. Plug the pluggable databases into the higher-version container database.

    Copy or move the pluggable database datafiles, pdb12101.xml postupgrade_fixup.sql, to the target location.

    Connect to the container database of the higher version. You are going to create a new pluggable database using the copied pluggable database datafiles.

```
SQL> startup
ORACLE instance started.
Database mounted.
Database opened.

SQL> show pdbs
    CON_ID CON_NAME                        OPEN MODE  RESTRICTED
---------- ------------------------------ ---------- ----------
         2 PDB$SEED                        READ ONLY  NO
         3 PDB121                          MOUNTED
```

You can see there is a pluggable database present already with the name PDB121. You cannot plug this pluggable database because it has the same name. So, choose a different name.

```
SQL>  create pluggable database pdb12102 using '/u02/oradata/CDB121/datafile/
pdb121/pdb12101.xml' source_file_name_convert=('/u01/app/oracle/oradata/CDB121
01/2EBB328E7A451883E0530F02000AE9E5/datafile/','/u02/oradata/CDB121/datafile/
pdb121/') nocopy;
```

Here the pluggable database is created with the name pdb12102. This means while plugging the database to a different container, you have the flexibility of changing the name.

In the previous example PDB121 datafiles, the XML files are copied to /u02/oradata/CDB121/datafile/pdb121.

The pluggable database has been created using the copied datafiles, and you have used the source_file_name_convert parameter to denote that the datafile location needs to be changed to /u02/oradata/CDB121/datafile/pdb121. Also, you used nocopy, which means the existing datafile at this location can be used. There is no need to copy the datafiles to the OMF location.

```
SQL> show pdbs

    CON_ID CON_NAME                        OPEN MODE  RESTRICTED
---------- ------------------------------ ---------- ----------
         2 PDB$SEED                        READ ONLY  NO
         3 PDB121                          MOUNTED
         4 PDB12102                        MOUNTED
```

6. Execute the upgrade steps.

    You can see the new pluggable database pdb121C2 has been created and it is in mount state. Remember, though, it is plugged into the higher-version container database. Still, the pluggable database's dictionary is 12.1.0.1.0. It needs to be upgraded. If you try to open the database in read-write mode, you will get a warning message, and the database will be opened in migrate mode.

    ```
    SQL> alter pluggable database pdb12102 open;
    Warning: PDB altered with errors.

    SQL> show pdbs

        CON_ID CON_NAME                        OPEN MODE  RESTRICTED
    ---------- ------------------------------ ---------- ----------
             2 PDB$SEED                        READ ONLY  NO
             3 PDB121                          MOUNTED
             4 PDB12102                        MIGRATE    YES
    ```

The pluggable database dictionary needs to be upgraded to 12.1.0.2.0 through catupgrd.sql.
Invoke catctl.pl to upgrade this particular pluggable database to a higher version. Using the -c option, you can specify the desired PDB to execute the upgrade scripts.

```
[oracle@Server admin]$ /u01/app/oracle/product/12.1.0/perl/bin/perl catctl.pl -n 4 -c
pdb12102 -l /u01/app/oracle/pdb_upgrade_log  catupgrd.sql
```

```
Argument list for [catctl.pl]
SQL Process Count        n = 4
SQL PDB Process Count    N = 0
Input Directory          d = 0
Phase Logging Table      t = 0
Log Dir                  l = /u01/app/oracle/pdb_upgrade_log
Script                   s = 0
Serial Run               S = 0
Upgrade Mode active      M = 0
Start Phase              p = 0
End Phase                P = 0
Log Id                   i = 0
Run in                   c = pdb12102
Do not run in            C = 0
Echo OFF                 e = 1
No Post Upgrade          x = 0
Reverse Order            r = 0
Open Mode Normal         o = 0
Debug catcon.pm          z = 0
Debug catctl.pl          Z = 0
Display Phases           y = 0
Child Process            I = 0

catctl.pl version: 12.1.0.2.0
Oracle Base              = /u01/app/oracle

Analyzing file catupgrd.sql
Log files in /u01/app/oracle/pdb_upgrade_log
catcon: ALL catcon-related output will be written to /u01/app/oracle/pdb_upgrade_log/
catupgrd_catcon_12390.lst
catcon: See /u01/app/oracle/pdb_upgrade_log/catupgrd*.log files for output generated by
scripts
catcon: See /u01/app/oracle/pdb_upgrade_log/catupgrd_*.lst files for spool files, if any
Number of Cpus         = 1
Parallel PDB Upgrades = 2
SQL PDB Process Count = 2
SQL Process Count     = 4

[CONTAINER NAMES]

CDB$ROOT
PDB$SEED
PDB121
PDB12102
PDB Inclusion:[PDB12102] Exclusion:[]
```

```
Start processing of PDB12102
[/u01/app/oracle/product/12.1.0/perl/bin/perl catctl.pl -n 2 -c 'PDB12102' -l /u01/app/
oracle/pdb_upgrade_log -I -i pdb12102 catupgrd.sql]

Argument list for [catctl.pl]
SQL Process Count      n = 2
SQL PDB Process Count  N = 0
Input Directory        d = 0
Phase Logging Table    t = 0
Log Dir                l = /u01/app/oracle/pdb_upgrade_log
Script                 s = 0
Serial Run             S = 0
Upgrade Mode active    M = 0
Start Phase            p = 0
End Phase              P = 0
Log Id                 i = pdb12102
Run in                 c = PDB12102
Do not run in          C = 0
Echo OFF               e = 1
No Post Upgrade        x = 0
Reverse Order          r = 0
Open Mode Normal       o = 0
Debug catcon.pm        z = 0
Debug catctl.pl        Z = 0
Display Phases         y = 0
Child Process          I = 1

catctl.pl version: 12.1.0.2.0
Oracle Base        = /u01/app/oracle

Analyzing file catupgrd.sql
Log files in /u01/app/oracle/pdb_upgrade_log
catcon: ALL catcon-related output will be written to /u01/app/oracle/pdb_upgrade_log/
catupgrdpdb12102_catcon_12492.lst
catcon: See /u01/app/oracle/pdb_upgrade_log/catupgrdpdb12102*.log files for output generated
by scripts
catcon: See /u01/app/oracle/pdb_upgrade_log/catupgrdpdb12102_*.lst files for spool files, if
any
Number of Cpus       = 1
SQL PDB Process Count = 2
SQL Process Count    = 2
```

```
[CONTAINER NAMES]

CDB$ROOT
PDB$SEED
PDB121
PDB12102
PDB Inclusion:[PDB12102] Exclusion:[]


-------------------------------------------------------
Phases [0-73]          Start Time:[2016_03_27 13:35:13]
Container Lists Inclusion:[PDB12102] Exclusion:[NONE]
-------------------------------------------------------

Serial    Phase #: 0    PDB12102 Files: 1    Time: 11s
Serial    Phase #: 1    PDB12102 Files: 5
.

.
Serial    Phase #:70    PDB12102 Files: 1    Time: 6s
Serial    Phase #:71    PDB12102 Files: 1    Time: 0s
Serial    Phase #:72    PDB12102 Files: 1    Time: 2s
Serial    Phase #:73    PDB12102 Files: 1    Time: 0s


-------------------------------------------------------
Phases [0-73]          End Time:[date time]
Container Lists Inclusion:[PDB12102] Exclusion:[NONE]

SQL> show pdbs

    CON_ID CON_NAME                          OPEN MODE  RESTRICTED
---------- ------------------------------- ---------- ----------
         2 PDB$SEED                          READ ONLY  NO
         3 PDB121                            MOUNTED
         4 PDB12102                          MOUNTED
```

After the upgrade, the pluggable database is in mount state. If catupgrd.sql has to be executed in multiple pluggable databases, you can specify this using –c 'PDB1,PDB2'.

Start the pluggable database and execute utlrp.sql.

```
SQL> alter session set container=pdb12102;
Session altered.

SQL> @?/rdbms/admin/utlrp.sql

    Check the Database component's version and its status
SQL> col comp_id format a10
SQL> col comp_name format a30
SQL> col version format a10
SQL> col status format a8

SQL> select substr(comp_id,1,15) comp_id,substr(comp_name,1,30) comp_
name,substr(version,1,10) version,status from dba_registry;
```

```
COMP_ID     COMP_NAME                        VERSION     STATUS
----------  ------------------------------   ----------  --------
DV          Oracle Database Vault            12.1.0.2.0  VALID
APEX        Oracle Application Express       4.2.5.00.0  VALID
OLS         Oracle Label Security            12.1.0.2.0  VALID
SDO         Spatial                          12.1.0.2.0  VALID
ORDIM       Oracle Multimedia                12.1.0.2.0  VALID
CONTEXT     Oracle Text                      12.1.0.2.0  VALID
OWM         Oracle Workspace Manager         12.1.0.2.0  VALID
XDB         Oracle XML Database              12.1.0.2.0  VALID
CATALOG     Oracle Database Catalog Views    12.1.0.2.0  VALID
CATPROC     Oracle Database Packages and T   12.1.0.2.0  VALID
JAVAVM      JServer JAVA Virtual Machine     12.1.0.2.0  VALID
XML         Oracle XDK                       12.1.0.2.0  VALID
CATJAVA     Oracle Database Java Packages    12.1.0.2.0  VALID
APS         OLAP Analytic Workspace          12.1.0.2.0  VALID
XOQ         Oracle OLAP API                  12.1.0.2.0  VALID
RAC         Oracle Real Application Cluste   12.1.0.2.0  OPTION OFF
```

Use catcon.pl to execute utlrp.sql to execute it in multiple pluggable databases using -c 'PDB1,PDB2'.

1) Perform the post-upgrade steps.

Execute post-fixup scripts in the upgraded pluggable databases by connecting to the pluggable database through SQL*Plus. Remember, fixup scripts have been created individually for each pluggable database

```
SQL> alter session set container=pdb12102;
Session altered.

SQL>@/u01/app/oracle/cfgtoollogs/preupgrade/pdbfiles/ post-upgrade_fixups.<PDBNAME>.sql
```

With this step, the pluggable database upgrade is completed.

Summary

In this chapter, we discussed multitenant database upgrades. You explored the upgrade steps for the container database upgrade and the pluggable database upgrade.

COMP_ID	COMP_NAME	VERSION	STATUS
DV	Oracle Database Vault	12.1.0.2.0	VALID
APEX	Oracle Application Express	4.2.5.00.08	VALID
OLS	Oracle Label Security	12.1.0.2.0	VALID
SDO	Spatial	12.1.0.2.0	VALID
OWM	Oracle Multimedia	12.1.0.2.0	VALID
CONTEXT	Oracle Text	12.1.0.2.0	VALID
OWM	Oracle Workspace Manager	12.1.0.2.0	VALID
XDB	Oracle XML Database	12.1.0.2.0	VALID
CATALOG	Oracle Database Catalog Views	12.1.0.2.0	VALID
CATPROC	Oracle Database Packages and Types	12.1.0.2.0	VALID
JAVAVM	JServer JAVA Virtual Machine	12.1.0.2.0	VALID
XML	Oracle XDK	12.1.0.2.0	VALID
CATJAVA	Oracle Database Java Packages	12.1.0.2.0	VALID
APS	OLAP Analytic Workspace	12.1.0.2.0	VALID
XOQ	Oracle OLAP API	12.1.0.2.0	VALID
RAC	Oracle Real Application Clusters	12.1.0.2.0	OPTION OFF

Use catcon.pl to execute utlrp.sql to recompile the invalid objects in the pluggable databases using –c "PDB1,PDB2".

3. Perform the post-upgrade steps.

Perform the post-upgrade steps in the upgraded pluggable databases by connecting to the pluggable database through SQL*Plus since the post-upgrade scripts have been created individually for each pluggable database.

SQL> alter session set container=pdb1pdb2;
Session altered.

SQL> @/app/oracle/cfgtoollogs/erorupgraue/catfiles/postupgrade_<groups>/PDBNAMEs.sql

With this step the pluggable database upgrade is complete.

Summary

In this chapter, we discussed multitenant database upgrades. You learned the upgrade steps for the container database upgrade and the pluggable database upgrade.

CHAPTER 11

∎∎∎

Pluggable Database Migrations

In a multitenant architecture you can move a pluggable database from one container database to another container database. This feature helps you make changes in the desired pluggable database. For example, as covered in Chapter 10, to upgrade a pluggable database, you unplug it from the lower version and plug it into a higher-version container database. Likewise, you can apply patches for the desired pluggable databases by installing the 12c software at a new location and patching the Oracle Home with the required patches. Then you create a container database in the newly patched Oracle Home. Finally, you unplug the pluggable database from the old container database and plug it into the newly patched container database. That's it. The pluggable database is patched now. Downtime is required just for unplugging and plugging it into the container database. You don't need additional storage because you use the existing datafiles of the pluggable database while plugging it into the higher version. Using the existing datafiles also means you do not need to move or copy the files, which will reduce the time for this operation.

The Need for Migration

In this chapter we will cover pluggable database migrations. Like with stand-alone databases, you might have a requirement to move your pluggable databases to a different environment because of hardware changes, operating system changes, or operating system bit conversion.

This chapter discusses how to move the pluggable database between different platforms. When you want to do a migration between platforms, you need to consider the endian format of the operating system. The endian format denotes the order in which the bytes of an integer are stored in memory. There are two endian formats: big and little. In big-endian format, the most significant bytes are stored in the lowest address with the following bytes in a sequentially higher address. The bytes appear in normal order when written from left to right. Little-endian format does the reverse. The least significant bytes are stored at the lowest address, with the increasingly significant bytes stored at increasing addresses. For example, the decimal number 260 (100000100 in binary) is stored as follows:

- *Big endian*: 00000001 00000100

- *Little endian*: 00000100 00000001

The operating system endian format can be either big or little. There are a variety of migration methods, such as export/import, Data Pump, transportable tablespace (TTS), GoldenGate, Create Table As Select (CTAS), RMAN convert database, Data Pump heterogeneous primary and standby, and Streams replication. We discussed these methods in detail in Chapter 5, and they all apply to pluggable databases also. Based on the endian format, the volume of data, and the available downtime, you need to choose the appropriate method. The endian format information can be retrieved v$transportable_platform, as shown in Table 11-1.

© Y V Ravikumar, K M Krishnakumar and Nassyam Basha 2017

N. Basha et al., *Oracle Database Upgrade and Migration Methods*, DOI 10.1007/978-1-4842-2328-4_11

Table 11-1. *Endian Format*

Platform	Endian Format
Solaris OE (32-bit)	Big
Solaris OE (64-bit)	Big
Microsoft Windows IA (32-bit)	Little
Linux IA (32-bit)	Little
AIX-based systems (64-bit)	Big
HP-UX (64-bit)	Big
HP Tru64 UNIX	Little
HP-UX IA (64-bit)	Big
Linux IA (64-bit)	Little
HP Open VMS	Little
Microsoft Windows IA (64-bit)	Little
IBM zSeries-based Linux	Big
Linux x86 64-bit	Little
Apple Mac OS	Big
Microsoft Windows x86 64-bit	Little
IBM Power-based Linux	Big
HP IA Open VMS	Little
Solaris operating system (x86)	Little
Solaris operating system (x86-64)	Little
Apple Mac OS (x86-64)	Little

Migration Steps

The following sections cover the migration steps.

Same Endian Format

A pluggable database can be migrated between platforms that have the same endian format. A pluggable database is unplugged from one platform and is plugged into the container database located on another platform with the same endian format. Here are the high-level steps to perform this migration:

1) Check the pluggable database. Ensure there are no datafiles that require recovery.

2) Unplug the pluggable database.

3) Move the pluggable database datafiles and XML file to the target platform. It can be sent in compressed format.

4) Unzip the compressed format file on the target server.

5) Create a new pluggable database using the copied datafiles.

We'll now discuss these steps with an example. Let's try to migrate the pluggable database from the Solaris operating system (x86-64) to Linux x86 64-bit. According to V$TRANSPORTABLE_PLATFORM, both operating systems have the same little endian format. This method also works if both systems have the same big endian format but will not work if the endian formats on the two systems are different.

- *Source platform*: Solaris operating system (x86-64)
- *Destination platform*: Linux x86 64-bit
- *Database version*: 12.1.0.1.0
- *Database name*: cdb12101
- *Pluggable database name*: pdb12101

Step 1

Connect to the container database and check the pluggable database status. Verify that the files do not need recovery and get a list of files to support the pluggable database.

```
SQL> show pdbs
    CON_ID CON_NAME                         OPEN MODE   RESTRICTED
---------- ---------------------------- ---------- ----------
         2 PDB$SEED                         READ ONLY   NO
         3 PDB12101                         READ WRITE  NO

SQL> select * from v$recover_file where con_id=3;
no rows selected

SQL>  select * from v$backup where status!='NOT ACTIVE' and CON_ID=3;
no rows selected
SQL> select file_name from cdb_data_files where con_id=3;
FILE_NAME
        --------------------------------------------------------------------
        /u01/app/oracle/oradata/cdb12101/pdb12101/system01.dbf
        /u01/app/oracle/oradata/cdb12101/pdb12101/sysaux01.dbf
        /u01/app/oracle/oradata/cdb12101/pdb12101/users01.dbf
```

Step 2

Unplug the pluggable database. Note that this will cause downtime for applications needing access to the pluggable database.

```
SQL> alter pluggable database pdb12101 close;
Pluggable database altered.
SQL> alter pluggable database pdb12101 unplug into '/u01/app/oracle/pdb12101.xml';

Pluggable database altered.
```

Step 3

Move the pluggable database datafiles to the target platform of Linux x86-64. This can be done with traditional OS utilities such as scp.

The pluggable database datafiles need to be transferred to the target platform. In the current example, you copy the datafile to the target platform, and after you ensure that the migration is successfully done, you drop the pluggable database from the source database. To avoid an individual datafile transfer, you can zip it as a single zip file or compress it using the tar command. This will also help you avoid binary corruption during the transfer.

The folder called backup has been created, and the datafiles are copied to the backup folder.

```
$ cp system01.dbf backup/
$ cp sysaux01.dbf backup/
$ cp users01.dbf backup/
$ tar cvf backup.tar backup/
```

Transfer backup.tar to the target platform.

```
$ scp backup.tar oracle@new_host:/home/oracle/backup.tar
```

Step 4

The next step is to plug into the target database.
Connect to the target container database on the Linux X86-64 platform.

```
$ sqlplus "/ as sysdba"
SQL> show pdbs
    CON_ID CON_NAME                       OPEN MODE  RESTRICTED
---------- ------------------------------ ---------- ----------
         2 PDB$SEED                       READ ONLY  NO
```

The backup.tar file is copied to the target server and extracted at /u02/oradata/CDB121/ datafile/12101.

```
tar xvf backup.tar
```

Step 5

Create a new pluggable database using the copied pluggable database files.

```
SQL> create pluggable database pdb_sol using '/u02/oradata/CDB121/datafile/12101/pdb12101.
xml' source_file_name_convert=('/u01/app/oracle/oradata/cdb12101/pdb12101/','/u02/oradata/
CDB121/datafile/12101/') nocopy;
Pluggable database created.
```

The pdb12101.xml file has the old location of database files. On the target server, the datafiles are copied to a different location: /u02/oradata/CDB121/datafile/121C1. To change the location of datafiles, use the SOURCE_FILE_NAME_CONVERT parameter. We are using the existing files available at the location in this example; hence, we've used nocopy. Note that in this example we have created a pluggable database with the name pdb_sol.

```
SQL> show pdbs
    CON_ID CON_NAME                           OPEN MODE  RESTRICTED
---------- ------------------------------ ---------- ----------
         2 PDB$SEED                           READ ONLY  NO
         3 PDB_SOL                            MOUNTED
SQL> alter pluggable database pdb_sol open;
Pluggable database altered.
SQL> alter session set container=pdb_sol;
Session altered.
SQL> select file_name from dba_data_files;
FILE_NAME
--------------------------------------------------------------------------------
/u02/oradata/CDB121/datafile/12101/system01.dbf
/u02/oradata/CDB121/datafile/12101/sysaux01.dbf
/u02/oradata/CDB121/datafile/12101/users01.dbf
```

In this exercise, you have plugged into the 12.1.0.1.0 container database. You can also plug into the higher-version 12.1.0.2.0 container database. In that case, you need to open the pluggable database in upgrade mode after plugging into the 12.1.0.2.0 version and execute the catupgrd.sql script like you do in a multitenant upgrade (covered in Chapter 10). Let's try that as well.

- *Source platform*: Solaris operating system (x86-64)

- *Destination platform*: Linux x86 64-bit

- *Database version*: 12.1.0.1.0

- *Database name*: cdb12101

- *Pluggable database name*: pdb12101

- *Target container database version*: 12.1.0.2.0

Connect to the 12.1.0.2.0 container database.

```
SQL> select banner from v$version;
BANNER
--------------------------------------------------------------------Oracle Database 12c
Enterprise Edition Release 12.1.0.2.0 - 64bit Production
PL/SQL Release 12.1.0.2.0 - Production
CORE    12.1.0.2.0      Production
TNS for Linux: Version 12.1.0.2.0 - Production
NLSRTL Version 12.1.0.2.0 - Production
SQL> show pdbs
    CON_ID CON_NAME                           OPEN MODE  RESTRICTED
---------- ------------------------------ ---------- ----------
         2 PDB$SEED                           READ ONLY  NO
```

The source pluggable database files are copied to /u02/oradata/CDB121/datafile/12101/pdb12102/.

```
SQL> create pluggable database pdb12102 using '/u02/oradata/CDB121/datafile/12101/pdb12101.
xml' source_file_name_convert=('/u01/app/oracle/oradata/cdb12101/pdb12101/','/u02/oradata/
CDB121/datafile/12101/pdb12102/') nocopy;
Pluggable database created.

SQL> show pdbs
    CON_ID CON_NAME                          OPEN MODE  RESTRICTED
---------- ------------------------------- ---------- ----------
         2 PDB$SEED                          READ ONLY  NO
         3 PDB12102                          MOUNTED
```

Remember, the source pluggable database version was 12.1.0.1.0, and you plugged into the 12.1.0.2.0 container database. Hence, you need to open the pluggable database in upgrade mode. Trying to open in normal mode will throw a warning and open it in migrate mode.

```
SQL> alter pluggable database pdb12102 open;
Warning: PDB altered with errors.
SQL> show pdbs

    CON_ID CON_NAME                          OPEN MODE  RESTRICTED
---------- ------------------------------- ---------- ----------
         2 PDB$SEED                          READ ONLY  NO
         3 PDB12102                          MIGRATE    YES
```

Execute the catupgrd.sql script on PDB12102 like you did in Chapter 10.

Different Endian Format

If the pluggable database is migrated from a different platform, you cannot migrate the whole database like you did when the platforms had the same endian format. Let's experience it through some practical steps.

In this example, the pluggable database is unplugged from the container database available in Solaris Sparc and tries to plug in to the container database located on the Linux x86-64 platform, as shown in Table 11-2.

Table 11-2. *Endian Format*

Platform Name	Endian Format
Solaris OE (64-bit)	Big
Linux x86 64-bit	Little

These platforms have different endian formats, so if you try to plug the database files retrieved from Solaris Sparc 64-bit to the Linux x86 64-bit database (like you did earlier in the chapter), then you get the ORA-65134 error shown here:

```
SQL> show pdbs
    CON_ID CON_NAME                        OPEN MODE   RESTRICTED
---------- ----------------------------- ----------  ----------
         2 PDB$SEED                        READ ONLY   NO
         3 PDBORCL                         MOUNTED

SQL> create pluggable database pdbsol using '/u01/app/oracle/oradata/solpdb/backup/
pdbsol121.xml' source_file_name_convert=('/u02/app/oracle/oradata/solpdb/','/u01/app/oracle/
oradata/solpdb/backup/') nocopy;
create pluggable database pdbsol using '/u01/app/oracle/oradata/solpdb/backup/pdbsol121.xml'
source_file_name_convert=('/u02/app/oracle/oradata/solpdb/','/u01/app/oracle/oradata/solpdb/
backup/') nocopy
*
ERROR at line 1:
ORA-65134: endian mismatch
```

The endian mismatch error is thrown. You need to convert the datafiles endian format and then plug the database into container database. But you cannot convert all the datafiles, including the SYSTEM and SYSAUX tablespaces. Doing that throws the ORA-19928 error, as shown here:

```
RMAN> convert from platform 'Solaris[tm] OE (64-bit)'
2> parallelism 2 datafile
'/u01/app/oracle/oradata/solpdb/backup/system01.dbf' format
'/u01/app/oracle/oradata/solpdb/backup_convert/system01.dbf';

Starting conversion at target at 25-MAR-16
using channel ORA_DISK_1
using channel ORA_DISK_2
channel ORA_DISK_1: starting datafile conversion
input file
name=/u01/app/oracle/oradata/solpdb/backup/o1_mf_system_chb1x2f7_.dbf
RMAN-00571:
RMAN-00569: ERROR MESSAGE STACK FOLLOWS
RMAN-00571: ===========================================================
RMAN-03009: failure of conversion at target command on ORA_DISK_1 channel at
ORA-19928: CONVERT of data files with undo segments between different Endian is not
supported.
```

Error ORA-19928 is thrown because the endian conversion is not supported on datafiles with UNDO segments.

So, for different endian formats, the available options are export/import, Data Pump, transportable tablespace (TTS), GoldenGate, Create Table As Select (CTAS) and Data Guard heterogeneous primary and standby (on certain supported platforms).

The steps are the same as you do for a stand-alone database. We discussed these methods in detail in Chapter 2 and Chapter 5. As an example, you will see how to achieve a different-endian migration through the TTS method.

The steps are the same as the stand-alone database TTS migration, except that you will be working on pluggable databases. There is no difference in steps, which is the beauty of the multitenant architecture.

You can consider the same platform combination.

```
PLATFORM_NAME              ENDIAN_FORMAT
Solaris[tm] OE (64-bit)    Big
Linux x86 64-bit           Little
Source database version: 12.1.0.1.0
Target database version: 12.1.0.1.0
Container database name: CDB12101
Pluggable database name: PDB12101
```

Kindly note you are going to migrate all the tablespaces of the pluggable database.

Steps

Here are the steps:

1) Connect to the source pluggable database. Ensure there are no files that require recovery.

```
SQL> select tablespace_name, online_status status from dba_data_files;
TABLESPACE_NAME                  STATUS
-------------------------------  ---------
SYSTEM                           ONLINE
SYSAUX                           ONLINE
TEMP                             ONLINE
USERS                            ONLINE
TEST                             ONLINE
USER_TEST                        ONLINE
```

2) This PDB has three nonadministrative tablespaces (USERS, TEST, and USER_TEST), and it needs to be migrated. Execute the transport tablespace check procedure for those tablespaces.

```
SQL> EXEC SYS.DBMS_TTS.TRANSPORT_SET_CHECK(ts_list => 'USERS,TEST,USER_
TEST',incl_constraints => TRUE);
PL/SQL procedure successfully completed.

SQL> Select * from transport_set_violations;
no rows selected
```

3) Create a logical directory to store the metadata dump.

```
SQL> create directory tts_dir as '/u01/app/oracle';
Directory created.
```

4) Make the nonadministrative tablespaces read-only.

```
SQL> alter tablespace users read only;
Tablespace altered.
SQL> alter tablespace test read only;
Tablespace altered.
SQL> alter tablespace user_test read only;
Tablespace altered.
```

5) Take an export dump for the metadata of the nonadministrative tablespaces.

```
$ expdp userid=\'sys@pdb12101 as sysdba\' directory=tts_dir transport_
tablespaces=USERS,TEST,USER_TEST
dumpfile=pdb_tablespace_metadata.dmp logfile=pdb_tablespace_metadata.log

Export: Release 12.1.0.1.0 - Production
Password:

Connected to: Oracle Database 12c Enterprise Edition Release 12.1.0.1.0 - 64bit
Production
With the Partitioning, OLAP, Advanced Analytics and Real Application Testing
options
Starting "SYS"."SYS_EXPORT_TRANSPORTABLE_01":  userid="sys/********@pdb12101 AS
SYSDBA" directory=tts_dir
transport_tablespaces=USERS,TEST,USER_TEST dumpfile=pdb_tablespace_metadata.dmp
logfile=pdb_tablespace_metadata.log
Processing object type TRANSPORTABLE_EXPORT/PLUGTS_BLK
Processing object type TRANSPORTABLE_EXPORT/STATISTICS/MARKER
Processing object type TRANSPORTABLE_EXPORT/POST_INSTANCE/PLUGTS_BLK
Master table "SYS"."SYS_EXPORT_TRANSPORTABLE_01" successfully loaded/unloaded
******************************************************************************
Dump file set for SYS.SYS_EXPORT_TRANSPORTABLE_01 is:
  /u01/app/oracle/pdb_tablespace_metadata.dmp
******************************************************************************
Datafiles required for transportable tablespace TEST:
  /u01/app/oracle/oradata/CDB12101/2F7F515DFA5519FEE054005056042305/datafile/
o1_mf_test_cj249nsz_.dbf
Datafiles required for transportable tablespace USERS:
  /u01/app/oracle/oradata/CDB12101/2F7F515DFA5519FEE054005056042305/datafile/
o1_mf_users_chz98kp9_.dbf
Datafiles required for transportable tablespace USER_TEST:
  /u01/app/oracle/oradata/CDB12101/2F7F515DFA5519FEE054005056042305/datafile/
o1_mf_user_tes_cj249wrg_.dbf
Job "SYS"."SYS_EXPORT_TRANSPORTABLE_01" successfully completed
```

6) Copy the datafiles of tablespaces and export the metadata dump (/u01/app/
oracle/pdb_tablespace_metadata.dmp) to the target server.

7) Connect to the target container database. Create a pluggable database for
adopting the source pluggable database files.

8) Convert the copied datafile endian format.

```
RMAN> convert from platform 'Solaris[tm] OE (64-bit)'
2> parallelism 2 datafile
3> '/u01/app/oracle/oradata/CDB12C/pdbsol/o1_mf_test_cj2f2fn7_.dbf' format
4> '/u01/app/oracle/oradata/CDB12C/pdbsol/convert/test01.dbf';
Starting conversion at target using target database control file instead of
recovery catalog
allocated channel: ORA_DISK_1
channel ORA_DISK_1: SID=46 device type=DISK
allocated channel: ORA_DISK_2
channel ORA_DISK_2: SID=1 device type=DISK
channel ORA_DISK_1: starting datafile conversion
input file name=/u01/app/oracle/oradata/CDB12C/pdbsol/o1_mf_test_cj2f2fn7_.dbf
converted datafile=/u01/app/oracle/oradata/CDB12C/pdbsol/convert/test01.dbf
channel ORA_DISK_1: datafile conversion complete, elapsed time: 00:00:07
Finished conversion at target

RMAN> convert from platform 'Solaris[tm] OE (64-bit)'
2> parallelism 2 datafile
3> '/u01/app/oracle/oradata/CDB12C/pdbsol/o1_mf_users_cj2f2kkb_.dbf' format
4> '/u01/app/oracle/oradata/CDB12C/pdbsol/convert/users01.dbf';
Starting conversion at target
using channel ORA_DISK_1
using channel ORA_DISK_2
channel ORA_DISK_1: starting datafile conversion
input file name=/u01/app/oracle/oradata/CDB12C/pdbsol/o1_mf_users_cj2f2kkb_.dbf
converted datafile=/u01/app/oracle/oradata/CDB12C/pdbsol/convert/users01.dbf
channel ORA_DISK_1: datafile conversion complete, elapsed time: 00:00:07
Finished conversion at target

RMAN> convert from platform 'Solaris[tm] OE (64-bit)'
2> parallelism 2 datafile
3> '/u01/app/oracle/oradata/CDB12C/pdbsol/o1_mf_user_tes_cj2f2y0p_.dbf' format
4> '/u01/app/oracle/oradata/CDB12C/pdbsol/convert/user_test01.dbf';
Starting conversion at target
using channel ORA_DISK_1
using channel ORA_DISK_2
channel ORA_DISK_1: starting datafile conversion
input file name=/u01/app/oracle/oradata/CDB12C/pdbsol/o1_mf_user_tes_cj2f2y0p_.
dbf
converted datafile=/u01/app/oracle/oradata/CDB12C/pdbsol/convert/user_test01.dbf
channel ORA_DISK_1: datafile conversion complete, elapsed time: 00:00:06
Finished conversion at target
```

9) Import the metadata dump into the pluggable database by specifying the datafile location.

```
$ impdp userid=\'sys@PDB12c as sysdba\' directory=tts_dir  dumpfile=pdb_
tablespace_sol_metadata.dmp logfile=pdb_tablespace_metadata.log
transport_datafiles='/u01/app/oracle/oradata/CD312C/pdbsol/convert/test01.dbf','/
u01/app/oracle/oradata/CDB12C/pdbsol/convert/users01.dbf','/u01/app/oracle/
oradata/CDB12C/pdbsol/convert/user_test01.dbf'

Import: Release 12.1.0.2.0 - Production

Connected to: Oracle Database 12c Enterprise Edition Release 12.1.0.2.0 - 64bit
Production
With the Partitioning, OLAP, Advanced Analytics and Real Application Testing
options
Master table "SYS"."SYS_IMPORT_TRANSPORTABLE_01" successfully loaded/unloaded
Starting "SYS"."SYS_IMPORT_TRANSPORTABLE_01":  userid="sys/********@PDB12c AS
SYSDBA" directory=tts_dir dumpfile=pdb_tablespace_sol_metadata.dmp
logfile=pdb_tablespace_metadata.log
transport_datafiles=/u01/app/oracle/oradata/CDB12C/pdbsol/convert/test01.dbf,/
u01/app/oracle/oradata/CDB12C/pdbsol/convert/users01.dbf,/u01/app/oracle/oradata/
CDB12C/pdbsol/convert/user_test01.dbf
Processing object type TRANSPORTABLE_EXPORT/PLUGTS_BLK
Processing object type TRANSPORTABLE_EXPORT/POST_INSTANCE/PLUGTS_BLK
Job "SYS"."SYS_IMPORT_TRANSPORTABLE_01" successfully completed
```

10) Check dba_datafiles to see whether these transported datafiles became part of the pluggable database.

```
SQL> select tablespace_name, file_name from dba_data_files;


TABLESPACE_NAME
------------------------------
FILE_NAME
--------------------------------------------------------------------------------
SYSTEM
/u01/app/oracle/oradata/CDB12C/301F4BE623CD0F65E0530100007F4F24/datafile/o1_mf_
system_cjn86ynl_.dbf

SYSAUX
/u01/app/oracle/oradata/CDB12C/301F4BE623CD0F65E0530100007F4F24/datafile/o1_mf_
sysaux_cjn86yns_.dbf

TEST
/u01/app/oracle/oradata/CDB12C/pdbsol/convert/test01.dbf
```

```
USERS
/u01/app/oracle/oradata/CDB12C/pdbsol/convert/users01.dbf

USER_TEST
/u01/app/oracle/oradata/CDB12C/pdbsol/convert/user_test01.dbf
```

Summary

In this chapter, we discussed endian formats and then explored the steps to migrate a database on platforms with the same and different endian formats.

CHAPTER 12

■■■

Oracle Database Patching Strategies

In this chapter, you'll learn about patching. Sometimes you may think that everything is perfect from the application side, but your database is not working properly. It throws unnecessary warnings and errors or produces unexpected results. The issue could be at the database binary level or at the database level. This improper behavior is called a *bug*. It is a failure or fault in the program that makes it behave in unintended ways. A fix, called a *patch*, has to be applied to the bug. In other words, a patch is a piece of code that fixes a bug or improves the software. Patching is adding or modifying something at the binary or database level to apply bug fixes or to add required changes. Regular patching also helps the database software be strong enough to handle external vulnerabilities. Oracle releases security fixes four times per year, and applying these patches should be part of the database administrator's routine.

New database versions include fixes for the bugs identified in current and previous versions. But it is not possible to upgrade the database software every time you need to fix a bug. An upgrade is a planned execution, but to fix bugs in the current database version, you need to use patching.

The following are the purposes of patching:

1) To improve the software's vulnerability by applying security fixes

2) To get bug fixes

Usually the required patches will be recommended by Oracle Support after diagnosing any issues. In addition, the same database version on different platforms may not have the same bugs. So, patches are released according to database version and platform.

Patches are available only at the My Oracle Support (MOS) site. This means patches are available only to customers who have a current maintenance contract. If a database version is in Extended support, then patches will be available only to Extended support customers. Again, while downloading a patch, you will need to choose the appropriate platform and version.

A patch might fix a single bug or multiple bugs, depending on how it was built. Each patch will have its own unique number. Usually a patch will be delivered as a ZIP file that includes fixes and a readme file. You should always read the readme file that accompanies the patch because this file will contain the patch installation instructions.

© Y V Ravikumar, K M Krishnakumar and Nassyam Basha 2017
N. Basha et al., *Oracle Database Upgrade and Migration Methods*, DOI 10.1007/978-1-4842-2328-4_12

What a Patch Contains

Usually a patch is delivered as a ZIP file. After it is extracted, you will notice that a folder has been created with a patch number. Inside that is a folder called `files`, which will have bug fixes, and a folder called the `etc` folder, which will have information about the expected database components. A readme file has the patch apply steps for the user. We'll discuss this topic with an example.

```
Downloaded Patch zip file : p18202441_121020_Linux-x86-64.zip
```

In this example, the patch number is 18202441. It was developed for database version 12.1.0.2.0 for the Linux x86-64 platform. After unzipping the patch, the following folder will be created:

```
$ ls -lrt
drwxrwxr-x 4 oracle oinstall    18202441
```

Inside the folder

```
oracle@localhost:~/patch/18202441$ ls -lrt
-rw-rw-r-- 1 oracle oinstall README.txt
drwxr-xr-x 3 oracle oinstall  files
drwxr-xr-x 3 oracle oinstall etc
```

The file `README.txt` will contain the steps to apply this patch. If a patch requires any specific requirement, that will be documented here. This file also contains instructions on how to roll back the patch and any known issues with the patch. It is vitally important to read the patch's readme file.

The `files` folder will have the bug fixes; usually it will be a software binary.

```
$ ls -lrt files/lib/libserver12.a/kdu.o
-rw-r--r-- 1 oracle oinstall 522040  files/lib/libserver12.a/kdu.o
```

This denotes that a bug has a fix and is delivered in the `kdu.o` file and that it needs to be placed in the Oracle Home in the `$ORACLE_HOME/lib/libserver12.a` archive. If the archive already has a `kdu.o` object file, then it will be replaced.

The `etc` folder contains two files: `inventory.xml` and `actions.xml`.

inventory.xml

This file will list the expected platform, database version, components that have to be patched, and whether a database shutdown is required. Note that the readme file contains much of this information, so the DBA is not required to actually read the `inventory.xml` file. Let's see what the 18202441 patch expects from Oracle Home.

```
<oneoff_inventory>
    <opack_version version="13.1.0.1.1"/>
    <reference_id number="18202441"/>
    <unique_patch_id>18790138</unique_patch_id>
    <cannot_autorollback>false</cannot_autorollback>
    <date_of_patch year="2015" month="Apr" day="7" time="10:39:33 hrs" zone="PST8PDT"/>
    <base_bugs>
        <bug number="18202441" description="LOGMINER SHOWS INCORRECT VALUE IN WHERE
        CLAUSE"/>
    </base_bugs>
```

```
<required_components>
    <component internal_name="oracle.rdbms" version="12.1.0.2.0" opt_req="0"/>
</required_components>
<os_platforms>
    <platform name="Linux x86-64" id="226"/>
</os_platforms>
<executables>
    <executable path="%ORACLE_HOME%/bin/oracle"/>
</executables>
<instance_shutdown>true</instance_shutdown>
<instance_shutdown_message></instance_shutdown_message>
<online_rac_installable>true</online_rac_installable>
<run_as_root>false</run_as_root>
<sql_migrate>false</sql_migrate>
<wls_prereq_oneoffs></wls_prereq_oneoffs>
<prereq_oneoffs></prereq_oneoffs>
<coreq_oneoffs></coreq_oneoffs>
<overlay_oneoffs></overlay_oneoffs>
<patch_type value="singleton"/>
<patch_language value="en"/>
<product_family value="db"/>
<patching_model value="one-off"/>
<auto>false</auto>
<translatable>false</translatable>
<applicable_product/>
<products></products>
<update_components></update_components>
</oneoff_inventory>
```

Here are some important points to note (these are expectations by the patch from the current Oracle Home).

- *Opatch tool version*: 13.1.0.1.1

- *Database component*: oracle.server with version 12.1.0.2.0 (but this is optional as opt_req is set to 0)

- *OS platform* : Linux x86-64

- *Instance shutdown*: Required

- *In RAC can I install online*: Yes

- *Can you install as root user*: No

- *Any prerequisite patch*: Not applicable

- *Patch applicable*: Database family

actions.xml

This file has the actions required for applying the patch.

```
<oneoff_actions>
    <oracle.rdbms version="12.1.0.2.0" opt_req="0">
        <archive name="libserver12.a" path="%ORACLE_HOME%/lib" object_name="lib/
libserver12.a/kdu.o"/>
        <make change_dir="%ORACLE_HOME%/rdbms/lib" make_file="ins_rdbms.mk" make_
target="ioracle"/>
    </oracle.rdbms>
</oneoff_actions>
```

The patch will update the $ORACLE_HOME/lib/libserver12.a/kdu.o file with the file provided by this patch and perform relinking on ioracle. The Opatch tool applies the patch. It will read the actions.xml file and perform the actions mentioned in that file.

You'll see in this chapter how the patching works in the background, the patching conflicts, and the types of patches, as well as any new concepts introduced in 12c in this chapter.

How Patching Works

Patching is the process of applying bug fixes either at the Oracle Home binary level or at the database level.

- *Binary level*: The patch accesses the existing Oracle Home binary to supply the bug fixes. Hence, the binary should be free from modification. Patching will either make changes in existing binary or add some additional object files to the binary. After adding or modifying additional contents to existing object files, the binary may need to be relinked for that particular modification. As you saw in Chapter 2, while doing relinking, the database services should be shut down. This means that while patching at the binary level, you will have database downtime.

- *Database level*: Usually SQL files will be delivered that contain the bug fix. Basically it performs changes at the database object level. For some patches, a utility called datapatch will apply the SQL files to the database.

Before going to see how the patching works, you should know about Oracle inventories, the Opatch tool, types of patches, and conflicts.

Central Inventory

There are two inventories created when an Oracle database is installed in a server. They are the central inventory and the local inventory.

The central inventory will have information about the Oracle products installed on the server. Some documentation refers to this as the oraInventory. When you are installing a new product, the Oracle Universal Installer (OUI) updates the existing central inventory regarding the software installation. If the central inventory doesn't exist on the server, in the case when this is the first installation, then the first central inventory will be created. The installation will then utilize the available central inventory. The central inventory location is pointed at by the file oraInst.loc. This file will be available by default in /etc or /var/opt/oracle on Unix platforms. In the Windows operating system, oraInst is defined in the registry at HKEY_LOCAL_MACHINE-> SOFTWARE-> ORACLE.

```
$ cat oraInst.loc
inventory_loc=/u01/app/oraInventory
inst_group=oinstall
```

As per the previous oraInst.loc file, the central inventory location is /u01/app/oraInventory, and it is owned by the oinstall group. The central inventory has the file inventory.xml, which has a list of all Oracle Homes installed on the server, and this file will be located in the folder $ORACLE_BASE/oraInventory/ContentsXML.

```
$ more inventory.xml
<?xml version="1.0" standalone="yes" ?>
<!-- Copyright (c) 1999, 2010, Oracle. All rights reserved. -->
<!-- Do not modify the contents of this file by hand. -->
<INVENTORY>
<COMPOSITEHOME_LIST>
</COMPOSITEHOME_LIST>
<VERSION_INFO>
   <SAVED_WITH>10.2.0.5.0</SAVED_WITH>
   <MINIMUM_VER>2.1.0.6.0</MINIMUM_VER>
</VERSION_INFO>
<HOME_LIST>
<HOME NAME="OraDb11g_home1" LOC="/u01/app/oracle/product/11.2.0" TYPE="O" IDX="2"/>
<HOME NAME="OraDb10g_home1" LOC="/u01/app/oracle/product/10.2.0" TYPE="O" IDX="3"/>
<HOME NAME="OraDB12Home1" LOC="/u01/app/oracle/product/12.1.0/dbhome_1" TYPE="O" IDX="1"/>
<HOME NAME="DB10g_home" LOC="/oradata/10.2.0" TYPE="O" IDX="4"/>
</HOME_LIST>
</INVENTORY>
```

You can see this inventory.xml file shows that the current server has Oracle Database 10g, 11g, and 12c products.

This shows that the central inventory was created when Oracle Database 10.2.0.5.0 got installed, and later it was updated by other installations done on this server.

HOME_NAME denotes a unique name to differentiate it from other installations. The value can be automatically chosen or provided by the user. LOC denotes the location of the installation. In other words, it defines ORACLE_HOME. IDX is the index value to uniquely identify the home in the central inventory.

Have you ever noticed that during installation it reported an error stating that the chosen installation location is already used by another Oracle product? For example, Figure 12-1 shows an error when 11.2.0.3.0 tried to install in a location where another 11.2.0.3.0 installation was already in place. The OUI checks the central inventory to know the installed products and their location. If the chosen Oracle Home location conflicts with the central inventory, it will throw the error shown in Figure 12-1.

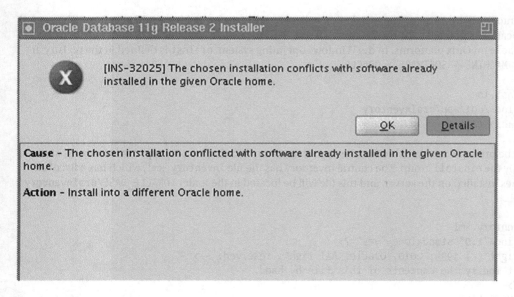

Figure 12-1. *Conflict with existing installation*

Figure 12-2 shows the error when 11.2.0.4.0 was attempted to be installed in a location where 11.2.0.3.0 was installed already.

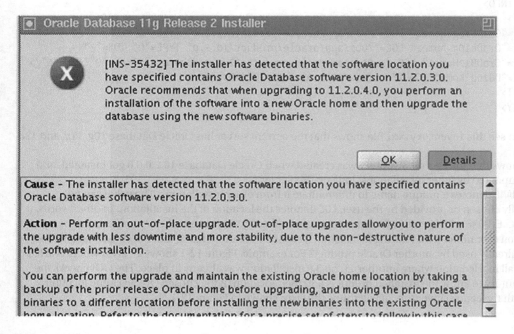

Figure 12-2. *Version 11.2.0.4.0 installation on 11.2.0.3.0 home*

Since 11.2.0.4.0 was attempted to be installed in a 11.2.0.3.0 location, the installation process thinks the binary upgrade was tried here and recommends installing it in a different location.

Re-creation Steps

If the central inventory is deleted mistakenly, then from any installed Oracle Home you can invoke the central inventory creation steps. In the previous example, you have 10g, 11g, and 12c homes. Let's say the /u01/app/oraInventory folder has been removed.

```
oracle@localhost:/u01/app$ mv oraInventory oraInventory_bkp
oracle@localhost:/u01/app$ ls -lrt
drwxrwx---  7 oracle oinstall 4096 oraInventory_bkp
drwxrwxrwx 17 oracle oinstall 4096 oracle
```

You choose an 11.2 Oracle Home to re-create the central inventory. Move to the $ORACLE_HOME/oui/bin directory and use the Oracle Universal Installer command-line utility to re-create the inventory and attach this home to that inventory.

```
$ pwd
/u01/app/oracle/product/11.2.0/oui/bin
$./runInstaller -silent -ignoreSysPrereqs -attachHome ORACLE_HOME="<Oracle_Home_Location>"
ORACLE_HOME_NAME="<Name_Of _Oracle_Home>"
```

attachHome specifies to add this Oracle Home to the central inventory. runInstaller will get the central inventory location using the oraInst.loc file. If the central inventory doesn't exist in that location, then it will be created. In this case, the central inventory is not available at /u01/app. Hence, it will be created.

```
/u01/app/oracle/product/11.2.0/oui/bin$ ./runInstaller -silent -ignoreSysPrereqs -attachHome
ORACLE_HOME="/u01/app/oracle/product/11.2.0" ORACLE_HOME_NAME="Oracle_11g_db_home"
Starting Oracle Universal Installer...

Checking swap space: must be greater than 500 MB.   Actual 4092 MB     Passed
The inventory pointer is located at /etc/oraInst.loc
The inventory is located at /u01/app/oraInventory
'AttachHome' was successful.

$ ls -lrt /u01/app/oraInventory
drwxrwx--- 2 oracle oinstall logs
drwxrwx--- 2 oracle oinstall ContentsXML
```

You can see the central inventory is created in /u01/app/oraInventory. Let's see what inventory.xml contains now:

```
$ cat /u01/app/oraInventory/ContentsXML/inventory.xml
<?xml version="1.0" standalone="yes" ?>
<!-- Copyright (c) 1999, 2011, Oracle. All rights reserved. -->
<!-- Do not modify the contents of this file by hand. -->
<INVENTORY>
<VERSION_INFO>
   <SAVED_WITH>11.2.0.3.0</SAVED_WITH>
   <MINIMUM_VER>2.1.0.6.0</MINIMUM_VER>
```

```
</VERSION_INFO>
<HOME_LIST>
<HOME NAME="Oracle_11g_db_home" LOC="/u01/app/oracle/product/11.2.0" TYPE="O" IDX="1"/>
</HOME_LIST>
<COMPOSITEHOME_LIST>
</COMPOSITEHOME_LIST>
</INVENTORY>
```

You can observe the changes that occurred in the new central inventory. SAVED_WITH changed to 11.2.0.3.0 because the inventory got created using the 11.2.0.3.0 version. It has information only about the 11.2.0.3.0 home. This means you have to add other Oracle Homes into the central inventory using the attachHome command. Let's add 12c and 10g homes using the same step.

```
$ ./runInstaller -silent -ignoreSysPrereqs -attachHome ORACLE_HOME="/u01/app/oracle/
product/12.1.0/dbhome_1/" ORACLE_HOME_NAME="Oracle_12c_db_home"
Starting Oracle Universal Installer...

Checking swap space: must be greater than 500 MB.    Actual 4092 MB    Passed
The inventory pointer is located at /etc/oraInst.loc
The inventory is located at /u01/app/oraInventory
'AttachHome' was successful.

$ ./runInstaller -silent -ignoreSysPrereqs -attachHome ORACLE_HOME="/oradata/10.2.0/"
ORACLE_HOME_NAME="Oracle_10g_db_home"
Starting Oracle Universal Installer...

Checking swap space: must be greater than 500 MB.    Actual 4092 MB    Passed
The inventory pointer is located at /etc/oraInst.loc
The inventory is located at /u01/app/oraInventory
'AttachHome' was successful.
```

Let's see the inventory.xml file now:

```
cat /u01/app/oraInventory/ContentsXML/inventory.xml
<?xml version="1.0" standalone="yes" ?>
<!-- Copyright (c) 1999, 2011, Oracle. All rights reserved. -->
<!-- Do not modify the contents of this file by hand. -->
<INVENTORY>
<VERSION_INFO>
   <SAVED_WITH>11.2.0.3.0</SAVED_WITH>
   <MINIMUM_VER>2.1.0.6.0</MINIMUM_VER>
</VERSION_INFO>
<HOME_LIST>
<HOME NAME="Oracle_11g_db_home" LOC="/u01/app/oracle/product/11.2.0" TYPE="O" IDX="1"/>
<HOME NAME="Oracle_12c_db_home" LOC="/u01/app/oracle/product/12.1.0/dbhome_1/" TYPE="O"
IDX="2"/>
<HOME NAME="Oracle_10g_db_home" LOC="/oradata/10.2.0/" TYPE="O" IDX="3"/>
</HOME_LIST>
<COMPOSITEHOME_LIST>
</COMPOSITEHOME_LIST>
</INVENTORY>
```

All Oracle Homes are registered with the same central inventory.

Here you may doubt whether you can have more than one central inventory on the same server. Say 10*g* and 11*g* are in one central inventory and 12*c* is in a different central inventory. The answer is yes. You can have multiple central inventories. But oraInst.loc can have only one central inventory location. During patching, oraInst.loc will be referred to in order to identify the central inventory. So, if the correct central inventory location is not pointed to in oraInst.loc, then an error will be thrown.

The other question that usually goes along with this is, if you have multiple homes, how do you move the Oracle Home from one central inventory to another central inventory? The proper procedure is to remove the home from the current central inventory and add it to the new central inventory.

How to Remove from the Central Inventory

Like with the attachHome command, you have detachHome remove the Oracle Home from the central inventory.

```
$ ./runInstaller -silent -ignoreSysPrereqs -detachHome ORACLE_HOME="/oradata/10.2.0/"
ORACLE_HOME_NAME="Oracle_10g_db_home"
Starting Oracle Universal Installer...

Checking swap space: must be greater than 500 MB.   Actual 4092 MB     Passed
The inventory pointer is located at /etc/oraInst.loc
The inventory is located at /u01/app/oraInventory
'DetachHome' was successful.
```

Here you removed the 10*g* Oracle Home from the central inventory. Let's check the oraInst.loc file.

```
<HOME_LIST>
<HOME NAME="Oracle_11g_db_home" LOC="/u01/app/oracle/product/11.2.0" TYPE="O" IDX="1"/>
<HOME NAME="Oracle_12c_db_home" LOC="/u01/app/oracle/product/12.1.0/dbhome_1/" TYPE="O"
IDX="2"/>
</HOME_LIST>
```

Let's remove the 11*g* home as well and check the inventory.

```
./runInstaller -silent -ignoreSysPrereqs -detachHome ORACLE_HOME="/u01/app/oracle/
product/11.2.0" ORACLE_HOME_NAME="Oracle_11g_db_home"     Starting Oracle Universal
Installer...

Checking swap space: must be greater than 500 MB.   Actual 4092 MB     Passed
The inventory pointer is located at /etc/oraInst.loc
The inventory is located at /u01/app/oraInventory
'DetachHome' was successful.
```

Let's check the inventory.xml file.

```
$ cat /u01/app/oraInventory/ContentsXML/inventory.xml
<?xml version="1.0" standalone="yes" ?>
<!-- Copyright (c) 1999, 2011, Oracle. All rights reserved. -->
<!-- Do not modify the contents of this file by hand. -->
<INVENTORY>
<VERSION_INFO>
```

```
    <SAVED_WITH>11.2.0.3.0</SAVED_WITH>
    <MINIMUM_VER>2.1.0.6.0</MINIMUM_VER>
</VERSION_INFO>
<HOME_LIST>
<HOME NAME="Oracle_12c_db_home" LOC="/u01/app/oracle/product/12.1.0/dbhome_1/" TYPE="O"
IDX="2"/>
<HOME NAME="Oracle_11g_db_home" LOC="/u01/app/oracle/product/11.2.0" TYPE="O" IDX="1"
REMOVED="T"/>
</HOME_LIST>
<COMPOSITEHOME_LIST>
</COMPOSITEHOME_LIST>
</INVENTORY>
```

You can see that the 11*g* home is present in the central inventory. But it has REMOVED=T, which denotes that the Oracle Home is removed from the central inventory. You may think, why didn't the same think happen for 10*g*? That is because this inventory was created using the 11*g* home.

If ORACLE_HOME is removed mistakenly using rm -rf or in Windows using the Shift+Del key, then you need to remove the reference using detachHome from the central inventory. Otherwise, the central inventory will unnecessarily hold this reference, and you cannot install any other products at this location.

Local Inventory

The local inventory is located in each Oracle Home. The central inventory will have information about all the installed Oracle products in the server, whereas the local inventory will have information about the components installed in that particular Oracle Home. When we say the database software is installed, we mean that its components such as JDK, EM, Server, LDAP, OLAP, and networking are also installed in that Oracle Home. This local inventory will have information about those installed components along with this Oracle Home. The local inventory will be located at $ORACLE_HOME/inventory/ContentsXML/comps.xml.

Here is part of comps.xml:

```
$ cat $ORACLE_HOME/inventory/ContentsXML/comps.xml
<?xml version="1.0" standalone="yes" ?>
<!-- Copyright (c) 1999, 2014, Oracle and/or its affiliates.
All rights reserved. -->
<!-- Do not modify the contents of this file by hand. -->
<PRD_LIST>
<TL_LIST>
<COMP NAME="oracle.server" VER="12.1.0.2.0" BUILD_NUMBER="0" REP_VER="0.0.0.0.0"
RELEASE="Production" INV_LOC="Components/oracle.server/12.1.0.2.0/1/" LANGS="en" XML_INV_
LOC="Components21/oracle.se
rver/12.1.0.2.0/" ACT_INST_VER="12.1.0.2.0" DEINST_VER="11.2.0.0.0" INSTALL_TIME="2015.
Aug.18 04:14:33 UTC" INST_LOC="/u01/app/oracle/product/12.1.0/dbhome_1/oracle.server">
   <EXT_NAME>Oracle Database 12c</EXT_NAME>
   <DESC>Installs an optional preconfigured starter database, product options, management
   tools, networking services, utilities, and basic client software for an Oracle Database
   server. This option
 also supports Automatic Storage Management database configuration.</DESC>
   <DESCID>COMPONENT_DESC</DESCID>
   <STG_INFO OSP_VER="10.2.0.0.0"/>
```

```
<CMP_JAR_INFO>
    <INFO NAME="filemapObj" VAL="Components/oracle/server/v12_1_0_2_0/filemap.xml"/>
    <INFO NAME="helpDir" VAL="Components/oracle/server/v12_1_0_2_0/help/"/>
    <INFO NAME="actionsClass" VAL="Components.oracle.server.v12_1_0_2_0.CompActions"/>
    <INFO NAME="resourceClass" VAL="Components.oracle.server.v12_1_0_2_0.resources.
    CompRes"/>
    <INFO NAME="identifiersXML" VAL="Components/oracle/server/v12_1_0_2_0/identifiers.
    xml"/>
    <INFO NAME="contextClass" VAL="Components.oracle.server.v12_1_0_2_0.CompContext"/>
    <INFO NAME="fastCopyLogXML" VAL="Components/oracle/server/v12_1_0_2_0/fastCopyLog.
    xml"/>
```

The previous portion shows the component oracle.server. There are other database components such as oracle.swd.oui.core, oracle.sysman.ccr, oracle.rdbms.rat, oracle.ovm, and oracle.ons.eons.

The DESC tag shows the description of that database component.

The local inventory is the heart of Oracle Home. It will also have the information about installed patches. When a patch is installed, an entry will be created in comps.xml for that patch. You will later see in this chapter how the entry is created while applying the patch.

Remember, like the central inventory, the local inventory should not be manually edited or modified. Unlike the central inventory, the local inventory cannot be re-created, and its location cannot be altered. If the local inventory is corrupted, then it has to be restored from backup or the Oracle software has to be installed again at a different location with the necessary patches applied.

Using the Opatch Tool

Opatch is a tool provided by Oracle to install patches. This tool will automatically get installed during the database software installation. Opatch will be located in the $ORACLE_HOME/OPatch folder. Unlike other binaries in the Oracle Home, this utility can be downloaded separately for each database version and platform. The Opatch tool is not part of Oracle installation relinking process; hence, it can be upgraded at any time without downtime. This tool version will be different from oracle database version. Oracle keeps releasing new versions for the Opatch tool for the supported database versions. It can be downloaded from the My Oracle Support (MOS) site using patch number 6880830. It is common to need to upgrade Opatch in your Oracle Home directory over time.

Any patch's readme file will often contain the minimum Opatch version number needed to apply that patch.

Consider you have installed the 12.1.0.1.0 Oracle Home on Linux x86-64. The default Opatch tool version available with the 12.1.0.1.0 installation is 12.1.0.1.3. This information can be identified through the following:

```
$ $ORACLE_HOME/OPatch/opatch version
OPatch Version: 12.1.0.1.3
```

If you search patch 6880880 on the My Oracle Support site, you can see that Opatch version 12.1.0.1.10 is available, which is higher than what you have.

Note that Opatch is released at the database release level. This means for the 12c version, Opatch is the same as for Oracle 12.1.0.1.0 and 12.1.0.2.0. Download this patch; the file name will be p6880880_121010_Linux-x86-64.zip.

Extract the patch; it will create the OPatch folder.

To upgrade the Opatch tool available in the Oracle Home, simply replace the folder with this extracted folder.

1) Unzip the downloaded Opatch tool. Unzipping will create OPatch folder.

```
$ unzip p6880880_121010_Linux-x86-64.zip
```

2) Move the existing Opatch tool in the Oracle Home into a different name to be on the safe side.

```
$ mv $ORACLE_HOME/OPatch $ORACLE_HOME/OPatch_bkp
```

3) Move the extracted Opatch folder into the Oracle Home.

```
$ cp -r OPatch/ $ORACLE_HOME/
```

4) Check the Opatch version.

```
$ $ORACLE_HOME/OPatch/opatch version
OPatch Version: 12.1.0.1.10
```

You can now see that the Opatch tool has been upgraded to version 12.1.0.1.10. It is always recommended that you upgrade the Opatch tool before applying any patches. The patches often require a certain version of Opatch or higher.

The Opatch tool can be used for three purposes.

- You know information about the Oracle Home, and the existing installed patches will be stored in the local inventory. Reading the local inventory comps.xml file will be difficult to understand. Using Opatch, you can retrieve the inventory details in readable form. The lsinventory (list inventory) argument is used to get the inventory details.

```
$ $ORACLE_HOME/OPatch/opatch lsinventory
Oracle Interim Patch Installer version 11.2.0.3.0
Oracle Home       : /u01/app/oracle/product/11.2.0
Central Inventory : /u01/app/oraInventory
   from           : /u01/app/oracle/product/11.2.0/oraInst.loc
OPatch version    : 11.2.0.3.0
OUI version       : 11.2.0.3.0
Log file location : /u01/app/oracle/product/11.2.0/cfgtoollogs/opatch/opatch<Date><Time>.log

Lsinventory Output file location : /u01/app/oracle/product/11.2.0/cfgtoollogs/opatch/
lsinv/<Date><Time>..txt

--------------------------------------------------------------------------------
Installed Top-level Products (1):

Oracle Database 11g                                      11.2.0.3.0
There is 1 product installed in this Oracle Home.
```

```
Interim patches (1) :

Patch  13923374     : applied on <Date><Time>
Unique Patch ID:  14847207
Patch description:  "Database Patch Set Update : 11.2.0.3.3 (13923374)"

Sub-patch  13696216; "Database Patch Set Update : 11.2.0.3.2 (13696216)"
Sub-patch  13343438; "Database Patch Set Update : 11.2.0.3.1 (13343438)"
   Bugs fixed:
     13419660, 10350832, 13632717, 14063281, 12919564, 13467683, 13588248
```

From the previous output, you can see that the Opatch lsinventory shows the Oracle Home location and central inventory location, the pointer for the central inventory location, the Opatch version, the Oracle Universal Installer (OUI) information, and the log file location where current execution will be logged. The Oracle Home information will be displayed every time Opatch is invoked. It lists the products installed in the Oracle Home and the patches installed in the Oracle Home.

If you want to see each individual database component installed in the Oracle Home, execute -detail along with lsinventory.

```
$ $ORACLE_HOME/OPatch/opatch lsinventory -detail
```

The lsinventory information will include individual database components installed in the Oracle Home along with their version.

```
Installed Products (136):
Agent Required Support Files            10.2.0.4.3
Assistant Common Files                  11.2.0.3.0
Bali Share                              1.1.18.0.0
Buildtools Common Files                 11.2.0.3.0
Character Set Migration Utility         11.2.0.3.0
```

The previous output shows 136 database components/products are installed in the Oracle Home.

Also, the output below shows the installed patches in detail, such as what files are touched by this patch.

```
Patch  13923374     : applied on <Date><Time>
Unique Patch ID:  14847207
Patch description:  "Database Patch Set Update : 11.2.0.3.3 (13923374)"
Sub-patch  13696216; "Database Patch Set Update : 11.2.0.3.2 (13696216)"
Sub-patch  13343438; "Database Patch Set Update : 11.2.0.3.1 (13343438)"
   Bugs fixed:
     13419660, 10350832, 13632717, 14063281, 12919564, 13467683, 13588248
     13420224, 12646784, 12861463, 12834027, 13036331, 12380299, 13499128
     12998795, 13492735, 12829021, 13503598, 10133521, 12718090, 13742433
     12905058, 12401111, 13742434, 12849688, 13362079, 12950644, 13742435
     12917230, 13923374, 12879027, 12535346, 12588744, 11377623, 13916709
     12847466, 13340388, 13528551, 13366202, 12894807, 13981051, 13343438
     12582664, 12748240, 12797765, 12923168, 13466801, 13772618, 11063191
     13070939, 13035804, 12797420, 13041324, 12976376, 13742437, 14062795
     13035360, 13742438, 13326736, 13332439, 14038787, 14062796, 12913474
     13001379, 13370330, 14062797, 13742436, 9873405, 14062794, 9858539
```

```
    12960925, 12662040, 9703627, 12617123, 13338048, 12938841, 12658411
    12620823, 12656535, 12845115, 14062793, 12764337, 12678920, 13354082
    14062792, 12612118, 9761357, 13742464, 13457582, 13527323, 12780983
    12780098, 13502183, 13696216, 11840910, 13903046, 13554409, 13657605
    13103913, 14063280
Files Touched:
    /kgl.o --> ORACLE_HOME/lib/libgeneric11.a
    /kgl2.o --> ORACLE_HOME/lib/libgeneric11.a
    /kgl4.o --> ORACLE_HOME/lib/libgeneric11.a
    ins_net_client.mk --> ORACLE_HOME/network/lib/client_sharedlib
    /ktb.o --> ORACLE_HOME/lib/libserver11.a
    /kks.o --> ORACLE_HOME/lib/libserver11.a
    /kks1.o --> ORACLE_HOME/lib/libserver11.a
```

- The Opatch tool performs patch installation and rollback. We'll discuss this later in this chapter.

- The Opatch tool can also perform other prerequisite checks before applying a patch. We will discuss this during the patch installation.

Types of Patches

Oracle has provided a variety of patches, each with different purposes: patch set updates (PSUs), security patch update (SPUs), one-off or interim patches, and more. All patches are available only for users with a valid support contract, and these patches can be downloaded only at the My Oracle Support site.

Patch Set Update (PSU)

PSU patches are released every quarter for the database versions that are under the patching period. The PSU will include security fixes plus one-off fixes that Oracle Support has deemed to be safe for production environments. It is a superset of SPU. PSU patches are cumulative. This means the latest PSU will contain the fixes of the PSU patches released earlier. The last digit in the Oracle database version denotes the PSU level. For example, 12.1.0.2.1 denotes PSU level 1. Recently Oracle has changed PSU naming convention. The last digit will have PSU release date. For example 12.1.0.2.0 July PSU name is 12.1.0.2.160719. The last digit denotes that PSU is released on 19th July,2016.

Once a new database version is released, from the next quarter the PSU will be released for that Oracle version. PSU patches are released only for Unix platforms. Starting with the Oracle 12c release, Oracle no longer provides the SPU. Furthermore, if the DBA applies the PSU, they cannot apply the SPU the following quarter this is because SPU is subset of PSU. So if the PSU is applied, they should continue with the PSU every quarter thereafter.

Security Patch Update (SPU)

SPU patches will have only security fixes. These patches are also released every quarter, and like the PSUs, these patches are cumulative. Organizations can follow either the SPU cycle or the PSU cycle. But from the PSU cycle, they cannot go to the SPU cycle because the PSU is a superset of CPU patches. SPU patches are also released only for Unix/Linux platforms.

Bundle Patches

The Windows platform has only bundle patches. This is equivalent to the PSU of Unix/Linux platforms. Like the PSU and SPU, the bundle patch will be released every quarter and also whenever required. Bundle patches are cumulative.

One-Off Patches

In addition to the PSU and CPU patches, there are patches developed to fix specific bugs. Those are called one-off patches. This type of patch will be released based on need and will be released for database versions that are covered under the patching period. A one-off patch should be applied only when you see a bug and Oracle Support recommends applying the patch.

Proactive Bundle Patches

From 12c (12.1.0.2.), Oracle has introduced Proactive bundle patches. These are different from Windows Bundle patches. This patch includes fixes for both Engineered Systems and for DB In-memory. It is super set of PSU patch. It includes all the fixes of PSU. This patch can be applied to Engineered and also non Engineered system and also applicable for both RAC and non-RAC configurations. It could be considered as a high level quarterly patch.

This is applicable to enterprise edition. For standard edition database PSU needs to be installed. In case PSU has been already installed and we want to install Proactive Bundle patch, then existing PSU needs to be rolled back and then apply Proactive bundle patches. We cannot mix both PSU and Proactive bundle patch in the same oracle home.

Conflicts

When you apply a patch, it will modify the Oracle Home binary to apply the fixes. If another patch touches the same binary to apply its own fix, then a conflict will occur. It is called a *binary conflict* because one patch may lose the changes of the other patch, and vice versa. You require fixes of both patches. You cannot lose any bug fix. In that case, you will require a merge patch, which will have the fixes of both with no conflicts. You may need to contact Oracle Support to find out about the merge patch details, or you can use the MOS conflict checker tool to find the merge patch details.

Suppose you are applying a patch that fixes 10 bugs and later at some time you apply a patch that fixes 20 bugs, including the 10 bugs fixed by the old patch. In that case, the new patch becomes a superset patch, and the old patch will be called a subset patch. In this case, the old patch can be rolled back, and the new patch can be applied. You will not be losing any bug fixes in this way. Another good example for a superset and subset combination is PSU and SPU patches. If the SPU is already applied and you are going to apply the latest PSU, then the installed SPU, which is a subset patch, can be rolled back and the superset patch can be applied.

Overlay Patches

At times you might come across a situation where you have installed a patch for fixing a bug and you are trying to install the PSU patch that conflicts with your existing patch. You cannot roll back the existing patch; also, the PSU doesn't include your bug fix, so you cannot consider the PSU as the superset. What should you do?

This is where you need overlay patches. These patches are built to overcome the conflict with the PSU. Suppose you have a 12.1.0.2.0 Oracle Home and you have applied patch A of the 12.1.0.2.0 version. Now you are trying to apply PSU 12.1.0.2.1 (remember that the last digit denotes the PSU level). You find that patch A has a conflict with PSU 12.1.0.2.1. You should report this conflict to Oracle Support. They'll deliver an overlay patch of patch A with version 12.1.0.2.1. This means the new patch A has been developed with version 12.1.0.2.1, which is compatible with PSU 12.1.0.2.1, and this new patch will not have a conflict with the 12.1.0.2.1 PSU. Roll back patch A first and then apply the PSU patch. Then apply patch A of version 12.1.0.2.1. Kindly note that overlay patches are installed on top of the respective PSU. If the PSU patch is rolled back, then the overlay patch sitting on that PSU will also be rolled back. So, be sure before rolling back PSU patches. Get the list of overlay patches and see whether you have the equivalent of those patches in the base version. In the previous example, when you roll back the 12.1.0.2.1 PSU, the overlay patch called patch A will be rolled back along with that. You need to apply patch A of the 12.1.0.2.0 version again or you will lose the bug fix.

Patch Apply Strategies (Online and Offline Patching)

In this section, we'll discuss how to apply a patch and what happens in the background while applying a patch.

A patch has some bug fixes in it. While applying the patch, it has to be placed in the Oracle Home at the appropriate place so that the bug fix will get applied to it. In other words, you can say the binary that has the bug will be altered or modified or replaced by the patch to place the right binary there. If you are applying PSU/SPU patches, then apply the latest PSU/SPU patch because they are cumulative in nature. In case you've planned to apply one-off patches, ensure that the patch is recommended by Oracle Support or applying it may have an adverse effect.

Download the patch from My Oracle Support. Usually the downloaded patch will have the name format p<patch_number>_<database_version>_<platform_name>.zip.

Once a patch is downloaded, move the ZIP file to the appropriate server. Suppose the patch is meant for a Linux X86-64 server; then transfer the patch ZIP file to the Linux x86-64 server. Transferring unzipped contents to the server may corrupt the patch files. Once the transfer is completed, check the integrity of the patch. This will help to ensure that the patch is not corrupted. An integrity check can be done through the MD5 sum and SHA-1 values.

For example, 6880880 of version 12.1.0.1 for Linux x86-64 is p6880880_121010_Linux-x86-64.zip. My Oracle Support reports its SHA-1 and MD5 values as follows:

```
SHA-1   xxxxx
MD5     xxxxx
```

When the patch is transferred to Linux x86-64, let's cross-check the values using shell commands. Compare the values to the information from My Oracle Support. If the values differ, you will most likely have to download the patch again.

```
$ md5sum p6880880_121010_Linux-x86-64.zip
```

```
$ sha1sum p6880880_121010_Linux-x86-64.zip
```

Once the integrity is checked, it can be unzipped. Unzipping the downloaded patch ZIP file will create a folder with the name of the patch. The downloaded folder will contain patch files and the README.txt file. This readme will have a description of this patch, whether this patch is RAC rolling installable, the installation steps, the de-installation steps, and the bugs fixed by this patch.

Before applying the patch, you need to do some prerequisite checks. Ask yourself these questions:

- Can this patch be applied online? This means the patch doesn't require any downtime. It can be applied when the database is up.

- Does this patch conflict with any existing installed patches? If this patch tries to modify some binaries that have already been modified by other patches for bug fixes, then conflict will occur. If there is a conflict, it is recommended that you contact Oracle Support and get a merge patch.

- Does the Oracle Home have all the required components for this patch? This check will be done at the local inventory.

- Does the Oracle Home mount point have enough free space to apply the patch? Sometimes the patch will have more fixes to apply and its size will be bigger.

- If you planned to apply multiple patches to Oracle Home, do these patches have conflict among themselves?

These prerequisite checks can be done **online** before applying a patch. Performing these prerequisite checks will help to reduce downtime and unexpected errors. Say a patch should be applied offline and the database has been shut down, but you haven't done a prerequisite check. You find that the patch apply steps fail because the patch has a conflict with an existing installed patch. In that case, you need to contact Oracle Support to get the merge patch details. If a merge patch is not already available for this conflict, then a new one has to be developed, which will take time based on the complexity. The downtime will continue in vain without the patch being applied. If you had done the conflict prerequisite check up front, then you could have approached Oracle Support with the conflict information in advance and the required merge patch could have been collected before the patch apply. This scenario is just an example. There are many more benefits of doing prerequisite checks.

Let's spend some time here getting to know the steps to perform these prerequisite checks. First you'll download and extract the patch. You have a folder with the name of the patch. It's called `patch_folder`.

1) To check whether the patch can be applied through the online method, use this:

   ```
   $ORACLE_HOME/OPatch/opatch query -is_online_patch <patch_folder>
   ```

   This will analyze the patch and let you know whether the patch can be applied online, as shown here:

   ```
   Patch is an online patch: false
   ```
   To check whether the patch is rolling applicable, use this:

   ```
   $ORACLE_HOME/OPatch/opatch query -is_rolling_patch <patch_folder>
   ```

   The result can be true or false.

   ```
   Patch is a rolling patch: true
   ```

2) To know whether the patch has any conflicts with the other installed patches, use this:

   ```
   $ORACLE_HOME/OPatch/opatch prereq CheckConflictAgainstOHWithDetail –ph <patch_folder>
   ```

The result shows whether the prerequisite check was successful or failed.

Does the patch getting applied require any prerequisite patches? If this condition is there, it will be displayed as follows:

```
"Interim patch <patch_number> requires prerequisite patch(es) [<[patch_number>] which are
not present in the Oracle Home.
Apply prerequisite patch(es) [<patch_number>] before applying interim patch <patch_number>.
```

Summary of Conflict Analysis

This section shows whether the patch getting applied has a conflict with any installed patches. If there are any conflicts present, they will be listed.

The following patches have conflicts. Please contact Oracle Support and get the merged patch of the patches.

```
<Patch numbers which has conflict>
Following patches will be rolled back from Oracle Home on application of the patches in the
given list :
        <patch_number which is getting applied>
        Conflicts/Supersets for each patch are:
Patch : <patch_number which is getting applied>
        Conflict with <existing patch which is getting conflicted>
        Conflict details:
        <which file is getting conflict>
```

For example, say you planned to apply 13923374 and 13004894 is already applied in the Oracle Home. You perform a conflict prerequisite check for 13923374. The results are as follows:

```
Following patches have conflicts. Please contact Oracle Support and get the merged patch of
the patches:
13004894, 13923374
Conflicts/Supersets for each patch are:
Patch : 13923374

        Conflict with 13004894
        Conflict details:
        /u01/app/oracle/product/11.2.0/lib/libserver11.a:/qke.o
```

3) Patching will be accessing binaries that are part of some database components, so before applying the patch, check the installed database components of the Oracle Home. As you know, the local inventory will have information about the installed database components. Before applying the patch, you need to check whether the required database component is present in the Oracle Home or else there's no need to apply the patch. This can be checked as follows:

```
$ORACLE_HOME/OPatch/opatch prereq CheckApplicable -ph <patch_directory>
Invoking prereq "checkapplicable"
Prereq "checkApplicable" for patch <patch_number> passed/failed.
```

For example, you can do the testing for patch 13923374 with this:

```
$ $ORACLE_HOME/OPatch/opatch prereq CheckApplicable -ph /home/oracle/
patch/13923374/

Invoking prereq "checkapplicable"

Prereq "checkApplicable" for patch 13343438 passed.

Prereq "checkApplicable" for patch 13696216 passed.
```

```
Patch 13923374: Optional component(s) missing :
[ oracle.network.cman, 11.2.0.3.0 ]

Prereq "checkApplicable" for patch 13923374 passed.
```

To see what components are expected by the patch, open the file <patch_directory>/etc/config/ inventory.xml. The required components will be between the required_components tags, as shown here:

```
<required_components>
        <component internal_name="oracle.rdbms" version="11.2.0.3.0"
opt_req="0"/>
    </required_components>
```

opt_req has the value 0, which means it's an optional component.

4) To check whether the Oracle Home mount point has the required free space, execute a prerequisite check as follows:

```
$ORACLE_HOME/OPatch/opatch prereq CheckSystemSpace  -ph <patch_directory>

$ $ORACLE_HOME/OPatch/opatch prereq CheckSystemSpace  -ph /home/oracle/
patch/13923374/

Invoking prereq "checksystemspace"

Prereq "checkSystemSpace" passed.

OPatch succeeded.
```

5) Check the conflicts between patches before they get applied. For example, say you planned to apply patch A and patch B. Before applying the patches, let's check whether these patches have a conflict among themself. This check is mandatory or you'll get a conflict message when applying the second patch.

To check for conflicts, you place the unzipped contents of both patch ZIP files into a single folder. Say /u01/app/oracle/patches has the patches 12749597, 14692386, and 17487358 that you have planned to apply. You want to check whether these patches have conflicts among themselves.

```
$ ls
12749597  14692386  17487358
$ $ORACLE_HOME/OPatch/opatch prereq CheckConflictAmongPatchesWithDetail -phBaseDir /home/
oracle/patch/patches/
Invoking prereq "checkconflictamongpatcheswithdetail"
ZOP-40: The patch(es) has conflicts with other patches installed in the Oracle Home (or)
among themselves.
Prereq "checkConflictAmongPatchesWithDetail" failed.
Summary of Conflict Analysis:
There are no patches that can be applied now.
```

```
Following patches have conflicts. Please contact Oracle Support and get the merged patch of
the patches :
12749597, 14692386, 17487358
Conflicts/Supersets for each patch are:
Patch : 12749597
        Conflict with 14692386
        Conflict details:
        /u01/app/oracle/product/12.1.0/dbhome_1/rdbms/admin/dbmsobj.sql

        Conflict with 17487358
        Conflict details:
        /u01/app/oracle/product/12.1.0/dbhome_1/rdbms/admin/dbmsobj.sql
Patch : 14692386
        Conflict with 12749597
        Conflict details:
        /u01/app/oracle/product/12.1.0/dbhome_1/rdbms/admin/dbmsobj.sql

        Conflict with 17487358
        Conflict details:
        /u01/app/oracle/product/12.1.0/dbhome_1/rdbms/admin/dbmsobj.sql


Patch : 17487358

        Conflict with 12749597
        Conflict details:
        /u01/app/oracle/product/12.1.0/dbhome_1/rdbms/admin/dbmsobj.sql

        Conflict with 14692386
        Conflict details:
        /u01/app/oracle/product/12.1.0/dbhome_1/rdbms/admin/dbmsobj.sql

OPatch succeeded.
```

The previous message shows that the patches have conflicts among themselves. Hence, you should apply the merge patch with the fixes of all the patches, not the individual patches.

6) You can perform all the prerequisites in one step with the Analyze option. This option will perform all the patch apply steps virtually and provide the results.

```
[oracle@Server 21948354]$ /u01/app/oracle/product/12.1.0/OPatch/opatch apply
-analyze
Oracle Interim Patch Installer version 12.1.0.1.10
Copyright (c) 2016, Oracle Corporation.  All rights reserved.

Oracle Home       : /u01/app/oracle/product/12.1.0
Central Inventory : /u01/app/oraInventory
   from           : /u01/app/oracle/product/12.1.0/oraInst.loc
OPatch version    : 12.1.0.1.10
OUI version       : 12.1.0.2.0
Log file location : /u01/app/oracle/product/12.1.0/cfgtoollogs/opatch/opatch.log
```

Verifying environment and performing prerequisite checks...
OPatch continues with these patches: 21948354

Do you want to proceed? [y|n]
y
User Responded with: Y
All checks passed.
[Report: skip "rm -rf /u01/app/oracle/product/12.1.0/ccr"]
[Report: skip unzipping "/u01/app/oracle/product/12.1.0/OPatch/ocm/ocm.zip"]
Provide your email address to be informed of security issues, install and
initiate Oracle Configuration Manager. Easier for you if you use your My
Oracle Support Email address/User Name.
Visit http://www.oracle.com/support/policies.html for details.
Email address/User Name:

You have not provided an email address for notification of security issues.
Do you wish to remain uninformed of security issues ([Y]es, [N]o) [N]: y

[Report: Skip calling "/bin/sh /u01/app/oracle/product/12.1.0/ccr/bin/setupCCR
-R /u01/app/oracle/product/12.1.0/.patch_storage/ocmRespFile -S OPatch -V
12.1.0.1.10" under "/u01/app/oracle/product/12.1.0/ccr/bin"]

Please shutdown Oracle instances running out of this ORACLE_HOME on the local
system.
(Oracle Home = '/u01/app/oracle/product/12.1.0')
Is the local system ready for patching? [y n]
y
User Responded with: Y
Backing up files...
Applying sub-patch '21948354' to OH '/u01/app/oracle/product/12.1.0'
Users request no RAC file generation. Do not create MP files.

Skip patching component oracle.rdbms.deconfig, 12.1.0.2.0 and its actions.
The actions are reported here, but are not performed.
Skip patching component oracle.xdk, 12.1.0.2.0 and its actions.
The actions are reported here, but are not performed.
Skip patching component oracle.tfa, 12.1.0.2.0 and its actions.
The actions are reported here, but are not performed.
Skip patching component oracle.rdbms, 12.1.0.2.0 and its actions.
The actions are reported here, but are not performed.
Skip patching component oracle.rdbms.dbscripts, 12.1.0.2.0 and its actions.
The actions are reported here, but are not performed.
Skip patching component oracle.xdk.parser.java, 12.1.0.2.0 and its actions.
The actions are reported here, but are not performed.
Skip patching component oracle.rdbms.rsf, 12.1.0.2.0 and its actions.
The actions are reported here, but are not performed.
Skip patching component oracle.xdk.rsf, 12.1.0.2.0 and its actions.
The actions are reported here, but are not performed.

```
ApplySession skipping inventory update.
Users request no RAC file generation.  Do not create MP files.
Composite patch 21948354 successfully applied.
Log file location: /u01/app/oracle/product/12.1.0/cfgtoollogs/opatch/<date>.
logOPatch succeeded.
```

The output shows the patch has passed all the required prerequisites, and the patch can be applied without any issues.

Patch Apply Steps

Once you are sure that the patch prerequisites are successful, you can proceed by applying the patch. It is always advisable to perform the patching in preproduction environments before proceeding to production. This will help in identifying any issues while applying the patch and also let you know whether this patch solves your problem, in other words, fixes the bug. After applying a patch in a test environment, verify the application functionality. Ensure that the bug fix resolved the issue and you didn't face any new issues. The verification check list can be the same as you do for post-upgrade checks.

Note that the preproduction environment should have the same patches installed as production or doing testing in preproduction will not be fruitful.

As part of patch apply consider at this stage, the patch ZIP file has been extracted, and it creates a folder with the name of the patch number. You have performed a prerequisite check and there are no conflicts, and you have ensured enough free space is available to apply the patch.

Check whether the patch can be applied online or whether offline mode is required. Let's first discuss how to apply a patch in offline mode.

Applying Patch in Offline Mode

When a patch requires offline mode, shut down Oracle Database and all database-related services such as the listener, Enterprise Manager Database Express, and Database Control. The binary should be free from modifications. In Microsoft Windows, stop the Oracle-related services using the Services window.

Set the ORACLE_HOME and PATH environment variables to the Oracle Home that is getting patched. Move to patch_directory and invoke Opatch with the apply argument. In the following example, you are applying 18202441 to the 12.1.0.1 Oracle Home.

```
$ $ORACLE_HOME/OPatch/opatch apply
Oracle Interim Patch Installer version 12.1.0.1.10
Oracle Home          : /u01/app/oracle/product/12.1.0/dbhome_1
Central Inventory : /u01/app/oraInventory
   from              : /u01/app/oracle/product/12.1.0/dbhome_1/oraInst.loc
OPatch version    : 12.1.0.1.10
OUI version       : 12.1.0.2.0
Log file location : /u01/app/oracle/product/12.1.0/dbhome_1/cfgtoollogs/
opatch/18202441_<date>/apply<date.time>.log

Verifying environment and performing prerequisite checks...
OPatch continues with these patches:   18202441

Do you want to proceed? [y|n]
y
User Responded with: Y
```

```
All checks passed.
Provide your email address to be informed of security issues, install and
initiate Oracle Configuration Manager. Easier for you if you use your My
Oracle Support Email address/User Name.
Visit http://www.oracle.com/support/policies.html for details.
Email address/User Name:

You have not provided an email address for notification of security issues.
Do you wish to remain uninformed of security issues ([Y]es, [N]o) [N]:  Y

Please shutdown Oracle instances running out of this ORACLE_HOME on the local system.
(Oracle Home = '/u01/app/oracle/product/12.1.0/dbhome_1')

Is the local system ready for patching? [y|n]
y
User Responded with: Y
Backing up files...
Applying interim patch '18202441' to OH '/u01/app/oracle/product/12.1.0/dbhome_1'

Patching component oracle.rdbms, 12.1.0.2.0...
Patch 18202441 successfully applied.
Log file location: /u01/app/oracle/product/12.1.0/dbhome_1/cfgtoollogs/
opatch/18202441_<Date>/apply<date-time>.log

OPatch succeeded.
```

Using the previous example, we will discuss the activities happening in the background while applying the patch.

```
$ORACLE_HOME/OPatch/opatch apply
Oracle Interim Patch Installer version 12.1.0.1.10
Oracle Home       : /u01/app/oracle/product/12.1.0/dbhome_1
Central Inventory : /u01/app/oraInventory
   from           : /u01/app/oracle/product/12.1.0/dbhome_1/oraInst.loc
OPatch version    : 12.1.0.1.10
OUI version       : 12.1.0.2.0
Log file location : /u01/app/oracle/product/12.1.0/dbhome_1/cfgtoollogs/
opatch/18202441_<date>/apply<date.time>.log
```

First the Opatch tool collects the Oracle Home details. For that, it read the /etc/oraInst.loc file and get the central inventory location. The central inventory will have a list of all the Oracle Home details along with their index number. Using these values, it connects to the Oracle Home and verifies the index number. If the index number doesn't match between the local and central inventory files or the central inventory doesn't have the patching Oracle Home information, then the patch will terminate at the first step.

```
Verifying environment and performing prerequisite checks...
```

Once the first phase is successful, it'll perform prerequisite checks that include verifying the platform, the sufficient free space, any active process related to Oracle Home, whether the required database components are installed in the Oracle Home, and conflicts with the installed Oracle Home.

```
Backing up files...
```

Once the prerequisites are met, it will start taking a backup of the files that it is going to modify. This backup will be used when you roll back the patch. If you roll back a patch, then the changes made by the patch have to be rolled back. For that reason, the Opatch tool keeps the backup of binaries that are modified by the patch in the $ORACLE_HOME/.patch_storage folder. This is a hidden folder that resides inside the Oracle Home. If you applied more patches, then this folder would become huge in size. You should not delete the contents of this folder. Doing that will create problems when you try to roll back.

```
Applying interim patch '18202441' to OH '/u01/app/oracle/product/12.1.0/dbhome_1'
```

After taking a backup, it starts modifying the binaries as mentioned in the patch's actions.xml file. The real patching happens at this stage.

```
Patching component oracle.rdbms, 12.1.0.2.0...
```

Once the patch files are placed at the Oracle Home, it has to be relinked to take effect. Relinking will be done on the required components based on files that the patch has replaced.

```
Patch 18202441 successfully applied.
```

Once relinking is successful, the Opatch tool updates the patch information in the inventory and also verifies whether the patch information was updated properly in the Oracle inventory.

To verify whether the patch was applied and the inventory was updated, invoke opatch lsinventory.

```
$ORACLE_HOME/OPatch/opatch lsinventory
Oracle Interim Patch Installer version 12.1.0.1.10
Oracle Home       : /u01/app/oracle/product/12.1.0/dbhome_1
Central Inventory : /u01/app/oraInventory
   from           : /u01/app/oracle/product/12.1.0/dbhome_1/oraInst.loc
OPatch version    : 12.1.0.1.10
OUI version       : 12.1.0.2.0
Log file location : /u01/app/oracle/product/12.1.0/dbhome_1/cfgtoollogs/opatch/<Date><Time>
.log
Lsinventory Output file location : /u01/app/oracle/product/12.1.0/dbhome_1/cfgtoollogs/
opatch/lsinv/lsinventory<Date><Time>.txt


--------------------------------------------------------------------------------
Local Machine Information::
Hostname: localhost.localdomain
ARU platform id: 226
ARU platform description:: Linux x86-64

Installed Top-level Products (1):

Oracle Database 12c                 12.1.0.2.0
There are 1 products installed in this Oracle Home.
Interim patches (1) :
Patch  18202441     : applied on <Date><Time>
Unique Patch ID:  18790138
   Created on <Date><Time>
   Bugs fixed:
     <Bug_number>
```

Lsinventory shows that the patch has been applied successfully.

Patching in Online Mode

In the previous example, the patch was applied offline. Oracle Database was shut down to apply the patch because the patch required the binary to be free from modification. In online patching, database services can be functional. Patching doesn't require relinking, and hence the binary can be actively used by processes. Opatch has to be invoked as follows for online patching:

```
$opatch apply online -connectString <SID>:<USERNAME>:<PASSWORD>:<NODE>
```

- The SID denotes the database connection string.

- The username and password of database user who has the SYSDBA privilege should be given.

- The node denotes the host name.

Here's an example. We apply online patch called patchA:

```
$ORACLE_HOME/OPatch/opatch  apply online -connectString prim:sys:sys
Oracle Interim Patch Installer version 11.2.0.3.0

Oracle Home       : /u01/app/oracle/product/11.2.0
Central Inventory : /u01/app/oraInventory
   from           : /u01/app/oracle/product/11.2.0/oraInst.loc
OPatch version    : 11.2.0.3.0
OUI version       : 11.2.0.3.0
Log file location : /u01/app/oracle/product/11.2.0/cfgtoollogs/
opatch/patchA_<date>_<time>/apply_<date>_<time>_1.log

The patch should be applied/rolled back in '-all_nodes' mode only.
Converting the RAC mode to '-all_nodes' mode.
Applying interim patch 'patchA' to OH '/u01/app/oracle/product/11.2.0'
Verifying environment and performing prerequisite checks...
All checks passed.
Provide your email address to be informed of security issues, install and
initiate Oracle Configuration Manager. Easier for you if you use your My
Oracle Support Email address/User Name.
Visit http://www.oracle.com/support/policies.html for details.
Email address/User Name:

You have not provided an email address for notification of security issues.
Do you wish to remain uninformed of security issues ([Y]es, [N]o) [N]:  y
Backing up files...

Patching component oracle.rdbms, 11.2.0.3.0...
Installing and enabling the online patch 'bug<patch_number>.pch', on database 'prim'.
```

```
Verifying the update...
Patch patchA successfully applied
Log file location: /u01/app/oracle/product/11.2.0/cfgtoollogs/opatch/patchA_<date>_<time>/
apply<date>_<time>_1.log

OPatch succeeded.
```

You can see the patch output is similar to offline mode. But in addition to the normal activity, it has called bug<patch_number>.pch to apply the patch online.

If there are multiple databases created in this Oracle Home, then it can be invoked as follows:

```
$opatch apply online -connectString <SID>:<USERNAME>:<PASSWORD>:<NODE>,<SID>:<USERNAME>:<PA
SSWORD>:<NODE>
```

The online patch can also be applied offline if you have any required downtime.
Either offline or online, follow the readme for the patch apply steps.

Post-Patch Steps

Some patches may require you to induce a fix at the database level. For that, the patch will deliver SQL files. You need to execute the SQL file after the Opatch apply process has been completed successfully. In 12*c* you need to execute datapatch to complete any database-related tasks. The missing post-patch script may not give fixes at the database level.

Patch Rollback

Sometimes you need to roll back installed patches. This might be because an applied patch is not delivering a required bug fix or it produces some other issue or you are planning to apply a superset patch.

When a patch is getting rolled back, the changes done by the patch should be revoked. Suppose a file is changed by the patch, then when rolling back, it should replace the original file. For that reason, while applying a patch, the patch takes a backup of files that it is going to change. The backup is stored in the hidden folder $ORACLE_HOME/.patch_storage. This folder should not get deleted or you cannot roll back the patch.

If the patch is applied through the offline method, then it should be rolled back in offline mode. The same mode should be followed for apply and rollback. Before rolling back, the patch binary should be free for offline patching.

1) Shut down the Oracle Home and other related services.

2) Invoke opatch rollback –id <list of patches to be rolled back>.

3) Start the database and invoke any post-patch actions if necessary.

```
$ /u01/app/oracle/product/12.1.0/OPatch/opatch rollback -id 20703000
Oracle Interim Patch Installer version 12.1.0.1.10
Copyright (c) 2016, Oracle Corporation.  All rights reserved.

Oracle Home       : /u01/app/oracle/product/12.1.0
Central Inventory : /u01/app/oraInventory
   from           : /u01/app/oracle/product/12.1.0/oraInst.loc
OPatch version    : 12.1.0.1.10
```

```
OUI version       : 12.1.0.2.0
Log file location : /u01/app/oracle/product/12.1.0/cfgtoollogs/opatch/20703000_<date>/
rollback<date>.log

RollbackSession rolling back interim patch '20703000' from OH '/u01/app/oracle/
product/12.1.0'

Please shutdown Oracle instances running out of this ORACLE_HOME on the local system.
(Oracle Home = '/u01/app/oracle/product/12.1.0')

Is the local system ready for patching? [y|n]
y
User Responded with: Y

Patching component oracle.rdbms, 12.1.0.2.0...
RollbackSession removing interim patch '20703000' from inventory
Log file location: /u01/app/oracle/product/12.1.0/cfgtoollogs/opatch/20703000_<date>/
rollback<date>.log
OPatch succeeded.
```

Opatch Debug

If you want to see the Opatch debug information, then set the OPATCH_DEBUG flag to true before invoking the apply command.

```
export OPATCH_DEBUG=TRUE
```

For the C shell, you can use the setenv command.

In Windows, use SET OPATCH_DEBUG=TRUE.

This will show debug information for any Opatch commands executed after that. The debug information will be useful when there are issues in Opatch command execution and the error is not self-explanatory.

PSU and SPU Patching

You have seen how to patch with one-off patches so far. In this section, you'll see the patching steps for PSU and SPU patches. As you know, there are PSU and SPU patches released every quarter. These patches have to be applied offline, which means that database services should be down. The prerequisite checks are the same as one-off patching. The only difference is that a one-off patch will have a single patch. But PSU and SPU patches are cumulative; they will include the patches released before. For example, 11.2.0.4 got released for Linux x86-64 in August 2013. The latest 11.2.0.4.0 PSU patch will have all the PSU patches released after August 2013.

When you extract a PSU patch, it will create a folder in the PSU patch number. Inside the folder you will notice separate folders for each previous PSU patch. The Opatch apply process has to be called from the parent folder.

For example, version 12.1.0.2.0 (October 2015 PSU) has been downloaded. Its downloaded patch ZIP name is p21359755_121020_Linux-x86-64.zip. Once you unzip the patch, you can see the following folders:

```
$ unzip p21359755_121020_Linux-x86-64.zip
$ls
README.txt
20299023   ---- 12.1.0.2.3 PSU
20831110   ---- 12.1.0.2.4 PSU
19769480   ---- 12.1.0.2.2 PSU
21359755   ---- 12.1.0.2.5 PSU
README.html
```

In PSU patching, you need to know some attributes of it.

PSU patches come in two kinds: composite and noncomposite.

- *Composite PSUs*: Some database versions such as 11.2.0.3 and 11.2.0.4 have PSU patches as composite. In the composite model, the only missing PSU on that Oracle Home will be applied. Suppose you applied the January 2015 PSU last and now you are applying the January 2016 PSU. The missing PSUs April 2015, July 2015, and October 2015 will get applied. Since this type of patch applies only the missing patches, the amount of time to apply the patch will be less. In turn, the downtime is less while applying composite PSU patches. This model has been around since the 11.2.0.2.0 version. This model will also be of more benefit for overlay patches. Say you have installed an overlay patch on top of 11.2.0.3.2 and now you are applying the 11.2.0.3.4 PSU patch; in this model the patch will not roll back the existing 11.2.0.3.2, and hence your overlay patch will not be rolled back. Only the 11.2.0.3.3 and 11.2.0.3.4 PSUs will get applied.

- *Noncomposite PSUs*: In this model, when the PSU patch gets applied, it will replace all the existing PSUs and apply the new PSU patch. This means it will roll back the existing PSU and apply the PSU that is executed. In this case, it will take longer to apply the patch, which means you will have more downtime. It will not check the existing patches. Simply roll back the existing PSU and apply the PSU that is being applied. The PSU being applied should be earlier than the PSU that is already installed.

  This noncomposite model also impacts overlay patches. When the existing PSU patch is getting rolled back, the attached overlay patches also will get rolled back. You need to contact Oracle Support to get a new overlay patch for the PSU being applied. This means every quarter you need to contact Oracle Support to get an overlay patch for the latest PSU.

PSU Patch Apply Steps

In PSU patching, like one-off patches, you need to perform prerequisite checks. The PSU should not conflict with any existing installed patches. Once all the prerequisites are met, you can follow these steps to apply the patch:

1) Shut down all the databases of the chosen Oracle Home.

2) Stop all the database-related services such as the listener and emctl of that Oracle Home.

3) Ensure the Oracle owner has logged into the system.

4) From the unzipped patch folder, invoke opatch apply to apply the patch to the Oracle Home.

5) Once the patch is applied and relinking has been completed, invoke `opatch lsinventory` to check that the patch information has been updated in the inventory.

6) Start the database in normal mode or upgrade mode as mentioned in the readme.

7) Execute the post-patch SQL script `catbundle.sql` (up to the 11g R2 version), which will perform post-patch executions. It also updates `registry$database` with the patch information. For 12c, execute the `datapatch` command to execute the post-patch steps.

Because the patch apply steps for one-off patches and PSU patches are the same, we will discuss only the post-patch steps for PSU patch execution. Up to 11g R2, the PSU patch requires execution of the `catbundle.sql` script for post-patch execution. This script modifies the data dictionary to induce the fixes at the database level and registers this PSU execution in the data dictionary.

Start the database and then invoke the `catbundle.sql` execution as the sys user.

In 12c, post-patch execution is done through the `datapatch` tool, which is delivered in the Opatch folder. This tool is smart enough to find all the modified SQL files placed by the patch and executes those SQL files. We'll discuss datapatch later in this chapter in detail.

```
[oracle@Server OPatch]$ ./datapatch -verbose
SQL Patching tool version 12.1.0.2.0 on <Date><Time>

Log file for this invocation: /u01/app/oracle/cfgtoollogs/sqlpatch/
sqlpatch_12803_<date>_<time>/sqlpatch_invocation.log

Connecting to database...OK
Bootstrapping registry and package to current versions...done
Determining current state...done
Current state of SQL patches:
Bundle series PSU:
ID 5 in the binary registry and not installed in the SQL registry
Adding patches to installation queue and performing prereq checks...
Installation queue:
  Nothing to roll back
The following patches will be applied:
  21359755 (Database Patch Set Update : 12.1.0.2.5 (21359755))
Installing patches...
Patch installation complete.  Total patches installed: 1
Validating logfiles...
Patch 21359755 apply: SUCCESS
  logfile: /u01/app/oracle/cfgtoollogs/sqlpatch/21359755/19194568/21359755_apply_<ORACLE_
SID>_<date><time>.log (no errors)
```

How to Confirm the PSU Patch Apply Is Successful

The PSU patch apply process can be confirmed in three ways.

1) Execute the Opatch lsinventory to see the list of patches applied. If a PSU patch is successfully applied, it will have been updated in the inventory.

```
$ORACLE_HOME/OPatch/opatch lsinventory
[oracle@Server 21359755]$ $ORACLE_HOME/OPatch/opatch lsinventory
Oracle Interim Patch Installer version 12.1.0.1.10
Copyright (c) 2016, Oracle Corporation.  All rights reserved.
Oracle Home        : /u01/app/oracle/product/12.1.0
Central Inventory : /u01/app/oraInventory
   from            : /u01/app/oracle/product/12.1.0/oraInst.loc
OPatch version    : 12.1.0.1.10
OUI version       : 12.1.0.2.0
Log file location : /u01/app/oracle/product/12.1.0/cfgtoollogs/opatch/
opatch<date><time>1.log

Lsinventory Output file location : /u01/app/oracle/product/12.1.0/cfgtoollogs/
opatch/lsinv/lsinventory date><time>.txt
Local Machine Information::
Hostname: Server.localdomain
ARU platform id: 226
ARU platform description:: Linux x86-64
Installed Top-level Products (1):
Oracle Database 12c                                              12.1.0.2.0
There are 1 products installed in this Oracle Home.
Interim patches (1) :
Patch  21359755     : applied on Sun Feb 28 10:28:09 GMT 2016
Unique Patch ID:  19194568
Patch description:  "Database Patch Set Update : 12.1.0.2.5 (21359755)"
   Created on 21 Oct 2015, 02:52:58 hrs PST8PDT
Sub-patch  20831110; "Database Patch Set Update : 12.1.0.2.4 (20831110)"
Sub-patch  20299023; "Database Patch Set Update : 12.1.0.2.3 (20299023)"
Sub-patch  19769480; "Database Patch Set Update : 12.1.0.2.2 (19769480)"
```

2) Along with lsinventory, you can use the bugs_fixed argument. This will show the descriptions of patches applied.

```
$ORACLE_HOME/OPatch/opatch lsinventory –bugs_fixed
[oracle@Server 21359755]$ $ORACLE_HOME/OPatch/opatch lsinventory -bugs_fixed |
grep -i psu
```

3) Once the post-patch script catbundle.sql has successfully completed, then the patch information will be recorded in registry$history. By querying that table, you can confirm the patch has been applied successfully. In 12c you invoke datapatch, and you can see the patch details in registry$sqlpatch.

PSU Rollback

Like one-off patches, a PSU patch can be rolled back.

For example, you can roll back patch 21948354.

```
[oracle@Server OPatch]$ ./opatch rollback -id 21948354
Oracle Interim Patch Installer version 12.1.0.1.10
Copyright (c) 2016, Oracle Corporation.  All rights reserved.


Oracle Home        : /u01/app/oracle/product/12.1.0
Central Inventory  : /u01/app/oraInventory
    from           : /u01/app/oracle/product/12.1.0/oraInst.loc
OPatch version     : 12.1.0.1.10
OUI version        : 12.1.0.2.0
Log file location  : /u01/app/oracle/product/12.1.0/cfgtool_logs/
opatch/21948354_<date>/<date>.log


Patches will be rolled back in the following order:
   21948354
The following patch(es) will be rolled back: 21948354
Sub-patches of a composite series are being rolled back. The system will be returned to a
state where 19769480,20299023,20831110,21359755 and all its fixes will still remain, because
the patch(es) were installed before patch(es) 21948354 were applied.
The following bug fixes will be removed:
20794034,19490948,19689979,19902195,19869255,21787056,17655240,21517440,21300341,20173897,21
668627,21526048,16887946,17551063,19879746,20101006,20618595,22092979,20318889,19326908,1897
3548,18799063,20877664,21756699,21875360,18886413,21188532,20869721,20890311,20446883,205094
82,17890099,20588502,19604659,20951038,18799993,19141838


Please shutdown Oracle instances running out of this ORACLE_HOME on the local system.
(Oracle Home = '/u01/app/oracle/product/12.1.0')


Is the local system ready for patching? [y|n]
y
User Responded with: Y


Rolling back patch 21948354...
RollbackSession rolling back interim patch '21948354' from OH '/u01/app/oracle/
product/12.1.0'


Patching component oracle.rdbms.deconfig, 12.1.0.2.0...
Patching component oracle.xdk, 12.1.0.2.0...
Patching component oracle.tfa, 12.1.0.2.0...
Patching component oracle.rdbms, 12.1.0.2.0...
Patching component oracle.rdbms.dbscripts, 12.1.0.2.0...
Patching component oracle.xdk.parser.java, 12.1.0.2.0...
Patching component oracle.rdbms.rsf, 12.1.0.2.0...
Patching component oracle.xdk.rsf, 12.1.0.2.0...
RollbackSession removing interim patch '21948354' from inventory
Log file location: /u01/app/oracle/product/12.1.0/cfgtoollogs/opatch/21948354_
Apr_05_2016_05_42_02/rollback2016-04-05_05-42-02AM_1.log


OPatch succeeded.
```

The rollback operation lists the bugs that will get rolled back by this operation. You might think that PSU patches are cumulative, so if you install the 11.2.0.4.2 PSU and then install the 11.2.0.4.4 PSU, then when you roll back 11.2.0.4.4 PSU, it will roll back 11.2.0.4.2 PSU also.

That's not the case. It will leave the 11.2.0.4.2 PSU. At the same time, you should see whether the PSU patch is composite or noncomposite.

Start the database and invoke datapatch to roll back the transactions at the database level.

```
$ ./datapatch -verbose
SQL Patching tool version 12.1.0.2.0
Copyright (c) 2015, Oracle.  All rights reserved.

Log file for this invocation: /u01/app/oracle/cfgtoollogs/sqlpatch/sqlpatch_<date>/sqlpatch_
invocation.log

Connecting to database...OK
Note:  Datapatch will only apply or rollback SQL fixes for PDBs
       that are in an open state, no patches will be applied to closed PDBs.
       Please refer to Note: Datapatch: Database 12c Post Patch SQL Automation
       (Doc ID 1585822.1)
Bootstrapping registry and package to current versions...done
Determining current state...done

Current state of SQL patches:
Bundle series PSU:
  ID 5 in the binary registry and ID 160119 in PDB CDB$ROOT, ID 160119 in PDB PDB$SEED, ID
160119 in PDB PDB12102

Adding patches to installation queue and performing prereq checks...
Installation queue:
  For the following PDBs: CDB$ROOT PDB$SEED PDB12102
    The following patches will be rolled back:
      21948354 (Database Patch Set Update : 12.1.0.2.160119 (21948354))
    Nothing to apply

Installing patches...
Patch installation complete.  Total patches installed: 3

Validating logfiles...
Patch 21948354 rollback (pdb CDB$ROOT): SUCCESS
  logfile: /u01/app/oracle/cfgtoollogs/sqlpatch/21948354/19553095/21948354_rollback_CDB121_
CDBROOT_<date>.log (no errors)
Patch 21948354 rollback (pdb PDB$SEED): SUCCESS
  logfile: /u01/app/oracle/cfgtoollogs/sqlpatch/21948354/19553095/21948354_rollback_CDB121_
PDBSEED_<date>.log (no errors)
Patch 21948354 rollback (pdb PDB12102): SUCCESS
  logfile: /u01/app/oracle/cfgtoollogs/sqlpatch/21948354/19553095/21948354_rollback_CDB121_
PDB12102_<date>.log (no errors)
SQL Patching tool complete.
```

For versions older than 12c, you need to start the database and execute $ORACLE_HOME/rdbms/admin/catbundle_PSU_<database SID>_ROLLBACK.sql.

SPU Patching

SPU patches are always a noncomposite model. They will replace the existing patch and apply the new one. They will have security fixes as molecules. Mostly the SPU will not conflict with the existing installed patches. If there is a conflict, then contact Oracle Support, which will release the merge patch for the conflicts. The conflict is resolved through merge patches, so even when you roll back the SPU patch, the merge patch will stay there. Like with a PSU, an SPU is a cumulative patch, and it will be applied offline. It will contain security fixes as molecules.

Note that since Oracle 12*c*, only PSU patches are released. SPU patches are available only for pre-12*c* versions. Also, SPUs are only subset patches. If a PSU patch is already installed, you cannot install the SPU patch on top of it.

Let's see the SPU patch installation through an example.

You can apply SPU patch 21972320 (11.2.0.4.160119) with these steps:

1) Shut down the Oracle Home and its related services.

2) Perform the prerequisite checks and apply the patch.

3) Perform the post-install steps.

```
$opatch napply -skip_subset -skip_duplicate
Oracle Interim Patch Installer version 11.2.0.3.11
Copyright (c) 2016, Oracle Corporation.  All rights reserved.

Oracle Home       : /oradata/11.2.0.4.0
Central Inventory : /u01/app/oraInventory
   from           : /oradata/11.2.0.4.0/oraInst.loc
OPatch version    : 11.2.0.3.11
OUI version       : 11.2.0.4.0
Log file location : /oradata/11.2.0.4.0/cfgtoollogs/opatch/opatch2016-04-09_16-02-30PM_1.log

Verifying environment and performing prerequisite checks...
OPatch continues with these patches:    17811429  17811438  17811447  18203835  18203837
18203838  19463893  19544839  19584068  19972564  19972566  19972568  20142975  20506715
20631274  21051833  21051840  21051852  21051858  21051862  21179898  21538558  21538567
21972320  22195441  22195448  22195457  22195465  22195477  22195485  22195492  22321741
22321756

Do you want to proceed? [y|n]
y
User Responded with: Y
All checks passed.
Provide your email address to be informed of security issues, install and
initiate Oracle Configuration Manager. Easier for you if you use your My
Oracle Support Email address/User Name.
Visit http://www.oracle.com/support/policies.html for details.
Email address/User Name:
You have not provided an email address for notification of security issues.
Do you wish to remain uninformed of security issues ([Y]es, [N]o) [N]:y
Please shutdown Oracle instances running out of this ORACLE_HOME on the local system.
(Oracle Home = '/oradata/11.2.0.4.0')
```

```
Is the local system ready for patching? [y|n]

User Responded with: Y
Backing up files...
Applying interim patch '17811429' to OH '/oradata/11.2.0.4.0'

Patching component oracle.rdbms, 11.2.0.4.0...

Verifying the update...
Applying interim patch '17811438' to OH '/oradata/11.2.0.4.0'

Patching component oracle.rdbms, 11.2.0.4.0...

Verifying the update...
Applying interim patch '17811447' to OH '/oradata/11.2.0.4.0'

Patching component oracle.rdbms, 11.2.0.4.0...

Patching component oracle.sdo, 11.2.0.4.0...

Patching component oracle.sdo.locator, 11.2.0.4.0...
Verifying the update...
.
.
.
Patches 17811429,17811438,17811447,18203835,18203837,18203838,19463893,19544839,19584068,199
72564,19972566,19972568,20142975,20506715,20631274,21051833,21051840,21051852,21051858,21051
862,21179898,21538558,21538567,21972320,22195441,22195448,22195457,22195465,22195477,2219548
5,22195492,22321741,22321756 successfully applied.
OPatch Session completed.
Log file location: /oradata/11.2.0.4.0/cfgtoollogs/opatch/opatch2016-04-09_16-02-30PM_1.log
```

The security molecules one by one get applied.

After the Opatch execution, start the database and execute the SQL script catbundle.sql.

```
SQL> @?/rdbms/admin/catbundle.sql cpu apply
```

This will apply security fixes to the database and register the SPU patch apply steps in registry$history.

```
select action, action_time, bundle_series from registry$history
ACTION          ACTION_TIME             BUNDLE_SER
------          ---------------         ----------
APPLY           <data and time>         CPU
```

Rolling back the SPU patch is the same as with the PSU patch. Shut down the database and execute the rollback command.

```
$ORACLE_HOME/OPatch/opatch rollback -id <patch_number of SPU patch>
```

After rolling back the patch at binary level, start the database and execute script catbundle_CPU_<databsae SID>_rollback.sql

Patch Apply Steps in RAC and Data Guard Environments

So far you have seen patching in a stand-alone database environment. Say a database associated with Real Application Clusters (RAC) and Data Guard (DG) also needs to be patched. The steps here are a little different from what you saw earlier. Let's discuss patching in an RAC environment first.

Patching in an RAC Environment

As you know, RAC has multiple nodes for achieving high availability. It has a Grid Infrastructure (GI) home and a database (DB) home in all nodes. Patching has to be done in all nodes. Patches have been built either only for the Grid home or for the database home or for both. This is based on the bug fixes delivered in the patch. The patch has to be applied on the appropriate homes. Here we will discuss how the PSU patching is done in an RAC environment.

Opatch provides an auto option to apply the patches in an RAC environment. Using this option, the patch can be automatically applied to both the GI and DB homes. This is the preferred method of applying a patch in an RAC environment. The opatch auto command has to be executed by the operating system with root privileges. Some of the binaries in the Grid home are owned by root. If the GI home or DB home is not shared among the nodes, then opatch has to be executed in all nodes. But at the same time, this utility should not be run in parallel on the nodes.

To patch the GI home and all Oracle RAC database homes of the same version, use this:

```
# opatch auto <UNZIPPED_PATCH_LOCATION> -ocmrf <ocm response file>
```

The Oracle Configuration Manager (OCM) response file will have the OCM connection settings. It can be created by executing $ORACLE_HOME/OPatch/ocm/bin/emocmrsp.

The opatch command should be executed from the Grid home

```
$./emocmrsp
OCM Installation Response Generator 10.3.7.0.0 - Production
Copyright (c) 2005, 2012, Oracle and/or its affiliates.  All rights reserved.
Provide your email address to be informed of security issues, install and
initiate Oracle Configuration Manager. Easier for you if you use your My
Oracle Support Email address/User Name.
Visit http://www.oracle.com/support/policies.html for details.
Email address/User Name:
You have not provided an email address for notification of security issues.
Do you wish to remain uninformed of security issues ([Y]es, [N]o) [N]:  y
The OCM configuration response file (ocm.rsp) was successfully created.
```

Specifying the response file will mean you won't be asked for this information while applying the patch. Here you are trying to achieve patch automation, and hence specifying the OCM response file is mandatory.

Let's discuss the patching with an example. Here you are trying to apply patch 13919095: GRID INFRASTRUCTURE PATCH SET UPDATE 11.2.0.3.3 (INCLUDES DB PSU 11.2.0.3.3) on Grid 11.2.0.3.0 setup.

- *Grid home version*: 11.2.0.3.0

- *Database home version*: 11.2.0.3.0

The Grid PSU has two kinds of patches: Grid component PSUs and database PSUs. Both the patches will be applied on both the Grid and database homes.

We have logged as the root user to invoke opatch auto.

```
[root@rac1 patch]# opatch auto /home/oracle/patch -ocmrf /u01/app/11.2.0/grid/OPatch/ocm/
bin/ocm.rsp

Executing /u01/app/11.2.0/grid/perl/bin/perl /u01/app/11.2.0/grid/OPatch/crs/patch11203.
pl -patchdir /home/oracle -patchn patch -ocmrf /u01/app/11.2.0/grid/OPatch/ocm/bin/ocm.rsp
-paramfile /u01/app/11.2.0/grid/crs/install/crsconfig_params

This is the main log file: /u01/app/11.2.0/grid/cfgtoollogs/opatchauto<date>.log

This file will show your detected configuration and all the steps that opatchauto attempted
to do on your system:
/u01/app/11.2.0/grid/cfgtoollogs/opatchauto<date>.report.log

Starting Clusterware Patch Setup
Using configuration parameter file: /u01/app/11.2.0/grid/crs/install/crsconfig_params

Stopping RAC /u01/app/oracle/product/11.2.0/dbhome_1 ...
Stopped RAC /u01/app/oracle/product/11.2.0/dbhome_1 successfully

patch /home/oracle/patch/13919095/custom/server/13919095  apply successful for home  /u01/
app/oracle/product/11.2.0/dbhome_1

patch /home/oracle/patch/13923374  apply successful for home  /u01/app/oracle/
product/11.2.0/dbhome_1

Stopping CRS...
Stopped CRS successfully

patch /home/oracle/patch/13919095  apply successful for home  /u01/app/11.2.0/grid
patch /home/oracle/patch/13923374  apply successful for home  /u01/app/11.2.0/grid

Starting CRS...
CRS-4123: Oracle High Availability Services has been started.

Starting RAC /u01/app/oracle/product/11.2.0/dbhome_1 ...
Started RAC /u01/app/oracle/product/11.2.0/dbhome_1 successfully

opatch auto succeeded.
```

First the patch performs the prerequisite checks at both the Grid and database homes. It stops Cluster Services on the local home and then applies patches to the database home. Once the database home patching is successful, it moves to the Grid home. After applying patches to the Grid and DB homes, the high availability services will be started.

In the previous example, you have the GI and database homes with version 11.2.0.3.0. But RAC could have different versions for the GI and DB versions. At the same time, the GI home should have a higher version than the database home.

In this case, you need to apply different patches. Suppose the GI home is 11.2.0.3.0 and the database home is 11.2.0.2.0. GI will ask for the 11.2.0.3.0 PSU, and the database will require the 11.2.0.2.0 PSU. In that case, you cannot patch both the homes at the same time. You need to apply individual patches. But patching can be done through the opatch auto option.

To patch only the GI home, use this:

```
# opatch auto <UNZIPPED_PATCH_LOCATION> -oh <GI_HOME> -ocmrf <ocm response file>
```

To patch one or more Oracle RAC database homes, use this:

```
# opatch auto <UNZIPPED_PATCH_LOCATION> -oh <oracle_home1_path>, <oracle_home2_path> -ocmrf
<ocm response file>
```

To roll back the patch from the GI home and each Oracle RAC database home, use this:

```
# opatch auto <UNZIPPED_PATCH_LOCATION> -rollback -ocmrf <ocm response file>
```

To roll back the patch from the GI home, use this:

```
# opatch auto <UNZIPPED_PATCH_LOCATION> -oh <path to GI home> -rollback -ocmrf <ocm response
file>
```

To roll back the patch from the Oracle RAC database home, use this:

```
# opatch auto <UNZIPPED_PATCH_LOCATION> -oh <path to RAC database home> -rollback -ocmrf
<ocm response file>
```

Once the patch has been applied successfully at the binary level, the post-patch SQL scripts have to be applied in the database. Pre-12c requires `catbundle.sql` execution in the database, and 12c requires datapatch execution. The command opatch auto will automatically perform the post-patch executions.

Patching in a Data Guard Environment

Data Guard is an Oracle high availability solution that replicates data to remote databases. In Data Guard, there will be a primary database and one or more standby databases. The primary database transactions will be transferred to the standby database through archived redo logs or a real-time apply. In general, the primary and standby will be located in different data centers. If the primary database is lost or disconnected, the standby database can take up the primary role. You learned about Data Guard in Chapter 2. Here we'll discuss Data Guard from a patching perspective.

Usually the primary and the standby will be on the same database version and patch level. Patches have to be applied on the primary and standby. At the binary level, you apply both database homes separately, but post-patch executions will be done at the primary site, and they get transferred to the standby database through the log transport.

1) Stop the media recovery process at the standby database.

2) Shut down the primary database and apply the patch at the binary level.

3) Shut down the standby database and apply the patch at the binary level.

4) Start the standby database in mount mode. Do not start managed recovery.

5) Start the primary database.

6) Apply any SQL scripts if required.

7) Start the media recovery process at the standby site.

Some patches offer the convenience of being able to apply the standby first. In that case, you can apply the patch on the standby at the binary level, and you can observe whether the patch is getting applied successfully and the bug fix is appropriate. In this case, the primary won't be affected. But some patches will not have this provision. So, before applying the patch, you need to verify this.

PSU/SPU Patch Apply in a Data Guard Environment

Follow these steps:

1) On the primary, disable the log shipping.

2) Stop the media recovery process and shut down the standby databases.

3) Apply the patches to the standby Oracle Homes.

4) Start the standby databases.

5) Shut down the primary database.

6) Apply the patches to the primary database.

7) Start the primary database.

8) Start the media recovery process on the standby databases.

9) Enable the log shipping on the primary database.

10) Execute post-patch executions on the primary database. The changes happening on the primary database will be transferred to all the standby databases.

Datapatch

Until 12*c*, the patch-post installation scripts are executed manually in the database. For example, the PSU patch installation requires catbundle.sql execution at the database level. After applying the patch at the binary level through Opatch, the database has to be started, and the post-installation scripts have to be executed manually. Missing this script execution will not get the fixes into the database level, and also the patch information will not be registered in the database. After the 12*c* patches, the post-installation step is automated by datapatch. This means you don't need to execute catbundle.sql.

The datapatch utility is available inside the $ORACLE_HOME/OPatch folder. After the patch is installed at the binary level, the datapatch utility can be invoked. It completes the post-patch SQL actions for RDBMS patches. The datapatch utility is smart enough to identify the post-patch SQL scripts and execute them. Though you install multiple patches and then invoke datapatch, the utility will complete the post-steps of all the patches in a single execution. It maintains a repository where the information about the installed patches and post-execution details are stored. Remember, datapatch is applicable only to patching with the post-patch SQL steps.

These are the options available with datapatch:

```
%sqlpatch_parameters,
db - database name
apply {patch1, patch2,..patchN} - Specified patches to consider to apply
rollback {patch1, patch2,..patchN} - Specified patches to consider to rollback
force - Run the apply scripts forcibly though the execution is not required
prereq - Run only prerequisite checks, do not perform actual execution
```

pdbs <pdb1,pdb2,..pdbN) - Specify particular PDB to execute the scripts
verbose - Enable verbose mode
bundle_series –This option will be specified for only bundle patches
help - Helping instructions for datapatch tool
debug - To show debug information
upgrade_mode_only – Consider only patches that require upgrade mode

Let's look at an example. Patch 21948354, which was a PSU released January 15 for 12.1.0.2.0, has been applied to the Oracle Home at the binary level. The Opatch lsinventory output shows the patch has been installed and registered in the inventory.

```
$ /u01/app/oracle/product/12.1.0/OPatch/opatch lsinventory
Oracle Home        : /u01/app/oracle/product/12.1.0
Central Inventory : /u01/app/oraInventory
   from             : /u01/app/oracle/product/12.1.0/oraInst.loc
OPatch version    : 12.1.0.1.10
OUI version       : 12.1.0.2.0
Log file location : /u01/app/oracle/product/12.1.0/cfgtoollogs/opatch/opatch<Date><Time>.log
Lsinventory Output file location : /u01/app/oracle/product/12.1.0/cfgtoollogs/opatch/
lsinv/<Date><Time>.txt
Local Machine Information::
Hostname: Server.localdomain
ARU platform id: 226
ARU platform description:: Linux x86-64
Installed Top-level Products (1):

Oracle Database 12c                                        12.1.0.2.0
There are 1 products installed in this Oracle Home.
Interim patches (1) :
Patch  21948354       : applied on <Date><Time>
Unique Patch ID:  19553095
Patch description:   "Database Patch Set Update : 12.1.0.2.160119 (21948354)"
```

Start the database. If it is a multitenant database, then start all the pluggable databases as well. Invoke the datapatch tool available in the $ORACLE_HOME/OPatch folder.

```
./datapatch -verbose
SQL Patching tool version 12.1.0.2.0 Copyright (c) 2015, Oracle.  All rights reserved.

Log file for this invocation: /u01/app/oracle/cfgtoollogs/sqlpatch/
sqlpatch_10275_2016_04_05_05_57_31/sqlpatch_invocation.log

Connecting to database...OK
Note:  Datapatch will only apply or rollback SQL fixes for PDBs
       that are in an open state, no patches will be applied to closed PDBs.
       Please refer to Note: Datapatch: Database 12c Post Patch SQL Automation    (Doc ID
       1585822.1)
Bootstrapping registry and package to current versions...done
Determining current state...done
```

```
Current state of SQL patches:
Bundle series PSU:
  ID 160119 in the binary registry and ID 5 in PDB CDB$ROOT, ID 5 in PDB PDB$SEED, ID 5 in
PDB PDB12102

Adding patches to installation queue and performing prereq checks...
Installation queue:
  For the following PDBs: CDB$ROOT PDB$SEED PDB12102
    Nothing to roll back
    The following patches will be applied:
      21948354 (Database Patch Set Update : 12.1.0.2.160119 (21948354))

Installing patches...
Patch installation complete.  Total patches installed: 3

Validating logfiles...
Patch 21948354 apply (pdb CDB$ROOT): SUCCESS
  logfile: /u01/app/oracle/cfgtoollogs/sqlpatch/21948354/19553095/21948354_apply_CDB121_
CDBROOT_<date>.log (no errors)
Patch 21948354 apply (pdb PDB$SEED): SUCCESS
  logfile: /u01/app/oracle/cfgtoollogs/sqlpatch/21948354/19553095/21948354_apply_CDB121_
PDBSEED_<date>..log (no errors)
Patch 21948354 apply (pdb PDB12102): SUCCESS
  logfile: /u01/app/oracle/cfgtoollogs/sqlpatch/21948354/19553095/21948354_apply_CDB121_
PDB12102_<date>..log (no errors)
SQL Patching tool complete
[oracle@Server OPatch]$
```

In the previous example, the script is executed in a multitenant database, and the datapatch utility executes the installation scripts in the container and all the open pluggable databases. If any pluggable databases are not open during execution, then the datapatch utility can be executed for that PDB alone when it is open. To confirm the patch apply, query the DBA_REGISTRY_SQLPATCH table.

```
SQL> select patch_id, action_time, action from DBA_REGISTRY_SQLPATCH;

  PATCH_ID      ACTION_TIME                     Action
-------------------------------------------------------
  21948354      <data and time>                 APPLY
```

Queryable Patch Inventory

Information about the installed patches in an Oracle Home is stored in the local inventory. You use the Opatch tool to read the local inventory and provide the information in a readable manner. For example, you execute the Opatch lsinventory. This will list all the installed patches in the Oracle Home. For that you need to log in to the database server and execute the opatch command as the Oracle Home owner. It is not possible to retrieve the patch information from the remote system. This has been overcome in the Oracle 12c version, which introduced a new option to access the patch information at a database level. This makes it possible to retrieve inventory information at the SQL prompt.

The DBMS_QOPATCH PL/SQL package does the job of viewing the installed patched information. This package has procedures and functions that will access the inventory and provide real-time data. The output will be in XML format.

For example, to check the lsinventory information, execute the following:

```
SQL> set long 20000
SQL> select dbms_qopatch.GET_OPATCH_LSINVENTORY from dual;
GET_OPATCH_LSINVENTORY
--------------------------------------------------------------------------------
<?xml version="1.0" encoding="US-ASCII" standalone='yes'?>
<InventoryInstance>
  <oracleHome>
    <UId>OracleHome-b0e4f043-a1ce-40f0-a383-b0cc26e2444a</UId>
    <targetTypeId>oracle_home</targetTypeId>
    <inventoryLocation>/u01/app/oraInventory</inventoryLocation>
    <isShared>false</isShared>
    <patchingModel>oneoff</patchingModel>
    <path>/u01/app/oracle/product/12.1.0</path>
  </oracleHome>
  <osPlatform id="226">

    <UId>FlexibleDataType-23832551-6e65-43e2-968b-f32c67a-14d4</UId>
    <hostName>Server.localdomain</hostName>
    <version>Linux x86-64</version>
  </osPlatform>
  <patches>
```

The previous format is in XML. It can be converted using the xmltransform function.

```
SQL> select xmltransform(DBMS_QOPATCH.GET_OPATCH_LSINVENTORY,
 DBMS_QOPATCH.GET_OPATCH_XSLT) from dual;

Oracle Querayable Patch Interface 1.0
--------------------------------------------------------------------------------

Oracle Home        : /u01/app/oracle/product/12.1.0
Inventory          : /u01/app/oraInventory
--------------------------------------------------------------------------------
Installed Top-level Products (1):
                              12.1.0.2.0
Interim patches:

Patch   18202441:   applied on <Date and Time>
Unique Patch ID: 18790138
  Patch Description:
  Created on    : <Date and Time>

 Bugs fixed:
        18202441
  Files Touched:

    /kdu.o
    ins_rdbms.mk
```

Table 12-1 shows some of the other available functions with examples. The steps are executed for PSU patch 21948354.

Table 12-1. *Available Functions*

Function/Procedure	Description	Argument	Example
GET_OPATCH_PREQS	Gets patch prerequisite details	Patch number	SQL> select xmltransform(DBMS_QOPATCH.GET_OPATCH_PREQS('21948354'), DBMS_QOPATCH.GET_OPATCH_XSLT) from dual; Output: This patch needs patches: 19769480 20299023 20831110 21359755
GET_OPATCH_BUGS	Returns the bugs fixed by installed paches		SQL> select xmltransform(DBMS_QOPATCH.GET_OPATCH_BUGS, DBMS_QOPATCH.GET_OPATCH_XSLT) from dual; Output: Bugs fixed: 20794034 19490948 19689979 19902195 19869255 21787056 17655240
GET_OPATCH_COUNT	Number of patches installed in the Oracle Home		select xmltransform(DBMS_QOPATCH.GET_OPATCH_COUNT, DBMS_QOPATCH.GET_OPATCH_XSLT) from dual; Output: Interim patches: (5)
GET_OPATCH_DATA	Gets specific patch details	Patch number	SQL> select xmltransform(DBMS_QOPATCH.GET_OPATCH_DATA('21948354'), DBMS_QOPATCH.GET_OPATCH_XSLT) from dual; Output: Patch Information: 21948354: applied on <date and time> Created on : <date and time> Bugs fixed: 20794034 19490948 19689979 19902195 19869255 21787056 17655240
GET_OPATCH_FILES	Files touched by the patch	Patch number	SQL> select xmltransform(DBMS_QOPATCH.GET_OPATCH_FILES('21948354'), DBMS_QOPATCH.GET_OPATCH_XSLT) from dual; Output: Patch Id : 21948354 ins_rdbms.mk xmlpatch xmldiff

Table 12-1. (*continued*)

Function/Procedure	Description	Argument	Example
GET_OPATCH_INSTALL_INFO	Oracle Home and central inventory details		SQL> select xmltransform(DBMS_QOPATCH.GET_OPATCH_INSTALL_INFO, DBMS_QOPATCH.GET_OPATCH_XSLT) from dual; Output: Oracle Home : /u01/app/oracle/product/12.1.0 Inventory : /u01/app/oraInventory
GET_OPATCH_LIST	Provides details about all patches including their description and bug fixed by the patch and files touched by the patch		select xmltransform(DBMS_QOPATCH.GET_OPATCH_LIST, DBMS_QOPATCH.GET_OPATCH_XSLT) from dual; Patch(sqlpatch) 21948354: \<date and time> Unique Patch ID: 19553095 Patch Description: Database Patch Set Update : 12.1.0.2.160119 (21948354) Created on : \<date and time> Bugs fixed: 20794034 19490948 19689979 19902195 19869255 21787056 17655240 Files Touched: ins_rdbms.mk xmlpatch
GET_SQLPATCH_STATUS	Provides details about individual patch apply details		SQL> exec dbms_qopatch.get_sqlpatch_status; Output: Patch Id : 21359755 Action : APPLY Action Time : \<Time it got applied> Description : Database Patch Set Update : 12.1.0.2.5 (21359755) Logfile :\<log location> Status : SUCCESS
IS_PATCH_INSTALLED	Gets specific patch installed in the Oracle Home	Patch number	SQL> select xmltransform(DBMS_QOPATCH.IS_PATCH_INSTALLED('21948354'), DBMS_QOPATCH.GET_OPATCH_XSLT) from dual; Output: Patch Information: 21948354: applied on 2016-04-05T05:54:59+01:00

CHAPTER 13

■■■

Database Downgrades

So far in this book we have been talking about database upgrades. Let's now look at a situation that would lead you to a database downgrade. Say your database was upgraded successfully but it is encountering unexpected issues after the upgrade; say either that the database performance is degrading or that an application is having some unexpected issues with the upgraded database. You don't have much time to debug the issue, so what options do you have to go back to the old version? Well, you can downgrade.

You know a database upgrade is going to a higher version. A *downgrade* is just the reverse—going back to the previous database version before the upgrade took place. The downgrade rolls back the changes that happened in the database upgrade and removes objects created during the upgrade.

In general, a downgrade happens rarely in production because you would have tested the database upgrade well in your preproduction environments. But sometimes production gives you different results than test instances and you may want to go back to an old version. So, it is advisable to test the downgrade procedure as well in the preproduction environment.

You may get a doubt that if you already took a backup of the database before upgrading, then why would you need to do a downgrade? Sure, you can use the database backup to go back to the old version, but remember, it takes time to restore a backup based on the database size and environment. Also, the DBA will require assistance from the storage team to make the necessary arrangements to access the backup storage drive. If your database is huge, then you cannot afford this time to restore. In addition, if you restore from a backup, you will not be able to roll forward past the upgrade time; any transactions that took place after the upgrade will be lost. If you do downgrade, even weeks or months later, you won't lose those transactions after the upgrade.

Limitations of Downgrading

Downgrading does have some limitations, as follows:

- The downgrade procedure makes changes only at the data dictionary level. So, it can be used only for databases upgraded through the DBUA or the manual method.

- The downgrade procedure is applicable to databases that have been successfully upgraded. This means that all the database components in the upgraded database are valid and there are no any invalid sys or system objects. The downgrade procedure cannot be used for databases that failed during upgrade.

- The COMPATIBLE parameter value should not have been changed after the upgrade. For this reason, it is often a good idea to delay changing COMPATIBLE until well after the upgrade time and after it has been established that a downgrade will not be performed.

© Y V Ravikumar, K M Krishnakumar and Nassyam Basha 2017

N. Basha et al., *Oracle Database Upgrade and Migration Methods*, DOI 10.1007/978-1-4842-2328-4_13

547

- Downgrading is just an option to go back to the old version. It doesn't guarantee that the database will be in the same state as it was before the upgrade. It may retain some higher-version objects, and some upgrade changes are not reversible.

- With a downgrade it is possible only to go the immediate old version. Suppose the 11.2.0.1.0 database is upgraded to 12c with an intermediate upgrade to 11.2.0.4.0 (as a 12c upgrade requires a minimum database version of 11.2.0.2.0). Then a downgrade is possible only to 11.2.0.4.0, not to 11.2.0.1.0.

- A downgrade is not supported for Enterprise Manager Database Control or Database Express.

Say you have upgraded a 11.2.0.4.0 database to a 12c version 12.1.0.2.0 and the COMPATIBLE parameter has not been changed after the upgrade. It still has the value 11.2. You want to downgrade the database to the 11.2.0.4.0 version.

1) First check the database components' status.

```
SQL> col comp_name format a30
SQL> select comp_name, version, status from dba_registry;

COMP_NAME                           VERSION        STATUS
------------------------------      ------------   ----------
Oracle Database Vault               12.1.0.2.0     VALID
Oracle Application Express          4.2.5.00.08    VALID
Oracle Label Security               12.1.0.2.0     VALID
Spatial                             12.1.0.2.0     VALID
Oracle Multimedia                   12.1.0.2.0     VALID
Oracle Text                         12.1.0.2.0     VALID
Oracle Workspace Manager            12.1.0.2.0     VALID
Oracle XML Database                 12.1.0.2.0     VALID
Oracle Database Catalog Views       12.1.0.2.0     VALID
Oracle Database Packages and Types  12.1.0.2.0     VALID
JServer JAVA Virtual Machine        12.1.0.2.0     VALID
Oracle XDK                          12.1.0.2.0     VALID
Oracle Database Java Packages       12.1.0.2.0     VALID
OLAP Analytic Workspace             12.1.0.2.0     VALID
Oracle OLAP API                     12.1.0.2.0     VALID
```

2) Check the sys and system user objects. There should not be any invalid objects.

```
SQL> select owner, object_name, object_type, status from dba_objects where owner
in ('SYS','SYSTEM') and status!='VALID';
No rows selected
```

3) Shut down the database and all the database-related services.

```
SQL> shutdown immediate
Database closed.
Database dismounted.
ORACLE instance shut down.
```

4) Take a database backup. It is always good to take a backup before making any
    changes. If the downgrade fails for some reason, you can always get back to the
    previous state by using a backup.

5) Start the database in downgrade mode in the 12.1.0.2.0 version.

```
SQL> startup downgrade
ORACLE instance started.

Total System Global Area 3909091328 bytes
Fixed Size                  2931520 bytes
Variable Size             872416448 bytes
Database Buffers         3019898880 bytes
Redo Buffers               13844480 bytes
Database mounted.
Database opened.
```

6) Execute catdwgrd.sql as the sys user to downgrade the components.

```
SQL>@?/rdbms/admin/catdwgrd.sql
```

7) Shut down the database.

```
SQL> shutdown immediate
Database closed.
Database dismounted.
ORACLE instance shut down.
```

8) Change the environment variables to the 11.2.0.4.0 home and start the database
    in upgrade mode using the 11.2.0.4.0 Oracle Home.

```
SQL> startup upgrade
ORACLE instance started.

Total System Global Area 3891630080 bytes
Fixed Size                  2259160 bytes
Variable Size             838862632 bytes
Database Buffers         3036676096 bytes
Redo Buffers               13832192 bytes
Database mounted.
Database opened.
```

9) Execute `catrelod.sql` to reload all the components to the 11.2.0.4.0 version.

```
SQL> @?/rdbms/admin/catrelod.sql
```

10) Execute `utlrp.sql`.

```
SQL> @?/rdbms/admin/utlrp.sql
```

11) Check the database components' versions and their status.

```
COMP_NAME                              STATUS      VERSION
-------------------------------------- ----------- ----------
Oracle Database Packages and Types     VALID       11.2.0.4.0
Oracle Database Catalog Views          VALID       11.2.0.4.0
JServer JAVA Virtual Machine           VALID       11.2.0.4.0
Oracle XDK                             VALID       11.2.0.4.0
Oracle Database Java Packages          VALID       11.2.0.4.0
Oracle Text                            VALID       11.2.0.4.0
Oracle XML Database                    VALID       11.2.0.4.0
Oracle Workspace Manager               VALID       11.2.0.4.0
OLAP Analytic Workspace                VALID       11.2.0.4.0
OLAP Catalog                           VALID       11.2.0.4.0
Oracle OLAP API                        VALID       11.2.0.4.0
Oracle Multimedia                      VALID       11.2.0.4.0
Spatial                                VALID       11.2.0.4.0
Oracle Application Express             VALID       3.2.1.00.1
OWB                                    VALID       11.2.0.4.0
```

Downgrade Steps for Multitenant Databases

Let's consider the same exercise for multitenant databases. In the multitenant model, the container database and all the pluggable databases have to be downgraded. For this example, you are upgrading a multitenant database from 12.1.0.1.0 to 12.1.0.2.0. The pluggable databases are also upgraded to 12.1.0.2.0. Now you are going to downgrade it to the 12.1.0.1.0 version.

1) First check the database components' status at the container level.

```
SQL>  col comp_name format a30
SQL> select comp_name, version, status from dba_registry;

COMP_NAME                        VERSION           STATUS
-------------------------------  ---------------   ----------
Oracle Database Vault            12.1.0.2.0        VALID
Oracle Application Express       4.2.5.00.08       VALID
Oracle Label Security            12.1.0.2.0        VALID
Spatial                          12.1.0.2.0        VALID
Oracle Multimedia                12.1.0.2.0        VALID
Oracle Text                      12.1.0.2.0        VALID
Oracle Workspace Manager         12.1.0.2.0        VALID
```

```
Oracle XML Database                    12.1.0.2.0          VALID
Oracle Database Catalog Views          12.1.0.2.0          VALID
Oracle Database Packages and Types     12.1.0.2.0          VALID
JServer JAVA Virtual Machine           12.1.0.2.0          VALID
Oracle XDK                             12.1.0.2.0          VALID
Oracle Database Java Packages          12.1.0.2.0          VALID
OLAP Analytic Workspace                12.1.0.2.0          VALID
Oracle OLAP API                        12.1.0.2.0          VALID

SQL> select owner, object_name, status from dba_objects where owner in
('SYS','SYSTEM') and status!='VALID' ;


no rows selected

SQL> show pdbs

    CON_ID CON_NAME                        OPEN MODE  RESTRICTED
---------- ------------------------------  ---------- ----------
         2 PDB$SEED                        READ ONLY  NO
         3 PDB12101                        READ WRITE NO
SQL> alter session set container=PDB12101;

Session altered.

SQL> select comp_name, version, status from dba_registry;

COMP_NAME                             VERSION                  STATUS
------------------------------------  -----------------------  -----------
Oracle Database Vault                 12.1.0.2.0               VALID
Oracle Label Security                 12.1.0.2.0               VALID
Spatial                               12.1.0.2.0               VALID
Oracle Multimedia                     12.1.0.2.0               VALID
Oracle Text                           12.1.0.2.0               VALID
Oracle Workspace Manager              12.1.0.2.0               VALID
Oracle XML Database                   12.1.0.2.0               VALID
Oracle Database Catalog Views         12.1.0.2.0               VALID
Oracle Database Packages and Types    12.1.0.2.0               VALID
JServer JAVA Virtual Machine          12.1.0.2.0               VALID
Oracle XDK                            12.1.0.2.0               VALID
Oracle Database Java Packages         12.1.0.2.0               VALID
OLAP Analytic Workspace               12.1.0.2.0               VALID
Oracle OLAP API                       12.1.0.2.0               VALID
```

2) Check the sys and system user objects. There should not be any invalid objects.

```
SQL> select owner, object_name, status from dba_objects where owner in
('SYS','SYSTEM') and status!='VALID' ;

no rows selected
```

3) Shut down the database and all the database-related services.

```
SQL> shutdown immediate
Database closed.
Database dismounted.
ORACLE instance shut down.
```

4) Start the container and pluggable databases in downgrade mode.

```
SQL> startup downgrade
ORACLE instance started.

Total System Global Area 1660944384 bytes
Fixed Size                  2925072 bytes
Variable Size            1056968176 bytes
Database Buffers          587202560 bytes
Redo Buffers               13848576 bytes
Database mounted.
Database opened.
SQL> show pdbs

    CON_ID CON_NAME                       OPEN MODE  RESTRICTED
---------- ------------------------------ ---------- ----------
         2 PDB$SEED                       MIGRATE    YES
         3 PDB12101                       MOUNTED

SQL> alter pluggable database all open downgrade;

Pluggable database altered.

SQL> show pdbs

    CON_ID CON_NAME                       OPEN MODE  RESTRICTED
---------- ------------------------------ ---------- ----------
         2 PDB$SEED                       MIGRATE    YES
         3 PDB12101                       MIGRATE    YES
```

5) Execute catdwgrd.sql first on the pluggable databases and then on the container database. The pluggable database and root database have their own dictionary, and the downgrade procedure should be done on all databases. The downgrade procedure will make changes in the data dictionary, and after its execution, the data dictionary might not be in a consistent state. Suppose if the downgrade procedure was done first on the container database CDB$ROOT. Then its data dictionary might be at an invalid state that will affect the downgrade steps of the pluggable database. So, first execute the downgrade steps on the pluggable database and then perform the steps on the root database.

```
SQL> alter session set container=PDB121;
```

```
Session altered.
SQL> @?/rdbms/admin/catdwgrd.sql

SQL> alter session set container=PDB$SEED;

Session altered.

SQL> @?/rdbms/admin/catdwgrd.sql
```

Execute at the container level.

```
Sql> connect sys/<password> as sysdba
Sql> @?/rdbms/admin/catdwgrd.sql
```

6) Shut down the database.

```
SQL> shutdown immediate;
Database closed.
Database dismounted.
ORACLE instance shut down.
```

7) Start the database using the 12.1.0.1.0 Oracle Home in upgrade mode. The pluggable databases also have to be started in upgrade mode.

```
SQL> startup upgrade
ORACLE instance started.

Total System Global Area 3891630080 bytes
Fixed Size                   2259160 bytes
Variable Size              838862632 bytes
Database Buffers          3036676096 bytes
Redo Buffers                13832192 bytes
Database mounted.
Database opened.
Sql> alter pluggable database all open upgrade;
Pluggable database altered.
```

8) Execute `catrelod.sql` in the container and all the pluggable databases.

```
Sql> @?/rdbms/admin/catrelod.sql

SQL> alter session set container=PDB121;

Session altered.
SQL> @?/rdbms/admin/ catrelod.sql

SQL> alter session set container=PDB$SEED;

Session altered.

SQL> @?/rdbms/admin/catrelod.sql
```

9) Execute `utlrp.sql` in the container and all the pluggable databases.

10) Check the database components' version and status on the container and on all the pluggable databases.

Downgrade Steps Using Database Flashback

A database flashback is one of the fallback options to get a database back to a previous state. Usually you use database flashback when tables are dropped accidentally or wrong data is inserted mistakenly. Using flashback, you can take the database to a time in the past to recover the data.

You can also consider Point in time recovery as one of the fallback option. But doing a point-in-time recovery (PITR) requires time and storage. Using a database flashback, you can take the database back easily to the state it was in before the changes took place. For a database flashback, the database should be enabled with archivelog and flashback modes. You can also create a restore point and flash back the database to that restore point. Remember, though, that a flashback operates on the whole database; you cannot revert changes that took place for a particular object through a database flashback. From the upgrade perspective, you will be creating a restore point before the upgrade, and at any time you can get the database back to that restore point. But note in this method that any changes that happened after the upgrade are reverted.

Let's see the steps in detail.

- *Source database version*: 11.2.0.4.0

- *Upgraded database version*: 12.1.0.2.0

Upgrade Steps

Database 11.2.0.4.0 is planned to be upgraded to 12.1.0.2.0. The pre-upgrade scripts were executed, and all the checks were successful. The database is ready for an upgrade.

1) Shut down the 11.2.0.4.0 database.

```
SQL> shutdown immediate;
Database closed.
Database dismounted.
ORACLE instance shut down.
```

2) Start the database in mount state and enable flashback mode. If the database is not in archivelog mode, change it to archive log before enabling flashback mode.

```
SQL> startup mount
ORACLE instance started.
Total System Global Area 1653518336 bytes
Fixed Size                  2253784 bytes
Variable Size            1023413288 bytes
Database Buffers          620756992 bytes
Redo Buffers                7094272 bytes
Database mounted.
```

Make sure db_recovery_file_dest_size and db_recovery_file_dest parameters are set.

```
SQL> alter database archivelog;
Database altered.

SQL>  alter database flashback on;
Database altered.
```

3) Start the database.

```
SQL> alter database open;
Database altered.
```

4) Create a guaranteed restore point. There are two kinds of restore points: normal and guaranteed. The advantage of creating a guaranteed restore point is that it never ages out of the control file, and it can be explicitly dropped. It will retain the required flashback logs to rewind the database to the restore point.

```
SQL> create restore point before_upgrade guarantee flashback database;
Restore point created.
SQL> select scn, GUARANTEE_FLASHBACK_DATABASE,NAME from v$restore_point;
SCN             GUARANTEE_FLASHBACK_DATABASE             NAME
-----           -------------------------------------    -----------
970673          YES                                      BEFORE_UPGRADE
```

5) Perform the database upgrade with either the DBUA or through a manual upgrade.

Downgrade Steps

The database upgrade has completed successfully. For some reason, you want to go back to the old version.

1) First make sure the database has been upgraded successfully and its components are in a valid state.

```
SQL> select comp_name, version,status from dba_registry;

COMP_NAME                     VERSION              STATUS
---------------------         ------------------   --------------------

Oracle Application Express    4.2.5.00.08          VALID
Spatial                       12.1.0.2.0           VALID
Oracle Multimedia             12.1.0.2.0           VALID
Oracle XML Database           12.1.0.2.0           VALID
Oracle Text                   12.1.0.2.0           VALID
Oracle Workspace Manager      12.1.0.2.0           VALID
Oracle Database Catalog Views 12.1.0.2.0           VALID
Oracle Database Packages and Types  12.1.0.2.0     VALID
JServer JAVA Virtual Machine  12.1.0.2.0           VALID
```

```
Oracle XDK                          12.1.0.2.0        VALID
Oracle Database Java Packages       12.1.0.2.0        VALID
OLAP Analytic Workspace             12.1.0.2.0        VALID
Oracle OLAP API                     12.1.0.2.0        VALID
```

2) Shut down the 12.1.0.2.0 database.

```
SQL> shutdown immediate
Database closed.
Database dismounted.
ORACLE instance shut down.
```

3) Start the database in mount state.

```
SQL> startup mount
ORACLE instance started.

Total System Global Area 1660944384 bytes
Fixed Size                  2925072 bytes
Variable Size            1006636528 bytes
Database Buffers          637534208 bytes
Redo Buffers               13848576 bytes
Database mounted.
```

4) Flash back the database to the restore point Before_upgrade.

```
SQL> flashback database to restore point before_upgrade;
Flashback complete.
```

5) Shut down the database.

```
SQL> shutdown immediate;
ORA-01109: database not open

Database dismounted.
ORACLE instance shut down.
```

6) Change ORACLE_HOME to the 11.2.0.4.0 database home and start the database in
    mount state using the 11.2.0.4.0 binaries.

```
sqlplus "/ as sysdba"

SQL*Plus: Release 11.2.0.4.0 Production

Copyright (c) 1982, 2013, Oracle.  All rights reserved.

Connected to an idle instance.

SQL> startup mount
ORACLE instance started.
```

```
Total System Global Area 1653518336 bytes
Fixed Size                   2253784 bytes
Variable Size             1006636072 bytes
Database Buffers           637534208 bytes
Redo Buffers                 7094272 bytes
Database mounted.
```

7) Open the database using the resetlogs option.

```
SQL> alter database open resetlogs;

Database altered.
```

8) Now the database version is 11.2.0.4.0, and the upgrade changes have been rolled back. This can be confirmed by using dba_registry.

```
SQL> select comp_name, version, status from dba_registry;


COMP_NAME                                                      VERSION
STATUS
--------------------------------------------              -------------        ---
---
Oracle Application Express                                     3.2.1.00.12
VALID
Oracle Enterprise Manager                                     11.2.0.4.0
VALID
OLAP Catalog                                                  11.2.0.4.0
VALID
Spatial                                                       11.2.0.4.0
VALID
Oracle Multimedia                                            11.2.0.4.0
VALID
Oracle XML Database                                          11.2.0.4.0
VALID
Oracle Text                                                  11.2.0.4.0
VALID
Oracle Expression Filter                                     11.2.0.4.0
VALID
Oracle Rules Manager                                         11.2.0.4.0
VALID
Oracle Workspace Manager                                     11.2.0.4.0
VALID
Oracle Database Catalog Views                                11.2.0.4.0
VALID
Oracle Database Packages and Types                           11.2.0.4.0
VALID
JServer JAVA Virtual Machine                                 11.2.0.4.0
VALID
Oracle XDK                                                    11.2.0.4.0
VALID
```

```
Oracle Database Java Packages                      11.2.0.4.0
VALID
OLAP Analytic Workspace                            11.2.0.4.0
VALID
Oracle OLAP API                                    11.2.0.4.0
VALID
```

The database has been downgraded to the previous version of 11.2.0.4.0.

Downgrade Steps Using Database Flashback for Multitenant Databases

Let's try the same exercise for a multitenant database.

- *Source database version*: 12.1.0.1.0 CDB

- *Upgraded database version*: 12.1.0.2.0 CDB

Upgrade Steps

The flashback steps are the same as you would use for a normal non-CDB database.

1) Shut down the 12.1.0.1.0 multitenant database.

```
SQL> shutdown immediate
Database closed.
Database dismounted.
ORACLE instance shut down.
```

2) Start the database in mount state and enable flashback mode. if the database is not in archivelog mode, change it to archive log before enabling flashback mode.

```
SQL> startup mount
ORACLE instance started.

Total System Global Area 1653518336 bytes
Fixed Size                  2289016 bytes
Variable Size            1056965256 bytes
Database Buffers          587202560 bytes
Redo Buffers                7061504 bytes
Database mounted.
SQL> show pdbs
```

```
     CON_ID CON_NAME                          OPEN MODE  RESTRICTED
---------- ------------------------------ ---------- ----------
          2 PDBSSEED                                  MOUNTED
          3 PDB12101                                  MOUNTED

SQL> alter database archivelog;
Database altered.

SQL> alter database flashback on;
Database altered.
```

3) Start the database.

```
SQL> alter database open;
Database altered.
```

4) Create a guaranteed restore point.

```
SQL> create restore point before_12c_upgrade guarantee flashback database;
Restore point created.
SQL> SELECT NAME, SCN, TIME, DATABASE_INCARNATION# DBI,GUARANTEE_FLASHBACK_
DATABASE GFD,  STORAGE_SIZE FROM v$restore_point;
NAME                    SCN       TIME
-----------             -------   ----------------------------------
    DBI                 GFD       STORAGE_SIZE
----------------        -------   ----------------------------------

BEFORE_12C_UPGRADE      1785514   23-APR-16 07.20.42.000000000 AM
         2              YES       52428800
```

5) Perform a database upgrade using either the DBUA or a manual upgrade.

Downgrade Steps

The database upgrade has completed successfully. For some reason, you want to go back to the old version.

1) First make sure the database has been upgraded successfully and its components are in a valid state.

```
SQL> select comp_name, version, status from dba_registry;


COMP_NAME                             VERSION            STATUS
------------------------------        ----------------   ----------
Oracle Database Vault                 12.1.0.2.0         VALID
Oracle Application Express            4.2.5.00.08        VALID
Oracle Label Security                 12.1.0.2.0         VALID
Spatial                               12.1.0.2.0         VALID
Oracle Multimedia                     12.1.0.2.0         VALID
Oracle Text                           12.1.0.2.0         VALID
Oracle Workspace Manager              12.1.0.2.0         VALID
```

```
Oracle XML Database                  12.1.0.2.0          VALID
Oracle Database Catalog Views        12.1.0.2.0          VALID
Oracle Database Packages and Types   12.1.0.2.0          VALID
JServer JAVA Virtual Machine         12.1.0.2.0          VALID
Oracle XDK                           12.1.0.2.0          VALID
Oracle Database Java Packages        12.1.0.2.0          VALID
OLAP Analytic Workspace              12.1.0.2.0          VALID
Oracle OLAP API                      12.1.0.2.0          VALID

SQL> alter session set container=PDB12101;

Session altered.

SQL> col comp_name format a10
SQL> col status format a5
SQL> select comp_name, status, version from dba_registry;

COMP_NAME                            STATUS VERSION
-------------------------------      ------ ---------
Oracle Database Vault                VALID  12.1.0.2.0
Oracle Application Express           VALID  4.2.5.00.08
Oracle Label Security                VALID  12.1.0.2.0
Spatial                              VALID  12.1.0.2.0
Oracle Multimedia                    VALID  12.1.0.2.0
Oracle Text                          VALID  12.1.0.2.0
Oracle Workspace Manager             VALID  12.1.0.2.0
Oracle XML Database                  VALID  12.1.0.2.0
Oracle Database Catalog Views        VALID  12.1.0.2.0
Oracle Database Packages and Types   VALID  12.1.0.2.0
JServer JAVA Virtual Machine         VALID  12.1.0.2.0
Oracle XDK                           VALID  12.1.0.2.0
Oracle Database Java Packages        VALID  12.1.0.2.0
OLAP Analytic Workspace              VALID  12.1.0.2.0
Oracle OLA P API                     VALID  12.1.0.2.0
```

2)   Shut down the 12.1.0.2.0 database.

```
SQL> shutdown immediate;
Database closed.
Database dismounted.
ORACLE instance shut down.
```

3)   Start the database in mount state.

```
SQL> startup mount
ORACLE instance started.
```

```
Total System Global Area 1660944384 bytes
Fixed Size                   2925072 bytes
Variable Size             1056968176 bytes
Database Buffers           587202560 bytes
Redo Buffers                13848576 bytes
Database mounted.
```

4) Flash back the database to the restore point Before_12c_upgrade.

```
SQL> flashback database to restore point BEFORE_12C_UPGRADE;
Flashback complete.
```

5) Shut down the database.

```
SQL> shutdown immediate
ORA-01109: database not open

Database dismounted.
ORACLE instance shut down.
```

6) Change ORACLE_HOME to the 12.1.0.1.0 database home and start the database in mount state using the 12.1.0.1.0 binaries.

```
$ sqlplus "/ as sysdba"


SQL*Plus: Release 12.1.0.1.0 Production
Copyright (c) 1982, 2013, Oracle.  All rights reserved.
Connected to an idle instance.

SQL> startup mount
ORACLE instance started.

Total System Global Area 1653518336 bytes
Fixed Size                   2289016 bytes
Variable Size             1056965256 bytes
Database Buffers           587202560 bytes
Redo Buffers                 7061504 bytes
Database mounted.
```

7) Open the database using the resetlogs option.

```
SQL> alter database open resetlogs;

Database altered.
```

8) Now the database version is 12.1.0.1.0, and the upgrade changes have been rolled back. This can be confirmed using dba_registry of the container and pluggable databases.

```
SQL> col comp_name format a15
SQL> col status format a5
SQL> select comp_name, status, version from dba_registry;

COMP_NAME                        STATUS  VERSION
---------------                  ------  ------------
Oracle Database Vault            VALID   12.1.0.1.0
Oracle Application Express       VALID   4.2.0.00.27
Oracle Label Security            VALID   12.1.0.1.0
Spatial                          VALID   12.1.0.1.0
Oracle Multimedia                VALID   12.1.0.1.0
Oracle Textt                     VALID   12.1.0.1.0
Oracle Workspace Manager         VALID   12.1.0.1.0
Oracle XML Database              VALID   12.1.0.1.0
Oracle Database  Catalog Views   VALID   12.1.0.1.0
Oracle Database Packages Types   VALID   12.1.0.1.0
JServer JAVA Virtual Machine     VALID   12.1.0.1.0
Oracle XDK                       VALID   12.1.0.1.0
Oracle Database  Java Packages   VALID   12.1.0.1.0
OLAP Analytic Workspace          VALID   12.1.0.1.0
Oracle OLAP API                  VALID   12.1.0.1.0

SQL> show pdbs

    CON_ID CON_NAME                        OPEN MODE  RESTRICTED
---------- ------------------------------ ---------- ----------
         2 PDB$SEED                        READ ONLY  NO
         3 PDB12101                                   MOUNTED
SQL> alter pluggable database all open;
Pluggable database altered.

SQL> alter session set container=PDB12101;
Session altered.

SQL>  select comp_name, status, version from dba_registry;

COMP_NAME                        STATUS   VERSION
-----------------------------    -------- -----------
Oracle Database  Vault           VALID    12.1.0.1.0
Oracle Application Express       VALID    4.2.0.00.27
Oracle Label Security            VALID    12.1.0.1.0
Spatial                          VALID    12.1.0.1.0
Oracle Multimedia                VALID    12.1.0.1.0
Oracle Text                      VALID    12.1.0.1.0
Oracle Workspace Manager         VALID    12.1.0.1.0
Oracle XML Database              VALID    12.1.0.1.0
Oracle Database Catalog Views    VALID    12.1.0.1.0
```

```
Oracle Database Packages and Types    VALID    12.1.0.1.0
JServer JAVA Virtual Machine          VALID    12.1.0.1.0
Oracle XDK                            VALID    12.1.0.1.0
Oracle Database Java Packages         VALID    12.1.0.1.0
OLAP Analytic Workspace               VALID    12.1.0.1.0
Oracle OLAP API                       VALID    12.1.0.1.0
```

Known Issues

The downgraded database may not have the same number of objects or the same database state as before. This is just one option to go back to the old database version.

Summary

In this chapter, we discussed how to roll back the upgrade changes in a database without losing data through the downgrade steps. A downgrade can be used when the upgraded database is not feasible for the environment.

CHAPTER 14

▪▪▪

Oracle Database Upgrades in Oracle Database Release 12.2

Oracle Database Release 12.2 is currently the latest version (12.1.0.2 0) of Oracle Database. This version has introduced a new set of features for upgrading that we will discuss in this chapter.

Upgrading to the 12.2 Release (12.2.0.1.0)

We'll discuss upgrading to Oracle Database R2 (12.2.0.1.0) through the Database Upgrade Assistant (DBUA) and via a manual upgrade, which will upgrade the data dictionary along with the data to the higher version. For other methods like TTS and Data Pump, the steps are the same as for 12*c* R1. Here we will discuss only a stand-alone database upgrade. For Real Application Cluster (RAC) and Data Guard (DG) environments, you can follow the steps documented in Chapters 7 and 8.

The minimum required version to upgrade to Oracle Database 12.2 (for the DBUA and manual upgrade methods) is Oracle Database 11.2.0.3.0. If the database version is less than 11.2.0.3.0, then an intermediate upgrade is required to upgrade to either 11.2.0.3.0, 11.2.0.4.0, 12.1.0 1.0, or 12.1.0.2.0. The minimum required versions for these intermediate upgrade versions are covered in Chapter 2.

As a first step, you need to make sure the database has met all the pre-upgrade checklists. You can verify this was done through the pre-upgrade output summary.

Pre-upgrade Checks: What's New in 12.2

As you know, the first step in the database upgrade is making sure that the database has met all the prerequisites. You can verify this through the pre-upgrade script execution output. For Oracle Database 12*c* Release 1, the pre-upgrade script was delivered as preupgrade.sql. In 12*c* Release 2, it has been enhanced and released as a Java archive file named preupgrade.jar. You can execute it at the command line, and you don't require SQL*Plus connectivity like you did in earlier releases. This script is available in the directory <12.2 ORACLE_HOME>/rdbms/admin. Since it is a JAR file, you require a Java compiler to execute it. By default, a Java compiler has been provided by Oracle in the directory $ORACLE_HOME/jdk/bin. ORACLE_HOME denotes the Oracle Home of the lower/source database version.

Here is the syntax of the pre-upgrade execution:

```
$ORACLE_HOME/jdk/bin/java –jar <12.2.0 ORACLE_HOME>/rdbms/admin/preupgrade.jar {Parameters}
The below Parameters can be used.
[TERMINAL|FILE] [TEXT|XML] [DIR <dirname> | -DIR <dirname>]
[-c <whitelistOfPdbs>] [-C <blacklistOfPdbs]
```

© Y V Ravikumar, K M Krishnakumar and Nassyam Basha 2017
N. Basha et al., *Oracle Database Upgrade and Migration Methods*, DOI 10.1007/978-1-4842-2328-4_14

```
[-u <username>] [-p <password>]
[-exec|-loadonly]
[-oh <oracle_home>] [-sid <oracle_sid>] [-help]
```

Terminal|File : This option denotes the script output location. By default, the value is File. If the value is Terminal, then the output will be shown in terminal and also the scripts & logs will be stored in preupgrade directory. Option 'File' will not show the output in terminal.

TEXT|XML : By default the output is text. If XML output is required, we can choose 'XML' option.

-DIR : It denotes the output directory location. If DIR output is not declared, then it will check ORACLE_BASE and creates output files there ($ORACLE_BASE/cfgtoollogs/<db_unique_name>/preupgrade). If DIR and ORACLE_BASE is not defined then output files will be created at $ORACLE_HOME/cfgtoollogs/<db_unique_name>/preupgrade directory.

[-c <whitelistOfPdbs>] [-C <blacklistOfPdbs>]: It is applicable when source database is a Multitenant database. '-c' option denotes PDB where preupgrade script needs to be executed. '-C' denotes the PDBs to be excluded from the execution.

[-u <username>] [-p <password>] : User credentials that we want to use to connect as SYSDBA to the database to perform the pre-upgrade checks. If Local OS authentication is not available (login user not part of OSDBA group), then this option will be useful.

[-oh <oracle_home>] [-sid <oracle_sid>] : This option is to specify desired Oracle home and database to execute pre-upgrade script. If these are not specified then pre-upgrade routine will collect these details from environment variables.

Let's examine the output with an example.

Let's look at an example.

- *Source database version*: 12.1.0.2.0

- *Database name*: cdb12102 (a multitenant database)

- *PDB name*: PDB1

- *ORACLE_HOME location*: /u02/product/12.1.0/dbhome_1/

You need to execute the pre-upgrade script for an Oracle Database 12*c* R1 (12.1.0.2.0) multitenant database.

Steps

Here are the steps:

1) First log in as the Oracle Home 12.1.0.2.0 owner and set the required environment variables for your platform (for example, ORACLE_HOME, PATH, ORACLE_BASE, and ORACLE_SID) to the 12.1.0.2.0 home.

2) Since it is a multitenant database, make sure all the pluggable databases are open. If the pluggable database is in closed state, then the pre-upgrade script will not get executed for that PDB.

To check the status of all pluggable databases, execute the following:

```
SQL> show pdbs;
```

To open all pluggable databases, execute the following:

```
SQL> alter pluggable database all open;
```

To open any particular pluggable database, execute the following:

```
SQL> alter pluggable database <Name> open;
```

3) Execute preupgrde.jar.

```
$ORACLE_HOME/jdk/bin/java –jar $<12.2 oracle home>/rdbms/admin/preupgrade.jar
```

Here the –DIR option is not used, but ORACLE_BASE environment variable is defined as /u01, and hence the output is like this:

```
$ /u02/product/12.1.0/dbhome_1/jdk/bin/java -jar /u01/app/oracle/product/12.2.0/
rdbms/admin/preupgrade.jar
```

Here are the files generated by the pre-upgrade script:

```
/u01/cfgtoollogs/cdb12102/preupgrade/preupgrade.log
/u01/cfgtoollogs/cdb12102/preupgrade/preupgrade_fixups.sql
/u01/cfgtoollogs/cdb12102/preupgrade/postupgrade_fixups.sql
```

The output file contains pre-upgrade information for the container and PDB$SEED and PDB1 databases. Also, the folder /u01/cfgtoollogs/cdb12102/preupgrade contains the same set of files (the pre-upgrade output, the pre-upgrade fixup script, and post-upgrade fixup scripts) for the container, PDB$SEED, and PDB1 databases.

Let's review the pre-upgrade log generated while executing preupgrade.jar to the cdb12102 multitenant database.

1) First it lists the preupgrade.jar version and container database details.

```
Upgrade-To version: 12.2.0.1.0


========================================
Status of the database prior to upgrade
========================================


          Database Name:  CDB12102
         Container Name:  CDB$ROOT
           Container ID:  1
                Version:  12.1.0.2.0
             Compatible:  12.1.0.0.0
              Blocksize:  8192
               Platform:  Linux x86 64-bit
          Timezone File:  18
      Database log mode:  NOARCHIVELOG
               Readonly:  FALSE
                Edition:  EE
```

2) It then lists the container database component details.

```
Oracle Component                  Upgrade Action      Current Status
----------------                  --------------      --------------
Oracle Server                     [to be upgraded]    VALID
JServer JAVA Virtual Machine      [to be upgraded]    VALID
Oracle XDK for Java               [to be upgraded]    VALID
Real Application Clusters         [to be upgraded]    OPTION OFF
Oracle Workspace Manager          [to be upgraded]    VALID
OLAP Analytic Workspace           [to be upgraded]    VALID
Oracle Label Security             [to be upgraded]    VALID
Oracle Database Vault             [to be upgraded]    VALID
Oracle Text                       [to be upgraded]    VALID
Oracle XML Database               [to be upgraded]    VALID
Oracle Java Packages              [to be upgraded]    VALID
Oracle Multimedia                 [to be upgraded]    VALID
Oracle Spatial                    [to be upgraded]    VALID
Oracle Application Express        [to be upgraded]    VALID
Oracle OLAP API                   [to be upgraded]    VALID
```

3) It also lists the tasks to be done before the upgrade. Fixes marked as AUTOFIXUP will be done by the pre-upgrade fixup script. Other fixes have to be executed manually.

```
==============
BEFORE UPGRADE
==============

    Run <preupgradeLogDirPath>/preupgrade_fixups_CDB_ROOT.sql to complete all
    of the BEFORE UPGRADE action items below marked with '(AUTOFIXUP)'.

    REQUIRED ACTIONS
    ================
    + Adjust TABLESPACE SIZES as needed.
                                            Auto      12.2.0.1.0
        Tablespace              Size        Extend    Min Size      Action
        ----------              ----------  --------  ----------    ------

        SYSAUX                  740 MB      ENABLED     1640 MB     None
        SYSTEM                  790 MB      ENABLED     1291 MB     None
        TEMP                     60 MB      ENABLED      150 MB     None
        UNDOTBS1                 95 MB      ENABLED      400 MB     None

    Note that 12.2.0.1.0 minimum sizes are estimates.
    If you plan to upgrade multiple pluggable databases concurrently,
    then you must ensure that the UNDO tablespace size is equal to at least
    the number of pluggable databases that you upgrade concurrently,
    multiplied by that minimum.  Failing to allocate sufficient space can
    cause the upgrade to fail.

    + Update NUMERIC INITIALIZATION PARAMETERS to meet estimated minimums.
```

```
Parameter                         12.2.0.1.0 minimum
---------                         ------------------
memory_target*                         3881828352
```

* These minimum memory/pool sizes are recommended for the upgrade process

4) Then you'll see the recommended tasks before the upgrade.

```
RECOMMENDED ACTIONS
===================
+ (AUTOFIXUP) Gather SYS schema and stale data dictionary statistics prior
  to database upgrade in off-peak time using:

  EXECUTE DBMS_STATS.GATHER_DICTIONARY_STATS;

  EXECUTE DBMS_STATS.GATHER_SCHEMA_STATS('SYS');

  Dictionary statistics do not exist or are stale (not up-to-date).

  Dictionary statistics help the Oracle optimizer find efficient SQL
  execution plans and are essential for proper upgrade timing. Oracle
  recommends gathering dictionary statistics in the last 24 hours before
  database upgrade.
```

5) Then you'll see information related to the upgrade.

```
INFORMATION ONLY
================
+ Consider upgrading APEX manually, before the database upgrade.

  The database contains APEX version 4.2.0.00.27 and will need to be
  upgraded to at least version 5.0.4.00.12.

  To reduce database upgrade time, you can upgrade APEX manually before
  the database upgrade. Refer to My Oracle Support Note 1088970.1 for
  information on APEX installation upgrades.
```

6) Then you'll see lists about tasks to be done after the upgrade. Fixes marked
    AUTOFIXUP will be done by the post-upgrade fixup script. Other fixes have to be
    executed manually.

```
=============
AFTER UPGRADE
=============

  Run <preupgradeLogDirPath>/postupgrade_fixups_CDB_ROOT.sql to complete all
  of the AFTER UPGRADE action items below marked with '(AUTOFIXUP)'.

REQUIRED ACTIONS
================
```

None

```
RECOMMENDED ACTIONS
===================
+ Upgrade the database time zone version using the DBMS_DST package.

    The database is using timezone datafile version 18 and the target
    12.2.0.1.0 database ships with timezone datafile version 26.

    Oracle recommends using the most recent timezone data.  For further
    information, refer to My Oracle Support Note 1585343.1.

+ (AUTOFIXUP) Gather dictionary statistics after the upgrade using the
    command:

        EXECUTE DBMS_STATS.GATHER_DICTIONARY_STATS;

    Oracle recommends gathering dictionary statistics after upgrade.

    Dictionary statistics provide essential information to the Oracle
    optimizer to help it find efficient SQL execution plans. After a
    database upgrade, statistics need to be re-gathered as there can now be
    tables that have significantly changed during the upgrade or new tables
    that do not have statistics gathered yet.

+ Gather statistics on fixed objects two weeks after the upgrade using the
    command:

        EXECUTE DBMS_STATS.GATHER_FIXED_OBJECTS_STATS;

    This recommendation is given for all preupgrade runs.

    Fixed object statistics provide essential information to the Oracle
    optimizer to help it find efficient SQL execution plans.  Those
    statistics are specific to the Oracle Database release that generates
    them, and can be stale upon database upgrade.
```

After executing the pre-upgrade script, take a backup of the database. This step is mandatory if the upgrade is not successful and you want to go back to the old version.

Upgrade Emulation

Oracle Database upgrade emulation is one of the new features released in 12*c* R2. In 12*c* Release 1, you can do a database upgrade using a parallel process. You can allocate more SQL processes to perform this parallel action for the upgrade. But you don't have the provision to verify that before the upgrade all the allocated SQL process will be used, and you cannot test how the resource allocation choices go through during the upgrade. Suppose you allocate four parallel processes to perform the upgrade (using the –n option of the catctl.pl command). You will come to know its usage only when the real upgrade is in progress. During the upgrade, you can specify many arguments with catctl.pl. For example, the –C option is defined to exclude the listed PDBs from the upgrade. Is there a way to verify before the upgrade that the upgrade will go only with the specified arguments? Yes, it is possible. In 12c Release 2, this difficulty is overcome through upgrade emulation. You can invoke the upgrade parallel script catctl.pl with the -E option, which will emulate the upgrade process and provide output logs. There is no real-time upgrade that happens when you invoke this option. The output will show how the allotted parallel processes are going to work. But remember, before invoking this, the database should have been started in upgrade mode using the 12.2 binaries. This means you require downtime to execute this. So, this option will help before executing the real upgrade. It can also be considered as a pre-upgrade task to verify how the resource allocation happens.

Here's an example:

```
$ORACLE_HOME/perl/bin/perl catctl.pl -E -n 4 -N 2 -l /u01/app/oracle  catupgrd.sql
```

Here the upgrade has been invoked with the –E (Emulation) option with four parallel SQL processes and two parallel SQL processes for the PDB upgrade. The log file location is /u01/app/oracle. The execution generates output like a real-time upgrade. We will discuss only the important points in the output.

```
Number of Cpus          = 1
Database Name           = cdb12102
DataBase Version        = 12.1.0.2.0
Parallel SQL Process Count (PDB)       = 2
Parallel SQL Process Count (CDB$ROOT) = 4
Concurrent PDB Upgrades                = 2
Generated PDB Inclusion:[PDB$SEED PDB1 PDB2 PDB3]
Components in [CDB$ROOT]
    Installed [APEX APS CATALOG CATJAVA CATPROC CONTEXT DV JAVAVM OLS ORDIM OWM SDO XDB XML
XOQ]
Not Installed [EM MGW ODM RAC WK]


-----------------------------------------------------
Phases [0-117]            Start Time:[2016_10_12 06:56:41]
Container Lists Inclusion:[CDB$ROOT] Exclusion:[NONE]
-----------------------------------------------------
***********   Executing Change Scripts   ***********
Serial   Phase #:0    [CDB$ROOT] Files:1    Time: 1s
**************   Catalog Core SQL   **************
Serial   Phase #:1    [CDB$ROOT] Files:5    Time: 0s
Restart  Phase #:2    [CDB$ROOT] Files:1    Time: 0s
***********  Catalog Tables and Views  ***********
Parallel Phase #:3    [CDB$ROOT] Files:19   Time: 1s
Restart  Phase #:4    [CDB$ROOT] Files:1    Time: 0s
************  Catalog Final Scripts  ************
Serial   Phase #:5    [CDB$ROOT] Files:6    Time: 0s
****************  Catproc Start  ****************
Serial   Phase #:6    [CDB$ROOT] Files:1    Time: 1s
```

In the previous output, you can see the number of parallel SQL processes involved for the CDB (-n option) and PDBs (-N option). This output carries the same number of SQL processes that you specified in the command. The output also has information about the PDBs that are going to be upgraded and about the installed database components. You can also see the description of each phase, which explains exactly what the phase is contributing to the upgrade.

```
*************** Summary report ****************
Serial   Phase #:115  [CDB$ROOT] Files:1    Time: 0s
Serial   Phase #:116  [CDB$ROOT] Files:1    Time: 0s
Serial   Phase #:117  [CDB$ROOT] Files:1    Time: 0s
Phases [0-117]            End Time:[2016_10_12 06:57:09]
Container Lists Inclusion:[CDB$ROOT] Exclusion:[NONE]
------------------------------------------------------

Start processing of PDB$SEED
[/u01/app/oracle/product/12.2.0/perl/bin/perl catctl.pl -E -n 2 -N 2 -l /u01/app/oracle -I
-i pdb_seed -c 'PDB$SEED' catupgrd.sql]

Start processing of PDB1
[/u01/app/oracle/product/12.2.0/perl/bin/perl catctl.pl -E -n 2 -N 2 -l /u01/app/oracle -I
-i pdb1 -c 'PDB1' catupgrd.sql]

Argument list for [catctl.pl]
Run in                  c = PDB$SEED
Do not run in           C = 0
Input Directory         d = 0
```

From the previous piece of output, you can see that the upgrade summary report for CDB$ROOT has been executed in phases 115, 116, and 117. This means 117 phases are involved in the container database upgrade. After the container database upgrade, it starts upgrading the PDB$SEED and PDB1 databases. In the output, you can see the value for each argument specified for the catctl.pl command.

Upgrade emulation is helpful in the following cases:

- When you want to test how the upgrade parameter selections are carried out. For example, you use the –c option with the catctl.pl command to specify which PDBs should be upgraded. Using the emulation option, you can verify before the upgrade that only the specified PDBs with the option –c will be considered for upgrade. As another example, say you specify the option –l for the log file direction location. Using emulation, you can confirm where the log file is going to be created.

- When you want to check the PDB upgrade priority order. In 12c R2 you have the provision to specify the order in which PDBs have to be upgraded. Suppose you have three PDBs, say, PDB1, PDB2, and PDB3. You want to complete the PDB upgrade in this order: first PDB3, then PDB1, and finally PDB2. In 12.2 you have option to specify the order. That order can be tested using emulation as follows:

```
catctl -E -L priority_list_name catupgrd.sql
```

priority_list_name is a file that has a priority list order, as shown here:

```
1,CDB$ROOT
2,PDB$SEED
3,PDB3
4,PDB1
5,PDB2
```

Say this order is saved in the text file priority.lst. Then invoke catctl.pl from the $ORACLE_HOME/rdbms/admin directory, as shown here:

```
/u01/app/oracle/product/12.2.0/perl/bin/perl catctl.pl -E -L priority.lst -n 2 catupgrd.sql
```

In the log, you can see at the end how the PDB order was followed.

```
Run file is [/u01/app/oracle/product/12.2.0/cfgtoollogs/cdb12102/upgrade20160926085741/
catctl_priority_run.lst]
0,CDB$ROOT
-------------------------------------------------------
1,PDB$SEED
-------------------------------------------------------
3,PDB3
-------------------------------------------------------
4,PDB1
-------------------------------------------------------
5,PDB2

        Time: 18s For CDB$ROOT
        Time: 80s For PDB(s)

Grand Total Time: 98s
 LOG FILES: (/u01/app/oracle/product/12.2.0/cfgtoollogs/cdb12102/upgrade20160926085741/
catupgrd*.log)
```

We will discuss more about priority order in upcoming sections.

- To obtain more information about the resource allocation choices, you use the -n
  and -N options.

- You know that the 12c database upgrade gets executed in multiple phases. The total
  number of phases varies between database versions. Using the emulation option,
  you get to know how many phases are involved in the database upgrade and how
  many SQL files are executed in each phase.

- The emulation output will show the phases involved in upgrading each database
  component. For example, the XDB-related scripts are executed in phases 58 to 71.
  We will discuss the output log when we talk about manual upgrades.

The emulation option does not perform a real-time upgrade. Hence, you cannot consider this option to
be simulating a real upgrade. This option can be used to check only the previously listed points.

Now that you have an understanding of upgrade emulation, you'll learn how to upgrade to Oracle 12c
R2. Next we'll cover the DBUA and command-line/manual database upgrade methods.

Database Upgrade Assistant

The DBUA is an Oracle-automated upgrade utility. It is a wizard to perform upgrade tasks automatically with
multiple user-friendly options. Refer to Chapter 2 for more details if needed. In this chapter, you will see only
the new features released with version 12.2 of the DBUA. Kindly refer to Chapter 2 if you want information
about the upgrade steps or any concepts not available in this chapter.

Here are the DBUA upgrade best practices:

- Execute the pre-upgrade script and validate the results. Fix issues prior to the
  upgrade. Though this script will be executed by the DBUA, it is better to execute and
  correct the database before upgrading to reduce the downtime.

- Take a database backup before invoking the DBUA. Though the DBUA has the option to take an RMAN backup, it will be an offline backup. So, it is better to take it before. Remember, database downtime starts when the DBUA starts executing its steps. Hence, taking a backup before the DBUA starts will reduce the downtime window.

- Ensure that the administrative tablespaces have enough storage to grow. The pre-upgrade results will show the expected size for those tablespaces. If tablespaces are not auto-extensible, then adjust the size of the datafiles to the required size.

- Make the user tablespaces read-only. The DBUA has a check box to choose this option, and in the manual upgrade method you could make schema-based tablespaces read-only using the –T option. Setting tablespaces to read-only or offline ensures that those tablespaces will not be altered during upgrade. After upgrade, any tablespaces changed to read-only or offline will be made online and read-only.

- If the database is archivelog enabled, make sure the archivelog destination has sufficient space to hold all the archived logs that are generated during the upgrade.

- If the RAC database is getting upgraded, leave the cluster_database parameter as TRUE.

- If the database has been restored manually and you are retrying the DBUA for the upgrade, then remove the $ORACLE_HOME/cfgtoollogs/dbua/logs/Welcome_SID.txt file.

Upgrade Steps

The 12.2 DBUA utility is available at $ORACLE_HOME/bin. The DBUA has to be invoked through the Oracle Home owner or error PRKH-1014 will be thrown (Current user "<username>" is not the oracle owner user "<oracle home owner>" of oracle home "<oracle home location>"). The DBUA first collects all the databases installed in the current system, as shown in Figure 14-1. You can see the list of databases and the text boxes for the login credentials at the bottom.

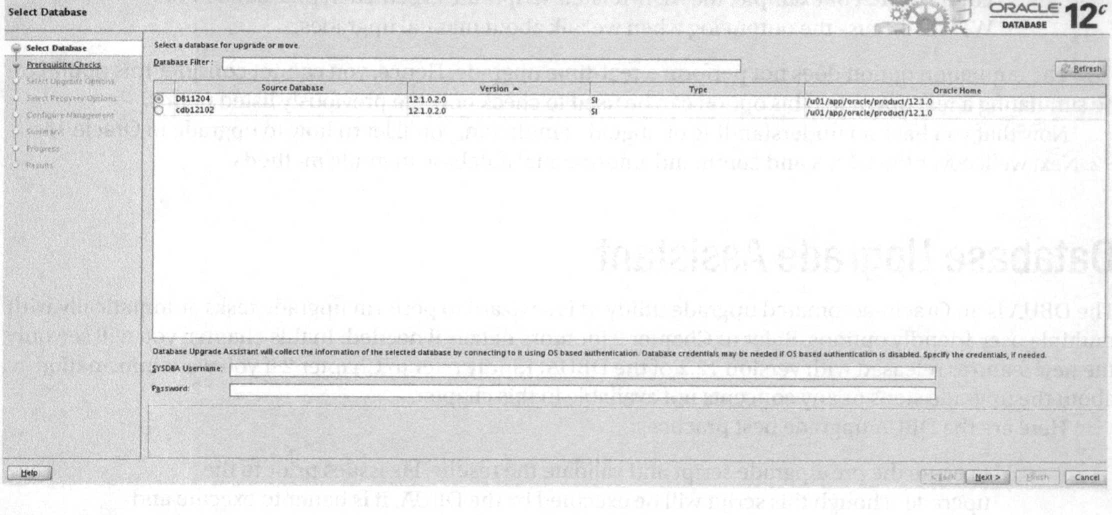

Figure 14-1. *DBUA, database selection page*

If the database is not listed here, then it could be that the database details are not available in the /etc/ oratab file. Suppose you know that the DBUA can operate on the database and only the entry is not available in /etc/oratab. In that case, invoke the DBUA using the –sid option as follows:

```
$dbua –sid <db_name> -oracleHome <Oracle home location>
```

Here's an example:

```
[oracle@Server Desktop]$ dbua -sid cdb12102 -oracleHome /u02/product/12.1.0/dbhome_1/
```

The DBUA will show the database in the list, as shown in Figure 14-1. In the example, if the cdb12102 database was not shown, then invoking dbua -sid cdb12102 -oracleHome /u02/product/12.1.0/ dbhome_1/ would show cdb12102 in the list.

This first page also has a database filter to select the database from the list of databases. In addition to that, it has the option to specify the sysdba username and its password if local OS authentication was disabled. Say for some reason SQLNET.AUTHENTICATION_SERVICES=(NONE) in sqlnet.ora, then local OS authentication is not possible. By specifying the SYSDBA username and password, you can proceed with your upgrade.

Once the database is chosen for upgrade, the next page (shown in Figure 14-2) will list the pluggable databases associated with the chosen database. This is applicable only when the chosen database is a multitenant container database.

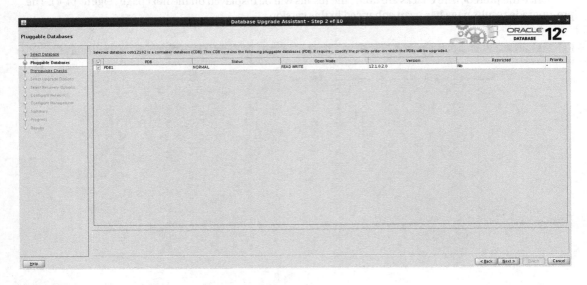

Figure 14-2. *DBUA, pluggable database information*

If the pluggable database is in a close state, that will be opened in read-write mode. All PDBs listed in this page will get upgraded. In 12.2 you can specify the priority order in which pluggable databases have to be upgraded. You can see the Priority column in the DBUA, which is editable. It accepts a numeric value, and the priority will be in ascending order. PDBs that have the same priority order will be upgraded in parallel. If you have multiple PDBs, then this will be helpful. You can see in Figure 14-3 that the container database has three pluggable database, and its priority for upgrade can be set here.

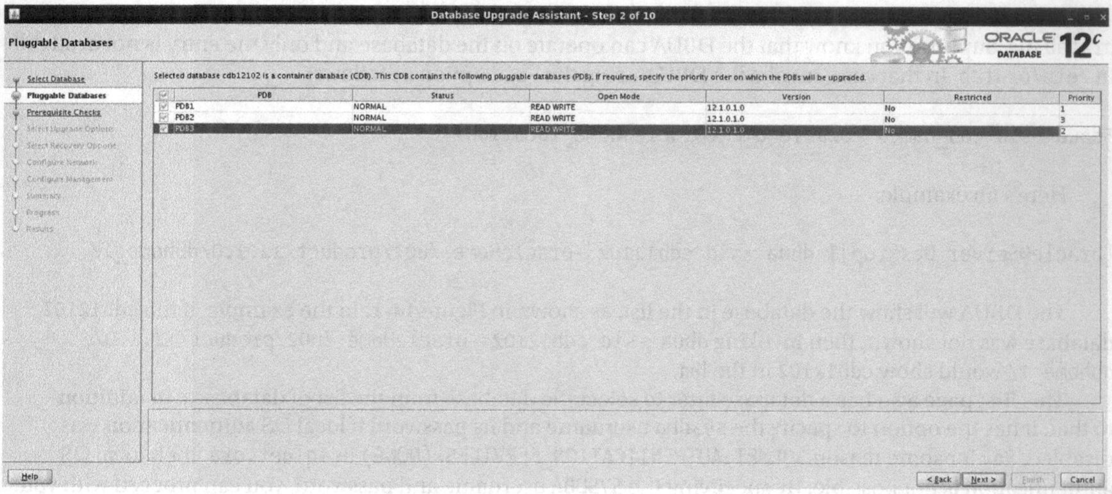

Figure 14-3. *DBUA, pluggable database priority setting*

The next page (shown in Figure 14-4) is the Prerequisite Checks page.

Once the prerequisite checks are done, the results will be displayed on the next page (Figure 14-4). The pre-upgrade results page has been enhanced in this version.

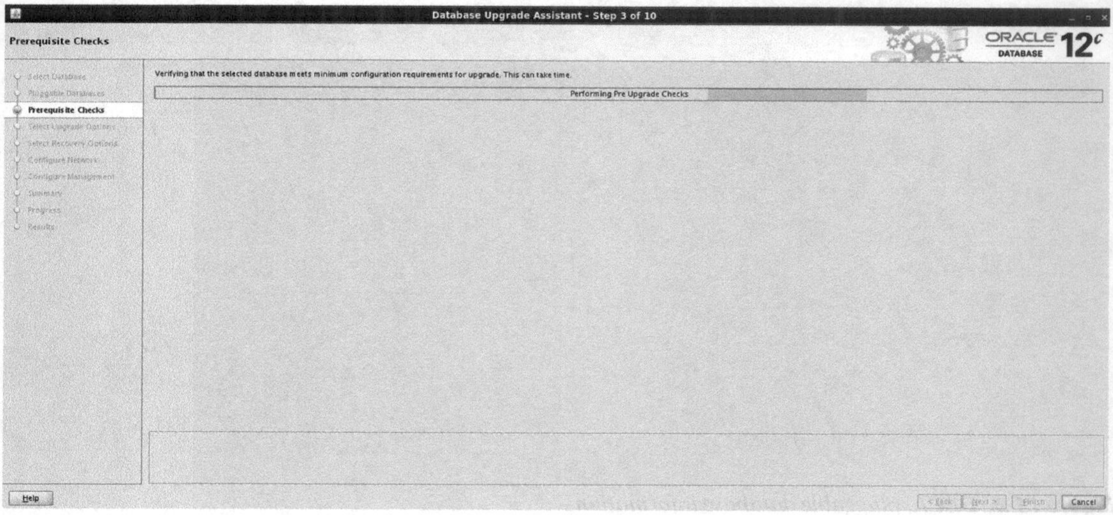

Figure 14-4. *DBUA, Prerequisite Checks page*

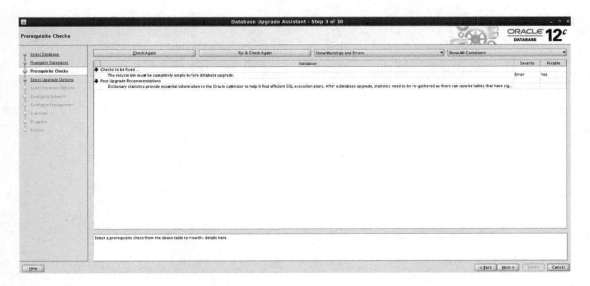

Figure 14-5. *DBUA, prerequisite results*

The prerequisite script will be executed in the container and in all pluggable databases. The results will be shown as common. If you want to check the prerequisite results of a particular database, then choose the database in the Show All Containers drop-down list, as shown in Figure 14-6.

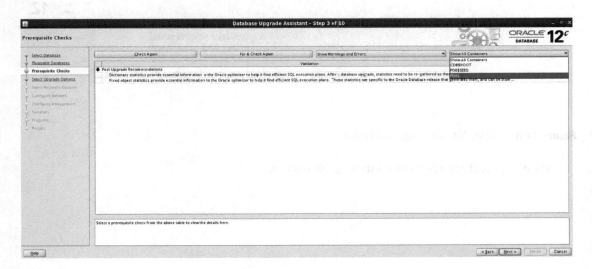

Figure 14-6. *DBUA, pre-upgrade check results for specific database*

Suppose there is an error in the pre-upgrade results; then you should check its severity. In Figure 14-5 you can see that an error is thrown because its Recycle Bin is not empty and its Fixable column is YES. It denotes this error can be fixed by the DBUA. Click Fix & Check Again, which will fix the error and automatically rerun the pre-upgrade script and display its results (Figure 14-7).

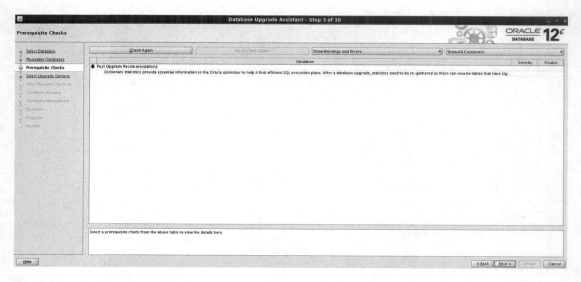

Figure 14-7. DBUA, preupgrade results after executing fixup scripts

A drop-down box is available to show only errors or both warnings and errors (Figure 14-8).

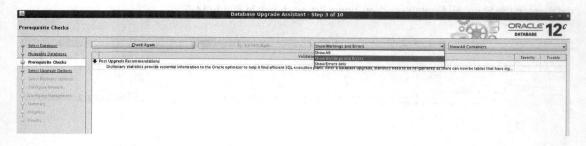

Figure 14-8. DBUA, lists warnings and errors

The next page (Figure 14-9) shows the upgrade options.

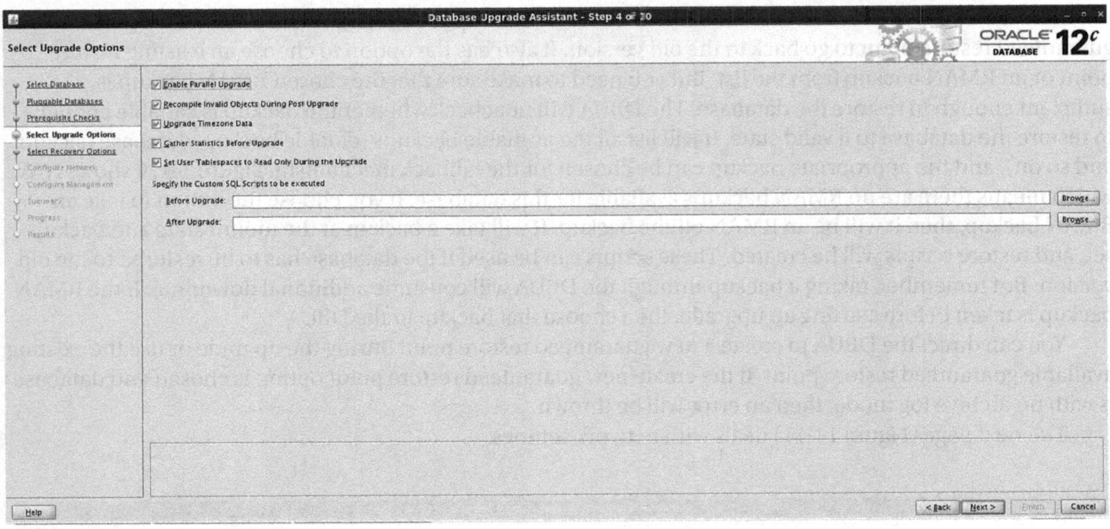

Figure 14-9. *DBUA, upgrade options*

Like with the previous release, you have the option to recompile invalid objects after a database upgrade, do a time zone upgrade, gather statistics before the upgrade, and set user tablespaces (nonadministrative tablespaces) to read-only during the upgrade. In addition, you have ability to perform the upgrade in parallel or do a serial upgrade. You can also specify custom SQL scripts to execute before and after the upgrade. The next page, shown in Figure 14-10, talks about the recovery options available with the DBUA.

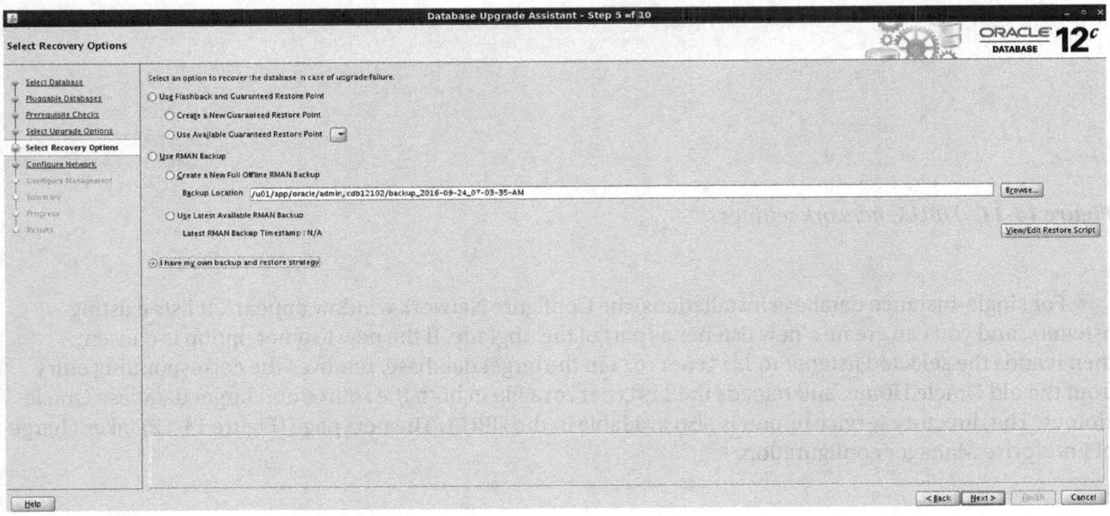

Figure 14-10. *DBUA, recovery options*

Like with the previous release, the DBUA has the fallback options of RMAN backup and flashback guaranteed restore point to go back to the old version. It also has the option to choose an existing restore point or an RMAN backup from the list. But you need to make sure that the chosen RMAN backup is sufficient enough to restore the database. The DBUA will not check whether the backup is capable enough to restore the database to a valid state. It will list all the available backups (datafile backup, database backup, and so on), and the appropriate backup can be chosen for the fallback mechanism. Figure 14-10 shows N/A, which means there are no RMAN backups available for this database. If you choose the option to take an RMAN backup, then it will be an RMAN offline backup. It will take a backup at the mount state and backup set, and restore scripts will be created. These scripts can be used if the database has to be restored to the old version. But remember, taking a backup through the DBUA will consume additional downtime. If the RMAN backup is taken before starting an upgrade, then choose that backup in the DBUA.

You can direct the DBUA to create a new guaranteed restore point during the upgrade or use the existing available guaranteed restore point. If the create new guaranteed restore point option is chosen and database is with no archive log mode, then an error will be thrown.

The next page (Figure 14-11) deals with network settings.

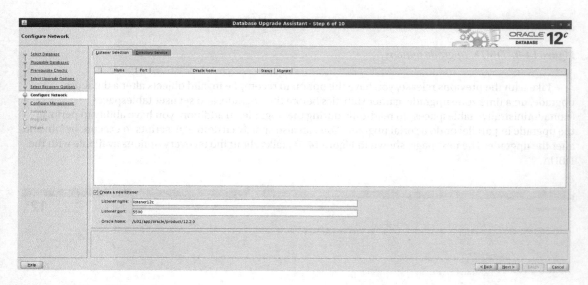

Figure 14-11. *DBUA, network settings*

For single-instance database installations, the Configure Network window appears. It lists existing listeners, and you can create a new listener as part of the upgrade. If the new listener option is chosen, then it adds the selected listener to `listener.ora` in the target database, removes the corresponding entry from the old Oracle Home, and reloads the `listener.ora` file in both the source and target database Oracle Homes. The directory service option is also available in the DBUA. The next page (Figure 14-12) takes charge of Enterprise Manager configuration.

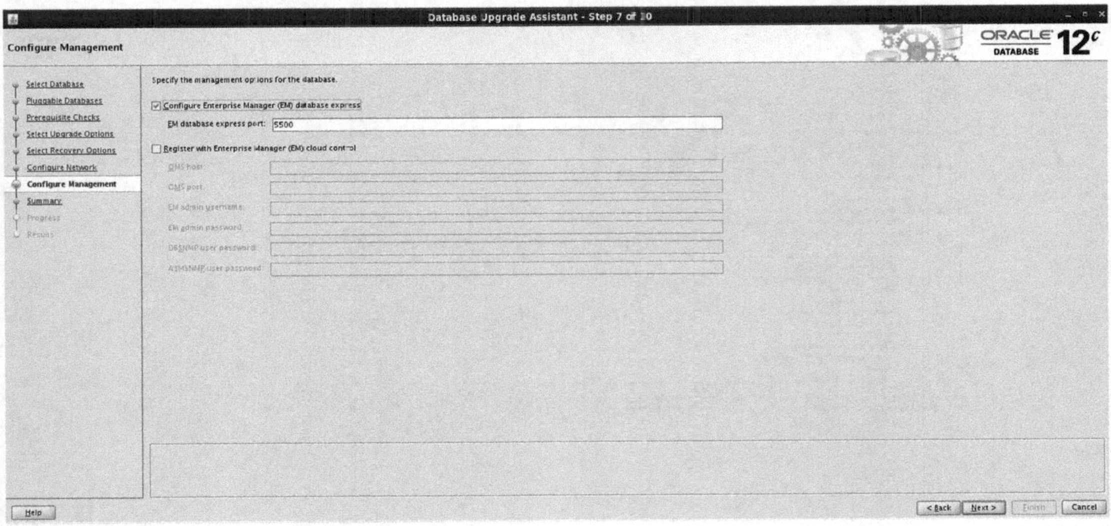

Figure 14-12. *DBUA, Enterprise Manager configuration*

The DBUA has the option to configure this database to be part of EM Cloud Control or EM Database Express.

Once all the parameters are specified, the DBUA summary page will be shown, as in Figure 14-13.

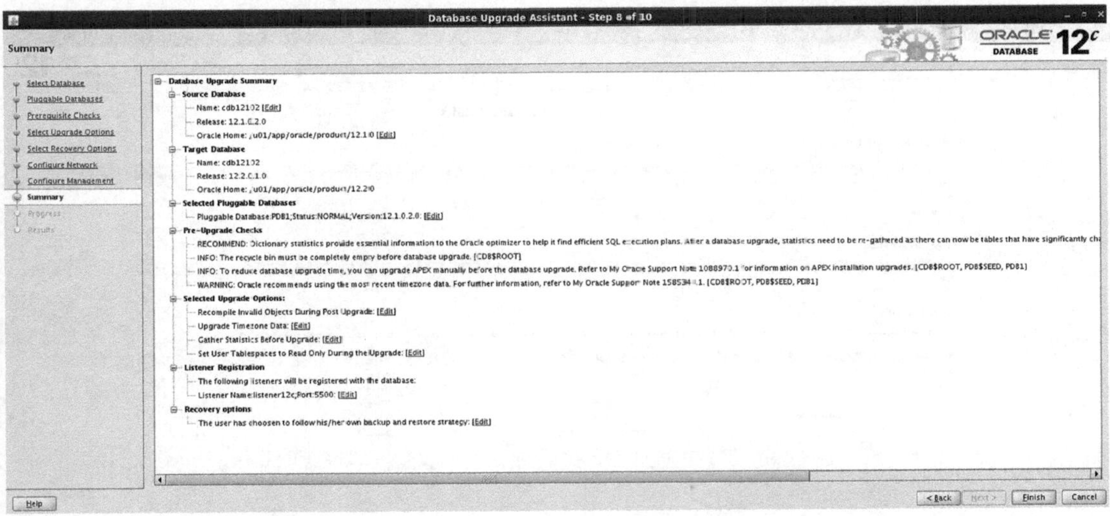

Figure 14-13. *DBUA, Summary page*

On the Summary page you can see details about the source database, the target database, and the other chosen options. Also there are Edit links available to modify the chosen option.

Once you click the Finish button, the database upgrade progress starts, as shown in Figure 14-14.

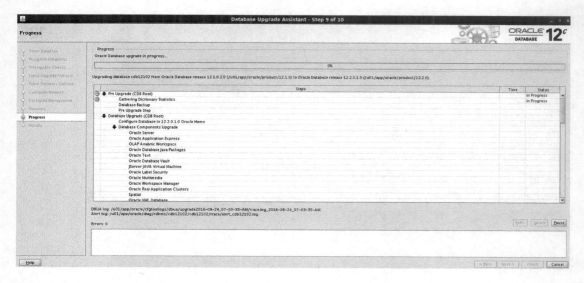

Figure 14-14. *DBUA, upgrade progress*

DBUA runs `catctl.pl`, which runs the upgrade process in parallel. It optimizes the utilization of CPU resources to hasten the upgrade and minimize downtime.

After the database upgrade has completed successfully, the upgrade results will be published (Figure 14-15).

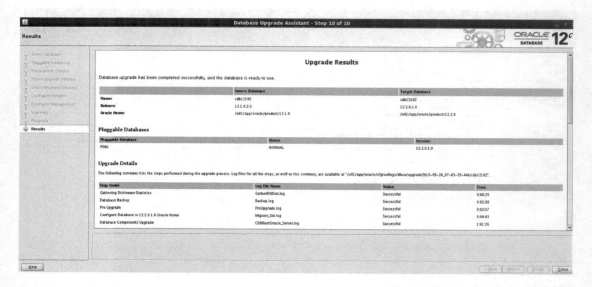

Figure 14-15. *DBUA, upgrade results*

In the upgrade results window, you can see the post-upgrade database status, each upgrade step and its status, and the completion time.

DBUA in Silent Mode

It is possible to execute the DBUA in silent mode where the graphical user interface (GUI) is not possible or desired. In silent mode the user interface is not available, and all the necessary upgrade options should be specified at the command line. To start the DBUA in silent mode, include -silent with dbua as follows:

```
dbua -silent -sid <db_name>
```

Let's discuss the new options available in 12.2 for a silent upgrade.

- -pdbs: Specify a comma-separated list with the names of the pluggable databases (PDBs) that will be upgraded. Specify -sid | -dbName along with the pdbs option.

- -pdbsWithPriority: You know the priority option is enabled in 12.2. With this option, specify a comma-separated list of pluggable databases (PDBs) to be upgraded along with their corresponding priorities. Here is the format: <pdb name>:<upgrade priority>,<pdb name>:<upgrade priority>.

New 12.2 DBUA Features

Here's a summary of the new features in 12.2 DBUA:

- Prioritized PDB upgrade execution

- Provision to specify sysdba username and password details in case local authentication is not available

- Filter box to filter required database from the list of available databases

- Pre-upgrade output displayed in the DBUA in a better way

- In the upgrade log you can see the phases responsible for each database upgrade component upgrade in detail. Using this information you can reexecute the upgrade steps for a particular database component if required. For example, XDB-related scripts are executed in phases 58 to 71. If XDB fails during upgrade, you can reexecute the upgrade from phase 58.

Manual Database Upgrade/Command-Line Upgrade

As you know, a manual database upgrade is another method to upgrade a database and its data dictionary to a higher database version. In this method, all the upgrade steps are done manually.

As a first step, execute the pre-upgrade script and evaluate the output. Make sure there are no warnings or errors in the pre-upgrade script output. The upgrade checklists are the same as earlier versions, which were discussed in Chapter 2. Hence, we won't elaborate much about that in this chapter.

Here are the best practices of a manual database upgrade:

1) Update the target Oracle Home to the latest patch set update before the upgrade.

2) Take a backup of Oracle Database.

3) Gather database statistics to reduce the database downtime.

4) Verify the materialized view refreshes are complete before the upgrade.

5) Ensure there are no datafiles in backup mode.

6) Make sure there are no datafiles that require media recovery.

7) Resolve outstanding distributed transactions before the upgrade.

8) Purge the Recycle Bin before the upgrade.

9) Save the Oracle Enterprise Manager Database Control configuration and data.

10) If used, remove Database Control with emremove.sql.

11) Disable Oracle Database Vault.

You can find the steps and SQL commands for these best practices in Chapter 2.

In Oracle Database 12c Release 1, the parallel upgrade utility catctl.pl was introduced. This utility reduces the total amount of time by upgrading the database dictionary in parallel by using multiple SQL processes. Performing an upgrade in parallel through multiple SQL processes enables you to take advantage of the available CPU. This utility needs to be executed using Perl libraries. But the catctl.pl command for upgrading is a lengthy one, and the Perl binary location has to be specified for the catctl command. Oracle has improvised this step in 12.2. To perform a manual upgrade in 12.2, you can use the shell command dbupgrade. It internally calls catctl.pl from the command line, instead of requiring you to run it from Perl.

The dbupgrade shell command is located in the $ORACLE_HOME/bin directory. It will accept command-line arguments. You can provide command-line arguments that are valid for catctl.pl to this shell command. If no arguments are specified, then dbupgrade invokes the following command:

```
$ORACLE_HOME/perl/bin/perl -I$ORACLE_HOME/perl/lib $ORACLE_HOME/rdbms/admin/catctl.pl
$ORACLE_HOME/rdbms/admin/catupgrd.sql
Else
$ORACLE_HOME/perl/bin/perl -I$ORACLE_HOME/perl/lib $ORACLE_HOME/rdbms/admin/catctl.pl
"<Arguments>" $ORACLE_HOME/rdbms/admin/catupgrd.sql
```

The script Catctl.pl is still valid to upgrade to the 12.2 version. But it needs to be invoked using Perl libraries. The arguments available with dbupgrade or catctl.pl in 12.2 are as follows:

```
catctl [-c QuotedSpaceSeparatedInclusionListOfPDBs]
               [-C QuotedSpaceSeparatedExclusionListOfPDBs]
               [-d Directory]
               [-e EchoOff]
               [-E Simulate]
               [-F Forced cleanup]
               [-i Identifier]
               [-l LogDirectory]
               [-L PriorityList]
               [-M UpgradeMode]
               [-n Processes]
               [-N PDB Processes]
               [-p StartPhase]
               [-P EndPhase]
               [-R UpgradeAutoResume]
               [-s Script]
               [-S SerialUpgrade]
               [-T ReadOnlyTablespaces]
               [-u UserName]
               [-y DIsplayPhases]
               [-z CatconDebug]
               [-Z 1 CatctlDebug]
               FileName
```

- -c denotes the PDBs where `catupgrd.sql` has to be executed.

- -C denotes the PDBs to be excluded from execution.

- -d denotes the directory where `catupgrd.sql` is located.

- -E denotes that you simulate the upgrade.

- -F forces a cleanup of previous upgrade errors.

- -i is an identifier to create spool log files.

- -l is a log directory where spool files have to be placed.

- -L is a new option introduced in 12.2. It is for the PDB priority list for the upgrade. Lower-priority numbers will be upgraded first. CDB\$ROOT and PDB\$SEED are always priorities 1 and 2 and cannot be changed. For other PDBs, the priority can be set. PDB priorities must start at 1, as shown here:

```
1,PDB1
1,PDB2
2,PDB3
2,PDB4
```

This denotes PDB1 and PDB2 have to be upgraded first in parallel and then PDB3 and PDB4. To make it faster, the priority information can be recorded in a text file and passed as an argument to this option.

- -M: If this is specified, then CDB\$ROOT is set to upgrade mode when upgrading all the containers, or it will be opened in normal mode.

- -n: This is the maximum number of parallel SQL processes to use to upgrade the database. The multitenant database defaults to the total number of CPUs on the system. The traditional database defaults to 4.

- -N: This is a new argument in 12.2. It is the maximum number of parallel SQL process to use per PDB during the upgrade in a multitenant environment. This is ignored for traditional databases. By default its value is 2 and maximum it can accept 8 and minimum will be 1. The maximum number of parallel PDB upgrade equals to divided by the value of -N.

Suppose you have 10 PDBs, -n (the number of parallel SQL processes) is specified as 10, -N (the number of parallel SQL processes for PDB) has a value of 2, and all PDBs have the same priority. Then the number of parallel PDB upgrades is 10/2 = 5. This means five PDBs can be upgraded in parallel, and two SQL processes will be acting on each PDB for the upgrade.

- -p: This denotes the start phase for the upgrade execution.

- -P: This denotes the stop phase where the execution should stop.

- -R: This automatically resumes an upgrade from the first failed phase. It is turned off by default. It is mutually exclusive with the argument -p (start phase).

- -s: This is the SQL script to initialize the session.

- -T: This places user tablespaces in read-only mode.

- -u: This is the username to connect to database. It prompts for a password during execution.

- -y: This displays phases only.

- -z: This turns on production catcon.pm debugging information while running this script.

- -Z: This turns on catctl debug tracing while running this script.

These options are new in 12.2:

```
[-E Simulate]
[-F Forced cleanup]
[-L PriorityList]
[-M UpgradeMode]
[-N PDB Processes]
[-R UpgradeAutoResume]
[-T ReadOnlyTablespaces]
[-z CatconDebug]
[-Z 1 CatctlDebug]
```

Upgrade Steps

Here are the upgrade steps:

1) Make sure the database backup has been taken.

2) Ensure the 12.2 Oracle Home has been patched with the latest PSU patches/ proactive bundle patches.

3) Ensure the pre-upgrade script is executed on the source database. There are no warnings or errors in the pre-upgrade output, and the pre-upgrade fixup script has been executed.

4) Make sure the best practices of the manual upgrade process have been followed.

5) Shut down the database.

6) Copy the init parameter file, password file, and other required files to the 12.2 Oracle Home. In Windows, the new service has been created in the 12.2 Oracle Home.

7) Start the database in upgrade mode. If it is a multitenant database, start the pluggable database also in upgrade mode.

8) Execute catctl.pl with the –E option to emulate the database upgrade. The output will show whether the PDB priority is being followed and whether the resource allocation (-n and –N arguments) is properly utilized.

9) Invoke the dbupgrade script to perform the database upgrade. Specify the desired arguments with dbupgrade.

10) Execute post-upgrade fixup scripts.

11) Verify the database component status at the container database level and pluggable database level for multitenant databases.

Let's discuss further with an example.

- *Source database version*: 12.1.0.2.0

- *Source database name*: CDB12102

- *PDB name*: PDB1, PDB2, PDB3

Here are the steps:

1) Say the pre-upgrade script has been executed as follows and there are no errors or warnings in the output:

```
$ $ORACLE_HOME/jdk/bin/java -jar /u01/app/oracle/product/12.2.0/rdbms/admin/
preupgrade.jar
```

All PDBs are open and you are going to upgrade all the PDBs.

2) Copy the password file and init file to the 12.2 Oracle Home.

```
cp orapwcdb12102 <12.2 oracle home>/dbs
cp initcdb12102.ora <12.2 oracle home>/dbs
```

3) Start the database in upgrade mode using the 12.2 Oracle Home and also start the PDB in upgrade mode.

```
$ sqlplus "/ as sysdba"

SQL*Plus: Release 12.2.0.1.0 Production

SQL> startup upgrade
ORACLE instance started.

Total System Global Area 1660944384 bytes
Fixed Size                   8793448 bytes
Variable Size              989856408 bytes
Database Buffers           654311424 bytes
Redo Buffers                 7983104 bytes
Database mounted.
Database opened.
SQL> alter pluggable database all open upgrade;
Pluggable database altered.
```

Check the pluggable database status using the following query:

```
SQL> show pdbs

    CON_ID CON_NAME                       OPEN MODE  RESTRICTED
---------- ------------------------------ ---------- ----------
         2 PDB$SEED                       MIGRATE    YES
         3 PDB1                           MIGRATE    YES
         4 PDB2                           MIGRATE    YES
         5 PDB3                           MIGRATE    YES
```

4) Exit from sqlprompt.

5) Invoke dbupgrade with the required arguments.

```
$dbupgrade
```

As you know, if you don't specify any arguments, then dbupgrade will call catctl.pl as follows:

```
$ORACLE_HOME/perl/bin/perl -I$ORACLE_HOME/perl/lib $ORACLE_HOME/rdbms/admin/catctl.pl
$ORACLE_HOME/rdbms/admin/catupgrd.sql
```

Here's an example for running a parallel upgrade on multiple PDBs:

```
$dbupgrade -n 4 -N 2 -l $ORACLE_HOME/diagnostics
```

The previous command utilizes four parallel SQL processes and two parallel SQL processes per PDB. This means 4/2=2; two PDBs can be upgraded in parallel.

If you have more PDBs and CPUs, then these values can be changed according to the requirements. Once the upgrade is successful, complete the post-upgrade tasks.

Post-upgrade Tasks

Here are the steps:

1) Execute utlrp.sql at the container and pluggable database levels. This can be done by executing through catcon.pl, which was discussed in Chapter 2.

   ```
   $ORACLE_HOME/perl/bin/perl catcon.pl -b utlrplog utlrp.sql
   ```

2) Check the database component status through the post-upgrade status tool.

Execute the utlu122s.sql script available in the <12.2 oracle home>/rdbms/admin folder as the sysdba user. This will collect the database component version and status. The sample output will be as follows:

```
          Oracle Database 12.2 Post-Upgrade Status Tool
                       [CDB$ROOT]


Component                        Current     Version    Elapsed Time
Name                             Status      Number     HH:MM:SS

Oracle Server                    VALID       12.2.0.1.0  00:19:48
JServer JAVA Virtual Machine     VALID       12.2.0.1.0  00:10:23
Oracle Real Application Clusters OPTION OFF  12.2.0.1.0  00:00:00
Oracle Workspace Manager         VALID       12.2.0.1.0  00:01:19
OLAP Analytic Workspace          VALID       12.2.0.1.0  00:00:36
Oracle OLAP API                  VALID       12.2.0.1.0  00:00:19
Oracle Label Security            VALID       12.2.0.1.0  00:00:12
Oracle XDK                       VALID       12.2.0.1.0  00:02:21
Oracle Text                      VALID       12.2.0.1.0  00:00:57
```

```
Oracle XML Database                 VALID       12.2.0.1.0  00:02:23
Oracle Database Java Packages       VALID       12.2.0.1.0  00:00:19
Oracle Multimedia                   VALID       12.2.0.1.0  00:03:30
Spatial                             VALID       12.2.0.1.0  00:09:09
Oracle Application Express          VALID       5.0.4.00.12 00:17:15
Oracle Database Vault               VALID       12.2.0.1.0  00:00:35
Final Actions                                               00:03:47
Post Upgrade                                                00:00:21
Post Compile                                                00:00:38
```

Total Upgrade Time: 01:14:15 [CDB$ROOT]

Database time zone version is 18. It is older than current release timezone version 26. Time zone upgrade is needed using the DBMS_DST package.

Summary Report File = /u01/app/oracle/product/12.2.0/cfgtoollogs/cdb12102/ upgrade20160927154536/upg_summary.log

You can see in the summary that it talks about the container name, its database component version, its status, the time spent for the upgrade, and the time zone version.

The status VALID denotes the component is valid with no errors. OPTION OFF denotes the component is not installed or linked with the server. If utlrp.sql is not executed, then the component status will be UPGRADED. This denotes that a component has completed upgrading with no errors.

3) Check the status of SYS and SYSTEM schema objects. There should not be any invalid objects in the database dictionary. If invalid objects are there, execute $ORACLE_HOME/rdbms/admin/utlrp.sql to recompile the objects.

4) Execute patch-post script execution if a patch is installed in the 12.2 Oracle Home before upgrading.

5) Modify oratab to reflect the 12.2 Oracle Home for the upgraded database.

6) Perform a time zone file version upgrade.

7) Upgrade the tables depending on the Oracle-maintained types. From Oracle 12.2, you must manually upgrade tables having Oracle-maintained types like AQ queue tables. You can identify whether any table with an Oracle-maintained type requires an upgrade using the following query:

    Sql> select owner, table_name from dba_tab_cols where data_upgraded='NO';

If the query returns any rows, then execute the following

    Sql> @$ORACLE_HOME/rdbms/admin/utluptabdata.sql

This SQL file will collect all such tables and perform the upgrade. Or you can upgrade each table by executing this:

    Sql> alter table <schema>.<table> upgrade including data;

8) Enable the new extended datatype capability. Enabling the database to take advantage of the new enhancement capabilities released in higher versions requires some actions. For example, Oracle 12*c* has introduced the max_string_ size parameter. By setting this parameter to Extended, you set the max value for the datatypes VARCHAR2, NVARCHAR2, and RAW to 32,676 bytes. In a standard type, it will have a value of 4,000 bytes. If you need to extend the capability, then the compatible parameter value has to be changed to 12.0.0, and the parameter max_string_size should have the value Extended.

9) Upgrade the STATS table. If the statistics tables are created using DBMS_STATS. CREATE_STAT_TABLE, then upgrade the statistics table by running DBMS_STATS. UPGRADE_STAT_TABLE.

   Run Sql> execute dbms_stats.upgrade_stat_table('<schema>','<stat_ table>');.

10) Upgrade the Oracle Application Express configuration.

11) Enable Oracle Database Vault.

12) You can set the compatible parameter value to 12.2. But this change could be done after performing all the application testing with the database. This parameter change is not irreversible. Hence, proper testing is required before doing the change.

Oracle 12.2 New Manual Upgrade Features

Here are the new features:

1) The pre-upgrade script has been changed to preupgrade.jar, and it will be executed from the command prompt.

2) The PDB upgrade priority can be chosen.

3) The upgrade process can be checked through emulation.

4) The upgrade command has been simplified by executing only the $ORACLE_HOME/ bin/dbupgrade script. It will call the Perl script catctl.pl internally.

Pluggable Database Upgrade

In the previous section, we discussed how to upgrade the container database through the DBUA and manual methods. You saw that all the pluggable databases associated with the container database were upgraded. Most of the time this is not the case; you usually will need to upgrade just a certain pluggable database, not all of them. In that case, you should not touch the container database; only the desired pluggable database has to be upgraded.

The pluggable database upgrade steps in 12.2 are the same as 12.1.

Pluggable Database Upgrade Steps

Here are the steps:

1) Execute the pre-upgrade script for the pluggable databases chosen for the upgrade. You can do this by executing preupgrade.jar on those particular pluggable databases.

   ```
   Preupgrade.jar:
   $ORACLE_HOME_12.1/bin/java -jar $ORACLE_HOME_12.2/rdbms/admin/preupgrade.jar dir
   {/tmp} -c <PDB list>
   ```

2) Execute the pre-upgrade fixup scripts in the pluggable database.

   ```
   Sql> alter session set container=<PDB_name>;
   Sql>@<preupgrade_fixup script.sql>
   ```

3) Verify that the pre-upgrade output doesn't have any warnings or errors.

4) Follow the best practices documented for a manual database upgrade.

5) Take a backup of the pluggable database before the upgrade.

6) Close the pluggable database.

7) Unplug the pluggable database from the container database. Note the PDB XML file.

8) Drop the pluggable database, but keep the datafiles of that PDB.

9) Connect to the 12.2 Oracle Home container database.

10) Create a new pluggable database by plugging into the lower-version 12*c* R1 pluggable database.

11) Open the pluggable database using the upgrade option.

12) Right now the PDB is with the lower version. Upgrade it either using the DBUA or using the manual method.

13) If a manual upgrade is done, then complete the post-upgrade PDB steps.

Let's discuss the PDB upgrade with an example.

```
Source database Name: cdb12102
Source database version: 12.1.0.2.0
PDB name: PDB1, PDB2
12.2 CDB Name: CDB122
```

You can assume PDB1 is getting upgraded. The pre-upgrade script has been executed on PDB1, and you have verified that there are no warnings or errors. A backup has been taken. Its database component version and status have been checked.

```
SQL> select comp_name, version, status from dba_registry  ;

COMP_NAME                        VERSION                     STATUS
-------------------------------- --------------------------- -----------
Oracle Database Vault            12.1.0.2.0                  VALID
Oracle Application Express       4.2.0.00.27                 VALID
Oracle Label Security            12.1.0.2.0                  VALID
Spatial                          12.1.0.2.0                  VALID
Oracle Multimedia                12.1.0.2.0                  VALID
Oracle Text                      12.1.0.2.0                  VALID
Oracle Workspace Manager         12.1.0.2.0                  VALID
Oracle XML Database              12.1.0.2.0                  VALID
Oracle Database Catalog Views    12.1.0.2.0                  VALID
Oracle Database Packages and Types 12.1.0.2.0                VALID
JServer JAVA Virtual Machine     12.1.0.2.0                  VALID
Oracle XDK                       12.1.0.2.0                  VALID
Oracle Database Java Packages    12.1.0.2.0                  VALID
OLAP Analytic Workspace          12.1.0.2.0                  VALID
Oracle OLAP API                  12.1.0.2.0                  VALID
Oracle Real Application Clusters 12.1.0.2.0                  OPTION OFF
```

Close the PDB.

```
SQL> alter pluggable database pdb1 close;

Pluggable database altered.
```

Unplug the pluggable database PDB1.

```
SQL> alter pluggable database pdb1 unplug into '/u01/app/oracle/pdb1.xml';

Pluggable database altered.
```

Drop the pluggable database, keeping the datafiles. If you don't specify the keep option, then the datafiles will be deleted.

```
SQL> drop pluggable database pdb1 keep datafiles;

Pluggable database dropped.
```

Target side
Connect to the 12.2 Oracle database CDB122 and check the existing pluggable databases.

```
SQL> show pdbs

    CON_ID CON_NAME                       OPEN MODE  RESTRICTED
---------- ------------------------------ ---------- ----------
         2 PDB$SEED                       READ ONLY  NO
         3 PDB1                           MOUNTED
```

You can see that already there is a pluggable database in 12.2 with the PDB1 name, so you need to plug in the pluggable database with a different name.

```
SQL> create pluggable database pdb122 using '/u01/app/oracle/pdb1.xml';

Pluggable database created.
```

While plugging into the database, you may get the error "ORA-65346: the PDB version is lower or components (APEX) are missing in CDB." This denotes the 12.2 CDB doesn't have APEX installed. You can configure APEX in the existing 12.2 database using the DBCA.

If the 12.2 database is on a different server, then you need to copy the datafiles of the pluggable database and pdb1.xml to the different server.

Open the newly created PDB122 database in migrate mode as its dictionary is still with the 12.1.0.2.0 version.

```
SQL> show pdbs
```

CON_ID	CON_NAME	OPEN MODE	RESTRICTED
2	PDB$SEED	READ ONLY	NO
3	PDB1	MOUNTED	
4	PDB122	MIGRATE	YES

This PDB122 database can be upgraded through the DBUA or via a manual upgrade. Let's first see the DBUA method.

Invoke the 12.2 version of the DBUA.

You can see the 12.2.0.1.0 database cdb122 on the first page. You can confirm this through the version parameter and Oracle Home path (Figure 14-16). Choose the CDB122 database and click Next.

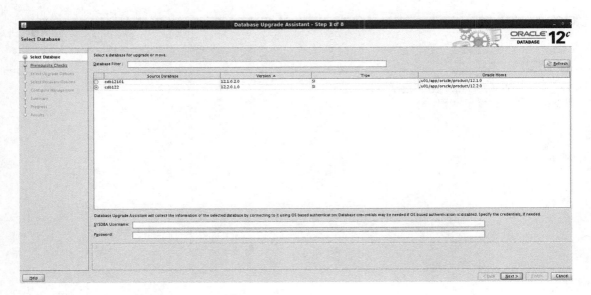

Figure 14-16. DBUA, 12.2 container database selection

In the next screen, you can see the pluggable database associated with the cdb12102 CDB, as shown in Figure 14-17.

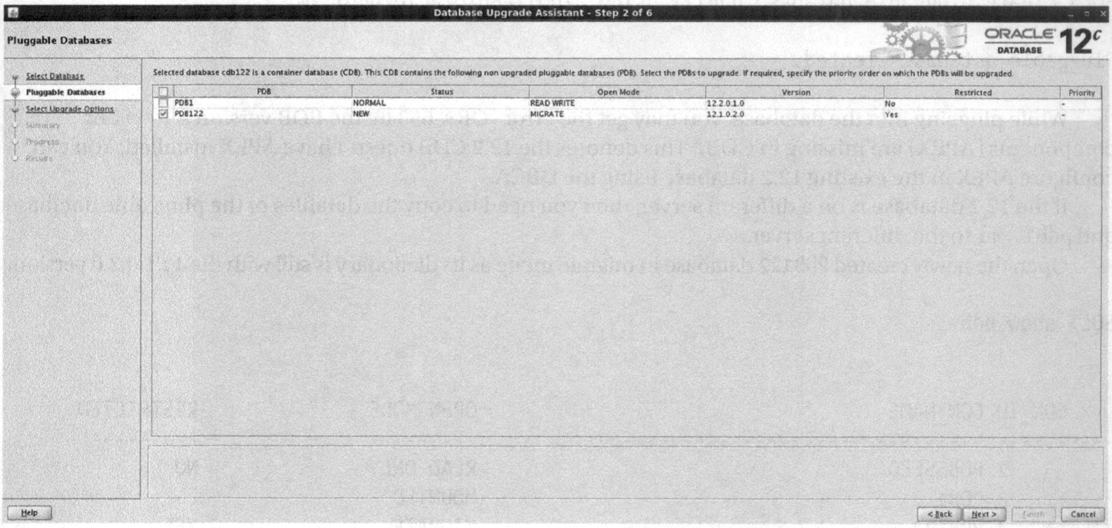

Figure 14-17. *DBUA, pluggable database selection*

As shown in Figure 14-17, you can see the PDB122 database is in Migrate state with version 12.1.0.2.0, and this particular pluggable database has to be upgraded to 12.2 version. Click Next.

On the next screen (Figure 14-18) you can see the PDB upgrade options.

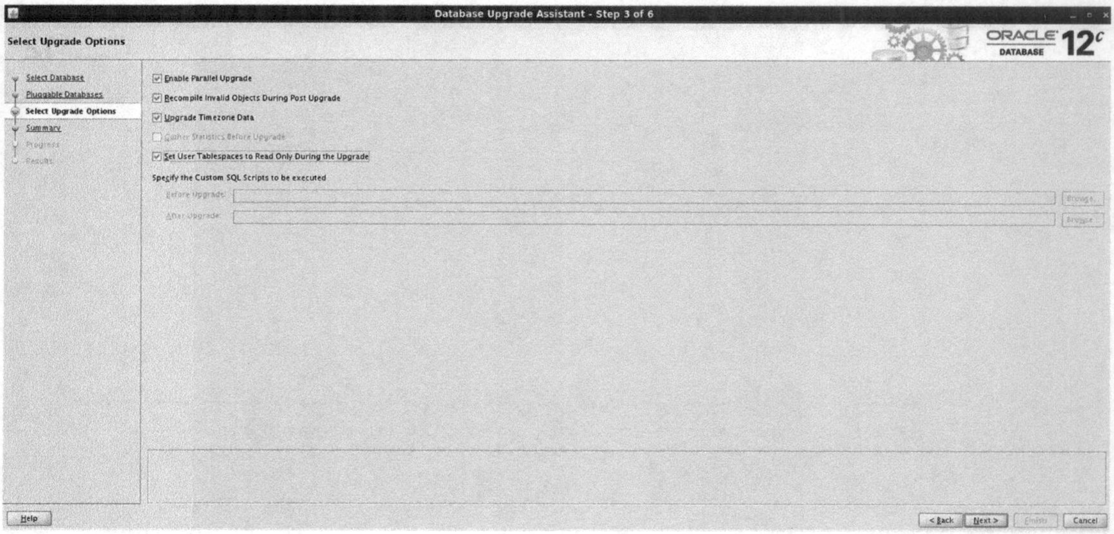

Figure 14-18. *DBUA, PDB upgrade options*

You can see that the options Gather Statistics and Custom SQL Scripts are grayed out, which means they are applicable for a CDB upgrade.

Click Next. You can see the PDB upgrade summary, as shown in Figure 14-19.

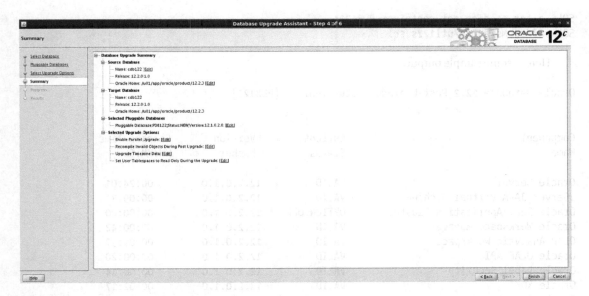

Figure 14-19. *DBUA, PDB upgrade summary*

The Summary page shows the source and target database details, which are the same because only the PDB is getting upgraded. This also shows the selected upgrade options for PDB.

Click Finish. This will start the upgrade progress, as shown in Figure 14-20.

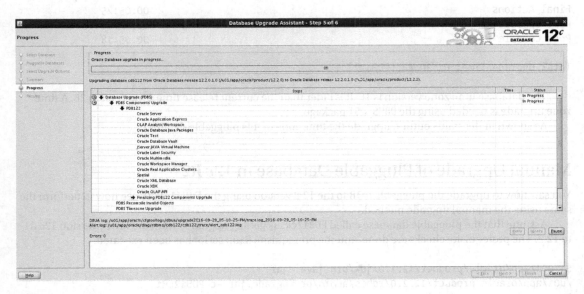

Figure 14-20. *DBUA, PDB upgrade progress*

Similar to the container database upgrades, the DBUA performs the upgrade for the PDB in a parallel way. Once the upgrade is completed, check the pluggable database upgrade status by executing utlu122s.sql in the pluggable database.

```
SQL> alter session set container=PDB122;
SQL> @?/rdbms/admin/utl122s.sql
```

Here is some sample output:

```
Oracle Database 12.2 Post-Upgrade Status Tool      [PDB122]
```

Component Name	Current Status	Version Number	Elapsed Time HH:MM:SS
Oracle Server	VALID	12.2.0.1.0	00:24:01
JServer JAVA Virtual Machine	VALID	12.2.0.1.0	00:09:31
Oracle Real Application Clusters	OPTION OFF	12.2.0.1.0	00:00:00
Oracle Workspace Manager	VALID	12.2.0.1.0	00:00:42
OLAP Analytic Workspace	VALID	12.2.0.1.0	00:01:57
Oracle OLAP API	VALID	12.2.0.1.0	00:00:20
Oracle Label Security	VALID	12.2.0.1.0	00:00:14
Oracle XDK	VALID	12.2.0.1.0	00:02:17
Oracle Text	VALID	12.2.0.1.0	00:01:04
Oracle XML Database	VALID	12.2.0.1.0	00:02:32
Oracle Database Java Packages	VALID	12.2.0.1.0	00:00:18
Oracle Multimedia	VALID	12.2.0.1.0	00:03:08
Oracle Application Express	VALID	5.0.4.00.12	00:21:07
Oracle Database Vault	VALID	12.2.0.1.0	00:01:18
Final Actions			00:05:25
Post Upgrade			00:02:16
Post Compile			00:05:18

```
Total Upgrade Time: 01:30:44 [PDB122]
```

The database time zone version is 18. It is older than the current release time zone version 26. A time zone upgrade is needed using the DBMS_DST package.

As shown in the status output, upgrade the time zone of this pluggable database.

Manual Upgrade of Pluggable Database in 12c R2

You saw how to upgrade the pluggable PDB to the 12.2 version using the DBUA. Let's see how to perform the same using the manual upgrade method.

Assume that the pluggable database called PDB12cR1 is getting upgraded from the lower-version 12c R1 to 12.2. The prerequisite checks are done, and the prerequisite fixup script has been executed.

```
$ /u01/app/oracle/product/12.1.0/jdk/bin/java -jar
/u01/app/oracle/product/12.2.0/rdbms/admin/preupgrade.jar -c PDB12cR1
Preupgrade generated files:
    /u01/app/oracle/cfgtoollogs/cdb12101/preupgrade/preupgrade.log
    /u01/app/oracle/cfgtoollogs/cdb12101/preupgrade/preupgrade_fixups.sql
```

```
    /u01/app/oracle/cfgtoollogs/cdb12101/preupgrade/postupgrade_fixups.sql

SQL> alter session set container=pdb12cR1;
Session altered.

SQL> @/u01/app/oracle/cfgtoollogs/cdb12101/preupgrade/preupgrade_fixups.sql
Executing Oracle PRE-Upgrade Fixup Script

Auto-Generated by:      Oracle Preupgrade Script
                        Version: 12.2.0.1.0 Build: 1
Generated on:           2016-09-29 17:32:40

For Source Database:     CDB12101
Source Database Version: 12.1.0.2.0
For Upgrade to Version:  12.2.0.1.0

Executing in container:  PDB12CR1

                        Fixup
Check Name              Status  Further DBA Action
----------              ------  ------------------
dictionary_stats        Passed  None
apex_upgrade_msg        Failed  Manual fixup recommended.

PL/SQL procedure successfully completed.

Session altered.
```

The APEX upgrade message is showing as failed. You can do the APEX upgrade later also. PDB12c1R1 has been unplugged now.

```
SQL> alter pluggable database pdb12cR1 close;
Pluggable database altered.

SQL> alter pluggable database pdb12cr1 unplug into '/u01/app/oracle/pdb12cR1.xml';
Pluggable database altered.
```

Target 12.2 Environment

Now PDB12cR1 is getting plugged into the 12.2 CDB with the name PDB12cR2. The PDB name can be changed while plugging into the higher version. The only restriction is that the name should be unique for that CDB.

```
SQL> create pluggable database pdb12cR2 using '/u01/app/oracle/pdb12cR1.xml';
Pluggable database created.

SQL> show pdbs
```

```
    CON_ID CON_NAME                              OPEN MODE  RESTRICTED
---------- ------------------------------     ---------- ----------
         2 PDB$SEED                             READ ONLY  NO
         3 PDB1                                 READ WRITE NO
         4 PDB12CR2                             MOUNTED
```

Start PDB12cR2 in Upgraded Mode

Use this command:

```
SQL> alter pluggable database pdb12cR2 open upgrade;
Pluggable database altered.
```

```
SQL> show pdbs
```

```
    CON_ID CON_NAME                              OPEN MODE  RESTRICTED
---------- ------------------------------     ---------- ----------
         2 PDB$SEED                             READ ONLY  NO
         3 PDB1                                 READ WRITE NO
         4 PDB12CR2                             MIGRATE    YES
```

Invoke the dbupgrade script from the shell or a command prompt and specify the PDB name to upgrade using the -c option.

```
$dbupgrade -n 4 -N 2 -l $ORACLE_HOME/diagnostics -c PDB12cR2
```

Ensure that there are no other PDBs getting upgraded at the same time. If there is any other pluggable database upgrade already in progress in the same container database, then you will get an error.

```
Unexpected error encountered in catctlGetUpgLockFile; Exiting due to another upgrade process
running.
Unable to lock file /tmp/cdb122.dat
```

Here cdb122 is the container database name.

Once the upgrade has completed, execute the utlrp.sql and post-fixup scripts of the pluggable database.

Query dba_registry to check the database component version and status.

You also need to upgrade the time zone of the pluggable database.

Downgrade 12.2 to Earlier Versions

As discussed in Chapter 13, you may at some point need to downgrade the databases to previous versions or releases from where they were upgraded. This means you need to roll back the upgrade changes happening in the database. Mostly you will choose to do this when you want to go back to an old version and you don't want to lose the changes that took place after the upgrade. Remember that the downgrade method discussed here is applicable only to databases upgraded through the DBUA or the command line (basically the data dictionary upgrade method). To use the downgrade option, the compatible parameter should not have been changed after the upgrade.

Note that the downgrade method is possible only for successfully upgraded databases. If an intermediate upgrade has happened to upgrade to 12.2, then the downgrade procedure will return the database to the intermediate version. For example, if the upgrade was from 11.2.0.1.0 to 12.2, then an intermediate upgrade would have been done because 11.2.0.3.0 is the minimum required version for 12.2. Suppose 11.2.0.1.0 was upgraded first to 11.2.0.4.0 and then it was upgraded to 12.2; then the downgrade will get the database to 11.2.0.4.0, not to 11.2.0.1.0.

There is a restriction that a 12.2 pluggable database can be downgraded to the 12.1.0.2 version, not to the 12.1.0.1.0 version.

Prerequisites

Here are the prerequisites:

1) If Database Vault is enabled, then disable Database Vault before the downgrade.

2) If the database uses Oracle Label Security and it is getting downgraded to release 11.2 or earlier, then run the Oracle Label Security (OLS) preprocess script olspredowngrade.sql in the new Oracle Database 12c Oracle Home.

3) If unified auditing is enabled, then back up and purge the unified audit trail.

4) If the time zone version is upgraded as part of the database upgrade, then install the same higher time zone version at the source Oracle Home.

Downgrade Steps for the Entire Container Database

Here are the steps:

1) Take a backup of the container and all pluggable databases. Right now the database is in upgrade state, and it is advisable to take a backup in this situation. If the downgrade procedure fails, you can restore the backup.

2) Start the container and pluggable databases in downgrade mode.

```
SQL> startup downgrade
ORACLE instance started.

Total System Global Area 1912602624 bytes
Fixed Size                  8794120 bytes
Variable Size            1845497848 bytes
Database Buffers           50331648 bytes
Redo Buffers                7979008 bytes
Database mounted.
Database opened.
SQL> show pdbs

    CON_ID CON_NAME                       OPEN MODE  RESTRICTED
---------- ------------------------------ ---------- ----------
         2 PDB$SEED                       MIGRATE    YES
         3 PDB1                           MOUNTED
SQL> alter pluggable database all open downgrade;
Pluggable database altered.
```

```
SQL> show pdbs
    CON_ID CON_NAME                          OPEN MODE   RESTRICTED
---------- ------------------------------ ---------- ----------
         2 PDB$SEED                           MIGRATE     YES
         3 PDB1                               MIGRATE     YES
```

3) Execute catdwgrd.sql on the pluggable database first and then execute it on the container database. You can also use catcon.pl to execute catdwgrd.sql. But you should use the -r option with catcon.pl, which will change the execution order. This will execute first in the pluggable database and then the container database.

```
$ORACLE_HOME/perl/bin/perl catcon.pl -b catdowngrade -r catdwgrd.sql
```

4) Shut down the database in the 12.2 home.

5) Start the container database and pluggable databases in upgrade mode using the previous Oracle version binaries.

```
SQL> startup upgrade
ORACLE instance started.
Total System Global Area  301989888 bytes
Fixed Size                  2923680 bytes
Variable Size             243270496 bytes
Database Buffers           50331648 bytes
Redo Buffers                5464064 bytes
Database mounted.
Database opened.
SQL> show pdbs

    CON_ID CON_NAME                          OPEN MODE   RESTRICTED
---------- ------------------------------ ---------- ----------
         2 PDB$SEED                           MIGRATE     YES
         3 PDB1                               MOUNTED
SQL> alter pluggable database all open upgrade;

SQL> show pdbs

    CON_ID CON_NAME                          OPEN MODE   RESTRICTED
---------- ------------------------------ ---------- ----------
         2 PDB$SEED                           MIGRATE     YES
         3 PDB1                               MIGRATE     YES
```

6) Execute catrelod.sql in the container database followed by all the pluggable databases. It can be done by invoking catcon.pl.

```
/u01/app/oracle/product/12.1.0.2.0/perl/bin/perl catcon.pl -b catreload catrelod.sql
```

7) Check the status of the database components in the database registry.

Note that the database downgrade is just an option to go back to the old version. It doesn't guarantee that the database will return 100 percent the same as it was in the previous version. There could be some higher-version objects retained after the downgrade.

Summary

This chapter was the most demanding chapter in this book because it contains the new upgrade features of the 12c Release 2. We covered the new features and explained how the PDBs are involved, and we gave examples of downgrading a database from 12.2 to a lower version.

Index

A

actions.xml, 506
Advanced queues (AQ), 218
Automatic Memory Management (AMM), 3
Automatic Storage Management (ASM), 3, 32, 34, 97
  benefits of, 278
  CDB and PDBs, 277–278
  datafiles, redo logs and control files, 279
  environment, 277
  OEM (*see* Oracle Enterprise Manager (OEM))
  Recovery Manager (RMAN)
    ASMCMD prompt, 315
    backup database, 312
    locations, 312, 319–320
    log program, 310
    output, 316–318
    primary container database, 313
    restore file, 314
    spfile restore, 316
    tablespace creation, 321
    truncated output, 312
Automatic Undo Management (AUM), 3

B

Bug fixes, 3
Bundle patches, 517

C

Catalog Control Perl Program (catctl.pl),
    54, 73–75, 137
Cluster file system (CFS), 324
Cluster verification utility (CUV), 336
Cold backup
  additional attribute, 176
  copying, 176
  12c RDBMS Home, 178, 180
  crosscheck, 172
  database configuration, 173
  database files, 171

database size, 171
directories, 173
log mode, 171
Oracle base, 174
OWB, 180
PL/SQL block, 180
prerequisites check, 175
pre-upgrade script, 172
RMAN utility, 171
target server, 173
users, 175
Compatibility matrix, 12–13
Container database (CDB), 8, 448
  catcon.pl script, 455
  container and pluggable databases, 457
  database upgrade, 463
  DBUA (*see* Database Upgrade Assistant (DBUA))
  error log file, 456
  mandatory arguments, 454
  output-generated files, 455
  parameters, 455
  pdb$seed databases, 457
  post-upgrade tasks, 479
  pre-upgrade script execution, 455
  preupgrd.sql, 456
  stand-alone database upgrade, 454
  upgrade steps, 468
Create Table As Select (CTAS), 249
  advantages and disadvantages, 127
  12c method, 137
  CTAS *vs.* COPY, 127
  enable supplementary logging, 136
  initiate flashback, 137
  logical standby database, 136
  logical to physical standby, 138
  Order By, 130–131
  parallel usage, 130
  requirements, 128, 130
  restore point, 135
  starting MRP, 138
  switchover, 137–139
  transient logical standby, 131, 133–135

© Y V Ravikumar, K M Krishnakumar and Nassyam Basha 2017
N. Basha et al., *Oracle Database Upgrade and Migration Methods*, DOI 10.1007/978-1-4842-2328-4

12*c* Upgrade script execution
    the catupgrd.sql execution, 73
    parallelism, 73
    phases, 74–75
    post-upgrade steps, 75
    time zone, 75, 77–78
    upgrade statistics table, 79

■ D

Database administrator, 10–11
Database backup
    production, 169
    restore, 169
    scenario, 169
    techniques, 170
    troubleshooting, 169
    upgrading, 170
Database downtime, 163, 165
Database flashback, 554
Database manual upgrade
    method, 61
    prerequisites, 61–62
    pre-upgrade tasks, 62
Database migration, 16
Database Release 12.2, 565
    DBUA (*see* Database Upgrade Assistant
        (DBUA))
    downgrade method, 598
        prerequisites, 599
        steps, 599–601
    emulation, 570
    manual database/command-line
        upgrade, 583
        argument option, 585
        catctl.pl script, 584
        dbupgrade command, 584
        features, 590
        manual database upgrade, 583
        postupgrade tasks, 588
        SQL processes, 585
        upgrade steps, 586
    pluggable database upgrade, 590
        container database selection, 593–594
        manual upgrade method, 596
        output, 596
        PDB12cR2 (upgraded mode), 598
        PDB upgrade options, 594
        progress, 595
        summary, 595
        target 12.2 environment, 597
        upgrade steps, 591–593
    pre-upgrade checks, 565
    R2 (12.2.0.1.0) upgrade, 565
    steps, 566

Database support level, 4
Database upgrade, 1, 3
    benefits, 4–5
    engineers, 9, 11
    hurdles, 5–6
    items, 7–8
    practices, 14–16
    types, 6–7
Database Upgrade Assistant (DBUA), 341, 346
    activities performed by, 26
    assistant, 22–23
    authenticated SSL users, 70, 79
    comparison methods, 161
    CONNECT role
        database link with password, 67–68
        materialized views, 68
        privileges, 67
    CTAS (*see* Create Table As Select (CTAS))
    database selection, 458
    datafiles, 49–50
        location, 71–72
        options, 461
        status, 67
    data pump
        expdp and impdp, 85
        parallel, 85
    disable cron/scheduled jobs, 69
    disable vault, 68
    enable vault, 79
    Estimate_only, 85
    execution method, 63
    features, 151–152
    flashback and guarantee restore point, 52–54
    flashback restore point, 70
    flash recovery area, 70
    full transportable export/import
        data pump, 139–140
        description, 139
        prerequisites, 140
        time-consuming process, 139
        transportable tablespace method, 139
        upgrade steps, 140–149
    11*g* R2 and 12*c* R1, 79
    11*g* R2 and 12*c* R1 DBUA, 59–61
    hidden/underscore parameters, 70
    incorrect/physical binary corruption, 19
    known issues, 57
    limitations, 56, 152
    log files, 56
    management options, 460
    manual processes, 154
    manualupgrade (*see* Database manual
        upgrade)
    network configuration, 461
    Network_link, 85

new offline RMAN backup, 50–52
number of actions, 165
Oracle
    binary relinking, 19–21
    GoldenGate (*see* Oracle GoldenGate)
    installation, 151
    software binaries, 19
OS libraries, 19
PDB list, 459
post-upgrade (*see also* Post-upgrade fixup script)
    steps, 54–56
practices, 26, 28
prerequisites, 23
pre-upgrade
    12*c* execution method, 63–64
    checks, 25–26
    fixup script, 65–66
    script execution, 62
    steps, 54
PSU patches installation, 71
recovery options, 462
recycle bin
    outstanding distributed transactions, 69
    sysdba user, 69
Remap datafile, 85
sample restore script, 31–33, 35, 37, 39–40, 42,
    44, 46–49
screen, 458
silent mode, 57–58
steps, 573
stop and reattach job, 86–87
summarization, 462
SYS and SYSTEM schema objects, 56
Sys and system tablespace, 69
Sysaux tablespace, 69
time zone version, 67
traditional export/import
    compatibility version matrix, 81–82
    export utility, 81
    import utility, 81
    the 9*i* database, 81
TTS (*see* Transportable tablespace (TTS))
types of, 21–22
upgrade
    compatibility matrix, 24
    method, 162–163
    options, 460
    progress, 463
    results, 459
    script execution, 72–74 (*see also* 12*c*
      Upgrade script execution)
upgrade steps, 28–31, 54, 71, 82–84, 87, 89–90
    container execution, 577
    enterprise manager configuration, 581
    features, 583

    lists warnings and errors, 578
    network settings, 580
    options, 579
    page summarization, 581
    pluggable database information, 575
    prerequisite checks page, 576
    preupgrade results, 578
    priority setting, 576
    recovery options, 579
    results, 577, 582
    selection page, 574
    silent mode, 583
    upgrade progress, 582
version, 86
window, 56
Data Guard environment
    DBMS_ROLLING (*see* DBMS_ROLLING
      database)
    overview, 381
    patching environment, 539
    PSU/SPU patch, 540
    RDBMS 11.2.0.4-DBUA 12.1.0.2
      post-upgrade tasks, 405
      pre-upgrade steps, 382
      review, 384
      rolling upgrades, 382
      transport lag, 382
    rolling database upgrades, 381
    upgrade section
      broker configuration, 389
      database name, 393–394
      EM/cloud control, 396
      FRA locations, 396–397
      GUI mode, 401–402
      listener contents, 397–398
      LOCAL_LISTENER, 392
      parallelism option, 395
      prerequisite check, 394–395
      results, 402–404
      RMAN backup configuration, 398–399
      standby database, 390
      summarization, 399–401
      tnsnames.ora file, 404
      upgrade Oracle database, 393
Datapatch, 540
Data pump
    departition, 221
    features, 155, 218
    import method, 220
    imp tool, 155
    limitations, 155
    meaning, 217
    merge, 221
    parameters, 156
    partition, 220

Data pump (*cont.*)
REMAP_DATAFILES, 222
REMAP_TABLESPACE, 222
REUSE_DATAFILES, 222
Solaris Sparc platform, 219
target database, 155
traditional export/import, 155
traditional method, 156
working process, 218
DBMS_ROLLING database, 410
12*c*, 411
11*g* vs. DBMS_ROLLING, 410
Downgrades
database flashback, 554
downgrade steps, 555, 559
issues, 563
multitenant database, 558
non-CDB database, 558
upgrade steps, 554
limitations, 547–548
multitenant database, 550
database flashback, 558
issues, 563
steps, 559
11.2.0.4.0 version, 548
Dynamic link libraries (DLLs), 19

■ **E**

E-Business Suite (EBS), 425
database upgrade process, 428
apps home, 438
completion, 438
components status, 440
cr9idata.pl execution, 439
database-12*c* version, 441
database home, 438
enterprise edition, 430
Grid options page, 429
installation options and
progress, 429, 437
inventory details, 431
location, 431, 434
MGDSYS schema, 440
prerequisite check page, 431, 435
pre-upgrade scripts, 439
product language, 430
security updates page, 428
shutdown (server process and
services), 439
summary page, 432–433, 436
sys.enabled$indexes drop table, 439
SYS/SYSTEM schema objects, 440
post-upgrade steps, 427, 442
prerequisite check page, 425–426

pre-upgrade steps, 426
upgrade steps, 427
Emulation, 570
Enterprise Manager (EM), 20, 36, 45, 48, 62–63,
65–66, 70

■ **F**

Flash Recovery Area (FRA), 70, 324
Full transportable export/import, 139–140, 146
features, 157
limitations, 158

■ **G**

Grid Infrastructure (GI)
ASM and database instances, 338–339
automatic storage management, 329
cluster nodes, 336–338
CVU pre-upgrade check tool, 324
execution steps (ORAchk)
orachk.zip, 326
report files, 328
system information, 327
GIMR database, 340
GIMR option, 335
global and nodes settings, 331
methods, 323
MGMTDB status, 340
node selection page, 330
ORAchk tool, 326
Oracle base and software location, 330
Oracle Enterprise Manager Cloud
Control 13c
cluster database, 379
environment configuration, 378
locations of, 378
OEM cloud control, 379
software location, 380
parallel upgrade script
catupgrd.log script, 370
catupgrd.sql script, 369
components, 372
database status, 376–377
DBMS_DST scripts, 374
factors, 369
locations, 372
log files, 370
srvctl commands, 376
stack-cluster components, 377
status, 373
upg_tzv_apply.sql, 375
utlrp.sql script, 373
utlu121s.sql, 371
v$timezone_file output, 373

prerequisites, 323
RAC database (11*g* to 12*c*)
    action nodes, 360
    Clusterware, 341
    database software installation, 356
    DBUA, 341, 346–347
    EM Database Express port, 350
    executing prerequisite checks, 348
    execution, 360–368
    factors, 352
    failure, 350
    global settings and grid options, 344, 358
    installation options, 341
    locations, 343, 358
    nodes selection page, 342, 357
    ORAC database installation, 342, 356
    ORACLE_HOME and database version, 347
    parameter changes, 355
    parallellism option, 349
    prerequisite checks, 344
    pre-upgrade script, 360
    preupgrd.sql, 359
    results button, 353–354
    root.sh script, 345
    script root.sh, 358
    source code, 356
    source database and target database, 351
    summarization, 351
    time duration and status, 353
    upgrade progress, 352
    validation results, 348
RAC instances (rac1 and rac2), 338
real application testing, 328
rolling method, 340–341
runInstaller execution, 328–329
script execution, 331–334
software components, 335–336
status of, 324
Grid Infrastructure Management Repository
    (GIMR), 340

■ **H**

Heterogeneous standby databases, 268
Hot backup (user-managed)
    alter database, 182
    backup mode, 184
    database altered, 187
    datafile, 180
    directories, 183
    invalid objects, 189
    manual method, 188
    My Oracle support, 189
    ORACLE_HOME, 185
    pfile locations, 185

    pfile/spfile, 184
    pre-upgrade check, 182
    redo data, 181
    RMAN, 181
    server location, 183
    source server page, 186
    target server (ORA-U2), 186, 187
    TNS entries, 190

■ **I, J, K**

Integrated Extract Capture mode, 121
inventory.xml, 504

■ **L**

Local inventory, 512
Logical Backup (expdp/impdp), 190–191
Logical change record (LCR), 270

■ **M**

Manual/command-line upgrade
    catupgrd.sql, 152
    features, 153
    ORA-01722, 152
    pre-upgrade steps, 152
Master control process (MCP), 218
Migration, 213
    Create Table As Select (CTAS), 249
    data pump
        departition, 221
        features, 218
        import method, 220
        meaning, 217
        merge, 221
        partition, 220
        REMAP_DATAFILES, 222
        REMAP_TABLESPACE, 222
        REUSE_DATAFILES, 222
        Solaris Sparc platform, 219
        working process, 218
    export/import utilities
        dump, 213
        export, 214
        import, 216
        output, 215–216
        source and target, 214
        steps, 214
    GoldenGate (*see* Oracle GoldenGate)
    heterogeneous standby databases, 268
    methods, 213
    Oracle Streams, 270
    overview, 213
    target database, 213

Migration (*cont.*)
   transportable tablespaces, 223
   transportdatabase (*see* Transport database
      method)
Multitenant database, 3
   architecture, 447
   CDB (*see* Container database (CDB))
   dictionary, 448–449
   downgrades, 550
   lower-version database, 450
      container database, 452
      conversion, 450
      noncdb_to_pdb.sql, 453
      read-only mode, 451
      shutdown, 452
      SQL queries, 451
      TEMPFILE REUSE, 453
      /tmp/12cNoCDB.xml, 453
      XML file, 451
   PDB (*see* Pluggable database (PDB))
   process and memory, 448
   root database, 448
My Oracle Support (MOS), 62

■ **N**

Network administrator, 11
Network file system (NFS), 324

■ **O**

Offline patching, 524
One-off patches, 517
Online patching, 527
Opatch tool, 513
Oracle Configuration Manager (OCM), 537
Oracle database, 1
Oracle Enterprise Manager (OEM)
   administration tab, 305
   agent deployment summaries, 300
   ASM locations, 307
   cloud control and admin server, 298
   components, 299
   container, seed and pluggable
         databases, 304
   database and host credentials option, 305
   Database Configuration Assistant
         (DBCA), 301–303
   database server, 297–298
   datafiles, control files and redo log files, 304
   fast recovery area locations, 306
   log programs, 308–309
   migration status, 308, 310
   minimum downtime option, 306

OMS, 299
repository database, 299
review, 307
RMAN report option, 309
schedule option, 306
status, 300–301
Oracle GoldenGate (OGG), 98, 104–105, 107, 109,
      114–116, 120–121, 123, 126
   advantages, 98
   bulkload method, 246
   CDB, 98
   configuration, 232
   configuration (target database), 243
   conjunction, 98
   description, 98
   environment setup, 228, 239
   extract process definition, 240
   flashback_scn option, 241
   info command, 241
   IT organizations, 98
   marker setup script, 233
   Oracle 12c for Oracle GoldenGate 12c, 113–114,
         116–119
   Oracle 11g, 119
   parameters, 233
   PDB, 98
   pdb12c and Oracle 11g, 120–126
   planning phase, 98–105
   replicat, 240
   source database, 229
   source database (Oracle 11g), 105–111
   target database (Oracle 12c), 111–113, 230
Oracle installation, 151
Oracle Label Security (OLS), 68, 599
Oracle Management Server (OMS), 299
Oracle RAC Configuration Audit Tool
      (ORAchk), 326

■ **P**

Patching
   actions.xml, 506
   binary level, 506
   bugs, 503
   bundle patches, 517
   central inventory, 506
      11.2.0.3.0 home, 508
      installation, 508
      oraInst.loc file, 507
      remove, 511
   conflicts, 517
   contains, 504
   database level, 506
   Data Guard environment, 539–540

datapatch, 540
inventory.xml, 504
local inventory, 506, 512
one-off patches, 517
Opatch tool, 513
overlay patches, 517–518
patch set update, 516
PSU (*see* Patch set updates (PSUs))
query inventory, 542
RAC, 537
re-creation steps, 509
security patch update, 516
strategies (online and offline), 518
    conflict analysis, 519–520
    offline mode, 524
    online mode, 527
    Opatch debug, 529
    patch steps, 524
    post-patch steps, 528
    rollback, 528
Patch set updates (PSUs), 516
attributes, 530
composite, 530
conformation, 532
noncomposite, 530
overview, 529
patches, 71, 73, 82
patch steps, 530
rollback, 533
Platform, 167
Pluggable database (PDB), 448, 479, 491
backup files, 480
catctl.pl, 485
different endian format
    container database, 496
    datafile format, 500
    dba_datafiles, 501–502
    export dump, 499
    import metadata dump, 501
    metadata dump, 498
    ORA-65134 error, 497
    platform combination, 498
    read-only, 499
    source files, 498
    SYSTEM and SYSAUX tablespaces, 497
    transport tablespace check, 498
    TTS, 497
Endian format, 492
    backup folder, 494
    catupgrd.sql script, 495
    container database, 493
    12.1.0.2.0 container database, 495
    high-level steps, 492
    new database creation, 494

target database, 494
    unplug program, 493
migrations, 491
pre-upgrade steps, 482–483
source container database, 483
upgrade steps, 479–480, 485
Post-upgrade fixup script
database backup, 66
source database, 66
statistics collection, 66
Prerequisites, 191

Q

Quality of service (QoS) management, 340

R

Real Application Clusters (RAC), 278, 537
Real Application Testing (RAT), 161, 328
Recovery Manager (RMAN)
ASMCMD prompt, 315
backup database, 201–210, 312
locations, 312, 319–320
log program, 310
output 316–318
primary container database, 313
restore script, 51, 314
spfile restore, 316
tablespace creation, 321
truncated output, 312
Registry components
12c database, 191
datafiles, 193
expdp, 196–197
impdp 197–201
metadata, 193
NLS settings, 192
objects count, 191–192
target database, 194
Relinking process, 20

S

Security patch update (SPUs), 516, 535
Source database version, 166
Storage administrator, 11
Streams, 270
Supporting environment, 4
SYSAUX tablespace presence, 25
SYS schema, 195
System administrator, 11
System architect, 11
SYSTEM tablespace, 166

■ T

Trace File Analyzer (TFA), 323
Transient logical standby
    block-by-block copy, 158
    DBUA, 158
    features, 159
    limitations, 159
    lower version, 158
    primary database, 158
    source database, 158
    Switchover, 159
Transparent Data Encryption (TDE), 97
Transportable database (TDB), 90
Transportable tablespace (TTS), 21, 90–92, 94,
       96–98, 101, 127, 139, 141, 147–148, 223, 497
    advantages, 98
    database's nonadministrative tablespaces, 90
    database version, 156
    datafile, 156
    definition, 90
    features, 157
    limitations, 97, 157
    prerequisites, 91–97
    tablespace set, 90–91
    things to consider, 91

Transport database method
    external objects, 253
    migrate steps, 253
        backup and restore, 266–267
        control file, 264, 267–268
        creation script, 262
        conversion script, 258–259, 263
        datafiles, 260
        Endian format, 254
        init parameter file, 262
        read-only mode, 254, 265
        resetlogs option, 257
        RMAN backup sets, 261
        RMAN prompt, 254–255
        target server, 257, 266
        tempfile, 258
        transport script, 255–257
        transportscript.sql, 259
    preparatory steps, 253
    requirements, 252

■ U, V, W, X, Y, Z

Unsupported features, 166
User objects, 166

Get the eBook for only $4.99!

Why limit yourself?

Now you can take the weightless companion with you wherever you go and access your content on your PC, phone, tablet, or reader.

Since you've purchased this print book, we are happy to offer you the eBook for just $4.99.

Convenient and fully searchable, the PDF version enables you to easily find and copy code—or perform examples by quickly toggling between instructions and applications.

To learn more, go to http://www.apress.com/us/shop/companion or contact support@apress.com.

All Apress eBooks are subject to copyright. All rights are reserved by the Publisher, whether the whole or part of the material is concerned, specifically the rights of translation, reprinting, reuse of illustrations, recitation, broadcasting, reproduction on microfilms or in any other physical way, and transmission or information storage and retrieval, electronic adaptation, computer software, or by similar or dissimilar methodology now known or hereafter developed. Exempted from this legal reservation are brief excerpts in connection with reviews or scholarly analysis or material supplied specifically for the purpose of being entered and executed on a computer system, for exclusive use by the purchaser of the work. Duplication of this publication or parts thereof is permitted only under the provisions of the Copyright Law of the Publisher's location, in its current version, and permission for use must always be obtained from Springer. Permissions for use may be obtained through RightsLink at the Copyright Clearance Center. Violations are liable to prosecution under the respective Copyright Law.